The Science of Mental Health

Volume 7

Personality and Personality Disorder

Series Content

The Science of Mental Health

Volume 7

Personality and Personality Disorder

Edited with introductions by

Steven Hyman
National Institute of Mental Health

ROUTLEDGE
New York/London

Published in 2001 by

Routledge
29 West 35th Street
New York, NY 10001

Published in Great Britain by
Routledge
11 New Fetter Lane
London EC4P 4EE

Routledge is an Imprint of Taylor & Francis Books, Inc.

Printed in the United States of America on acid-free paper.

10 9 8 7 6 5 4 3 2 1

Library of Congress Cataloging-in-Publication Data

The science of mental health / edited with introductions by Steven Hyman.
p. cm.
Includes bibliographical references.
ISBN 0-8153-3743-4 (set)
1. Mental health. I. Hyman, Steven E.
RA790 .S435 2002
616.89--dc21

2001048491

ISBN 0-8153-3743-4 (set)
ISBN 0-8153-3744-2 (v.1)
ISBN 0-8153-3745-0 (v.2)
ISBN 0-8153-3746-9 (v.3)
ISBN 0-8153-3747-7 (v.4)
ISBN 0-8153-3748-5 (v.5)
ISBN 0-8153-3749-3 (v.6)
ISBN 0-8153-3750-7 (v.7)
ISBN 0-8153-3751-5 (v.8)
ISBN 0-8153-3752-3 (v.9)
ISBN 0-8153-3753-1 (v.10)

Contents

Treatment

Introduction

One of the most challenging areas of behavioral research is the study of personality and personality disorders. The main challenge can be stated directly: it is difficult to know with certainty which personality traits are fundamental and which are complex elaborations of fundamental traits. Without good models of basic traits, it is difficult to perform other types of studies, ranging from meaningful measurements of variation in the population to studies of genetic or environmental susceptibility factors to studies of the pathogenesis of disordered forms of personality. This type of problem can be described as a struggle to "carve nature at the joints." Although it is important to understand the richness of variation of personality within the normal range, a public health problem results from what are called personality disorders. The core concept of a personality disorder as described in the American Psychiatric Association's *Diagnostic and Statistical Manual of Mental Disorders,* 4th edition (DSM-IV), is an enduring pattern of inner experience and behavior that deviates markedly from the expectations of the individual's culture. This pattern is long-lasting, inflexible, and pervasive across a broad range of personal and social situations. It leads to clinically significant distress or impairment in social, occupational, or other important areas of functioning. The pattern is stable and of long duration, and its onset can be traced back at least to adolescence or early adulthood.[1]

There is no disagreement that individuals with personality disorders have marked impairments in social and occupational functioning, and those with personality disorders that are characterized by severe emotional lability and distress are very high utilizers of psychiatric and general medical services. However, there is strong disagreement over how personality disorders should be described and classified, their boundaries with normalcy, how many disorders there might be, and their relationship to such better understood illnesses as depression and anxiety disorders. The major debate is between dimensional and syndromal approaches to classification. Dimensional approaches assume that a catalog of fundamental traits can be identified and that personality disorders represent quantitative extremes on one or more dimensions of personality. A syndromal approach is far more consistent with typical medical practice, which often conceptualizes illnesses in terms of clusters of typical symptoms and signs (in general medicine, these clusters are understood to derive from an identifiable pathophysiologic process; such processes for mental disorders have not yet been identified). The syndromal approach is used by the DSM-IV. However, the syndromes listed in the manual are poorly validated. Many if not most real-world individuals with a personality disorder qualify for multiple diagnoses. Many investigators argue that even if clinicians think intuitively in terms of syndromes, dimensional approaches are more likely to lead to a valid classification system. Different approaches to the description and classification of personality variants and disorders included in this volume are those of Cloninger (1987), Costa and McCrae (1992), Goldberg (1990), and Widiger and Costa (1994).

Within the syndromal approach of the DSM-IV, the disorder that is arguably the most clinically significant (in terms of impairment, distress, and utilization of services) and the best studied is borderline personality disorder. Based on DSM-IV criteria, this disorder is characterized by a pervasive pattern of instability of interpersonal relationships, self-image, and emotion and marked impulsivity beginning by early adulthood and present in a variety of contexts. The DSM-IV requires at least five of nine symptoms: (1) frantic efforts to avoid real or imagined abandonment; (2) a pattern of unstable and intense interpersonal relationships; (3) identity disturbance (markedly and persistently unstable sense of self); (4) potentially self-damaging impulsivity; (5) recurrent suicidal behavior, gestures, or threats or self-mutilating behavior; (6) affective instability; (7) chronic feelings of emptiness; (8) inappropriate, intense anger or difficulty controlling anger; (9) transient, stress-related paranoid ideation or severe dissociative symptoms. Research has found that borderline personality disorder appears to run in families and that the course of this disorder is often punctuated by episodes of major depression. Research on risk factors has raised the question of whether early childhood trauma may play an important role (Gunderson and Sabo, 1993).

The other well-researched personality disorder is antisocial personality disorder. It is characterized by a pervasive pattern of disregard for and violation of the rights of others and begins early in life. (The DSM-IV says prior to age 15.) The DSM-IV requires a childhood history of conduct disorder and three or more symptoms from a list of seven: (1) failure to conform to social norms with respect to lawful behaviors, as indicated by repeatedly performing acts that are grounds for arrest; (2) deceitfulness, as indicated by repeated lying, use of aliases, or conning others for personal profit or pleasure; (3) impulsivity or failure to plan ahead; (4) irritability and aggressiveness, as indicated by repeated physical fights or assaults; (5) reckless disregard for the safety of self or others; (6) consistent irresponsibility, as indicated by repeated failure to sustain consistent work behavior or honor financial obligations; and (7) lack of remorse, as indicated by being indifferent to or rationalizing having hurt, mistreated, or stolen from another. There is considerable evidence that antisocial personality disorder runs in families, and substantial work on life course informs prevention and early intervention research. One classic analysis examines the implications of onset of antisocial behavior early in life or limited to adolescence (Moffitt, 1993).

Whether one is examining normal variations in personality or personality disorders, genes seem to play a significant role as susceptibility factors. Much of the work on the role of genes and environment in personality utilizes twin designs. In such designs concordance for the trait of interest is typically compared between pairs of identical (monozygotic) versus fraternal (dizygotic) twins. Both types of twin pairs are assumed to share similar environments, while they differ in their degree of genetic similarity. Monozygotic twins share 100 percent of their DNA, whereas dizygotic twins share, on average, 50 percent. Thus if a trait has a genetic component, monozygotic twin pairs should be more similar to each other than dizygotic twin pairs. An even more powerful design for distinguishing genetic from environmental influences is the study of twins reared apart (Bouchard et al., 1990; Tellegen et al., 1988).

Overall, the twin data derived from studies of personality variation (Bouchard et al., 1990; Hewitt et al., 1997; Plomin, 1990), personality disorders (Torgersen et al., 2000), and psychiatric illness more generally (Kendler et al., 1993) find that genes have an important effect on personality (controlling approximately 50 percent of the variance for many personality traits) but exert their influence in interaction with nongenetic factors. One striking, if contentious, argument made by many of the behavioral geneticists who use twin designs to study personality is that the significant nongenetic factors derive not from the shared familial environment (which might reflect socioeconomic status, general parenting style, or the number of books in the house) but from unshared environmental factors. Although there is still disagreement over this interpretation (Maccoby, 2000), there has been increasing study of familial events that might be unique to a single child, such as abuse (Johnson et al., 1999) or factors that occur outside the shared family environment. The difficulty with many studies of abuse is that they are retrospective and often liable to recall bias unless good records are available. Prospective studies are difficult but important. Harris (1995) has argued that under normal circumstances the critical unshared environmental factor in personality development is not related to the family at all but is supplied by peer groups (Harris et al., 1995). Sampson et al. (1999) have not studied personality development per se, but their work suggests that even larger social groupings, such as neighborhoods, may have an impact on outcomes for children.

An entirely separate line of research relevant to personality and personality disorders is the study of brain structures and circuits involved in personality traits. The neurologic method, studying individuals with damage to specific brain regions and correlating behavioral abnormalities with the lesion, has underscored the importance of the human prefrontal cortex in what might be described as social and moral behavior (Bechara et al., 1994; Damasio et al., 1990). Other information on the relationship of brain regions and brain circuits to personality traits is increasingly coming from human neuroimaging, although this type of investigation is in its early stages. A summary of current thinking about violence, for example, which integrates information from neuroimaging, neurochemistry, and other sources, is reviewed by Davidson et al. (2000). While the understanding and classification of personality and personality disorders are contentious and the study of pathogenesis of personality disorders is in its early stages, the development of effective treatments for personality disorders may be at an earlier stage still. There have been almost no adequate studies of pharmacologic treatments of personality disorders. A review of the pharmacology of borderline personality disorder is included (Soloff, 2000), but the goal of pharmacologic treatment is control of symptoms. In general the strategy is to target drugs to individual symptoms or groups of symptoms reminiscent of other illnesses (for example, depression). There are no pharmacologic treatments for the core symptoms of any personality disorder, and the current treatments seem to help individuals only moderately, and often with side effects. Psychodynamic psychotherapies have traditionally been used in the treatment of personality disorders, but they have not been studied in modern clinical trials. A specific behavioral therapy that has been developed and tested for the treatment of borderline personality disorder is called dialectical behavior therapy (Koerner and Linehan, 2000). Nonetheless, newer and more effective treatments for individuals with personality disorders are much needed. Whether such treatments can be developed absent a better classification system and absent clues to pathogenesis, such as genetic variants that produce risk, is an open question.

Reference

1. American Psychiatric Association. *Diagnostic and Statistical Manual of Mental Disorders,* 4th ed. Washington, D.C.: American Psychiatric Press, 1994.

News and Views

A Systematic Method for Clinical Description and Classification of Personality Variants

A Proposal

C. Robert Cloninger, MD

• A systematic method for clinical description and classification of both normal and abnormal personality variants is proposed based on a general biosocial theory of personality. Three dimensions of personality are defined in terms of the basic stimulus-response characteristics of novelty seeking, harm avoidance, and reward dependence. The possible underlying genetic and neuroanatomical bases of observed variation in these dimensions are reviewed and considered in relation to adaptive responses to environmental challenge. The functional interaction of these dimensions leads to integrated patterns of differential response to novelty, punishment, and reward. The possible tridimensional combinations of extreme (high or low) variants on these basic stimulus-response characteristics correspond closely to traditional descriptions of personality disorders. This reconciles dimensional and categorical approaches to personality description. It also implies that the underlying structure of normal adaptive traits is the same as that of maladaptive personality traits, except for schizotypal and paranoid disorders.

(*Arch Gen Psychiatry* 1987;44:573-588)

Current approaches to the description and diagnosis of personality disorders have serious practical and conceptual limitations. First, an individual often has features characteristic of more than one personality disorder when discrete categories are specified, as in current classifications of the American Psychiatric Association[1] or the World Health Organization.[2] Second, clinical distinctions between maladaptive personality traits and personality disorders are somewhat arbitrary because of the graded nature of variation in social and cognitive styles, as well as the graded nature of severity of adaptive impairment. Third, adaptive impairment depends on both situational and temperamental variables, so the same temperament may lead to successful achievement in one social or occupational setting and to disability and distress in another setting. Fourth, the behaviors that are typically chosen as criterion variables in a particular culture are obviously not socially desirable or admirable; consequently, direct questioning often leads to guarded and defensive responses, even when the individual is aware of others' perception of his behavior.

Partly as a result of such fundamental problems, the criteria and categories that are used to assess personality and its adaptive consequences have often fluctuated based on contemporary fashion rather than fact. Different categories for personality diagnosis are recommended in the third edition of the *Diagnostic and Statistical Manual of Mental Disorders (DSM-III)* and in the *International Classification of Diseases* (ICD). Such problems have been acknowledged in the development of systems such as *DSM-III*,[3-5] but they have not been solved by such acknowledgment. For example, the different categories for personality disorder are meant to serve as "prototypes" or examples of clinical groups that have traditionally been distinguished rather than truly discrete pathophysiological entities with natural diagnostic boundaries.[5] However, this begs the fundamental question of whether personality variation is categorical or dimensional, and ultimately fails in practice, as do all appeals to tradition or authority when there is no consensus about what the traditional categories are or should be. The inadequacy of reliance on traditional prototypes was recently vividly illustrated by the sociopolitical nature of the discussion about the addition of some new categories to *DSM-III*.[6] Furthermore, the choice of categories and criterion variables in *DSM-III* appears culturebound or ethnocentric to clinicians in other countries (V. K. Varma, MD, personal communication, 1986).

In contrast, research on normal personality traits has usually measured variation along continuous dimensions

Accepted for publication Dec 5, 1986.

From the Departments of Psychiatry and Genetics, Washington University School of Medicine and The Jewish Hospital of St Louis.

Reprint requests to The Jewish Hospital of St Louis, 216 S Kingshighway Blvd, PO Box 14109, St Louis, MO 63178 (Dr Cloninger).

that are based on either quantitative clinical ratings or scores on self-report inventories.[7-10] The observed variation in "normal" or adaptive personality traits generally follows an approximately gaussian distribution in general population samples.[11,12] There has been little or no evidence of bimodality or multimodality, as would be expected if adaptive personality variation was influenced by discrete disease processes.[13,14] A bewildering array of different scales have been described, but these are highly redundant with one another. Empirical factor analyses consistently indicate that there are three major dimensions of normal personality variation in the general population.[8-10] The well-known scales of the Eysencks distinguish between the three dimensions of neuroticism, extraversion-introversion, and psychoticism, or tough-mindedness.[8] Three dimensions, similar to those described by the Eysencks, consistently emerge when the many different inventories of normal personality variation are factor analyzed. In other words, normal personality traits can be well described by variation along three dimensions that are normally distributed and uncorrelated with one another.

Similarly, three independent dimensions arise when responses to questions measuring *DSM-III* personality disorder categories are factor analyzed.[15] However, no systematic relationship has been described between the three major dimensions of normal (adaptive) personality traits and the three dimensions of abnormal (maladaptive) personality. For example, factor analyses of the Millon Clinical Multiaxial Inventory reveal factors for being "negativistic-avoidant," "paranoid," and "asocial-avoidant," which do not correspond well to adaptive traits.[15] On the other hand, if the characteristics associated with the extremes of the Eysencks' three dimensions of adaptive personality traits ("neurotic" vs "stable," "extravert" vs "introvert," and "tough-minded" vs "tender-minded") are combined, the resulting combinations do not correspond closely with traditional descriptions of personality disorders.

One major difficulty in integrating work on adaptive and maladaptive traits is related to a fundamental limitation of factor analysis. The limitation is that extrastatistical information is needed to specify the structure of the underlying biologic and social variability in personality traits. Factor analysis can determine only the number of dimensions, not their underlying causal structure, location, or "rotation" in space. In other words, descriptive data about behavior are not sufficient to permit any strong preference among alternative ways of summarizing descriptive behavioral data. For example, Tellegen[9] has suggested that variation in personality is better summarized by three behavioral dimensions he labeled as "positive emotionality," "negative emotionality," and "constraint." It is difficult to justify a preference between the factor structures of the Eysencks and Tellegen on descriptive grounds alone, and neither system seems to have a simple relationship to traditional categories of personality disorder. Gray[16,17] has used observations about the effects of antianxiety drugs on personality to argue that the structure described by the Eysencks does not correspond well to underlying biologic variation. For example, drugs that reduce scores on measures of neuroticism, such as alcohol, barbiturates, and the benzodiazepines, also consistently reduce scores on measures of introversion, suggesting that these dimensions share biologic determinants even though the Eysencks' model assumes they are independent processes. Such experimental biologic information can help to choose among an infinite number of alternative sets of three dimensions.

However, another difficulty arises that complicates the use of biologic data to make choices about the structure of behavioral variation. This second difficulty is that the structure of the observed behavioral variation may not be the same as the structure of the underlying biologic variation because social learning and environmental factors also influence behavior. The phenotypic structure may differ from the underlying biogenetic structure because observed behavioral variation, ie, phenotypic variation, is the result of the interaction of genetic and environmental influences.[18,19] The heritabilities of adaptive personality traits consistently have been estimated to be between 40% and 60%,[20] so genetic and environmental factors have roughly equal importance in determining behavioral responses. In fact, the structure of the underlying biogenetic variation does not correspond closely with the phenotypic structure because the systems that are genetically independent have shared environmental determinants.[18] Thus, additional information is needed to specify the structure of biogenetic and socioenvironmental factors for assessments of personality to have optimal utility for either biologic or social approaches to prevention and treatment.

Allport[21] defined personality as "the dynamic organization within the individual of those psychophysical systems that determine his unique adjustments to his environment." Likewise, Thorpe[22] defined learning as "the organization of behavior as a result of individual experience." Individuals are said to learn when they perceive and change their behavior as a result of their perceptions. Therefore, individual differences in the adaptive systems involved in the reception, processing, and storing of information about the environment define "personality."[23,24] Unfortunately, factor-analytic approaches to the characterization of personality have made little progress toward specifying the psychophysical systems involved in such learning, either in terms of the underlying neural systems or in terms of the relevant social and environmental stimuli involved in personality development and change. Studies of personality trait structure have not been well integrated with learning theory or with the remarkable recent advances in knowledge about the neurobiology of motivation and learning.[25-27] At the same time, neurobiologic and learning studies are often difficult to interpret because they neglect robust findings about the multidimensional structure of personality.

To address these fundamental problems constructively, herein I describe a unified biosocial theory of personality that provides a systematic approach to the description and classification of personality variants. More specifically, I show that the overlap among the different traditional categories of personality disorder is orderly and systematically predictable from available knowledge of the biogenetic structure underlying basic patterns of adaptive response to danger, novelty, and reward.

A GENERAL THEORY OF PERSONALITY

Recently, I presented a unified biosocial theory of personality and its role in the development of anxiety states based on a synthesis of information from family studies, studies of longitudinal development, and psychometric studies of personality structure, as well as neuropharmacologic and neuroanatomical studies of behavioral conditioning and learning in man and other animals.[24] Based on this synthesis, I hypothesized that there were three dimensions of personality that are genetically independent and that have predictable patterns of interaction in their adaptive responses to specific classes of environmental stimuli.

The three underlying genetic dimensions of personality are called *novelty seeking*, *harm avoidance*, and *reward dependence*. Novelty seeking is hypothesized to be a heritable tendency toward intense exhilaration or excitement in

Table 1.—Three Major Brain Systems Influencing Stimulus-Response Characteristics

Brain System (Related Personality Dimension)	Principal Monoamine Neuromodulator	Relevant Stimuli	Behavioral Response
Behavioral activation (novelty seeking)	Dopamine	Novelty	Exploratory pursuit
		Potential reward	Appetitive approach
		Potential relief of monotony or punishment	Active avoidance, escape
Behavioral inhibition (harm avoidance)	Serotonin	Conditioned signals for punishment, novelty, or frustrative nonreward	Passive avoidance, extinction
Behavioral maintenance (reward dependence)	Norepinephrine	Conditioned signals for reward or relief of punishment	Resistance to extinction

response to novel stimuli or cues for potential rewards or potential relief of punishment, which leads to frequent exploratory activity in pursuit of potential rewards as well as active avoidance of monotony and potential punishment. Harm avoidance is a heritable tendency to respond intensely to signals of aversive stimuli, thereby learning to inhibit behavior to avoid punishment, novelty, and frustrative nonreward. Reward dependence is hypothesized to be a heritable tendency to respond intensely to signals of reward (particularly verbal signals of social approval, sentiment, and succor), and to maintain or resist extinction of behavior that has previously been associated with rewards or relief from punishment. These three dimensions reflect variation in three brain systems described in Table 1. Further description and supporting data are presented below.

Genetic variation in each dimension follows a gaussian, or normal, distribution, with most people having intermediate values. Harm avoidance serves as a modulating influence on both novelty-seeking and reward-seeking behavior, leading to inhibition of exploration of unfamiliar or uncertain situations as well as passive avoidance of punishment and nonreward. As a result of this modulatory influence, environmental influences on harm-avoidant behavior are shared among the three dimensions. More specifically, in response to novel stimuli, the novelty-seeking dimension leads to active-approach behavior, whereas the harm-avoidance dimension leads to inhibited or passively avoidant behavior. The resulting behavior is the balance between these influences on active approach and passive avoidance. Likewise, in response to frustrative nonreward, reward dependence predisposes to continued reward-seeking behavior, whereas harm avoidance predisposes to extinction of behavior; again, the resulting behavior is the balance between these influences on maintenance and extinction. Furthermore, reward dependence predisposes to maintenance of familiar activities that have been rewarded previously, whereas novelty seeking leads to initiation of unfamiliar activities that are potentially rewarding. Thus, the genetic variation is independent, but correlated environmental variation leads to a different structure of the observed behavior.[24]

Individuals who are higher than average in novelty seeking and average in the other two dimensions are characterized as impulsive, exploratory, fickle, excitable, quick-tempered, extravagant, and disorderly. They are readily engaged in new interests and activities, but they tend to neglect details and are quickly distracted or bored. Also they are easily provoked to prepare for fight or flight. In contrast, individuals who are lower than average in novelty seeking and average on the other two dimensions are characterized as only slowly engaged in new interests, often become preoccupied with narrowly focused details, and require considerable thought before making decisions. They are typically described as reflective, rigid, loyal, stoic, slow-tempered, frugal, orderly, and persistent.

These novelty-seeking traits are thought to reflect variation in the brain's "incentive," or behavioral activation, system.[24] Dopaminergic cell bodies in the midbrain receive inputs from several sources and then project impulses to the forebrain, thereby acting as the final common pathway for the behavioral activation system.[25,28,29] This behavioral activation is associated with exploration of novel environmental stimuli, pursuit of and approach to potential rewards, active avoidance of monotony or potential punishment, and escape from punishment. Such behavioral activation is associated with a particular pattern of physiological arousal, particularly an increased heart rate and decreased sensation threshold.[30,31]

This activation of purposeful behavior requires both sensorimotor integration and direction of behavior toward novel or pleasurable stimuli. In mammals, dopaminergic projections to the forebrain play a central role in all these functions via nigrostriatal projections, mesolimbic projections (from the ventral tegmentum to limbic structures, including the septum, nucleus accumbens, and amygdala), and mesofrontal projections (from the ventral tegmentum to the neocortex, including the mesial frontal, anterior cingulate, and entorhinal areas).[32] The amygdala is involved in active avoidance responses and preparation for fight or flight in conjunction with the cortex and the hypothalamus. Inputs to the dopaminergic cell bodies include ascending paths in the reticular formation, descending paths from the hypothalamus, and feedback from the cerebral cortex via the amygdala and caudate.

Self-stimulation with electrodes at sites of dopaminergic neurons is rapid and accompanied by marked locomotor activation and positive reinforcement of eliciting behavior in animals and reports of the subjective experience of pleasure and satisfaction in humans.[25,28-30,33,34] Lesions of noradrenergic neurons in the locus ceruleus do not affect self-stimulatory behavior, at least not with continuous reinforcement schedules.[25,29,35,36] Spontaneous exploratory motor behavior by mammals in a novel environment is dependent on the integrity of mesolimbic dopaminergic projections.[35] Dopamine-depleting lesions in the nucleus accumbens or the ventral tegmentum lead to neglect of novel environmental stimuli and reduce both spontaneous

Table 2.—Summary of Novelty-Seeking Scale

+3	*Severely High:* Consistently seeks thrilling adventures and exploration; disorderly and unpredictable; intolerant of structure and monotony regardless of consequences; decisions and opinions based on vague global impressions and intuitions; consistently plays roles for dramatic effect so that real feelings and beliefs are uncertain; consistently spends on impulse in absence of external constraints; interests and friendships shift rapidly with the latest influence without any sustained commitments
+2	*Moderately High:* Usually seeks exhilaration from thrilling ventures and exploration of unfamiliar places and situations; intolerant of structure and routine, trying to break rules and introduce change; easily excitable and quick tempered and engaged with new ideas, activities, or people; strongly prefers to act on intuitive hunches and frequently has to revise these decisions; skilled and convincing at role playing and dramatic exaggeration; prefers impulse spending but able to save for special occasions
+1	*Mildly High:* Prefers pursuit of exciting thrills and exploration to familiar routines unless benefits from stable routines are highly likely; tolerates structure and discipline without much difficulty; more excitable and easily engaged than average and more easily becomes disinterested and bored by monotony; prefers quick decisions based on hunches and impressions rather than detailed analysis; mildly histrionic and convincing in dramatic role playing; prefers to spend on impulse without a budget but responsibly avoids major debt
0	*Average:* Equally tolerant of novelty and routine with choices depending on what appears most beneficial; balanced use of both logical analysis and intuition; average amount of role playing and attention to saving; average excitability and rate of engagement/disengagement with people, activities, or ideas
−1	*Mildly Low:* Prefers to stay with familiar routines unless benefits from new venture are highly likely; orderly and well organized but does not usually try to impose stable structures; slower to become excited or attached than average; enjoys thrills and novelty when encountered but does not seek them out; usually prefers logical analysis over intuitive hunches but also often acts on first impressions; limited role playing or dramatic exaggeration but will often lie or disguise feelings to spare others' feelings; prefers to save and budget but not obviously stingy or frugal
−2	*Moderately Low:* Prefers to stay with familiar routines unless benefits from new ventures are nearly certain; orderly and disciplined, usually trying to impose stable structure and organization; reserved and controlled, slowly becomes excited, angry, or enthusiastic or interested and attached; prefers detailed analysis over quick intuitive impressions but sometimes uses impressions tentatively; limited role playing and dramatic exaggeration; strong preference for saving and spending according to budgets over impulse spending
−3	*Severely Low:* Resists nearly all attempts to modify familiar routines; disinterested in novelty and exploratory pursuits regardless of potential benefits; highly orderly and well organized, trying to impose stable structure and consistent routine; highly controlled, rarely becoming angry or excited quickly; analytical decision maker who always requires detailed analysis of complete information, consistently direct and honest without role playing or exaggeration; highly frugal with consistent effort to save and budget; loyal and stoical, highly slow to form and change interests and social attachments

activity and investigative behavior, but partial lesions may lead to hyperactivity.[25] Dopamine agonists, such as amphetamines and cocaine as well as alcohol, opiates, and opioid neuropeptides, lead to facilitation of dopaminergic transmission and behavioral activation, whereas dopamine blockers, such as haloperidol, lead to reduced exploratory behavior and anhedonia or reduced responsiveness to positive reinforcement.[35] Such behavioral activation by dopamine and its agonists depends on the integrity of the nucleus accumbens, but not the caudate nucleus.[34] Other supporting neurophysiological, neuroanatomical, and biochemical data are reviewed elsewhere.[24,25,36]

A seven-point scale for clinical rating of novelty seeking is summarized in Table 2. An interview and a self-report questionnaire for obtaining ratings are described later. Average is rated as 0 with mild (1), moderate (2), and extreme (3) deviations from the mean specified in both directions. These values are meant to approximate standard scores rounded to the nearest integer between +3 and −3. In other words, in a general population the highest 1% are expected to have scores of +3, the next highest 6% have moderate ratings of +2, another 24% have mildly elevated ratings of +1, and the middle 38% have average ratings of 0.

Individuals who are higher than average in harm avoidance and average on the other two dimensions are characterized as cautious, tense, apprehensive, fearful, inhibited, shy, easily fatigable, and apprehensive worriers. Those who are lower than average in harm avoidance and average on the other two dimensions are confident, relaxed, optimistic, carefree, uninhibited, outgoing, and energetic. A seven-point scale for clinical ratings of harm avoidance is summarized in Table 3.

These harm-avoidant traits are thought to reflect variation in the brain's "punishment," or behavioral inhibition system, which includes the septohippocampal system, serotonergic projections from the raphe nuclei in the brain stem, and cholinergic projections to the frontal neocortex from the ventral tegmental area and the basal nucleus of Meynert.[24] Ascending serotonergic neurons from the raphe nuclei project to the limbic system, including the septum and hippocampus, as well as to the prefrontal cortex. Gray[16,17] and Warburton[37] have suggested that the septohippocampal system functions as a comparator, checking predicted against actual events, and then interrupting behavior when the unexpected is encountered. Ascending serotonergic projections from the dorsal raphe nuclei to the substantia nigra inhibit nigrostriatal dopaminergic neurons and are essential for conditioned inhibition of activity by signals of punishment and frustrative nonreward.[38] In response to novel stimuli that are not paired with rewards or relief of punishment, cholinergic projections from the ventral tegmental area and the basal nucleus of the amygdala excite the frontal cortex and stimulate release of stress hormones such as corticotropin and cortisol.[37] In turn, frontostriatal projections reduce exploratory activity by inhibiting dopaminergic neurons in the caudate nucleus.[35]

Benzodiazepines and other antianxiety drugs do *not* block the acquisition of aversive responses by "classic" conditioning, in which a neutral stimulus is learned to predict an aversive stimulus.[16,39] However, antianxiety drugs block the expression of behavioral inhibition acquired by "operant" or "instrumental" conditioning, in which a particular behavioral response is learned to predict punishment or omission of rewards.[16,39] Furthermore, antianxiety drugs block the increase in electrodermal activity that occurs in anticipation of both classically and operantly conditioned aversive stimuli.[30] Benzodiazepines disinhibit avoidance conditioning by γ-aminobutyric acid–ergic inhibition of serotonergic neurons originating in the dorsal raphe nuclei.[40,41] Other neuropharmacologic, neuroanatomical, and biochemical data are reviewed elsewhere.[34,36]

Individuals who are higher than average in reward dependence and average on the other two dimensions are clinically characterized as eager to help and please others, persistent, industrious, warmly sympathetic, sentimental, and sensitive to social cues and personal succor but able to

Table 3.—Summary of Harm-Avoidance Scale

+3	*Severely High:* Nearly always fearful and anticipating harm even with reassurance and supportive circumstances; extremely pessimistic and inhibited by unfamiliar situations, strangers, and minor risks; highly fatigable so that activities must be limited to minimize effort required
+2	*Moderately High:* Noticeably inhibited and tense even under ordinary circumstances; frequent worrying far in advance about minor difficulties; moderately pessimistic and negativistic; easily tired so that extra rest and relaxation is needed on most days; slow to recuperate from physical exertion, emotional stress, or minor illness
+1	*Mildly High:* Usually worried that things will not go well even under ordinary circumstances; inhibited and tense unless there is high probability of friendly support; mildly fatigable with need for occasional extra periods of rest and relaxation
0	*Average:* Transient worries and tension in proportion to objective risks; no prolonged rumination; avoids risk of serious personal injury nearly always but willing to take calculated moderate risks occasionally; average energy level and recuperative/adaptive ability
−1	*Mildly Low:* Uninhibited and calm under ordinary circumstances with some inhibition and/or tension in face of serious harm or personal injury that is highly probable; occasional worry in advance about minor problems; somewhat more energetic and rapidly recuperative/adaptive than average
−2	*Moderately Low:* Uninhibited and carefree unless others call attention to dangers that are severe and nearly certain; confident and optimistic with rare anticipatory worries about severe risks but not minor problems; moderately high energy level and rapid recuperative/adaptive ability
−3	*Severely Low:* Highly uninhibited, calm, and carefree even when confronted with unfamiliar situations, strangers, or imminent risk of personal injury; confident and optimistic with no worry in advance of difficulties; minimal reluctance to risk personal injury; highly energetic with rapid recuperative ability following exertion and rapid adaptation to changes in routine

delay gratification with the expectation of eventually being rewarded. In contrast, those who are lower than average in reward dependence are socially detached, emotionally cool, practical, tough-minded, and emotionally independent in what they choose to do. Individuals who are low in reward dependence do respond to practical rewards such as money, but are insensitive to verbal signals of social reinforcement and quickly become indifferent and terminate activities or relations that are no longer gratifying. In contrast, highly reward-dependent individuals are highly sensitive to praise and social cues and also persist in their craving for gratification in the same or similar ways long after reinforcement by actual rewards is withdrawn because of reinforcement by secondary signals of approval. A seven-point scale for clinical ratings of reward dependence is summarized in Table 4.

These reward-dependent traits are thought to reflect variation in a third major brain system that is postulated to facilitate acquisition of conditioned signals of reward or relief from punishment, and thereby also to increase resistance to extinction of previously rewarded behavior.[24] Norepinephrine appears to be the major neuromodulator for this system, and may play a critical role in the learning and memory of new paired associations.[42] The major ascending noradrenergic pathways arise from the locus ceruleus in the pons and project to the hypothalamus and limbic structures, including the amygdala, septum, and hippocampal formation, and then branch throughout the entire neocortex.[43] The number of noradrenergic neurons is small, but they project to nearly every brain region with elaborately branched axons that have highly collaterized networks of fine preterminal fibers with many varicosities. These varicosities are loaded with synaptic vesicles that store norepinephrine, but only about 5% form actual synapses in the cerebral cortex. The remainder secrete norepinephrine into the surrounding neuropil to modulate the general level or "tone" of neuronal activity or response to other inputs.[44] More specifically, stimulation of the locus or its dorsal bundle, or direct application of norepinephrine, has two effects on a target area: the spontaneous firing rate of affected neurons is inhibited, but their response to other afferents is increased.[45] Thus, the "signal to noise ratio" is increased, allowing relevant or important stimuli to stand out from irrelevant stimuli.

Extensive studies of a variety of conditioning and learning paradigms in human and other mammals suggest that the effects of noradrenergic deficits are rather specific. In rodents, long-term partial reduction of norepinephrine release in the forebrain by lesions of the locus ceruleus or its dorsal bundle leads to increased resistance to extinction of previously rewarded behavior[16,46] and to improved responses to *conditioned* signals of relief of punishment in two-way active avoidance tasks.[16] Mason and Iversen[46] have reported that in rodents, resistance to extinction is increased if the lesion is made before acquisition of the rewarded response but not if it is made after the response is acquired. Reduced noradrenergic activity in the dorsal bundle or lesions of the locus ceruleus do *not* consistently impair the initial acquisition of behavioral responses to *unconditioned* rewards or relief from punishment in animals.[16] In humans, short-term reduction of norepinephrine release by acute infusion of the α_2-presynaptic agonist clonidine selectively impairs paired-associate learning, particularly the acquisition of novel associations.[42] This deficit in learning new associations is similar to the circumscribed learning deficit characteristic of patients with destructive lesions of the locus ceruleus, as occurs in many subjects with Korsakoff's amnestic syndrome.[47,48] Arginine vasopressin and norepinephrine metabolite levels are reduced in the cerebrospinal fluid of patients with such lesions.[49] Vasopressin enhances memory when injected immediately after learning trials, but this enhancement is dependent on an intact dorsal noradrenergic bundle.[50,51]

These findings in humans indicate that norepinephrine release leads to enhancement of the formation of conditioned associations in general. However, studies of rodents indicate a greater or more consistent effect of the noradrenergic system on the formation of conditioned signals of reward or relief of punishment, rather than conditioned signals of punishment or frustrative nonreward.[16] This difference may be attributable to the inhibition of the locus ceruleus by serotonergic activity at the onset of punishment or omission of expected rewards.[37,52] Consequently, under natural conditions the enhancement of paired-associate learning by norepinephrine release will occur mainly at the onset of rewards or the offset of punishment.

Verbal indications of approval (eg, "That's good") may be regarded as conditioned signals of reward. There are individual differences in responsiveness to such signals, and verbal conditioning of social reinforcement is impaired in humans who are low in reward dependence, including both primary psychopaths[53] and obstinate obsessionals.[54] Individuals with reduced basal activity in the dorsal noradrenergic bundle (and, hence, greater sensitivity to norepinephrine) are expected to respond to signals of social sentiment and to persist in reward-seeking behavior even when frustrated, whereas those with higher basal noradrenergic activity (and, hence, lower sensitivity to norepinephrine) are more practical and quickly stop activity that is no longer gratifying. In this way, the resistance to extinction of intermittently rewarded behavior may determine individual differences in perseverance and responsiveness to verbal conditioning.

The behavioral maintenance and activation systems act in concert so that the dopaminergic activation system influences approach and initial acquisition of rewarded behavior and the noradrenergic maintenance system influences the rate of extinction of previously rewarded behavior. In contrast, the behavioral maintenance system functions in counterbalance with the behavioral inhibition system, since

Table 4.—Summary of Reward Dependence Scale

+3	*Severely High:* Highly dependent on emotional supports and intimacy with others; highly sensitive to social cues and responsive to social pressure; highly sentimental, crying very easily; industrious, ambitious overachiever who pushes self to exhaustion; extremely sensitive to rejection from even minor slights, leading to reward-seeking behaviors such as overeating; highly persistent in craving for gratification even when frustrated in attempts to obtain expected recognition or benefits
+2	*Moderately High:* Close intimate relations are desired nearly always; cries easily in sentimental situations; pushes self to maximal efforts but not exhaustion; sensitive to major rejection always and minor slights usually, but perseveres in activities long after they are no longer gratifying or rewarded
+1	*Mildly High:* More warm and emotionally open than average, preferring intimacy over privacy; usually conforms to social pressure because of a desire to be liked and to please; usually sympathetic and helpful; usually industrious and mildly ambitious; sensitive to major rejections but not minor slights
0	*Average:* Average emotional warmth and social attachment; average ambition, industriousness, and sensitivity to rejection or frustrative nonreward
−1	*Mildly Low:* Maintains regular social contacts but with minimal intimacy; usually resists social pressures but occasionally acts based on sympathetic sentiment; occasionally responds to encouragement to work hard to please others and to attain rewards; only occasional and transient upset in response to rejection or frustration
−2	*Moderately Low:* Seldom confides personal feelings in others, occasionally wants social support and acts based on sympathetic sentiment; works to please others seldom and then only due to practical benefits; quickly stops activities and relations that are no longer gratifying
−3	*Severely Low:* Socially detached, never sharing intimate feelings with others, content to be alone; independent nonconformist, practical and self-determined; minimal ambition and motivation to please others; cynical, alienated, and insensitive to social cues and pressures; does only what is immediately gratifying, stopping other activities as soon as they cease to be rewarding

Fig 1.—Interaction of two personality dimensions, novelty seeking and harm avoidance.

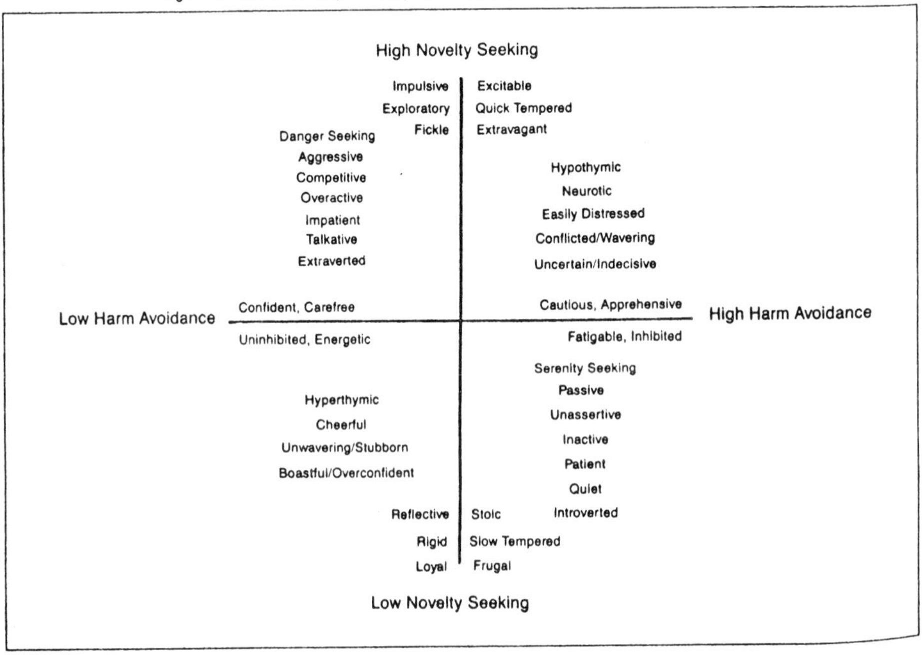

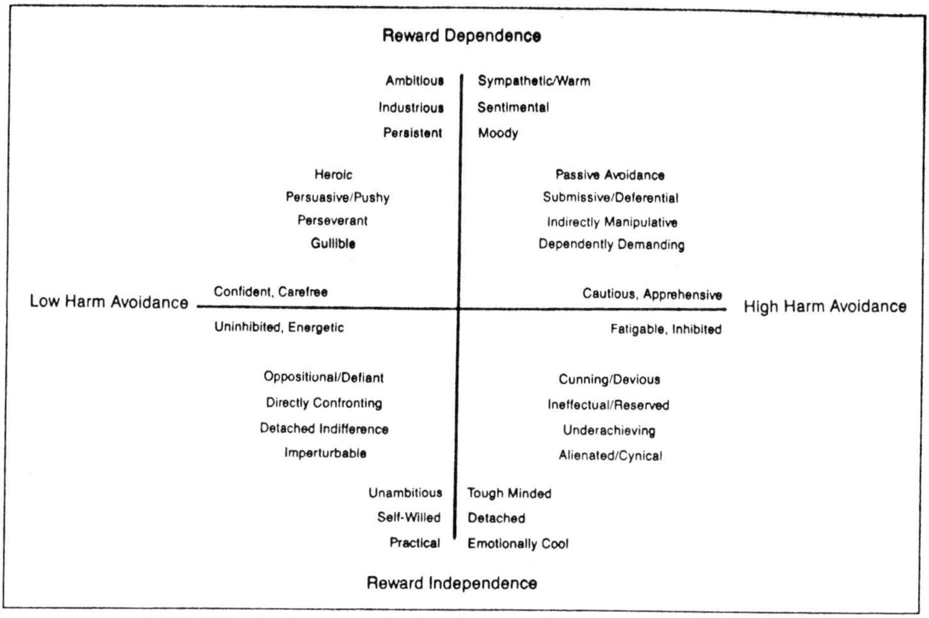

Fig 2.—Interaction of two personality dimensions, reward dependence and harm avoidance.

Fig 3.—Interaction of two personality dimensions, novelty seeking and reward dependence.

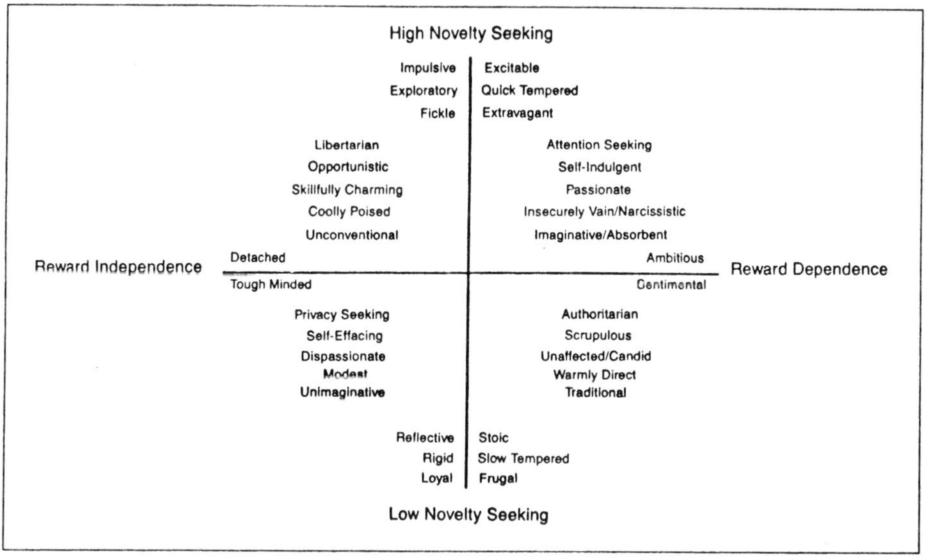

each has opposite effects on the rate of extinction in response to punishment or frustrative nonreward. For example, increased serotonergic activity at the onset of punishment leads to inhibition of noradrenergic neurons in the locus ceruleus.[52] Likewise, the behavioral activation system functions in counterbalance with the behavioral inhibition system, since each has opposite effects on approach to unfamiliar or uncertain situations and other novel stimuli, and serotonergic neurons inhibit nigrostriatal dopaminergic neurons.

The biogenetic predisposition to the stimulus-response characteristics of each of these three systems appears to be independently set in each individual, but the systems are functionally interconnected. As a result of these interconnections, the systems interact to give rise to integrated patterns of differential responses to punishment, reward, and novelty. These functional interactions give rise to the wide variation in personal response characteristics that are observed in social behavior in different situations. In other words, the same response level on one dimension is expressed in different ways depending on the response level on the other dimensions.

The interactions of the three personality dimensions are summarized in Figs 1 through 3. For example, in Fig 1 an individual who is high in novelty seeking will usually show behavior that is impulsive, danger seeking, and aggressive if he is also low in harm avoidance, whereas he will usually show conflicted or neurotic behavior, with inhibition or worrisome "second thoughts" checking his initial impulses, if he is also high in harm avoidance. On the other hand, an individual who is low in harm avoidance will usually be cheerful, boastful, and overconfident if he is also low in novelty seeking. Since average values are most frequent, the description of behavior associated with each dimension will be dominated by the characteristics mentioned earlier, but at least one of these combinations of extreme values are expected to occur about as often as deviations on only one dimension.

While the same response level may be expressed in different ways depending on other traits, the same adjective may be used to describe different combinations of personality traits.[56] For example, the word "sociable" may be used to describe different response patterns. An individual may be described as sociable if he is readily engaged when meeting new people (as someone who is high in novelty seeking and average on other dimensions), if he is confident and uninhibited with strangers (as someone who is low in harm avoidance and average on other dimensions), or if he is warm and socially sympathetic (as someone who is high in reward dependence and average on the other dimensions). As a result, the rating of each underlying dimension from observed or self-reported behavior requires attention to the interaction of the dimensions with one another. Description and rating is a problem of pattern recognition that must take into account a wide range of responses in a variety of situations.

EMPIRICAL TESTS OF THE PROPOSED STRUCTURAL MODEL

Given my concern about the ambiguity of descriptive terms, I developed a set of specific self-report questions based on the theoretical model. To quantify behavioral variation on each dimension separately, questions were specified that were theoretically expected to involve minimal interaction among the dimensions. In practice, this meant that questions were chosen to evaluate the behaviors that were thought to be characteristic of individuals deviant on one dimension and average on the others. Questions that could be answered "true" or "false" were written to distinguish different degrees of deviation from the mean, as summarized in Tables 2 through 4. For example, two questions assessing the rapid, intuitive decision-making characteristic of novelty seekers are "I prefer to make decisions only after considerable thought" (true in individuals who are below the mean on novelty seeking, so false indicates novelty seeking), and "I often act on hunches, momentary whims, or my intuition without making a detailed analysis of facts" (true in individuals who are above the mean on novelty seeking, so true indicates novelty seeking). An 80-item inventory, called the *Tridimensional Personality Questionnaire* (TPQ), was developed and administered to a group of 101 sophomore medical students along with several other tests over a one-month period. The results of these tests will be described in detail elsewhere. Briefly, the students had average means and variances on the Eysenck extraversion and neuroticism scales, but had low means and restricted variances in psychoticism or tough mindedness.[8] On Tellegen's *Multidimensional Personality Questionnaire* (MPQ),[9] they had high mean and restricted variance on achievement, and they had a low mean and restricted variance on alienation.

Table 5.—Tridimensional Personality Questionnaire Scale Means, SDs, and Reliabilities in 101 Medical Students

Scale	No. of Items	Mean Score	SD	Internal Consistency, α	Test-Retest Reliability*
Harm avoidance	26	8.3	4.9	.84	.92
Novelty seeking	28	12.9	4.6	.77	.85
Reward dependence	26	17.4	3.6	.65	.87

*Pearson correlations on tests given one week apart.

Table 6.—Intercorrelations Among the Tridimensional Personality Questionnaire Scales in Medical Students*

Scale	Harm Avoidance (*P*)	Novelty Seeking (*P*)	Reward Dependence (*P*)
Harm avoidance	...	−.14 (.14)	+.16 (.11)
Novelty seeking	−.29 (.01)	...	+.04 (.68)
Reward dependence	+.19 (.06)	+.02 (.82)	...

*Product-moment correlations are given at the first test (N = 101) above the diagonal and at retest (N = 90) below the diagonal.

The distribution of scores was approximately trivariate normal and had reliabilities comparable with those of commonly used tests (Table 5). The intercorrelations among scales were negligible or weak (Table 6). The weak correlations observed were consistent with those expected theoretically: novelty seeking is inhibited by harm avoidance, so these behavioral scales have a weak negative correlation, whereas high reward dependence leads to repeated exposure to frustrative nonreward, thus predisposing weakly to sensitization,[34] so there is a weak positive correlation between reward-dependent and harm-avoidant behavior.

Tellegen's MPQ measures 11 primary phenotypic factors, many of which were expected to involve substantial interactions among the underlying dimensions proposed herein. The observed pattern of relations (Table 7) agreed remarkably well with the expected patterns depicted in Figs 1 through 3. Feelings of well-being (happy, optimistic) were associated with low harm avoidance, particularly when novelty seeking was not high, as shown in Fig 1. In contrast, the combination of low harm avoidance and high novelty seeking was associated with social potency (assertiveness) and impulsiveness (lack of control), as predicted in Fig 1. On the MPQ, danger seeking was also associated largely with low harm-avoidance alone. High resistance to extinction of rewarded behavior, indicated by the combination of high reward dependence and low harm avoidance, was associated with achievement (perseverance, hard work) and social closeness (warm sociability), as predicted in Fig 2. Traditionalism (authoritarian, conventional) is

Table 7.—Partial Regressions of MPQ Primary Scales on TPQ Scales (Decimals Omitted)*

	Partial Regression Weights on TPQ			Multiple R^2		
MPQ Scales	Harm Avoidance	Novelty Seeking	Reward Dependence	TPQ	EPQ	MPQ
Well-being	−66†	−08	02	48	53	68
Social potency	−50†	29‡	05	25	38	64
Achievement	−25†	−14	25‡	14	03	33
Social closeness	−28†	−03	66†	29	18	18
Stress reaction	78†	57†	35‡	54	74	67
Alienation	04	02	08	02	07	44
Aggression	04	18‡	−12	07	14	48
Impulsiveness	−25†	70†	−01	52	18	54
Danger seeking	−30‡	08	−23	11	08	45
Traditionalism	00	−29‡	16	08	07	43
Absorption	−12	49†	20	16	19	46

*MPQ indicates Multidimensional Personality Questionnaire; TPQ, Tridimensional Personality Questionnaire; and EPQ, Eysenck Personality Questionnaire.
†$P<.01$.
‡$P<.05$.

Table 8.—Basic Stimulus-Response Characteristics of Traditional Personality Categories

Personality Disorder	Novelty Seeking	Harm Avoidance	Reward Dependence
Antisocial	High	Low	Low
Histrionic	High	Low	High
Passive-aggressive	High	High	High
Explosive	High	High	Low
Obsessional	Low	High	Low
Schizoid	Low	Low	Low
Cyclothymic	Low	Low	High
Passive-dependent	Low	High	High

associated with low novelty seeking, particularly when combined with high reward dependence, as predicted in Fig 3. Absorbency was developed to understand hypnotic susceptibility and is associated with high novelty seeking, especially in combination with high reward dependence, as predicted in Fig 3. The tendency to be nervous and easily distressed (stress reaction) was associated with high scores on all three dimensions of the TPQ, as predicted.[24] Alienation was expected to be low in individuals who are high in reward dependence and low in harm avoidance (Fig 2); this is consistent with the low mean and restricted variance in this medical student sample, but the restricted variance makes detailed interpretation impossible here.

The amount of variability in these behaviors that is explained by the TPQ is similar to that explained by the Eysenck Personality Questionnaire overall (Table 7). However, the proportion of variability explained (multiple R^2) by the TPQ or the Eysenck questionnaire differs from scale to scale, much as they do when the three higher order factor scales of the MPQ are used to predict the values of their individual components (Table 7).

These initial empirical results support the basic structural model of personality proposed herein, and indicate that reliable and clinically relevant assessments can be made with brief self-report instruments.

DIAGNOSIS OF PERSONALITY VARIANTS

To describe and diagnose personality variants systematically, a clinical interview schedule was also developed. This schedule, called the Tridimensional Interview of Personality Style (TIPS), includes seven questions about the response patterns or traits that are characteristic of each of the three basic dimensions and four questions for each of the six pairwise combinations shown in Figs 1 through 3. Each question has a hierarchy of six additional probes specified to allow rating on a seven-point scale. These probes are an expanded set of those used in the self-report TPQ. Each trait is rated for two periods (the past year and the midteens) to assess age at onset and developmental change. In addition, advantages and/or problems associated with each trait are evaluated separately so that response style is not confounded with adaptive success or impairment.

Altogether, the TIPS yields ratings of impairment, inflexibility, or distress in nine clusters of traits that, in varying combinations, make up the criteria for personality disorders. The personality disorders defined in this way include extreme variants on each of the three dimensions, extreme variants on two dimensions, and extreme variants on only one dimension. I will first describe the items used to assess the three basic dimensions of response to novel, aversive, and rewarding stimuli. Next I will describe the six second-order clusters of traits arising from the combination of deviations on two dimensions. Finally, I will describe the eight third-order clusters of traits arising from the combination of deviations on all three dimensions.

ASSESSMENT OF BASIC STIMULUS-RESPONSE CHARACTERISTICS

The basic patterns of response to novelty, punishment, and reward are assessed by variation in the three dimensions of novelty seeking, harm avoidance, and reward dependence briefly described above. The eight possible combinations of deviations on these three dimensions correspond closely to traditional descriptions of personality disorders that have been most consistently presented. This correspondence is summarized in Table 8 to help guide the reader to what follows, but the description of the interrelationship between basic response characteristics and traditional personality categories will be developed in stages in the following sections.

The first stage of this description is a summary of traits characterizing each of the three basic response dimensions. In the TIPS, each dimension is assessed by seven bipolar traits. In other words, each trait varies from high to low. In the following summaries, the two poles of each trait are separately described.

High vs Low Novelty Seeking

High novelty seeking is part of the characteristics of the antisocial, histrionic, passive-aggressive, and explosive personality disorders. Low novelty seeking is part of the characteristics of the obsessional, passive-dependent, cyclothymic, and schizoid personalities. Either extreme variant can also occur alone.

1. Frequent exploratory thrill-seeking and intolerance of familiar routine *vs* resistance to changes in familiar routine.
2. Disorderly or unconventional rule breaking *vs* highly regimented discipline and order.
3. Excitable and quick tempered *vs* stoical and slow tempered.
4. Fickle (attachments quickly formed and dissolved) *vs* loyal (attachments slowly formed and dissolved regardless of advantages or disadvantages).
5. Often acts immediately on momentary whims or quickly formed intuitive impressions or is distractible and impersistent *vs* often acts too slowly and only after considerable thought, methodical reflection, and planning with a preoccupation with organizational details.
6. Frequent dramatization and preference for talking over listening *vs* preference for listening over talking and restricted ability at role playing or dramatization.
7. Extravagant spending so has difficulty saving or delaying gratification *vs* frugal saving and budgeting so has difficulty enjoying buying things for oneself.

High vs Low Harm Avoidance

High harm avoidance is part of the characteristics of obsessional, passive-dependent, passive-aggressive, and explosive personality

Table 9.—Clusters of Personality Traits Associated With Various Combinations of Basic Stimulus-Response Characteristics

Personality Cluster	Basic Stimulus-Response Characteristics: Novelty Seeking	Harm Avoidance	Reward Dependence
Impulsive	High	Low	...
vs			
Rigid	Low	High	...
Hyperthymic	Low	Low	...
vs			
Hypothymic	High	High	...
Scrupulous	Low	...	High
vs			
Opportunistic	High	...	Low
Narcissistic	High	...	High
vs			
Self-effacing	Low	...	Low
Passive-avoidant	...	High	High
vs			
Oppositional	...	Low	Low
Gullible	...	Low	High
vs			
Alienated	...	High	Low

disorders. Low harm avoidance is part of the characteristics of antisocial, histrionic, schizoid, and cyclothymic personalities. Either variant can also occur alone.

1. Frequent anticipatory worrying and inhibitory apprehension requiring reassurance even under ordinary circumstances *vs* carefree lack of inhibition even when the situation calls for caution.
2. Tension and worry when dealing with unfamiliar tasks or situations *vs* overconfident and lacking in appropriate caution when dealing with unfamiliar tasks.
3. Shyness (inhibited withdrawal from strangers that limits social activity or enjoyment) *vs* carefree lack of inhibition around strangers.
4. Preference for quiet inactivity because of overstimulation by excitement or activities involving risk of physical injury *vs* preference for stimulation by activities with risk of physical injury rather than quiet inactivity.
5. Pessimistic, with frequent negative expectations *vs* optimistic, with frequent positive expectations.
6. Easy fatigability that limits physical exertion *vs* high energy level with quick recovery from exertion.
7. Slow adaptation to change and slow recovery from minor illness, stress, or changes in familiar routines *vs* rapid adaptation and recovery from minor illness, stress, or changes in familiar routines.

High vs Low Reward Dependence

High reward dependence is part of the characteristics of passive-dependent, cyclothymic, histrionic, and passive-aggressive personalities. Low reward dependence is part of the characteristics of antisocial, explosive, obsessional, and schizoid personalities. Either variant can occur alone.

1. Social vulnerability associated with ready tendency to openly reveal personal intimacies *vs* social detachment with tendency to remain aloof and distant without revealing personal intimacies.
2. Need for praise and approval of others with excessive tendency to conform to peer pressures *vs* independent nonconformist with resistance to peer pressures.
3. Highly sympathetic and easily exploited by sentimental appeals *vs* practical tough-minded detachment from social sentiment.
4. Intensely driven, frequently pushing self to point of exhaustion *vs* lack of industry and initiative, frequently quitting before maximal effort has been expended.
5. Marked persistence in previously rewarded behavior despite frustration of efforts *vs* rapid termination of activities that are not immediately gratifying with feelings of indifference or lack of persistent ambition for delayed rewards.
6. Marked sensitivity to social cues of approval or rejection, loss, and frustrative nonreward with persistent craving for gratification in similar ways *vs* insensitivity to social cues of approval or rejection, loss, and frustrative nonreward with rapid development of indifference to relationships that become ungratifying.
7. Excessive reward-seeking behavior in response to rejection or frustration (such as overeating, overworking, increased sexual activity, or unnecessary buying) *vs* cynical social alienation and preference to be alone.

Six Second-Order Clusters of Personality Traits

Deviations on two basic dimensions in the same individual give rise to integrated patterns of basic responses that are associated with distinctive behavioral clusters. The possible combinations of deviations on pairs of dimensions are summarized in Table 9. Descriptions of the associated clusters of personality traits are summarized in the following sections, which are summaries of items specified in the TIPS. As before, each trait is bipolar, and each pole is separately described.

Impulsive-Aggressive vs Rigid-Patient

The impulsive-aggressive pole results from high novelty seeking and low harm avoidance, as in histrionic and antisocial personalities. The rigid-patient pole results from low novelty seeking and high harm avoidance, as in passive-dependent and obsessional personalities. The impulsive-aggressive pole corresponds to broad concepts of antisociality, whereas the rigid-patient pole corresponds to broad concepts of obsessionality. Each variant can also occur alone.

1. Danger-seeking behavior or impulsive acts involving high risk of personal injury *vs* safety- and serenity-seeking behavior or preoccupation with maintaining order and safety by means of attention to rules and organizational details.
2. Highly aggressive and competitive behavior, including offensive initiation of violence, bullying, or forceful domination of others *vs* highly passive and unassertive behavior and inability to tolerate conflict or violence.
3. Highly impatient and easily annoyed by short delays or need for even brief periods of quiet inactivity either at work or at leisure *vs* highly patient and able to wait in contented silence and inactivity for prolonged periods.
4. Reckless and quick decisions are often made without regard to later consequences *vs* decision making is avoided, postponed, or deferred to others as a result of concern about making mistakes and/or rigid preoccupation with trivial details.

Hyperthymic vs Hypothymic

The hyperthymic pole results from low novelty seeking and harm avoidance, as in cyclothymic and schizoid disorders. The hypothymic pole results from high novelty seeking and harm avoidance, as in passive-aggressive and explosive disorders. Each variant can also occur alone.

1. Hyperthymia or cheerful overoptimism with a tendency to underestimate the need for caution and alarm *vs* hypothymia or easily distressed and pessimistic with a tendency to overestimate the need for alarm and caution.
2. Unwavering and stubbornly methodical regardless of danger *vs* frequent conflicted wavering or indecision due to worrisome "second thoughts."
3. Boastful or bragging overconfidence even in unfamiliar situations for which the individual is unprepared or untrained *vs* low self-confidence and pessimistic self-doubt even in situations for which the individual is well prepared.
4. Expresses disagreement openly and assertatively but slow to become angry *vs* quickly becomes angry but often keeps anger partially bottled up because of fear to express anger fully and openly.

Scrupulous-Authoritarian vs Opportunistic-Libertarian

The scrupulous-authoritarian pole results from the combination of low novelty seeking and high reward dependence, and is part of the characteristics of cyclothymic and passive-dependent personalities. The opportunistic-libertarian pole results from the combi-

Table 10.—Personality Clusters Associated With Traditional Categories

Personality Disorder	Second-Order Personality Clusters: Impulsive vs Rigid	Hyperthymic vs Hypothymic	Scrupulous vs Opportunistic	Narcissistic vs Self-Effacing	Passive-Avoidant vs Oppositional	Gullible vs Alienated
Antisocial	Impulsive	. . .	Opportunistic	. . .	Oppositional	. . .
Histrionic	Impulsive	. . .	. . .	Narcissistic	. . .	Gullible
Passive-aggressive	. . .	Hypothymic	. . .	Narcissistic	Passive-avoidant	. . .
Explosive	. . .	Hypothymic	Opportunistic	. . .	. . .	Alienated
Obsessional	Rigid	. . .	. . .	Self-effacing	. . .	Alienated
Schizoid	. . .	Hyperthymic	. . .	Self-effacing	Oppositional	. . .
Cyclothymic	. . .	Hyperthymic	Scrupulous	. . .	. . .	Gullible
Passive-dependent	Rigid	. . .	Scrupulous	. . .	Passive-avoidant	. . .

nation of high novelty seeking and low reward dependence and is part of the characteristics of antisocial and explosive personalities. Each variant can also occur alone.

1. Authoritarian insistence on traditional values and principles *vs* libertarian demand for autonomy regardless of disruptive social consequences.
2. Scrupulous and overly conscientious *vs* opportunistic or acting for own advantage without regard to traditional principles or consequences.
3. Highly earnest with unaffected candor and lack of social artifice *vs* pathologic lying or enjoyment in charming or misleading others for its own sake without regard for truth or personal advantage.
4. Readily able to delay gratification, work hard, and sacrifice to achieve postponed benefits *vs* seldom able to delay gratification, work hard, and sacrifice for postponed benefits.

Narcissistic vs Self-effacing

The narcissistic pole results from high novelty seeking and high reward dependence; it is one of the characteristics of histrionic and passive-aggressive personalities. The self-effacing pole results from low novelty seeking and low reward dependence; it is one of the characteristics of obsessional and schizoid disorders. Each variant can also occur alone, as in narcissistic personality disorder.

1. Excessive attention seeking *vs* excessive privacy seeking.
2. Prodigal (reckless, wasteful, extravagant) self-indulgence *vs* excessive self-effacement or rigid insistence on sacrifice and sharing with others without regard to sentiment or self-interest.
3. Excessively demonstrative and affectionate *vs* restricted ability to express warm feelings.
4. Preoccupation and frequent deep absorbency in fantasy and imagined experiences, possibly including trancelike states, mystical or paranormal experiences, other dissociative states or identity disturbances *vs* restricted ability to be deeply involved in fantasy, imagined experiences, art, or music, or to appreciate nature.

Passive-Avoidant vs Oppositional

The passive-avoidant pole results from high reward dependence and harm avoidance, as in passive-aggressive and passive-dependent personalities. The oppositional pole results from low reward dependence and harm avoidance, as in antisocial and schizoid disorders. Either variant can also occur alone.

1. Highly submissive, deferential, and ingratiating *vs* highly oppositional, defiant, and argumentative.
2. Indirectly manipulative using indirect methods of resistance such as pouting, postponing or delaying effective action, intentional forgetting, or inefficiency *vs* direct argument and confrontation in an offensive argumentative way.
3. Lonely and socially avoidant out of fear of rejection *vs* content and socially indifferent when isolated or alone.
4. Frequent fear of failure with ambivalence or conflicting feelings about the uncertain benefit of hard work vs the social shame and disapproval of giving up *vs* confident indifference to issues about long-term success, doing whatever is independently considered desirable and practical and no more or less.

Gullible-Heroic vs Alienated-Cowardly

The gullible-heroic pole results from high reward dependence and low harm avoidance, as in histrionic and cyclothymic personalities. The alienated-cowardly pole results from low reward dependence and high harm avoidance, as in obsessional and explosive personalities. Individuals who are alienated view the world warily as an unfriendly place, but they are not suspicious in the sense of actively seeking confirmation of preconceived ideas that they are special targets for harm or abuse. Either variant can occur alone.

1. Excessive heroic risk-taking, such as risking own life to save total strangers, *vs* cowardly or self-protective behavior in which devious methods are used to avoid jeopardy to self, even to help family or friends.
2. Excessively gullible, trusting, and easily exploited by others, even after being cheated or rejected *vs* alienated and cynically dispassionate with the feeling that others cannot be trusted not to harm or take advantage.
3. Markedly pushy, domineering, or persuasive *vs* socially ineffectual, reserved, and unable to influence others.
4. Perseverance and fortitude or the ability to persist calmly and firmly in the face of difficulty, misfortune, danger, or opposition *vs* excessive tendency to give up quickly in response to difficulty, misfortune, danger, or opposition.

EIGHT THIRD-ORDER CLUSTERS OF PERSONALITY TRAITS

The clusters of traits described in the preceding section can be combined to define personality disorders that correspond closely to descriptions of traditional clinical categories (summarized in Table 10). This provides a simple and systematic way to decompose the overlap among various traditional categories. It provides a more accurate account of the pattern of overlap among categories than does separation into three nonoverlapping groups of categories, such as the "anxious," "erratic," and "odd" clusters suggested in *DSM-III*. It also provides a systematic method for defining diagnostic criteria for personality disorder. The suggested systematic method is to use ratings of both the basic response characteristics and the second-order characteristics described above. The second-order characteristics are not adequate when used alone because similar patterns can result when an individual is moderately high on two dimensions or when an individual is extremely high on one dimension and not too low on the other dimension. Accordingly, use of both the basic and the second-order characteristics minimizes overlap between categories and thereby increases the descriptive value and discriminative power of the diagnostic criteria. Criteria for antisocial personality disorder are presented here in detail as an example of this approach, and others are easily elaborated from Tables 8 through 10 based on this example.

Antisocial Personality Disorder

The individual's current and long-term functioning is characterized by the combination of features described in **A** and **B** below.

This characteristic behavior is not limited to episodes of illness and causes significant impairment in social or occupational functioning, or prominent inflexibility in behavior and attitudes that restricts life-style, or subjective distress in particular situations leading to changes in life-style.

A. Impairment, restriction, or distress in each of the following three adaptive patterns.
   1. Difficulty from at least two of the seven traits characteristic of high novelty seeking.
   2. Difficulty from at least two of the seven traits characteristic of low reward dependence.
   3. Difficulty from at least two of the seven traits characteristic of low harm avoidance.
B. Impairment, restriction, or distress in each of the following three groups of adaptive patterns.
   1. The combination of high novelty seeking and low reward dependence, as evidenced by difficulty from at least one of the four traits in the opportunistic cluster.
   2. The combination of high novelty seeking and low harm avoidance, as evidenced by difficulty with at least one of the four traits in the impulsive aggressive cluster.
   3. The combination of low reward dependence and low harm avoidance, as evidenced by difficulty in at least one of the four traits in the oppositional cluster.

COMPARISON WITH TRADITIONAL DESCRIPTIONS

Antisocial Personality

Antisocial personality is defined here as the personality variant characterized by the basic response characteristics of high novelty seeking, low harm avoidance, and low reward dependence. This combination is associated with second-order traits of impulsive-aggressive, oppositional, and opportunistic behavior. This description is essentially identical to the traditional concept of the "primary psychopath" described by Cleckley[56] and others.[57]

Antisocial personality as defined here is a more narrow group than current *DSM-III* criteria based on the behavioral descriptions of Robins.[58] Robins' criteria correspond most closely to the second-order cluster of impulsive-aggressive traits, and do not distinguish well between individuals with high and low reward dependence. In other words, overt antisocial behavior is frequently seen in both antisocial personality and histrionic personality.[59-61] It is also occasionally seen in passive-aggressive or explosive personalities as defined here, particularly when the latter are complicated by abuse of alcohol and other drugs that reduce harm-avoidant behavior.[62]

Histrionic Personality

Histrionic personality is defined here in terms of the basic response patterns of high novelty seeking, low harm avoidance, and high reward dependence, which are associated with the second-order traits of being impulsive, gullible or emotionally vulnerable, and narcissistic. This corresponds closely to the *DSM-III* and ICD descriptions of histrionic or hysterical personality. These traditional groups are also characterized by their narcissistic traits (dramatic, attention-seeking, self-indulgent, vain), vulnerability and emotional dependence (dependent, seeking reassurance, warm, and charming), and impulsive-aggressive traits (craving for activity and excitement, angry outbursts, and suicidal behavior).[60]

The *DSM-III* description of borderline personality disorder also shows a similar combination of traits, with the emotional dependence and identity disturbance relatively more prominent than the narcissistic traits. It remains questionable whether borderline personality is really distinct from histrionic personality and other clinical groups.[63-65] Quantitative ratings along each basic response dimension would be useful to specify possible differences in the degree of deviation along one or more personality dimensions.

Passive-Aggressive Personality

Passive-aggressive personality is defined here in terms of the basic response characteristics of being high on all three dimensions, which is associated with second-order traits of being narcissistic, hypothymic, and passive-avoidant. The passive-avoidant trait cluster includes behavior that is deferential and ingratiating; use of indirect methods of manipulation such as pouting, postponing, forgetting, or inefficiency; social avoidance caused by fear of rejection; and frequent outbursts of verbal anger that are partially inhibited. Systematic description of patients with passive-aggressive personality shows that they are characterized by the full combination of traits described herein.[62] Passive-aggressive subjects were described as being high in novelty seeking ("impulsive," "sudden, unpremeditated action," "frequent outburts of verbal anger," "neglects responsibilities"), as well as high in both harm avoidance and reward dependence or passive-avoidant (no physical aggression but indirectly "manipulative"). As expected of individuals high in all three dimensions, they were easily distressed ("nervous") and moody ("gloomy, cries often"), without meeting full criteria for major depression.

The *DSM-III* currently defines the disorder only in terms of traits in the second-order passive-avoidant cluster. Consequently, this broad definition yields a highly heterogeneous group.[66] In particular, the broad *DSM-III* definition leads to overlap with passive-dependent personality, which differs in terms of novelty-seeking behavior. In contrast, the ICD does not distinguish sharply between explosive and passive-aggressive personalities, which differ in reward dependence.

Explosive Personality

Explosive personality is defined here in terms of the basic response characteristics of high novelty seeking, high harm avoidance, and low reward dependence, which are associated with the second-order traits of being alienated, opportunistic, and hypothymic. This corresponds to the ICD description of individuals who are characterized by their difficulty in inhibiting their outbursts of rage. These individuals are moody and experience frequent unfriendly feelings toward others. However, the ICD description does not sharply distinguish between hypothymic individuals who are socially involved or high in reward dependence (passive-aggressive) and those who are low in reward dependence or socially detached (explosive). To emphasize the utility of this distinction, I have elsewhere suggested that a more specific name for this group would be "explosive schizoid personality" to reduce heterogeneity in individuals who are called explosive or schizoid.[24] Furthermore, individuals who are low in reward dependence may be regarded as schizoid simply because they are emotionally cool and socially detached. However, this term either needs to be qualified by associated variation in other traits or should be used more restrictively.

Obsessional Personality

Obsessional personality is narrowly defined here in terms of the basic response characteristics of low novelty seeking, high harm avoidance, and low reward dependence, which is associated with the second-order traits of being rigid, alienated, and self-effacing. The second-order cluster of "rigid-patient" traits caused by the combination of low novelty seeking and high harm avoidance includes patient or unassertive behavior and preoccupation with maintaining order and safety by attention to rules and organizational details. The information-processing style associated with this second-order cluster corresponds closely to broad definitions of obsessional personality.[67,68] Here a further distinction is made between rigid individuals who are high in reward dependence (passive-dependent individuals who are also scrupulous and avoidant) and those who are low in reward dependence (obsessionals who are also self-effacing and alienated). This distinction corresponds closely to the traditional differentiation of "oral" or passive-dependent traits from "anal" or obsessional traits.[54,69] Traditional obsessional traits include being self-effacing (ie, unable to express warm emotions) and alienated (obstinate, self-willed, aloof), as well as rigid and orderly.[54] This traditional distinction is clinically important, because rigid individuals who are low in reward dependence are at greater risk for compulsive rituals than are those with passive-dependent personality.[70]

Obsessional and explosive personalities are alienated in that they cynically view the world as an unfriendly place for everyone in general, but they are not suspicious or paranoid in the sense of actively seeking confirmation of preconceived ideas that they have been singled out as special targets for harm or abuse. This distinction between paranoid and obsessional thinking has been well described by Shapiro.[71]

Schizoid Personality

Schizoid disorder is narrowly defined here in terms of being low on all three basic response dimensions, which is associated with the second-order traits of being oppositional, hyperthymic, and self-effacing. Schizoid individuals are highly resistant to social pressures to conform to the wishes of others because they are socially detached (low reward dependence), self-confident (low harm avoidance), and rigid (low novelty seeking). In addition, schizoid individuals are described as self-effacing because they prefer privacy and have a restricted ability to express warm feelings. This description corresponds closely with the definitions of schizoid personality in both the *DSM-III* and ICD, which require low reward dependence (emotional aloofness and absence of warm tender feelings for others, few friends, indifference to praise) and possibly low harm avoidance (indifference to criticism). However, despite the correspondence in concept, the *DSM-III* criteria do not strictly require anything but low reward dependence.

Accordingly, clinical groups identified with such a broad definition are highly heterogeneous.[63,64] Elsewhere, I have recommended that the term *imperturbable schizoid* be used to make clear the more restrictive definition suggested here.[24]

Cyclothymic Personality

Cyclothymic personality is defined here in terms of the basic response characteristics of low novelty seeking, low harm avoidance, and high reward dependence, which are associated with the second-order traits of being scrupulous and usually hyperthymic but gullible and vulnerable to frustration and rejection. Such individuals are warm and socially sympathetic but highly self-confident authoritarians. Although they are usually cheerful and optimistic, they are also moody or dysphoric in response to being cheated or rejected. This corresponds closely to classical descriptions of cyclothymic personality.[72,73]

However, current criteria in the *DSM-III* and ICD do not strictly distinguish between such a stable temperamental variant and mild endogenous mood disorder without the associated temperamental variant. In fact, in the *DSM-III*, cyclothymic disorder is listed only with affective disorders, not personality disorders. Reliable methods are available for identifying a broadly defined group of individuals with subclinical affective disorders.[74] However, it should be possible to distinguish between the personality disorder defined here and mild affective disorders without the associated personality variant. Individuals with the personality variant should have other personality traits that are not necessarily associated with mood disturbances. For example, cyclothymic personality should be associated with being frugal (low novelty seeking) and persistent (high reward dependence), with the dysphoric states being reactive to frustrative loss of expected rewards, rather than autonomous.

Passive-Dependent Personality

Passive-dependent personality is defined here in terms of the basic response characteristics of low novelty seeking, high harm avoidance, and high reward dependence, which is associated with second-order traits of being scrupulous, rigid, and passive-avoidant. Thus, the combination of high reward dependence and high harm avoidance is associated with such individuals being highly submissive, deferential, ingratiating, and highly sensitive to criticism, frustration, or punishment. This corresponds closely to descriptions of dependent personality in the *DSM-III* and ICD. However, obsessional traits of scrupulosity and rigidity are also prominent in this definition, but apparently are assigned to a separate category in the *DSM-III* and ICD. This full combination of traits corresponds closely to the triad of oral character traits.[54,69] The full triad has also been termed *anxious personality* based on the premorbid personalities of individuals with anxiety neurosis. Such individuals are described as having lifelong traits of being sensitive and socially sympathetic and overly conscientious or perfectionistic, and being neurotic introverts who are emotionally dependent and passively avoidant.[16,75,76] Passive-dependent personality is more strongly associated with anxiety neurosis (ie, anxiety states uncomplicated by compulsions), whereas obsessional personality is more strongly associated with obsessional neurosis,[70] so the distinction is clinically important.

THE CONCEPT OF AN INTERMEDIATE ADAPTIVE OPTIMUM

The close correspondence between traditional personality categories and those predicted as extreme variants of normal personality traits suggests that adaptive and maladaptive personality traits have the same underlying biogenetic structure. If the biogenetic structure for adaptive and maladaptive traits is the same, then what distinguishes normal from abnormal personalities? Consideration of the characteristics summarized in Figs 1 through 3 suggests that all extremes on these dimensions may be either an advantage or a disadvantage, depending on the situation. For example, an individual high in novelty seeking and low in harm avoidance may do well as an explorer or soldier, but would be ill-suited to work as an accountant, which requires careful and exact tabulation and long periods of tedious inactivity. The individuals who can adapt most flexibly to the full range of possible environmental situations are those who have average values on all three dimensions.

In other words, the adaptive optimum overall is expected to be for intermediate or nearly average values. Variants at either extreme (high or low) may excel in special situations but will be at a relative disadvantage overall. The expectation of an intermediate adaptive optimum is supported by the negative-feedback relationships described earlier between the systems for behavioral activation, maintenance, and inhibition. Also, an intermediate adaptive optimum is supported by the observed pattern of inheritance of adaptive personality traits in the general population.[19] The inheritance of such traits is consistent with additive polygenic and nonfamilial environmental effects, as expected when extreme high and extreme low values are equally disadvantageous overall. From an evolutionary perspective, balanced selection against either extreme results in the mean values and variability of the trait remaining stable across successive generations. Such balanced selection and intermediate adaptive optima may explain the persistence of extreme variants in the population.

Schizotypal and paranoid personality do not appear to be extreme variants of adaptive personality traits. Schizotypal and paranoid traits involve distorted or defective information processing regardless of the situation. This suggests that they would be more appropriately classified with schizophrenic and paranoid disorders.

IMPORTANCE OF SOCIAL LEARNING FOR SUCCESSFUL ADAPTATION

Polygenic contributions and nonfamilial environment, but not family environment or social learning, have been found to be substantial determinants of adaptive personality traits in random samples of the general population.[18,19] In contrast, adoption studies show that family environment and social learning do influence the risk of social impairment from personality disorders such as antisocial personality or histrionic personality. For example, the risk of antisocial behavior in adulthood is increased by low social status, lax or inconsistent discipline, instability of the early home environment, or being reared by a criminal parent, even when the biologic parent background is taken into account.[24,77-79] Similarly, social modeling of abnormal sick role behavior seems to increase the risk of disability from somatization in individuals with histrionic traits.[80] This suggests the hypothesis that personality disorders may be extreme variants of personality traits that are maladaptive because of inflexible responses to particular situations and additional influences from inconsistent or inappropriate social learning.

Elsewhere, I have reviewed evidence suggesting that aversive conditioning serves the maturation function of increasing harm-avoidant behavior and decreasing novelty seeking and reward dependence.[34] As a result of this sensitization or maturation process, individuals exposed to consistent aversive conditioning become more cautious, less exploratory and impulsive, and less sensitive to peer pressures. For examples, if a child who is high in novelty seeking and low in harm avoidance receives strict and consistent discipline, he is less likely to persist in extremely impulsive or aggressive behavior.

Conversely, a child who is high in harm avoidance and reward dependence is likely either to develop chronic anxiety from long-term sensitization in an aversive or hostile situation in which safety and danger cannot be reliably distinguished or to develop reactive depression from frustration when there is loss of control over rewards and gratification.[34] Such a child is most likely to avoid disability when provided with "desensitization" in a reassuring and consistently supportive environment. Modification of behavior in response to experience is an important adaptive mechanism, and may account for the importance of social opportunity and family environment in the risk of impairment from personality traits.

FREQUENCY OF PERSONALITY VARIANTS

The rating approach described here permits quantitative ratings of the three basic dimensions (Tables 1 through 3). It also permits identification of deviant clinical subgroups using explicit criteria. If the categorical approach is used, it is reasonable to question whether we need to identify variants besides the third-order clusters that correspond closely to the most consistently recognized traditional categories. For example, should we distinguish variants such as the second-order narcissistic, or avoidant, clusters? Some of these second-order clusters do appear in the *DSM-III* but others do not. Omission of some probably results from cultural biases and prior lack of a systematic method for defining categories.

The expected frequency of these second-order clusters in the general population suggests that they should be included in a comprehensive system. If the theoretical assumption of three independent normal distributions is granted, some simple calculations permit a guess about what we might expect for the frequency of different variants. Specifically, if we designate the proportion of the population with nearly average values on each one of the dimensions as p and the remainder on each one of the dimensions as q, then the frequency of being average on all three dimensions is p^3, the frequency of being nonaverage on only one dimension is $3p^2q$, the frequency of being nonaverage on exactly two dimensions is $3pq^2$, and the frequency of being nonaverage on all three dimensions is q^3. If about half of the population is nearly average ($p = q = ½$), then among every eight people in the general population we expect one to be nearly average on all three dimensions, three to be deviant (high or low) on one dimension, three to be deviant on two dimensions, and one to be deviant on all three. There are eight possible three-way combinations, and $6 \times 2 = 12$ possible two-way combinations. Therefore, about (⅛) × (⅛) or 2% of the population have each three-way combination, and (⅜) × (1/12) or 3% have each two-way combination. Such calculations should be considered at best as crude guesses because of the assumption of multivariate normality and the neglect of possible developmental modification from environmental contributions. Also, not all extreme variants will have enough disability to warrant a diagnosis of personality disorder. However, these calculations do suggest that the recognition of the second-order clusters is likely to be of as much practical importance as the recognition of the more traditional third-order clusters.

COMMENT

The close correspondence between extreme variants of normal personality traits and traditional personality disorders suggests that the underlying biogenetic structure of adaptive personality traits and maladaptive personality traits may be the same. The only observed exceptions are schizotypal and paranoid traits, which appear to be relatively discrete defects rather than adaptive variants. The relationship of personality variants to schizophrenic and affective psychoses has been discussed in more detail elsewhere.[24,36]

The degree of correspondence with traditional descriptions is surprising given the nonsystematic nature of the clinical approach to classification. Whether the general theory of personality described here is true, the hypothesis has heuristic value because it simplifies, systematizes, and quantifies the description and diagnosis of personality variants. The systematic method described here could be used to guide future revisions of the *DSM-III* and the ICD based on fundamental stimulus-response characteristics rather than culture bound traditions. This approach has a number of other implications for both clinical practice and research on personality and psychopathology.

Future Directions for Clinical Practice

The most basic implication of this approach is that quantitative ratings of personality dimensions can be used in conjunction with categorical labels. Use of the categorical labels is an efficient way of grouping individuals and of communicating descriptive information to others. However, quantitative ratings of the basic response characteristics may have fewer pejorative connotations and provide more information about the degree of response bias on each dimension. This encourages assessment of response patterns in individuals with successful adaptation as well as those with social impairments. Such assessment can be extremely helpful in patient management, whether that management is based on cognitive, behavioral, and/or pharmacologic approaches. In fact, the theoretical perspective described here is intended to integrate and unify psychosocial and neurobiologic approaches to patient assessment and treatment.

The TIPS was developed to aid clinicians in acquiring a thorough understanding of the concepts described herein. It can be adapted for clinical interviews by experienced clinicians, or it can be used by less experienced interviewers as a verbatim schedule or modified for use as a self-report instrument like the TPQ. Once the concepts are well understood, an experienced clinician can make assessments of a patient more efficiently in discussions that are individualized to the particular setting and subject. However, it is uncertain whether such individualized assessments are as reliable as standardized interviews or self-reports like the TPQ.

Future Directions for Research on Personality

The formulation of variation in personality in terms of basic patterns of response to conditioned signals of punishment, reward, and novelty should facilitate tests of the theory. First, further work applying the TIPS and TPQ in clinical and general population samples is needed to clarify the psychometric properties of the instruments and to develop versions for children. Clinical rating scales of personality in children have already been shown to have the same tridimensional structure demonstrated here in adults, to be moderately stable from the age of 10 years into adulthood, and to be predictive of adult behavioral adjustment.[81,82] Next, tests of the theoretical constructs can be carried out by correlating ratings of the personality dimensions with performance in both information-processing and conditioning paradigms designed to assess responses to novel, aversive, and rewarding stimuli. The neuroanatomic localization of such response functions could be assessed in part by positron-emission tomography or topographical analysis of event-related potentials of the electroencephalogram under a variety of stimulus conditions. Such studies should be carried out in populations that are successfully adapted, as well as impaired groups. Comparison of inheritance in both successfully adapted and impaired individuals could provide tests of the hypothesis that social learning and family environment are important determinants of the risk of psychopathology or functional impairment.

Research on clinical applications would also be warranted because of the implication that therapy can be specialized to take into account the particular response characteristics of the individual in treatment. Use of quantitative measures for such assessment should increase the power to test the effect of differences in personality traits on individual differences in response to treatment.

Overall, the theory outlined here should facilitate the integration of research in a number of specialty areas of psychology, psychiatry, and the neurosciences. This is meant to address the challenge that makes psychiatry such a unique field of clinical science: our need to understand how behavior is modified by experience or how man learns to adapt to changes in his environment. More practically, the method described here should simplify the efforts of clinicians to describe personality variation systematically. It is much easier to quantify variation along three dimensions that are systematically defined in terms of basic response characteristics than it is to try to remember the details of criteria for numerous arbitrary categories.

This work was supported in part by Research Scientist Award MH-00048 and grant MH-31302 from the National Institute of Mental Health, grant AA-03539 from the National Institute of Alcoholism and Alcohol Abuse, and a grant from the MacArthur Foundation Network on Risk and Protective Factors in Major Mental Disorders.

The commentary and cooperation of many colleagues and students is gratefully acknowledged. In particular, Morris Cloninger, MA, T. J. Crow, MD, Norman Garmezy, PhD, Irving Gottesman, PhD, Samuel B. Guze, MD, John C. Loehlin, PhD, and Auke Tellegen, PhD, were particularly helpful. Jonathan Goldberg, MA, assisted with computer programming.

References

1. American Psychiatric Association Task Force on Nomenclature and Statistics: *Diagnostic and Statistical Manual of Mental Disorders*, ed 3. Washington, DC, American Psychiatric Association, 1980.

2. World Health Organization: Classification of mental disorders, in *Manual of the International Classification of Diseases, Injuries, and Causes of Death (ICD 9)*. Geneva, World Health Organization, 1977, vol 1.

3. Frances A: The *DSM-III* personality disorders section: A commentary. *Am J Psychiatry* 1980;137:1050-1054.

4. Millon T: *Disorders of Personality, DSM III: Axis II*. New York, John Wiley & Sons Inc, 1981.

5. Widiger TA, Frances A: The *DSM-III* personality disorders: Perspectives from psychology. *Arch Gen Psychiatry* 1985;42:615-623.

6. Caplan PJ, Miller JB: Self-defeating and sadistic personality disorders: Needed additions to *DSM-III-R*? Presented at the 139th Annual Meeting of the American Psychiatric Association, Washington, DC, May 12, 1986.

7. Frances A: Categorical and dimensional systems of personality diagnosis: A comparison. *Compr Psychiatry* 1982;23:516-527.

8. Eysenck HJ, Eysenck SB: *Manual of the EPQ (Eysenck Personality Inventory)*. San Diego, Educational and Industrial Testing Service, 1976.

9. Tellegen A: Structures of mood and personality and their relevance to assessing anxiety, with an emphasis on self-report, in Tuma AH, Maser J: *Anxiety and the Anxiety Disorders*. Hillsdale, NJ, Lawrence Erlbaum Assoc Inc, 1985, pp 681-706.

10. Barrett JE Jr: Use of the M-N-T Inventory (Sjöbring personality dimensions) on an American population. *Acta Psychiatr Scand* 1972;48:501-509.

11. Essen-Möller E, Larsson H, Uddenberg CE, White G: Individual traits and morbidity in a Swedish rural population. *Acta Psychiatr Scand Suppl* 1956;100:1-160.

12. Hagnell O: *A Prospective Study of the Incidence of Mental Disorder*. Stockholm, Scandinavian University Books, Svenska Bokförlaget/Norstedts-Bonniers, 1966.

13. Kendell R: The choice of diagnostic criteria for biological research. *Arch Gen Psychiatry* 1982;39:1334-1339.

14. Cloninger CR, Martin RL, Guze SB, Clayton PJ: Diagnosis and prognosis in schizophrenia. *Arch Gen Psychiatry* 1985;40:15-25.

15. Flynn PM, McMahon RC: An examination of the factor structure of the Millon Clinical Multiaxial Inventory. *J Pers Assess* 1984;48:308-311.

16. Gray JA: *The Neuropsychology of Anxiety*. New York, Oxford University Press Inc, 1982.

17. Gray JA: Anxiety, personality and the brain, in Gale A, Edwards JA (eds): *Physiological Correlates of Human Behavior: III. Individual Differences and Psychopathology*. Orlando, Fla, Academic Press Inc, 1983, pp 31-43

18. Eaves L, Eysenck HJ: The nature of extraversion: A genetical analysis. *J Pers Soc Psychol* 1975;32:102-112.

19. Fulker DW: The genetic and environmental architecture of psychoticism, extraversion and neuroticism, in Eysenck HJ (ed): *A Model for Personality*. New York, Springer-Verlag NY Inc, 1981, pp 88-122.

20. Loehlin JC: Are personality traits differentially heritable? *Behav Genet* 1982;12:417-428.

21. Allport GW: *Personality: A Psychological Interpretation*. New York, Holt Rinehart & Winston, 1937.

22. Thorpe WH: *Learning and Instinct in Animals*. Cambridge, Mass,

Harvard University Press, 1956.
23. Cloninger CR, Gilligan SB: Neurogenetic mechanisms of learning: A phylogenetic perspective. *J Psychiatr Res*, in press.
24. Cloninger CR: A unified biosocial theory of personality and its role in the development of anxiety states. *Psychiatr Dev* 1986;3:167-226.
25. Stellar JR, Stellar E: *The Neurobiology of Motivation and Reward*. New York, Springer-Verlag NY Inc, 1985.
26. Thompson RF: The neurobiology of learning and memory. *Science* 1986;233:941-947.
27. Goelet P, Castellucci VF, Schacher S, Kandel ER: The long and the short of long-term memory: A molecular framework. *Nature* 1986;322: 419-422.
28. Wise RA: Action of drugs of abuse on brain reward systems. *Pharmacol Biochem Behav* 1980;13:213-223.
29. Routtenberg A: The reward system of the brain. *Sci Am* 1978; 239:154-164.
30. Fowles DC: The three arousal model: Implications of Gray's two factor learning theory for heart rate, electrodermal activity and psychopathy. *Psychophysiology* 1980;17:87-104.
31. Obrist TA: The cardiovascular-behavioral interaction—as it appears today. *Psychophysiology* 1976;13:95-107.
32. Moore RY, Bloom FE: Central catecholamine neuron systems: Anatomy and physiology of the dopamine systems. *Ann Rev Neurosci* 1978;1: 129-169.
33. Heath RG (ed): *The Role of Pleasure in Behavior*. New York, Harper & Row Publishers Inc, 1964.
34. Kelley A, Stinus L: Neuroanatomical and neurochemical substrates of affective behavior, in Fox NA, Davidson RJ (eds): *Affective Development: A Psychobiological Perspective*. Hillsdale, NJ, Lawrence Erlbaum Assoc Inc, pp 1-75.
35. Iversen SD: Brain dopamine systems and behavior, in Iversen LL, Iversen SD, Snyder SH (eds): *Handbook of Psychopharmacology*. New York, Plenum Publishing Corp, 1977, vol 8, pp 333-374.
36. Cloninger CR: *Personality and Psychopathology: A Unified Biosocial Theory*. New York, Oxford University Press Inc, in press.
37. Warburton DM: Stimulus selection and behavioral inhibition, in Iversen LL, Iversen SD, Snyder SH (eds): *Handbook of Psychopharmacology*, New York, Plenum Publishing Corp, 1977, vol 8, pp 385-432.
38. Thiebot M-H, Hamon M, Soubrie P: Serotonergic neurones and anxiety-related behavior in rats, in Trimble MR, Zarifian E (eds): *Psychopharmacology of the Limbic System*. New York, Oxford University Press Inc, 1984, pp 164-174.
39. Huppert FA, Iversen SD: Response suppression in rats: A comparison of response contingent and non-contingent punishment and the effect of the minor tranquilizer, chlordiazepoxide. *Psychopharmacologia* 1975;44: 67-75.
40. Stein L: Behavioral pharmacology of benzodiazepines, in Klein DF, Rabkin J (eds): *Anxiety: New Research and Changing Concepts*. New York, Raven Press, 1981, pp 201-214.
41. Sepinwall J, Cook L: Mechanism of action of the benzodiazepines: Behavioral aspects. *Fed Proc* 1980;39:3021-3031.
42. Frith CD, Dowdy J, Ferrier IN, Crow TJ: Selective impairment of paired associate learning after administration of a centrally-acting adrenergic agonist (clonidine). *Psychopharmacology* 1985;87:490-493.
43. Moore RY, Bloom FE: Central catecholamine neuron systems: Anatomy and physiology of the norepinephrine and epinephrine systems. *Ann Rev Neurosci* 1979;2:113-168.
44. Angevine JB Jr, Cotman CW: *Principles of Neuroanatomy*. New York, Oxford University Press Inc, 1981.
45. Segal M, Bloom FE: The action of norepinephrine in the rat hippocampus: IV. The effects of locus coeruleus stimulation on evoked hippocampal unit activity. *Brain Res* 1976;107:513-525.
46. Mason ST, Iversen ST: Theories of the dorsal bundle extinction effect. *Brain Res Rev* 1979;1:107-137.
47. McEntee WJ, Mair RG, Langlais PJ: Neurochemical pathology in Korsakoff's psychosis: Implications for other cognitive disorders. *Neurology* 1984;31:648-652.
48. Mair RG, McEntee WJ: Cognitive enhancement in Korsakoff's psychosis by clonidine: A comparison with L-dopa and ephedrine. *Psychopharmacology* 1986;88:274-280.
49. Mair RG, Langlais PJ, Mazurek MF, Beal MF, Martin JB, McEntee WJ: Reduced concentrations of arginine vasopressin and MHPG in lumbar CSF of patients with Korsakoff's psychosis. *Life Sci*, in press.
50. DeWeid D, Bohus B: Modulation of memory processes by neuropeptides of hypothalamic neurohypophyseal origin, in Brazier MAB (ed): *Brain Mechanisms in Memory and Learning: From the Single Neuron to Man*. New York, Raven Press, 1979, pp 139-149.
51. Kovacs GL, Bohus B, Versteeg DHG: Facilitation of memory consolidation by vasopressin: Mediation by terminals of the dorsal noradrenergic bundle? *Brain Res* 1979;172:73-85.
52. Crow TJ, Deakin JFW: Neurohumoral transmission, behavior, and mental disorder, in *Handbook of Psychiatry*. New York, Cambridge University Press, 1985, vol 5, Shepherd M (ed): *The Scientific Foundations of Psychiatry*, pp 137-182.
53. Spielberger CD, Kling JK, O'Hagan SEJ: Dimensions of psychopathic personality: Antisocial behavior and anxiety, in Hare RD, Schalling D (eds): *Psychopathic Behavior: Approaches to Research*. New York, John Wiley & Sons Inc, 1978, pp 23-46.
54. Pollak JM: Obsessive-compulsive personality: A review. *Psychol Bull* 1979;86:225-241.
55. Sjöbring H: Personality structure and development: A model and its application. *Acta Psychiatr Scand Suppl* 1973;244:1-204.
56. Cleckley H: *The Mask of Sanity*, ed 5. St Louis, CV Mosby Co, 1976.
57. Schalling D: Psychopathy-related personality variables and the psychophysiology of socialization, in Hare RD, Schalling D (eds): *Psychopathic Behavior: Approaches to Research*. New York, John Wiley & Sons Inc, 1978, pp 85-106.
58. Robins LN: *Deviant Children Grown Up: A Sociological and Psychiatric Study of Sociopathic Personality*. Baltimore, Williams & Wilkins, 1966.
59. Cloninger CR: The link between hysteria and sociopathy, in Akiskal HS, Webb WL (eds): *Psychiatric Diagnosis: Exploration of Biological Predictors*. New York, Spectrum Inc, 1978, pp 189-218.
60. Horowitz MJ: *Hysterical Personality*. New York, Jason Aronson Inc, 1977.
61. Bohman M, Cloninger CR, von Knorring AL, Sigvardsson S: An adoption study of somatoform disorders: III. Cross-fostering analysis and genetic relationship to alcoholism and criminality. *Arch Gen Psychiatry* 1984;41:872-878.
62. Small IF, Small JG, Alig VB, Moore DF: Passive-aggressive personality disorder: A search for a syndrome. *Am J Psychiatry* 1970;126:973-983.
63. Dahl A: A critical examination of empirical studies of the diagnosis of borderline disorders in adults. *Psychiatr Dev* 1985;3:1-29.
64. Torgersen S: Genetic and nosological aspects of schizotypal and borderline personality disorders: A twin study. *Arch Gen Psychiatry* 1984;41:546-554.
65. Berner W, Karlick-Bolten E: *DSM-III*-Personlichkeitsdiagnostik bei einer Gruppe chronischer Straftater. *Wien Klin Wochenschr* 1985;97: 555-561.
66. Perry JC, Flannery RB: Passive-aggressive personality disorder: Treatment implications of a clinical typology. *J Nerv Ment Dis* 1982;170: 164-173.
67. Reed GF: Obsessional personality disorder and remembering. *Br J Psychiatry* 1977;130:177-183.
68. Volans PJ: Styles of decision-making and probability appraisal in selected obsessional and phobic patients. *Br J Soc Clin Psychol* 1976;15: 305-317.
69. Gottheil E, Stone GC: Factor analytic study of orality and anality. *J Nerv Ment Dis* 1968;146:1-17.
70. Tyrer P, Casey P, Gall J: Relationship between neurosis and personality disorder. *Br J Psychiatry* 1983;142:404-408.
71. Shapiro D: *Neurotic Styles*. New York, Basic Books Inc Publishers, 1965.
72. Kretschmer E: *Physique and Character*, ed 2. New York, Harcourt Brace Jovanich Publishers, 1925.
73. Wetzel RD, Cloninger CR, Hong B, Reich T: Personality as a subclinical expression of affective disorder. *Compr Psychiat* 1980;21: 197-205.
74. Depue RA, Slater JF, Wolfstetter-Kausch H, Klein D, Gopleurd E, Farr D: A behavioral paradigm for identifying persons at risk for bipolar depressive disorders: A conceptual frame work and five validation studies. *J Abnorm Psychology* 1981;90:381-437.
75. Cloninger CR, Martin RL, Guze SB, Clayton PJ: A blind follow-up and family study of anxiety neurosis: Preliminary analysis of the St Louis 500, in Klein DF, Rabkin J (eds): *Anxiety: New Research and Changing Concepts*. New York, Raven Press, 1981, pp 137-150.
76. Noyes R Jr, Clancy J, Hoenk PR, Slymen DJ: The prognosis of anxiety neurosis. *Arch Gen Psychiatry* 1980;37:173-178.
77. Bohman M, Cloninger CR, Sigvardsson S, von Knorring A-L: Predisposition to petty criminality in Swedish adoptees: I. Genetic and environmental heterogeneity. *Arch Gen Psychiatry* 1982;39:1233-1241.
78. Cloninger CR, Sigvardsson S, Bohman M, von Knorring A-L: Predisposition to petty criminality in Swedish adoptees: II. Cross-fostering analysis of gene-environment interaction. *Arch Gen Psychiatry* 1982;39: 1242-1247.
79. Sigvardsson S, Cloninger CR, Bohman M, von Knorring A-L: Predisposition to petty criminality in Swedish adoptees: III. Sex differences and validation of the male typology. *Arch Gen Psychiatry* 1982;39:1248-1253.
80. Cloninger CR: Somatoform and dissociative disorders, in Winokur G, Clayton PJ (eds): *Medical Basis of Psychiatry*. Philadelphia, WB Saunders Co, 1986, pp 123-151.
81. Cloninger CR, Sigvardsson S, Bohman M: Childhood personality predicts alcohol abuse in young adults. *Alcoholism*, in press.
82. Sigvardsson S, Bohman M, Cloninger CR: Structure and stability of childhood personality: Prediction of later social adjustment. *J Child Psychol Psychiatry*, in press.
83. Cloninger CR: Neurogenetic adaptive mechanisms, in alcoholism. *Science*, in press.

Journal of Personality Disorders, 6(4), 343–359, 1992

THE FIVE-FACTOR MODEL OF PERSONALITY AND ITS RELEVANCE TO PERSONALITY DISORDERS

Paul T. Costa, Jr., and Robert R. McCrae

The five-factor model is a dimensional representation of personality structure that has recently gained widespread acceptance among personality psychologists. This article describes the five factors (Neuroticism, Extraversion, Openness, Agreeableness, and Conscientiousness); summarizes evidence on their consensual validity, comprehensiveness, universality, heritability, and longitudinal stability; and reviews several approaches to the assessment of the factors and their defining traits. In research, measures of the five factors can be used to analyze personality disorder scales and to profile the traits of personality-disordered patient groups; findings may be useful in diagnosing individuals. As an alternative to the current categorical system for diagnosing personality disorders, it is proposed that Axis II be used for the description of personality in terms of the five factors and for the diagnosis of personality-related problems in affective, interpersonal, experiential, attitudinal, and motivational areas.

Since the adoption of a multiaxial system of diagnosis for mental disorders (American Psychiatric Association, 1980), clinicians have been asked to indicate the presence or absence of personality disorders in their patients, usually in addition to other mental disorders. A set of 11 disorders have been identified and specific criteria established to diagnose each. These criteria include traits, current behaviors, and historical data intended to define a particular syndrome.

This categorical, medical model of personality disorders has frequently been criticized (e.g., Eysenck, Wakefield, & Friedman, 1983; Kato, 1988). Widiger and his colleagues, in particular, have argued that dimensional approaches are less arbitrary, more informative, and more consistent with empirical data on the nature of personality disorders (Trull, Widiger, & Guthrie, 1990; Widiger & Frances, in press). Further, dimensional

From the Gerontology Research Center, National Institute on Aging, NIH.

Address correspondence to Paul T. Costa, Jr., Laboratory of Personality and Cognition, Gerontology Research Center, 4940 Eastern Avenue, Baltimore, MD 21224.

Thanks are due to Thomas A. Widiger for comments on this paper.

An earlier version of this paper was presented at the NIMH Workshop on Assessment of Personality Disorders, March 1991, New York.

approaches to personality disorders emphasize continuity with normal variations in personality traits and, if adopted, could facilitate an integration of research on personality disorders with decades of research on normal personality structure and measurement.

The chief stumbling block to proponents of such an integration has been the lack of a universally accepted model of normal personality. Personality psychologists have created hundreds of scales to measure as many different constructs, and rivalry between different schools has often been intense (Kline & Barrett, 1983). It is hardly surprising that psychiatrists have been reluctant to adopt any of these models as the basis for the diagnosis of personality disorders. (Psychiatry's alternative has been clinical consensus regarding the clustering of behaviors that, in the aggregate, are believed to be pathological.)

In the past few years, however, rapid progress has been made toward a consensus on personality structure. Five basic factors have been found to recur in many different studies and appear to account for most of the variance in measures derived from a wide variety of personality theories. This article summarizes evidence on the validity, comprehensiveness, universality, heritability, and stability of these five factors, and reviews instruments for their assessment. We then describe a number of ways in which the five-factor model can be applied to research on and diagnosis of personality disorders.

THE FIVE-FACTOR MODEL OF PERSONALITY

Personality traits can be defined as "dimensions of individual differences in tendencies to show consistent patterns of thoughts, feelings, and actions" (McCrae & Costa, 1990, p. 23). The English language has terms for thousands of such traits (Allport & Odbert, 1936), and psychologists and psychiatrists have invented many more. Fortunately, there is enormous redundancy in these lists of traits, and for decades factor analysts have sought to summarize them by identifying underlying dimensions. In 1961 Tupes and Christal announced that five factors seemed adequate for representing the variance in observer ratings of traits selected to represent the full range of English-language trait terms, and the same five factors were later found in self-reports (Goldberg, 1980). Similar factors were found in studies of personality questionnaires (e.g., McCrae & Costa, 1985a, 1989b), and by 1990 it was clear to many psychologists that these five factors were indeed basic (Digman, 1990; John, 1990; Wiggins & Trapnell, in press). These factors, some of the names that have been used to describe them, and adjective-pair and questionnaire scale definers of the factors are listed in Table 1.

CONSENSUAL VALIDITY

The most fundamental question about the five factors is whether they are meaningful and scientifically useful constructs, or whether they are mere artifacts. Twenty years ago there was considerable skepticism about the reality of personality traits: Many psychologists thought that traits were

Table 1 Selected Labels and Definers of the Five Factors

Factor	Label	Adjective definers	NEO-PI-R facet scale definers
N	Neuroticism, Negative Affectivity vs. Emotional Stability	Calm—Worrying Even tempered—Temperamental Self-satisfied—Self-pitying Comfortable—Self-Conscious Unemotional—Emotional Hardy—Vulnerable	Anxiety Angry hostility Depression Self-consciousness Impulsiveness Vulnerability
E	Extraversion, Surgency, Social Activity vs. Introversion	Reserved—Affectionate Loner—Joiner Quiet—Talkative Passive—Active Sober—Fun loving Unfeeling—Passionate	Warmth Gregariousness Assertiveness Activity Excitement seeking Positive emotions
O	Openness to Experience, Intellect, Culture vs. Closedness	Down to earth—Imaginative Uncreative—Creative Conventional—Original Prefer routine—Prefer variety Uncurious—Curious Conservative—Liberal	Fantasy Aesthetics Feelings Actions Ideas Values
A	Agreeableness, Friendly Compliance, Socialization vs. Antagonism	Ruthless—Soft hearted Suspicious—Trusting Stingy—Generous Antagonistic—Acquiescent Critical—Lenient Irritable—Good natured	Trust Straightforwardness Altruism Compliance Modesty Tender mindedness
C	Conscientiousness, Will to Achieve, Constraint vs. Undirectedness	Negligent—Conscientious Lazy—Hardworking Disorganized—Well-Organized Late—Punctual Aimless—Ambitious Quitting—Persevering	Competence Order Dutifulness Achievement striving Self-discipline Deliberation

Note. Adapted from Costa, McCrae, & Dye, 1991; and McCrae & Costa, 1986. NEO-PI-R = Revised NEO Personality Inventory.

mere cognitive fictions with no basis in observable patterns of behavior (Mischel, 1968). People might *believe* that they were nervous, energetic, original, accommodating, or careful, but others around them might have quite different ideas about their characteristics; and the objective scientist, duly recording behaviors, might find no consistency at all in behavior.

This extreme view was never adopted by clinical psychologists or psychiatrists, who saw the consistency of behavior in their daily interactions with patients. But it was seriously entertained by social psychologists and, in turn, by personologists who wished to refute it (e.g., Block, 1977; Epstein,

1977). And refute it they did: There is now ample evidence that the dimensions of the five-factor model are not mere fictions but instead refer to observable differences in patterns of thought, feeling, and behavior.

Some studies have used naturalistic (Small, Zeldin, & Savin-Williams, 1983) or laboratory (Gifford & O'Connor, 1987) observation to validate self-reported personality traits. Another approach has been to examine agreement among observer ratings or between ratings and self-reports. Where reliable and valid instruments are used, the correspondence has been found to be substantial (Funder & Colvin, in press). McCrae and Costa (1989a) reported self/peer, spouse/peer, and peer/peer correlations ranging from .26 to .54 (median = .42) for the five factors of the NEO Personality Inventory (NEO-PI—Costa & McCrae, 1985, 1989), a questionnaire measure of the five-factor model; agreement between self and spouse was even higher, ranging from .53 to .60 (all $p < .001$).

These correlations are far from unity and considerably less than the reliabilities of the measures. Thus, self-reports and ratings are not interchangeable. They are, however, all meaningful and valid measures of traits, and even better measures might be obtained by aggregating them. The factors themselves refer to real, consensually validated aspects of human behavior that can be treated quantitatively. They are legitimate scientific phenomena.

COMPREHENSIVENESS

An optimal model of personality would account for all important individual differences in emotional, interpersonal, experiential, attitudinal, and motivational styles. Identifying and enumerating all such traits has been the central problem in studies of personality structure: How can we be sure that we have not overlooked important traits? There have been two major approaches to this problem.

The first was based on the lexical hypothesis (Norman, 1963). If a trait is truly important, it seems likely that over the course of the centuries, someone would have noticed it and given it a name. Every natural language, in fact, has many such terms; over 4,000 have been identified in English (Allport & Odbert, 1936) and several hundred of these are commonly used (Goldberg, 1981). It was in the analysis of traits culled from such lists that the five-factor model was first identified (see John, Angleitner, & Ostendorf, 1988, for a review), and more recent research using more representative selections of trait terms has confirmed that five factors are both necessary and sufficient to account for the covariation among these terms (Goldberg, 1990).

The second approach was both more widespread and more haphazard: Scales and inventories created by personality psychologists were analyzed to identify common factors (e.g., Coan, 1974; Costa & McCrae, 1980; French, 1953; Noller, Law, & Comrey, 1987). By 1968 Wiggins had concluded from such studies that two factors—Neuroticism (*N*) and Extraversion (*E*)—were indeed recurrent, and in 1980 Costa and McCrae suggested that a third factor, Openness (*O*), was also a basic dimension of personality. These three factors resembled three of the five factors identified in studies of natural language. An empirical comparison (McCrae & Costa, 1985b) confirmed their equivalence and suggested the need for questionnaire measures of the other two factors, Agreeableness (*A*) and Conscientiousness (*C*).

Based on these analyses, the NEO-PI was developed as a questionnaire measure of the five-factor model. Studies comparing NEO-PI scales to those found in a variety of standard personality questionnaires suggested that the same five factors found in natural language were also the basic dimensions underlying personality questionnaires (McCrae, 1989).

Among the questionnaires that have been related to the five-factor model are several intended to measure personality disorders. Wiggins and Pincus (1989) examined both the MMPI Personality Disorder Scales (MMPI-PDS—Morey, Waugh, & Blashfield, 1985) and the Personality Adjective Check List (PACL—Strack, 1987); they also used two measures of the five-factor model: the Interpersonal Adjective Scales—Big 5 Version (IASR-B5—Trapnell & Wiggins, 1990) and the NEO-PI. Joint factor analyses and cannonical correlations led them to the conclusion that the same five factors were found in both sets of instruments. Their findings were replicated by Costa and McCrae (1990), who examined the MMPI-PDS and the Millon Clinical Multiaxial Inventories (MCMI-I and -II—Millon, 1983, 1987). It appears from these studies that the five-factor model developed in studies of normal personality is fully adequate to account for the dimensions of abnormal personality as well (cf. Clark, Vorheis, & McEwen, in press).

In considering dimensional alternatives to the categorical system of the DSM-III-R, Widiger et al. (1991) mentioned as candidates the interpersonal circumplex and the dimensional systems of Cloninger, Eysenck, Millon, and Tellegen. Each of these has merit, but all are subsumed by the dimensions of the five-factor model (Costa & McCrae, 1990, in press-b; McCrae & Costa, 1985a, 1989c; Tellegen & Waller, in press). Only the five-factor model provides a comprehensive description of personality.

UNIVERSALITY

Culture doubtless affects the expression of personality—just as it influences forms of psychopathology—but the underlying structure of personality may be universal. This is an empirical question but one that has definitional implications. If personality structure varied substantially across cultures, how could a uniform system of personality disorders be meaningfully included in the *International Classification of Diseases?*

It would certainly be premature to suggest that the five-factor model (or any other model of personality) has been recovered in all the world's cultures and subcultures, but there is considerable evidence of its generality. Good to excellent replications in either the natural language or questionnaire measures have been reported for German (Ostendorf, 1990), Dutch (De Raad, Mulder, Kloosterman, & Hofstee, 1988), Japanese (Bond, Nakazato, & Shiraishi, 1975), Filipino (Church & Katigbak, 1989), and Chinese (Yang & Bond, 1990) samples. The inclusion of non-Indo-European-language cultures in this group is particularly telling because it suggests that the factor structure is not a product of the lexical system.

The five-factor model is universal in other ways as well. It has been reported in children (Digman & Inouye, 1986), college students (Goldberg, 1990), and older adults (McCrae & Costa, 1985b); in women as well as men;

and in non-White as well as White respondents (Costa, McCrae, & Dye, 1991).

HERITABILITY

Nothing in the definition of personality traits or personality disorders requires that they be heritable. But psychiatrists have a keen interest in questions of heritability, because heritable traits must have some biological basis that might provide an avenue of intervention. It appears that all five factors are substantially heritable.

By far the most research has been conducted on the two dimensions of *E* and *N* (see Eaves, Eysenck, & Martin, 1989, for a review), and the data leave no doubt that both these dimensions are substantially determined by genetic influences. The few studies that have examined Openness using behavior genetics models have also found evidence of heritability: Plomin and McClearn (1990) reported that 41% of the variance in NEO-PI Openness scores was attributable to additive genetic variance. Tellegen and Waller (in press) reported heritabilities of .55 and .50 for two scales of the Multidimensional Personality Questionnaire (MPQ), Harm Avoidance and Absorption, that are related to the negative and positive poles of *O*, respectively.

Eysenck (1990) has also reported heritability for a dimension he calls *Psychoticism*, which is related to low *A* and low *C* (McCrae & Costa, 1985a). The Achievement and Control scales of the MPQ, which are related to high *C*, showed heritabilities of about .40 (Tellegen & Waller, in press), and 29% of the variance in a short Swedish version of the NEO-PI *C* scale could be attributed to nonadditive genetic effects (Plomin & McClearn, 1990).

The factor about which there is the least consistent evidence on heritability is *A*. Using a short Swedish version of the NEO-PI *A* scale, Plomin and McClearn (1990) reported only 12% of the variance could be attributed to genetic effects, whereas 21% showed evidence of shared environmental effects. Loehlin (1987) conducted an analysis of items in the California Psychological Inventory (CPI) and found four heritable factors that he explicitly interpreted in terms of Norman's (1963) five-factor model. The missing factor was *A*, which may indicate that Agreeableness is not heritable—or which may simply reflect the fact that there is a relative absence of items measuring *A* in the CPI (McCrae, Costa, & Piedmont, in press).

Other studies have found evidence of strong heritability for *A*-related traits. Tellegen and Waller (in press) reported a heritability of .44 for MPQ Aggression, a trait related to low *A*. Rushton, Fulker, Neale, Nias, and Eysenck (1986) estimated heritabilities of .56 to .72 for scales measuring altruism, empathy, nurturance, and aggressiveness.

Each of the five factors has shown at least some evidence for heritability. Further research is needed here, especially for the *O*, *A*, and *C* factors, and new studies would profit by the inclusion of observer ratings as well as self-reports for assessing personality (Costa & McCrae, 1987). In the meantime, it is clear that the dimensions of the five-factor model have some biological basis that may make them of particular relevance to biosocial approaches to psychiatry (Cloninger, 1988).

LONGITUDINAL STABILITY

Personality disorders are characterized by inflexibility and distinguished in part from Axis I syndromes by their long-term persistence. Millon (1981) suggested that this stability was due, at least in part, to self-perpetuating features in the disorders. Avoidant individuals, for example, might shun the social contact that would otherwise give them social skills and confidence. This analysis seems to imply that normal personality traits are more malleable and more likely to change with age or corrective experience. If that were the case, proposals to link personality traits and personality disorders might be questionable.

There are certainly changes in personality between adolescence and age 30 (Siegler et al., 1990), although there is also considerable continuity. But after age 30, normal personality traits are highly stable (McCrae & Costa, 1990). Over long periods of time there are systematic declines in a few traits, notably activity level, but the mean levels of most traits are relatively constant over decades of adulthood (Costa et al., 1986).

With regard to the stability of individual differences—the extent to which individuals maintain the same rank ordering along different dimensions—there is also strong evidence of stability. For example, 6-year stability coefficients for self-reports on NEO-PI *N, E,* and *O* scales ranged from .73 to .87 for men and women; and 3-year stability coefficients for short *A* and *C* ranged from .55 to .84 (Costa & McCrae, 1988). Similar values have been found for periods of up to 30 years using other personality questionnaires that can be interpreted in the framework of the five-factor model (Block, 1977; Costa & McCrae, 1992b). Finally, studies of observer-rated personality also find stability of mean levels and individual differences (Costa & McCrae, 1988, 1992b). Seven-year retest correlations for peer ratings of *N, E, O, A,* and *C* were .74, .79, .79, .70, and .75, respectively.

ASSESSMENT OF THE FIVE FACTORS

The five-factor model will be useful in research and clinical practice only insofar as it can be accurately assessed. The simplest option would be global clinical judgments of standing on each of the five factors. The clinician might review the case history and observe the patient's behavior in the interview, and base ratings on this information. In the late phases of treatment, when the clinician has extensive knowledge about the patient, such ratings would be of great value as criteria against which to judge other measures of the five factors. Early in treatment they might be useful in helping the clinician organize his or her conception of the patient. For example, systematic assessment of all five factors might focus attention on the client's altruism or achievement striving—potential strengths that might have been overlooked when the major concern is the identification of psychopathology.

However, clinician ratings do not provide the clinician with new information, and they are likely to be limited in accuracy, especially in the early phases of treatment, precisely when knowledge of personality would be most helpful. Personality scales and inventories were designed to provide such information and have long been an integral part of clinical assessment (Costa & McCrae, 1992a). Clinicians who have customarily used instruments developed outside the tradition of the five-factor model may find it useful to reinterpret scales within this framework. For example, the Thoughtfulness scale of the Guilford–Zimmerman Temperament Survey (Guilford, Zimmerman, & Guilford, 1976), the Sentience scale of the Personality Research Form (Jackson, 1984), the Achievement via Independence scale of the CPI, and the Intuition scale of the Myers–Briggs Type Indicator (Myers & McCaulley, 1985) all measure aspects of Openness to Experience (McCrae, 1989); standing on this dimension can suggest the most effective form of psychotherapy (Miller, 1991).

Many inventories in widespread use do not assess the full range of traits. For example, measures of the interpersonal circumplex emphasize *E* and *A* but neglect traits in the domains of *N*, *O*, and *C* (McCrae & Costa, 1989c). Several instruments have been developed specifically to measure the five factors, including several different forms of adjective scales (Goldberg, 1990), the Revised Interpersonal Adjective Scales—Big Five version (IASR-B5—Trapnell & Wiggins, 1990), the Hogan Personality Inventory (HPI—Hogan, 1986), and the NEO Personality Inventory (NEO-PI—Costa & McCrae, 1985, 1989). These instruments are reviewed by Briggs (1992). Of these, only the NEO-PI has been used extensively in clinical practice; illustrations of its use are given in Miller (1991), Mutén (1991), Fagen et al. (1991), Costa and McCrae (1990, 1992a), and Clarkin and Sanderson (in press).

Two of these instruments provide additional information on more specific personality traits that are likely to be of interest. The IASR-B5 defines the *E* and *A* factors in terms of eight scales that assess octants of the interpersonal circumplex, a system widely used in clinical psychology and psychiatry (Wiggins & Pincus, 1989). The Revised NEO-PI (Costa, McCrae, & Dye, 1991) assesses all five factors of personality at two levels: Each of the factors is defined by six scales measuring specific traits (see Table 1); these facet scales are summed to provide broader domain scale scores. The domain scales are useful in forming a global impression of the patient's personality; the facet scales give more detailed information that may be crucial in making diagnostic distinctions.

Although self-report instruments have always been central to psychological assessment, they are not the only means of measuring the five factors, nor are they invariably the best. Self-reports are based on the self-concept, and when the self-concept is distorted by psychopathology—as, for example, in the inflated self-image of the narcissistic personality disorder—self-report data may not be trustworthy. An alternative is personality ratings by knowledgeable informants, typically spouses (Mutén, 1991). Because we know the five-factor model is consensually valid, observer ratings may be used with some confidence as a supplement or alternative to self-reports. Form R of the NEO-PI provides a standardized and validated instrument for gathering such data.

APPLICATIONS IN RESEARCH AND DIAGNOSIS

There are several ways in which the five-factor model can be profitably used in research on personality disorders, whether the investigator subscribes to the categorical model of DSM-III-R or seeks a dimensional alternative. The five factors provide basic descriptive data on personality traits that can be conceptualized in many different ways.

ANALYSES OF PERSONALITY DISORDER SCALES

Most research to date has examined correlations between the five factors and scales created specifically to measure features of personality disorders. The first such study was by Wiggins and Pincus (1989), showing common dimensions underlying normal personality and scales intended to measure the 11 personality disorders. A similar study was conducted by Costa and McCrae (1990). These studies demonstrated the necessity and sufficiency of the five factors in accounting for variance among personality disorder scales. They also provided specific information on each of the personality disorders. For example, they suggested that the often difficult distinction between Avoidant and Schizoid disorders can be made by attending to scores on *N:* Both Avoidant and Schizoid individuals are introverted, but Avoidant individuals are also emotionally unstable.

Such analyses also allow comparisons between different measures of the same disorder that may be helpful in evaluating their validity. Costa and McCrae (1990) showed that the Compulsive scale of the MCMI-I was negatively related to *N*, whereas the MMPI-PDS Compulsive scale was positively related to *N*. This reversal probably explains the lack of correlation between these two measures (McCann, 1989). Conceptually, one might argue that the most meaningful pattern of correlations with the five factors was found for the MCMI-II Compulsive scale, which was unrelated to *N* but strongly correlated with Conscientiousness.

Some researchers (Clark, 1990b; Livesley, 1991) have argued that the categories of DSM-III-R do not represent naturally covarying clusters of symptoms and have developed instruments that more faithfully reflect the actual associations among personality disorder symptoms. Clark, Vorheis, and McEwen (in press) have examined relations between measures of the five factors and the Schedule for Normal and Abnormal Personality (SNAP—Clark, 1990a). Their study showed links between all 12 symptom dimensions and one or more of the five factors, including associations between Suicide Potential and *N*, Exhibition and *E*, Schizotypal Thinking and *O*, Manipulativeness and low *A*, and Workaholism and *C*.

At a broader level, Cloninger (1977) has proposed a three-dimensional system for the description of personality and the classification of personality disorders. Correlations between the subscales of his instrument, the Tridimensional Personality Questionnaire, and the NEO-PI showed that Cloninger's factors may be considered combinations of the familiar five factors (Costa & McCrae, in press). Cloninger's Novelty Seeking is related chiefly to low *C*, and his Harm Avoidance is essentially equivalent to *N*. Reward Dependence, however, includes elements of all five factors and may prove difficult to interpret.

PERSONALITY PROFILES OF PD PATIENTS

It is one thing to say that scales intended to measure personality disorders can be interpreted in terms of the five factors. It is something else to say that patients diagnosed as having a disorder share distinctive personality profiles on measures of the five factors. To date there have been no studies in which instruments designed to measure the five factors were administered to psychiatric patients with different personality disorders. But Lyons, Merla, Ozer, and Hyler (1990) created scales from the items of the Personality Diagnostic Questionnaire (PDQ—Hyler et al., 1989) to measure four of the five factors and scored them on a psychiatric sample of whom about half had at least one diagnosable personality disorder. Results for the *E*, *A*, and *C* scales were consistent with the findings of Wiggins and Pincus (1989) and Costa and McCrae (1990); results with the PDQ *N* scale were less clear.

An obvious program of research would be to identify samples of individuals with each of the 11 DSM-III-R Axis II diagnoses (and the Sadistic and Self-Defeating disorders that have been cited as needing further study), administer measures of the five factors, and look for characteristic profiles. Researchers might choose to use two different measures of the five factors, including one that gives scores for more specific traits within the five domains. Ideally, self-reports would be supplemented by spouse or peer ratings, and clinical assessments on the five factors would also be obtained. The result of this ambitious program would be a comprehensive characterization of the personality disorders in terms of their constituent traits.

This research need not be exploratory. Based on the current literature and on conceptual analyses, specific hypotheses have been advanced about links between the personality disorders and the five factors and their component traits (Clarkin & Sanderson, in press; Widiger, Trull, & Costa, in press). Until they are superseded by the empirical data, these hypotheses may be clinically useful in suggesting diagnoses for individuals. At a minimum, they can be used to rule out some diagnoses: Patients who are warm, gregarious, and assertive are clearly not suffering from a Schizoid personality disorder.

A RECONCEPTUALIZATION OF AXIS II

The program of research outlined in the preceding section should provide definitive information on the personality characteristics of individuals with personality disorders *as defined by DSM-III-R*. But many researchers are dissatisfied with the current set of disorders. Livesley (1991) would have us return to the pool of symptoms and reconstitute the personality disorders along more empirically guided lines. Even this approach tacitly assumes the comprehensiveness of the pool of symptoms associated with DSM-III-R personality disorders, which is highly questionable. For example, very little attention has been paid to symptoms that reflect inflexible and maladaptive traits related to high or low Openness to Experience. Excessive or disordered Openness might lead to eccentric thinking, poor integration of the life structure, or weak ego boundries (McCrae & Costa, in press); excessive closedness might be seen in dogmatic thinking or an inability to adapt to changing social conditions. Again, it might be argued that the depression and anxiety associated with such chronic Axis I disorders as dysthymia and social phobia also belong in the pool of personality disorder symptoms because they too may be outcomes of personality traits (e.g., Keller, 1989).

We know little about the comprehensiveness of collections of personality disorder symptoms, but we know a great deal about the comprehensiveness of models of personality traits. It might, therefore, make sense to make a fresh start at defining Axis II. Instead of a classification of discrete personality disorders, Axis II could be used for (*a*) the description of personality and (*b*) the diagnosis of associated problems. The basic dimensions of Axis II would be the five factors, and every patient would be described in terms of his or her standing on each factor. The clinician would then determine whether the patient showed significant psychopathology related to these personality factors and, if so, assign corresponding diagnoses. Dimensional information would be embodied in the personality description; and categorical information, in the associated diagnostic codes.

This far-reaching proposal requires both illustration and discussion. By way of illustration, consider the hypothetical case of an individual who is brought for consultation by his wife because of marital difficulties. Both his own self-report and his wife's ratings suggest that he is average on *N*, very high on *E*, low on *O*, very low on *A*, and average on *C*. When the clinician is satisfied that these are reasonably valid descriptions (as the agreement between self-report and rating strongly suggests), they become the Axis II personality description.

The clinician then considers the individual's problems in living with reference to these dimensions. The very high *E* scores suggest that there may be interpersonal problems such as attention seeking and being inappropriately self-disclosing (Pincus & Wiggins, 1990), but those do not appear to be a difficulty in the present case, and no *E*-related diagnosis is coded. The very low *A* score suggests that there may be problems with self-centeredness and lack of empathy, and these are exactly the issues about which the patient's wife complains. The patient belittles his wife, makes plans without consulting her, and expects her to neglect her friends to spend time with his. He acknowledges the behaviors but fails to see why they are problematic, suggesting a sense of entitlement. The patient is given a diagnostic code of "low *A*—related maladjustment."

Although this patient shows some resemblance to individuals with a narcissistic personality disorder, he probably would not meet criteria for this diagnosis under DSM-III-R. Indeed, he might not meet criteria for any mental disorder, although he would certainly be a candidate for psychotherapy and the therapy would probably center on his interpersonal problems. He might be given a V61.10: Marital Problem code, but this diagnosis would fail to indicate that his marital problems stemmed from his personality. The proposed revision of Axis II would be more flexible and applicable to a wider range of patients than is the current categorical system. The new system would also have the advantage of focusing therapy on the symptom—the maladjustment—rather than on the underlying personality disposition with which it is associated. Personality traits are extraordinarily difficult to change (Costa & McCrae, 1986); symptoms may be more responsive to treatment.

Note that in this example mere extremeness of personality scores is not considered sufficient to warrant a diagnosis. Some high-*E* individuals have histrionic traits that cause difficulties in living, but many do not. High standing on a trait dimension implies, among other things, frequent occurrence of relevant behaviors, but what matters is not the frequency with which traits are manifested but the *appropriateness* of their manifestation. Attending parties every night shows extreme Extraversion, but unless it interferes with work and intimacy, it is not disordered behavior. Even such traits as self-centeredness and lack of empathy may be appropriate in the business world; they become problematic when they are also applied to the intimate context of marriage. This inappropriateness is, we think, what is meant when it is said that personality disorders stem from *inflexible* traits.

Our illustration assumes that the new Axis II manual will specify the sorts of maladjustments associated with each pole of each factor. The work of Livesley and Jackson (1986), Pincus and Wiggins (1990), Clark (1990b), and Millon (1990)—as well as the Symptom Index in the DSM-III-R—provide useful starting points in enumerating personality-related symptoms. Empirical studies would then show with which factor or factors each is associated.

In a previous publication (Costa & McCrae, 1990) we suggested that a sixth dimension of cognitive aberation might be needed to describe fully all the personality disorders. A simpler alternative might be to note that cognitive distortions are one of the ways in which personality can lead to maladjustments. For example, an individual very high in Openness might entertain unconventional ideas; if that person were also so introverted as to be socially isolated from the usual corrective feedback, he or she might develop what we would call schizotypal thinking.*

It might be argued that the use of Axis II for the description of aspects of personality that are not psychopathological is beyond the scope of a diagnostic and statistical manual. But Axes III and IV provide descriptive information on physical conditions and psychosocial stressors, and Kato (1988) has argued that Axis II be used for the classification of personality disorders "*together with personality traits of psychiatric significance*" (p. 171, emphasis added). And we would argue that all five factors are of psychiatric significance: some for understanding etiology, some for the selection of treatment, some for the prediction of therapy outcomes.

To return to our hypothetical case, this man's average standing on *N* and *C* suggests a relatively good prognosis: He will not be overwhelmed by chronic feelings of distress, and he is capable of working toward self-improvement. By contrast, his very low *A* score means that he may distrust the clinician and be skeptical about the process of psychotherapy itself; the clinician will need to work to win his cooperation. The very high *E* implies that he would be comfortable in group or client-centered therapy. The low *O*, however, means that he has little tolerance for unconventional approaches and may benefit more from directive and behavioral methods (Di Loretto, 1971; Miller, in press; Qualls & Sheehan, 1979).

Indeed, it is probably the treatment implications that will ultimately be of most significance in the integration of personality disorder research and the five-factor model. By assessing the five factors and their facets, the clinician learns not only where problems are likely to lie, but also how

*If a sixth dimension is needed for Axis II, perhaps it should be the other great dimension of individual differences, intelligence. This would be consistent with the current practice of diagnosing mental retardation on this axis.

patients may react to different approaches to treatment, how easily they will form a therapeutic alliance, and how diligently they will perform the work of therapy. Instead of seeing personality disorders as relatively rare and bizarre combinations of traits, clinicians will come to see personality as a key determinant of many kinds of psychopathology and a pervasive influence on the psychotherapeutic enterprise.

REFERENCES

Allport, G. W., & Odbert, H. S. (1936). Trait names: A psycho-lexical study. *Psychological Monographs, 47* (1, Whole No. 211).

American Psychiatric Association. (1980). *Diagnostic and statistical manual of mental disorders* (3rd ed.). Washington, DC: Author.

Block, J. (1977). Advancing the psychology of personality: Paradigmatic shift or improving the quality of research? In D. Magnusson & N. S. Endler (Eds.), *Personality at the cross-roads: Current issues in interactional psychology* (pp. 37–64). Hillsdale, NJ: Lawrence Erlbaum Associates.

Bond, M. H., Nakazato, H., & Shiraishi, D. (1975). Universality and distinctiveness in dimensions of Japanese person perception. *Journal of Cross-Cultural Psychology, 6*, 346–357.

Briggs, S. R. (1992). Assessing the five-factor model of personality description. In R. R. McCrae (Ed.), The five-factor model: Issues and applications [Special issue]. *Journal of Personality, 60*, 253–293.

Church, T. A., & Katigbak, M. S. (1989). Internal, external, and self-report structure of personality in a non-Western culture: An investigation of cross-language and cross-cultural generalizability. *Journal of Personality and Social Psychology, 57*, 857–872.

Clark, L. A. (1990a). *Preliminary manual for the Schedule for Normal and Abnormal Personality (SNAP)*. Submitted for publication.

Clark, L. A. (1990b). Toward a consensual set of symptom clusters for assessment of personality disorder. In J. N. Butcher & C. D. Spielberger (Eds.), *Advances in personality assessment* (Vol. 8, pp. 243–266). Hillsdale, NJ: Lawrence Erlbaum Associates.

Clark, L. A., Vorheis, L., & McEwen, J. L. (in press). Personality disorder symptomatology from the five-factor perspective. In P. T. Costa, Jr., & T. A. Widiger (Eds.), *Personality disorders and the five-factor model of personality*. Washington, DC: American Psychological Association.

Clarkin, J. F., & Sanderson, C. (in press). NEO-PI personality dimensions and treatment planning. In P. T. Costa, Jr., & T. A. Widiger (Eds.), *Personality disorders and the five-factor model of personality*. Washington, DC: American Psychological Association.

Cloninger, C. R. (1977). A systematic method for clinical description and classification of personality variants. *Archives of General Psychiatry, 44*, 573–588.

Cloninger, C. R. (1988). A unified biosocial theory of personality and its role in the development of anxiety states: A reply to communtaries. *Psychiatric Development, 2*, 83–120.

Coan, R. W. (1974). *The optimal personality*. New York: Columbia University Press.

Costa, P. T., Jr., & McCrae, R. R. (1980). Still stable after all these years: Personality as a key to some issues in adulthood and old age. In P. B. Baltes & O. G. Brim, Jr. (Eds.), *Life span development and behavior* (Vol. 3, pp. 65–102). New York: Academic Press.

Costa, P. T., Jr., & McCrae, R. R. (1985). *The NEO Personality Inventory manual*. Odessa, FL: Psychological Assessment Resources.

Costa, P. T., Jr., & McCrae, R. R. (1986). Personality stability and its implications for clinical psychology. *Clinical Psychology Review, 6*, 407–423.

Costa, P. T., Jr., & McCrae, R. R. (1987). On the need for longitudinal evidence and multiple measures in behavior-genetics studies of adult personality. *Behavioral and Brain Sciences, 10*, 22–23.

Costa, P. T., Jr., & McCrae, R. R. (1988). Personality in adulthood: A six-year longitudinal study of self-reports and spouse ratings on the NEO Personality Inventory. *Journal of Personality and Social Psychology, 54*, 853–863.

Costa, P. T., Jr., & McCrae, R. R. (1989). *The NEO-PI/NEO-FFI manual supple-*

ment. Odessa, FL: Psychological Assessment Resources.

Costa, P. T., Jr., & McCrae, R. R. (1990). Personality disorders and the five-factor model of personality. *Journal of Personality Disorders, 4,* 362–371.

Costa, P. T., Jr., & McCrae, R. R. (1992a). Normal personality assessment in clinical practice: The NEO Personality Inventory. *Psychological Assessment: A Journal of Consulting and Clinical Psychology, 4,* 5–13.

Costa, P. T., Jr., & McCrae, R. R. (1992b). Trait psychology comes of age. In T. B. Sonderegger (Ed.), *Nebraska Symposium on Motivation: Psychology and Aging* (pp. 169–204). Lincoln, NE: University of Nebraska Press.

Costa, P. T., Jr., & McCrae, R. R. (in press). The NEO Personality Inventory. In S. R. Briggs & J. Cheek (Eds.), *Personality measures* (Vol. 1). Greenwich, CT: JAI Press.

Costa, P. T., Jr., McCrae, R. R., & Dye, D. A. (1991). Facet scales for Agreeableness and Conscientiousness: A revision of the NEO Personality Inventory. *Personality and Individual Differences, 12,* 887–898.

Costa, P. T., Jr., McCrae, R. R., Zonderman, A. B., Barbano, H. E., Lebowitz, B., & Larson, D. M. (1986). Cross-sectional studies of personality in a national sample: 2. Stability in neuroticism, extraversion, and openness. *Psychology and Aging, 1,* 144–149.

De Raad, B., Mulder, E., Kloosterman, K., & Hofstee, W. K. (1988). Personality-descriptive verbs. *European Journal of Personality, 2,* 81–96.

Digman, J. M. (1990). Personality structure: Emergence of the five-factor model. *Annual Review of Psychology, 41,* 417–440.

Digman, J. M., & Inouye, J. (1986). Further specification of the five robust factors of personality. *Journal of Personality and Social Psychology, 50,* 116–123.

Di Loretto, A. O. (1971). *Comparative psychotherapy: An experimental analysis.* Chicago: Aldine–Atherton.

Eaves, L. J., Eysenck, H. J., & Martin, N. G. (1989). *Genes, culture, and personality: An empirical approach.* New York: Academic Press.

Epstein, S. (1977). Traits are alive and well. In D. Magnusson & N. S. Endler (Eds.), *Personality at the crossroads: Current issues in interactional psychology* (pp. 83–98). Hillsdale, NJ: Lawrence Erlbaum Associates.

Eysenck, H. J. (1990). Genetic and environmental contributions to individual differences: The three major dimensions of personality. In D. M. Buss (Ed.), Biological foundations of personality: Evolution, behavioral genetics, and psychophysiology [Special issue]. *Journal of Personality, 58,* 245–262.

Eysenck, H. J., Wakefield, J. A., Jr., & Friedman, A. F. (1983). Diagnosis and clinical assessment: The DSM-III. *Annual Review of Psychology, 34,* 167–193.

Fagan, P. J., Wise, T. N., Schmidt, C. W., Ponticas, Y., Marshall, R. D., & Costa, P. T., Jr. (1991). A comparison of five-factor personality dimensions in males with sexual dysfunction and males with paraphilia. *Journal of Personality Assessment, 57,* 434–448.

French, J. W. (1953). *The description of personality measurements in terms of rotated factors.* Princeton, NJ: Educational Testing Service.

Funder, D. C., & Colvin, C. R. (in press). Congruence of self and others' judgments of personality. In S. R. Briggs, R. Hogan, & W. H. Jones (Eds.), *Handbook of personality psychology.* New York: Academic Press.

Gifford, R., & O'Connor, B. (1987). The interpersonal circumplex as a behavior map. *Journal of Personality and Social Psychology, 52,* 1019–1026.

Goldberg, L. R. (1980, May). *Some ruminations about the structure of individual differences: Developing a common lexicon for the major characteristics of human personality.* Paper presented at the Western Psychological Association Convention, Honolulu, HI.

Goldberg, L. R. (1981). Language and individual differences: The search for universals in personality lexicons. In L. Wheeler (Ed.), *Review of personality and social psychology* (Vol. 2, pp. 141–165). Beverly Hills, CA: Sage.

Goldberg, L. R. (1990). An alternative "description of personality": The Big-Five factor structure. *Journal of Personality and Social Psychology, 59,* 1216–1229.

Guilford, J. S., Zimmerman, W. S., & Guilford, J. P. (1976). *The Guilford–Zimmerman Temperament Survey Handbook: Twenty-five years of research and application.* San Diego, CA: EdITS Publishers.

Hogan, R. (1986). *Hogan Personality Inventory manual.* Minneapolis, MN: National Computer Systems.

Hyler, S. E., Rieder, R. O., Williams, J. B.

W., Spitzer, R. L., Hendler, J., & Lyons, M. (1989). A comparison of self-report and clinical diagnosis of DSM-III personality disorders in 552 patients. *Comprehensive Psychiatry, 30,* 170–178.

Jackson, D. N. (1984). *Personality Research Form manual* (3rd ed.). Port Huron, MI: Research Psychologists Press.

John, O. P. (1990). The "Big Five" factor taxonomy: Dimensions of personality in the natural language and in questionnaires. In L. Pervin (Ed.), *Handbook of personality theory and research* (pp. 66–100). New York: Guilford Press.

John, O. P., Angleitner, A., & Ostendorf, F. (1988). The lexical approach to personality: A historical review of trait taxonomic research. *European Journal of Personality, 2,* 171–203.

Kato, M. (1988). Issues on diagnosing and classifying personality disorders. In J. E. Mezzich & M. von Cranach (Eds.), *International classification in psychiatry: Unity and diversity* (pp. 166–174). New York: Cambridge University Press.

Keller, M. (1989). Current concepts in affective disorders. *Journal of Clinical Psychology, 50,* 157–162.

Kline, P., & Barrett, P. (1983). The factors in personality questionnaires among normal subjects. *Advances in Behaviour Research and Therapy, 5,* 141–202.

Livesley, W. J. (1991). Classifying personality disorders: Ideal types, prototypes, or dimensions? *Journal of Personality Disorders, 5,* 52–59.

Livesley, W. J., & Jackson, D. N. (1986). The internal consistency and factorial structure of behaviors judged to be associated with DSM-III categories of personality disorders. *American Journal of Psychiatry, 143,* 1473–1474.

Loehlin, J. C. (1987). Heredity, environment, and the structure of the California Psychological Inventory. *Multivariate Behavioral Research, 22,* 137–148.

Lyons, M. J., Merla, M. E., Ozer, D. J., & Hyler, S. E. (1990, August). *Relationship of the "Big-Five" factors to DSM III personality disorders.* Paper presented at the American Psychological Association Annual Convention, Boston.

McCann, J. T. (1989). MMPI personality disorder scales and the MCMI: Concurrent validity. *Journal of Clinical Psychology, 45,* 365–369.

McCrae, R. R. (1989). Why I advocate the five-factor model: Joint analyses of the NEO-PI and other instruments. In D. M. Buss & N. Cantor (Eds.), *Personality psychology: Recent trends and emerging directions* (pp. 237–245). New York: Springer-Verlag.

McCrae, R. R., & Costa, P. T., Jr. (1985a). Comparison of EPI and Psychoticism scales with measures of the five-factor model of personality. *Personality and Individual Differences, 6,* 587–597.

McCrae, R. R., & Costa, P. T., Jr. (1985b). Updating Norman's "adequate taxonomy": Intelligence and personality dimensions in natural language and in questionnaires. *Journal of Personality and Social Psychology, 49,* 710–721.

McCrae, R. R., & Costa, P. T., Jr. (1989a). Different points of view: Self-reports and ratings in the assessment of personality. In J. P. Forgas & M. J. Innes (Eds.), *Recent advances in social psychology: An international perspective* (pp. 429–439). Amsterdam: Elsevier Science Publishers.

McCrae, R. R., & Costa, P. T., Jr. (1989b). Reinterpreting the Myers–Briggs Type Indicator from the perspective of the five-factor model of personality. *Journal of Personality, 57,* 17–40.

McCrae, R. R., & Costa, P. T., Jr. (1989c). The structure of interpersonal traits: Wiggins's circumplex and the five-factor model. *Journal of Personality and Social Psychology, 56,* 586–595.

McCrae, R. R., & Costa, P. T., Jr. (1990). *Personality in adulthood.* New York: Guilford Press.

McCrae, R. R., & Costa, P. T., Jr. (in press). Conceptions and correlates of Openness to Experience. In S. R. Briggs, R. Hogan, & W. H. Jones (Eds.), *Handbook of personality psychology.* New York: Academic Press.

McCrae, R. R., Costa, P. T., Jr., & Piedmont, R. L. (in press). Folk concepts, natural language, and psychological constructs: The California Psychological Inventory and the five-factor model. *Journal of Personality.*

Miller, T. (1991). The psychotherapeutic utility of the five-factor model of personality. *Journal of Personality Assessment, 57,* 415–433.

Millon, T. (1981). *Disorders of personality: DSM III: Axis II.* New York: Wiley.

Millon, T. (1983). *Millon Clinical Multiaxial Inventory manual* (3rd ed.). Minneapolis: Interpretive Scoring Systems.

Millon, T. (1987). *Manual for the MCMI-II* (2nd ed.). Minneapolis: National Computer Systems.

Millon, T. (1990). The disorders of personality. In L. A. Pervin (Ed.), *Handbook of personality: Theory and research* (pp. 339–370). New York: Guilford Press.

Mischel, W. (1968). *Personality and assessment.* New York: Wiley.

Morey, L. C., Waugh, M. H., & Blashfield, R. K. (1985). MMPI scales for DSM-III personality disorders: Their derivation and correlates. *Journal of Personality Assessment, 49,* 245–251.

Mutén, E. (1991). Self-reports, spouse ratings, and psychophysiological assessment in a behavioral medicine program: An application of the five-factor model. *Journal of Personality Assessment, 57,* 449–464.

Myers, I. B., & McCaulley, M. H. (1985). *Manual: A guide to the development and use of the Myers–Briggs Type Indicator.* Palo Alto, CA: Consulting Psychologists Press.

Noller, P., Law, H., & Comrey, A. L. (1987). Cattell, Comrey, and Eysenck personality factors compared: More evidence for the five robust factors? *Journal of Personality and Social Psychology, 53,* 775–782.

Norman, W. T. (1963). Toward an adequate taxonomy of personality attributes: Replicated factor structure in peer nomination personality ratings. *Journal of Abnormal and Social Psychology, 66,* 574–583.

Ostendorf, F. (1990). *Sprache und Persönlichkeitsstruktur: Zur Validität des Fünf-Faktoren-Modells der Persönlichkeit* [Language and personality structure: Toward the validation of the five-factor model of personality]. Regensburg: S. Roderer Verlag.

Pincus, A. L., & Wiggins, J. S. (1990). Interpersonal problems and conceptions of personality disorders. *Journal of Personality Disorders, 4,* 342–352.

Plomin, R., & McClearn, G. E. (1990). Human behavioral genetics of aging. In J. E. Birren & K. W. Schaie (Eds.), *Handbook of the psychology of aging* (3rd ed., pp. 67–78). New York: Academic Press.

Qualls, P. J., & Sheehan, P. W. (1979). Capacity for absorption and relaxation during electromyograph biofeedback and no-feedback conditions. *Journal of Abnormal Psychology, 88,* 652–662.

Rushton, J. P., Fulker, D. W., Neale, M. C., Nias, D. K. B., & Eysenck, H. J. (1986). Altruism and aggression: The heritability of individual differences. *Journal of Personality and Social Psychology, 50,* 1192–1198.

Siegler, I. C., Zonderman, A. B., Barefoot, J. C., Williams, R. B., Jr., Costa, P. T., Jr., & McCrae, R. R. (1990). Predicting personality in adulthood from college MMPI scores: Implications for follow-up studies in psychosomatic medicine. *Psychosomatic Medicine, 52,* 644–652.

Small, S. A., Zeldin, R. S., & Savin-Williams, R. C. (1983). In search of personality traits: A multimethod analysis of naturally occurring prosocial and dominance behavior. *Journal of Personality, 51,* 1–16.

Strack, S. (1987). Development and validation of an adjective checklist to assess the Millon personality types in a normal population. *Journal of Personality Assessment, 51,* 572–587.

Tellegen, A., & Waller, N. G. (in press). Exploring personality through test construction: Development of the Multidimensional Personality Questionnaire. In S. R. Briggs & J. M. Cheek (Eds.), *Personality measures: Development and evaluation* (Vol. 1). Greenwich, CT: JAI Press.

Trapnell, P. D., & Wiggins, J. S. (1990). Extension of the Interpersonal Adjective Scales to include the Big Five dimensions of personality. *Journal of Personality and Social Psychology, 59,* 781–790.

Trull, T. J., Widiger, T. A., & Guthrie, P. (1990). The categorical versus dimensional status of borderline personality disorder. *Journal of Abnormal Psychology, 99,* 40–48.

Tupes, E. C., & Christal, R. E. (1961). *Recurrent personality factors based on trait ratings* (USAF ASD Technical Report No. 61–97). Lackland Air Force Base, TX: U.S. Air Force.

Widiger, T. A., & Frances, A. J. (in press). Towards a dimensional model for the personality disorders. In P. T. Costa, Jr., & T. A. Widiger (Eds.), *Personality disorders and the five-factor model of personality.* Washington, DC: American Psychological Association.

Widiger, T. A., Trull, T. J., & Costa, P. T., Jr. (in press). Using the five-factor model for the diagnosis of personality disorders. In P. T. Costa, Jr., & T. A. Widiger (Eds.), *Personality disorders and the five-factor model of personality.* Washington, DC: American Psychological Association.

Widiger, T. A., Frances, A. J., Harris, M., Jacobsberg, L. B., Fyer, M., & Manning, D. (1991). Comorbidity among Axis II disorders. In J. Oldham (Ed.), *Axis II: New perspectives on validity* (pp. 165–194). Washington, DC: American Psychiatric Press.

Wiggins, J. S. (1968). Personality structure. In P. R. Farnsworth, M. R. Rosenzweig, &

J. T. Polefka (Eds.), *Annual Review of Psychology* (Vol. 19, pp. 293–350). Palo Alto, CA: Annual Reviews.
Wiggins, J. S., & Pincus, A. L. (1989). Conceptions of personality disorders and dimensions of personality. *Psychological Assessment: A Journal of Consulting and Clinical Psychology, 1*, 305–316.
Wiggins, J. S., & Trapnell, P. D. (in press). Personality structure: The return of the Big Five. In S. R. Briggs, R. Hogan, & W. H. Jones (Eds.), *Handbook of personality psychology*. New York: Academic Press.
Yang, K., & Bond, M. H. (1990). Exploring implicit personality theories with indigenous or imported constructs: The Chinese case. *Journal of Personality and Social Psychology, 58*, 1087–1095.

An Alternative "Description of Personality": The Big-Five Factor Structure

Lewis R. Goldberg
University of Oregon and Oregon Research Institute, Eugene

In the 45 years since Cattell used English trait terms to begin the formulation of his "description of personality," a number of investigators have proposed an alternative structure based on 5 orthogonal factors. The generality of this 5-factor model is here demonstrated across unusually comprehensive sets of trait terms. In the first of 3 studies, 1,431 trait adjectives grouped into 75 clusters were analyzed; virtually identical structures emerged in 10 replications, each based on a different factor-analytic procedure. A 2nd study of 479 common terms grouped into 133 synonym clusters revealed the same structure in 2 samples of self-ratings and in 2 samples of peer ratings. None of the factors beyond the 5th generalized across the samples. In the 3rd study, analyses of 100 clusters derived from 339 trait terms suggest their potential utility as Big-Five markers in future studies.

The variety of individual differences is nearly boundless, yet most of these differences are insignificant in people's daily interactions with others and have remained largely unnoticed. Sir Francis Galton may have been among the first scientists to recognize explicitly the fundamental lexical hypothesis—namely that the most important individual differences in human transactions will come to be encoded as single terms in some or all of the world's languages. Indeed, Galton (1884) attempted to tap "the more conspicuous aspects of the character by counting in an appropriate dictionary," and he "estimated that it contained fully one thousand words expressive of character, each of which has a separate shade of meaning, while each shares a large part of its meaning with some of the rest" (p. 181).

Galton's (1884) estimate of the number of personality-related terms in English was later sharpened empirically, first by Allport and Odbert (1936), who culled such terms from the second edition of *Webster's Unabridged Dictionary of the English Language,* and later by Norman (1967), who supplemented the earlier list with terms from the third edition. Galton's insight concerning the relations among personality terms has been mirrored in the efforts of later investigators to discover the nature of those relations, so as to construct a structural representation of personality descriptors (for historical reviews of such efforts, see John, 1990; John, Angleitner, & Ostendorf, 1988; and Wiggins & Trapnell, in press).

This project was supported by Grant MH-39077 from the National Institute of Mental Health.

I am enormously indebted to Sarah E. Hampson, Willem K. B. Hofstee, Oliver P. John, Henry Kaiser, Kevin Lanning, Dean Peabody, Tina K. Rosolack, and Auke Tellegen for their thoughtful suggestions.

Correspondence concerning this article should be addressed to Lewis R. Goldberg, Oregon Research Institute, 1899 Willamette Street, Eugene, Oregon 97401.

One of the first of these investigators was L. L. Thurstone, a pioneer in the development of factor analysis, and the report of his initial findings reads today with almost haunting clairvoyance:

> Sixty adjectives that are in common use for describing people . . . were given to each of 1300 raters. Each rater was asked to think of a person whom he knew well and to underline every adjective that he might use in a conversational description of that person. . . . The tetrachoric correlation . . . coefficients for the sixty personality traits were then analyzed by means of multiple factor methods and we found that *five* factors are sufficient to account for the coefficients.
>
> It is of considerable psychological interest to know that the whole list of sixty adjectives can be accounted for by postulating only *five* [italics added] independent common factors. . . . We did not foresee that the list could be accounted for by as few . . . factors. *This fact leads us to surmise that the scientific description of personality may not be quite so hopelessly complex as it is sometimes thought to be* (Thurstone, 1934, pp. 12-14 [italics added]).

The Big Five

One of the most influential scientists to apply empirical procedures to the task of constructing a personality taxonomy was Raymond B. Cattell, who began with a perusal of English personality-descriptive terms. Allport and Odbert (1936) had catalogued about 18,000 such terms and had divided them into four alphabetical lists, the first of which included approximately 4,500 terms that they had classified as stable traits. Cattell (1943) used this trait list as a starting point (adding some concepts gleaned from the psychological literature, including various aspects of psychopathology) to construct 171 scales, most of which were bipolar. Guided by the correlations among the 171 scales in some empirical analyses, Cattell (1943) developed a set of 35 bipolar clusters of related terms. Rating scales based on these clusters were then employed in various studies, in each of which the correlations among the variables were factored using oblique rotational procedures (Cattell, 1945).

Journal of Personality and Social Psychology 1990, Vol. 59, No. 6, 1216-1229

Cattell has repeatedly claimed to have identified at least a dozen oblique factors. However, when Cattell's variables were analyzed by orthogonal rotational methods, only five factors proved to be replicable (e.g., Digman & Takemoto-Chock, 1981; Fiske, 1949; Norman, 1963; Tupes & Christal, 1961). Similar five-factor structures based on other sets of variables have been reported by Borgatta (1964), Digman and Inouye (1986), and McCrae and Costa (1985, 1987).

These "Big-Five" factors have traditionally been numbered and labeled as follows: (I) Surgency (or Extraversion), (II) Agreeableness, (III) Conscientiousness (or Dependability), (IV) Emotional Stability (vs. Neuroticism), and (V) Culture. Alternatively, Factor V has been interpreted as Intellect (e.g., Digman & Takemoto-Chock, 1981; Peabody & Goldberg, 1989) and as Openness (e.g., McCrae & Costa, 1987).

Because the Big-Five factor structure was originally discovered in studies using Cattell's 35 variables, some critics have argued that these five factors have not been sufficiently generalized beyond that initial set of variables. Indeed, Waller and Ben-Porath (1987) have asserted

> Much of the evidence that has been offered in support of the five-factor model stems from an assemblage of cognate studies better thought of as demonstrating the reliability rather than the validity (or comprehensiveness) of the five-factor paradigm. In other words, we feel that many of these studies are better thought of as a series of quasi-literal replications, rather than conceptual validations of the five-factor model. (p. 887)

The present article is an attempt to rebut such arguments by demonstrating the generality of the Big-Five representation within sets of trait terms that are far more representative of the total English trait lexicon than were those included in any previous studies. The article begins with analyses of the most comprehensive pool of English trait-descriptive adjectives ever studied empirically. Specifically, 1,431 trait terms grouped into 75 clusters are used to (a) discover whether the Big-Five structure can be confirmed with these data, (b) determine the robustness of the structure across different procedures for factor extraction and rotation, and (c) examine the nature of any additional factors beyond the first five. In a second study employing 479 commonly used English trait adjectives, four different factor structures are compared, two based on samples of individuals describing themselves and two based on samples of individuals describing others whom they know well. The use of four independent samples permits an analysis of the across-sample generality of the factor structures, thus providing a crucial test of the dimensionality of English trait adjectives. Finally, a third study focuses on the refinement of 100 synonym clusters based on a pool of 339 common trait terms, to be available for use as Big-Five marker variables in future studies.

Study 1

Rationale and Background

This study was designed to investigate the structure of a nearly comprehensive set of common English trait adjectives, probably the largest subset of the total pool that has yet been studied in this way. Initially, Norman (1967) had investigated 2,800 trait terms selected from unabridged English dictionaries. Nonoverlapping sets of 200 terms were administered to samples of 100 university students (50 men and 50 women), who for each term (a) provided a definition (or indicated that they could not do so), (b) rated its social desirability, and (c) indicated the extent to which it characterized themselves and each of three peers. On the basis of these data, ambiguous terms and terms that were unfamiliar to the typical college student were culled from the set.

Later, Norman classified the remaining 1,431 terms into 75 categories based on his understanding of their similarities in meaning. In making his classifications, Norman began by sorting the terms into a few broad categories, and then he subsequently developed more fine-grained classifications within each of the initial categories. Table 1 lists the number of terms in each of his final 75 categories, along with a few terms as examples.

Method

From the 2,800 trait terms included in Norman (1967), Goldberg (1982) selected a subset of 1,710 (which included the 1,431 described earlier) to be included in a self-report inventory of trait-descriptive adjectives (see Goldberg, 1982, for the procedural details). Under instructions to work on this task for no more than an hour at a time, 187 college students (70 men and 117 women) described themselves on each of the 1,710 terms, using an 8-step rating scale ranging from *extremely inaccurate* to *extremely accurate* as a self-descriptor. After all omitted responses were given a middle (5) value in a transformed 1-9 rating scale, the responses for each subject in turn were standard scored, thereby eliminating all intersubject differences in their means and variances across the 1,710 items.

Responses to the terms in each of the Norman categories were aggregated to obtain 75 scale scores for every subject. The coefficient alpha reliability estimates for each of these variables, which are listed in Table 1, are quite high for scales constructed without recourse to any internal-consistency analyses: For the 74 scales including more than one item, 95% of the reliability coefficients were larger than .60, and 73% were at least .70; the median scale obtained a coefficient of .76. Because the scales vary markedly in their number of items and because coefficient alpha is highly sensitive to scale length, Table 1 also includes the mean intercorrelation among the items in each scale.

The variables are listed in Table 1 by the factor on which they had their highest loading in this first study, and within each factor by the size of their loadings on that factor. Consequently, the first variables listed for each factor (the factor definers) exemplify its core meaning and are likely to be the most robust across studies. On the other hand, the last variables listed for each factor, which are only peripherally related to its core content, may be equally related to other factors, and therefore the factor with which they are most highly related may tend to vary from study to study.

Results

Effects of different methods of factor extraction and rotation. At the outset, it is important to try to allay the qualms of any readers who assume that, in factor analysis, what one finds depends primarily on *how* one looks. If that were so, the general goal of developing a scientifically compelling taxonomy of individual differences could be a foolish quest, as Eysenck (1981) once argued:

> Correlational psychology cannot in the nature of things come up with objective, universally agreed dimensions or categories; there

Table 1
The 75 Categories in the Norman Taxonomy of 1,431 Trait-Descriptive Adjectives

Factor pole/category	Examples	No. terms	Reliability α	Reliability $\bar{r}$
I+				
Spirit	Jolly, merry, witty, lively, peppy	26	.88	.22
Talkativeness	Talkative, articulate, verbose, gossipy	23	.86	.21
Sociability	Companionable, social, outgoing	9	.77	.27
Spontaneity	Impulsive, carefree, playful, zany	28	.77	.11
Boisterousness	Mischievous, rowdy, loud, prankish	11	.78	.24
Adventure	Brave, venturous, fearless, reckless	44	.86	.12
Energy	Active, assertive, dominant, energetic	36	.77	.08
Conceit	Boastful, conceited, egotistical	13	.76	.20
Vanity	Affected, vain, chic, dapper, jaunty	5	.28	.07
Indiscretion	Nosey, snoopy, indiscreet, meddlesome	6	.55	.17
Sensuality	Sexy, passionate, sensual, flirtatious	12	.76	.20
I−				
Lethargy	Reserved, lethargic, vigorless, apathetic	19	.74	.13
Aloofness	Cool, aloof, distant, unsocial, withdrawn	26	.86	.19
Silence	Quiet, secretive, untalkative, indirect	22	.87	.23
Modesty	Humble, modest, bashful, meek, shy	18	.76	.15
Pessimism	Joyless, solemn, sober, morose, moody	19	.79	.17
Unfriendliness	Tactless, thoughtless, unfriendly	20	.70	.10
II+				
Trust	Trustful, unsuspicious, unenvious	20	.83	.19
Amiability	Democratic, friendly, genial, cheerful	29	.81	.13
Generosity	Generous, charitable, indulgent, lenient	18	.70	.11
Agreeableness	Conciliatory, cooperative, agreeable	17	.71	.13
Tolerance	Tolerant, reasonable, impartial, unbiased	19	.76	.14
Courtesy	Patient, moderate, tactful, polite, civil	17	.73	.14
Altruism	Kind, loyal, unselfish, helpful, sensitive	29	.76	.10
Warmth	Affectionate, warm, tender, sentimental	18	.82	.20
Honesty	Moral, honest, just, principled	16	.67	.11
II−				
Vindictiveness	Sadistic, vengeful, cruel, malicious	13	.79	.22
Ill humor	Bitter, testy, crabby, sour, surly	16	.75	.16
Criticism	Harsh, severe, strict, critical, bossy	33	.79	.10
Disdain	Derogatory, caustic, sarcastic, catty	16	.74	.15
Antagonism	Negative, contrary, argumentative	11	.75	.21
Aggressiveness	Belligerent, abrasive, unruly, aggressive	21	.79	.15
Dogmatism	Biased, opinionated, stubborn, inflexible	49	.78	.07
Temper	Irritable, explosive, wild, short-tempered	29	.86	.17
Distrust	Jealous, mistrustful, suspicious	8	.65	.19
Greed	Stingy, selfish, ungenerous, envious	18	.61	.08
Dishonesty	Scheming, sly, wily, insincere, devious	29	.80	.12
III+				
Industry	Persistent, ambitious, organized, thorough	43	.85	.12
Order	Orderly, prim, tidy	3	.62	.35
Self-discipline	Discreet, controlled, serious, earnest	17	.64	.10
Evangelism	Crusading, zealous, moralistic, prudish	13	.71	.16
Consistency	Predictable, rigid, conventional, rational	27	.77	.11
Grace	Courtly, dignified, genteel, suave	8	.73	.26
Reliability	Conscientious, dependable, prompt, punctual	11	.68	.16
Sophistication	Blasé, urbane, cultured, refined	16	.72	.14
Formality	Formal, pompous, smug, proud	13	.67	.13
Foresight	Aimful, calculating, farseeing, progressive	17	.62	.09
Religiosity	Mystical, devout, pious, spiritual	13	.86	.31
Maturity	Mature	1	—	—
Passionlessness	Coy, demure, chaste, unvoluptuous	4	.13	.04
Thrift	Economical, frugal, thrifty, unextravagant	4	.74	.42
III−				
Negligence	Messy, forgetful, lazy, careless	51	.90	.14
Inconsistency	Changeable, erratic, fickle, absent-minded	17	.72	.13
Rebelliousness	Impolite, impudent, rude, cynical	22	.81	.16
Irreverence	Nonreligious, informal, profane	9	.73	.23
Provinciality	Awkward, unrefined, earthy, practical	27	.63	.06
Intemperance	Thriftless, excessive, self-indulgent	13	.67	.13

Table 1 (*continued*)

Factor pole/category	Examples	No. terms	Reliability α	Reliability $\bar{r}$
IV+				
Durability	Tough, rugged, unflinching	11	.66	.15
Poise	Worriless, calm, stable, sedate, peaceful	23	.83	.18
Self-reliance	Confident, independent, resourceful	11	.71	.18
Callousness	Ruthless, insensitive, cold, stern	17	.78	.17
Candor	Frank, blunt, explicit, curt, terse	31	.69	.07
IV−				
Self-pity	Touchy, careworn, whiny, oversensitive	14	.77	.19
Anxiety	Fearful, nervous, fussy, unstable	30	.85	.16
Insecurity	Unconfident, self-critical, unpoised	17	.84	.24
Timidity	Cowardly, timid, unventurous, wary	14	.72	.15
Passivity	Docile, dependent, submissive, pliant	22	.80	.15
Immaturity	Naive, gullible, superstitious, childlike	18	.70	.11
V+				
Wisdom	Intelligent, philosophical, complex, deep	16	.72	.14
Originality	Insightful, clever, creative, curious	17	.78	.17
Objectivity	Alert, perceptive, logical, certain	23	.72	.10
Knowledge	Informed, literate, studious, intellectual	16	.80	.20
Reflection	Pensive, thoughtful, meditative	10	.63	.15
Art	Literary, poetic, artistic, musical	4	.49	.19
V−				
Imperceptivity	Simple, ignorant, dull, illogical, narrow	45	.85	.11

Note. The two estimates of internal consistency—the coefficient alpha value for the total scale and the mean interitem correlation ($\bar{r}$)—were based on the standardized (*Z*-scored) responses of 187 college students (70 men and 117 women) who described themselves using an inventory of 1,710 trait-descriptive terms.

> are innumerable, mathematically equivalent ways of rotating factors, for instance, and no statistical magic key (not even simple structure) can close the door on alternative solutions. . . . Alternative solutions and rotations are in principle, and usually in practice, not only possible but also appeal to different people. . . . The final factors never completely escape the shadow of . . . the selection of methods of extraction and rotation. (p. 13)

Eysenck argued that scientific agreement on a structural representation is impossible, in part because alternative methods of factor extraction and rotation will generate different factors. In an attempt to examine the extent to which factor structures are influenced by the particular methods that are used, the 75 Norman categories were analyzed using a wide variety of such procedures, specifically five methods of factor extraction (principal-components, principal-factors, alpha-factoring, image-factoring, and maximum-likelihood procedures), each rotated by an orthogonal (varimax) and an oblique (oblimin) algorithm.

Of the 3,750 total factor loadings (75 variables × 10 methods × 5 factors) generated by these analyses, in only 30 cases (fewer than 1%) was the highest loading on a different factor than the modal one; in those few cases, moreover, the variables loaded about equally on two factors, one of which was the modal one. This high degree of intermethod congruence can be quantified more precisely by correlating across the 187 subjects the factor scores derived from each of the 10 factoring methods. When averaged across the five corresponding factors in each pair of analyses, the mean correlation of the factor scores between the orthogonal and oblique rotational procedures (holding constant the method of factor extraction) ranged from .991 to .995, and the mean intercorrelations among the five methods of factor extraction (holding constant the procedure for rotation) ranged from .950 to .996. Table 2 lists the factor loadings from varimax rotations of both principal factors and principal components; the uniformity of the values in the table demonstrates the robustness of the solutions across these procedural variations.

Although it would be foolish to contend that factors are never influenced by the particular algorithm that is used, such procedural effects are typically quite small in size. For the data sets analyzed in this article, findings based on principal components have been compared with those based on principal factors, and orthogonal rotations have been compared with oblique ones. In none of these analyses have the findings changed in any substantial way as a function of the particular method used. As a consequence, this article will include only the varimax-rotated solutions based on an initial principal-components analysis of the variable intercorrelations. For convenience, however, these components will typically be referred to as "factors."

Effects of the number of factors rotated. The intercorrelations among the factor scores derived from the analyses described earlier were averaged across the 10 methods so as to provide mean congruence correlations for each of the five factors. These mean intermethod correlations for Factors I and II (.99 for both) and for Factors III and IV (.98 for both) were somewhat higher than that for Factor V (.96). Nonetheless, the latter factor (Intellect) remained invariant as more factors were rotated. Instead, Factor III bifurcated when six factors were rotated, providing a more homogeneous version of the Conscientiousness factor, plus one that included the more peripheral categories

Table 2
The 75 Norman Categories: Factor Loadings From Varimax Rotations of Principal Components and Principal Factors

	Factor									
	I		II		III		IV		V	
Factor pole/category	Com	Fac	Com	Fac	Com	Fac	Com	Fac	Com	Fac
Factor I: Surgency										
I+										
Spirit	79*	78*	23	22	02	02	05	05	01	01
Talkativeness	77*	75*	−07	−07	11	11	−08	−08	08	07
Sociability	75*	74*	24	24	17	17	18	18	04	04
Spontaneity	68*	67*	01	01	−37	−37	−14	−13	03	03
Boisterousness	63*	61*	−31	−31	−31	−31	02	02	−02	−02
Adventure	58*	57*	−14	−14	−31	−30	44	44	04	05
Energy	56*	55*	−19	−19	13	12	42	41	18	18
Conceit	46*	44*	−39	−37	00	−01	14	14	−09	−08
Vanity	41*	39*	−08	−07	31	28	−27	−24	−18	−17
Indiscretion	38*	36*	−32	−31	−12	−12	−16	−15	−07	−07
Sensuality	25*	24*	−17	−16	−01	−01	−13	−10	22	18
I−										
Lethargy	−78*	−77*	01	00	01	01	13	13	−27	−26
Aloofness	−78*	−76*	−16	−16	−11	−11	−06	−06	02	02
Silence	−76*	−75*	20	20	−12	−12	−18	−18	−17	−17
Modesty	−66*	−65*	44	44	−08	−08	−13	−13	01	01
Pessimism	−61*	−60*	−34	−33	07	07	−46	−45	09	08
Unfriendliness	−53*	−51*	−27	−26	−35	−34	17	16	−04	−03
Factor II: Agreeableness										
II+										
Trust	−25	−25	82*	81*	05	05	10	09	−10	−09
Amiability	41	41	69*	68*	08	08	22	22	−02	−02
Generosity	30	29	68*	66*	07	07	−14	−14	05	05
Agreeableness	06	06	68*	66*	11	11	−13	−13	00	−01
Tolerance	−37	−37	61*	60*	−30	−29	17	17	19	19
Courtesy	−25	−24	61*	60*	33	32	20	19	15	15
Altruism	26	25	56*	55*	36	36	−30	−30	15	14
Warmth	33	32	43*	43*	38	37	−41	−40	−04	−04
Honesty	−11	−11	33*	31*	27	26	18	16	11	11
II−										
Vindictiveness	−01	−01	−79*	−77*	00	00	08	08	−09	−09
Ill humor	00	00	−74*	−72*	−09	−09	−15	−15	03	03
Criticism	08	09	−73*	−72*	32	32	12	11	11	11
Disdain	12	12	−67*	−64*	−10	−10	−11	−10	14	13
Antagonism	−07	−06	−65*	−63*	−12	−13	−18	−17	01	00
Aggressiveness	30	29	−64*	−63*	−21	−21	30	29	−15	−14
Dogmatism	08	08	−63*	−61*	10	10	31	30	−20	−18
Temper	30	30	−58*	−57*	−28	−27	02	02	18	17
Distrust	−15	−14	−52*	−50*	−11	−11	−33	−31	25	22
Greed	−26	−25	−51*	−49*	03	02	−09	−09	−14	−13
Dishonesty	28	26	−42*	−39*	−06	−06	11	11	00	00
Factor III: Conscientiousness										
III+										
Industry	−11	−11	−13	−12	71*	70*	17	16	35	34
Order	−03	−02	−04	−03	68*	65*	−18	−17	01	01
Self-discipline	−30	−30	34	34	65*	64*	03	02	03	03
Evangelism	31	30	01	01	61*	58*	−07	−07	−25	−23
Consistency	−23	−23	−02	−02	59*	59*	45	43	−20	−19
Grace	27	26	23	23	59*	56*	−01	−01	14	13
Reliability	−05	−05	11	11	53*	51*	24	22	13	13
Sophistication	05	05	20	20	52*	49*	06	06	31	28
Formality	29	28	−25	−23	48*	45*	−15	−14	−17	−16
Foresight	00	01	14	14	49*	47*	16	15	44	41
Religiosity	−14	13	22	21	43*	40*	−10	−10	−21	−18
Maturity	−20	−18	17	17	35*	34*	31	29	11	11

Table 2 (*continued*)

	Factor									
	I		II		III		IV		V	
Factor pole/category	Com	Fac	Com	Fac	Com	Fac	Com	Fac	Com	Fac
Passionlessness	−11	−10	19	18	**31**[a]	29[a]	−13	−12	−23	−19
Thrift	−21	−19	17	16	26[a]	25[a]	09	08	13	12
III−										
Negligence	−04	−04	19	19	**−73**[a]	**−73**[a]	−10	−09	**−36**	**−35**
Inconsistency	−03	−03	05	05	**−62**[a]	**−61**[a]	**−50**	**−48**	−03	−04
Rebelliousness	13	12	**−54**	**−53**	**−55**[a]	**−55**[a]	09	09	**31**	**30**
Irreverence	−19	−18	−18	−17	**−53**[a]	**−50**[a]	08	08	28	25
Provinciality	−24	−23	06	05	**−53**[a]	**−49**[a]	08	07	−11	−10
Intemperance	16	14	−14	−14	**−44**[a]	**−42**[a]	−21	−20	−24	−22
					Factor IV: Emotional Stability					
IV+										
Durability	−06	−06	−10	−10	−01	−01	**79**[a]	**77**[a]	01	02
Poise	**−37**	**−37**	**42**	**42**	14	14	**61**[a]	**60**[a]	−01	00
Self-reliance	16	15	14	14	14	15	**51**[a]	**49**[a]	**39**	**37**
Callousness	**−46**	**−45**	**−45**	**−45**	−06	−06	**48**[a]	**47**[a]	−07	−06
Candor	20	19	03	03	11	11	**43**[a]	**39**[a]	18	17
IV−										
Self-pity	−14	−14	−05	−04	15	14	**−81**[a]	**−80**[a]	−04	−05
Anxiety	25	26	−26	−26	05	05	**−75**[a]	**−74**[a]	−05	−06
Insecurity	**−31**	**−30**	−05	−05	−21	−21	**−69**[a]	**−67**[a]	−11	−12
Timidity	**−42**	**−41**	16	16	05	05	**−60**[a]	**−58**[a]	−07	−08
Passivity	−01	−01	**39**	**38**	16	15	**−55**[a]	**−53**[a]	**−30**	**−30**
Immaturity	15	14	22	21	−26	−26	**−52**[a]	**−51**[a]	**−42**	**−41**
					Factor V: Intellect					
V+										
Wisdom	−02	−02	−10	−10	−06	−06	01	01	**75**[a]	**71**[a]
Originality	19	18	12	11	−09	−09	20	20	**70**[a]	**67**[a]
Objectivity	−05	−05	04	04	24	24	**46**	**44**	**60**[a]	**59**[a]
Knowledge	01	01	11	11	27	26	15	15	**60**[a]	**56**[a]
Reflection	**−43**	**−41**	15	14	−07	−07	**−32**	**−30**	**45**[a]	**41**[a]
Art	15	14	25	24	03	03	−08	−06	**42**[a]	**36**[a]
V−										
Imperceptivity	−18	−18	25	24	−21	−21	−17	−17	**−78**[a]	**−78**[a]

Note. All values equal to or greater than ±.30 are listed in boldface. These analyses are based on the standardized responses of 187 college students (70 men and 117 women) who described themselves using an inventory of 1,710 trait-descriptive terms. Decimal points are omitted. Com = components. Fac = factors.
[a] Highest factor loading of the variable in each analysis.

labeled Grace, Formality, Vanity, Sophistication, Order, Evangelism, and Religiosity (positive loadings) versus Provinciality, Irreverence, and Rebelliousness (negative loadings). When seven factors were rotated, the three Religiosity categories (Religiosity and Evangelism versus Irreverence) formed their own small factor.

Moreover, beyond these 7 factors, all additional ones were defined by only one or two variables (e.g., Thrift versus Intemperance, Sensuality versus Passionlessness), whereas the initial 7 factors remained nearly invariant across rotations of up to 13 factors. For this set of variables, then, the factor structures seem to be remarkably robust, regardless of the number of factors that are rotated. Thus, one can conclude from this first study that this five-factor structure seems to be nearly impervious to variations in the specific factor procedures that are used, and it remains quite stable across variations in the number of factors that are rotated.

Factor structures are, however, known to be especially sensitive to the selection of variables under analysis (Peabody & Goldberg, 1989). Indeed, the structural representation displayed in Table 2 shows some anomalies when compared with analyses of other sets of variables. Some of these anomalies can be traced to the use of unfortunate terms as category labels; for example, the trait adjectives *conceited, vain,* and *unfriendly* (which normally are highly related to the negative pole of Factor II) were unfortunately used as the labels for categories that combine aspects of Surgency (Factor I) and Disagreeableness (Factor II). Nonetheless, although one should expect some differences in factor structures from study to study, the basic meaning of the factors must remain constant if they are to be given the same labels. Specifically, to demonstrate the robustness of the Big-Five factor structure, it is necessary to show that the core variables associated with each factor (the factor definers in Table 2) play the same role when analyzed within other subsets of variables.

Study 2

Rationale and Method

For inclusion in other studies, Norman's 75 categories have two major disadvantages. In the first place, the 1,431 terms in that taxonomy are too numerous to be administered in a single testing session. In addition, all of the classification decisions were made by a single individual. To provide a more objective basis for such classifications, dictionaries and synonym finders were used to classify trait adjectives into clusters of quasi-synonyms. As the criteria for this sorting task, the terms in a cluster had to be independently judged by lexicographers as synonyms; in addition, their mean social-desirability ratings (Norman, 1967) had to fall within a reasonably narrow range. The result was a set of 133 synonym clusters based on 479 commonly used trait adjectives. These 479 terms, all of which had been included in the inventory of 1,710 trait adjectives (1,710-TDA), were augmented by some others to form inventories of 566 and 587 terms (for further details concerning the construction of these shorter inventories, see Goldberg, 1982).

Each of the 133 synonym clusters was treated as a personality scale. Separate factor analyses of these 133 variables were carried out within each of four samples, two of which provided self-descriptions and two of which provided peer descriptions. *Sample D* included the self-descriptions from those 187 subjects already described in Study 1, each of whom completed the 1,710-TDA. *Sample C* included 320 other college students who described themselves on the 587-TDA using the item format that was described in Studies 3 and 4 of Goldberg (1981b); four middle response options were provided (*average or neutral, it depends on the situation, don't know*; and *term unclear or ambiguous*), all of which were here given a midscale value of 0 on a scale ranging from −3 to +3. *Sample A* included 316 of the subjects from Sample C, who used the 587-TDA to describe someone of their sex and approximate age whom they knew well and liked. *Sample B* included 205 students in law school and in an upper-division psychology course, roughly one third of whom were randomly assigned to describe one of three types of peer targets: (a) "someone whom you know well and *like* as a person," (b) "someone whom you know well but *neither like nor dislike*," or (c) "someone whom you know well and *dislike* as a person." The targets were further specified in all three conditions to be "of the same sex as you are, and about your own age." Subjects in Sample B used the 566-TDA, with the same 8-step (transformed to 9-step) rating scale used by the subjects in Sample D. Ratings of the three types of targets were pooled in the analyses of Sample B.

Results

Self-ratings versus peer ratings. Because of space limitations, the findings from this study could not be presented in tabular form. Available from the author are the 133 variables analyzed in this study, including each of the terms in each cluster, the coefficient alpha reliability estimates, and the mean correlations among the items. Because each of the clusters was designed to include only quasi-synonyms, they were all quite short (averaging fewer than 4 items each), and therefore their reliability coefficients would be expected to be low. The median of these alpha coefficients turned out to be .54, which is quite high for scales of this length.

Also available from the author are tables presenting the factor loadings from varimax rotations of five principal components analyzed separately in each of the four samples. Within each sample, the Big-Five factor structure emerged quite clearly. Tucker's coefficient of factor congruence (Harman, 1967, p. 257) was used as a quantitative index of the similarity between the factors derived in each of the four samples. The mean congruence coefficients across the five factors ranged from .86 (Samples B vs. D) to .94 (Samples A vs. C) and averaged .91. Moreover, the overall factor congruence between the two samples of peer ratings (.93) and between the two samples of self-ratings (.91) was not appreciably higher than that between the self and peer samples (.90).

Of more theoretical interest, however, intersample congruence varied substantially by factor; the values for Factors I, II, and III were all about .95, whereas those for Factors IV and V were both about .85. These findings, which replicate those reported by Peabody and Goldberg (1989) based on a set of 57 bipolar scales selected to be representative of common trait adjectives (Peabody, 1987), reflect the differential distribution of variables associated with each of the Big-Five factors. Specifically, within any pool of variables that is based on a reasonably representative sampling of the English lexicon of trait adjectives, there will be substantially more variables associated with each of the first three factors than with each of the last two. For example, within the set of 133 synonym clusters there were, on average, twice as many variables associated with each of Factors I, II, and III than with each of Factors IV and V.

What lies beyond the Big-Five domains? The design of this study permits a critical examination of the five-factor representation, both because of the relatively large number of variables under study and because the simultaneous analysis of four samples permits a direct test of factor replicability. Specifically, as progressively more factors are rotated, one can discover how many factors remain invariant across the four samples.

When additional factors were rotated in each of the four samples, the results paralleled those from the analyses of the 75 Norman categories in Study 1: The five original factors remained virtually invariant. Of even more significance, none of the additional factors replicated across the four samples. In three of the samples, Religiosity (Religious and Reverent) and Nonreligiosity (Nonreligious and Irreverent) loaded highly in opposite directions on one additional factor, but the other variables associated with that factor varied from sample to sample. In summary, then, this search for replicable domains beyond the Big Five was not successful.

Study 3

Rationale

The inclusion in the 479 set of some peripheral terms such as those tapping Religiosity and Nonreligiosity, the inelegance of including among the 133 "clusters" a few single terms (for which there were no synonyms in the 1,710-TDA), and the low reliabilities of a few of the remaining clusters stimulated efforts to refine the set further. For this purpose, a new sample of subjects was used to develop a refined set of synonym clusters, and then two of the samples from Study 2 were used to provide independent evidence of their factor structure.

Derivation of the 100 Revised Clusters

As a first step, the 479 trait adjectives were ordered alphabetically and administered with instructions to describe oneself "as accurately as possible," using a 9-step rating scale where 1 = *extremely inaccurate as a self-description*, 5 = *I'm uncertain or the meaning of the term is unclear*, and 9 = *extremely accurate as a self-description*. Subjects in this study were 192 university undergraduates enrolled in an introductory course in personality who elected to complete a course-related battery of self-report measures for extra credit. Subjects responded to these measures semi-anonymously, using only numbers for identification. To correct for individual differences in their rating means and variances, the responses of each subject were standard (Z) scored across the items, and all analyses were carried out separately using both the original and the standard-scored response values.

For each of the original 133 synonym clusters that had been derived in Study 2, internal-consistency analyses were carried out separately within each data set. As would be expected, the clusters tended to be slightly more homogeneous when based on the original response values (M alpha = .55) than when based on the Z-scored data (M alpha = .48), demonstrating that part of the covariation in the original responses can be attributed to individual differences in usage of the rating scales. Consequently, the standard-scored data were used to cull out the least homogeneous items from each cluster, and in rare cases to add an item that had been excluded from another cluster. Through an iterative process, the least homogeneous clusters were eliminated, including all of the single items, and a few new synonym sets were formed.

The result is a set of 100 clusters based on 339 trait adjectives. Table 3 lists the terms in each of the clusters, as well as their coefficient alpha reliability estimates and mean item intercorrelations. Whereas the original 133 synonym clusters averaged 3.7 items, the corresponding length of the 100 revised clusters was 3.4. Moreover, as would be expected to occur in this derivation sample, the reliabilities of the new clusters were higher than the old ones; the mean alpha was raised from .55 to .66 (original responses) and from .48 to .61 (Z-scores), whereas the mean item intercorrelation was raised from .29 to .40 (original responses) and from .23 to .34 (Z-scores).

Five principal components were rotated by varimax separately within the original and Z-scored responses from this derivation sample, and clear versions of the Big-Five structure emerged; a table presenting both of these factor structures is available from Lewis R. Goldberg.

To provide independent replications of these factor structures, two of the data sets from Study 2 were used. The *self* sample included those 320 subjects in Sample C of Study 2 who used the 587-TDA to describe themselves. The *liked-peer* sample included a subset of 316 of those subjects (called Sample A in Study 2), who used the same inventory of 587 trait adjectives to describe someone of their own age and sex whom they knew well and liked.

Results

Table 4 presents the factor loadings from varimax rotations of five principal components separately in the *liked* and the *self* samples. The congruence coefficients between the corresponding factors in the two data sets were .97, .97, .97, .93, and .92 for Factors I through V, respectively. Moreover, when the factor scores based on the 100 clusters were related to those based on the original 133 synonym clusters derived in Study 2, the correlations were .99, .99, .98, .93, and .97 in the *liked* sample and .97, .98, .98, .93, and .96 in the *self* sample.

Clearly, then, the factors derived from the 100 clusters are virtually identical to those derived from the 133 clusters, even though the former are based on 140 fewer terms. Moreover, the 100 clusters provide essentially the same factor structure for self-descriptions as for descriptions of liked peers. And, finally, the factors displayed in Table 4 are nearly perfect examples of the Big-Five: Not only do each of the clusters load highly on the factor with which they are normally most highly associated, but instances of extreme factorial complexity are quite rare.

General Discussion

The major aim of this article has been to provide sufficient evidence to alleviate any qualms about the generality of the Big-Five structure. To this end, findings were presented to demonstrate factor robustness within a near-comprehensive set of 1,431 trait adjectives across a wide variety of factor-analytic procedures (Study 1), and within a representative set of 479 commonly used terms across samples of both self- and peer descriptions (Study 2). Moreover, in both studies it was possible to assess the overall dimensionality of the pool of common English trait adjectives by examining successively more factors beyond the initial five. In no case was any additional factor of any substantial size, and in Study 2 no additional factor demonstrated any significant amount of across-sample generality.

Consequently, it now seems reasonable to conclude that analyses of any reasonably large sample of English trait adjectives in either self- or peer descriptions will elicit a variant of the Big-Five factor structure, and therefore that virtually all such terms can be represented within this model. In other words, trait adjectives can be viewed as blends of five major features, features that relate in a gross way to Power, Love, Work, Affect, and Intellect (Peabody & Goldberg, 1989). These features are clearly dimensional, rather than categorical, in nature (Chaplin, John, & Goldberg, 1988). Moreover, it has been shown that it is possible to uncover a variant of the Big-Five structure from analyses of judgments of the semantic similarity among a representative selection of trait descriptors (Peabody & Goldberg, 1989).

Given that the Big-Five structure seems to characterize the relations among English trait adjectives, it is reasonable to try to discover its generality to other types of stimuli, as well as to other languages (Goldberg, 1981a). Although a preliminary taxonomy of common English trait nouns has been constructed

Table 3
The 100 Revised Synonym Clusters

Factor pole/cluster	Terms included	No. terms	α Raw	α Z	$\bar{r}$ Raw	$\bar{r}$ Z
I+						
Spirit	Enthusiastic, spirited, vivacious, zestful	4	.76	.71	.45	.38
Gregariousness	Extroverted, gregarious, sociable	3	.62	.58	.35	.31
Playfulness	Adventurous, mischievous, playful, rambunctious	4	.57	.55	.25	.24
Expressiveness	Communicative, expressive, verbal	3	.71	.67	.45	.40
Spontaneity	Carefree, happy-go-lucky, spontaneous	3	.64	.67	.37	.39
Unrestraint	Impetuous, uninhibited, unrestrained	3	.52	.49	.26	.24
Energy level	Active, energetic, vigorous	3	.75	.66	.50	.39
Talkativeness	Talkative, verbose, wordy	3	.68	.64	.42	.38
Assertion	Assertive, dominant, forceful	3	.61	.55	.34	.29
Animation	Demonstrative, exhibitionistic, flamboyant	3	.55	.48	.29	.24
Courage	Brave, courageous, daring	3	.71	.69	.46	.43
Self-esteem	Assured, confident, proud	3	.67	.65	.41	.38
Candor	Direct, frank, straightforward	3	.74	.73	.49	.48
Humor	Humorous, witty	2	.61	.58	.45	.42
Ambition	Ambitious, enterprising, opportunistic	3	.63	.54	.36	.28
Optimism	Cheerful, jovial, merry, optimistic	4	.71	.71	.38	.38
I−						
Aloofness	Seclusive, unsociable, withdrawn	3	.74	.68	.48	.41
Silence	Quiet, silent, untalkative	3	.80	.79	.57	.55
Reserve	Detached, reserved, secretive	3	.62	.55	.35	.29
Shyness	Bashful, shy, timid	3	.79	.77	.55	.52
Inhibition	Inhibited, restrained	2	.59	.58	.42	.41
Unaggressiveness	Unadventurous, unaggressive, uncompetitive	3	.56	.58	.29	.31
Passivity	Docile, passive, submissive	3	.60	.57	.34	.31
Lethargy	Lethargic, sluggish	2	.65	.49	.48	.33
Pessimism	Bitter, joyless, melancholic, moody, morose, pessimistic, somber	7	.79	.65	.35	.21
II+						
Cooperation	Accommodating, agreeable, cooperative, helpful, patient, peaceful, reasonable	7	.66	.68	.23	.25
Amiability	Amiable, cordial, friendly, genial, pleasant	5	.68	.68	.30	.30
Empathy	Considerate, kind, sympathetic, trustful, understanding	5	.72	.72	.36	.35
Leniency	Lenient, uncritical, undemanding	3	.50	.59	.24	.31
Courtesy	Courteous, diplomatic, polite, respectful, tactful	5	.75	.72	.39	.36
Generosity	Benevolent, charitable, generous	3	.59	.58	.33	.32
Flexibility	Adaptable, flexible, obliging	3	.45	.46	.21	.22
Modesty	Humble, modest, selfless, unassuming	4	.45	.48	.17	.19
Morality	Ethical, honest, moral, principled, sincere, truthful	6	.77	.74	.38	.35
Warmth	Affectionate, compassionate, sentimental, warm	4	.70	.66	.38	.34
Earthiness	Down-to-earth, earthy, folksy, homespun, simple	5	.49	.51	.16	.18
Naturalness	Casual, easygoing, informal, natural, relaxed	5	.57	.59	.21	.23
II−						
Belligerence	Antagonistic, argumentative, combative, quarrelsome	4	.78	.67	.47	.34
Overcriticalness	Faultfinding, harsh, unforgiving, unsympathetic	4	.66	.45	.33	.17
Bossiness	Bossy, demanding, domineering, manipulative	4	.73	.65	.41	.31
Rudeness	Abusive, disrespectful, impolite, impudent, rude, scornful	6	.75	.45	.34	.13
Cruelty	Cruel, ruthless, vindictive	3	.74	.55	.48	.29
Pomposity	Condescending, pompous, smug, snobbish	4	.71	.60	.39	.28
Irritability	Crabby, cranky, irritable, grumpy	4	.87	.82	.62	.55
Conceit	Boastful, conceited, egocentric, egotistical, vain	5	.83	.73	.50	.35
Stubbornness	Bullheaded, obstinate, stubborn	3	.64	.63	.38	.37
Distrust	Cynical, distrustful, skeptical, suspicious	4	.68	.60	.36	.28
Selfishness	Greedy, selfish, self-indulgent	3	.66	.57	.39	.30
Callousness	Cold, impersonal, insensitive	3	.72	.62	.47	.35
Surliness	Caustic, curt, flippant, gruff, surly	5	.79	.63	.44	.26
Cunning	Crafty, cunning, devious, sly	4	.76	.68	.45	.35

Table 3 (*continued*)

Factor pole/cluster	Terms included	No. terms	α Raw	α Z	$\bar{r}$ Raw	$\bar{r}$ Z
Prejudice	Bigoted, prejudiced	2	.68	.59	.51	.41
Unfriendliness	Unfriendly, ungracious, unkind	3	.76	.65	.52	.38
Volatility	Explosive, tempestuous, volatile	3	.68	.56	.42	.31
Stinginess	Miserly, stingy	2	.67	.56	.51	.39
Deceit	Deceitful, dishonest, underhanded, unscrupulous	4	.69	.45	.35	.17
Thoughtlessness	Inconsiderate, tactless, thoughtless	3	.69	.60	.45	.34
III+						
Organization	Orderly, organized, systematic	3	.84	.84	.63	.62
Efficiency	Concise, exacting, efficient, fastidious, self-disciplined	5	.61	.62	.24	.24
Dependability	Dependable, reliable, responsible	3	.85	.82	.66	.60
Precision	Meticulous, perfectionistic, precise	3	.71	.68	.46	.42
Persistence	Industrious, persistent, tenacious, thorough	4	.59	.52	.26	.21
Caution	Careful, cautious	2	.70	.66	.54	.50
Punctuality	Prompt, punctual	2	.86	.87	.76	.77
Decisiveness	Decisive, deliberate, firm, purposeful	4	.53	.46	.22	.17
Dignity	Dignified, formal, mannerly	3	.51	.47	.27	.23
Predictability	Consistent, predictable, steady	3	.60	.64	.34	.38
Thrift	Economical, thrifty	2	.68	.70	.51	.53
Conventionality	Conventional, traditional	2	.57	.54	.40	.37
Logic	Analytical, logical	2	.45	.43	.30	.28
III−						
Disorganization	Disorganized, haphazard, inefficient, scatterbrained, sloppy, unsystematic	6	.80	.73	.41	.32
Negligence	Careless, negligent, undependable, unconscientious, unreliable	5	.78	.67	.43	.30
Inconsistency	Erratic, inconsistent, unpredictable	3	.50	.44	.25	.21
Forgetfulness	Forgetful, absent-minded	2	.80	.77	.67	.63
Recklessness	Foolhardy, rash, reckless	3	.70	.58	.44	.31
Aimlessness	Aimless, unambitious	2	.56	.57	.39	.40
Sloth	Lazy, slothful	2	.52	.41	.36	.26
Indecisiveness	Indecisive, wishy-washy	2	.49	.50	.33	.34
Frivolity	Extravagant, frivolous, impractical	3	.61	.53	.34	.27
Nonconformity	Nonconforming, rebellious, unconventional	3	.46	.43	.22	.20
IV+						
Placidity	Passionless, unexcitable, unemotional	3	.63	.49	.36	.23
Independence	Autonomous, independent, individualistic	3	.52	.46	.27	.22
VI−						
Insecurity	Defensive, fretful, insecure, negativistic, self-critical, self-pitying	6	.78	.70	.36	.27
Fear	Anxious, fearful, nervous	3	.61	.48	.34	.24
Instability	Temperamental, touchy, unstable	3	.66	.53	.40	.28
Emotionality	Emotional, excitable	2	.57	.44	.40	.29
Envy	Envious, jealous	2	.73	.71	.57	.55
Gullibility	Gullible, naive, suggestible	3	.58	.56	.31	.29
Intrusiveness	Intrusive, meddlesome, nosey	3	.71	.60	.46	.33
V+						
Intellectuality	Contemplative, intellectual, introspective, meditative, philosophical	5	.74	.71	.36	.32
Depth	Complex, deep	2	.63	.55	.46	.38
Insight	Foresighted, insightful, perceptive	3	.59	.56	.35	.31
Intelligence	Bright, intelligent, smart	3	.81	.76	.60	.52
Creativity	Artistic, creative, imaginative, innovative, inventive	5	.84	.81	.53	.47
Curiosity	Curious, inquisitive	2	.61	.56	.46	.40
Sophistication	Cosmopolitan, cultured, refined, sophisticated, worldly	5	.74	.74	.37	.36
V−						
Shallowness	Shallow, unintellectual, unreflective	3	.63	.51	.36	.25
Unimaginativeness	Uncreative, unimaginative	2	.84	.84	.74	.73
Imperceptiveness	Imperceptive, unobservant	2	.52	.41	.35	.26
Stupidity	Dull, ignorant, unintelligent	3	.59	.49	.33	.25
M		3.4	.66	.61	.40	.34

Note. The two estimates of internal consistency—coefficient alpha and the mean interitem correlation ($\bar{r}$)—were based on the original (raw) and standardized (Z) responses of 192 college students who described themselves using an inventory of 479 terms.

Table 4
Varimax-Rotated Factor Loadings From the 100 Clusters in the Liked and the Self Samples

Factor pole/cluster	I Liked	I Self	II Liked	II Self	III Liked	III Self	IV Liked	IV Self	V Liked	V Self
Factor I: Surgency										
I+										
Spirit	.70*	.63*	.27	.35	.05	.08	-.07	-.09	.10	-.01
Gregariousness	.70*	.73*	.07	.13	-.06	-.03	.03	-.07	.02	.03
Playfulness	.61*	.58*	.01	.01	-.18	-.17	.00	.04	.10	-.10
Expressiveness	.58*	.60*	.09	.05	.04	-.01	-.07	-.08	.19	.21
Spontaneity	.58*	.48*	.26	.29	-.28	-.21	.11	.03	-.07	-.16
Unrestraint	.55*	.55*	-.01	.01	-.32	-.14	.17	.07	.07	.09
Energy level	.54*	.60*	.09	.18	.19	.16	.18	.15	.06	-.09
Talkativeness	.53*	.58*	-.02	-.05	-.14	-.09	-.24	-.14	-.06	-.00
Assertion	.49*	.56*	-.46	-.33	.14	.15	.24	.28	.11	.09
Animation	.46*	.45*	-.16	-.14	-.21	-.14	-.07	.02	.08	.11
Courage	.40	.45*	-.04	-.03	.06	.06	.42*	.33	.10	-.09
Self-esteem	.48*	.51*	-.07	.08	.25	.24	.44	.38	.08	.07
Candor	.44*	.34*	-.01	-.10	.12	.03	.29	.29	.06	.17
Humor	.35*	.21*	.29	.07	-.12	-.04	.08	-.07	.14	.17
Ambition	.37*	.42*	-.06	-.10	.36	.28	.29	.15	.19	.21
Optimism	.59*	.47	.50	.59*	.08	.01	.09	.07	-.03	-.05
I-										
Aloofness	-.78*	-.71*	-.07	-.13	-.01	-.07	.01	.13	-.02	.05
Silence	-.78*	-.75*	.18	.10	.14	.11	.08	.14	.05	-.04
Reserve	-.66*	-.53*	-.02	-.08	.04	.03	.00	.17	-.02	-.05
Shyness	-.66*	-.66*	.35	.20	.06	-.01	-.19	-.18	-.06	-.18
Inhibition	-.59*	-.64*	.16	.08	.15	.12	-.13	.01	-.13	-.08
Unaggressiveness	-.57*	-.62*	.46	.19	-.06	-.21	-.11	-.14	-.10	.05
Passivity	-.48*	-.48*	.33	.28	.01	-.07	-.35	-.20	-.27	-.32
Lethargy	-.46*	-.28	-.06	-.12	-.26	-.30*	-.07	-.15	-.10	-.19
Pessimism	-.55*	-.52*	-.37	-.35	-.09	-.02	-.29	-.24	-.07	-.06
Factor II: Agreeableness										
II+										
Cooperation	.04	-.06	.77*	.72*	.25	.27	.13	.15	.00	-.13
Amiability	.32	.24	.61*	.60*	.04	-.02	-.11	-.08	.08	.07
Empathy	.17	.04	.74*	.70*	.21	.16	-.21	-.18	.06	-.07
Leniency	-.19	-.21	.63*	.49*	-.10	-.15	.24	.16	-.18	-.16
Courtesy	.00	.04	.55*	.48*	.37	.38	-.23	-.14	.18	.08
Generosity	.16	.03	.56*	.48*	.02	.04	-.04	.03	.14	.06
Flexibility	.13	.05	.55*	.54*	.15	.05	.12	.11	.04	.03
Modesty	-.30	-.39	.56*	.40*	.12	.11	.08	.02	-.05	-.16
Morality	-.10	-.09	.50*	.48*	.45	.24	-.05	.25	.10	.01
Warmth	.37	.19	.54*	.50*	.09	.08	-.37	-.44	.13	.00
Earthiness	-.03	-.11	.45*	.40*	.08	.08	.18	.12	-.21	-.32
Naturalness	.22	.19	.45*	.44*	-.17	-.09	.35	.37	-.06	-.19
II-										
Belligerence	.10	.22	-.74*	-.56*	-.02	-.12	-.14	-.07	.01	-.11
Overcriticalness	-.11	-.19	-.70*	-.67*	.01	-.07	.08	.08	-.14	-.03
Bossiness	.34	.40	-.68*	-.54*	.07	.15	-.09	.04	.00	.06
Rudeness	-.04	-.07	-.63*	-.53*	-.29	-.29	.26	.28	-.16	-.07
Cruelty	.02	.05	-.59*	-.46*	-.02	.03	.13	.12	-.22	-.27
Pomposity	-.04	.05	-.54*	-.50*	-.06	.00	-.15	-.07	-.10	-.12
Irritability	-.13	-.18	-.61*	-.42*	-.04	-.07	-.30	-.41	-.05	-.06
Conceit	.14	.16	-.64*	-.43*	-.16	-.21	-.02	.02	.03	.21
Stubbornness	.08	.12	-.57*	-.35*	-.07	-.15	.00	-.07	.04	-.03
Distrust	-.29	-.35	-.53*	-.49*	-.13	-.12	-.02	-.01	.05	.14
Selfishness	-.01	-.05	-.51*	-.44*	-.22	-.18	-.13	-.18	.04	.22
Callousness	-.38	-.32	-.50*	-.48*	.00	-.05	.33	.42	-.17	-.01
Surliness	.02	.09	-.44*	-.37*	-.08	-.10	.07	.08	-.26	-.34
Cunning	.18	.23	-.41*	-.35*	-.10	.12	.07	.05	.08	.08
Prejudice	-.04	-.03	-.44*	-.34*	-.09	.01	.08	.04	-.17	-.08
Unfriendliness	-.33	-.38	-.41*	-.38*	-.19	-.26	.28	.30	-.14	-.07
Volatility	.23	.29*	-.41*	-.23	-.10	-.17	-.20	-.26	-.06	-.12
Stinginess	-.32*	-.04	-.31	-.36*	.04	.04	-.03	-.07	-.06	.04

Table 4 (*continued*)

Factor pole/cluster	I Liked	I Self	II Liked	II Self	III Liked	III Self	IV Liked	IV Self	V Liked	V Self
					Factor II: Agreeableness (*continued*)					
Deceit	.09	.02	**−.43**[a]	**−.31**[a]	**−.37**	−.10	.08	.02	−.21	−.17
Thoughtlessness	−.15	−.04	**−.49**[a]	**−.34**	**−.37**	**−.44**[a]	.27	.21	−.24	−.14
					Factor III: Conscientiousness					
III+										
Organization	−.09	−.08	.03	.02	**.71**[a]	**.74**[a]	−.02	.03	−.05	−.03
Efficiency	−.06	−.05	.03	.10	**.75**[a]	**.73**[a]	.19	.12	.10	.11
Dependability	.04	−.02	**.31**	.29	**.67**[a]	**.61**[a]	.12	−.02	.00	−.10
Precision	−.13	−.06	−.06	−.08	**.54**[a]	**.62**[a]	−.05	.09	.16	.14
Persistence	.13	.21	−.05	.00	**.56**[a]	**.52**[a]	**.31**	.24	.18	.15
Caution	−.26	−.24	.14	.10	**.55**[a]	**.42**[a]	−.13	−.02	.04	−.10
Punctuality	.00	−.07	.10	.08	**.58**[a]	**.40**[a]	.06	−.07	−.01	−.01
Decisiveness	.18	.19	−.09	−.02	**.56**[a]	**.51**[a]	**.39**	**.36**	.11	.06
Dignity	−.12	.00	.18	.05	**.53**[a]	**.54**[a]	−.18	−.18	.14	.02
Predictability	−.20	−.12	.20	.21	**.49**[a]	**.48**[a]	**.30**	.26	−.20	**−.31**
Thrift	−.22	−.10	.20	.10	**.49**[a]	**.43**[a]	.06	.13	−.16	−.09
Conventionality	−.21	−.15	.24	.09	**.41**[a]	**.37**	−.05	−.03	**−.33**	**−.42**[a]
Logic	−.11	−.14	.01	−.01	**.45**[a]	**.30**	.22	**.34**	**.34**	**.39**[a]
III−										
Disorganization	.05	−.08	−.02	.04	**−.81**[a]	**−.81**[a]	.00	−.02	−.04	−.08
Negligence	−.10	.03	−.22	−.12	**−.75**[a]	**−.68**[a]	−.04	.03	−.09	−.06
Inconsistency	.04	.09	−.22	−.17	**−.55**[a]	**−.54**[a]	−.19	−.12	.12	.21
Forgetfulness	−.10	−.09	−.05	.03	**−.55**[a]	**−.49**[a]	.00	−.15	−.01	.01
Recklessness	.20	.18	−.21	−.25	**−.55**[a]	**−.47**[a]	.01	.00	−.14	−.14
Aimlessness	**−.31**	−.26	.06	.12	**−.50**[a]	−.29[a]	−.07	.03	−.26	−.08
Sloth	−.20	−.26	−.15	−.10	**−.46**[a]	**−.42**[a]	.00	−.13	−.11	−.16
Indecisiveness	−.28	−.25	.04	.07	**−.45**[a]	**−.45**[a]	**−.35**	−.25	−.11	−.04
Frivolity	.14	.13	−.13	−.12	**−.45**[a]	**−.40**[a]	−.22	**−.32**	.06	−.01
Nonconformity	.11	.07	−.15	−.08	**−.42**[a]	**−.33**	.22	.24	**.36**	**.39**[a]
					Factor IV: Emotional Stability					
IV+										
Placidity	**−.49**	**−.37**	−.09	−.14	.04	.03	**.54**[a]	**.59**[a]	−.06	−.09
Independence	.14	.04	−.07	−.09	.21	.09	**.38**[a]	**.37**[a]	.26	**.31**
IV−										
Insecurity	**−.45**	**−.46**	**−.30**	−.28	−.15	−.11	**−.56**[a]	**−.53**[a]	.02	.04
Fear	−.15	−.21	−.08	−.08	.01	−.02	**−.55**[a]	**−.61**[a]	−.05	−.08
Instability	−.20	−.16	**−.42**	−.27	−.17	−.15	**−.53**[a]	**−.58**[a]	−.06	.11
Emotionality	**.37**	**.30**	.21	.10	−.05	−.07	**−.53**[a]	**−.59**[a]	.08	−.02
Envy	−.03	−.11	−.26	**−.30**	−.12	−.01	**−.49**[a]	**−.52**[a]	−.10	−.15
Gullibility	−.15	−.08	.27	.27	−.22	−.20	**−.37**[a]	**−.46**[a]	**−.32**	−.18
Instrusiveness	**.30**[a]	.17	−.24	−.27	−.15	−.13	−.18	−.29[a]	−.12	−.22
					Factor V: Intellect					
V+										
Intellectuality	−.27	−.21	.23	.14	.02	−.08	.09	.13	**.64**[a]	**.71**[a]
Depth	−.12	−.11	.11	.14	−.08	−.11	.02	−.02	**.62**[a]	**.58**[a]
Insight	.06	.00	.25	.14	.24	.18	.26	.07	**.50**[a]	**.39**[a]
Intelligence	−.05	.01	.19	.08	.19	.06	.24	.08	**.54**[a]	**.58**[a]
Creativity	.09	.09	.13	.01	.02	.05	.10	.12	**.59**[a]	**.55**[a]
Curiosity	.21	.11	.01	.03	.00	−.13	.11	.00	**.34**[a]	.24[a]
Sophistication	.08	.15	.12	−.01	.26	.29[a]	−.15	−.01	**.41**[a]	.29
V−										
Shallowness	−.10	−.03	−.09	−.04	−.06	−.04	.04	.01	**−.66**[a]	**−.67**[a]
Unimaginativeness	−.23	−.16	.04	.09	.09	−.03	.09	.02	**−.51**[a]	**−.49**[a]
Imperceptiveness	−.20	−.17	.08	.13	−.23	−.20	.06	.08	**−.49**[a]	**−.45**[a]
Stupidity	−.27	−.28	−.08	.10	−.07	−.16	.00	−.05	**−.49**[a]	**−.41**[a]

Note. All values equal to or greater than ±.30 are listed in boldface. The values are based on subject-standardized responses in the liked (n = 316) and the self (n = 320) samples.
[a] Highest factor loading of each variable.

(Goldberg, 1980), no empirical analyses of these terms have been undertaken. On the other hand, analyses of Dutch trait nouns are already under way (de Raad & Hoskens, 1990), and the first analyses of German trait adjectives suggest that the Big-Five structure may well characterize the terms in that closely related language (Angleitner, Ostendorf, & John, 1990; Ostendorf, 1990).

When one turns from single terms to multiword statements, the picture is less clear. In some factor analyses of scales from one or more personality inventories, the investigators have interpreted their findings in terms of the Big-Five structure (e.g., Noller, Law, & Comrey, 1987), as have some reviewers (e.g., Digman, 1990; John, 1990), whereas other investigators have not (e.g., Zuckerman, Kuhlman, & Camac, 1988). However, only in studies in which markers of the Big-Five structure have been included is it possible to discover the actual degree of convergence. To solve this problem, Costa and McCrae (1985) have used questionnaire statements to construct a personality inventory (the NEO Personality Inventory [NEO-PI]) based on the Big-Five structure, and these investigators have been actively trying to assimilate the scales from a host of other inventories within the Big-Five framework (e.g., Costa, Busch, Zonderman, & McCrae, 1986; Costa & McCrae, 1988; McCrae & Costa, 1985, 1987, 1989).

In addition, the scales included in the NEO-PI have also been used as Big-Five factor markers in an extensive study by Borkenau and Ostendorf (1989). In a sample of 300 German adults, these investigators analyzed 36 scales, including the 5 from the NEO-PI, 14 from the Personality Research Form (PRF; Jackson, 1967), 11 from the Freiburger Personality Inventory (FPI; Fahrenberg, Hampel, & Selg, 1984), 3 from the Eysenck Personality Inventory (EPI; Eysenck & Eysenck, 1964), and 3 measures of response bias. Within this set of scales, the congruence with the Big-Five structure was exquisite: Factor I was defined by the Extraversion scales of the FPI, EPI, and NEO-PI; Factor II by Agreeableness (NEO-PI), Nurturance (PRF), Social Orientation (FPI), and Affiliation (PRF) versus Aggression (PRF and FPI); Factor III by Achievement (PRF), Conscientiousness (NEO-PI), Endurance (PRF), Order (PRF), and Achievement Orientation (FPI) versus Impulsivity (PRF); Factor IV by Emotionality (FPI), Neuroticism (EPI), Edwards's (1957) Social Desirability scale, Proneness to Stress (FPI), Somatic Complaints (FPI), and Irritability (FPI); and Factor V by Openness (NEO-PI) and Understanding (PRF).

The 100 new synonym clusters developed in Study 3 provide another set of Big-Five markers, which might now be included in future investigations. An inventory of the 339 adjectives used to score the 100 clusters is roughly the same size as the NEO-PI, and they both take about the same amount of time for self-descriptions. On the other hand, it should probably be easier to collect descriptions of a target from knowledgeable informants using the adjective inventory than using the NEO-PI. A description of the development of a number of more economical sets of adjective-based Big-Five markers is the topic of another report (Goldberg, 1990).

References

Allport, G. W., & Odbert, H. S. (1936). Trait-names: A psycho-lexical study. *Psychological Monographs, 47*(1, Whole No. 211).

Angleitner, A., Ostendorf, F., & John, O. P. (1990). Towards a taxonomy of personality descriptors in German: A psycho-lexical study. *European Journal of Personality, 4,* 89–118.

Borgatta, E. F. (1964). The structure of personality characteristics. *Behavioral Science, 9,* 8–17.

Borkenau, P., & Ostendorf, F. (1989). Descriptive consistency and social desirability in self- and peer reports. *European Journal of Personality, 3,* 31–45.

Cattell, R. B. (1943). The description of personality: Basic traits resolved into clusters. *Journal of Abnormal and Social Psychology, 38,* 476–506.

Cattell, R. B. (1945). The description of personality: Principles and findings in a factor analysis. *American Journal of Psychology, 58,* 69–90.

Chaplin, W. F., John, O. P., & Goldberg, L. R. (1988). Conceptions of states and traits: Dimensional attributes with ideals as prototypes. *Journal of Personality and Social Psychology, 54,* 541–557.

Costa, P. T., Jr., Busch, C. M., Zonderman, A. B., & McCrae, R. R. (1986). Correlations of MMPI factor scales with measures of the five factor model of personality. *Journal of Personality Assessment, 50,* 640–650.

Costa, P. T., Jr., & McCrae, R. R. (1985). *The NEO Personality Inventory manual.* Odessa, FL: Psychological Assessment Resources.

Costa, P. T., Jr., & McCrae, R. R. (1988). From catalog to classification: Murray's needs and the five-factor model. *Journal of Personality and Social Psychology, 55,* 258–265.

de Raad, B., & Hoskens, M. (1990). Personality descriptive nouns. *European Journal of Personality, 4,* 131–146.

Digman, J. M. (1990). Personality structure: Emergence of the five-factor model. In M. R. Rosenzweig & L. W. Porter (Eds.), *Annual review of psychology* (Vol. 41, pp. 417–440). Palo Alto, CA: Annual Reviews.

Digman, J. M., & Inouye, J. (1986). Further specification of the five robust factors of personality. *Journal of Personality and Social Psychology, 50,* 116–123.

Digman, J. M., & Takemoto-Chock, N. K. (1981). Factors in the natural language of personality: Re-analysis, comparison, and interpretation of six major studies. *Multivariate Behavioral Research, 16,* 149–170.

Edwards, A. L. (1957). *The social desirability variable in personality assessment and research.* New York: Dryden.

Eysenck, H. J. (1981). General features of the model. In H. J. Eysenck (Ed.), *A model for personality* (pp. 1–37). New York: Springer-Verlag.

Eysenck, H. J., & Eysenck, S. B. G. (1964). *Manual of the Eysenck Personality Inventory.* London: University of London Press.

Fahrenberg, J., Hampel, R., & Selg, H. (1984). *Das Freiburger Persönlichkeitsinventar* [The Freiburg Personality Inventory]. Göttingen, Federal Republic of Germany: Hogrefe.

Fiske, D. W. (1949). Consistency of the factorial structures of personality ratings from different sources. *Journal of Abnormal and Social Psychology, 44,* 329–344.

Galton, F. (1884). Measurement of character. *Fortnightly Review, 36,* 179–185.

Goldberg, L. R. (1980). *A catalogue of 1947 nouns that can be used to describe personality and a taxonomy of 1342 nouns that are typically so used.* Unpublished report, Oregon Research Institute.

Goldberg, L. R. (1981a). Language and individual differences: The search for universals in personality lexicons. In L. Wheeler (Ed.), *Review of personality and social psychology* (Vol. 2, pp. 141–165). Beverly Hills, CA: Sage.

Goldberg, L. R. (1981b). Unconfounding situational attributions from uncertain, neutral, and ambiguous ones: A psychometric analysis of descriptions of oneself and various types of others. *Journal of Personality and Social Psychology, 41,* 517–552.

Goldberg, L. R. (1982). From Ace to Zombie: Some explorations in the language of personality. In C. D. Spielberger & J. N. Butcher (Eds.),

Advances in personality assessment (Vol. 1, pp. 203–234). Hillsdale, NJ: Erlbaum.
Goldberg, L. R. (1990). *Standard markers of the Big-Five factor structure.* Unpublished report, Oregon Research Institute.
Harman, H. H. (1967). *Modern factor analysis* (2nd ed.). Chicago: University of Chicago Press.
Jackson, D. N. (1967). *Personality Research Form Manual.* Goshen, NY: Research Psychologists Press.
John, O. P. (1990). The "Big Five" factor taxonomy: Dimensions of personality in the natural language and in questionnaires. In L. A. Pervin (Ed.), *Handbook of personality theory and research* (pp. 66–100). New York: Guilford Press.
John, O. P., Angleitner, A., & Ostendorf, F. (1988). The lexical approach to personality: A historical review of trait taxonomic research. *European Journal of Personality, 2,* 171–203.
McCrae, R. R., & Costa, P. T., Jr. (1985). Comparison of EPI and psychoticism scales with measures of the five-factor model of personality. *Personality and Individual Differences, 6,* 587–597.
McCrae, R. R., & Costa, P. T., Jr. (1987). Validation of the five-factor model of personality across instruments and observers. *Journal of Personality and Social Psychology, 52,* 81–90.
McCrae, R. R., & Costa, P. T., Jr. (1989). Reinterpreting the Myers-Briggs Type Indicator from the perspective of the five-factor model of personality. *Journal of Personality, 57,* 17–40.
Noller, P., Law, H., & Comrey, A. L. (1987). Cattell, Comrey, and Eysenck personality factors compared: More evidence for the five robust factors? *Journal of Personality and Social Psychology, 53,* 775–782.
Norman, W. T. (1963). Toward an adequate taxonomy of personality attributes: Replicated factor structure in peer nomination personality ratings. *Journal of Abnormal and Social Psychology, 66,* 574–583.
Norman, W. T. (1967). *2800 personality trait descriptors: Normative operating characteristics for a university population.* Ann Arbor: Department of Psychology, University of Michigan.
Ostendorf, F. (1990). *Sprache und Personlichkeitsstruktur: Zur Validitat des Funf-Faktoren-Modells der Personlichkeit* [Language and personality structure: On the validity of the five-factor model of personality]. Regensburg, Federal Republic of Germany: Roderer Verlag.
Peabody, D. (1987). Selecting representative trait adjectives. *Journal of Personality and Social Psychology, 52,* 59–71.
Peabody, D., & Goldberg, L. R. (1989). Some determinants of factor structures from personality-trait descriptors. *Journal of Personality and Social Psychology, 57,* 552–567.
Thurstone, L. L. (1934). The vectors of mind. *Psychological Review, 41,* 1–32.
Tupes, E. C., & Christal, R. E. (1961). *Recurrent personality factors based on trait ratings* (Technical Report No. ASD-TR-61-97). Lackland Air Force Base, TX: U.S. Air Force.
Waller, N. G., & Ben-Porath, Y. S. (1987). Is it time for clinical psychology to embrace the five-factor model of personality? *American Psychologist, 42,* 887–889.
Wiggins, J. S., & Trapnell, P. D. (in press). Personality structure: The return of the Big Five. In S. R. Briggs, R. Hogan, & W. H. Jones (Eds.), *Handbook of personality psychology.* San Diego, CA: Academic Press.
Zuckerman, M., Kuhlman, D. M., & Camac, C. (1988). What lies beyond E and N? Factor analyses of scales believed to measure basic dimensions of personality. *Journal of Personality and Social Psychology, 54,* 96–107.

Received September 5, 1989
Revision received March 7, 1990
Accepted June 19, 1990 ■

The Phenomenological and Conceptual Interface Between Borderline Personality Disorder and PTSD

John G. Gunderson, M.D., and Alex N. Sabo, M.D.

Objective: The authors explore the conceptual and phenomenological interface between posttraumatic stress disorder (PTSD) and borderline personality disorder as well as the therapeutic and research implications of this interface. Method: They systematically review the relevant empirical, conceptual, and clinical literature. Results: These seemingly separate disorders are related. Borderline personality disorder is often shaped in part by trauma, and individuals with borderline disorder are therefore vulnerable to developing PTSD. Conclusions: The authors draw a distinction between the enduring effects that traumas can have on formation (or change) of axis II personality traits (including those found in borderline personality disorder) and acute symptomatic reactions to trauma, called PTSD, that are accompanied by specific psychophysiological correlates. They describe the implications of these conclusions for DSM-IV, therapy, and future research.

(Am J Psychiatry 1993; 150:19–27)

This examination of the interface between borderline personality disorder and posttraumatic stress disorder (PTSD) should be placed in the perspective of examinations of two other axis I disorders with which borderline psychopathology has been linked. Previous examinations of the interface between borderline personality disorder and schizophrenia (1, 2) and affective disorder (3) have involved research that helped establish the present boundaries for the borderline construct but have not greatly enhanced understanding of the pathogenesis of this personality disorder. Our current review of the relationship between PTSD and borderline personality disorder indicates that viewing the link between borderline personality disorder and childhood trauma through the lens provided by PTSD can cast more substantial light on the pathogenesis of borderline personality disorder.

Borderline personality disorder and PTSD both became official diagnoses in 1980 with the appearance of DSM-III. Awareness of posttraumatic psychiatric consequences has been present since the Civil War, but it was the influx of casualties from the Vietnam conflict that led to its inclusion in our nosology. As a symptom complex with physiological correlates, triggered by an external event, PTSD entered the axis I section of DSM-III. The earlier literature on PTSD was largely derived from the study of combat veterans and included a variety of approaches to its treatment (4–7). In contrast, borderline personality disorder entered the axis II section of DSM-III as a type of personality organization. Its inclusion in DSM-III grew out of its already widespread use by psychoanalytic clinicians and the empirically based descriptive studies that clinical use of the concept had already prompted (8).

The emergence of both borderline personality disorder and PTSD as official diagnostic categories has been greeted by wide but not always discriminating use. For many clinicians a diagnosis of "borderline" remains synonymous with "severe" personality disorder (9, 10), which is akin to Kernberg's original use of the term (11). According to Vaillant (12), the diagnosis is used for any patient who evokes hostile countertransference reactions. In this respect, feminist clinicians have voiced the concern that overuse of the diagnosis of borderline personality disorder by male clinicians for female patients reflects a negative attitude toward these patients (13). When Morey and Ochoa (14) examined this concern empirically, they found it to be unjustified, but the idea that the diagnosis of borderline personality disorder is pejorative has doubtless fueled enthusiasm for using diagnoses that evoke more supportive attitudes—such as PTSD.

The use of PTSD has been encouraged by the fact that it is a relatively efficient way to make a diagnosis that is both discrete and understandable to patients and to third-party payers. Moreover, public awareness of child abuse and the current mental health climate has made it professionally shameful to overlook or minimize a history of abuse. Unfortunately, hurried clini-

Received June 25, 1991; revision received June 1, 1992; accepted June 26, 1992. From the Personality and Psychosocial Program, McLean Hospital. Address reprint requests to Dr. Gunderson, McLean Hospital, Belmont, MA 02178.

The authors thank Drs. Frances Arnold, James Chu, Jonathan Davidson, and Katherine Phillips for helpful comments.

TABLE 1. Studies of Childhood Trauma

Authors	Year	N[a]	Diagnoses of Comparison Subjects	Childhood Experiences of Subjects With Borderline Personality Disorder (%)			
				Separation/ Loss	Physical Abuse	Sexual Abuse	No Trauma
Soloff and Millward (17)	1983	45	Schizophrenia, depression	56–62[b]			
Akiskal et al. (18)	1985	100	Other personality disorder, bipolar disorder, depression	37[b]			
Links et al. (19)	1988	88	Subthreshold borderline criteria	25[b]	29[b]	26[b]	44[b]
Zanarini et al. (20)	1989	50	Other personality disorder, antisocial personality disorder	46[b]	46	26[b]	26
Herman et al. (21)	1989	24	Other personality disorder		71[b]	67[b]	19[b]
Johnson et al. (22)	1989	43	Other personality disorder, normal	40			
Ogata et al. (23)	1990	24	Depression		42	71[b]	21[b]
Shearer et al. (24)	1990	40			25	40	
Stone (25, 26)							
New York Hospital-Westchester Division study	1987	29			28	35	
New York Psychiatric Institute study	1990	206	Schizophrenia, schizoaffective disorder	37	11	17	45
Australian study	1987	15				47	
Westen et al. (27)	1990	23	Undefined		52	52[b]	
Paris and Zweig-Frank (28)	1992	78	Other personality disorder		70[b]	70[b]	27[b]

[a]Number of subjects with borderline personality disorder.
[b]Significantly higher than percent of comparison patients.

cians may too readily diagnose anyone who has had recent exposure to severe stress as having PTSD—despite the fact that fewer than a fourth of patients who experience such stress actually develop the axis I syndrome (15).

Although borderline personality disorder and PTSD had very different backgrounds before entering DSM-III, their interface was propelled into attention by the overlap in their DSM-III and DSM-III-R definitions and acquired great significance after Herman and van der Kolk (16) highlighted the role of childhood trauma in the formation of borderline psychopathology. Several studies have persuasively documented that many patients with borderline personality disorder have childhood histories of sexual and/or physical abuse (17–28) (table 1). Available epidemiologic data indicate that of the 2%–3% of the population with borderline personality disorder (29, 30), roughly one-third fulfill criteria for PTSD (29). The overlap between the phenomenology of borderline personality disorder and the phenomenology of PTSD raised the same questions about their relationship as had been previously raised about the relationship between borderline personality disorder and schizophrenia and affective disorder. Are they separate but comorbid conditions? Does one contribute to the development of the other? Do they share common etiological backgrounds to the point that they are variants of the same disorder, and, if so, is this overlap in etiology sufficient that the disorders should be classified together on either axis II or axis I?

In this paper we will review the phenomenological and conceptual interface between borderline personality disorder and PTSD and document that these seemingly separate diagnoses have a complicated relationship. We will also identify areas where available knowledge can lead clinicians to more discriminating use of these diagnoses and, perhaps, eventually lead to more effective treatment strategies. In this process, we will identify multiple areas that are in need of more study.

THE PHENOMENOLOGICAL INTERFACE: SYMPTOMS AND TRAITS

In 1987, Herman and van der Kolk (16) observed that the clinical presentation of patients with either PTSD or borderline personality disorder shared major disturbances in affect regulation, impulse control, reality testing, interpersonal relationships, and self-integration. We will show that their overlap in presentation can often mask distinctions found by taking careful longitudinal and developmental histories.

Many characteristics of PTSD, if enduring, could also represent traits that offer evidence for a disorder of personality. This includes four of the proposed DSM-IV avoidant criteria (C4–C7) and two of the arousal criteria (D2 and D4) for PTSD (31) (appendix 1). If these or other symptoms of PTSD emerge and persist after exposure to a severe stressor, they represent a personality change (not necessarily like borderline personality disorder) for which DSM-IV now offers a new category—personality change after catastrophic experience (32). If several of these symptoms, namely hypervigilance (D4), irritability (D2), and feeling detached or es-

TABLE 2: Perceptual Problems Reported in Studies of Patients With Borderline Personality Disorder

Authors	Year	N[a]	Reported Perceptual Problem							
				Dissociation			Paranoid Experience		
			Visual Illusions	Depersonalization	Derealization	Undefined	Ideation	Ideas of Reference	Undefined
George and Soloff (37)[b]	1986	30	33		37				
McGlashan (38)[b]	1987	81	12	9	9		11	9	
Widiger et al. (39)[b]	1987	27	21				12	25	
Frances et al. (40)	1984	26				30			
Chopra and Beatson (41)	1986	13		85	92				77
Jacobsberg et al. (42)	1986	22	36	73			73	77	
Links et al. (43)	1989	88		49					32
Silk et al. (44)	1990	24				37			37
Zanarini et al. (45)	1990	50	24	36	30		78	74	

[a]Number of subjects with borderline personality disorder.
[b]Patients with borderline personality disorder with comorbid schizotypal personality disorder were not included in study.

tranged (C5), were to emerge, endure, *and* be associated with an intense unstable relationship or self-destructiveness, the diagnosis of borderline personality disorder might wrongly be made. This mistake would reflect a failure to attend to the early onset requirement for a personality disorder diagnosis.

The overlap between PTSD and borderline personality disorder is further confounded by the fact that instability is central to the construct of borderline personality disorder and a number of its criteria. If certain traits (namely, borderline criteria 5, 6, and 8 and the newly proposed criterion 9 [appendix 1]) are not documented parts of enduring patterns, they could be considered symptoms rather than personality traits. Their use as criteria for a personality disorder rests on their having an early onset and their being persistent qualities that endure across many situations. Moreover, other criteria for borderline personality disorder (e.g., criteria 1 and 3), intended to describe ongoing stable traits, could also surface as symptomatic reactions to trauma and—if their durability is unappreciated—could then wrongly be seen as evidence for a disorder like PTSD, if not PTSD itself.

Although the phenomenology of borderline personality disorder and PTSD would seem to be very intertwined, clinicians can usually distinguish these disorders by applying a fundamental distinction between symptoms and traits. The prototypical patient with PTSD presents with a subjectively disturbing symptom complex occurring in reaction to exposure to a recognizable and extreme stress (combat, rape, assault, etc.). PTSD usually is not confused with borderline personality disorder if the patient has a history of reasonably healthy functioning and relationships. The prototypical patient with borderline personality disorder presents with a hunger for care and a history of repeatedly failed relationships that would be atypical for most patients with PTSD. Thus, disentangling the overlap in phenomenology involves taking a careful longitudinal history to distinguish the enduring patterns that constitute personality traits from the rapid, adult-onset, symptomatic occurrence of those phenomena which overlap.

Although a longitudinal perspective can often distinguish when phenomena are symptoms of PTSD or traits of borderline personality disorder, unusual perceptual phenomena such as dissociation, paranoid ideation, or visual illusions may offer a new overlap issue in DSM-IV. Both dissociative and paranoid experiences have been associated with borderline personality disorder since before DSM-III (33, 34) and well before its linkage to PTSD. These symptoms are understood as observable evidence of the vulnerable reality sense and reality testing that characterize borderline psychopathology (11, 35, 36). Indeed, the prevalence and discriminating power of these experiences (table 2) has led to their being proposed as a new ninth criterion for borderline personality disorder in DSM-IV (appendix 1) (9). Dissociative experiences might also be either a reexperiencing (B3) or avoidant (C5) criterion for PTSD (appendix 1), and paranoid experiences are identifiable in several PTSD criteria such as B4, D2, and D4 (appendix 1). For borderline patients such experiences are usually triggered by an interpersonal stimulus (46), such as the perception of being abandoned or rejected, an experience believed to reflect intolerance of being alone (35). The dissociative states of borderline personality disorder often involve depersonalization and derealization. Unlike such states in PTSD, the dissociative states of borderline personality disorder are not commonly associated with amnesia, fugue, or problems with concentration. Moreover, the borderline patient's dissociative episodes are usually more transient and milder than those of the patient with PTSD, which, in DSM-III-R, requires a month's duration. DSM-IV proposes that the more transient types of dissociative states found in borderline personality disorder should be distinguished from PTSD as a separate category—brief reactive dissociative disorder (31).

The most distinctive signals for the presence of PTSD are the reexperiencing symptoms—intrusive memories, recurrent nightmares, or flashbacks (criteria B1–B3). Their occurrence reflects sensitivity to trigger stimuli (internal or external cues, criterion B4), such as smell, body position, or window lighting, that symbolize or resemble an aspect of the traumatic experience. The presence of these aspects of PTSD is closely related to the severity of the stressor event and not closely related to premorbid vulnerability (47). It is our impression that although these reexperiencing symptoms are not typical of most borderline patients, the types of visual illusions experienced by some borderline patients (table 2) often appear after exposure to current stresses and—now that the connection between borderline personality disorder and trauma has been established—may overlap the flashbacks or illusions of reliving of PTSD (criterion B3). When reexperiencing symptoms occur in borderline patients, DSM-III-R considers their appearance to be evidence for a comorbid problem, namely, PTSD. The emergence of PTSD symptoms under such circumstances could also be considered an elaboration of borderline personality traits (e.g., mood reactivity, abandonment fears, and vulnerable reality testing) caused by the strains placed on usual defenses. In any event, vulnerability to such reexperiencing symptoms (and comorbid PTSD) will probably be found to join other features (i.e., promiscuity, dependent/masochistic relationships, chronic dysphoria, and dissociative experiences) that have been shown to distinguish patients with borderline personality disorder who have histories of childhood abuse from those who do not (23, 26).

There is considerable phenomenological overlap in the ways that both PTSD and borderline personality disorder can present, such as being desperate, impulsive, self-destructive, and angry. There are also fundamental distinctions between the traits belonging to borderline personality disorder and symptoms belonging to PTSD that can be identified by use of a longitudinal perspective. Although perceptual symptoms can occur with both disorders, these may be more transitory and relationship-related for borderline personality disorder and more directly associated with traumatic memories for patients with PTSD. This is an emerging area that still requires more empirical examination. Other empirically testable questions include the following: 1) Can the phenomenology of borderline psychopathology be divided into parts that do and do not represent posttraumatic consequences? 2) Do different types of childhood trauma (e.g., abandonment versus abuse) or do the ages, frequency, or relationship to the perpetrator have distinctive consequences in the phenomenology of patients with borderline personality disorder?

THE CONCEPTUAL INTERFACE: TRAUMA AND PERSONALITY

Borderline personality disorder has become part of the still-enlarging awareness of the high frequency and manifold effects of trauma. This linkage can be traced retrospectively to Adolph Stern's seminal 1938 paper on borderline psychopathology (48). He noted that "actual cruelty, neglect and brutality by the parents of many years' duration are factors found in these patients" (48). Although a few other clinicians subsequently noted a high frequency of incest (49, 50), most psychoanalytically oriented writers overlooked Stern's observation. Even before Herman and van der Kolk observed the overlap in the phenomenology of borderline personality disorder and PTSD, Browne and Finkelhor (51) reported that victims of sexual abuse develop a constellation of symptoms that clinicians could readily associate with borderline personality disorder—specifically, depression, substance abuse, revictimization, and self-destructiveness. Subsequently, the link of childhood abuse to self-destructiveness—the most prototypical borderline behavior (14, 35)—has been confirmed (52), and a link with dissociation has also been demonstrated (53). This work has set the stage for the examination of how such childhood experiences relate to developing borderline personality disorder.

Available epidemiologic evidence suggests that although 38% of the population is exposed to catastrophic stress, only about 9.2% ever experience a PTSD-like reaction (15). Hence, the PTSD construct is complicated by the issue of vulnerability. It has been observed that PTSD is more likely to occur in individuals who have had previous exposure to unusual stress (54) or who have maladaptive coping mechanisms (55) and other adjustment problems (56). Recently Breslau et al. (15) identified childhood separations, a family history of antisocial behavior, and being female as risk factors for developing PTSD. The majority (75%) of patients with borderline personality disorder are women (9), and many have had excessive exposure to childhood separation experiences (table 1); patients with borderline disorder also have a high rate of antisocial behavior in their first-degree relatives (57). Therefore, they are also vulnerable to PTSD. This vulnerability is verified by the fact that roughly a third of patients with borderline personality disorder meet DSM-III-R criteria for PTSD (29).

The abusive experiences of borderline patients occur significantly earlier—mainly in childhood or during latency (20, 21, 27)—and more often involve the child's caregivers (23, 24, 27, 28) than do the abusive experiences of other clinical populations. These characteristics of the trauma underscore their severity and the likelihood that they will exert enduring effects on the child's character. In response to such trauma, children can become emotionally detached, forget, and dissociate; children can even develop PTSD (58). Beyond such observable reactions, the traumas evoke immature or primitive defenses that can persist well after the stress is over (59). It seems likely that the image-distorting defenses such as denial, splitting, and projection found to typify borderline patients (11, 60, 61) are at least in part derivative of the childhood traumas that most borderline patients have experienced. Thus, a dialectical process occurs after trauma whereby stress causes poor coping mechanisms that predispose to more stress and to having more maladaptive reactions to such stress. Given that premorbid vulnerability plays a relatively small role in the development of PTSD in reaction to extreme stress (5, 62, 63), having borderline personality disorder doubtlessly represents such extreme vulnerability that even modest stress may evoke it.

In the language of object relations, trauma affects representations of the self (e.g., as bad or helpless) and of others (e.g., as punitive or powerful) that shape the child's future expectations, goals, and reactions. More globally, the traumatized child's type of attachments are characterized by approach-avoidance and "hyperalert watchfulness" (64, 65). These concepts are core aspects of the borderline personality disorder construct, and the terms are consistent with an axis II perspective.

In neurophysiological language, the model of "kindling" can be used to explicate this process (66). According to this model, childhood traumas leave lasting traces in the brain's neurophysiological regulatory system; these are subsequently represented by hypersensitivity to later stressors that are evocative of the original trauma—stressors that would otherwise not reach the threshold for eliciting the excitation observed (67, 68). These are also core aspects of the PTSD construct, and the terms are more consistent with an axis I perspective.

Although abnormal neurophysiology of serotonin has been proposed as a temperamental substrate for borderline personality disorder psychopathology to account for hostility and impulsivity (69), this abnormality could as readily be the "carrier" condition that results from early trauma. Patients with PTSD show greater sympathetic activity, hyperfunction of the hypothalamic-pituitary axis, and dysregulation of the endogenous opioid system (70). These neurophysiological "carriers" may be important determinants of whether disturbances of personality develop after later exposure to traumas (71). In fact, Kolb (72) postulated that neuronal change in PTSD leads to inescapable physiological disturbances that in turn distort body image, self-concept, and, ultimately, personality.

Because several studies (table 1) have found a high frequency of childhood trauma in subjects who develop borderline personality disorder, because family studies (25, 49, 73) have shown that borderline personality disorder develops without abuse or abandonment about 20%–40% of the time, and because a history of childhood abuse is also associated with many other types of psychopathology (74, 75), it seems safe to conclude that the role of abuse in the pathogenesis of borderline psychopathology, although important, is neither specific nor sufficient. Borderline psychopathology arises out of a history in which abusive experiences join other factors to help shape enduring aspects of the character. The abuse in such instances is symptomatic of more pervasive problems of enduring emotional neglect and extreme conflict with both parents (20, 19, 25, 73, 76). The impact of abusive experiences, like the impact of experiences of loss (77), is probably mediated by the exposure to a neglectful environment before and after the events. Supportive caregiving can greatly diminish the consequences of exposure to abuse and, presumably, other trauma and can result in healthy adaptation to the experience (78).

The clinical diagnosis of borderline personality disorder is apt for describing a personality whose warp and woof can be traced to a complex intermingling of familial emotional neglect and misunderstanding beginning in childhood—often amplified by and perhaps partly created by the occurrence of childhood traumas (21, 57, 79).

These comments highlight a broader conceptual issue. Psychoanalytic theory holds that personality is formed, to a great extent, from the interaction between the child's innate disposition (i.e., his or her constitution or temperament), early parenting experiences, and other childhood experiences. Early psychoanalytic theory sees personality developing as "compromise formations" from the conflicts between impulses and prohibitions. These compromise formations organize the way a child binds and channels energy and organize the child's experiences and expectations. The emergence of object relations theory has added weight to the issue of whether such prohibitions are offered by the primary caregiver and within a predictable empathic relationship. In any event, personality development is intimately connected to the developmental processes involving stress, restraint, and frustration, and what renders these developmental experiences traumatic as opposed to creative depends a great deal on whether, in retrospect, we believe the resultant character traits are adaptive or not. Beyond the more easily identifiable traumas of physical or sexual abuse, desertion, and abandonment are the less obvious "microtraumas" such as emotional neglect, humiliation, or misattribution of blame (80). The boundary between the situational events and interpersonal problems that are identifiable as traumatic and those which are identifiable as creative is intrinsically unclear and subtle. Those children who experience severe traumas, with or without developing childhood PTSD, will adapt in ways that represent compromise formations which allow them to creatively adapt and survive. Once created, these compromise formations represent consolidated coping patterns that, unfortunately, may subsequently prove maladaptive in other, nontraumatic contexts. The image-distorting defenses used by borderline patients exemplify such handicaps.

CONCLUSIONS

We have described how the axis I diagnosis of PTSD was developed to identify a syndrome occurring in adults as a result of exposure to extreme stress. It was not intended to describe a childhood-initiated developmental process. Predisposing factors in personality (immature defenses or coping mechanisms), a family history of antisocial behavior, early separation experiences, and exposure to previous sustained traumas all make people with borderline personality disorder more likely to develop PTSD in response to later stress. Borderline personality disorder exemplifies a type of personality whose formation is often partly shaped by childhood traumas—a type of personality that is keenly vulnerable to developing PTSD in response to what might for others be subthreshold stressors. Having noted this, we think that these findings have implications for our diagnostic system, for treatment, and for future research.

The interface between borderline personality disorder and PTSD has several implications for DSM-IV. First, the proposed changes in the criteria for borderline personality disorder (defining persistent self-image distortions in criterion 3 and, as discussed, adding a ninth criterion reflecting cognitive/perceptual disturbance) highlight phenomena with associations to childhood trauma. We believe that this will usefully anchor the phenomenology of this personality disorder in its pathogenesis—as well as giving recognition to clinically important features (9). Second, DSM-IV should better convey the reciprocal relationship between severity of the stressor and premorbid vulnerability in developing PTSD. The emergence of PTSD symptoms after exposure to only a mild stressor should alert clinicians to the need to clarify vulnerability issues, and borderline personality disorder should specifically be cited as a known form of vulnerability. Moreover, the DSM-IV description of borderline personality disorder should cite PTSD as a common comorbid and complicating condition, as proposed by Davidson and Foa (81). Third, emphasis should be given to the distinctions between axis II traits of borderline personality disorder and axis I symptoms of PTSD by urging attention to their onset and duration. Fourth, added weight should be given to the reexperiencing subset of PTSD criteria in view of their relative independence from vulnerability. Clinicians should be urged to distinguish when the avoidant or arousal criteria of PTSD become enduring traits as opposed to reactive symptoms. Fifth, when PTSD symptoms become enduring traits as a result of adult stress, the reaction should be identified—regardless of how borderline personality disorder-like the illness seems—as personality change after catastrophic experience (32).

The enhanced understanding of the interface between borderline personality disorder and PTSD also has implications for treatment. Clinicians should be aware that their countertransference reactions may be operative when they use either of these diagnoses. Misuse of either PTSD or borderline personality disorder may reflect sympathy or dislike, respectively, as countertransference problems. The hazards associated with dislike of a patient with borderline personality disorder may have impelled the current enthusiasm for sympathy for the patient with PTSD.

Acknowledgment of the past traumas of borderline patients, accompanied by appreciation for the adaptive value of the ways in which the person managed the experience as either a child or an adult, can help the borderline patient attach to a therapist and ally with therapeutic goals (61, 79). Because recognition of a history of childhood trauma encourages a more supportive attitude, this can diminish the frequency with which borderline patients drop out of psychotherapy due to negative reactions to early interpretations or confrontations (82, 83). It can also lead to a more cautious and discriminating approach to family involvement (79).

Recognition of PTSD as a comorbid condition for borderline patients (i.e., those whose traumas are evoked and being reexperienced) should encourage the use of support groups. Such groups have proven effective in diminishing the pathological impact of trauma (5, 80). This use of groups contrasts with the usual unresponsiveness to group therapy referrals that has characterized most patients with borderline personality disorder (35, 84). Patients with borderline personality disorder and comorbid PTSD might also respond to medications directed at the reexperiencing symptoms such as propranolol (85, 86) or phenelzine (87). Conversely, recognition of comorbid borderline personality disorder may help explain variations in the response to medications among patients with PTSD (88).

Beyond these ways in which the recognition of trauma can inform treatment of borderline personality disorder, it is also important in later stages of treatment that a focus on traumas not deflect attention from the characterologic vulnerability issues (e.g., aggressive and secondary gain motives) that often complicate dysfunctional behaviors. This process differentiates here-and-now from past experiences of neglect or abuse and is needed in order to help modify the borderline patient's maladaptive character structure.

We have already identified a number of empirical questions that still surround the interface between borderline personality disorder and PTSD. First, could borderline psychopathology develop from repeated childhood exposure to abuse in the context of a reasonably healthy family? Second, do childhood histories of sustained neglect and periodic trauma predictably lead to developing borderline personality disorder? Third, can the neurophysiological changes associated with the PTSD syndrome also be found as sequelae to childhood trauma in the neurophysiological substrate of borderline personality disorder? If so, can these changes be altered pharmacologically in ways that diminish the character-forming consequences of trauma in children or the duration of the PTSD symptoms when they emerge in borderline adults? Finally, do borderline patients with histories of severe/sustained abuse differ significantly in their prognosis and/or treatment response from those without such histories? If they do, does this signify that the borderline construct should be narrowed to exclude patients whose character did not develop out of such trauma? If this should happen, borderline personality disorder would become a prototype for a personality disorder with a description strongly anchored in the medical tradition of being etiologically based and therapeutically specific. It might then assume a place alongside yet another axis I condition, multiple personality disorder.

In this paper we have examined the relationship between an axis I disorder, PTSD, and an axis II disorder, borderline personality disorder. In the process, the limitations of such a division and the complexities of the interface between them have been uncovered. Unlike the previous examinations of the interface between borderline personality disorder and other axis I disorders, we found that trauma offers an important perspective on its pathogenesis. As with other axis I/axis II divisions, the presence of seemingly separate but related categories in our diagnostic system provides a structure and a stimulant for further research. We have identified some directions that can be taken to further illuminate this interface.

REFERENCES

1. Gunderson JG, Singer MT: Defining borderline patients: an overview. Am J Psychiatry 1975; 132:1–10
2. Spitzer RL, Endicott J, Gibbon M: Crossing the border into borderline personality and borderline schizophrenia: the development of criteria. Arch Gen Psychiatry 1979; 36:17–24
3. Gunderson JG, Phillips KA: A current view of the interface between borderline personality disorder and depression. Am J Psychiatry 1991; 148:967–975
4. Garber J, Seligman ME (eds): Human Helplessness: Theory and Applications. New York, Academic Press, 1980
5. Grinker RR, Spiegel JP: Men Under Stress. Philadelphia, Blakiston, 1945
6. Horowitz MJ: Stress Response Syndromes. New York, Jason Aronson, 1976
7. Kardiner A: The Traumatic Neuroses of War. New York, Harper, 1941
8. Gunderson JG: Empirical studies of the borderline diagnosis, in Psychiatry 1982: The American Psychiatric Association Annual Review. Edited by Grinspoon L. Washington, DC, American Psychiatric Press, 1982
9. Gunderson JG, Zanarini MC, Kisiel CL: Borderline personality disorder: a review of data on DSM-III-R descriptions. J Personality Disorders 1991; 5:340–352
10. Nurnberg HG, Raskin M, Levine PE, Pollack S, Siegel O, Prince R: The comorbidity of borderline personality disorder and other DSM-III-R axis II personality disorders. Am J Psychiatry 1991; 148:1371–1377
11. Kernberg O: Borderline personality organization. J Am Psychoanal Assoc 1967; 15:641–685
12. Vaillant GE: The beginning of wisdom is never calling a patient borderline. J Psychotherapy Res Practice 1992; 1:117–134
13. Henry KA, Cohen CI: The role of labeling processes in diagnosing borderline personality disorder. Am J Psychiatry 1983; 140: 1527–1529
14. Morey LC, Ochoa ES: An investigation of adherence to diagnostic criteria: clinical diagnosis of the DSM-III personality disorders. J Personality Disorders 1989; 3:180–192
15. Breslau N, Davis GC, Andreski P, Peterson E: Traumatic events and posttraumatic stress disorder in an urban population of young adults. Arch Gen Psychiatry 1991; 48:216–222
16. Herman J, van der Kolk BA: Traumatic antecedents of borderline personality disorder, in Psychological Trauma. Edited by van der Kolk BA. Washington, DC, American Psychiatric Press, 1987
17. Soloff PH, Millward JW: Developmental histories of borderline patients. Compr Psychiatry 1983; 24:574–588
18. Akiskal HS, Chen SE, Davis GC, Puzantian VR, Kashgarian M, Bolinger JM: Borderline: an adjective in search of a noun. J Clin Psychiatry 1985; 46:41–48
19. Links PS, Steiner M, Offord DR, Eppel A: Characteristics of borderline personality disorder: a Canadian study. Can J Psychiatry 1988; 33:336–340
20. Zanarini MC, Gunderson JG, Marino MF, Schwartz EO, Frankenburg FR: Childhood experiences of borderline patients. Compr Psychiatry 1989; 30:18–25
21. Herman JL, Perry JC, van der Kolk BA: Childhood trauma in borderline personality disorder. Am J Psychiatry 1989; 146: 490–495
22. Johnson C, Tobin D, Enright A: Prevalence and clinical characteristics of borderline patients in an eating disordered population. J Clin Psychiatry 1989; 50:9–15
23. Ogata SN, Silk KR, Goodrich S, Lohr NE, Westen D, Hill EM: Childhood sexual and physical abuse in adult patients with borderline personality disorder. Am J Psychiatry 1990; 147:1008–1013
24. Shearer SL, Peters CP, Quaytman MS, Ogden RL: Frequency and correlates of childhood sexual and physical abuse histories in adult female borderline patients. Am J Psychiatry 1990; 147: 214–216
25. Stone MH: Abuse and abusiveness in borderline personality disorder, in Family Environment and Borderline Personality Disorder. Edited by Links P. Washington, DC, American Psychiatric Press, 1990
26. Stone MH: Incest in the borderline patient, in Incest-Related Syndromes of Adult Psychopathology. Edited by Kluft RP. Washington, DC, American Psychiatric Press, 1990
27. Westen D, Ludolph P, Misle B, Ruffins S, Block MJ: Physical and sexual abuse in adolescent girls with borderline personality disorder. Am J Orthopsychiatry 1990; 60:55–66
28. Paris J, Zweig-Frank H: A critical review of the role of childhood sexual abuse in the etiology of borderline personality disorder. Can J Psychiatry 1992; 37:125–128
29. Swartz M, Blazer D, George L, Winfield I: Estimating the prevalence of borderline personality disorder in the community. J Personality Disorders 1990; 4:257–272
30. Coryell W, Zimmerman M: DSM-III personality disorder diagnoses in a nonpatient sample. Arch Gen Psychiatry 1989; 46: 682–689
31. American Psychiatric Association Task Force on DSM-IV: DSM-IV Options Book: Work in Progress 9/1/91. Washington, DC, APA, 1991
32. Shea T: Enduring personality change after catastrophic experience: a review of the literature, in DSM-IV Sourcebook. Edited by Widiger T. Washington, DC, American Psychiatric Press (in press)
33. Gunderson JG, Carpenter WT Jr, Strauss JS: Borderline and schizophrenic patients: a comparative study. Am J Psychiatry 1975; 132:1257–1264
34. Gunderson JG: The relatedness of borderline schizophrenic disorders. Schizophr Bull 1979; 5:17–22
35. Gunderson JG: Borderline Personality Disorder. Washington, DC, American Psychiatric Press, 1984
36. Frosch J: Psychotic character versus borderline. Int J Psychoanal 1988; 69:347–357
37. George A, Soloff PH: Schizotypal symptoms in patients with borderline personality disorders. Am J Psychiatry 1986; 143:212–215
38. McGlashan TH: Testing DSM-III symptom criteria for schizotypal and borderline personality disorders. Arch Gen Psychiatry 1987; 44:143–148
39. Widiger TA, Trull TJ, Hurt SW, Clarkin J, Frances A: A multidimensional scaling of the DSM-III personality disorders. Arch Gen Psychiatry 1987; 44:557–563
40. Frances A, Clarkin JF, Gilmore M, Hurt SW, Brown R: Reliability of criteria for borderline personality disorder: a comparison of DSM-III and the Diagnostic Interview for Borderline Patients. Am J Psychiatry 1984; 141:1080–1084
41. Chopra HD, Beatson JA: Psychotic symptoms in borderline personality disorder. Am J Psychiatry 1986; 143:1605–1607
42. Jacobsberg LB, Hymowitz P, Barasch A, Frances AJ: Symptoms of schizotypal personality disorder. Am J Psychiatry 1986; 143: 1222–1227
43. Links PS, Steiner M, Mitton J: Characteristics of psychosis in borderline personality disorder. Psychopathology 1989; 22: 188–193
44. Silk KR, Westen D, Lohr NE, Benjamin J, Gold L: DSM-III and DSM-III-R schizotypal symptoms in borderline personality disorder. Compr Psychiatry 1990; 31:103–110
45. Zanarini MC, Gunderson JG, Frankenburg FR: Cognitive features of borderline personality disorder. Am J Psychiatry 1990; 147:57–63
46. Sternbach SE, Judd PH, Sabo AN, McGlashan T, Gunderson JG: Cognitive and perceptual distortions in borderline personality

disorder and schizotypal personality disorder in a vignette sample. Compr Psychiatry 1992; 33:186–189
47. True WR, Rice J, Eisen SA, Goldberg J, Lyons MJ, Nowak MS: A twin study of genetic and environmental contributions to liability for posttraumatic stress symptoms. Arch Gen Psychiatry (in press)
48. Stern A: Psychoanalytic investigation and therapy in the borderline group of neuroses. Psychoanal Q 1938; 7:467–489
49. Walsh F: The family of the borderline patient, in The Borderline Patient. Edited by Grinker R, Werble B. New York, Jason Aronson, 1977
50. Stone MH: Borderline syndromes: a consideration of subtypes and an overview, directions for research. Psychiatr Clin North Am 1981; 4:3–24
51. Browne A, Finkelhor D: Impact of sexual abuse: a review of the research. Psychol Bull 1986; 99:66–77
52. van der Kolk BA, Perry JC, Herman JL: Childhood origins of self-destructive behavior. Am J Psychiatry 1991; 148:1665–1671
53. Chu JA, Dill DL: Dissociative symptoms in relation to childhood physical and sexual abuse. Am J Psychiatry 1990; 147: 887–892
54. Green BL, Grace MC, Gleser GC: Identifying survivors at risk: long-term impairment following the Beverly Hills Supper Club Fire. J Consult Clin Psychol 1985; 53:672–678
55. Gleser GC, Green BL, Winget CN: Prolonged Psychosocial Effects of Disaster: A Study of Buffalo Creek. New York, Academic Press, 1981
56. McCahill TW, Meyer LC, Fischman AM: The Aftermath of Rape. Lexington, Mass, DC Heath, 1979
57. Gunderson JG, Zanarini MC: Pathogenesis of borderline personality disorder, in American Psychiatric Press Review of Psychiatry, vol 8. Edited by Tasman A, Hales RE, Frances AJ. Washington, DC, American Psychiatric Press, 1989
58. Lyons JA: Posttraumatic stress disorder in children and adolescents: a review of the literature. Developmental and Behavioral Pediatrics 1987; 8:349–356
59. Vaillant GE, Bond M, Vaillant CO: An empirically validated hierarchy of defense mechanisms. Arch Gen Psychiatry 1986; 43: 786–794
60. Bond M, Gardiner ST, Christian J, Sigel JJ: An empirical examination of defense mechanisms. Arch Gen Psychiatry 1983; 40: 333–338
61. Saunders EA, Arnold F: Borderline Personality Disorder and Childhood Abuse: Revisions in Clinical Thinking and Treatment Approach: Work in Process 59. Wellesley, Mass, Stone Center, 1991
62. Rabkin JG, Struening EL: Life events, stress and illness. Science 1976; 194:1013–1020
63. Shore JH, Tatum EL, Vollmer WM: Psychiatric reactions to disaster: the Mount St Helens experience. Am J Psychiatry 1986; 143:590–595
64. Bowlby J: Violence in the family as a disorder of the attachment and caregiving systems. Am J Psychoanal 1984; 44:9–27
65. Bowlby J: Developmental psychiatry comes of age. Am J Psychiatry 1988; 145:1–10
66. Meyersburg HA, Post RM: An holistic developmental view of neural and psychological processes: a neurobiologic-psychoanalytic integration. Br J Psychiatry 1979; 135:139–155
67. van der Kolk BA, Greenberg MS: The psychobiology of the trauma response: hyperarousal, constriction, and addiction to traumatic reexposure, in Psychological Trauma. Edited by van der Kolk BA. Washington, DC, American Psychiatric Press, 1987
68. Southwick SM, Krystal JH, Johnson DR, Charney DS: Neurobiology of posttraumatic stress disorder, in American Psychiatric Press Review of Psychiatry, vol 11. Edited by Tasman A, Riba MR. Washington, DC, American Psychiatric Press, 1992
69. Coccaro EF, Siever LJ, Klar HM, Maurer G, Cochrane K, Cooper TB, Mohs RC, Davis KL: Serotonergic studies in patients with affective and personality disorders: correlates with suicidal and impulsive aggressive behavior. Arch Gen Psychiatry 1989; 46:587–599
70. Friedman MJ: Biological approaches to the diagnosis and treatment of posttraumatic stress disorder. J Traumatic Stress 1991; 4:67–91
71. DeFazio VJ: Dynamic perspectives on the nature and effects of combat stress, in Stress Disorders Among Vietnam Veterans: Theory, Research and Treatment. Edited by Figley CR. New York, Brunner/Mazel, 1978
72. Kolb LC: A neurophysiological hypothesis explaining posttraumatic stress disorders. Am J Psychiatry 1987; 144:989–995
73. Gunderson JG, Kerr J, Englund E: The families of borderlines: a comparative study. Arch Gen Psychiatry 1980; 37:27–33
74. Herman J: Sequelae of prolonged and repeated trauma: evidence for a complex posttraumatic syndrome (DESNOS): a review of the literature, in DSM-IV Sourcebook. Edited by Widiger T. Washington, DC, American Psychiatric Press (in press)
75. Terr LC: Childhood traumas: an outline and overview. Am J Psychiatry 1991; 148:10–20
76. Zweig-Frank H, Paris J: Parents' emotional neglect and overprotection according to the recollections of patients with borderline personality disorder. Am J Psychiatry 1991; 148:648–651; correction, 148:1282
77. Kendler KS, Neale MG, Kessler RC, Heath AC, Eaves LJ: Childhood parental loss and adult psychopathology in women: a twin study perspective. Arch Gen Psychiatry 1992; 49:109–116
78. Featherman J: Factors relating to the quality of adult adjustment in female victims of child sexual abuse. Developments, spring 1992, p 1
79. Perry JC, Herman JL, van der Kolk BA, Hoke LA: Psychotherapy and psychological trauma in borderline personality disorder. Psychiatr Annals 1990; 20:33–43
80. Moses R: Adult psychic trauma: the question of early predisposition and some detailed mechanisms. Int J Psychoanalysis 1978; 59:353–363
81. Davidson J, Foa E: Diagnostic issues in posttraumatic stress disorder: considerations for the DSM-IV. J Abnorm Psychol 1991; 100:346–355
82. Gunderson J, Frank A, Ronningstam ER, Wachter S, Lynch F, Wolf PJ: Early discontinuance of borderline patients from psychotherapy. J Nerv Ment Dis 1989; 177:38–42
83. Kolb JE, Gunderson JG: Book review, OF Kernberg, MA Selzer, HW Koenigsberg, AC Carr, AH Appelbaum: Psychodynamic Psychotherapy of Borderline Patients. Int Rev Psychoanalysis 1990; 17:513–516
84. Stone MH, Weissman R: Group therapy with borderline patients, in Contemporary Perspectives in Group Psychotherapy. Edited by Slavinska-Haly IV. London, Routledge & Kegan Paul, 1984
85. Famularo R, Kinscherff R, Fenton T: Propranolol treatment for childhood posttraumatic stress disorder, acute type: a pilot study. Am J Dis Child 1988; 142:1244–1247
86. Kolb LC, Burns BC, Griffiths S: Propranolol and clonidine in the treatment of posttraumatic stress disorders, in Posttraumatic Stress Disorder: Psychological and Biological Sequelae. Edited by van der Kolk BA. Washington, DC, American Psychiatric Press, 1984
87. Frank JB, Kosten TR, Giller EL Jr, Dan E: A randomized clinical trial of phenelzine and imipramine for posttraumatic stress disorder. Am J Psychiatry 1988; 145:1289–1291
88. Davidson J, Kindler H, Smith R, Mahorney SL, Lipper S, Hammett E, Saunders WB, Cavenar JO: Treatment of posttraumatic stress disorder with amitriptyline and placebo. Arch Gen Psychiatry 1990; 47:259–266

APPENDIX 1. Proposed DSM-IV Criteria for Borderline Personality Disorder and PTSD From *DSM-IV Options Book: Work in Progress 9/1/91* (31)

Criteria for Borderline Personality Disorder

Pervasive pattern of instability of interpersonal relationships, as indicated by five or more of the following:

1. Frantic efforts to avoid real or imagined abandonment
2. Pattern of unstable, intense interpersonal relationships

3. Identity disturbance: persistent self-image distortions (e.g., feeling that one does not exist or embodies evil) (this criterion involves significant changes from DSM-III-R)
4. Impulsiveness in potentially self-damaging areas (e.g., substance abuse)
5. Recurrent self-destructive threats, gestures, or behavior
6. Affective instability; marked reactivity of mood (e.g., intense episodic dysphoria)
7. Chronic feelings of emptiness
8. Inappropriate, intense, or uncontrolled anger
9. Transient, stress-related dissociative or paranoid ideation (this criterion involves significant changes from DSM-III-R)

Criteria for PTSD

A. Exposure to traumatic event or severe stress

B. Reexperience of the traumatic event in one or more of the following ways:

1. Recurrent and intrusive recollections (images, thoughts, perceptions) of the event
2. Recurrent distressing dreams of the event
3. Acting or feeling as if event were recurring (flashbacks or illusions of reliving the event)
4. Intense psychological reaction to internal or external cues symbolizing or resembling the event
5. Physiological reactivity to internal or external cues symbolizing or resembling the event

C. Persistent avoidance of stimuli associated with the event, indicated by two or more of the following:

1. Avoidance of thoughts and feelings associated with the trauma
2. Avoidance of activities associated with the trauma
3. Inability to recall the trauma
4. Diminished interest in significant activities
5. Feeling detached or estranged
6. Restricted affect (e.g., unable to have loving feelings)
7. Sense of a limited future

D. Persistent arousal symptoms, indicated by two or more of the following:

1. Difficulty falling or staying asleep
2. Irritability
3. Difficulty concentrating
4. Hypervigilance
5. Exaggerated startle response

E. Duration (symptoms for 1 month or more or 3 months or more or subspecify as acute or chronic) (these criteria involve significant changes from DSM-III-R)

Annu. Rev. Psychol. 1998. 49:229–58

RECONCILING PROCESSING DYNAMICS AND PERSONALITY DISPOSITIONS

Walter Mischel

Department of Psychology, Columbia University, New York, New York 10027;
e-mail: wm@psych.columbia.edu

Yuichi Shoda

Department of Psychology, University of Washington, Seattle, Washington 98195;
e-mail: yshoda@u.washington.edu

KEY WORDS: traits, person-situation interactions, cognitive-affective system, personality stability, dispositions, dynamics, social cognition

ABSTRACT

Developments in personality-social psychology, in social cognition, and in cognitive neuroscience have led to an emerging conception of personality dynamics and dispositions that builds on diverse contributions from the past three decades. Recent findings demonstrating a previously neglected but basic type of personality stability allow a reconceptualization of classic issues in personality and social psychology. It reconstrues the nature and role of situations and links contextually sensitive processing dynamics to stable dispositions. It thus facilitates the reconciliation within a unitary framework of dispositional (trait) and processing (social cognitive–affective–dynamic) approaches that have long been separated. Given their history, however, the realization of this promise remains to be seen.

CONTENTS

0066-4308/98/0201-0229$08.00

INTRODUCTION

Throughout the history of the field, two different approaches to personality have competed (often bitterly) in the search for an adequate theory of the person as an individual and of the important differences between persons. In this chapter we ask if they can be reconciled in light of developments within personality-social-cognitive psychology in the past three decades and make the case that the answer is affirmative—at least theoretically, although the depths of the splits that have occurred have made such reconciliation difficult to realize.

TWO APPROACHES TO PERSONALITY: PROCESSING DYNAMICS AND BEHAVIORAL DISPOSITIONS

In one approach, personality is construed as a system of mediating units (e.g. encodings, expectancies, goals) and psychological processes or cognitive-affective dynamics, conscious and unconscious, that interact with the situation. In this view, in the past twenty years, the basic question has been to understand how the person functions psychologically in terms of the mediating processes that underlie stable individual differences in social behavior and that can make sense of intra-individual variability across situations (e.g. Bandura 1986; Cantor 1994; Cantor & Kihlstrom 1987; Higgins 1990, 1996; Mischel 1973, 1984, 1990; Pervin 1990a,b).

The second approach, dispositional or trait theory, in recent years personified in the Big Five approach (e.g. Costa & McCrae 1997; Wiggins & Trapnell 1997), posits broad stable traits, factors, or behavioral dispositions as its basic units. Its fundamental goal is to characterize individuals in terms of a comprehensive but finite, preferably small set of stable dispositions that remain invariant across situations and that are distinctive for the individual, determining a wide range of important behaviors (e.g. Allport 1937, Funder 1991, Goldberg 1993, Wiggins & Pincus 1992). Thus, traditionally, as textbooks regularly teach, the processing approach tends to focus on the interaction of the specific situation with the social-cognitive-emotional processing system of the individual. The dispositional approach, in contrast, focuses on the broad stable characteristics that differentiate individuals consistently, seeking evidence for the breadth and durability of these differences across diverse situations.

Divergent Goals

The uneasy, often even antagonistic relationship between these two approaches over many decades in part reflects that their advocates tend to be committed passionately to different goals that seem to be in intrinsic conflict and even mutually preemptive. Consequently, the field has long been divided into two subdisciplines, pursuing two distinct sets of goals—either personality processes or personality dispositions—with different agendas and strategies that often seem in conflict (Cervone 1991; Cronbach 1957, 1975; Mischel & Shoda 1994). Currently these debates on the relative virtues and limitations of these alternatives occupy center stage in personality theory, with special issues and handbooks devoted both to explicating the distinctive contributions of each of the two approaches and to pointing out the limitations of the other side, as each either critiques or ignores the other (e.g. Cervone 1991, Funder 1991, Goldberg 1993, Pervin 1994, Wiggins & Pincus 1992). A good example of this dualistic approach to personality is seen in pursuit of the question of whether human personality is malleable or stable over the life course, with trait conceptions of personality generally demonstrating stability and process conceptions of personality typically finding change (Heatherton & Weinberger 1994, Heatherton & Ambady 1993).

Two Fields—Or One?

The most common, and often justified, critique of processing approaches is that they neglect the stable dispositional differences between individuals and thus bypass a core aspect of the personality construct. Studies conducted within these approaches tend to focus on the effects of situational characteristics on people in general, and as a consequence they are often viewed as underemphasizing the role of individual differences, or even as relegating them to the role of unwanted, "error" variance. They thus are easily criticized as losing the person and the phenomena of personality in their focus on processes. Objecting to such a neglect, Funder (1991), for example, advocates a return to an intuitively appealing neo-Allportian global dispositional approach, reminding advocates of processing approaches that people are characterizable in broad dispositional terms, as in the person who is always (or mostly) miserable-and-complaining, and arguing that such information has potential explanatory as well as predictive value (Funder 1994). A failure to take account of such differences in temperament or other dispositions on which people differ would at the least highly constrain any personality theory and risks creating an oxymoron.

Even assuming, however, the existence of broad temperamental and other pervasive human characteristics, the question still remains: What is the nature of the basic invariances that form the core of each person's personality? What are the intra-individual dynamics and psychological processes that mediate between these invariances and their experiential and behavioral expression? As Epstein (1994) put it, articulating his concerns about trait theory generally and the Big Five in particular, "a description of surface attributes, although useful for some purposes, provides a poor basis for understanding process. If one wishes to understand what makes people tick, and what to do about their offbeat ticking, a more dynamic interactive approach capable of elucidating cause-and-effect relations is necessary" (p. 121).

PERSONALITY AT THE CROSSROADS

Given this history, the field is now at a major choice point: to try to carve an overarching framework that integrates the two disciplines to pursue both goals within one field, or to show that such an integration is impossible or unconstructive. Absent such a reconciliation, personality psychology is likely to continue to split itself in half, as the partitions that separate basic processes and individual differences in its mainstream journal already institutionalize, at best indifferent to each other, at worst undermining each other, and in either case risking making it more difficult to become a cumulative coherent science.

A vivid illustration of the unfortunate consequences of this division can be found in research on coping with stress, which traditionally has been pursued either in a dispositional framework—*coping styles*—or in a *coping processes* approach (e.g. Lazarus 1993). The styles approach assumes that each person is characterized by a type of coping strategy consistently across a wide range of situations. It measures the individuals' typical coping strategy, either by reports of typical strategy use or by averaging behavior in multiple situations into a single coping style index. The process approach, on the other hand, focuses on what people do in a specific stressful encounter, focusing on the change over time and across situations, and asks: What type of coping strategies do people use in what situations?

While each approach makes a contribution, they leave an important gap. One casualty, for example, is the phenomenon of flexibility in adaptation of coping styles (Chiu et al 1995, Shoda 1996). As the process approach stresses, such flexibility may be valuable because no single type of coping behavior is effective in all situations. For example, sometimes it is better to blunt anxiety-provoking events and sometimes it is better to monitor for them, and it is important to discriminate which one to use and when (Chiu et al 1995, Miller 1987). Therefore, a person with a situationally invariant global coping style is bound to be less effective in at least some situations. To capture such differences among individuals in flexible use of coping styles in response to different situational characteristics, however, requires a perspective that focuses on stable individual differences in coping that is situationally contextualized and process connected, "specifying meaningful patterning and regularities in person-environment transactions" (Coyne & Gottlieb 1996, p. 971). That is, it will require the integration of both approaches.

This point is also relevant to, and is being taken increasingly seriously in, behavioral medicine and health psychology (Baumeister & Heatherton 1996; Miller et al 1996a,b; Taylor & Aspinwall 1996). Likewise, the interactional, indeed transactional, perspective has allowed an analysis of emotions as "responses to the appraised person-environment *relationship*" (emphasis in original) that has reinvigorated the research in that area (e.g. Smith & Pope 1992, p. 32). And in the same vein, current analyses of the self construe it as experienced and defined in part in relation to significant others, again requiring a transactional dynamic perspective (e.g. Andersen et al 1997). Any personality theory that wishes to be relevant to these areas also needs to take that perspective into account. The message here is easy to misconstrue. Dispositions, no matter how conceptualized, are key aspects of the personality construct. The point is that personality theory needs to analyze dispositions in a way that allows us to understand how individuals interact with situations and, most importantly, to identify and assess the dynamic intra-individual processes that underlie these interactions.

Steps Toward Reconciliation

To reconcile the two approaches to personality requires first an understanding of their differences. Some of these differences sound greater than they are and seem more to be matters of differential emphases and preferred levels of analysis than fundamental incompatibilities. Indeed there are grounds for reconciliation. It has long been recognized that the existence of overall enduring important differences between individuals in such qualities as temperament, chronic mood and affective states, and skills does not necessarily create any theoretical conflict with processing approaches (e.g. Cantor 1994; Mischel 1968, 1973, 1990, 1993; Pervin 1990a,b). Nor are process-oriented approaches incompatible with evidence for substantial genetic contributions to personality. On the contrary, they assume such contributions and incorporate them into the framework (Mischel 1993, Mischel & Shoda 1995).

Rather than denying the importance of individual differences in personality and behavior, processing approaches have helped to identify diagnostic situations in which such differences, for example with regard to aggressive tendencies or self-control abilities, are likely to become particularly visible (e.g. Baumeister et al 1993, Shoda et al 1990, Wright & Mischel 1987).

Other process-oriented researchers have examined the stable correlates and consequences of individual differences in such social cognitive person variables as the goals and personal projects pursued over time (e.g. Cantor 1994, Cantor & Fleeson 1994), the person's beliefs and goal structures (Weary & Edwards 1994), and the type of focus primed in goal pursuit such as gain-oriented versus loss-avoidant (Higgins 1996b,c). They even have probed the implications of the person's own implicit theories about personality in terms of stable traits versus modifiable processes have and shown the importance of these theories for how individuals experience their worlds and act within them (e.g. Dweck & Leggett 1988, Dweck et al 1995; Y Hong, C Chiu & CS Dweck, submitted for publication).

Studies of basic cognitive-attentional processes during self-control efforts in young children in the past decade also have identified dramatic threads of long-term continuity and stability in the course of development (e.g. Mischel et al 1989). The results show significant and substantial links between seconds of delay of gratification in certain diagnostic laboratory situations in preschool and behavioral outcomes years later in adolescence and early adulthood (e.g. Mischel et al 1989, Shoda et al 1990). For example, seconds of preschool delay time significantly predicted verbal and quantitative scores on the Scholastic Aptitude Test (SAT) administered in adolescence (Shoda et al 1990). It also correlated significantly with parental ratings of competencies, including ability to use and respond to reason, planfulness, ability to handle stress, ability to delay gratification, self-control in frustrating situations, and ability to concentrate without becoming distracted. The preschoolers' self-control strategies in the delay of gratification situations, in turn, seem to be foreshadowed by the types of strategies they use in certain mother-toddler interactions three years earlier (Sethi & Shoda 1997). Such levels of stability and meaningful networks of associated developmental outcomes seem clearly indicative of long-term personality coherence. They also provide support for the construct of social-emotional intelligence (Cantor & Kihlstrom 1987, Goleman 1995, Mischel et al 1996, Salovey & Mayer 1990). Provocative, albeit still tentative, connections to findings on temperament and attention processes early in life are also emerging (e.g. Rothbart et al 1995).

Moves toward integration also are visible from at least some dispositional theorists who increasingly seem to allow room for the contextualized, situation-bound expressions of traits, and who seek to incorporate motivational and processing-dynamic concepts into their models (e.g. Revelle 1995). In one direction is the trait-state distinction, with emphasis on the state that is evoked with the particular context as influencing the behavior within that situation, whereas the broader trait disposition is seen as underlying the types of states likely to be readily activated within the person. Research in this vein increasingly is aimed at specifying the boundary conditions within which traits will be selectively activated (e.g. Stemmler 1997). Most notably, a quiet but potentially profound transformation may be occurring in the very definition of personality dispositions. For many researchers, the construct seems to be moving away from the global and uncontextualized trait construct, criticized thirty years earlier for the empirically unviable assumption of cross-situational consistency (Mischel 1968), to: "likelihood and rates of change in behavior in response to particular situational cues" (Revelle 1995, p. 315)—a definition independent of cross-situational consistency that any process theorist could happily accept.

A viable theoretical reconciliation requires crossing many conceptual and methodological barriers that underlie the historical divisions. That calls, first of all, for a framework for an adequately rich and comprehensive processing model. Such a framework must be capable of dealing with the complexity of human personality and the cognitive-affective dynamics, conscious and unconscious—both "cool" and "hot," cognitive and emotional—that underlie the individual's distinctive, characteristic internal states and external behavioral expressions (see Metcalfe & Jacobs 1998). It also requires a reconceptualization of the situation in psychological terms that captures the interaction of context with the dynamic processing system in the generation of those distinctive behavioral expressions. And it requires a conceptual and methodological bridge from the dynamic processing system that characterizes individuals idiographically (when $N = 1$) to the characterization and classification of dispositional types and subtypes nomothetically (when N = many). We consider below some of the most relevant developments.

Evolving Models of Processing Dynamics

Attempts to build a theory of processing dynamics that respects the complexity of the human mind and its often contrary, conflictful, perplexing behavioral expressions, in the tradition pioneered by Freud and advanced over the century by such theorists as Henry Murray, Gardner Murphy, Kurt Lewin, and George Kelly, continue and seem to be having a resurgence in contemporary personality-social psychology (see Cervone 1991, Gollwitzer & Bargh 1996, Higgins & Kruglanski 1996, Mischel et al 1996, Pervin 1990a,b). Although there are many differences among particular processing models in specific variables, they share a focus on the social-cognitive-emotional mediating processes that underlie, motivate, and guide behavior. Many use language and theoretical constructs that draw extensively on social, cognitive, and social learning theories and concepts as well as on self theories and research (e.g. Bandura 1982, 1986; Baumeister & Heatherton 1996; Cantor 1990, 1994; Dodge 1986, 1993; Downey & Walker 1989; Dweck & Leggett 1988; Fiske & Taylor 1991; Higgins 1987, 1996b,c; Kihlstrom & Cantor 1984; Markus & Kitayama 1991; Mischel 1973, 1990; Scheier & Carver 1988a,b; Shoda & Mischel 1993; Vallacher & Wegner 1987). They tend to be predominantly "social cognitive" in their theoretical language, but they also are sensitive to the role of automatic and unconscious processing (e.g. Kihlstrom 1987, 1990; Uleman & Bargh 1989) and to the goals and motivations that underlie behavior (e.g. Gollwitzer & Bargh 1996, Pervin 1989, Read & Miller 1989a,b, Westen 1990) in interaction with the situation or psychological context.

Most of these approaches draw heavily on information processing models and it is here that some particularly exciting developments for personality theory have unfolded. In recent years models of information processing have become available that promise to have some of the richness and complexity needed to make them relevant for a dynamic conception of personality. Going beyond the "cool cognitions" of the early models based on serial, central, and logical computing analogues, they take account of the fact that personally important information processing is affect-laden, encompassing not just cool cognitions but hot representations and emotional states (e.g. Kahneman & Snell 1990, Smith & Lazarus 1990) that impact profoundly on decisions and behaviors (e.g. Mischel & Shoda 1995, Wright & Mischel 1982).

A key development that makes such processing models germane for the analysis of cognitive-affective personality dynamics is a shift in their focus. The focus now is not just on how much of a particular unit (e.g. self-efficacy expectations or anxiety states or achievement goals) a person has, but also on how the units relate to each other within that person, forming a unique network of interconnections that functions as an organized whole. Such a dynamic interacting processing system can operate rapidly in parallel at multiple levels of accessibility, awareness, and automaticity, able to exceed the limitation of conscious awareness (Kihlstrom 1990). It goes beyond the conceptualization of the individual as a bundle of mediating variables or as a flow chart of discrete procedures and decision rules to a more parallel and distributed (rather than serial, centralized) processing system. It is also congruent with the insights coming from cognitive neuroscience in the past decade, such as the neural network theories and connectionist models (e.g. Anderson 1996, Kandel & Hawkins 1992, Rumelhart & McClelland 1986). The unifying theme is that the key to complex human information processing is in the organization of the relationships among the units through which they are interassociated. These developments make it possible to begin to conceptualize social information processing as a dynamic organized network of interconnected and interacting cognitions and affects (e.g. Kunda & Thagard 1996, Read & Miller 1998, Shoda & Mischel 1998, Shultz & Lepper 1996), operating at various levels of awareness (e.g. Westen 1990).

AN EMERGING CONCEPTION OF THE INDIVIDUAL: THE COGNITIVE-AFFECTIVE PERSONALITY SYSTEM

Growing out of these contributions, a unifying framework has emerged (articulated in Mischel & Shoda 1995) called the cognitive-affective processing system approach, reviewed next.

Individual Differences in Chronic Accessibility of Units

In the cognitive-affective personality system (CAPS) approach, individual differences are seen as reflecting in part difference in the chronic accessibility or activation levels of the particular mental-emotional representations—the cognitions and affects—the person has available. For twenty-five years these types of cognitive-emotional mediating units have been conceptualized in terms of five relatively stable person variables on which individuals differ in processing self-relevant information (Mischel 1973). In the intervening years, these units have been enriched, modified, and supplemented by extensive research (reviewed in Mischel & Shoda 1995, Mischel et al 1996) and are summarized in Table 1. These units refer to various types of mental events— thoughts and affects—that become activated characteristically and stably within a given individual in relation to certain features of situations or of the self.

Note that affects and goals, as well as encodings, expectancies, and beliefs, and competencies and self-regulatory plans and strategies constitute the types

Table 1 Types of cognitive-affective units in the personality mediating system[a]

1. Encodings: Categories (constructs) for the self, people, events, and situations (external and internal).
2. Expectancies and Beliefs: About the social world, about outcomes for behavior in particular situations, about self-efficacy.
3. Affects: Feelings, emotions, and affective responses (including physiological reactions).
4. Goals and Values: Desirable outcomes and affective states; aversive outcomes and affective states; goals, values, and life projects.
5. Competencies and Self-Regulatory Plans: Potential behaviors and scripts that one can do, and plans and strategies for organizing action and for affecting outcomes and one's own behavior and internal states.

[a]From Mischel & Shoda (1995). Reprinted with permission.

of units within the CAPS system. Individual differences in chronic accessibility are reflected in the finding that, for example, some individuals tend to encode ambiguous negative events as instances of personal rejection (e.g. Downey & Feldman 1996), whereas others may be prone to feel angry even when they hear a mumbled greeting (e.g. Dodge 1993), and others characteristically experience irritability and distress (e.g. Eysenck & Eysenck 1985).

Individual Differences in Stable Organization of Relations

In this type of CAPS model, stable individual differences also, and importantly, reflect the distinctive organization of relationships among the cognitions and affects, which characterizes how they change in their salience, or activation, over time and in relation to different situations. It is this organization that guides and constrains the activation of the particular cognitions, affect, and actions that are available within the system in relation to one another and to situational features. And it is this organization that constitutes the basic stable structure of personality and that underlies and reflects the person's characteristic distinctiveness. This stable organization or network of interrelations is conceptualized as the product of the individual's cognitive social learning history in interaction with the biological history, such as temperamental, and genetic-biochemical determinants (e.g. Plomin et al 1994, Posner 1997, Rothbart et al 1994, Wachs & King 1994).

The stable structure of personality emerges in the course of development, and it reflects both experience and genetics, generating the distinctive stable patterns of behavior characteristic of the individual (Mischel & Shoda 1995). The system is intrinsically interactive with the social world in which it is contextualized, and it is continuously activated, partly by external features, partly by its own internal cognitive and affective activities—such as its fantasy, daydreaming, planning, and self-regulatory attempts (Mischel et al 1996, Shoda & Mischel 1998). In turn, the behaviors that the personality system generates impact on the social world, partly shaping and selecting the interpersonal situations the person subsequently faces in a dynamic transaction (Buss 1987).

To recapitulate, the CAPS analysis begins with the assumption that individuals differ stably in the chronic accessibility or activation levels of the particular mental representations available to them (e.g. Higgins 1996a, Higgins & Bargh 1987, Mischel 1973) but adds a second assumption—namely, stable individual differences in the distinctive organization of relationships among the cognitions and affects available in the system. The latter is consistent with the emerging connectionist models of social information processing (Read & Miller 1994) as well as with contemporary models of the biological bases of human information processing (e.g. Anderson 1996, Rumelhart & McClelland 1986) and of the brain (e.g. Crick & Koch 1990, Churchland & Sejnowski 1992, Edelman 1987, Kandel & Hawkins 1992).

Dynamic, Transactional System: The Active/Proactive Person

A schematic, highly simplified illustration of such a personality system is in Figure 1, which shows that a personality system is characterized by the available cognitive and affective units (Table 1), organized in a distinctive network of interrelations. When certain configurations of situation features are experienced by an individual, a characteristic subset of cognitions and affects (shown schematically as *circles*) becomes activated through this distinctive network of connections in the encoding process. Within any individual a rich system of interconnections among the cognitive and affective units guides and constrains further activation of other units throughout the network, ultimately activating plans, strategies, and potential behaviors in the behavior generation process. Within each person, the organization of this system is assumed to be stable and unique. In this type of system, mediating units become activated in relation to some situation features, are deactivated or inhibited in relation to others, and are not affected by the rest. That is, the connections among units within the stable network that characterizes the person may be positive, increasing the activation, or negative (shown as *broken lines* in Figure 1), which decreases the activation. It should be evident that in this view the personality system is active and indeed proactive, not just reactive—a system that anticipates, influences, rearranges, and changes situations as well as reacts to them. Thus the personality system and the behavior it generates selects, modifies, and shapes the environment in reciprocal transactions (see Mischel & Shoda 1995, Figure 5, p. 264).

Incorporating Context

One important implication of this view of personality is that individuals may differ characteristically in the particular situational features (e.g. being teased, being approached socially) that are the salient active ingredients for them (Mischel & Shoda 1995). When they are present, they activate the individual's distinctive dynamics, i.e. their predictable characteristic pattern of cognitive, affective, and behavioral reactions to those situations. However, these dynamics are not just activated by external features of situations (as when milk that is spilled on an adolescent in line at the cafeteria is encoded as a violation) (cf Dodge 1993) but also by feedback from one's own cognitions and affects activated by such internal events as one's affective state and thoughts, such as "when sad," "when lonely" (Wright & Mischel 1988), and from situations that are simply imagined or anticipated (e.g. Cantor et al 1982). Thus, to reiterate, there also are internal feedback loops within the system through which self-generated stimuli (as in thinking, fantasy, daydreaming) activate their distinctive pathways of connections (e.g. Shoda & Mischel 1998). The behaviors the person constructs may in turn affect the interpersonal environment and social ecology, which changes the situational features that are encountered subsequently, in continuous transactions, that connects the behavioral patterns constructed by the personality system back to the situations encountered (e.g. Dodge 1986, 1993, 1997a,b).

The System in Action: Identifying Dynamics and Linking Them to Dispositional Types

To illustrate such a system in action, consider a person for whom potentially conflictful social interactions reliably activate rejection expectancies. When beginning to discuss a troublesome relationship issue with a romantic partner, for example, the individual's anxious expectations thus trigger scripts such as scanning for evidence of imminent rejection and focusing on those features of the situation most likely to provide such evidence (Downey & Feldman 1996). These expectations, affects, and behaviors interact and combine to lower the individual's threshold for perceiving rejection. Ambiguous partner behavior thus may be perceived as rejection, leading, within this distinctive processing system, to the activation of behavioral scripts for hostility (Ayduk et al 1997). The individual's enacted hostility can elicit partner rejection and, ultimately, relationship erosion, thus fulfilling and maintaining rejection expectations in a positive feedback loop reflecting dynamic interaction between the individual's cognitive-affective processing system and features of the environment (Downey et al 1997). Note that behavior generation ultimately depends both on the situational features and on the cognitive-affective organization of the system. When the relevant situational features are present, characteristic processes become activated in a predictable pattern.

A particular noteworthy characteristic of this pattern is that hostile behavior becomes activated specifically in relation to perceived rejection from a roman-

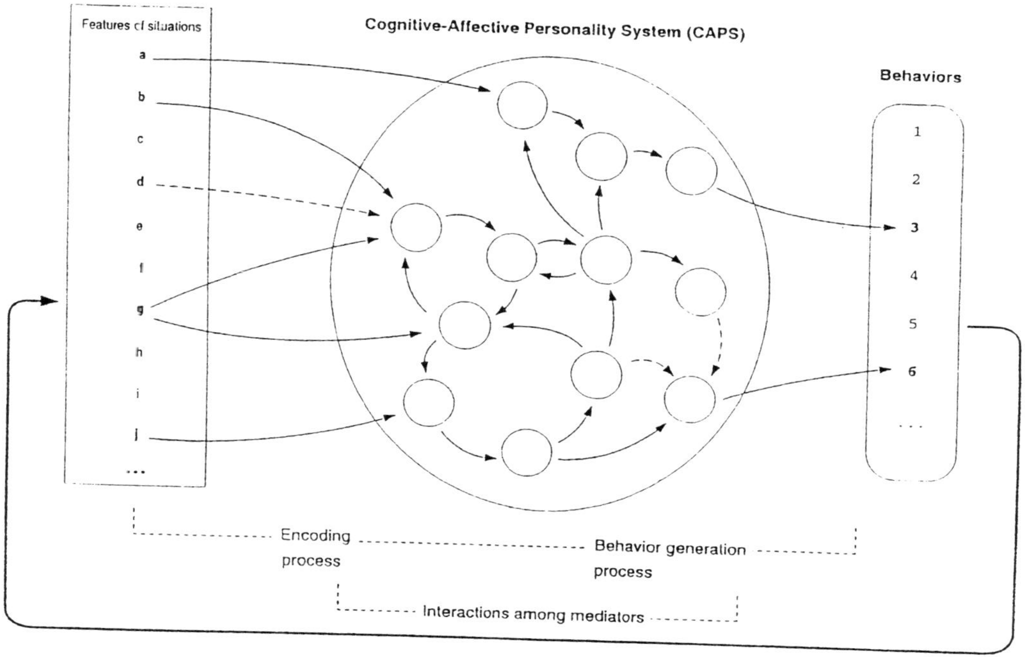

Figure 1 Simplified illustration of types of cognitive-affective mediating processes that generate an individual's distinctive behavior patterns. Situational features activate a given mediating unit (the encoding process), which activates specific subsets of other mediating units through a stable network of relations that characterize an individual, generating distinctive cognition, affect, and behavior in response to different situations. The relation may be positive (*solid line*), which increases the activation, or negative (*dashed line*), which decreases the activation. (Adapted from Mischel & Shoda 1995, Figure 4, p. 254.)

tic partner. The same individual can behave exceptionally caringly in other situations (e.g. early in the relationship). Linking this type of processing dynamic to the dispositional construct—in this case rejection sensitivity (Downey & Feldman 1996)—requires identifying the people who share these cognitive-affective unit organization by assessing the similarity in the *if...then* patterns that characterize them in their intimate relationships (Downey & Feldman 1996, Wright & Mischel 1987). Such a strategy allows construction of dispositional taxonomies based on the shared dynamic processes that underlie the distinctive *if...then* behavioral signatures that can distinguish a particular dynamic prototype.

This example illustrates that although intra-individual dynamics exist within a given individual, they need not just be studied idiographically with $N = 1$. By categorizing dynamics into types, one can work at a level when $N =$ many, applying an idiographic person-centered framework to do nomothetic research (Shoda et al 1994). This approach allows one to focus not just on the average overall differences between persons on particular dimensions but also on the characteristic ways they behave distinctively in relation to particular types of contexts. Note also that observers' dispositional judgments in fact depend on the *if...then* patterns in which the behavior unfolds in context (Shoda et al 1994), not just on the mean level of a type of behavior observed (e.g. average level of friendly behaviors). If the pattern changes, so does the dispositional judgment (Shoda et al 1989).

COMPLEX BEHAVIORAL EXPRESSIONS OF THE PERSONALITY SYSTEM'S STABILITY

By definition, an information processing system like CAPS is sensitive to changing external and internal conditions. Just as one can say that "if it changes, it must be processes" (Folkman & Lazarus 1985), the reverse in this case may be true: If it is a processing system, then it must respond to changing conditions. But an important and often unrecognized point here is that changes in the behavioral expression of a processing system do not imply that the structure of the system itself is unstable or inconsistent. An extremely stable pattern and organization may characterize and constrain the surface changes in the individual's behavior. As in a musical piece, the notes played at any moment may change, but they follow a pattern that reflects the underlying structure of the composition. Thus the consistency and stability in the underlying structure of the processing system may be reflected in patterns of change in the observable behavior (Larsen 1989). During the past decade, several empirical approaches to operationalizing consistency at a higher level have been proposed and explored, as indicated below.

Variations Across Situations: Stable Individual Differences in Situation-Behavior If...Then Relations

It follows from the assumptions of the CAPS model that the behavioral variation in relation to changing situations in part constitutes a potentially meaningful reflection of the personality system itself. Whereas different cognitions, affects, and behaviors become activated as the situation and its features change, the interconnections among them remain unchanged across situations. That is, the personality system determines the relationships between the types of situations encountered and the cognitive, affective, and behavioral responses. As the *if's* change, so do the *then's*, but the relationship between them is stable as long as the personality system remains unchanged.

This assumption leads this approach to expect characteristic, predictable patterns of variation in the individual's behavior across situations. If personality is a stable system that processes the information about the situations, external or internal, then it follows that as individuals encounter different situations, their behaviors should vary across the situations, reflecting important differences among them in their psychological by active features (Mischel & Shoda 1995). Over time this will generate distinctive *if...then* situation-behavior profiles of characteristic elevation and shape like those illustrated in Figure 2. To illustrate with a simple example, suppose that in situation A people rarely initiate personal interactions, whereas in situation B such interactions are relatively frequent. Suppose also that Person 1 tends to become irritated when she thinks she is being ignored, whereas person 2 is happier when he is left alone, and even becomes irritated when people tell him personal stories. Then Person 1 will become irritated in situation A, but not in situation B; Person 2 will show the opposite *if...then* pattern, irritated in situation B but not in A. These affects further activate other cognitions and feelings in each situation, following the pathways of activation distinctive for each person. These individual differences reflect the particular acquired meanings of the situational features in terms of the cognitions and affects associated with them, so that even if both people are similar in their overall levels of "irritability," they will display distinctive, predictable patterns of behavioral variability in their *if...then* signatures.

Consistent with the clinical wisdom of such classic processing theories as Freud's conception of psychodynamics, clues about peoples' underlying processing dynamics and qualities—the construals and goals, the motives and passions, that drive the individual—may be seen not only in its overall average frequency but also in when and where the person manifests a type of behavior. In short, this type of model expects that the stable patterns of situation-behavior relationships that unfold provide a key to the personality—an expression of personality coherence, not a source of error to be eliminated systemati-

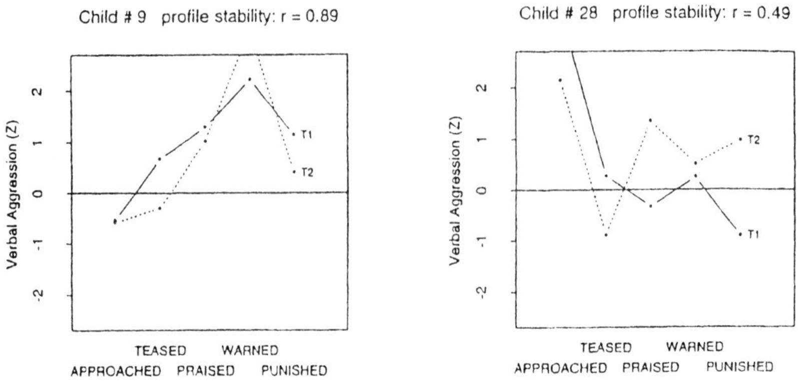

Figure 2 Illustrative intra-individual, situation-behavior profiles for verbal aggression in relation to five situations in two time samples (*solid* and *dotted lines*). Data are shown in standardized scores (*Z*) relative to the normative levels of verbal aggression in each situation. (From Shoda et al 1994, Figure 1, p. 678.)

cally by aggregating out the situation. It thus broadens the concept of the invariances in the expression of personality to include the profile of situation-behavior relations that might characterize the person, not just the overall average level of particular types of behavior aggregated across diverse situations.

Empirical Evidence for Stable If...Then Profiles

These theoretical expectations have received direct empirical support in a series of studies of the social behavior (e.g. "verbal aggression," "compliance") of children who were systematically observed in relation to the interpersonal situations in which the behavior occurred in vivo in a residential summer camp setting (e.g. Shoda et al 1993a, 1994). To illustrate, some children were found to be consistently more verbally aggressive than others when warned by an adult but were much less aggressive than most peers when peers approached them positively. In contrast, another group of children with a similar overall average level of aggression were distinguished by a striking and opposite pattern: They were more aggressive than any other children when peers approached them positively, but were exceptionally unaggressive when warned by an adult. To test the overall hypothesis, the profile stabilities for each individual were ipsatively computed, and the statistical significance of the group mean stability was tested. The results were highly significant for such behaviors as verbal aggression and compliance (Shoda et al 1994).

It is noteworthy that in classic trait approaches to behavioral dispositions, such intra-individual variations in a type of behavior across situations (after the main effects of situations are removed by standardization) is assumed to reflect only intrinsic unpredictability or measurement error. From that perspective, the stability of the intra-individual pattern of variation should on average be zero. The obtained findings obviously contradict this expectation and reveal that meaningfully patterned behavioral expressions of personality, contextualized within particular situations, characterize individuals. They yield distinctive profiles of variability for particular types of behavior, forming a behavioral signature of personality (Shoda et al 1994). Note that such profiles, illustrated in Figure 2, have a meaningful shape as well as elevation. They reflect when a given individual becomes particularly angry or depressed, anxious or relieved, in a stable pattern, such as the following: He A when X but B when Y, and does A most when Z. Ironically, by focusing on the effects of the situation on the organization of behavior in depth and detail it became possible to find this second type of personality stability, enriching rather than undermining the personality construct.

Behavioral Roots of Self-Perceived Consistency

Recent evidence shows that these more-complex manifestations of personality stability and coherence also are linked to self-perceptions of consistency. It is noteworthy that the individual's self-perception of consistency with regard to a dimension of behavior or trait in recent research has been related to the intra-individual *if...then* profile stability, not to the level of cross-situational consistency. This was found in a reanalysis by Mischel & Shoda (1995) of the Carleton College field study (Mischel & Peake 1982). In that study, college students were repeatedly observed on campus in various situations relevant to their conscientiousness in the college setting (such as in the classroom, in the dormitory, in the library), assessed over repeated occasions in the semester. Students who perceived themselves as consistent did not show greater consistency cross-situationally than did those who perceived themselves as variable in conscientiousness.

Mischel & Shoda (1995) reexamined those data to test the hypothesis that the students' self-perceptions of consistency would be related to the stability of their situation-behavior profiles. As the first set of two columns of Figure 3 show (and as reported in Mischel & Peake 1982), those who perceived themselves as consistent (the first light column) did not show greater overall cross-situational consistency than those who did not. Note, however, that for individuals who perceived themselves as consistent (the second set of columns), the average situation-behavior profile stability correlation was near 0.5, but it was trivial for those who viewed themselves as inconsistent. It is the stability in the situation-behavior profiles, not the cross-situational consistency of behavior, that seems to underlie the perception of consistency.

In sum, such stable situation-behavior profiles reflect characteristic intra-individual patterns in how the person relates to different psychological conditions, forming a sort of behavioral signature of personality (Shoda et al 1994). Most striking is not so much that this type of behavioral signature of personality exists but rather that it has so long been treated as error and purposefully removed by simply averaging behavior over diverse situations. Whereas such aggregation was intended to capture personality, it actually can remove data that can alert us to the individual's most distinctive qualities and unique intra-individual patterning.

The Personality Paradox Demystified

The types of *if...then* situation-behavior relations that a dynamic personality system like CAPS necessarily generates has important implications for the field, particularly the classic "personality paradox" (Bem & Allen 1974). As Bem & Allen noted two decades ago, on the one hand, the person's behavior across situations yields only modest cross-situational consistency coefficients (Hartshorne & May 1928, Newcomb 1929), but on the other hand, personality theory's fundamental assumption, and our intuition, insist that personality surely is stable (e.g. Bem & Allen 1974; Heatherton & Weinberger 1994; Krahe 1990; Mischel 1968; Moskowitz 1982, 1994).

This paradox dissolves, however, by recognizing that the variability of behaviors within individuals across situations is neither all "error" nor is it "due to the situation rather than to the person." Instead, it is at least partly an essential expression of the enduring but dynamic personality system itself and its stable underlying organization. Thus the person's behaviors in a domain will necessarily change from one type of situation to another because when the *if* changes, so will the *then*, even when the personality structure remains entirely unchanged. Just how the individual's behavior and experience change across situations is part of the essential expression of personality (Mischel & Shoda 1995) and becomes a key focus for personality assessment. From this perspective, the person's ability to make subtle discriminations among situations and to take these cues into account in the self-regulation of behavior in order to adapt it to changing situational requirements is a basic aspect of social competence, not a reflection of inconsistency (Chiu et al 1995, Shoda et al 1993a). This type of discriminative facility seems to be a component of social intelligence, a sensitivity to the subtle cues in the situation that influences behavior. Such discriminative facility, for example, by encoding spontaneously social information in conditional versus global dispositional terms, was found to predict the quality of the person's social interaction (Chiu et al 1995). Indeed such *discriminative facility* is an index of adaptive behavior and constructive func-

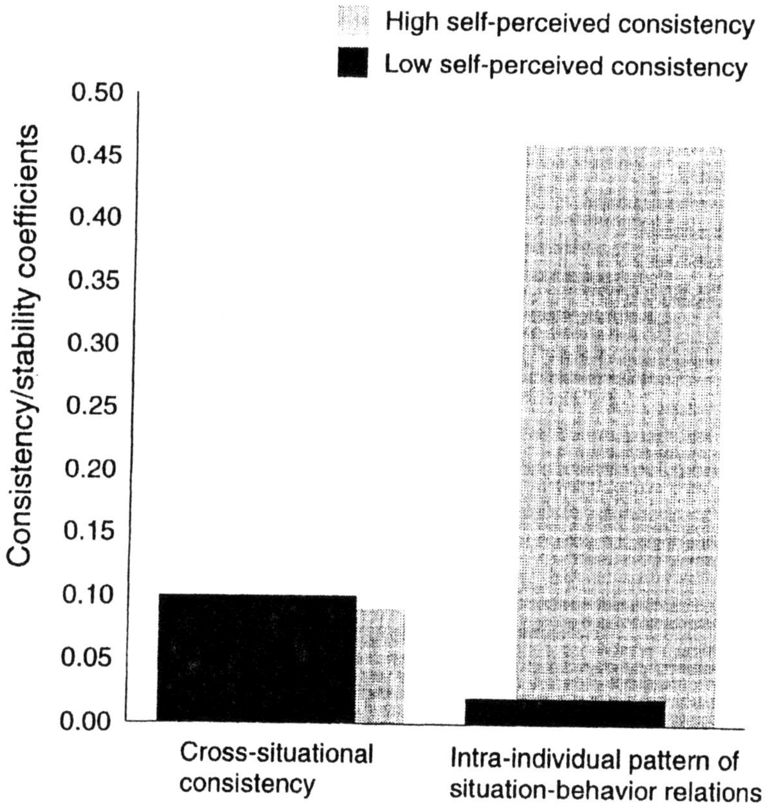

Figure 3 Self-perceived consistency and the organization of behavior. Cross-situational consistency and the stability of person-situation profiles for people high versus low in perceived consistency in conscientiousness (based on data in Mischel & Peake 1982). (From Mischel & Shoda 1995, Figure 3, p. 251.)

tioning, whereas consistency regardless of subtle contextual cues can be a sign of rigidity (Chiu et al 1995).

Redefining Situations in Terms of Active Psychological Ingredients: The Ifs and Thens of Personality

Situations have been difficult to incorporate into personality theory in part because they have been defined in nominal rather than psychological terms (e.g. "playground," "arts and crafts"). Specific nominal situations, like school playground, however, may provide information about individual differences only in relation to such specific places and be of limited interest if they are not generalizable beyond them.

In the CAPS approach, one seeks to analyze situations in terms of their *active ingredients* or *psychological features*, i.e. those in relation to which the person's characteristic dynamics become activated (Mischel & Shoda 1995, Shoda et al 1994). In the case of rejection-sensitive individuals (Downey & Feldman 1996), for example, such features include criticism or lack of attention in the context of an intimate relationship. In the presence of those diagnostic psychological ingredients, regardless of the nominal setting (at school, at home), the characteristic dynamics and their typical behavioral expressions should become activated and predictable. For example, individuals characterized by dynamics in which angry feelings and aggressive impulses become activated in relation to aversive and frustrating experiences tend to show their prototypic behavior depending on competency demands of the situation (Wright & Mischel 1987). By identifying and classifying diverse nominal situations in terms of their functional equivalence with regard to psychological features (e.g. the types of competencies they demand), it becomes possible to specify the types of diagnostic conditions in which characteristic dynamics and their behavioral expressions will be seen.

To identify such potentially diagnostic *if*s, one can analyze the open-ended descriptions provided by people who know each other well (Wright & Mischel 1988). Such analyses suggest that even children tend to spontaneously qualify their characterizations of people they know well with conditional modifiers. These modifiers point to the psychological circumstances, both interpersonal (e.g. when teased by peers) and intrapsychic (e.g. when mad) in which the individual's characteristic behaviors (e.g. verbal aggression) are expressed and contextualized.

In addition to identifying the relevant *if*s, an analysis of intra-individual dynamics also requires specifying the *then*s. Research from many directions is providing relevant strategies for the assessment of experiences and behaviors (Cervone & Williams 1982, Mischel 1993, Mischel et al 1996). The strategies encompass systematic time sampling of tasks, behavior, and perceptions at the moment in the everyday course of life (e.g. Cantor et al 1991, Moskowitz et al 1994), self-reports of reactions to daily stressors (e.g. Bolger & Shilling 1991), sampling of physical symptoms and emotional reactions to them (Larsen & Kasimatis 1991) as well as records of personal strivings and well-being (Emmons 1991), and therapeutic interventions to facilitate emotional processing of traumatic events (Foa & Riggs 1993). All these methods allow systematic analyses of the types of *if*s and *then*s significant in the lives of individuals, relevant to different characteristic behavioral patterns generated by the underlying system.

Stable Patterns of Change over Time

Evidence for stability in the patterning of change also comes from studies of the frequency and regularity of daily mood changes over time when individuals are assessed repeatedly (Larsen 1987, 1989). For example, some college students reliably exhibit a pronounced weekly pattern of change in their affects, while others do not (Larsen & Kasimatis 1990). And for some individuals, different affects covary over time so that on some days they might experience most of the negative affects, while on others the positive affects occur. Other individuals, however, are characterized by the fact that their affects do not covary to a high degree, so that on some days they may be happy but not necessarily contented, and on other days they are sad but not angry. Such differences in the degree to which distinct affects covary in turn have been related to emotional reactivity, and among men to psychosomatic complaints (Larsen & Cutler 1996). In a related direction, research by Cantor and colleagues has pioneered ways to make visible the types of psychosocial dynamics that underlie the coping process as people pursue their life projects over time (e.g. Cantor & Fleeson 1994).

CROSSING THE GAP?

So far we have considered the links from dynamics to dispositions. It is, of course, also possible to reconcile the two approaches to personality by starting on the other end and trying to identify the dynamic processes that characterize members of dispositional types. Such a route is particularly appealing to the degree that there is consensus about the dispositional types themselves. Historically and currently such consensus is widely seen as essential for the field of personality psychology. Indeed, the subjective sense of well-being in the field has swung over the years in a series of cycles from depression to euphoria, back and forth, in direct relation to the perceived degree of agreement achieved (or claimed) for that consensus.

From Dispositions to Dynamics

The most popular candidate for such consensus and durability in recent years has been the Big Five approach. Hailed by its enthusiasts as a quiet revolution (e.g. Goldberg 1992), its claim of an achieved consensus for representing the structure of different personalities in terms of the Big Five factors has been widely embraced. This reception is understandable in a field tired of self-criticism and eager to go beyond a potentially endless array of intercorrelated personality constructs to a small set of factors or basic dispositions. Consequently, the Big Five provides a promising taxonomy that could be linked to the types of processing dispositions conceptualized within the CAPS approach. This connection certainly merits exploration.

Concurrently, however, there also are signs of disagreements in the consensus, and growing concern about the limitations of the approach. In a special journal issue devoted to an analysis of current trait theory and the Big Five approach, for example, Pervin (1994) reviews the claims about the Big Five (e.g. Brody 1988, Goldberg 1993, Wiggins & Pincus 1992) and finds them remarkably discrepant from the data. Pervin's critique is only one strong voice in a chorus of many, all expressing diverse concerns lest the contributions of this approach be lost among the exaggerated and even preemptive claims made by overenthusiastic advocates. Especially worrisome is the slippage from the summary meaning of trait terms to the causal-explanatory meaning that seems to have developed as the Big Five, originally presented as psycholexical descriptive dimensions about behavior, metaphorphize into the basic units used to explain what underlies and generates those behaviors (see also John & Robins 1993, McAdams 1992). Localizing someone in the factor space defined by psycholexical dimensions does not necessarily help to explain and predict why and when a person behaves in characteristic ways. The goal of explanation in personality psychology includes understanding the intra-individual psychological mediating dynamic processes that underlie individual differences. As Block put it, after a penetrating critique of the Big Five on conceptual, empirical, and methodological grounds, "my final most ambitious suggestion is that, in the conceptual/empirical arguments to be made for specific dimensions, of whatever number, these constructs be situated within a coherent, *intra-individual* theoretical framework" (emphasis in original) (1995, p. 210).

Because the Big Five are cast at a highly general, global, unconditionalized level, it is understandable that their empirical links to specific behavioral outcomes, such as performance measures, are modest. Relevant to this, for example, Pervin (1994) questions Goldberg's (1993, p. 31) assertion that "reviews of the literature have concluded that personality measures when classified within the Big-Five domains, are systematically related to a variety of criteria of job performance" and that they are "valid predictors" that show incremental validities over measures of cognitive ability for predicting job proficiency. To illustrate, the best correlations averaged 0.22 for conscientiousness (for the other four trait factors the estimated true correlations ranged from 0.00 to 0.18). To those who still remember how those types of correlations felt when they were first noted in 1968 (e.g. Mischel 1968, Peterson 1968), not to mention earlier (e.g. Vernon 1964), Pervin's conclusion will seem familiar: "What is clear...is that the personality measures did not show incremental validity over measures of cognitive ability for the measures of core job proficiency.... In areas such as this, I'm still not sure that we have gone much beyond the .30

correlation barrier between trait measures and measures of behavior" (1994, p. 108).

However, such critiques may apply only to the degree that dispositional approaches focus on traits at a very high level of abstraction in which they are not contextualized in relation to the situations in which they function. While the trait construct seems to have become less global and more contextualized for some personologists (e.g. Baumeister et al 1993, Bornstein et al 1996, Larsen 1989, Revelle 1995, Stemmler 1997), such movement toward the conditionalization of dispositions is, of course, contradicted to the degree that researchers focus exclusively on the abstract, broad level of analysis of the Big Five approach without also incorporating more contextualized levels and dispositional subtypes.

The encouraging news, however, for the goal of reconciling dispositional and processing approaches is that a number of researchers are showing how dispositions like those in the Big Five can be analyzed in terms of the cognitive-affective process dynamic characteristic of them. For example, attempts to forge a link between trait and process orientations to personality are exemplified in research by Bolger to delineate several of the processes whereby neuroticism leads to heightened distress (Bolger 1990, Bolger & Schilling 1991, Bolger & Zuckerman 1995). In a series of studies using a daily diary methodology, Bolger and colleagues (1996) found that neuroticism affects distress through increasing both exposure and reactivity to stressful events, especially interpersonal conflict. Furthermore, neuroticism-related differences in reactivity seem to be due in part to differential choice of coping efforts (e.g. high neuroticism people were more likely to use confrontative coping) and differential effectiveness of those efforts (e.g. when used by high neuroticism people, self-control was ineffective in reducing depression).

The search for types of people who differ in the types of behavior they show in relation to different types of situations is also facilited by a triple typology model and methodology developed by Vansteelandt & Mechelen (1997). Drawing on the conditional analysis of dispositions proposed by Wright & Mischel (1987) and Mischel & Shoda (1995), the triple typology model of individual differences yields typologies of person, situation, and behavior classes. Their method simultaneously identifies clusters of people, situations, and behaviors such that each cluster of people is characterized by distinctive *if...then* relations, using the clusters of situation identified as the units of *ifs* and the clusters of behaviors indentified as the units of *thens*. This method makes it possible, for example, to differentiate subtypes of hostile people in terms of the types of hostile behavior they are likely to manifest in different types of frustrating situations (Vansteelandt & Mechelen 1997).

Genetic Determinants of Cognitive-Affective Dynamics

The individual's cognitive-affective processing system arises in the course of development from a foundation that is both biochemical and psychosocial, genetically guided, as well as shaped by experience and learning in the course of development (Mischel & Shoda 1995). To link processing dynamics and predispositions requires clarifying not only the structure and organization of the cognitive-affective-behavioral processing system but also its biochemical-genetic foundations (Saudino & Plomin 1996). These individual differences in genetic foundations presumably affect how people construe or encode—and shape—their environments, which in turn produce important person-context interactions throughout the life course (Plomin 1994, Plomin et al 1997, Rutter 1997, Saudino & Plomin 1996). Dispositions like those identified in the Big Five approach may be a useful step in that direction, a promising guide for where to look, but it is unlikely to be the conclusion.

The study of the biochemical foundations of dispositions, although still at an early phase, already points to some temperamental characteristics that seem particularly important influences on the structure and organization of CAPS. These largely heritable characteristics, such as activity level, visible early in development, seem particularly relevant to the person's emotional life (e.g. Bates & Wachs 1994, Buss & Plomin 1984, Plomin et al 1990), and they are likely to have important, albeit complex, links to emotional-attentional-self-regulatory processes (e.g. Posner 1997, Rothbart et al 1994, 1997). Theoretically, these influences should be manifested not just in the mean levels of particular types of behavior as traditional dispositional approaches expect, but also in the patterns of stable *if...then* relations in which they are expressed, as dynamic processing approaches predict, in ways that are contextualized and interactive with features of situations.

Personality as a Unified Field

To the degree that the boundary between dispositional and process approaches to personality becomes fuzzy and even evaporates, there are theoretical implications for the study of personality that need to be made explicit. Suppose, for example, that the *if...then* relationship, rather than the unconditionalized global trait, becomes a basic unit in personality assessment and theory. Then the analyses of just how and why variation in the situation is predictably linked to variation in the characteristic response pattern distinctive for the person becomes a fundamental route for personality assessment. That requires recognition of the high cost of decontextualizing personality. It highlights the need for collaboration rather than confrontation with disciplines bifurcated from personality psychology, such as cognitive and social psychology, by a historical definition of personality that pits it against the situation rather than rooting it within it.

Traditionally, the "situation" has been deliberately eliminated in the assessment of personality in order to distill those stable aspects that characterize the individual, no matter what the context, i.e. across diverse situations. From that perspective, the analysis of situations and of what determines behavior within them becomes the province of social psychology (pioneered by Floyd Allport), whereas the study of individuals and individual differences regardless of the situation becomes the mission of personality psychology, founded by Gordon Allport (the other brilliant brother in the team that created this partition of the two fields). This division seems to have served both disciplines well for many of their early years, but it may have outlived its usefulness, with the boundaries becoming increasingly fuzzy as social psychologists focus on person-situation interactions and personality psychologists incorporate the role of situations into the analysis of dispositions (e.g. Higgins & Kruglanski 1996).

As Gordon Allport (1937, p. 61) emphasized since the start of the field, the stable intra-individual patterns that characterize each person are at the core of personality, yet curiously much of modern personality psychology has searched for dispositions while losing those internal processes and dynamics. The two goals of personality psychology, to understand both dispositions and dynamics, have long had separate histories driven by different conceptions and commitments, more in competition than in the service of building a cumulative coherent science of personality. Might both goals be enhanced if pursued as two sides of the same unitary system within one field?

ACKNOWLEDGMENT

Preparation of this chapter and the research for it by the authors were supported in part by Grants MH39349 and MH45994 to Walter Mischel from the National Institute of Mental Health.

Literature Cited

Allport GW. 1937. *Personality: A Psychological Interpretation*. New York: Holt, Rinehart & Winston

Andersen SM, Reznik I, Chen S. 1997. The self in relation to others: motivational and cognitive underpinnings. In *The Self Across Psychology: Self-Recognition, Self Awareness, and the Self-Concept*, ed. JG Snodgrass, RL Thompson, pp. 233–75. New York: NY Acad. Sci.

Anderson JR. 1996. (1983). *The Architecture of Cognition*. Mahwah, NJ: Erlbaum

Ayduk O, Downey G, Testa A, Shoda Y, Ying Y. 1997. Does rejection elicit hostility in

rejection sensitive women? *Soc. Cogn.* In press
Bandura A. 1982. Self-efficacy mechanism in human agency. *Am. Psychol.* 37:122–47
Bandura A. 1986. *Social Foundations of Thought and Action: A Social Cognitive Theory.* Englewood Cliffs, NJ: Prentice Hall
Bates JE, Wachs TD, eds. 1994. *Temperament: Individual Differences at the Interface of Biology and Behavior.* Washington, DC: Am. Psychol. Assoc.
Baumeister RF, Heatherton TF. 1996. Self-regulation failure: an overview. *Psychol. Inq.* 7:1–15
Baumeister RF, Heatherton TF, Tice D. 1993. When ego threats lead to self-regulation failure: negative consequences of high self-esteem: *J. Pers. Soc. Psychol.* 64: 141–56
Bem DJ, Allen A. 1974. On predicting some of the people some of the time: the search for cross-situational consistencies in behavior. *Psychol. Rev.* 81:506–20
Block J. 1995. A contrarian view of the five-factor approach to personality description. *Psychol. Bull.* 117:187–215
Bolger N. 1990. Coping as a personality process: a prospective study. *J. Pers. Soc. Psychol.* 59:525–37
Bolger N, Schilling EA. 1991. Personality and the problems of everyday life: the role of neuroticism in exposure and reactivity to daily stressors. *J. Pers.* 59:355–86
Bolger N, Zuckerman A. 1995. A framework for studying personality in the stress process. *J. Pers. Soc. Psychol.* 69:890–902
Bornstein RF, Riggs MJ, Hill EL, Calabrese C. 1996. Activity, passivity, self-denigration, and self-promotion: toward an interactionist model of interpersonal dependency. *J. Pers.* 64:637–73
Brody N. 1988. *Personality: In Search of Individuality.* New York: Academic
Buss AH, Plomin R. 1984. *Temperament: Early Developing Personality Traits.* Hillsdale, NJ: Erlbaum
Buss DM. 1987. Selection, evocation and manipulation. *J. Pers. Soc. Psychol.* 53: 1214–21
Cantor N. 1990. From thought to behavior: "having" and "doing" in the study of personality and cognition. *Am. Psychol.* 45: 735–50
Cantor N. 1994. Life task problem-solving: situational affordances and personal needs. Presidential address Soc. Pers. Soc. Psychol. (Div. 8 Am. Psychol. Assoc.), 1993, Toronto, Can. *Pers. Soc. Psychol. Bull.* 20:235–43
Cantor N, Fleeson W. 1994. Social intelligence and intelligent goal pursuit: a cognitive slice of motivation. In *Integrative Views of Motivation, Cognition, and Emotion. Nebr. Symp. Motiv.*, ed. W Spaulding, 41:125–79. Lincoln: Univ. Nebr. Press
Cantor N, Kihlstrom JF. 1987. *Personality and Social Intelligence.* Englewood Cliffs, NJ: Prentice Hall
Cantor N, Mischel W, Schwartz JC. 1982. A prototype analysis of psychological situations. *Cogn. Psychol.* 14:45–77
Cantor N, Norem J, Langston C, Zirkel S, Fleeson W, Cook-Flannagan C. 1991. Life tasks and daily life experience. *J. Pers.* 59:425–51
Cervone D. 1991. The two disciplines of personality psychology: review of Handbook of Personality: Theory and Research. *Psychol. Sci.* 2:371–77
Cervone D, Williams SL. 1982. Social cognitive theory and personality. In *Modern Personality Psychology: Critical Reviews and New Directions*, ed. GV Caprara, GL Van Heck, pp. 200–52. New York: Harvester Wheatsheaf/Simon & Schuster
Chiu C, Hong Y, Mischel W, Shoda Y. 1995. Discriminative facility in social competence: conditional versus dispositional encoding and monitoring-blunting of information. *Soc. Cogn.* 13:49–70
Churchland PS, Sejnowski TJ. 1992. *The Computational Brain.* Cambridge, MA: MIT Press
Costa PT, McCrae RR. 1997. Longitudinal stability of adult personality. In *Handbook of Personality Psychology*, ed. R Hodan, J Johnson, S Briggs, pp. 269–90. San Diego, CA: Academic
Coyne JC, Gottlieb BH. 1996. The mismeasure of coping by checklist. *J. Pers.* 64: 959–91
Crick F, Koch C. 1990. Towards a neurobiological theory of consciousness. *Semin. Neurosci.* 2:263–75
Cronbach LJ. 1957. The two disciplines of scientific psychology. *Am. Psychol.* 12: 671–84
Cronbach LJ. 1975. Beyond the two disciplines of scientific psychology. *Am. Psychol.* 30:116–27
Dodge KA. 1986. A social information processing model of social competence in children. *Cogn. Perspect. Child. Soc. Behav. Dev., Minn. Symp. Child Psychol.* 18: 77–125
Dodge KA. 1993. Social-cognitive mechanisms in the development of conduct disorder and depression. *Annu. Rev. Psychol.* 44:559–84

Dodge KA. 1997a. *Testing developmental theory through prevention trials*. Presented at Bienn. Meet. Soc. Res. Child Dev., Apr., Washington, DC

Dodge KA. 1997b. *Early peer social rejection and acquired autonomic sensitivity to peer conflicts: conduct problems in adolescence*. Presented at Bienn. Meet. Soc. Res. Child Dev., Apr., Washington, DC

Downey G, Feldman S. 1996. Implications of rejection sensitivity for intimate relationships. *J. Pers. Soc. Psychol.* 70:1327–43

Downey G, Freitas A, Michaelis B, Khouri H. 1997. The self-fulfilling prophecy in close relationships: Do rejection sensitive women get rejected by their partners? Dep. Psychol., Columbia Univ., NY. Unpubl. manuscr.

Downey G, Walker E. 1989. Social cognition and adjustment in children at risk for psychopathology. *Dev. Psychol.* 25:835–45

Dweck CS, Chiu C, Hong Y. 1995. Implicit theories and their role in judgments and reactions: a world from two perspectives. *Psychol. Inq.* 6:267–85

Dweck CS, Leggett EL. 1988. A social-cognitive approach to motivation and personality. *Psychol. Rev.* 95:256–73

Edelman GM. 1987. *Neural Darwinism: The Theory of Neuronal Group Selection*. New York: Basic Books

Emmons RA. 1991. Personal strivings, daily life events, and psychological and physical well-being. *J. Pers.* 59:453–72

Epstein S. 1994. Trait theory as personality theory: Can a part be as great as the whole? *Psychol. Inq.* 5:120–22

Eysenck HJ, Eysenck MW. 1985. *Personality and Individual Differences: A Natural Science Approach*. New York: Plenum

Fiske ST, Taylor SE. 1991. *Social Cognition*. New York: McGraw-Hill. 2nd ed.

Foa E, Riggs D. 1993. Post-traumatic stress disorder in rape victims. In *American Psychiatric Press Review of Psychiatry*, ed. J Oldham, M Riba, A Tasman, 12:273–303. Washington, DC: Am. Psychiatr.

Folkman S, Lazarus RS. 1985. If it changes it must be a process: study of emotion and coping during three stages of a college examination. *J. Pers. Soc. Psychol.* 48: 150–70

Funder DC. 1991. Global traits: a neo-Allportian approach to personality. *Psychol. Sci.* 2:31–39

Funder DC. 1994. Explaining traits. *Psychol. Inq.* 5:125–27

Goldberg LR. 1992. The development of markers for the Big-Five factor structure. *Psychol. Assess.* 4:26–42

Goldberg LR. 1993. The structure of phenotypic personality traits. *Am. Psychol.* 48: 26–34

Goleman D. 1995. *Emotional Intelligence*. New York: Bantam

Gollwitzer PM, Bargh JA, eds. 1996. *The Psychology of Action: Linking Cognition and Motivation to Behavior*. New York: Guilford

Hartshorne H, May MA. 1928. *Studies in Deceit: Studies in the Nature of Character*, Vol. 1. New York: Macmillan

Heatherton TF, Ambady N. 1993. Self-esteem, self-prediction, and living up to commitments. In *Self-Esteem: The Puzzle of Low Self-Regard*, ed. RF Baumeister, pp. 131–45. New York: Plenum

Heatherton TF, Weinberger JL, eds. 1994. *Can Personlity Change?* Washington, DC: Am. Psychol. Assoc.

Higgins ET. 1987. Self-discrepancy: a theory relating self and affect. *Psychol. Rev.* 94: 319–40

Higgins ET. 1990. Personality, social psychology, and person-situation relations: standards and knowledge activation as a common language. See Pervin 1990a, pp. 301–38

Higgins ET. 1996a. Knowledge activation: accessibility, applicability, and salience. See Higgins & Kruglanski 1996, pp. 133–68

Higgins ET. 1996b. Ideals, oughts, and regulatory focus: affect and motivation from distinct pains and pleasures. See Gollwitzer & Bargh 1996, pp. 91–114

Higgins ET. 1996c. Emotional experiences: the pains and pleasures of distinct regulatory systems. In *Emotion: Interdisciplinary Perspectives*, ed. RD Kavanaugh, B Zimmerberg, S Fein, pp. 203–41. Mahwah, NJ: Erlbaum

Higgins ET, Bargh JA. 1987. Social cognition and social perception. *Annu. Rev. Psychol.* 38:369–425

Higgins ET, Kruglanski AW, eds. 1996. *Social Psychology: Handbook of Basic Principles*. New York: Guilford

John OP, Robins RW. 1993. Gordon Allport: father and critic of the Five-Factor model. In *Fifty Years of Personality Psychology*, ed. KH Craik, pp. 215–36. New York: Plenum

Kahneman D, Snell J. 1990. Predicting utility. In *Insights in Decision Making: A Tribute to Hillel J. Eihorn*, ed. RM Hogarth, pp. 295–310. New York: Univ. Chicago Press

Kandel ER, Hawkins RD. 1992. The biological basis of learning and individuality. *Sci. Am.* 267:78–86

Kihlstrom JF. 1987. The cognitive unconscious. *Science* 237:1445–52
Kihlstrom JF. 1990. The psychological unconscious. See Pervin 1990a, pp. 445–64
Kihlstrom JF, Cantor N. 1984. Mental representations of the self. In *Advances in Experimental Social Psychology. Theorizing in Social Psychology: Special Topics*, ed. L Berkowitz, 17:2–40. New York: Academic
Krahe B. 1990. *Situation Cognition and Coherence in Personality: An Individual-Centered Approach*. Cambridge, England: Cambridge Univ. Press
Kunda Z, Thagard P. 1996. Forming impressions from sterotypes, traits, and behaviors: a parallel-constraint-satisfaction theory. *Psychol. Rev.* 103:284–308
Larsen RJ. 1987. The stability of mood variability: a spectral analytic approach to daily mood assessments. *J. Pers. Soc. Psychol.* 52:1195–204
Larsen RJ. 1989. A process approach to personality psychology: utilizing time as a facet of data. In *Personality Psychology: Recent Trends and Emerging Directions*, ed. D Buss, N Cantor, pp. 177–93. New York: Springer-Verlag
Larsen RJ, Cutler SE. 1996. The complexity of individual emotional lives: a within-subject analysis of affect structure. *J. Soc. Clin. Psychol.* 15:206–30
Larsen RJ, Kasimatis M. 1990. Individual differences in entrainment of mood to the weekly calendar. *J. Pers. Soc. Psychol.* 58:164–71
Larsen RJ, Kasimatis M. 1991. Day-to-day physical symptoms: individual differences in the occurrence, duration, and emotional concomitants of minor daily illnesses. *J. Pers.* 59:387–423
Lazarus RS. 1993. Coping theory and research: past, present, and future. *Psychosom. Med.* 55:234–47
Markus HR, Kitayama S. 1991. Culture and the self: implications for cognition, emotion, and motivation. *Psychol. Rev.* 98: 224–53
McAdams DP. 1992. The Five-Factor model in personality. *J. Pers.* 60:329–61
Metcalfe J, Jacobs WJ. 1998. Emotional memory: the effects of stress on "cool" and "hot" memory systems. In *Psychology of Learning and Motivation: Advances in Research and Theory*, ed. DL Medin, 38: In press. San Diego, CA: Academic
Miller SM. 1987. Monitoring and blunting: validation of a questionnaire to assess styles of information seeking under threat. *J. Pers. Soc. Psychol.* 52:345–53
Miller SM, Mischel W, O'Leary A, Mills M. 1969. From human papillomavirus (HPV) to cervical cancer: psychosocial processes in infection, detection, and control. *Ann. Behav. Med.* 18:219–28
Miller SM, Shoda Y, Hurley K. 1996b. Applying cognitive-social theory to health-protective behavior: breast self-examination in cancer screening. *Psychol. Bull.* 119: 70–94
Mischel W. 1968. *Personality and Assessment*. New York: Wiley. Republished 1996. Mahwah, NJ: Erlbaum
Mischel W. 1973. Toward a cognitive social learning reconceptualization of personality. *Psychol. Rev.* 80:252–83
Mischel W. 1984. On the predictability of behavior and the structure of personality. In *Personality and the Prediction of Behavior*, ed. RA Zucker, J Aronoff, AI Rabin, pp. 269–305. New York: Academic
Mischel W. 1990. Personality dispositions revisited and revised: a view after three decades. See Pervin 1990a, pp. 111–34
Mischel W. 1993. *Introduction to Personality*. Fort Worth, TX: Harcourt Brace Jovanovich. 5th ed.
Mischel W, Cantor N, Feldman S. 1996. Principles of self-regulation: the nature of willpower and self-control. See Higgins & Kruglanski 1996, pp. 329–60
Mischel W, Peake PK. 1982. Beyond déjà vu in the search for cross-situational consistency. *Psychol. Rev.* 89:730–55
Mischel W, Shoda Y. 1994. Personality psychology has two goals: Must it be two fields? *Psychol. Inq.* 5:156–58
Mischel W, Shoda Y. 1995. A cognitive-affective system theory of personality: reconceptualizing situations, dispositions, dynamics, and invariance in personality structure. *Psychol. Rev.* 102:246–68
Mischel W, Shoda Y, Rodriguez ML. 1989. Delay of gratification in children. *Science* 244:933–38
Moskowitz DS. 1982. Coherence and cross-situational generality in personality: a new analysis of old problems. *J. Pers. Soc. Psychol.* 43:754–68
Moskowitz DS. 1994. Cross-situational generality and the interpersonal circumplex. *J. Pers. Soc. Psychol.* 66:921–33
Moskowitz DS, Suh EJ, Desaulniers J. 1994. Situational influences on gender differences in agency and communion. *J. Pers. Soc. Psychol.* 66:753–61
Newcomb TM. 1929. *Consistency of Certain Extrovert-Introvert Behavior Patterns in 51 Problem Boys*. New York: Columbia Univ., Teach. Coll., Bur. Publ.

Pervin LA, ed. 1989. *Goal Concepts in Personality and Social Psychology*. Hillsdale, NJ: Erlbaum

Pervin LA, ed. 1990a. *Handbook of Personality: Theory and Research*. New York: Guilford

Pervin LA. 1990b. Goal concepts: themes, issues, and questions. See Pervin 1990a, pp. 473–79

Pervin LA. 1994. A critical analysis of current trait theory. *Psychol. Inq.* 5:103–13

Peterson DR. 1968. *The Clinical Study of Social Behavior*. New York: Appleton

Plomin R. 1994. *Genetics and Experience: The Developmental Interplay Between Nature and Nurture*. Newbury Park, CA: Sage

Plomin R, Chipuer HM, Loehlin JC. 1990. Behavioral genetics and personality. See Pervin 1990a, pp. 225–43

Plomin R, DeFries JC, McClearn GE, Rutter M. 1997. *Behavioral Genetics*. New York: Freeman. 3rd ed.

Plomin R, Owen MJ, McGuffin P. 1994. The genetic basis of complex human behaviors. *Science* 264:1733–39

Posner MI. 1997. *Cognitive neuroscience and the development of attention*. Presented at Bienn. Meet. Soc. Res. Child Dev., Apr., Washington, DC

Read SJ, Jones DK, Miller LC. 1990. Traits as goal-based categories: the importance of goals in the coherence of dispositional categories. *J. Pers. Soc. Psychol.* 58: 1048–61

Read SJ, Miller LC. 1989a. The importance of goals in personality: toward a coherent model of persons. In *Social Intelligence and Cognitive Assessments of Personality. Advances in Social Cognition*, ed. RS Wyer, TK Srull, 2:163–74. Hillsdale, NJ: Erlbaum

Read SJ, Miller LC. 1989b. Inter-personalism: toward a goal-based theory of persons in relationships. See Pervin 1989, pp. 413–72

Read SJ, Miller LC. 1993. Rapist or "regular guy": explanatory coherence in the construction of mental models of others. *Pers. Soc. Psychol. Bull.* 19:526–40

Read SJ, Miller LC. 1994. Dissonance and balance in belief systems: the promise of parallel constraint satisfaction processes and connectionist modeling approaches. In *Beliefs, Reasoning, and Decision Making: Psycho-Logic in Honor of Bob Abelson*, ed. RC Schank, E Langer, pp. 209–35. Hillsdale, NJ: Erlbaum

Read SJ, Miller LC, eds. 1998. *Connectionist Models of Social Reasoning and Social Behavior*. Mahwah, NJ: Erlbaum. In press

Revelle W. 1995. Personality processes. *Annu. Rev. Psychol.* 46:295–328

Rothbart MK, Derryberry D, Posner MI. 1994. A psychobiological approach to the development of temperament. See Bates & Wachs 1994, pp. 83–116

Rothbart MK, Posner MI, Gerardi GM. 1997. *Effortful control and the development of temperament*. Presented at Bienn. Meet. Soc. Res. Child Dev., Apr., Washington, DC

Rothbart MK, Posner MI, Hershey KL. 1995. Temperament, attention, and developmental psychopathology. In *Manual of Developmental Psychopathology*, ed. D Cicchetti, DJ Cohen, 1:315–40. New York: Wiley

Rumelhart DE, McClelland JL. 1986. *Parallel Distributed Processing: Explorations in the Microstructure of Cognition: Foundations*, Vol. 1. Cambridge, MA: MIT Press/ Bradford Books

Salovey P, Mayer JD. 1990. Emotional intelligence. *Imagin. Cogn. Pers.* 9:185–211

Saudino KJ, Plomin R. 1996. Personality and behavioral genetics: Where have we been and where are we going? *J. Res. Pers.* 30:335–47

Scheier MF, Carver CS. 1988a. A model of behavioral self-regulation: translating intention into action. In *Advances in Experimental Social Psychology: Social Psychological Studies of the Self: Perspectives and Programs*, ed. L Berkowitz, 21: 303–46. San Diego: Academic

Scheier MF, Carver CS. 1988b. Individual differences in self-concept and self-process. In *The Self in Social Psychology*, ed. DM Wegner, RR Vallacher, pp. 229–51. New York: Oxford Univ. Press

Sethi A, Shoda Y. 1997. *The relationships between maternal responsivity, secure base behavior, and emotion regulation: a molecular analysis*. Presented at Bienn. Meet. Soc. Res. Child Dev., Apr., Washington, DC

Shoda Y. 1996. Discriminative facility as a determinant of coping. *Am. Psychol. Soc., 8th, San Francisco*

Shoda Y, Mischel W. 1993. Cognitive social approach to dispositional inferences: What if the perceiver is a cognitive-social theorist? *Pers. Soc. Psychol. Bull.* 19:574–85

Shoda Y, Mischel W. 1998. The person as a cognitive-affective activation network: characteristic patterns of behavior variation emerging from a stable personality structure. See Read & Miller 1998, pp. 175–208

Shoda Y, Mischel W, Peake PK. 1990. Pre-

dicting adolescent cognitive and self-regulatory competencies from preschool delay of gratification: identifying diagnostic conditions. *Dev. Psychol.* 26:978–86
Shoda Y, Mischel W, Wright JC. 1989. Intuitive interactionism in person perception: effects of situation-behavior relations on dispositional judgments. *J. Pers. Soc. Psychol.* 56:41–53
Shoda Y, Mischel W, Wright JC. 1993a. The role of situational demands and cognitive competencies in behavior organization and personality coherence. *J. Pers. Soc. Psychol.* 65:1023–35
Shoda Y, Mischel W, Wright JC. 1993b. Links between personality judgments and contextualized behavior patterns: situation-behavior profiles of personality prototypes. *Soc. Cogn.* 11:399–429
Shoda Y, Mischel W, Wright JC. 1994. Intraindividual stability in the organization and patterning of behavior: incorporating psychological situations into the idiographic analysis of personality. *J. Pers. Soc. Psychol.* 67:674–87
Shultz TR, Lepper MR. 1996. Cognitive dissonance reduction as constraint satisfaction. *Psychol. Rev.* 103:219–40
Smith CA, Lazarus RS. 1990. Emotion and adaptation. See Pervin 1990a, pp. 609–37
Smith CA, Pope LK. 1992. Appraisal and emotion: the interactional contributions of dispositional and situational factors. In *Emotion and Social Behavior. Review of Personality and Social Psychology*, ed. MS Clark, 14:32-62. Newbury Park, CA: Sage
Stemmler G. 1997. Selective activation of traits: boundary conditions for the activation of anger. *Pers. Individ. Differ.* 22: 213–33
Taylor SE, Aspinwall LG. 1996. Mediating and moderating processes in psychosocial stress: appraisal, coping, resistance, and vulnerability. In *Psychosocial Stress: Perspectives on Structure, Theory, Life-Course, and Methods*, ed. HB Kaplan, pp. 71–110. San Diego, CA: Academic
Uleman JS, Bargh JA, eds. 1989. *Unintended Thought.* New York: Guilford
Vallacher RR, Wegner DM. 1987. What do people think they're doing? Action identification and human behavior. *Psychol. Rev.* 94:3–15
Vansteelandt K, Mechelen IV. 1997. Individual difference in situation-behavior profiles: a triple typology model. *Res. Rep. No. 97-2*, pp. 1–33. Catholic Univ. Leuven, Dep. Psychol., Leuven, Belg.
Vernon PE. 1964. *Personality Assessment: A Critical Survey.* New York: Wiley
Wachs TD, King B. 1994. Behavioral research in the brave new world of neuroscience and temperament: a guide to the biologically perplexed. See Bates & Wachs 1994, pp. 307–36
Weary G, Edwards JA. 1994. Individual differences in causal uncertainty. *J. Pers. Soc. Psychol.* 67:308–18
Westen D. 1990. Psychoanalytic approaches to personality. See Pervin 1990a, pp. 21–65
Wiggins JS, Pincus AL. 1992. Personality: structure and assessment. *Annu. Rev. Psychol.* 43:473–504
Wiggins JS, Trapnell PD. 1997. Personality structure: the return of the Big Five. In *Handbook of Personality Psychology*, ed. R Hogan, J Johnson, S Briggs, pp. 737–65. San Diego, CA: Academic
Wright J, Mischel W. 1982. Influence of affect on cognitive social learning person variables. *J. Pers. Soc. Psychol.* 43:901–14
Wright JC, Mischel W. 1987. A conditional approach to dispositional constructs: the local predictability of social behavior. *J. Pers. Soc. Psychol.* 53:1159–77
Wright JC, Mischel W. 1988. Conditional hedges and the intuitive psychology of traits. *J. Pers. Soc. Psychol.* 55:454–69

Psychological Review
1993, Vol. 100, No. 4, 674-701

0033-295X/93/$3.00

Adolescence-Limited and Life-Course-Persistent Antisocial Behavior: A Developmental Taxonomy

Terrie E. Moffitt

A dual taxonomy is presented to reconcile 2 incongruous facts about antisocial behavior: (a) It shows impressive continuity over age, but (b) its prevalence changes dramatically over age, increasing almost 10-fold temporarily during adolescence. This article suggests that delinquency conceals 2 distinct categories of individuals, each with a unique natural history and etiology: A small group engages in antisocial behavior of 1 sort or another at every life stage, whereas a larger group is antisocial only during adolescence. According to the theory of *life-course-persistent* antisocial behavior, children's neuropsychological problems interact cumulatively with their criminogenic environments across development, culminating in a pathological personality. According to the theory of *adolescence-limited* antisocial behavior, a contemporary maturity gap encourages teens to mimic antisocial behavior in ways that are normative and adjustive.

There are marked individual differences in the stability of antisocial behavior. Many people behave antisocially, but their antisocial behavior is temporary and situational. In contrast, the antisocial behavior of some people is very stable and persistent. Temporary, situational antisocial behavior is quite common in the population, especially among adolescents. Persistent, stable antisocial behavior is found among a relatively small number of males whose behavior problems are also quite extreme. The central tenet of this article is that temporary versus persistent antisocial persons constitute two qualitatively distinct types of persons. In particular, I suggest that juvenile delinquency conceals two qualitatively distinct categories of individuals, each in need of its own distinct theoretical explanation.

Of course, systems for classifying types of antisocial persons have been introduced before (e.g., American Psychiatric Association, 1987; Chaiken & Chaiken, 1984; Hare, Hart, & Harpur, 1991; Jesness & Haapanen, 1982; Lahey et al., 1990; Megargee, 1976; Moffitt, 1990a; Quay, 1966; Warren, 1969). However, none of these classifications has acquired the ascendancy necessary to guide mainstream criminology and psychopathology research. Indeed, "general" theories of crime (e.g., Gottfredson & Hirschi, 1990), comparisons of delinquent versus nondelinquent groups (e.g., Feehan, Stanton, McGee, Silva, & Moffitt, 1990), and arraying samples of subjects along antisocial dimensions (e.g., Fergusson, Horwood, & Lloyd, 1991) remain the status quo.

Previous antisocial classification schemes may have failed to capture the imaginations of social scientists because, although they provided more or less accurate behavioral descriptions of antisocial subtypes, they offered relatively little in the way of etiological or predictive validity (Morey, 1991). A classification becomes a taxonomy if it engenders assertions about origins and outcomes by weaving a nomological net of relationships between the taxa and their correlates (Meehl & Golden, 1982). A taxon carries a network of meaning over and above a behavioral description; it includes implications for etiology, course, prognosis, treatment, and relations with other taxa. Previous classifications of antisocial behavior have not been extended into theories, and "it is theory that provides the glue that holds a classification together and gives it both its scientific and its clinical relevance" (Millon, 1991, p. 257; Quine, 1977). In this article, I elaborate on the distinction between temporary and persistent antisocial behavior and offer a pair of new developmental theories of criminal behavior that are based on this distinction. The theories are accompanied by refutable predictions.

If correct, this simple typology can serve a powerful organizing function, with important implications for theory and research on the causes of crime. For delinquents whose criminal activity is confined to the adolescent years, the causal factors may be proximal, specific to the period of adolescent development, and theory must account for the *dis*continuity in their lives. In contrast, for persons whose adolescent delinquency is merely one inflection in a continuous lifelong antisocial course, a theory of antisocial behavior must locate its causal factors early in their childhoods and must explain the continuity in their troubled lives.

The dual taxonomy (and its two theories) that I propose in

Work on this article was supported by the Violence and Traumatic Stress Branch of the National Institute of Mental Health (Grants MH43746, MH45070, and MH45548) and by the Program on Human Development and Antisocial Behavior, a joint project of the MacArthur Foundation and the National Institute of Justice. During writing, I was hosted by the Institute for Personality Assessment and Research of the University of California at Berkeley.

Without the persistent help of Avshalom Caspi, this article would not have been done. Other colleagues also helped to hone the ideas: Thomas Achenbach, Robert Cairns, Felton Earls, David Farrington, Bill Henry, Ben Lahey, Richard Linster, Rolf Loeber, Gerald Patterson, Steven Raudenbusch, Albert Reiss, Jr., Lee Robins, Robert Sampson, Richard Tremblay, Christy Visher, and Jennifer White. Ericka Overgard prepared the figures and edited the article.

Correspondence concerning this article should be addressed to Terrie E. Moffitt, Department of Psychology, University of Wisconsin at Madison, Madison, Wisconsin 53706-1611.

this article is best introduced with reference to the mysterious relationship between age and antisocial behavior. This relationship is at once the most robust and least understood empirical observation in the field of criminology.

Age and Antisocial Behavior

When official rates of crime are plotted against age, the rates for both prevalence and incidence of offending appear highest during adolescence; they peak sharply at about age 17 and drop precipitously in young adulthood. The majority of criminal offenders are teenagers; by the early 20s, the number of active offenders decreases by over 50%, and by age 28, almost 85% of former delinquents desist from offending (Blumstein & Cohen, 1987; Farrington, 1986). With slight variations, this general relationship between age and crime obtains among males and females, for most types of crimes, during recent historical periods and in numerous Western nations (Hirschi & Gottfredson, 1983). A prototype of the empirical curve of criminal offenses over age is shown in Figure 1.

Until recently, research on age and crime has relied on official data, primarily arrest and conviction records. As a result, the left-hand side of the age–crime curve has been censored. Indeed, in many empirical comparisons between early-onset and late-onset antisocial behavior, *early* has been artifactually defined as mid-adolescence on the basis of first police arrest or court conviction (cf. Farrington, Loeber, Elliott, et al., 1990; Tolan, 1987). However, research on childhood conduct disorder has now documented that antisocial behavior begins long before the age when it is first encoded in police data banks. Indeed, it is now known that the steep decline in antisocial behavior between ages 17 and 30 is mirrored by a steep incline in antisocial behavior between ages 7 and 17 (Loeber, Stouthamer-Loeber, Van Kammen, & Farrington, 1989; Wolfgang, Figlio, & Sellin, 1972). This extension to the age–crime curve is plotted in Figure 2. Furthermore, we may venture across disciplinary boundaries to add developmental psychologists' reports of childhood aggression (Pepler & Rubin, 1991) and mental health researchers' reports of conduct disorder (Kazdin, 1987) to criminologists' studies of self-reported delinquency and official crime. So doing, it becomes obvious that manifestations of antisocial behavior emerge very early in the life course and remain present thereafter.

With the advent of alternate measurement strategies, most notably self-reports of deviant behavior, researchers have learned that arrest statistics merely reflect the tip of the deviance iceberg (Hood & Sparks, 1970; Klein, 1989). Actual rates of illegal behavior soar so high during adolescence that participation in delinquency appears to be a normal part of teen life (Elliott, Ageton, Huizinga, Knowles, & Canter, 1983). With the liberty of some artistic license, the curved line plotted in Figure 3 may be taken to represent what is currently known about the prevalence of antisocial behaviors over the life course.

Although there is widespread agreement about the curve of crime over age, there are few convincing explanations for the shape of the curve. Until recently, scholars still disagreed about whether the adolescent peak represented a change in prevalence or a change in incidence: Does adolescence bring an increment

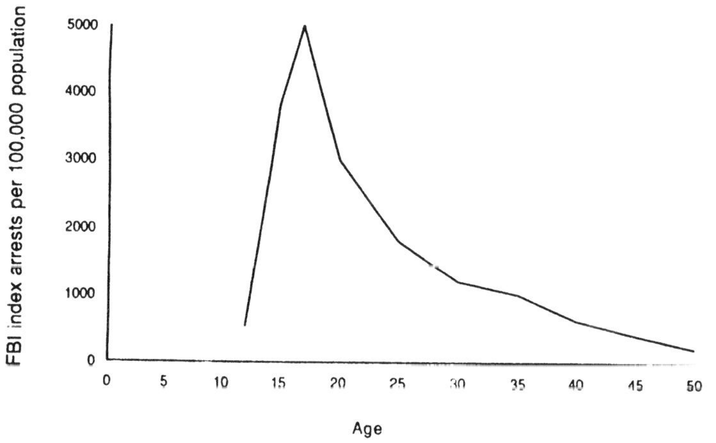

Figure 1. Age-specific arrest rates for United States Federal Bureau of Investigation's (FBI) index offenses in 1980. (Index offenses include homicide, forcible rape, robbery, aggravated assault, burglary, larceny, and auto theft. From "Criminal Career Research: Its Value for Criminology" by A. Blumstein, J. Cohen, and D. P. Farrington, 1988, *Criminology, 26,* p. 11. Copyright 1988 by the American Society of Criminology. Adapted by permission.)

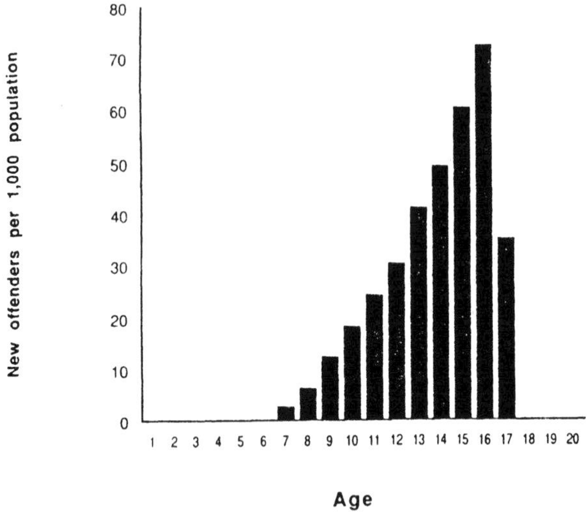

Figure 2. The rate of new male offenders at each age per 1,000 male population. (Onset of offending was defined as the age at which a child was first taken into custody and designated delinquent by the police. Rates are based on a cohort of 9,945 boys born in 1945 in Philadelphia, Pennsylvania. From *Delinquency In a Birth Cohort* (p. 132) by M. E. Wolfgang, R. M. Figlio, and T. Sellin, 1972, Chicago: The University of Chicago Press. Copyright 1972 by The University of Chicago. Adapted by permission.)

in the number of people who are willing to offend or does the small and constant number of offenders simply generate more criminal acts while they are adolescent? Empirical evaluations now suggest that the former explanation is correct. In his English study of offense rates over age, Farrington (1983) showed that the adolescent peak reflects a temporary increase in the number of people involved in antisocial behavior, not a temporary acceleration in the offense rates of individuals. This finding has been replicated in American samples (Wolfgang, Thornberry, & Figlio, 1987). The small human figures under the curve of Figure 3 portray these changes in prevalence.

But whence the increase in the prevalence of offenders? One possibility is that some phenomenon unique to adolescent development causes throngs of new adolescent offenders to temporarily join the few stable antisocial individuals in their delinquent ways. Figure 3 depicts the typological thesis to be argued here. A small group of persons is shown engaging in antisocial behavior of one sort or another at every stage of life. I have labeled these persons *life-course-persistent* to reflect the continuous course of their antisocial behavior. A larger group of persons fills out the age–crime curve with crime careers of shorter duration. I have labeled these persons *adolescence-limited* to reflect their more temporary involvement in antisocial behavior. Thus, timing and duration of the course of antisocial involvement are the defining features in the natural histories of the two proposed types of offenders.

Two oft-cited rules of thumb asserted by Robins (1978) seem to simultaneously assert and deny the life-course stability of antisocial behavior: "Adult antisocial behaviour virtually *requires* childhood antisocial behaviour [yet] most antisocial youths do *not* become antisocial adults" (p. 611). In fact, research has shown that antisocial behavior is remarkably stable across time and circumstance for some persons but decidedly unstable for most other people.

The stability of antisocial behavior is closely linked to its extremity. The extreme frequency of crime committed by a very few males is impressive; it has been repeatedly shown that the most persistent 5% or 6% of offenders are responsible for about 50% of known crimes (see Farrington, Ohlin, & Wilson, 1986, for a review). In their study of 10,000 men, Wolfgang et al. (1972) found that 6% of offenders accounted for more than half of the crimes committed by the sample; relative to other offenders, these high-rate offenders began their criminal careers earlier and continued them for more years. The relationship between stability and extremity is found in samples of children as well. In his analysis of a sample of third-grade boys, Patterson (1982) found that the most aggressive 5% of the boys constituted the most persistent group as well; 39% of them ranked above the 95th percentile on aggression 10 years later, and 100% of them were still above the median. Similarly, Loeber (1982) has reviewed research showing that stability of youngsters' antisocial behavior across time is linked with stability across situations

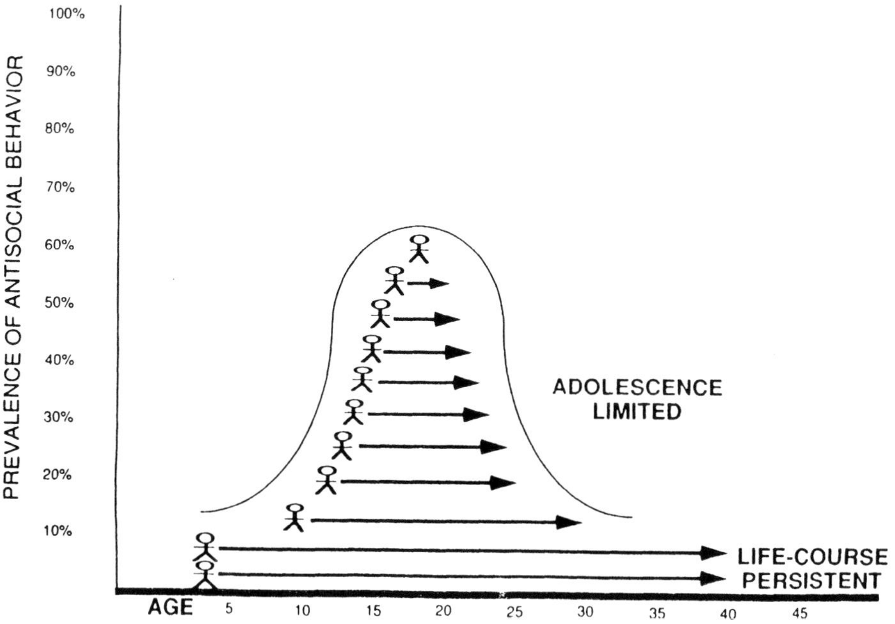

Figure 3. Hypothetical illustration of the changing prevalence of participation in antisocial behavior across the life course. (The solid line represents the known curve of crime over age. The arrows represent the duration of participation in antisocial behavior by individuals.)

and that both forms of stability are characteristic of a relatively small group of persons with extremely antisocial behavior.

Thus, in defiance of regression to the mean, a group of extremely antisocial persons remain extreme on measures taken at later ages and in different situations. Among other persons, however, temporary and situational manifestations of antisocial behavior (even to severe levels) may be quite common.

This point is vividly illustrated in a longitudinal investigation of a representative cohort of 1,037 New Zealand children born in 1972–1973. In this sample, I compared the base rates of persistent and temporary antisocial behavior problems (Moffitt, 1991). I identified a group of boys whose antisocial behavior was rated above average at each of seven biennial assessments (ages 3, 5, 7, 9, 11, 13, and 15). The boys were also rated as very antisocial by three different reporting agents (parents, teachers, and self). Five percent of the boys in the sample met these selection criteria. As a group, their mean antisocial ratings were more than a standard deviation above the norm for boys at every age. In contrast, fully two thirds of the remaining boys were rated above average on antisocial checklists as well but at only one or two ages or by only one reporter, illustrating that stability cannot be inferred from cross-sectional measures of extremity (Henry, Moffitt, Robins, Earls, & Silva, 1993). A disproportionate amount of the measured stability in the New Zealand sample could be attributed to the 5% of boys whose antisocial behavior was both extreme and consistent. For example, when these few boys were excluded from calculations, the 8-year stability coefficient for teacher ratings was reduced from .28 (R^2 = .078) to .16 (R^2 = .025), indicating that 5% of the sample accounted for 68% of the sample's stability. (If antisocial behavior had been a stable characteristic throughout the sample, with most boys retaining their relative standing in the group across time, then excluding the top 5% of the sample should not have affected the stability coefficient.) In summary, there appear to be noteworthy individual differences in the stability of antisocial behavior.

I have already alluded to the small number of persons in the general population whose antisocial behavior is life-course-persistent. In fact, epidemiological research has shown that there is remarkable uniformity in the prevalence rates of different manifestations of severe antisocial behavior: Regardless of their age, under 10% of males warrant an "official" antisocial designation. For example, about 5% of preschool boys are considered by their parents or caretakers to be "very difficult to manage" (McGee, Partridge, Williams, & Silva, 1991). The prevalence of conduct disorder among elementary-school-aged boys has been found to be between 4% and 9% in several countries (Costello, 1989; Rutter, Tizard, & Whitmore, 1970). About 6% of boys are first arrested by police as preteens (Moffitt & Silva, 1988c; Wolfgang et al., 1972); such early arrest is important because it is the best predictor of long-term recidivistic offending. The rate of conviction for a violent offense in young adult males is between 3% and 6% (Moffitt, Mednick, & Gabrielli, 1989), and about 4% of male adolescents self-report sustained careers of serious violence (three or more violent offenses per year for 5 years; Elliott, Huizinga, & Morse, 1986). Finally, the prevalence of men with antisocial personality disorder is estimated at about 4% to 5% (Davison & Neale, 1990; Robins, 1985).

It is possible, of course, that the persons who constitute these epidemiological statistics at different ages are all different individuals. However, the longitudinal data suggest otherwise: It is more likely that the remarkable constancy of prevalence rates reflects the reoccurrence of the same life-course-persistent individuals in different antisocial categories at different ages. Robins (1966, 1978) has shown that there are virtually no subjects with adult antisocial personality disorder who did not also have conduct disorder as children. White, Moffitt, Earls, Robins, and Silva (1990) found notable continuity from disobedient and aggressive behavior at age 3 to later childhood conduct disorder and thence to arrest by police in the early teen years. Loeber (1982) reviewed research that pinpoints a first arrest between ages 7 and 11 as particularly important for predicting long-term adult offending. Hare and McPherson (1984) have reported that a conviction for violence in the early 20s is characteristic of almost all men who become diagnosed with antisocial (psychopathic) personality disorder.

There are still gaps in the epidemiological database: each of the earlier cited studies connected only two or three points in the life course. Nonetheless, the consistency is impressive: A substantial body of longitudinal research consistently points to a very small group of males who display high rates of antisocial behavior across time and in diverse situations. The professional nomenclature may change, but the faces remain the same as they drift through successive systems aimed at curbing their deviance: schools, juvenile-justice programs, psychiatric treatment centers, and prisons. The topography of their behavior may change with changing opportunities, but the underlying disposition persists throughout the life course.

Whereas a few males evidence antisocial behavior that emerges in toddlerhood and is persistent thereafter, the majority of boys who become antisocial first do so during adolescence (Elliott, Knowles, & Canter, 1981). This tidal wave of adolescent onset has been studied in the aforementioned representative sample of New Zealand boys (Moffitt, 1991). Between ages 11 and 15, about one third of the sample joined the delinquent lifestyles of the 5% of boys who had shown stable and pervasive antisocial behavior since preschool. As a group, these adolescent newcomers to antisocial ways had not formerly exceeded the normative levels of antisocial behavior for boys at ages 3, 5, 7, 9, or 11. Despite their lack of prior experience, by age 15, the newcomers equaled their preschool-onset antisocial peers in the variety of laws they had broken, the frequency with which they broke them, and the number of times they appeared in juvenile court (Moffitt, 1991). On the basis of such commonly used indexes of adolescent delinquency, the two delinquent groups were indistinguishable. Thus, if the sample was viewed only as an adolescent cross section, researchers would lose sight of the two delinquent groups' very different developmental histories, seeing only delinquents and nondelinquents.

Indeed, researchers and practitioners cannot yet effectively assign individual delinquent adolescents to meaningful subtypes on the basis of cross-sectional "snapshots" of their antisocial behavior during adolescence (Loeber & LeBlanc, 1990; Moffitt, 1990a). Again, the New Zealand sample provides an example: At age 15, both the childhood-persistent and adolescent-onset groups had members who scored more than 5 standard deviations above the mean on self-report delinquency, and by age 19 both groups had some members with more than 50 convictions for crimes in the New Zealand courts. Elliott and Huizinga (1984) reported similarly poor classification in a representative sample of American teens. They attempted to discriminate, at the time of first arrest, individual future career offenders from adolescence-limited offenders. Discrimination could not be improved beyond chance by entering the kinds of information typically available to officials: type of current offense, age, sex, race, class, involvement with delinquent peers, and attitudes toward deviance. Addition of measures of the extremity of self-reported delinquency and emotional problems improved prediction only 7% beyond chance. Earlier, I noted that the stability of antisocial behavior implies its extremity but that extremity does not imply stability; measures of the frequency or seriousness of adolescent offending will not discriminate very well between life-course-persistent and adolescence-limited delinquents. On the basis of their study and others, Elliott and Huizinga concluded that there is "no effective means for discriminating between the serious career offenders and nonserious offenders" (p. 98). A notable feature of the taxonomy introduced in this article is that knowledge of a subject's preadolescent behavior is *required* for making the differential diagnosis between the life-course-persistent and adolescence-limited types of antisocial teenager. Longitudinal designs are needed to collect the lifetime repeated measures that are needed to distinguish individual differences in the developmental course of antisocial behavior.[1]

I have argued in this section that juvenile delinquency conceals two categories of people. A very large group participates in antisocial behavior during adolescence. A much smaller group,

[1] It may be countered that research has distinguished delinquent subtypes that are based on cross-sectional information. For example, the delinquent behaviors of the life-course-persistent type may be distinguished by relatively more overt aggression, whereas the adolescence-limited type may show relatively more covert offending under peer influence. I agree. Factor-analytic studies have revealed an aggressive "undersocialized" factor and a "socialized" peer-oriented factor (Quay, 1964a, 1964b, 1966), and meta-analytic studies have revealed "overt" and "covert" offense patterns (Loeber & Schmaling, 1985). However, such scale pairs are highly and positively correlated in adolescent samples, in which the evidence for offense versatility outweighs evidence for offense specialization (Klein, 1984; Robins, 1978). Cross-sectional classification has not proven effective at the level of the individual. My assertion that developmental history is needed for confident classification is buttressed by the repeated finding that age of onset of antisocial

who continues serious antisocial behavior throughout adulthood, is the same group whose antisocial behavior was stable across the years from early childhood. The categories remain hypothetical types, because no longitudinal study has yet repeatedly measured antisocial behavior in a representative sample of the same individuals from preschool to midlife. I describe in the next sections the two hypothetical types of antisocial youth: life-course-persistent and adolescence-limited. I argue that the two groups differ in etiology, developmental course, prognosis, and, importantly, classification of their behavior as either pathological or normative. The goal of this article is to proffer a description of the two types in the form of a set of testable predictions.

Life-Course-Persistent Antisocial Behavior

My account of the life-course-persistent antisocial type follows this plan: In the first section, *Continuity of Antisocial Behavior Defined*, I provide a definition and description of persistent antisocial behavior. In the second section, *Beginnings: Neuropsychological Risk for Difficult Temperament and Behavioral Problems*, I present the hypothesis that persistent antisocial behavior has its origins in an interaction between children's neuropsychological vulnerabilities and criminogenic environments. In the third section, *Maintenance and Elaboration Over the Life Course: Cumulative Continuity, Contemporary Continuity, and Narrowing Options for Change*, I introduce the cumulative and contemporary processes that maintain antisocial behavior across time and that expand antisocial behavior into a pervasive adult life-style. In the fourth section, I summarize the theory's perspective on continuity, and in the fifth section, I make a case that life-course-persistent antisocial behavior is a form of psychopathology.

Continuity of Antisocial Behavior Defined

As implied by the label, continuity is the hallmark of the small group of life-course-persistent antisocial persons. Across the life course, these individuals exhibit changing manifestations of antisocial behavior: biting and hitting at age 4, shoplifting and truancy at age 10, selling drugs and stealing cars at age 16, robbery and rape at age 22, and fraud and child abuse at age 30; the underlying disposition remains the same, but its expression changes form as new social opportunities arise at different points in development. This pattern of continuity across age is matched also by cross-situational consistency: Life-course-persistent antisocial persons lie at home, steal from shops, cheat at school, fight in bars, and embezzle at work (Farrington, 1991; Loeber, 1982; Loeber & Baicker-McKee, 1989; Robins, 1966, 1978; White et al., 1990).

The concept of behavioral coherence, or *heterotypic continuity*, is invoked here to extend observations of continuity beyond the mere persistence of a single behavior to encompass a variety of antisocial expressions that emerge as development affords new opportunities. Heterotypic continuity refers to continuity of an inferred trait or attribute that is presumed to underlie diverse phenotypic behaviors (Kagan, 1969). As Kagan and Moss (1962) suggested, a specific behavior in childhood might not be predictive of phenotypically similar behavior later in adulthood, but it may still be associated with behaviors that are *conceptually* consistent with the earlier behavior.

Examples of heterotypic continuities have been reported by Ryder (1967), who found that childhood aggression, physical adventurousness, and nonconformity were related to adult sexual behavior. Another example of coherence is provided in a 22-year follow-up study of men and women who had been rated as aggressive by their peers in late childhood (Huesmann, Eron, Lefkowitz, & Walder, 1984). As adults, the men were likely to commit serious criminal acts, abuse their spouses, and drive while intoxicated, whereas the women were likely to punish their offspring severely. Another example of personality coherence is the finding that the developmental antecedents of erratic work histories may be found in phenotypically dissimilar attributes of difficult temperament in childhood (Caspi, Elder, & Bem, 1987). In addition, in their hallmark study, West and Farrington (1977) observed that stealing, alcohol abuse, sexual promiscuity, reckless driving, and violence were linked across the life course. The prognosis for the life-course-persistent person is bleak: Drug and alcohol addiction; unsatisfactory employment; unpaid debts; homelessness; drunk driving; violent assault; multiple and unstable relationships; spouse battery; abandoned, neglected, or abused children; and psychiatric illness have all been reported at very high rates for offenders who persist past the age of 25 (Farrington & West, 1990; Robins, 1966; Sampson & Laub, 1990). Thus, this theory of life-course-persistent antisocial behavior predicts continuity across the entire life course but allows that the underlying disposition will change its manifestation when age and social circumstances alter opportunities.

Although reports of the continuity of antisocial styles from childhood to young adulthood abound, the outcomes of antisocial individuals during midlife have seldom been examined. The pattern of official crime over age (Figure 1) implies that criminal offending all but disappears by midlife,[2] but there is no reason to expect that life-course-persistents miraculously assume prosocial tendencies after an antisocial tenure of several decades. Indeed, criminal psychopaths decrease their number of arrestable offenses at about age 40, but the constellation of antisocial personality traits described by Cleckley (1976) per-

behavior problems is the single best predictor of adult criminal outcomes (Farrington, Loeber, Elliott, et al., 1990).

[2] The conclusion that crime ceases in midlife may be premature: it is based on cross-sectional age comparisons of arrest and conviction rates. There are at least four reasons to doubt the conclusions that have been based on this method. First, official records underestimate the amount of true crime. Second, there may be justice-system biases toward underarrest and prosecution of older persons. Third, death and imprisonment may selectively remove persistent offenders from official crime statistics. Fourth, cross-cohort comparisons may mistake generational effects for age effects (Rowe & Tittle, 1977). Thus, until longitudinal researchers collect self-reports of crime in the same individuals from adolescence to old age, the midlife disappearance of crime will remain an empirical question.

sists in male samples at least until age 69 (Harpur & Hare, 1991). As I argue in the third section of this article (*Maintenance*), an analysis of the cumulative developmental forces underlying the continuity of aggression from childhood to adulthood will predict continuity on into midlife as well. Beyond young adulthood, the antisocial disposition of life-course-persistents may be expressed in a form that is simply not yet well measured by epidemiological surveys of official crime: One such possibility is neglect and abuse of family members. Consistent with this hypothesis, Farrington and West (1990) found that half of the persistent offenders in the Cambridge longitudinal study self-reported having hit their spouses when they were interviewed at age 32. Fagan and Wexler (1987) reviewed studies showing that spouse battery is often preceded by a history of violence against strangers. Also, crime statistics show that, whereas property crimes peak in the teen years and drop thereafter, family violence offenses show a steady increase with age (Gottfredson & Hirschi, 1986). Research is needed that follows offenders into late adulthood while measuring multiple indicators of an antisocial life-style.

Beginnings: Neuropsychological Risk for Difficult Temperament and Behavioral Problems

If some individuals' antisocial behavior is stable from preschool to adulthood as the data imply, then investigators are compelled to look for its roots early in life, in factors that are present before or soon after birth. It is possible that the etiological chain begins with some factor capable of producing individual differences in the neuropsychological functions of the infant nervous system. Factors that influence infant neural development are myriad, and many of them have been empirically linked to antisocial outcomes.

One possible source of neuropsychological variation that is linked to problem behavior is disruption in the ontogenesis of the fetal brain. Minor physical anomalies, which are thought to be observable markers for hidden anomalies in neural development, have been found at elevated rates among violent offenders and subjects with antisocial personality traits (Fogel, Mednick, & Michelson, 1985; E. Kandel, Brennan, & Mednick, 1989; Paulhus & Martin, 1986). Neural development may be disrupted by maternal drug abuse, poor prenatal nutrition, or pre- or postnatal exposure to toxic agents (Needleman & Beringer, 1981; Rodning, Beckwith, & Howard, 1989; Stewart, 1983). Even brain insult suffered because of complications during delivery has been empirically linked to later violence and antisocial behavior in carefully designed longitudinal studies (E. Kandel & Mednick, 1991; Szatmari, Reitsma-Street, & Offord, 1986). In addition, some individual differences in neuropsychological health are heritable in origin (Borecki & Ashton, 1984; Martin, Jardine, & Eaves, 1984; Plomin, Nitz, & Rowe, 1990; Tambs, Sundet, & Magnus, 1984; Vandenberg, 1969). Just as parents and children share facial resemblances, they share some structural and functional similarities within their nervous systems. After birth, neural development may be disrupted by neonatal deprivation of nutrition, stimulation, and even affection (Cravioto & Arrieta, 1983; Kraemer, 1988; Meany, Aitken, van Berkel, Bhatnagar, & Sapolsky, 1988). Some studies have pointed to child abuse and neglect as possible sources of brain injury in the histories of delinquents with neuropsychological impairment (Lewis, Shanok, Pincus, & Glaser, 1979; Milner & McCanne, 1991; Tarter, Hegedus, Winsten, & Alterman, 1984).

There is good evidence that children who ultimately become persistently antisocial do suffer from deficits in neuropsychological abilities. I have elsewhere reviewed the available empirical and theoretical literatures; the link between neuropsychological impairment and antisocial outcomes is one of the most robust effects in the study of antisocial behavior (Moffitt, 1990b; Moffitt & Henry, 1991; see also Hirschi & Hindelang, 1977). Two sorts of neuropsychological deficits are empirically associated with antisocial behavior: verbal and "executive" functions. The verbal deficits of antisocial children are pervasive, affecting receptive listening and reading, problem solving, expressive speech and writing, and memory. In addition, executive deficits produce what is sometimes referred to as a comportmental learning disability (Price, Daffner, Stowe, & Mesulam, 1990), including symptoms such as inattention and impulsivity. These cognitive deficits and antisocial behavior share variance that is independent of social class, race, test motivation, and academic attainment (Moffitt, 1990b; Lynam, Moffitt, & Stouthamer-Loeber, 1993). In addition, the relation is not an artifact of slow-witted delinquents' greater susceptibility to detection by police; undetected delinquents have weak cognitive skills too (Moffitt & Silva, 1988a).

The evidence is strong that neuropsychological deficits are linked to the kind of antisocial behavior that begins in childhood and is sustained for lengthy periods. In a series of articles (Moffitt, 1990a; Moffitt & Henry, 1989; Moffitt & Silva, 1988b), I have shown that poor verbal and executive functions are associated with antisocial behavior, if it is extreme and persistent. In these studies, adolescent New Zealand boys who exhibited symptoms of both conduct disorder and attention-deficit disorder with hyperactivity (ADDH) scored very poorly on neuropsychological tests of verbal and executive functions and had histories of extreme antisocial behavior that persisted from age 3 to age 15. Apparently, their neuropsychological deficits were as long standing as their antisocial behavior; at ages 3 and 5 these boys had scored more than a standard deviation below the age norm for boys on the Bayley and McCarthy tests of motor coordination and on the Stanford-Binet test of cognitive performance. Contrast groups of boys with single diagnoses of either conduct disorder or ADDH did not have neuropsychological deficits or cognitive–motor delays, but neither were their behavior problems stable over time.

In a study designed to improve on measurement of executive functions (White, Moffitt, Caspi, Jeglum, Needles, & Stouthamer-Loeber, in press), we gathered data on self-control and impulsivity for 430 Pittsburgh youths. Twelve measures were taken from multiple sources (mother, teacher, self, and observer) by using multiple methods (rating scales, performance tests, computer games, Q sorts, and videotaped observations). A linear composite of the impulsivity measures was strongly related to the 3-year longevity of antisocial behavior, even after controlling for IQ, race, and social class. Boys who were very delinquent from ages 10 to 13 scored significantly higher on impulsivity than both their nondelinquent and temporarily delinquent age-mates. Taken together, the New Zealand and Pittsburgh longitudinal studies suggest that neuropsychological dysfunctions that manifest themselves as poor scores on tests of language and self-control—and as the inattentive, overactive, and impulsive symptoms of ADDH—are linked with the early childhood emergence of aggressive antisocial behavior and with its subsequent persistence.

Neuropsychological variation and the "difficult" infant. Before describing how neuropsychological variation might constitute risk for antisocial behavior, it is useful to define what is meant here by neuropsychological. By combining *neuro* with *psychological*, I refer broadly to the extent to which anatomical structures and physiological processes within the nervous system influence psychological characteristics such as temperament, behavioral development, cognitive abilities, or all three. For example, individual variation in brain function may engender differences between children in activity level, emotional reactivity, or self-regulation (temperament); speech, motor coordination, or impulse control (behavioral development); and attention, language, learning, memory, or reasoning (cognitive abilities).

Children with neurological difficulties severe enough to constitute autism, severe physical handicap, or profound mental retardation are usually identified and specially treated by parents and professionals. However, other infants have subclinical levels of problems that affect the difficulty of rearing them, variously referred to as difficult temperament, language or motor delays, or mild cognitive deficits. Compromised neuropsychological functions are associated with a variety of consequences for infants' cognitive and motor development as well as for their personality development (Rothbart & Derryberry, 1981). Toddlers with subtle neuropsychological deficits may be clumsy and awkward, overactive, inattentive, irritable, impulsive, hard to keep on schedule, delayed in reaching developmental milestones, poor at verbal comprehension, deficient at expressing themselves, or slow at learning new things (Rutter, 1977, 1983; Thomas & Chess, 1977; Wender, 1971).

Hertzig (1983) has described an empirical test of the proposed relationship between neurological damage and difficult behavior in infancy. She studied a sample of 66 low-birth-weight infants from intact middle-class families. Symptoms of brain dysfunction detected during neurological examinations were significantly related to an index of difficult temperament taken at ages 1, 2, and 3 (Thomas & Chess, 1977; the index comprised rhythmicity, adaptability, approach–withdrawal, intensity, and mood). The parents of the children with neurological impairment and difficult temperament more often sought help from child psychiatrists as their children grew up, and the most frequent presenting complaints were immaturity, overactivity, temper tantrums, poor attention, and poor school performance. Each of these childhood problems has been linked by research to later antisocial outcomes (cf. Moffitt, 1990a, 1990b). Importantly, the impairments of the children with neural damage were not massive; their mean IQ score was 96 (only 4 points below the population mean). Hertzig's study showed that even subtle neurological deficits can influence an infant's temperament and behavior, the difficulty of rearing the infant, and behavioral problems in later childhood.

Child–environment covariation in nature: A source of interactional continuity. Up to this point, I have emphasized in this article the characteristics of the developing child as if environments were held constant. Unfortunately, children with cognitive and temperamental disadvantages are not generally born into supportive environments, nor do they even get a fair chance of being randomly assigned to good or bad environments. Unlike the aforementioned infants in Hertzig's (1983) study of temperament and neurological symptoms, most low-birth-weight infants are not born into intact, middle-class families. Vulnerable infants are disproportionately found in environments that will not be ameliorative because many sources of neural maldevelopment co-occur with family disadvantage or deviance.

Indeed, because some characteristics of parents and children tend to be correlated, parents of children who are at risk for antisocial behavior often inadvertently provide their children with criminogenic environments (Sameroff & Chandler, 1975). The intergenerational transmission of severe antisocial behavior has been carefully documented in a study of three generations (Huesmann et al., 1984). In that study of 600 subjects, the stability of individuals' aggressive behavior from age 8 to age 30 was exceeded by the stability of aggression across the generations: from grandparent to parent to child. Thus, with regard to risk for antisocial behavior, nature does not follow a 2×2 design with equal cell sizes.

Parents and children resemble each other on temperament and personality. Thus, parents of children who are difficult to manage often lack the necessary psychological and physical resources to cope constructively with a difficult child (Scarr & McCartney, 1983; Snyder & Patterson, 1987). For example, temperamental traits such as activity level and irritability are known to be partly heritable (Plomin, Chipuer, & Loehlin, 1990). This suggests that children whose hyperactivity and angry outbursts might be curbed by firm discipline will tend to have parents who are inconsistent disciplinarians; the parents tend to be impatient and irritable too. The converse is also true: Empirical evidence has been found for a relationship between variations in parents' warmth and infants' easiness (Plomin, Chipuer, & Loehlin, 1990).

Parents and children also resemble each other on cognitive ability. The known heritability of measured intelligence (Plomin, 1990; Loehlin, 1989) implies that children who are most in need of remedial cognitive stimulation will have parents who may be least able to provide it. Moreover, parents' cognitive abilities set limits on their own educational and occupational attainment (Barrett & Depinet, 1991). As one consequence, families whose members have below-average cognitive capacities will often be least able financially to obtain professional interventions or optimal remedial schooling for their at-risk children.

Even the social and structural aspects of the environment may be stacked against children who enter the world at risk. Plomin and Bergeman (1990) have shown that there are genetic components to measures that are commonly used by developmental psychologists to assess socialization environments. For example, the Home Observation for Measurement of the Environment scale, the Moos Family Environment scales, and the

Holmes and Rahe scales of stressful life events all revealed the influence of heritable factors when they were examined with behavior genetic research designs (Plomin & Bergeman, 1990). Vulnerable children are often subject to adverse homes and neighborhoods because their parents are vulnerable to problems too (cf. Lahey et al., 1990).

Importantly, although examples from behavior genetics research have been cited in the previous three paragraphs, the perverse compounding of children's vulnerabilities with their families' imperfections does not require that the child's neuropsychological risk arise from any genetic disposition. In fact, for my purposes, it is immaterial whether parent–child similarities arise from shared genes or shared homes. A home environment wherein prenatal care is haphazard, drugs are used during pregnancy, and infants' nutritional needs are neglected is a setting where sources of children's neuropsychological dysfunction that are clearly environmental coexist with a criminogenic social environment.

Problem child–problem parent interactions and the emergence of antisocial behaviors. I believe that the juxtaposition of a vulnerable and difficult infant with an adverse rearing context initiates risk for the life-course-persistent pattern of antisocial behavior. The ensuing process is a transactional one in which the challenge of coping with a difficult child evokes a chain of failed parent–child encounters (Sameroff & Chandler, 1975). The assertion that children exert important effects on their social environments is useful in understanding this hypothetical process (Bell & Chapman, 1986). It is now widely acknowledged that personality and behavior are shaped in large measure by interactions between the person and the environment (cf. Buss, 1987; Plomin, DeFries, & Loehlin, 1977; Scarr & McCartney, 1983). One form of interaction may play a particularly important role both in promoting an antisocial style and in maintaining its continuity across the life course: *Evocative* interaction occurs when a child's behavior evokes distinctive responses from others (Caspi et al., 1987).

Children with neuropsychological problems evoke a challenge to even the most resourceful, loving, and patient families. For example, Tinsley and Parke (1983) have reviewed literature showing that low-birth-weight, premature infants negatively influence the behavior of their caretakers; they arrive before parents are prepared, their crying patterns are rated as more disturbing and irritating, and parents report that they are less satisfying to feed, less pleasant to hold, and more demanding to care for than healthy babies. Many parents of preterm infants hold unrealistic expectations about their children's attainment of developmental milestones, and these may contribute to later dysfunctional parent–child relationships (Tinsley & Parke, 1983). More disturbing, an infant's neurological health status has been shown to be related to risk for maltreatment and neglect (Friedrich & Boriskin, 1976; Frodi et al., 1978; Hunter, Kilstrom, Kraybill, & Loda, 1978; Milowe & Lowrie, 1964; Sandgrund, Gaines, & Green, 1974).

Numerous studies have shown that a toddler's problem behaviors may affect the parents' disciplinary strategies as well as subsequent interactions with adults and peers (Bell & Chapman, 1986; Chess & Thomas, 1987). For example, children characterized by a difficult temperament in infancy are more likely to resist their mothers' efforts to control them in early childhood (Lee & Bates, 1985). Similarly, mothers of difficult boys experience more problems in their efforts to socialize their children. Maccoby and Jacklin (1983) showed that over time these mothers reduce their efforts to actively guide and direct their children's behavior and become increasingly less involved in the teaching process. In a study of unrelated mothers and children, K. E. Anderson, Lytton, and Romney (1986) observed conduct-disordered and nonproblem boys interacting with mothers of conduct-disordered and nonproblem sons in unrelated pairs. The conduct-disordered boys evoked more negative reactions from both types of mothers than did normal boys, but the two types of mothers did not differ from each other in their negative reactions. It may well be that early behavioral difficulties contribute to the development of persistent antisocial behavior by evoking responses from the interpersonal social environment, responses that exacerbate the child's tendencies (Goldsmith, Bradshaw, & Rieser-Danner, 1986; Lytton, 1990). "The child acts; the environment reacts; and the child reacts back in mutually interlocking evocative interaction" (Caspi et al., 1987, p. 308).

Such a sequence of interactions would be most likely to produce lasting antisocial behavior problems if caretaker reactions were more likely to exacerbate than to ameliorate children's problem behavior. To my knowledge, students of child effects have not yet tested for interactions between child behavior and parental deviance or poor parenting, perhaps because very disadvantaged families are seldom studied with such designs. Nonetheless, some data suggest that children's predispositions toward antisocial behavior may be exacerbated under deviant rearing conditions. In the New Zealand longitudinal study, there was a significant interaction effect between children's neuropsychological deficit and family adversity on one type of delinquent act: aggressive confrontation with a victim or adversary. Among the 536 boys in the sample, the 75 boys who had both low neuropsychological test scores and adverse home environments earned a mean aggression score more than four times greater than that of boys with either neuropsychological problems or adverse homes (Moffitt, 1990b). The index of family adversity included parental characteristics such as poor mental health and low intelligence as well as socioeconomic status. Behavior-genetic adoption studies of antisocial behavior often report a similar pattern of findings, wherein the highest rates of criminal outcomes are found for adoptees whose foster parents, as well as their biological parents, were deviant (e.g., Mednick, Gabrielli, & Hutchings, 1984). Thus, children's predispositions may evoke exacerbating responses from the environment and may also render them more vulnerable to criminogenic environments.

If the child who "steps off on the wrong foot" remains on an ill-starred path, subsequent stepping-stone experiences may culminate in life-course-persistent antisocial behavior. For life-course-persistent antisocial individuals, deviant behavior patterns later in life may thus reflect early individual differences that are perpetuated or exacerbated by interactions with the social environment: first at home, and later at school. Quay (1987) summarized this as "this youth is likely to be at odds with everyone in the environment, and most particularly with those who must interact with him on a daily basis to raise, educate, or otherwise control him. . . . This pattern is the most troublesome to society, seems least amenable to change, and has the most pessimistic prognosis for adult adjustment" (p. 121).

However, inauspicious beginnings do not complete the story. In the New Zealand study, for example, a combination of preschool measures of antisocial behavior and cognitive ability was able to predict 70% of the cases of conduct disorder at age 11 but at the cost of a high false-positive rate (White et al., 1990). The next section explores the specific interactional processes that nourish and augment the life-course-persistent antisocial style beyond childhood.

Maintenance and Elaboration Over the Life Course: Cumulative Continuity, Contemporary Continuity, and Narrowing Options for Change

In the previous section, the concept of evocative person–environment interaction was called on to describe how children's difficult behaviors might affect encounters with their parents. Two additional types of interaction may help to explain how the life-course-persistent individual's problem behavior, once initiated, might promote its own continuity and pervasiveness. *Reactive* interaction occurs when different youngsters exposed to the same environment experience it, interpret it, and react to it in accordance with their particular style. For example, in interpersonal situations where cues are ambiguous, aggressive children are likely to mistakenly attribute harmful intent to others and then act accordingly (Dodge & Frame, 1982). *Proactive* interaction occurs when people select or create environments that support their styles. For example, antisocial individuals appear to be likely to affiliate selectively with antisocial others, even when selecting a mate. Some evidence points to nonrandom mating along personality traits related to antisocial behavior (Buss, 1984), and there are significant spouse correlations on conviction for crimes (e.g., Baker, Mack, Moffitt, & Mednick, 1989).

The three types of person–environment interactions can produce two kinds of consequences in the life course: *cumulative consequences* and *contemporary consequences* (Caspi & Bem, 1990). Early individual differences may set in motion a downhill snowball of cumulative continuities. In addition, individual differences may themselves persist from infancy to adulthood, continuing to influence adolescent and adult behavior in a proximal contemporary fashion. Contemporary continuity arises if the life-course-persistent person continues to carry into adulthood the same underlying constellation of traits that got him into trouble as a child, such as high activity level, irritability, poor self-control, and low cognitive ability.

The roles of cumulative and contemporary continuities in antisocial behavior have been explored by Caspi, Bem, and Elder (1989; Caspi et al., 1987), using data from the longitudinal Berkeley Guidance Study. They identified men who had a history of temper tantrums during late childhood (when tantrums are not developmentally normative). Then they traced the continuities and consequences of this personality style across the subsequent 30 years of the subjects' lives and into multiple diverse life domains: education, employment, and marriage. A major finding was that hot-tempered boys who came from middle-class homes suffered a progressive deterioration of socioeconomic status as they moved through the life course. By age 40, their occupational status was indistinguishable from that of men born into the working class. A majority of them held jobs of lower occupational status than those held by their fathers at a comparable age. Did these men fail occupationally because their earlier ill-temperedness started them down a particular path (cumulative consequences) or because their current ill-temperedness handicapped them in the world of work (contemporary consequences)?

Cumulative consequences were implied by the effect of childhood temper on occupational status at midlife: Tantrums predicted lower educational attainment, and educational attainment, in turn, predicted lower occupational status. Contemporary consequences were implied by the strong direct link between ill-temperedness and occupational stability. Men with childhood tantrums continued to be hot-tempered in adulthood, where it got them into trouble in the world of work. They had more erratic work lives, changing jobs more frequently and experiencing more unemployment between ages 18 and 40. Ill-temperedness also had a contemporary effect on marital stability. Almost half (46%) of the men with histories of childhood tantrums had divorced by age 40 compared with only 22% of other men.

Elsewhere, I describe in detail some of the patterns of interaction between persons and their social environments that may promote antisocial continuity across time and across life domains (Caspi & Moffitt, in press-b). Two sources of continuity deserve emphasis here because they narrow the options for change. These processes are (a) failing to learn conventional prosocial alternatives to antisocial behavior and (b) becoming ensnared in a deviant life-style by crime's consequences. These concepts have special implications for the questions of why life-course-persistent individuals fail to desist from delinquency as young adults and why they are so impervious to intervention.

A restricted behavioral repertoire. This theory of life-course-persistent antisocial behavior asserts that the causal sequence begins very early and the formative years are dominated by chains of cumulative and contemporary continuity. As a consequence, little opportunity is afforded for the life-course-persistent antisocial individual to learn a behavioral repertoire of prosocial alternatives. Thus, one overlooked and pernicious source of continuity in antisocial behavior is simply a lack of recourse to any other options. In keeping with this prediction, Vitaro, Gagnon, and Tremblay (1990) have shown that aggressive children whose behavioral repertoires consist almost solely of antisocial behaviors are less likely to change over years than are aggressive children whose repertoires comprise some prosocial behaviors as well.

Life-course-persistent persons miss out on opportunities to acquire and practice prosocial alternatives at each stage of development. Children with poor self-control and aggressive behavior are often rejected by peers and adults (Coie, Belding, & Underwood, 1988; Dodge, Coie, & Brakke, 1982; Vitaro et al., 1990). In turn, children who have learned to expect rejection are likely in later settings to withdraw or strike out preemptively, precluding opportunities to affiliate with prosocial peers

(Dodge & Newman, 1981; Dodge & Frame, 1982; LaFrenier & Sroufe, 1985; Nasby, Hayden, & DePaulo, 1980). Such children are robbed of chances to practice conventional social skills. Alternatively, consider this sequence of narrowing options: Behavior problems at school and failure to attain basic math and reading skills place a limit on the variety of job skills that can be acquired and thereby cut off options to pursue legitimate employment as an alternative to the underground economy (Farrington, Gallagher, Morley, Ledger, & West, 1986; Maughan, Gray, & Rutter, 1985; Moffitt, 1990a). Simply put, if social and academic skills are not mastered in childhood, it is very difficult to later recover lost opportunities.

Becoming ensnared by consequences of antisocial behavior. Personal characteristics such as poor self-control, impulsivity, and inability to delay gratification increase the risk that antisocial youngsters will make irrevocable decisions that close the doors of opportunity. Teenaged parenthood, addiction to drugs or alcohol, school dropout, disabling or disfiguring injuries, patchy work histories, and time spent incarcerated are *snares* that diminish the probabilities of later success by eliminating opportunities for breaking the chain of cumulative continuity (Cairns & Cairns, 1991; J. Q. Wilson & Herrnstein, 1985). Similarly, labels accrued early in life can foreclose later opportunities; an early arrest record or a "bad" reputation may rule out lucrative jobs, higher education, or an advantageous marriage (Farrington, 1977; Klein, 1986; West, 1982). In short, the behavior of life-course-persistent antisocial persons is increasingly maintained and supported by narrowing options for conventional behavior.

Interventions with life-course-persistent persons have met with dismal results (Lipton, Martinson, & Wilks, 1975; Palmer, 1984; Sechrest, White, & Brown, 1979). This is not surprising, considering that most interventions are begun relatively late in the chain of cumulative continuity. The forces of continuity are formidable foes (Caspi & Moffitt, in press-a). After a protracted deficient learning history, and after options for change have been eliminated, efforts to suppress antisocial behavior will not automatically bring prosocial behavior to the surface in its place. Now-classic research on learning shows conclusively that efforts to extinguish undesirable behavior will fail unless alternative behaviors are available that will attract reinforcement (Azrin & Holz, 1966). My analysis of increasingly restricted behavioral options suggests the hypothesis that opportunities for change will often be actively transformed by life-course-persistents into opportunities for continuity: Residential treatment programs provide a chance to learn from criminal peers, a new job furnishes the chance to steal, and new romance provides a partner for abuse. This analysis of life-course-persistent antisocial behavior anticipates disappointing outcomes when such antisocial persons are thrust into new situations that purportedly offer the chance "to turn over a new leaf."

The Reason for Persistence: Traits, Environments, and Developmental Processes

According to some accounts of behavioral continuity, an ever-present underlying trait generates antisocial outcomes at every point in the life span (e.g., Gottfredson & Hirschi, 1990). By other accounts, antisocial behavior is sustained by environmental barriers to change (e.g., Bandura, 1979, pp. 217–224). In this theory of life-course-persistent antisocial behavior, neither traits nor environments account for continuity.

True, the theory begins with a trait: variation between individuals in neuropsychological health. The trait is truly underlying in that it seldom comes to anyone's attention unless an infant is challenged by formal examinations; it is manifested behaviorally as variability in infant temperament, developmental milestones, and cognitive abilities.

Next, the theory brings environments into play. Parents and other people respond to children's difficult temperaments and developmental deficits. In nurturing environments, toddlers' problems are often corrected. However, in disadvantaged homes, schools, and neighborhoods, the responses are more likely to exacerbate than amend. Under such detrimental circumstances, difficult behavior is gradually elaborated into conduct problems and a dearth of prosocial skills. Thus, over the years, an antisocial personality is slowly and insidiously constructed. Likewise, deficits in language and reasoning are incrementally elaborated into academic failure and a dearth of job skills. Over time, accumulating consequences of the youngster's personality problems and academic problems prune away the options for change.

This theory of life-course-persistent antisocial behavior emphasizes the constant process of reciprocal interaction between personal traits and environmental reactions to them. The original attribute is thus elaborated on during development, to become a syndrome that remains conceptually consistent, but that gains new behavioral components (Caspi & Bem, 1990). Through that process, relatively subtle childhood variations in neuropsychological health can be transformed into an antisocial style that pervades all domains of adolescent and adult behavior. It is this infiltration of the antisocial disposition into the multiple domains of a life that diminishes the likelihood of change.

When in the life course does the potential for change dwindle to nil? How many person–environment interactions must accumulate before the life-course-persistent pattern becomes set? I have argued that a person–environment interaction process is needed to predict emerging antisocial behavior, but after some age will the "person" main effect predict adult outcomes alone? An answer to these questions is critical for prevention efforts. The well-documented resistance of antisocial personality disorder to treatments of all kinds seems to suggest that the life-course-persistent style is fixed sometime before age 18 (Suedfeld & Landon, 1978). Studies of crime careers reveal that it is very unusual for males to first initiate crime after adolescence, suggesting that if an adult is going to be antisocial, the pattern must be established by late adolescence (Elliott, Huizinga, & Menard, 1989).[3] At the same time, efforts to predict antisocial outcomes

[3] Between 9% and 22% of males not arrested as juveniles are arrested as adults, suggesting that adult-onset offenders constitute between 5% and 15% of all males (for a review see Farrington, Ohlin, & Wilson, 1986). However, estimates that are based on such official data are too high because most offenders engage in crime for some time before they are first arrested. Longitudinal studies of self-report delinquency show that only 1% to 4% of males commit their first criminal offense after age

from childhood conduct problems yield many errors (e.g., White et al., 1990). These errors seem to suggest that antisocial styles become set sometime after childhood.

Unfortunately, the extant longitudinal database does not provide a sound basis for conclusions. Typically, childhood behavior problems are assessed at only one time point from a single source, thereby lumping the many children who are temporarily or situationally aggressive with the few children who are on a persistent and pervasive trajectory. Outcomes are also typically assessed at a single point, often during late adolescence when temporary delinquents and future persisters are lumped together. According to my theory, such predictive designs should yield large numbers of false positives and false negatives. Analyses should ask, when between preschool and late adolescence can *stable–pervasive* antisocial behavior problems best predict antisocial outcomes among adults?

Life-Course-Persistent Antisocial Behavior as Psychopathology

The life-course-persistent antisocial syndrome, as described here, has many characteristics that, taken together, suggest psychopathology. For example, the syndrome is statistically unusual; much research converges to suggest that it is characteristic of about 5% of males (Robins, 1985). Its rarity is thus consistent with a simple statistical definition of abnormality.

The theoretical syndrome is also characterized by tenacious stability across time and in diverse circumstances. This high-probability response style is relied on even in situations where it is clearly inappropriate or disadvantageous (Caspi & Moffitt, in press-b), especially if there is a very limited repertoire of alternative conventional behaviors (Tremblay, 1991). Life-course-persistent antisocial behavior is thus maladaptive in the sense that it fails to change in response to changing circumstances.

The syndrome of life-course-persistent antisocial behavior described here has a biological basis in subtle dysfunctions of the nervous system (Moffitt, 1990b). (I reiterate my assertion that biological origins are in no way deterministic. Rather, individual variations in nervous system health provide raw material for subsequent person–environment interactions.)

The syndrome is associated with other mental disorders. There is good evidence that such "comorbidity" is associated with long-term continuity. An impressive body of research documents an overlap between persistent forms of antisocial behavior and other conditions of childhood such as learning disabilities and hyperactivity (cf. Moffitt, 1990a). Three studies (Elliott, Huizinga, & Menard, 1989; Farrington, Loeber, & Van Kammen, 1990; Moffitt, 1990a) have now shown that the presence of multiple behavioral disorders predicts persistence of illegal behavior over the course of years. This proliferation of mental disorders is common among life-course-persistent antisocial persons. For example, in the Epidemiological Catchment Area (ECA) study of mental disorders among 19,000 adults, over 90% of the cases with antisocial personality disorder had at least one additional psychiatric diagnosis. (Evidence of onset before adulthood is required for the diagnosis of antisocial personality disorder, confirming persistence in the ECA cases.) The comorbid conditions that disproportionately affected antisocial adults were mania, schizophrenia, drug and alcohol abuse, depression, and anxiety disorders (Robins & Regier, 1991).

Of course, no one or two of these parameters is enough to warrant the classification of life-course-persistent antisocial behavior as psychopathology. Nonetheless, when taken together they form a more persuasive argument that persons whose antisocial behavior is stable and pervasive over the life course may constitute a category that is distinct from persons whose antisocial behavior is short term and situational.

17 (Elliott, Huizinga, & Menard, 1989). Adult-onset crime is not only very unusual, but it tends to be low rate, nonviolent (Blumstein & Cohen, 1987), and generally not accompanied by the many complications that attend a persistent and pervasive antisocial life-style (Farrington, Loeber, Elliott, et al., 1990).

Adolescence-Limited Antisocial Behavior

My account of the adolescence-limited antisocial type will follow this plan: In the first section, *Discontinuity: The Most Common Course of Antisocial Behavior,* I provide a definition and description of this ubiquitous form of antisocial behavior. In the second section, *Beginnings: Motivation, Mimicry, and Reinforcement,* I present three etiological hypotheses. Adolescence-limited antisocial behavior is motivated by the gap between biological maturity and social maturity, it is learned from antisocial models who are easily mimicked, and it is sustained according to the reinforcement principles of learning theory. In the third section, I answer the question, *Why doesn't every teenager become delinquent?* In the fourth section, *Desistence From Crime: Adolescence-Limiteds Are Responsive to Shifting Reinforcement Contingencies,* I explain how temporary delinquents come to be exempted from the processes of continuity. In the fifth section, *Adolescence-Limited Delinquency and Secular Change,* I locate adolescence-limited delinquency in its recent historical context. In the sixth section, I make a case that the antisocial behavior of adolescence-limited delinquents is best regarded as adaptive social behavior.

Discontinuity: The Most Common Course of Antisocial Behavior

As implied by the proffered label, discontinuity is the hallmark of teenaged delinquents who have no notable history of antisocial behavior in childhood and little future for such behavior in adulthood. However, the brief tenure of their delinquency should not obscure their prevalence in the population or the gravity of their crimes. In contrast with the rare life-course-persistent type, adolescence-limited delinquency is ubiquitous. Several studies have shown that about one third of males are arrested during their lifetime for a serious criminal offense, whereas fully four fifths of males have police contact for some minor infringement (Farrington, Ohlin, & Wilson, 1986). Most of these police contacts are made during the adolescent years. Indeed, numerous rigorous self-report studies have now documented that it is statistically aberrant to refrain from crime during adolescence (Elliott et al., 1983; Hirschi, 1969; Moffitt & Silva, 1988c).

Compared with the life-course-persistent type, adolescence-limited delinquents show relatively little continuity in their antisocial behavior. Across age, change in delinquent involvement is often abrupt, especially during the periods of onset and desistence. For example, in my aforementioned longitudinal study of a representative sample of boys, 12% of the youngsters were classified as new delinquents at age 13; they had no prior history of antisocial behavior from age 5 to age 11. Between age 11 and age 13, they changed from below the sample average to 1.5 standard deviations above average on self-reported delinquency (Moffitt, 1990a). By age 15, another 20% of this sample of boys had joined the newcomers to delinquency despite having no prior history of antisocial behavior (Moffitt, 1991). Barely into mid-adolescence, the prevalence rate of markedly antisocial boys had swollen from 5% at age 11 to 32% at age 15. When interviewed at age 18, only 7% of the boys denied all delinquent activities. By their mid-20s, at least three fourths of these new offenders are expected to cease all offending (Farrington, 1986).

Adolescence-limited delinquents may also have sporadic, crime-free periods in the midst of their brief crime "careers." Also, in contrast with the life-course-persistent type, they lack consistency in their antisocial behavior across situations. For example, they may shoplift in stores and use drugs with friends but continue to obey the rules at school. Because of the chimeric nature of their delinquency, different reporters (such as self, parent, and teacher) are less likely to agree about their behavior problems when asked to complete rating scales or clinical interviews (Loeber, Green, Lahey, & Stouthamer-Loeber, 1990; Loeber & Schmaling, 1985).

These observations about temporal *in*stability and cross-situational *in*consistency are more than merely descriptive. They have implications for a theory of the etiology of adolescence-limited delinquency. Indeed, the flexibility of most delinquents' behavior suggests that their engagement in deviant life-styles may be under the control of reinforcement and punishment contingencies.

Unlike their life-course-persistent peers, whose behavior was described as inflexible and refractory to changing circumstances, adolescence-limited delinquents are likely to engage in antisocial behavior in situations where such responses seem profitable to them, but they are also able to abandon antisocial behavior when prosocial styles are more rewarding. They maintain control over their antisocial responses and use antisocial behavior only in situations where it may serve an instrumental function. Thus, principles of learning theory will be important for this theory of the cause of adolescence-limited delinquency.

A theory of adolescence-limited delinquency must account for several empirical observations: modal onset in early adolescence, recovery by young adulthood, widespread prevalence, and lack of continuity. Why do youngsters with no history of behavior problems in childhood suddenly become antisocial in adolescence? Why do they develop antisocial problems rather than other difficulties? Why is delinquency so common among teens? How are they able to spontaneously recover from an antisocial life-style within a few short years?

Just as the childhood onset of life-course-persistent persons compelled me to look for causal factors early in their lives, the coincidence of puberty with the rise in the prevalence of delinquent behavior compels me to look for clues in adolescent development. Critical features of this developmental period are variability in biological age, the increasing importance of peer relationships, and the budding of teenagers' self-conscious values, attitudes, and aspirations. These developmental tasks form the building blocks for a theory of adolescence-limited delinquency.

Beginnings: Motivation, Mimicry, and Reinforcement

Why do adolescence-limited delinquents begin delinquency? The answer advanced here is that their delinquency is "social mimicry" of the antisocial style of life-course-persistent youths. The concept of social mimicry is borrowed from ethology. Social mimicry occurs when two animal species share a single niche and one of the species has cornered the market on a resource that is needed to promote fitness (Moynihan, 1968). In such circumstances, the "mimic" species adopts the social behavior of the more successful species to obtain access to the valuable resource. For example, cowbird chicks, who are left by their mothers to be reared in the nests of unsuspecting parent birds, learn to behave like the parent birds' own true chicks and thus stimulate the parents to drop food their way. Social mimicry may also allow some species to safely pass among a more successful group and thus share access to desired resources. For example, some monkey species have learned to mimic bird calls. One such species of monkeys, rufous-naped tamarins, is able to share the delights of ripe fruit after a tree has been located by tyrant flycatchers, whose superior avian capacities in flight and distance vision better equip them to discover bearing trees. Similarly, zebras are sensitive to the social signals of impalas and gazelles and thus benefit from the latter species' superior sensitivity to approaching predators (E. O. Wilson, 1975).

If social mimicry is to explain why adolescence-limited delinquents begin to mimic the antisocial behavior of their life-course-persistent peers, then, logically, delinquency must be a social behavior that allows access to some desirable resource. I suggest that the resource is mature status, with its consequent power and privilege.

Before modernization, biological maturity came at a later age, social adult status arrived at an earlier age, and rites of passage more clearly delineated the point at which youths assumed new roles and responsibilities. In the past century, improved nutrition and health care have decreased the age of biological maturity at the rate of three tenths of a year per decade (Tanner, 1978; Wyshak & Frisch, 1982). Simultaneously, modernization of work has delayed the age of labor-force participation to ever later points in development (Empey, 1978; Horan & Hargis, 1991; Panel on Youth of the President's Science Advisory Committee, 1974). Thus, secular changes in health and work have lengthened the duration of adolescence. The ensuing gap leaves modern teenagers in a 5- to 10-year role vacuum (Erikson, 1960). They are biologically capable and compelled to be sexual beings, yet they are asked to delay most of the positive aspects of adult life (see Buchanan, Eccles, & Becker, 1992, for a review of studies of the compelling influence of pubertal hormones on teens' behavior and personality). In most American states, teens are not allowed to work or get a driver's license before age 16, marry or vote before age 18, or buy alcohol before age 21, and they are admonished to delay having children and establishing their own private dwellings until their education is completed at age 22, sometimes more than 10 years after they attain sexual maturity. They remain financially and socially dependent on their families of origin and are allowed few decisions of any real import. Yet they want desperately to establish intimate bonds with the opposite sex, to accrue material belongings, to make their own decisions, and to be regarded as consequential by adults (Csikszentmihalyi & Larson, 1984). Contemporary adolescents are thus trapped in a *maturity gap*, chronological hostages of a time warp between biological age and social age.

This emergent phenomenology begins to color the world for most teens in the first years of adolescence. Steinberg has shown that, between ages 10 and 15, a dramatic shift in youngsters' self-perceptions of autonomy and self-reliance takes place. Moreover, the timing of the shift for individuals is connected with their pubertal maturation (Steinberg, 1987; Steinberg & Silverberg, 1986; Udry, 1988). At the time of biological maturity, salient pubertal changes make the remoteness of ascribed social maturity painfully apparent to teens. This new awareness coincides with their promotion into a high school society that is numerically dominated by older youth. Thus, just as teens begin to feel the discomfort of the maturity gap, they enter a social reference group that has endured the gap for 3 to 4 years and has already perfected some delinquent ways of coping with it. Indeed, several researchers have noted that this life-course transition into high school society may place teens at risk for antisocial behavior. In particular, exposure to peer models, when coupled with puberty, is an important determinant of adolescence-onset cases of delinquency (Caspi, Lynam, Moffitt, & Silva, 1993; Magnusson, 1988; Simmons & Blyth, 1987).

Life-course-persistent youngsters are the vanguard of this transition. Healthy adolescents are capable of noticing that the few life-course-persistent youths in their midst do not seem to suffer much from the maturity gap. (At a prevalence rate of about 5%, one or two such experienced delinquents in every classroom might be expected.) Already adept at deviance, life-course-persistent youths are able to obtain possessions by theft or vice that are otherwise inaccessible to teens who have no independent incomes (e.g., cars, clothes, drugs, or entry into adults-only leisure settings). Life-course-persistent boys are more sexually experienced and have already initiated relationships with the opposite sex.[4] Life-course-persistent boys appear relatively free of their families of origin; they seem to go their own way, making their own rules. As evidence that they make their own decisions, they take risks and do dangerous things that parents could not possibly endorse. As evidence that they have social consequence in the adult world, they have personal attorneys, social workers, and probation officers; they operate small businesses in the underground economy; and they have fathered children (Weiher, Huizinga, Lizotte, & Van Kammen, 1991). Viewed from within contemporary adolescent culture, the antisocial precocity of life-course-persistent youths becomes a coveted social asset (cf. Finnegan, 1990a, 1990b; Jessor & Jessor, 1977; Silbereisen & Noack, 1988). Like the aforementioned bird calls that were mimicked by hungry tamarin monkeys, antisocial behavior becomes a valuable technique that is demonstrated by life-course-persistents and imitated carefully by adolescence-limiteds. The effect of peer delinquency on the onset of delinquency is among the most robust facts in criminology research (Elliott & Menard, in press; Jessor & Jessor, 1977; Reiss, 1986; Sarnecki, 1986). However, is there evidence consistent with a social mimicry interpretation? I describe the evidence in the next section.

Social mimicry and the relationships between life-course-persistent and adolescence-limited delinquents. One hypothesized by-product of the maturity gap is a shift during early adolescence by persistent antisocial youth from peripheral to more influential positions in the peer social structure. This shift should occur as aspects of the antisocial style become more interesting to other teens. In terms of its epidemiology, delinquent participation shifts from being primarily an individual psychopathology in childhood to a normative group social behavior during adolescence and then back to psychopathology in adulthood. Consider that the behavior problems of the few pioneering antisocial children in an age cohort must develop on an individual basis; such early childhood pioneers lack the influence of delinquent peers (excepting family members). However, near adolescence, a few boys join the life-course-persistent ones, then a few more, until a critical mass is reached when almost all adolescents are involved in some delinquency with age peers. Elliott and Menard (in press) have analyzed change in peer group membership from age 11 to age 24 in a national probability sample. Their data show a gradual population drift from membership in nondelinquent peer groups to membership in delinquent peer groups up to age 17; the trend reverses thereafter. For example, 78% of 11-year-olds reported no or minimal delinquency among their friends. In contrast, 66% of 17-year-olds reported substantial delinquency on the part of the friends in their group.

The word *friends* in the previous sentence seems to imply a personal relationship between life-course-persistents and adolescence-limiteds that is implausible. Much evidence suggests that, before adolescence, life-course-persistent antisocial children are ignored and rejected by other children because of their unpredictable, aggressive behavior (Coie et al., 1988; Dodge et al., 1982). After adolescence has passed, life-course-persistent adults are often described as lacking the capacity for loyalty or friendship (Cleckley, 1976; Robins, 1985). At first, these observations may seem contrary to my assertion that life-course-persistents assume social influence over youths who admire and emulate their style during adolescence. However, it is important to recall that social mimicry required no exchange of affection between the successful birds and their monkey mimics. In this theory, adolescents who wish to prove their maturity need only

[4] Several longitudinal studies have shown that a history of antisocial behavior predicts early sexual experience for males relative to their age peers (Elliott & Morse, 1987; Jessor, Costa, Jessor, & Donovan, 1983; Weiher, Huizinga, Lizotte, & Van Kammen, 1991). Specifically, almost all of the sexual experience of an early adolescent cohort is concentrated among the most seriously delinquent 5% of its boys (Elliott & Morse, 1987).

notice that the style of life-course-persistents resembles adulthood more than it resembles childhood. Then they need only observe antisocial behavior closely enough and long enough to imitate it successfully. What is contended is that adolescence-limited youths should regard life-course-persistent youths as models, and life-course-persistent teens should regard themselves as magnets for other teens. Neither perception need involve reciprocal liking between individuals.

A modeling role would imply that measures of exposure to delinquent peers (e.g., knowledge of their delinquent behavior or time spent in proximity to them) should be better predictors of self-delinquency than measures of relationship quality (e.g., shared attitudes or attachment to delinquent peers). Few studies have parsed peer-delinquency effects into separate components, but two findings consistent with this prediction have been reported from the National Youth Survey, a representative sample of more than 1,500 teens. Agnew (1991) examined relationship characteristics in interaction with levels of peer delinquency. He argued that attachment to peers should encourage deviance if peers are delinquent but discourage it if they are not. Agnew's results showed that such interaction terms were good predictors. However, the results also showed that time spent with delinquent peers was a stronger unique predictor of self-delinquency than the interaction between peer attachment and peer crime. Warr and Stafford (1991) found that the knowledge of friends' delinquent behavior was 2.5 to 5 times more important for self-delinquency than friends' attitudes about delinquency. (This pattern has been replicated in another sample by Nagin & Paternoster, 1991.) Moreover, the effect of peer delinquency was direct; it was not mediated by influencing the respondents' attitudes to be more like those of deviant peers. These findings are not consistent with the notion that teens take up delinquency after pro-delinquency attitudes are transferred in the context of intimate social relations. Rather, Warr and Stafford concluded that the data on peer effects are best interpreted in terms of imitation or vicarious reinforcement.

A magnet role would imply that children who were rejected and ignored by others should experience newfound "popularity" as teens, relative to their former rejected status. That is, life-course-persistent youth should encounter more contacts with peers during adolescence when other adolescents draw near so as to imitate their life-style. Some research is consistent with this interpretation. For example, in a study of 450 students in middle school, aggressive youths who were rejected by their peers reported that they did not feel lonely, whereas submissive rejected youths did feel lonely (Parkhurst & Asher, 1992). Similarly, aggressive seventh-graders in the Carolina Longitudinal Study were rated as popular as often as nonaggressive youths by both teachers and themselves and were as likely as other youths to be nuclear members of peer groups (Cairns, Cairns, Neckerman, Gest, & Gariépy, 1988). In their review of peer-relationship studies, Coie, Dodge, and Kupersmidt (1990) noted that the relationship between overt aggression and peer rejection is weaker or absent in adolescent samples compared with child samples. Findings such as these suggest that aggressive teens experience regular contacts with peers, however short-lived. Similarly, in the Oregon Youth Study, rejection by peers at age 10 was prognostic of greater involvement with delinquent peers 2 years later (Dishion, Patterson, Stoolmiller, & Skinner, 1991). Although the Oregon researchers interpreted their results as suggesting that aggressive children seek delinquent friends, their data are equally consistent with my interpretation that aggressive youths begin to serve as a magnet for novice delinquents during early adolescence. Definitive sociometric research must follow up aggressive–rejected children to test whether they develop networks in adolescence that include late-onset delinquents of the adolescence-limited type.

Researchers from the Carolina Longitudinal Study have carefully documented that boys with an aggressive history do participate in peer networks in adolescence but that the networks are not very stable (Cairns et al., 1988). Consistent with a social mimicry hypothesis, delinquent groups have frequent membership turnover. In addition, the interchanges between network members are characterized by much reciprocal antisocial behavior (Cairns et al., 1988). Reiss and Farrington (1991) have shown that the most experienced high-rate young offenders tend to recruit different co-offenders for each offense.

Life-course-persistents serve as core members of revolving networks, by virtue of being role models or trainers for new recruits (Reiss, 1986). They exploit peers as drug customers, as fences, as lookouts, or as sexual partners. Such interactions among life-course-persistent and adolescence-limited delinquents may represent a symbiosis of mutual exploitation. Alternatively, life-course-persistent offenders need not even be aware of all of the adolescence-limited youngsters who imitate their style. Unlike adolescence-limited offenders, who appear to need peer support for crime, life-course-persistent offenders are willing to offend alone (Knight & West, 1975). The point is that the phenomena of "delinquent peer networks" and "co-offending" during the adolescent period do not necessarily connote supportive friendships that are based on intimacy, trust, and loyalty, as is sometimes assumed. Social mimicry of delinquency can take place if experienced offenders actively educate new recruits. However, it can also take place if motivated learners merely observe antisocial models from afar.

Reinforcement of delinquency by its "negative" consequences. For teens who become adolescence-limited delinquents, antisocial behavior is an effective means of knifing-off childhood apron strings and of proving that they can act independently to conquer new challenges (Erikson, 1960). Hypothetical reinforcers for delinquency include damaging the quality of intimacy and communication with parents, provoking responses from adults in positions of authority, finding ways to look older (such as by smoking cigarettes, being tattooed, playing the big spender with ill-gotten gains), and tempting fate (risking pregnancy, driving while intoxicated, or shoplifting under the noses of clerks). None of these putative reinforcers may seem very pleasurable to the middle-aged academic, but each of the aforementioned consequences is a precious resource to the teenager and can serve to reinforce delinquency. Bloch and Niederhoffer (1958) have offered an anthropological perspective: "It is almost as if the contemporary young person, in the absence of puberty rituals and ordeals, is moved to exclaim: If you don't care to test us, then we will test ourselves!" (p. 28).

I suggest that every curfew violated, car stolen, drug taken, and baby conceived is a statement of personal independence and thus a reinforcer for delinquent involvement. Ethnographic interviews with delinquents reveal that proving maturity and autonomy are strong personal motives for offending (e.g., Goldstein, 1990). Such hypothetical reinforcing properties have not been systematically tested for most types of delinquent acts. However, epidemiological studies have confirmed that adolescent initiation of tobacco, alcohol, and drug abuse are reinforced because they symbolize independence and maturity to youth (D. Kandel, 1980; Mausner & Platt, 1971).

In summary, in this narrative account of the etiology of adolescent-onset delinquency I have emphasized three conditions: motivation, mimicry, and reinforcement. I have suggested that a secular change in the duration of adolescence has generated an age-dependent motivational state. In addition, life-course-persistent antisocial models must be available so that their delinquent behaviors can be imitated. Finally, adolescents' fledgling attempts to mimic antisocial styles will continue if they are socially reinforced by the "negative consequences" of crime.

Why Doesn't Every Teenager Become Delinquent?

The proffered theory of adolescence-limited delinquency regards this sort of delinquency as an adaptive response to contextual circumstances. As a consequence, the theory seems to predict that every teen will engage in delinquency. Data from epidemiological studies using the self-report method suggest that almost all adolescents do commit some illegal acts (Elliott et al., 1983). In addition, even studies using official records of arrest by police find surprisingly high prevalence rates (for a review see Farrington, Ohlin, & Wilson, 1986). Nevertheless, some youths commit less delinquency than others, and a small minority abstains completely. Unfortunately, almost no research sheds light on the characteristics of teens who abstain from antisocial behavior altogether. Speculations are thus ill-informed by empirical observations. However, some predictions may be derived from the present theory of adolescence-limited delinquency. The predictions center on two theoretical prerequisites for adolescent-onset delinquency: the motivating maturity gap and antisocial role models. Some youths may skip the maturity gap because of late puberty or early initiation into adult roles. Others may find few opportunities for mimicking life-course-persistent delinquent models.

Some youths who refrain from antisocial behavior may, for some reason, not sense the maturity gap and therefore lack the hypothesized motivation for experimenting with crime. Perhaps such teens experience very late puberty so that the gap between biological and social adulthood is not signaled to them early in adolescence. For example, Caspi and Moffitt (1991) have shown that girls who do not menstruate by age 15 tend not to become involved in delinquency; in fact they evidence fewer than normal behavior problems as teens. Perhaps other abstainers belong to cultural or religious subgroups in which adolescents are given legitimate access to adult privileges and accountability. In his vivid ethnographic account of "old heads" and teenaged boys in a poor black neighborhood, Anderson (1990) described how mature community leaders drew certain boys into their own work and social lives, deliberately and publicly initiating the boys into manhood (and preventing delinquent involvement).

Some nondelinquent teens may lack structural opportunities for modeling antisocial peers. Adolescent crime rates are generally lower in rural areas than in inner-city areas (Skogan, 1979, 1990). Teens in urban areas are surrounded by a greater density of age peers (and have readier unsupervised access to them through public transportation and meeting venues such as parks and shopping malls) than are teens in relatively isolated rural areas. For instance, Sampson and Groves (1989) determined that the strongest community-level correlate of local rates of robbery and violence was the presence of "unsupervised groups of teenagers hanging out and making a nuisance" (p. 789). In that study, more traditional community correlates of crime, such as socioeconomic status, residential mobility, and ethnicity, were mediated by the teenaged social scene. School structures may also constrain or facilitate access to life-course-persistent models. Caspi et al. (1993) found that early puberty was associated with delinquency in girls but only if they had access to boys through attending coed high schools. Girls who were enrolled in girls' schools did not engage in delinquency. In that study, the difference in delinquent involvement between coed and single-sex school settings could not be explained by any personal or family characteristics that may have influenced how the girls came to be enrolled in their schools; access to delinquent role models was clearly the best explanation for the girls' behavior problems.

Youths may also be excluded from opportunities to mimic antisocial peers because of some personal characteristics that make them unattractive to other teens or that leave them reluctant to seek entry to newly popular delinquent groups. Shedler and Block (1990) found such an effect on the use of illegal drugs. They compared the personality styles of three adolescent groups: teens who abstained from trying any drug, teens who experimented with drugs, and teens who were frequent heavy drug users. Adolescents who experimented were the best adjusted teens in the sample. As expected, frequent users were troubled teens, who were alienated and antisocial. However, the abstainers were also problem teens: They were "relatively tense, overcontrolled, emotionally constricted, . . . somewhat socially isolated and lacking in interpersonal skills" (p. 618). This personality style was not a consequence of failing to try drugs. Rather, it was an enduring personality configuration. At age 7, these abstainers had been prospectively described by raters as "overcontrolled, timid, fearful and morose . . . , they were not warm and responsive, not curious and open to new experience, not active, not vital, and not cheerful" (pp. 619–620). Similarly, Farrington and West (1990) reported that boys from criminogenic circumstances who did not become delinquent seemed nervous and withdrawn and had few or no friends. These provocative findings remind us that deviance is defined in relationship to its normative context. During adolescence, when delinquent behavior becomes the norm, nondelinquents warrant our scientific scrutiny.

In summary, this theory of adolescence-limited delinquency suggests that adolescents who commit no antisocial behavior at all have either (a) delayed puberty, (b) access to roles that are respected by adults, (c) environments that limit opportunities for learning about delinquency, (d) personal characteristics that exclude them from antisocial peer networks, or (e) all four. Research is needed to determine whether or not abstaining from delinquency is necessarily a sign of good adolescent adjustment.

Desistence From Crime: Adolescence-Limiteds Are Responsive to Shifting Reinforcement Contingencies

By definition, adolescence-limited delinquents generally do not maintain their delinquent behavior into adulthood. The account of life-course-persistent persons I made earlier in this article required an analysis of maintenance factors. In contrast, this account of adolescence-limited delinquents demands an analysis of desistence: Why do adolescence-limited delinquents desist from delinquency? This theory's answer: Healthy youths respond adaptively to changing contingencies. If motivational and learning mechanisms initiate and maintain their delinquency, then, likewise, changing contingencies can extinguish it.

Preoccupied with explaining the origins of crime, most theories of delinquency have neglected to address the massive shift in the prevalence of criminal involvement between adolescence and adulthood. Gove (1985) reviewed six of the most influential theories of deviance: labeling theory, conflict theory, differential association theory, control theory, anomie theory, and functional theory. He concluded, "All of these theoretical perspectives either explicitly or implicitly suggest that deviant behavior is an amplifying process that leads to further and more serious deviance" (p. 118). A general application of an amplifying process to all delinquency is inconsistent with the empirical observation that desistence from crime is the normative pattern.

Waning motivation and shifting contingencies. In contrast with amplifying theories, the present maturity-gap theory does anticipate desistence. With the inevitable progression of chronological age, more legitimate and tangible adult roles become available to teens. Adolescence-limited delinquents gradually experience a loss of motivation for delinquency as they exit the maturity gap. Moreover, when aging delinquents attain some of the privileges they coveted as teens, the consequences of illegal behavior shift from rewarding to punishing, *in their perception.* An adult arrest record will limit their job opportunities, drug abuse keeps them from getting to work on time, drunk driving is costly, and bar fights lead to accusations of unfit parenthood. Adolescence-limited delinquents have something to lose by persisting in their antisocial behavior beyond the teen years.

There is some evidence that many young adult offenders weigh the relative rewards from illegal and conventional activities when they contemplate future offending. In a study of three samples, the effect of age on criminal participation was mediated by young men's expectations about whether illegal earnings would exceed earnings from a straight job (Piliavin, Thornton, Gartner, & Matsueda, 1986). Important for this theory, research shows that "commitment costs" are among the factors weighed by young adults when they decide to discontinue offending. In the criminological subfield of perceptual deterrence research, commitment costs are defined as a person's judgment that past accomplishments will be jeopardized or that future goals will be foreclosed (Williams & Hawkins, 1986). Criminal behavior incurs commitment costs if it risks informal sanctions (disapproval by family, community, or employer) as well as formal sanctions (arrest or conviction penalty). Given that very few delinquent acts culminate in formal sanctions, perceptual deterrence theories consider informal sanctions as keys to deterrence. Paternoster and colleagues have tested the proposed effects of commitment costs and informal sanctions in a follow-up study of 300 young adults. They found that criminal offending 1 year later was best predicted by prospective indexes of commitment costs ($r = -.23$) and informal sanctions ($r = -.40$). Those variables outdid gender, perceived risk of arrest, grade point average, and peer attachment (Paternoster, Saltzman, Waldo, & Chiricos, 1983).[5]

Options for change. Consistent with this motivational analysis, the antisocial behavior of many delinquent teens has been found to decline after they leave high school (Elliott & Voss, 1974), join the army (Elder, 1986; Mattick, 1960), marry a prosocial spouse (Sampson & Laub, 1990), move away from the old neighborhood (West, 1982), or get a full-time job (Sampson & Laub, 1990). As these citations show, links between the assumption of adult roles and criminal desistence have been observed before. The issue left unaddressed by theory is why are some delinquents able to desist when others are not? What enables adolescence-limited delinquents to make these (often abrupt) transitions away from crime? Why do adolescence-limited delinquents come to realize that they have something to lose, whereas life-course-persistent delinquents remain undeterred? Here, two positions are advanced: Unlike their life-course-persistent counterparts, adolescence-limited delinquents are relatively exempt from the forces of (a) cumulative and (b) contemporary continuity.

First, without a lifelong history of antisocial behavior, the forces of cumulative continuity have had fewer years in which to gather the momentum of a downhill snowball. Before taking up delinquency, adolescence-limited offenders had ample years to develop an accomplished repertoire of prosocial behaviors and basic academic skills. These social skills and academic achievements make them eligible for postsecondary education, good marriages, and desirable jobs.

[5] Deterrence effects on crime are controversial. However, most past studies of deterrence have few implications for my theory of desistence among adolescence-limited delinquents for several reasons: (a) Some compare aggregate-level crime rates across places or periods that differ on severity of formal penalties. Such designs ignore the influence of individuals' perceptions about the certainty of sanctions. (b) Some use cross-sectional correlations between past offending and current perceptions of sanction certainty. Such designs evaluate the effects of experience on perceptions, not the effect of perceptions on future offending. They show only that experienced criminals know that the risk of arrest is inconsequential. (c) Most focus on the severity and certainty of formal legal sanctions, ignoring informal sanctions from the broader social context. People have concerns about nonlegal problem consequences of illicit behaviors, whether they expect to get caught or not (Nagin & Paternoster, 1991). (d) Most fail to study general samples during the age when the desistence process peaks, instead studying high school students or midlife prison inmates. Only the study by Paternoster et al. (1983) has compared prospective measures of individual perceptions of formal and informal sanctions on the later offending behavior of young adult subjects.

The availability of alternatives to crime may explain why some adolescence-limited delinquents desist later than others. (As shown in Figure 1, the desistence portion of the age–crime curve slopes more gradually than the abrupt criminal initiation portion.) Although the forces of cumulative continuity build up less momentum over the course of their relatively short crime careers, many adolescence-limited youths will fall prey to many of the same snares that maintain continuity among life-course-persistent persons. Those whose teen forays into delinquency inadvertently attracted damaging consequences may have more difficulty desisting. A drug habit, an incarceration, interrupted education, or a teen pregnancy are snares that require extra effort and time from which to escape. Thus, this theory predicts that variability in age at desistence from crime should be accounted for by the cumulative number and type of ensnaring life events that entangle persons in a deviant life-style.

Second, in stark contrast with the earlier account of life-course-persistent offenders, personality disorder and cognitive deficits play no part in the delinquency of adolescence-limited offenders. As a result, they are exempt from the sources of contemporary continuity that plague their life-course-persistent counterparts. In general, these young adults have adequate social skills, they have a record of average or better academic achievement, their mental health is sturdy, they still possess the capacity to forge close attachment relationships, and they retain the good intelligence they had when they entered adolescence. One study of girls who grew up in institutional care has illustrated that individual differences influence which adolescents are able to attain prosocial outcomes in young adulthood (Quinton & Rutter, 1988). In that study, some girls reared in institutions were able to escape adversity for advantage through marriage to a supportive husband, but a constellation of individual psychological attributes determined which girls were able to marry well.

At the crossroads of young adulthood, adolescence-limited and life-course-persistent delinquents go different ways. This happens because the developmental histories and personal traits of adolescence-limiteds allow them the option of exploring new life pathways. The histories and traits of life-course-persistents have foreclosed their options, entrenching them in the antisocial path. To test this hypothesis, research must examine conditional effects of individual histories on opportunities for desistence from crime.

Adolescence-Limited Delinquency and Secular Change

I have suggested that adolescence-limited delinquency is a by-product of modernization, an adolescent adaptation to a maturity gap engendered by the opposing social forces of improved health and a smaller, better educated work force. If this theory is correct, then secular changes should have rendered the age–crime curve relatively steeper with increasing modernization. The theory predicts that, in contemporary preindustrial nations and in earlier historical periods, the age–crime curve should have a flatter kurtosis; in other words, it will lack the characteristic sharp peak between the ages of 15–18.

Empirical data support this prediction. Greenberg (1985) compared crime statistics from the mid-1800s to 1980s in the United States, France, Norway, and Holland. He also made cross-cultural comparisons between India and Uganda and more industrialized nations. The results show that the steepness of the age–crime curve is indeed greatest during recent times and among modern nations. Farrington (1986) compared the relationship between age and crime for English males using British Home Office statistics from 1938, 1961, and 1983. His results, reproduced in Figure 4, show that the rate of offending by adolescents increased considerably over this historical period.

Diverse factors may be influential in accounting for the changing nature of the age–crime curve (J. Q. Wilson, 1983). However, I suggest that many of these factors are the very features of modernization and modernity invoked in this theory of adolescence-limited delinquency. The earlier age of puberty and the extension of the period of childhood are generally overlooked as by-products of modernization, but they have important implications for the experience of youths. The years between 1938 and 1983, covered in the study by Farrington (1986), also witnessed an incremental displacement of sons by their mothers as the family's secondary breadwinners (Modell, Furstenberg, & Hershberg, 1976). The shift of work away from farms, trades, and small family businesses to factories and service industries has stopped adolescents from sharing the daily lives of older relatives. As Anderson (1990) has observed, fewer and fewer "old heads" are initiating young proteges into the adult world. Teens are less well-integrated with adults than ever before. What has emerged is an age-bounded ghetto (Schwendinger & Schwendinger, 1985) from within which it seems advantageous to mimic deviant behavior.

Important for this theory, additional data suggest that secular changes may have influenced the age pattern of some crimes but not all. A comparison of the age–crime curve for data from the Federal Bureau of Investigation's *Uniform Crime Reports* for 1940, 1960, and 1980 showed that the adolescent peakedness of the curves for most crimes increased in a linear fashion over the 40-year period (Steffensmeier, Allan, Harer, & Streifel, 1989). However, the authors noted that

> the shift toward more peaked distributions is greater for some types of offenses than for others. The shifts are comparatively small for the person crimes and for those property offenses primarily involving older offenders (e.g., fraud and forgery), while the shifts are moderate to substantial for the youth-oriented, low-yield property offenses (e.g., robbery and burglary), public order offenses, and the substance abuse offenses. (p. 823)

Steffensmeier's finding of different curves for different offenses is consistent with the distinction I have made between two hypothetical types of offenders. On the one hand, life-course-persistent offenders (with mild neuropsychological impairment, poor self-control, pathological interpersonal relationships, weak connections to other people, and a lifelong antisocial personality configuration) should account for violence against persons as well as for crimes committed in late life. On the other hand, adolescence-limited offenders should account primarily for crimes that serve to meet adolescents' lust for acknowledgment and privilege: theft, vandalism, public order, and substance abuse.

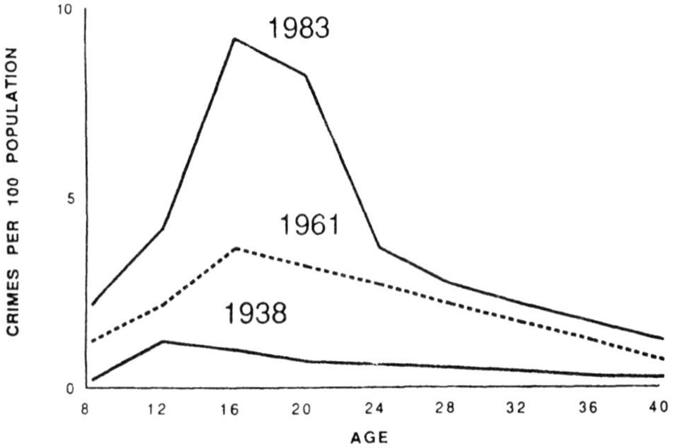

Figure 4. The relationship between age and crime for English males. (The graphs show the rate of findings of guilt and cautions per 100 population for indictable offenses in the years 1938, 1961, and 1983, as reported by the British Home Office. From "Age and Crime" by D. P. Farrington, 1986, *Crime and Justice: An Annual Review of Research, 7*, p. 192. Copyright 1986 by The University of Chicago. Adapted by permission.)

Adolescence-Limited Antisocial Behavior Is Not Pathological Behavior

In an earlier section, it was contended that life-course-persistent antisocial behavior represented an especially pernicious and tenacious form of psychopathology. My view of adolescence-limited delinquency is strikingly different: Its prevalence is so great that it is normative rather than abnormal. It is flexible and adaptable rather than rigid and stable; most delinquent careers are of relatively short duration because the consequences of crime, although reinforcing for youths caught inside the maturity gap, become punishing to youths as soon as they age out of it. Instead of a biological basis in the nervous system, the origins of adolescence-limited delinquency lie in youngsters' best efforts to cope with the widening gap between biological and social maturity. Moreover, neither this theory nor the empirical evidence suggests that there are links between mental disorders and short-term adolescent delinquency.

According to this theory of adolescence-limited delinquency, the behavior of youths who make the transition to delinquent groups near adolescence is readily understood as a group social phenomenon, it does not represent individual-level deviance. Quay (1987) concurred:

> A second pattern . . . involves behavior of a less overtly aggressive and interpersonally alienated nature. In fact, good peer relations in the context of delinquency are at the core of this pattern. . . . There is little, if any, reason to ascribe psychopathology to youths manifesting this pattern; it may well represent an adjustive response to environmental circumstances. (p. 131)

It is my stance that individual characteristics will not predict adolescence-limited offending; it is a product of an interaction between age and historical period. True, past studies have reported low to moderate correlations between adolescent delinquency and individual difference variables (such as IQ). However, none of these studies excluded life-course-persistent subjects before analysis. Thus, it remains unclear whether the obtained correlations represent linear monotonic relationships between variables or "outlier" effects of the extreme scores of life-course-persistent subjects. For example, in the New Zealand sample, the often-reported 8-point IQ difference (Hirschi & Hindelang, 1977) between delinquents and nondelinquents obtains, but it is the pooled result of a 1-point mean deficit for adolescence-onset delinquents and a 17-point mean deficit for childhood-onset delinquents. The same pattern obtains for measures of reading achievement and impulsivity (Moffitt, 1990a; White et al., in press).

The Evidence and the Alternatives

In this theory of adolescence-limited delinquency, I have made several novel propositions. I have suggested that adolescence-onset delinquency constitutes social mimicry of a pathological type of antisocial child. I have suggested that the motivation for such mimicry follows from a maturity gap between biological adulthood and ascribed adulthood. I have suggested that delinquent mimicry is reinforced by its own consequences while a youth is inside the maturity gap. I have suggested that those consequences lose their rewarding properties after youths age out of the gap, extinguishing delinquency. All three of the components of this theory are needed to support my assertion that adolescence-limited delinquency is not psychopathology. Because of the newness of this set of hypotheses, there is yet no literature of studies specifically designed to test them. Nonetheless, it was possible to glean from the existing literature empirical evidence in support of most aspects of the theory.

There is some evidence for the mimicry component. A drift into delinquent peer relationships does match the timing of the maturity gap. As predicted, most teens appear to engage in delinquency because they are simply aware of delinquent peer behavior, not because they share attitudes or close friendships with delinquents. Conversely, the most experienced early-onset delinquents do interact with other adolescents, albeit briefly and with their trademark antisocial style.

There is some evidence for the motivational component. The maturity gap has widened during this century, and, as predicted by the theory, the change has coincided with a differential increase in teen crime. After puberty, youngsters' thoughts do turn increasingly to proving their own adultness, and, as predicted by the theory, the particular types of crimes that increased among adolescents this century are ones that satisfy wishes for adult privileges.

There is less evidence for the reinforcement component. Research suggests that youngsters take up drug and alcohol use because it makes them feel independent, but studies of the symbolic reward value of other delinquent acts have not yet been reported. There is better evidence that the informal consequences of crime become deterrents after young adults exit the maturity gap. As predicted, young adults' desistence from crime is influenced by their expectancies of informal sanctions from family, employer, and community.

To date, almost no studies have discriminated childhood-onset persistent delinquents from adolescence-onset delinquents and then examined the specific correlates of delinquency in the latter group. Because the available literature mixes the two types of delinquents, it is difficult to evaluate the predictions from this theory against extant findings. However, in evaluating the empirical foundation for this theory of adolescence-limited delinquency, it is helpful to contrast the theory with its most favored predecessors: control theories and social learning theories.

Control theories of delinquency point to weak social controls, such as lax supervision by adults or weak bonds to parents, as the causes of burgeoning delinquency (e.g., Hirschi, 1969). The database for control theories is a cross-sectional correlation between measures of delinquency and supervision in adolescent samples. Research has yet to demonstrate that parenting practices change before teen's interest in problem behavior begins.[6] More critical, control theories do not explain why antisocial behavior per se is the outcome of weakened social control systems. Why do unsupervised teens not mow lawns for the elderly? Why don't weakly attached youths gather in groups to do more algebra homework? In answer, social control theories rely on the philosophical assumption that all humans are inherently antisocial; crime must thus emerge spontaneously, by default, whenever social controls are weakened. A taxonomic theory cannot afford the luxury of this philosophical premise about the universal mainsprings of human behavior. I offer instead an answer that links individual motivation for crime to its ecological context: Algebra homework does not make a statement about independence; it does not assert that a youth is entitled to be taken seriously. Crime does. How do pubescent teens come to know about antisocial behavior and its effects? I have suggested that they vicariously observe the life-styles of the life-course-persistent youths in their midst. Control theories assert that, in the absence of any such models, innocents would invent delinquency.

Calling on learning theory to explain juvenile delinquency, as I have done in this section, is not unique. Social learning theories have suggested that delinquency follows the learning of attitudes conducive to crime (e.g., Sutherland & Cressey, 1978). However, social learning theories of delinquency have not asked, why do so many people learn the attitudes at the same life stage? Why do they learn them so rapidly? What suddenly motivates that learning? What reinforces it? Who are the "teachers"? Why are deviant attitudes unlearned so readily a few years later? Social learning theories describe aspects of the process by which an individual acquires delinquent skills. However, without a motivational component, social learning theories do not address the inescapable epidemiological facts about adolescent delinquency. This developmental analysis of adolescence-limited delinquency invokes the maturity gap as an explanation for the motivation and timing of adolescence-limited delinquency. The concept of social mimicry is borrowed to explain why healthy adolescents adopt the style of youths who have been antisocial since early childhood. Thus, this narrative attempts to answer some questions begged by earlier theories.

Comparing These Two Theories With Others

Students of antisocial behavior have been blessed with a number of thoughtful theories. As a group, the theories have tended to be "general" theories of crime; each extends its causal explanation to all offenders.

General theories that summon sociological processes to explain crime and delinquency have provided valuable insights about the proximal mechanisms that promote juvenile delinquency (e.g., Becker, 1968; Cloward & Ohlin, 1960; Hagan, 1987; Hirschi, 1969; Lemert, 1967; Shaw & McKay, 1942; Sutherland & Cressey, 1978). However, sociologists have trained their lenses on the adolescent age period, when the peak prevalence of criminal involvement occurs, and when antisocial behavior is most easily studied with survey methods (Hagan, Gillis, & Simpson, 1985; Sampson & Laub, 1992). Historically, reliance on legal definitions of antisocial behavior and record sources of data kept delinquency researchers focused on the adolescent onset of illegal behavior. Consequently, many delinquency theories have failed to address the stability of antisocial

[6] Indeed, some research indicates that changes in parental behavior may be a *child effect*. Steinberg (1981, 1987) has shown that pubertal maturation precedes emotional distance and less authoritarian parenting. There is much evidence for the activational effects of pubertal hormones on problem behavior and on escalation of parent–child conflict (Buchanan, Eccles, & Becker, 1992). In the Oregon Youth Study, parental monitoring and discipline fell to insignificance as predictors of delinquent outcome when the child's prior antisocial behavior was entered first (Dishion, Patterson, Stoolmiller, & Skinner, 1990).

behavior that begins *before* adolescence, during early childhood. In addition, most sociological theories invoke amplifying causal mechanisms that seem to ignore the empirical facts about the enormous amount of desistence from crime that happens soon *after* adolescence (Gove, 1985). Causal factors such as low social class, unemployment, cultural approval for violence, and deviant labels do not seem to remit contemporaneously with that undeniable downward shift in the prevalence of offenders during early adulthood.

General theories that invoke causal variables from personality psychology or biology have taught researchers much about how individual differences predispose toward crime (e.g., Bowlby, 1988; Buikhuisen, 1987; Cloninger, 1987; Eysenck, 1977; Gorenstein & Newman, 1980; Mednick, 1977). However, these theories, too, fail to provide a satisfying account. Because such theorists have trained their lenses on early childhood and adulthood (often to the neglect of adolescence), they have failed to anticipate the enormous surge in the prevalence of antisocial involvement that occurs *during* adolescence. Such theories typically rely on the stability of individual differences in traits such as impulsivity, neuroticism, autonomic nervous system reactivity, or low intelligence. Psychological theories cannot explain the onset and desistence of adolescent delinquency without positing compelling reasons for a sudden and dramatic population shift in criminogenic traits followed by return to baseline a few years later.

Despite the imperfect fit of many existing theories to the epidemiological facts, data in partial support of each theory abound. The resulting stalemate has engendered among students of crime a gentlemen's agreement to disagree. The dual taxonomy described in this article argues that this compromise may be needless. The competing theories may all be correct, but the processes they describe may fit better for different types of delinquents or may operate at different developmental stages in the natural history of antisocial behavior. Among the many mechanisms touted by this developmental taxonomy, few are brand new. What is new is the way in which many different theories of delinquency have been integrated under a taxonomic umbrella.

Indeed, this developmental taxonomy may serve to reconcile disagreements, controversies, and misunderstandings in research on antisocial behavior. For example, the developmental taxonomy may account for effects that appear, disappear, and reappear as a function of the age of research subjects. Behavior-genetic studies have shown that childhood aggression and adult crime are heritable, whereas juvenile delinquency is much less so (DiLalla & Gottesman, 1989; Edelbrock, Rende, Plomin, & Thompson, in press). Other correlates show also strong relationships to antisocial behavior when it is measured in children and adults but only weak relationships to antisocial behavior measured during adolescence. Such age-related fluctuations in effect size have been noticed for the associations among antisocial behavior and social class (Elliott & Huizinga, 1983), gender (Smith & Visher, 1980), and reading problems (B. Maughan, personal communication, October 1990; Murray, 1976).

These disappearing effects yield (unnecessary) controversy; they may be an inadvertent consequence of mixing apples with oranges when using adolescents as research samples. I have here proposed that the ratio of life-course-persistents to their social mimics will differ as a function of the age of the research sample. Samples of antisocial children and adults should contain relatively more life-course-persistent subjects, but in samples of delinquent teens, adolescence-limited subjects will far outnumber their persistent peers. Consequently, effect sizes for the correlates of persistent antisocial behavior should be attenuated in adolescent samples, and developmental interpretations of cross-sectional data will be confounded. Note one implication: Juvenile delinquents may not be the best group to study if researchers wish to detect the correlates of persistent crime or antisocial psychopathology.

Strategies for Research

Epidemiological Predictions

According to the theory, natural histories of antisocial behavior should be found at predictable prevalence rates in samples followed from childhood until adolescence. Less than 10% of males should show extreme antisocial behavior that begins during early childhood and is thereafter sustained at a high level across time and across circumstances, throughout childhood and adolescence. A much larger number of males, a majority, should show similar levels of antisocial behavior during the adolescent age period but should fail to meet research criteria for a childhood history of stable and pervasive problem behavior. Teenaged males who abstain from any and all delinquency should be relatively rare. False-positive subjects, who meet criteria for a stable and pervasive antisocial childhood history and yet recover (eschew delinquency) after puberty, should be extremely rare.

A specific research design is needed to evaluate whether these epidemiological parameters will be borne out. Samples should be representative to tap the population range of natural histories. The same individuals should be studied longitudinally to describe the trajectories of individuals as opposed to population shifts. Reports of antisocial behavior should be gathered from multiple sources to tap pervasiveness across circumstances. Antisocial behavior should be assessed repeatedly from childhood through adolescence to capture stability and change across time. Measures of antisocial behavior should be sensitive to developmental heterogeneity to tap individual differences while allowing for the emergence of new forms of antisocial behavior (e.g., automobile theft) or for the forsaking of old forms (e.g., tantrums).

If appropriate research designs fail to yield the predicted individual natural histories (or growth curves), at or near the predicted base rates, then the theory is wrong. However, if subjects are found who match the natural histories of this taxonomy, then the following hypotheses may be tested about differential predictors and outcomes.

Predictions About Differential Correlates of Life-Course-Persistent and Adolescence-Limited Antisocial Behavior

According to the theory, the life-course-persistent type has its origins in neuropsychological problems that assume measurable influence when difficult children interact with criminogenic home environments. Beginning in childhood, discipline problems and academic failures accumulate increasing momentum, cutting off opportunities to practice prosocial behavior. As time passes, recovery is precluded by maladaptive individual dispositions and narrowing life options, and delinquents are channeled into antisocial adult life-styles. Thus, the strongest prospective predictors of persistent antisocial behavior are anticipated to be measures of individual and family characteristics. These measures include health, gender, temperament, cognitive abilities, school achievement, personality traits, mental disorders (e.g., hyperactivity), family attachment bonds, child-rearing practices, parent and sibling deviance, and socioeconomic status, *but not age*.

According to the description of adolescence-limited delinquency, youths with little risk from personal or environmental disadvantage encounter motivation for crime for the first time when they enter adolescence. For them, an emerging appreciation of desirable adult privileges is met with an awareness that those privileges are yet forbidden. After observing their antisocial peers' effective solution to the modern dilemma of the maturity gap, youths mimic that delinquent solution. Perversely, the consequences of delinquency reinforce and sustain their efforts, but only until aging into adulthood brings a subjective shift in the valence of the consequences of crime. Then such offenders readily desist from crime, substituting the prosocial skills they practiced before they entered adolescence. This narrative suggests a direct contrast with the predictions made for persistent antisocial behavior. Individual differences should play little or no role in the prediction of short-term adolescent offending careers. Instead, the strongest prospective predictors of short-term offending should be knowledge of peer delinquency, attitudes toward adulthood and autonomy, cultural and historical context, *and age*.

If life-course-persistent and adolescence-limited delinquents, defined on the basis of their natural histories, do not show the predicted differential patterns of correlates, then the theory is wrong.

Predictions About Types of Offenses

According to the theory, the two types will engage in different patterns of offending. Adolescence-limited offenders should engage primarily in crimes that symbolize adult privilege or that demonstrate autonomy from parental control: vandalism, public order offenses, substance abuse, "status" crimes such as running away, and theft. Life-course-persistent offenders should spawn a wider variety of offenses, including types of crimes that are often committed by lone offenders. Thus, in addition to the aforementioned crime types, they should commit more of the victim-oriented offenses, such as violence and fraud.

If groups of life-course-persistent and adolescence-limited delinquents, defined on the basis of their natural histories, do not show the predicted differential patterns of antisocial behaviors, then the theory is wrong.

Predictions About Desistence From Crime

According to this theory, transition events in the life course are *not* unconditional determinants of desistence from crime. Indeed, events such as marriage, employment, or military service can provide opportunities for desistence, but such events can also provide opportunities for continuity. According to this theory, individuals' reactions to life-transition events will vary predictably, depending on their personal antisocial histories. Adolescence-limited delinquents can profit from opportunities for desistence, because they retain the option of successfully resuming a conventional life-style. Life-course-persistent delinquents may make transitions into marriage or work, but their injurious childhoods make it less likely that they can leave their past selves behind; they should select jobs and spouses that support their antisocial style, and they should express antisocial behavior at home and at work.

If life-course-persistent and adolescence-limited delinquents, defined on the basis of their natural histories, do not show the predicted differential responses to young-adulthood transitions, then the theory is wrong.

Predictions About Teenagers Who Abstain From Delinquency

I have proposed that adolescence-limited delinquency does not constitute pathology. Rather, it is social activity that is normative as well as understandable from the perspective of contemporary teens. If this assertion is true, the existence of people (however few) who abstain from all delinquency during their adolescent years requires explanation. Earlier, I suggested that adolescents who commit no antisocial behavior have either (a) pathological characteristics that exclude them from peer networks, (b) structural barriers that prevent them from learning about delinquency, or (c) no experience of the maturity gap (because of late puberty or early access to adult roles).

If adolescence-limited delinquents and abstainers, defined on the basis of their natural histories, do not differ in these predicted ways, then that part of the theory is wrong.

Predictions About the Longitudinal Stability of Antisocial Behavior

I have proposed that most adults who behave in an antisocial fashion are the same individuals who began antisocial behavior in early childhood. During the peak participation period of adolescence, those persistent individuals will be masked by the "noise" of their more numerous mimics. Following from this observation, estimates of the individual stability of antisocial behavior are expected to violate the *longitudinal law*, which states that relationships between variables become weaker as the time interval between them grows longer (Clarke & Clarke, 1984). One study has found evidence that the longitudinal law is violated in this way when antisocial behavior is studied in the same individuals over time. Stattin and Magnusson (1984) reported that adult crime was predicted more strongly by behavior at age 10 than by behavior between ages 15 and 17. This prediction awaits additional corroboration.

Conclusions

The bulk of research, including the longitudinal research, on antisocial behavior continues to be performed on adolescent subjects. This is unfortunate. If the taxonomy introduced here has merit, then studying offenders at the peak participation age offers the least favorable prospects for understanding the sort of antisocial subject who will develop an adult career of crime and violence. Researchers will learn more about the etiology of severe, persistent antisocial behavior if they single out childhood-onset persistent cases for study and if they begin their studies during infancy, or even prenatally, and follow the same individuals to adulthood. In the past, cross-sectional comparisons that lumped all delinquents together may have resulted in attenuated effect sizes. This probably obscured some potential causal factors from view and produced underestimates of the importance of others. Indeed, it is likely that most of the research findings cited in this article were attenuated. If the theory is correct, then the empirical footing for it could have been clearer if the distinction between persistent and temporary delinquents had been made in past research. In our past efforts to uncover the causes of persistent predatory crime, we have been studying many of the right variables but in the wrong subjects and at the wrong point in the life course.

Also unfortunate is that almost none of the contemporary theories of delinquency do a good job explaining delinquency that begins in adolescence and ends soon after. Our failure as a field to recognize the heterogeneity of adolescent delinquency may have caused us to overlook important theoretical variables, such as biological age, or structural factors in schools and neighborhoods that determine access to antisocial models. Research is needed that analyzes the roles of biological age and attitudes about maturity in the onset of teenaged delinquency. Delinquency theories are woefully ill-informed about the phenomenology of modern teenagers from their own perspective. I fear that we cannot understand adolescence-limited delinquency without first understanding adolescents.

References

Agnew, R. (1991). The interactive effect of peer variables on delinquency. *Criminology, 29*, 4 -72.

American Psychiatric Association. (1987). *Diagnostic and statistical manual of mental disorders* (3rd ed., rev.). Washington, DC: Author.

Anderson, E. (1990). *Streetwise*. Chicago: University of Chicago Press.

Anderson, K. E., Lytton, H., & Romney, D. M. (1986). Mothers' interactions with normal and conduct-disordered boys: Who affects whom? *Developmental Psychology, 22*, 604–609.

Azrin, N. H., & Holz, W. C. (1966). Punishment. In W. K. Honig (Ed.), *Operant behavior: Areas of research and application* (pp. 390–477). New York: Appleton-Century-Crofts.

Baker, L. A., Mack, W., Moffitt, T. E., & Mednick, S. A. (1989). Etiology of sex differences in criminal convictions in a Danish adoption cohort. *Behavior Genetics, 19*, 355–370.

Bandura, A. (1979). The social learning perspective: Mechanisms of aggression. In H. Toch (Ed.), *Psychology of crime and criminal justice* (pp. 193–236). Prospect Heights, IL: Waveland Press.

Barrett, G. V., & Depinet, R. L. (1991). A reconsideration of testing for competence rather than for intelligence. *American Psychologist, 46*, 1012–1024.

Becker, G. S. (1968). Crime and punishment: An economic approach. *Journal of Political Economy, 76*, 169–217.

Bell, R. Q., & Chapman, M. (1986). Child effects in studies using experimental or brief longitudinal approaches to socialization. *Developmental Psychology, 22*, 595–603.

Bloch, H. A., & Niederhoffer, A. (1958). *The gang: A study in adolescent behavior*. New York: Philosophical Library.

Blumstein, A., & Cohen, J. (1987). Characterizing criminal careers. *Science, 237*, 985–991.

Blumstein, A., Cohen, J., & Farrington, D. P. (1988). Criminal career research: Its value for criminology. *Criminology, 26*, 1–35.

Borecki, I. B., & Ashton, G. C. (1984). Evidence for a major gene influencing performance on a vocabulary test. *Behavior Genetics, 14*, 63–80.

Bowlby, J. (1988). Developmental psychiatry comes of age. *American Journal of Psychiatry, 145*, 1–10.

Buchanan, C. M., Eccles, J. S., & Becker, J. B. (1992). Are adolescents the victims of raging hormones: Evidence for activational effects of hormones on moods and behavior at adolescence. *Psychological Bulletin, 111*, 62–107.

Buikhuisen, W. (1987). Cerebral dysfunctions and persistent juvenile delinquency. In S. A. Mednick, T. E. Moffitt, & S. A. Stack (Eds.), *The causes of crime: New biological approaches* (pp. 168–184). Cambridge, England: Cambridge University Press.

Buss, D. M. (1984). Toward a psychology of person–environment correspondence: The role of spouse selection. *Journal of Personality and Social Psychology, 47*, 361–377.

Buss, D. M. (1987). Selection, evocation, and manipulation. *Journal of Personality and Social Psychology, 53*, 1214–1221.

Cairns, R. B., & Cairns, B. D. (1991). *Adolescence in our time: Lifelines and risks*. Unpublished manuscript.

Cairns, R. B., Cairns, B. D., Neckerman, H. J., Gest, S. D., & Gariépy, J.-L. (1988). Social networks and aggressive behavior: Peer support or peer rejection? *Developmental Psychology, 24*, 815–823.

Caspi, A., & Bem, D. J. (1990). Personality continuity and change across the life course. In L. Pervin (Ed.), *Handbook of personality theory and research* (pp. 549–575). New York: Guilford Press.

Caspi, A., Bem, D. J., & Elder, G. H., Jr. (1989). Continuities and consequences of interactional styles across the life course. *Journal of Personality, 57*, 375–406.

Caspi, A., Elder, G. H., & Bem, D. J. (1987). Moving against the world: Life-course patterns of explosive children. *Developmental Psychology, 23*, 308–313.

Caspi, A., Lynam, D., Moffitt, T. E., & Silva, P. A. (1993). Unraveling girls' delinquency: Biological, dispositional, and contextual contributions to adolescent misbehavior. *Developmental Psychology, 29*, 19–30.

Caspi, A., & Moffitt, T. E. (1991). Individual differences are accentuated during periods of social change: The sample case of girls at puberty. *Journal of Personality and Social Psychology, 61*, 157–168.

Caspi, A., & Moffitt, T. E. (in press-a). Continuity amidst change: A paradoxical theory of personality coherence. *Psychological Inquiry*.

Caspi, A., & Moffitt, T. E. (in press-b). The continuity of maladaptive behavior: From description to understanding in the study of antisocial behavior. In D. Cicchetti & D. Cohen (Eds.), *Manual of developmental psychopathology*. New York: Wiley.

Chaiken, M. R., & Chaiken, J. M. (1984). Offender types and public policy. *Crime and Delinquency, 30*, 195–226.

Chess, S., & Thomas, A. (1987). *Origins and evolution of behavior disorders: From infancy to early adult life*. Cambridge, MA: Harvard University Press.

Clarke, A. D. B., & Clarke, A. M. (1984). Constancy and change in the growth of human characteristics. *Journal of Child Psychology and Psychiatry, 25*, 191–210.

Cleckley, H. (1976). *The mask of sanity* (5th ed.). St. Louis, MO: Mosby.

Cloninger, C. R. (1987). A systematic method for clinical description and classification of personality variants. *Archives of General Psychiatry, 44*, 573–588.

Cloward, R. A., & Ohlin, L. E. (1960). *Delinquency and opportunity.* New York: Free Press of Glencoe.

Coie, J. D., Belding, M., & Underwood, M. (1988). Aggression and peer rejection in childhood. In B. Lahey & A. Kazdin (Eds.), *Advances in clinical child psychology* (Vol. 2, pp. 125–158). New York: Plenum Press.

Coie, J. D., Dodge, K., & Kupersmidt, J. (1990). Peer group behavior and social status. In S. R. Asher & J. D. Coie (Eds.), *Peer rejection in childhood* (pp. 17–59). Cambridge, England: Cambridge University Press.

Costello, E. J. (1989). Developments in child psychiatric epidemiology. *Journal of the American Academy of Child and Adolescent Psychiatry, 28,* 836–841.

Cravioto, J., & Arrieta, R. (1983). Malnutrition in childhood. In M. Rutter (Ed.), *Developmental neuropsychiatry* (pp. 32–51). New York: Guilford Press.

Csikszentmihalyi, M., & Larson, R. (1984). *Being adolescent: Conflict and growth in the teenage years.* New York: Basic Books.

Davison, G. C., & Neale, J. M. (1990). *Abnormal psychology* (5th ed.). New York: Wiley.

DiLalla, L. F., & Gottesman, I. I. (1989). Heterogeneity of causes for delinquency and criminality: Lifespan perspectives. *Development and Psychopathology, 1,* 339–349.

Dishion, T. J., Patterson, G. R., Stoolmiller, M., & Skinner, M. L. (1990). *An ecological analysis of boys' drift to antisocial peers: From middle childhood to early adolescence.* Unpublished manuscript, Oregon Social Learning Center, Eugene.

Dishion, T. J., Patterson, G. R., Stoolmiller, M., & Skinner, M. L. (1991). Family, school, and behavioral antecedents to early adolescent involvement with antisocial peers. *Developmental Psychology, 27,* 172–180.

Dodge, K. A., Coie, J. D., & Brakke, N. P. (1982). Behavior patterns of socially rejected and neglected preadolescents: The roles of social approach and aggression. *Journal of Abnormal Child Psychology, 10,* 389–410.

Dodge, K. A., & Frame, C. L. (1982). Social cognitive biases and deficits in aggressive boys. *Child Development, 53,* 629–635.

Dodge, K. A., & Newman, J. P. (1981). Biased decision-making processes in aggressive boys. *Journal of Abnormal Psychology, 90,* 375–379.

Edelbrock, C., Rende, R., Plomin, R., & Thompson, L. A. (in press). Genetic and environmental effects on competence and problem behavior in childhood and early adolescence. *Journal of Child Psychology and Psychiatry.*

Elder, G. H., Jr. (1986). Military times and turning points in men's lives. *Developmental Psychology, 22,* 233–245.

Elliott, D. S., Ageton, S. S., Huizinga, D., Knowles, B. A., & Canter, R. J. (1983). *The prevalence and incidence of delinquent behavior: 1976–1980* (The National Youth Survey Report No. 26). Boulder, CO: Behavioral Research Institute.

Elliott, D. S., & Huizinga, D. (1983). Social class and delinquent behavior in a national youth panel: 1976–1980. *Criminology, 21,* 149–177.

Elliott, D. S., & Huizinga, D. (1984, April). *The relationship between delinquent behavior and ADM problems.* Paper presented at the ADAMHA/OJJDP State-of-the-Art Research Conference on Juvenile Offenders with Serious Drug, Alcohol, and Mental Health Problems. Rockville, MD.

Elliott, D. S., Huizinga, D., & Menard, S. (1989). *Multiple problem youth: Delinquency, substance use, and mental health problems.* New York: Springer-Verlag.

Elliott, D. S., Huizinga, D., & Morse, B. (1986). Self-reported violent offending: A descriptive analysis of juvenile violent offenders and their offending careers. *Journal of Interpersonal Violence, 1,* 472–514.

Elliott, D. S., Knowles, B., & Canter, R. (1981). *The epidemiology of delinquent behavior and drug use among American adolescents: 1976–1980* (The National Youth Survey Project Report No. 14). Boulder, CO: Behavioral Research Institute.

Elliott, D., & Menard, S. (in press). Delinquent friends and delinquent behavior: Temporal and developmental patterns. In D. Hawkins (Ed.), *Some current theories of deviance and crime.* New York: Springer-Verlag.

Elliott, D. S., & Morse, B. J. (1987). Drug use, delinquency, and sexual activity. In C. Jones & E. McAnarney (Eds.), *Drug abuse and adolescent sexual activity, pregnancy, and parenthood* (pp. 32–60). Washington, DC: U.S. Government Printing Office.

Elliott, D. S., & Voss, H. L. (1974). *Delinquency and dropout.* Lexington, MA: Heath.

Empey, L. T. (1978). *American delinquency.* Homewood, IL: Dorsey Press.

Erikson, E. H. (1960). Youth and the life cycle. *Children Today, 7,* 187–194.

Eysenck, H. J. (1977). *Crime and personality.* London: Routledge.

Fagan, J., & Wexler, S. (1987). Crime at home and in the streets: The relationship between family and stranger violence. *Violence and Victims, 2,* 5–23.

Farrington, D. P. (1977). The effects of public labelling. *British Journal of Criminology, 17,* 112–125.

Farrington, D. P. (1983). Offending from 10 to 25 years of age. In K. Van Dusen & S. A. Mednick (Eds.), *Prospective studies of crime and delinquency* (pp. 17–38). Boston: Kluwer-Nijhoff.

Farrington, D. P. (1986). Age and crime. In M. Tonry & N. Morris (Eds.), *Crime and Justice: An Annual Review of Research* (Vol. 7, pp. 189–250). Chicago: University of Chicago Press.

Farrington, D. P. (1989). Early predictors of adolescent aggression and adult violence. *Violence and Victims, 4,* 79–100.

Farrington, D. P. (1991). Antisocial personality from childhood to adulthood. *The Psychologist, 4,* 389–394.

Farrington, D. P., Gallagher, B., Morley, L., Ledger, R. J., & West, D. J. (1986). Unemployment, school leaving and crime. *British Journal of Criminology, 26,* 335–356.

Farrington, D. P., Loeber, R., Elliott, D. S., Hawkins, D. J., Kandel, D. B., Klein, M. W., McCord, J., Rowe, D., & Tremblay, R. (1990). Advancing knowledge about the onset of delinquency and crime. In B. Lahey & A. Kazdin (Eds.), *Advances in clinical child psychology* (Vol. 13, pp. 283–342). New York: Plenum Press.

Farrington, D. P., Loeber, R., & Van Kammen, W. B. (1990). Long-term criminal outcomes of hyperactivity-impulsivity-attention deficit and conduct problems in childhood. In L. N. Robins & M. R. Rutter (Eds.), *Straight and devious pathways from childhood to adulthood* (pp. 62–81). Cambridge, England: Cambridge University Press.

Farrington, D., Ohlin, L., & Wilson, J. Q. (1986). *Understanding and controlling crime.* New York: Springer-Verlag.

Farrington, D. P., & West, D. J. (1990). The Cambridge study of delinquent development: A long-term follow-up of 411 London males. In H. J. Kerner & G. Kaiser (Eds.), *Kriminalitat* (pp. 117–138). New York: Springer-Verlag.

Feehan, M., Stanton, W., McGee, R., Silva, P. A., & Moffitt, T. E. (1990). Is there an association between lateral preference and delinquent behavior? *Journal of Abnormal Psychology, 99,* 198–201.

Fergusson, D. M., Horwood, L. J., & Lloyd, M. (1991). A latent class model of child offending. *Criminal Behaviour and Mental Health, 1,* 90–106.

Finnegan, W. (1990a, September). Out there, I. *The New Yorker,* pp. 51–86.

Finnegan, W. (1990b, November). Out there, II. *The New Yorker,* pp. 60–90.

Fogel, C. A., Mednick, S. A., & Michelson, N. (1985). Minor physical anomalies and hyperactivity. *Acta Psychiatrica Scandinavica, 72,* 551–556.

Friedrich, W. N., & Boriskin, J. A. (1976). The role of the child in abuse. *American Journal of Orthopsychiatry, 46,* 580–590.

Frodi, A. M., Lamb, M. E., Leavitt, L. E., Donovan, W. L., Neff, C., & Sherry, D. (1978). Fathers' and mothers' responses to the faces and cries of normal and premature infants. *Developmental Psychology, 14,* 490–498.

Goldsmith, H. H., Bradshaw, D. L., & Rieser-Danner, L. A. (1986). Temperament as a potential developmental influence on attachment. In J. V. Lerner & R. M. Lerner (Eds.), *Temperament and social interaction during infancy and childhood* (pp. 5–34). San Francisco: Jossey-Bass.

Goldstein, A. P. (1990). *Delinquents on delinquency.* Champaign, IL: Research Press.

Gorenstein, E. E., & Newman, J. P. (1980). Disinhibitory psychopathology: A new perspective and a model for research. *Psychological Review, 87,* 301–315.

Gottfredson, M., & Hirschi, T. (1986). The value of lambda would appear to be zero: An essay on career criminals, criminal careers, selective incapacitation, cohort studies, and related topics. *Criminology, 24,* 213–234.

Gottfredson, M., & Hirschi, T. (1990). *A general theory of crime.* Stanford, CA: Stanford University Press.

Gove, W. R. (1985). The effect of age and gender on deviant behavior: A biopsychosocial perspective. In A. Rossi (Ed.), *Gender and the life course* (pp. 115–144). Chicago: Aldine.

Greenberg, D. F. (1985). Age, crime, and social explanation. *American Journal of Sociology, 91,* 1–21.

Hagan, J. (1987). Class in the household: A power-control theory of gender and delinquency. *American Journal of Sociology, 92,* 788–816.

Hagan, J., Gillis, A. R., & Simpson, J. (1985). The class structure of gender and delinquency: Toward a power-control theory of common delinquent behavior. *American Journal of Sociology, 90,* 1151–1179.

Hare, R. D., Hart, S. D., & Harpur, T. J. (1991). Psychopathy and the *DSM-IV* criteria for antisocial personality disorder. *Journal of Abnormal Psychology, 100,* 391–398.

Hare, R. D., & McPherson, L. M. (1984). Violent and aggressive behavior by criminal psychopaths. *International Journal of Law and Psychiatry, 7,* 35–50.

Harpur, T. J., & Hare, R. D. (1991). *The assessment of psychopathy as a function of age.* Unpublished manuscript, University of British Columbia, Vancouver, British Columbia, Canada.

Henry, B., Moffitt, T. E., Robins, L. N., Earls, F., & Silva, P. A. (1993). Early family predictors of child and adolescent antisocial behavior: Who are the mothers of delinquents? *Criminal Behavior and Mental Health, 3,* 97–118.

Hertzig, M. (1983). Temperament and neurological status. In M. Rutter (Ed.), *Developmental neuropsychiatry* (pp. 164–180). New York: Guilford Press.

Hirschi, T. (1969). *Causes of delinquency.* Berkeley, CA: University of California Press.

Hirschi, T., & Gottfredson, M. (1983). Age and the explanation of crime. *American Journal of Sociology, 89,* 552–584.

Hirschi, T., & Hindelang, M. J. (1977). Intelligence and delinquency: A revisionist review. *American Sociological Review, 42,* 571–587.

Hood, R., & Sparks, R. (1970). *Key issues in criminology.* New York: McGraw-Hill.

Horan, P. M., & Hargis, P. G. (1991). Children's work and schooling in the late nineteenth-century family economy. *American Sociological Review, 56,* 583–596.

Huesmann, L. R., Eron, L. D., Lefkowitz, M. M., & Walder, L. O. (1984). Stability of aggression over time and generations. *Developmental Psychology, 20,* 1120–1134.

Hunter, R. S., Kilstrom, N., Kraybill, E. N., & Loda, F. (1978). Antecedents of child abuse and neglect in premature infants: A prospective study in a newborn intensive care unit. *Pediatrics, 61,* 629–635.

Jesness, C. F., & Haapanen, R. A. (1982). *Early identification of chronic offender.* Sacramento, CA: Department of Youth Authority.

Jessor, R., Costa, F., Jessor, L., & Donovan, J. E. (1983). Time of first intercourse: A prospective study. *Journal of Personality and Social Psychology, 44,* 608–626.

Jessor, R., & Jessor, S. L. (1977). *Problem behavior and psychosocial development: A longitudinal study of youth.* San Diego, CA: Academic Press.

Kagan, J. (1969). The three faces of continuity in human development. In D. A. Goslin (Ed.), *Handbook of socialization theory and research* (pp. 983–1002). Chicago: Rand McNally.

Kagan, J., & Moss, H. A. (1962). *Birth to maturity.* New York: Wiley.

Kandel, D. (1980). Drug and drinking behavior among youth. *Annual Review of Sociology, 6,* 235–285.

Kandel, E., Brennan, P. A., & Mednick, S. A. (1989). Minor physical anomalies and parental modeling of aggression predict to violent offending. *Acta Psychiatrica Scandanavica, 78,* 1–5.

Kandel, E., & Mednick, S. A. (1991). Perinatal complications predict violent offending. *Criminology, 29,* 519–530.

Kazdin, A. E. (1987). *Conduct disorders in childhood and adolescence.* Newbury Park, CA: Sage.

Klein, M. W. (1984). Offense specialization and versatility among juveniles: A review of the evidence. *British Journal of Criminology, 24,* 185–194.

Klein, M. W. (1986). Labelling theory and delinquency policy. *Criminal Justice and Behavior, 13,* 47–79.

Klein, M. (1989). Watch out for that last variable. In S. Mednick, T. Moffitt, & S. A. Stack (Eds.), *The causes of crime: New biological approaches* (pp. 25–41). Cambridge, England: Cambridge University Press.

Knight, B. J., & West, D. J. (1975). Temporary and continuing delinquency. *British Journal of Criminology, 15,* 43–50.

Kraemer, G. W. (1988). Speculations on the developmental neurobiology of protest and despair. In P. Simon, P. Soubrie, & D. Widlocher (Eds.), *Inquiry into schizophrenia and depression: Animal models of psychiatric disorders* (pp. 101–147). Basel, Switzerland: Karger.

LaFrenier, P., & Sroufe, L. A. (1985). Profiles of peer competence in the preschool: Interrelations between measures, influence of social ecology, and relation to attachment history. *Developmental Psychology, 21,* 56–69.

Lahey, B. B., Frick, P. J., Loeber, R., Tannenbaum, B. A., Van Horn, Y., & Christ, M. A. G. (1990). *Oppositional and conduct disorder: I. A meta-analytic review.* Unpublished manuscript.

Lee, C. L., & Bates, J. E. (1985). Mother-child interaction at age two years and perceived difficult temperament. *Child Development, 56,* 1314–1323.

Lemert, E. M. (1967). *Human deviance, social problems, and social control.* Englewood Cliffs, NJ: Prentice Hall.

Lewis, D. O., Shanok, S. S., Pincus, J. H., & Glaser, G. H. (1979). Violent juvenile delinquents: Psychiatric, neurological, psychological and abuse factors. *Journal of the American Academy of Child Psychiatry, 2,* 307–319.

Lipton, D., Martinson, R., & Wilks, J. (1975). *The effectiveness of correctional treatment: A survey of treatment evaluation studies.* New York: Praeger.

Loeber, R. (1982). The stability of antisocial and delinquent child behavior: A review. *Child Development, 53,* 1431–1446.

Loeber, R., & Baicker-McKee, C. (1989). *The changing manifestations of disruptive/antisocial behavior from childhood to early adulthood: Evolution or tautology?* Unpublished manuscript, Western Psychiatric Institute, University of Pittsburgh, Pittsburgh, PA.

Loeber, R., Green, S., Lahey, B., & Stouthamer-Loeber, M. (1990). Optimal informants on childhood disruptive behaviors. *Development and Psychopathology; 1,* 317–337.

Loeber, R., & LeBlanc, M. (1990). Toward a developmental criminology. In M. Tonry & N. Morris (Eds.), *Crime and justice* (Vol. 12, pp. 375–473). Chicago: University of Chicago Press.

Loeber, R., & Schmaling, K. B. (1985). Empirical evidence for overt and covert patterns of antisocial conduct problems: A metaanalysis. *Journal of Abnormal Child Psychology; 13,* 337–353.

Loeber, R., Stouthamer-Loeber, M., Van Kammen, W., & Farrington, D. P. (1989). Development of a new measure of self-reported antisocial behavior for young children: Prevalence and reliability. In M. Klein (Ed.), *Cross-national research in self-reported crime and delinquency* (pp. 203–226). Boston: Kluwer-Nijhoff.

Loehlin, J. C. (1989). Partitioning environmental and genetic contributions to behavioral development. *American Psychologist, 44,* 1285–1292.

Lynam, D., Moffitt, T., & Stouthamer-Loeber, M. (1993). Explaining the relation between IQ and delinquency: Class, race, test motivation, school failure, or self-control? *Journal of Abnormal Psychology; 102,* 187–196.

Lytton, H. (1990). Child and parent effects in boys' conduct disorder: A reinterpretation. *Developmental Psychology; 26,* 683–697.

Maccoby, E. E., & Jacklin, C. N. (1983). The "person" characteristics of children and the family as environment. In D. Magnusson & V. L. Allen (Eds.), *Human development: An interactional perspective* (pp. 75–92). San Diego, CA: Academic Press.

Magnusson, D. (1988). *Individual development from an interactional perspective: A longitudinal study.* Hillsdale, NJ: Erlbaum.

Martin, N. G., Jardine, R., & Eaves, L. J. (1984). Is there only one set of genes for different abilities? *Behavior Genetics, 14,* 355–370.

Mattick, H. W. (1960). Parolees in the army during World War II. *Federal Probation, 24,* 49–55.

Maughan, B., Gray, G., & Rutter, M. (1985). Reading retardation and antisocial behavior: A follow-up into employment. *Journal of Child Psychiatry and Psychology; 26,* 741–758.

Mausner, B., & Platt, E. S. (1971). *Smoking: A behavioral analysis.* Elmsford, NY: Pergamon Press.

McGee, R., Partridge, F., Williams, S. M., & Silva, P. A. (1991). A twelve-year follow up of preschool hyperactive children. *Journal of the American Academy of Child and Adolescent Psychiatry; 30,* 224–232.

Meany, M. J., Aitken, D. H., van Berkel, C., Bhatnagar, S., & Sapolsky, R. M. (1988). Effect of neonatal handling on age-related impairments associated with the hippocampus. *Science, 239,* 766–768.

Mednick, S. A. (1977). A bio-social theory of the learning of law-abiding behavior. In S. A. Mednick & K. O. Christiansen (Eds.), *Biosocial bases of criminal behavior* (pp. 1–8). New York: Gardner Press.

Mednick, S. A., Gabrielli, W. F., & Hutchings, B. (1984). Genetic influences in criminal behavior: Some evidence from an adoption cohort. *Science, 224,* 891–893.

Meehl, P. E., & Golden, R. R. (1982). Taxometric methods. In P. C. Kendall & J. N. Butcher (Eds.), *Handbook of research methods in clinical psychology* (pp. 127–181). New York: Wiley.

Megargee, E. (1976). The prediction of dangerous behavior. *Criminal Justice & Behavior, 3,* 3–21.

Millon, T. (1991). Classification in psychopathology: Rationale, alternatives, and standards. *Journal of Abnormal Psychology; 100,* 245–261.

Milner, J. S., & McCanne, T. R. (1991). Neuropsychological correlates of physical child abuse. In J. S. Milner (Ed.), *Neuropsychology of aggression* (pp. 131–145). Norwell, MA: Kluwer Academic.

Milowe, I. D., & Lowrie, R. S. (1964). The child's role in the battered child syndrome. *Journal of Pediatrics, 65,* 1079–1081.

Modell, J., Furstenberg, F. F., & Hershberg, T. (1976). Social change and transitions to adulthood in historical perspective. *Journal of Family History; 12,* 7–32.

Moffitt, T. E. (1990a). Juvenile delinquency and attention-deficit disorder: Developmental trajectories from age 3 to 15. *Child Development, 61,* 893–910.

Moffitt, T. E. (1990b). The neuropsychology of delinquency: A critical review of theory and research. In N. Morris & M. Tonry (Eds.), *Crime and justice* (Vol. 12, pp. 99–169). Chicago: University of Chicago Press.

Moffitt, T. E. (1991, September). *Juvenile delinquency: Seed of a career in violent crime, just sowing wild oats—or both?* Paper presented at the Science and Public Policy Seminars of the Federation of Behavioral, Psychological, and Cognitive Sciences, Washington, DC.

Moffitt, T. E., & Henry, B. (1989). Neuropsychological assessment of executive functions in self-reported delinquents. *Development and Psychopathology; 1,* 105–118.

Moffitt, T. E., & Henry, B. (1991). Neuropsychological studies of juvenile delinquency and violence: A review. In J. Milner (Ed.), *The neuropsychology of aggression* (pp. 67–91). Norwell, MA: Kluwer Academic.

Moffitt, T. E., Mednick, S. A., & Gabrielli, W. F. (1989). Predicting criminal violence: Descriptive data and predispositional factors. In D. Brizer & M. Crowner (Eds.), *Current approaches to the prediction of violence* (pp. 13–34). Washington, DC: American Psychiatric Association.

Moffitt, T. E., & Silva, P. A. (1988a). IQ and delinquency: A direct test of the differential detection hypothesis. *Journal of Abnormal Psychology; 97,* 330–333.

Moffitt, T. E., & Silva, P. A. (1988b). Neuropsychological deficit and self-reported delinquency in an unselected birth cohort. *Journal of the American Academy of Child and Adolescent Psychiatry; 27,* 233–240.

Moffitt, T. E., & Silva, P. A. (1988c). Self-reported delinquency: Results from an instrument for New Zealand. *Australian and New Zealand Journal of Criminology; 21,* 227–240.

Morey, L. C. (1991). Classification of mental disorder as a collection of hypothetical constructs. *Journal of Abnormal Psychology; 100,* 289–293.

Moynihan, M. (1968). Social mimicry: Character convergence versus character displacement. *Evolution, 22,* 315–331.

Murray, C. A. (1976). *The line between learning disabilities and juvenile delinquency.* Washington, DC: U.S. Department of Justice.

Nagin, D., & Paternoster, R. (1991). The preventive effects of the perceived risk of arrest: Testing an expanded conception of deterrence. *Criminology; 29,* 561–588.

Nasby, W., Hayden, B., & DePaulo, B. M. (1980). Attributional bias among aggressive boys to interpret unambiguous social stimuli as displays of hostility. *Journal of Abnormal Psychology; 89,* 459–468.

Needleman, H. L., & Beringer, D. C. (1981). The epidemiology of low-level lead exposure in childhood. *Journal of Child Psychiatry; 20,* 496–512.

Palmer, T. (1984). Treatment and the role of classification: A review of basics. *Crime and Delinquency; 30,* 245–267.

Panel on Youth of the President's Science Advisory Committee. (1974). *Transition to adulthood.* Chicago: University of Chicago Press.

Parkhurst, J. T., & Asher, S. R. (1992). Peer rejection in middle school: Subgroup differences in behavior, loneliness, and interpersonal concerns. *Developmental Psychology; 28,* 231–241.

Paternoster, R., Saltzman, L. E., Waldo, G. P., & Chiricos, T. G. (1983). Perceived risk and social control: Do sanctions really deter? *Law & Society Review, 17*, 457–479.

Patterson, G. R. (1982). *Coercive family process*. Eugene, OR: Castalia.

Paulhus, D. L., & Martin, C. L. (1986). Predicting adult temperament from minor physical anomalies. *Journal of Personality and Social Psychology, 50*, 1235–1239.

Pepler, D., & Rubin, K. (Eds.). (1991). *The development and treatment of childhood aggression*. Hillsdale, NJ: Erlbaum.

Piliavin, I., Thornton, C., Gartner, R., & Matsueda, R. (1986). Crime, deterrence, and rational choice. *American Sociological Review, 51*, 101–119.

Plomin, R. (1990). The role of inheritance in behavior. *Science, 248*, 183–188.

Plomin, R., & Bergeman, C. S. (1990). The nature of nurture: Genetic influence on "environmental" measures. *Behavioral and Brain Sciences, 14*, 373–386.

Plomin, R., Chipuer, H. M., & Loehlin, J. C. (1990). Behavioral genetics and personality. In L. A. Pervin (Ed.), *Handbook of personality theory and research* (pp. 225–243). New York: Guilford Press.

Plomin, R., DeFries, J. C., & Loehlin, J. C. (1977). Genotype-environment interaction and correlation in the analysis of human behavior. *Psychological Bulletin, 88*, 245–258.

Plomin, R., Nitz, K., & Rowe, D. C. (1990). Behavioral genetics and aggressive behavior in childhood. In M. Lewis & S. M. Miller (Eds.), *Handbook of developmental psychopathology* (pp. 119–133). New York: Plenum Press.

Price, B. H., Daffner, K. R., Stowe, R. M., & Mesulam, M. M. (1990). The comportmental learning disabilities of early frontal lobe damage. *Brain, 113*, 1383–1393.

Quay, H. C. (1964a). Dimensions of personality in delinquent boys as inferred from the factor analysis of case history data. *Child Development, 35*, 479–484.

Quay, H. C. (1964b). Personality dimensions in delinquent males as inferred from the factor analysis of behavior ratings. *Journal of Research in Crime and Delinquency, 1*, 33–37.

Quay, H. C. (1966). Personality patterns in preadolescent delinquent boys. *Educational and Psychological Measurements, 16*, 99–110.

Quay, H. C. (1987). Patterns of delinquent behavior. In H. C. Quay (Ed.), *Handbook of juvenile delinquency* (pp. 118–138). New York: Wiley.

Quine, W. V. O. (1977). Natural kinds. In S. P. Schwartz (Ed.), *Naming, necessity and natural kinds* (pp. 155–175). Ithaca, NY: Cornell University Press.

Quinton, D., & Rutter, M. (1988). *Parenting breakdown: The making and breaking of intergenerational links*. Aldershot, England: Avebury.

Reiss, A. J., Jr. (1986). Co-offender influences on criminal careers. In A. Blumstein, J. Cohen, J. A. Roth, & C. Visher (Eds.), *Criminal careers and career criminals* (pp. 121–160). Washington, DC: National Academy Press.

Reiss, A. J., Jr., & Farrington, D. P. (1991). Advancing knowledge about co-offending: Results from a prospective longitudinal survey of London males. *Journal of Criminal Law and Criminology, 82*, 360–395.

Robins, L. N. (1966). *Deviant children grown up*. Baltimore, MD: Williams & Wilkins.

Robins, L. N. (1978). Sturdy childhood predictors of adult antisocial behaviour: Replications from longitudinal studies. *Psychological Medicine, 8*, 611–622.

Robins, L. N. (1985). Epidemiology of antisocial personality. In J. O. Cavenar (Ed.), *Psychiatry* (Vol. 3, pp. 1–14). Philadelphia: Lippincott.

Robins, L. N., & Regier, D. A. (1991). *Psychiatric disorders in America*. New York: Free Press.

Rodning, C., Beckwith, L., & Howard, J. (1989). Characteristics of attachment organization and play organization in prenatally drug-exposed toddlers. *Development and Psychopathology, 1*, 277–289.

Rothbart, M. K., & Derryberry, D. (1981). Development of individual differences in temperament. In M. E. Lamb & A. L. Brown (Eds.), *Advances in developmental psychology* (Vol. 1, pp. 37–66). Hillsdale, NJ: Erlbaum.

Rowe, A. R., & Tittle, C. R. (1977). Life cycle changes and criminal propensity. *The Sociological Quarterly, 18*, 223–236.

Rutter, M. (1977). Brain damage syndromes in childhood: Concepts and findings. *Journal of Child Psychology and Psychiatry, 18*, 1–22.

Rutter, M. (Ed.). (1983). *Developmental neuropsychiatry*. New York: Guilford Press.

Rutter, M., Tizard, J., & Whitmore, K. (1970). *Education, health and behaviour*. London: Longman.

Ryder, R. G. (1967). Birth to maturity revisited: A canonical analysis. *Journal of Personality and Social Psychology, 1*, 168–172.

Sameroff, A., & Chandler, M. (1975). Reproductive risk and the continuum of caretaking casualty. In F. Horowitz, M. Hetherington, S. Scarr-Salapatek, & G. Siegel (Eds.), *Review of child development research* (Vol. 4, pp. 187–244). Chicago: University of Chicago Press.

Sampson, R. J., & Groves, W. B. (1989). Community structure and crime: Testing social disorganization theory. *American Journal of Sociology, 94*, 774–802.

Sampson, R. J., & Laub, J. H. (1990). Crime and deviance over the life course: The salience of adult social bonds. *American Sociological Review, 55*, 609–627.

Sampson, R. J., & Laub, J. H. (1992). Crime and deviance in the life course. *Annual Review of Sociology, 18*, 63–84.

Sandgrund, A. K., Gaines, R., & Green, A. (1974). Child abuse and mental retardation: A problem of cause and effect. *American Journal of Mental Deficiency, 79*, 327–330.

Sarnecki, J. (1986). *Delinquent networks*. Stockholm: National Council for Crime Prevention.

Scarr, S., & McCartney, K. (1983). How people make their own environments: A theory of genotype → environment effects. *Child Development, 54*, 424–435.

Schwendinger, H., & Schwendinger, J. S. (1985). *Adolescent subcultures and delinquency*. New York: Praeger.

Sechrest, L., White, S. O., & Brown, E. D. (Eds.). (1979). *The rehabilitation of criminal offenders: Problems and prospects*. Washington, DC: National Academy of Sciences.

Shaw, C. R., & McKay, H. D. (1942). *Juvenile delinquency and urban areas*. Chicago: University of Chicago Press.

Shedler, J., & Block, J. (1990). Adolescent drug use and psychological health. *American Psychologist, 45*, 612–630.

Silbereisen, R. K., & Noack, P. (1988). On the constructive role of problem behavior in adolescence. In N. Bolger, A. Caspi, G. Downey, & M. Moorehouse (Eds.), *Persons in context: Developmental processes* (pp. 152–180). Cambridge, England: Cambridge University Press.

Simmons, R. G., & Blyth, D. A. (1987). *Moving into adolescence: The impact of pubertal change and school context*. New York: Aldine de Gruyter.

Skogan, W. G. (1979). Crime in contemporary America. In H. D. Graham & T. R. Gurr (Eds.), *Violence in America: Historical and comparative perspectives* (pp. 375–391). Beverly Hills, CA: Sage.

Skogan, W. G. (1990). *Disorder and decline*. New York: Free Press.

Smith, D. A., & Visher, C. A. (1980). Sex and involvement in deviance/crime: A quantitative review of the empirical literature. *American Sociological Review, 45*, 691–701.

Snyder, J., & Patterson, G. (1987). Family interaction and delinquent behavior. In H. Quay (Ed.), *Handbook of juvenile delinquency* (pp. 216–243). New York: Wiley.

Stattin, H., & Magnusson, D. (1984). *The role of early aggressive behavior for the frequency, the seriousness, and the types of later criminal offenses* (report). Stockholm: University of Stockholm, Department of Psychology.

Steffensmeier, D. J., Allan, E. A., Harer, M. D., & Streifel, C. (1989). Age and the distribution of crime. *American Journal of Sociology, 94,* 803–831.

Steinberg, L. (1981). Transformations in family relations at puberty. *Developmental Psychology, 17,* 833–840.

Steinberg, L. (1987). Impact of puberty on family relations: Effects of pubertal status and pubertal timing. *Developmental Psychology, 23,* 451–460.

Steinberg, L., & Silverberg, S. B. (1986). The vicissitudes of autonomy in early adolescence. *Child Development, 57,* 841–851.

Stewart, A. (1983). Severe perinatal hazards. In M. Rutter (Ed.), *Developmental neuropsychiatry* (pp. 15–31). New York: Guilford Press.

Suedfeld, P., & Landon, P. B. (1978). Approaches to treatment. In R. Hare & D. Schalling (Eds.), *Psychopathic behaviour* (pp. 347–376). New York: Wiley.

Sutherland, E., & Cressey, D. R. (1978). *Criminology.* Philadelphia: Lippincott.

Szatmari, P., Reitsma-Street, M., & Offord, D. (1986). Pregnancy and birth complications in antisocial adolescents and their siblings. *Canadian Journal of Psychiatry, 31,* 513–516.

Tambs, K., Sundet, J. M., & Magnus, P. (1984). Heritability analysis of the WAIS subtests: A study of twins. *Intelligence, 8,* 283–293.

Tanner, J. M. (1978). *Fetus into man.* Cambridge, MA: Harvard University Press.

Tarter, R. E., Hegedus, A. M., Winsten, N. E., & Alterman, A. L. (1984). Neuropsychological, personality and familial characteristics of physically abused delinquents. *Journal of the American Academy of Child Psychiatry, 23,* 668–674.

Thomas, A., & Chess, S. (1977). *Temperament and development.* New York: Brunner/Mazel.

Tinsley, B. R., & Parke, R. D. (1983). The person-environment relationship: Lessons from families with preterm infants. In D. Magnusson & V. L. Allen (Eds.), *Human development: An interactional perspective* (pp. 93–110). San Diego, CA: Academic Press.

Tolan, P. H. (1987). Implications of age of onset for delinquency risk. *Journal of Abnormal Child Psychology, 15,* 47–65.

Tremblay, R. E. (1991). Aggression, prosocial behavior, and gender: Three magic words, but no magic wand. In D. Pepler & K. Rubin (Eds.), *The development and treatment of childhood aggression* (pp. 71–77). Hillsdale, NJ: Erlbaum.

Udry, J. R. (1988). Biological predispositions and social control in adolescent sexual behavior. *American Sociological Review, 53,* 709–722.

Vandenberg, S. G. (1969). A twin study of spatial ability. *Multivariate Behavioral Research, 4,* 273–294.

Vitaro, F., Gagnon, C., & Tremblay, R. E. (1990). Predicting stable peer rejection from kindergarten to grade one. *Journal of Clinical Child Psychology, 19,* 257–264.

Warr, M., & Stafford, M. (1991). The influence of delinquent peers: What they think or what they do? *Criminology, 29,* 851–866.

Warren, M. Q. (1969). The case for differential treatment of delinquents. *Annals of the American Academy of Political Science, 381,* 47–59.

Weiher, A., Huizinga, D., Lizotte, A. J., & Van Kammen, W. B. (1991). The relationship between sexual activity, pregnancy, delinquency, and drug abuse. In D. Huizinga, R. Loeber, & T. Thornberry (Eds.), *Urban delinquency and substance abuse: A technical report* (chapter 6). Washington DC: Office of Juvenile Justice and Delinquency Prevention.

Wender, P. H. (1971). *Minimal brain dysfunction in children.* New York: Wiley.

West, D. J. (1982). *Delinquency.* Cambridge, MA: Harvard University Press.

West, D. J., & Farrington, D. P. (1977). *The delinquent way of life.* New York: Crane Russak.

White, J., Moffitt, T. E., Caspi, A., Jeglum, D., Needles, D., & Stouthamer-Loeber, M. (in press). Measuring impulsivity and examining its relationship to delinquency. *Journal of Abnormal Psychology.*

White, J., Moffitt, T. E., Earls, F., Robins, L. N., & Silva, P. A. (1990). How early can we tell? Preschool predictors of boys' conduct disorder and delinquency. *Criminology, 28,* 507–533.

Williams, K. R., & Hawkins, R. (1986). Perceptual research on general deterrence: A review. *Law & Society Review, 20,* 545–572.

Wilson, E. O. (1975). *Sociobiology.* Cambridge, MA: Harvard University Press.

Wilson, J. Q. (1983). Crime and American culture. *The Public Interest, 70,* 22–48.

Wilson, J. Q., & Herrnstein, R. J. (1985). *Crime and human nature.* New York: Simon & Schuster.

Wolfgang, M. E., Figlio, R. M., & Sellin, T. (1972). *Delinquency in a birth cohort.* Chicago: University of Chicago Press.

Wolfgang, M. E., Thornberry, T. P., & Figlio, R. M. (1987). *From boy to man, from delinquency to crime.* Chicago: University of Chicago Press.

Wyshak, G., & Frisch, R. E. (1982). Evidence for a secular trend in age of menarche. *New England Journal of Medicine, 306,* 1033–1035.

Received June 29, 1992
Revision received January 4, 1993
Accepted January 15, 1993 ■

Journal of Abnormal Psychology
1994, Vol. 103, No. 1, 78-91

0021-843X/94/$3.00

Personality and Personality Disorders

Thomas A. Widiger and Paul T. Costa, Jr.

The mental disorders that most clearly relate to personality are the personality disorders. The purpose of this article is to review the support for the hypothesis that the personality disorders of the *Diagnostic and Statistical Manual of Mental Disorders* (3rd ed., rev.; American Psychiatric Association, 1987) represent variants of normal personality traits. We focus in particular on the efforts to identify the dimensions of personality that may underlie the personality disorders. We then illustrate the relationship of personality to personality disorders using the five-factor model, discuss conceptual issues in relating normal and abnormal personality traits, and consider methodological issues that should be addressed in future research.

The mental disorders that most clearly relate to personality are the personality disorders. It is becoming increasingly evident that the personality disorders identified in the revised third edition of the American Psychiatric Association's (APA) *Diagnostic and Statistical Manual of Mental Disorders* (*DSM-III-R*; APA, 1987) represent, for the most part, maladaptive variants of traits that are evident in all persons to varying degrees (Costa & Widiger, in press). Details regarding the weak construct validity for the *DSM-III-R* (and *DSM-IV*) categorical model of personality disorder classification are presented elsewhere (Widiger, 1992, 1993a; Widiger & Sanderson, in press-b). It is the purpose of this article to review the relationship between personality and personality disorders. We focus in particular on the efforts to identify the dimensions of personality that may underlie the *DSM-III-R* and *DSM-IV* personality disorders. We illustrate the relationship of personality to personality disorders through use of the dimensions of the five-factor model (FFM), discuss conceptual issues in relating normal and abnormal personality, and then consider methodological issues that should be addressed in future research.

Personality Disorder Dimensions

The *DSM-III-R* provides 11 officially recognized personality disorder (PD) diagnoses and two additional diagnoses within an appendix (APA, 1987). The *DSM* nomenclature, however, is rather unstable, with no compelling rationale for any particular set (Frances & Widiger, 1986). Four of the 11 disorders were new to the *DSM-III* (narcissistic, borderline, schizotypal, and avoidant; APA, 1980), and 2 more were included in the appendix to *DSM-III-R* (sadistic and self-defeating). Those 2 will be deleted entirely from the *DSM-IV*, passive–aggressive disorder will be moved to the appendix, and depressive PD will be added to the appendix. There have been many compelling proposals for other additions (e.g., Akiskal & Akiskal, 1992; Cooper, 1993; Hamlin, 1990). Two fundamental questions in this area are: What are the underlying maladaptive traits that make up the 11 PDs? and What is the relationship between the inflexible and maladaptive traits in the *DSM-III-R* criteria sets and so-called normal-range personality traits?

A variety of problems complicate the effort to identify the dimensions of personality that may underlie the *DSM-III-R* PD diagnoses. Many researchers have attempted to treat the 11 PDs as if they were single dimensions that could be rated in terms of severity (e.g., Dowson & Berrios, 1991; Hyler & Lyons, 1988; Widiger, Trull, Hurt, Clarkin, & Frances, 1987; Zimmerman & Coryell, 1990), but the categories currently defined on Axis II involve sets of symptoms and traits at inconsistent levels of complexity and specificity (Shea, 1992). Shea cited in particular Livesley, Jackson, and Schroeder's (1990) identification of two separable dimensions underlying the dependent PD criteria set (attachment-related behaviors and need for instrumental help), Hurt et al. (1990) showed that the eight borderline criteria form three clusters (identity, affectivity, and impulsivity), and Shea indicated how the passive–aggressive PD is confined to an indirect expression of hostility and assertion. Even when the criteria within a PD category refer to manifestations of a single underlying construct, they may vary in the narrowness or breadth of their assessment.

Another way of understanding this phenomenon is through reference to different levels of the trait hierarchy. As discussed by Harkness (1992), personality traits are organized hierarchically from molecular behavioral units, to first-order (or more specific) trait dimensions, to second- or higher order (global or general) trait dimensions. Many of the 11 PD categories represent unknown admixtures of different trait dimensions at varying levels of this hierarchy.

At the theoretical level, the lack of a comprehensive framework for exhaustively defining the domain of PD symptoms is another important obstacle (Frances & Widiger, 1986). A third problem is the variability in the persons making PD ratings:

Thomas A. Widiger, Psychology Department, University of Kentucky; Paul T. Costa, Jr., National Institute on Aging, Baltimore, Maryland.

We express our appreciation to Jerry Wiggins for providing unpublished data and to Lee Anna Clark, William Grove, and two anonymous reviewers for their helpful comments and suggestions with respect to an earlier version of the article.

Correspondence concerning this article should be addressed to Thomas A. Widiger, 115 Kastle Hall, Psychology Department, University of Kentucky, Lexington, Kentucky 40506-0044.

clinicians versus students versus adults residing in the community versus patients. A fourth problem is the variability in the criteria for factor extraction (e.g., eigenvalues over 1.0 versus visual inspection of scree plots versus theoretical expectations). For example, measures of PD symptoms involve a much larger range of variables (79 to 436) than do those that deal with measures of PD constructs, which tend to be identical to the number of categories in the *DSM* (i.e., 11–13). The latter analyses typically yield three or four factors, whereas the former tend to identify anywhere from 13 to 39 factors, which is not surprising because they involve so many more variables, for example, 100 (Livesley, Jackson, & Schroeder, 1992), 136 (Harkness, 1992), 137 (Hyler et al., 1990), 167 (Clark, 1990), and 436 (Livesley & Jackson, 1986). Examination of studies in which nearly identical numbers of variables (e.g., 136 in Harkness's [1992] study and 167 in Clark's [1990] study) were used reveals that even under this condition there can be divergent results (39 versus 23 factors, respectively). Hyler et al. also entered 137 variables but required a priori an 11-factor solution.

Attempts to Recover the DSM Clusters

Both the *DSM-III* (APA, 1980) and *DSM-III-R* organize the 11 PDs into three non-empirically based clusters: odd or eccentric (Cluster A), dramatic, emotional, or erratic (Cluster B), and anxious or fearful (Cluster C). The creation of these three clusters suggests an alternative to viewing each of the PDs as single entities that are distinct and mutually exclusive. However, when Kass, Skodol, Charles, Spitzer, and Williams (1985) factor analyzed PD ratings, they found four factors, not three as suggested by the *DSM*. Paranoid, schizoid, and schizotypal disorders loaded on the first factor, corresponding to Cluster A. Three of the four disorders placed in Cluster B—histrionic, narcissistic, and borderline—loaded on one factor, but antisocial PD did not have a significant loading. The avoidant, dependent, and passive-aggressive PDs loaded on a third factor corresponding roughly to Cluster C. The fourth factor was defined by compulsive PD ratings, with inverse, negative loadings from the borderline and antisocial PDs. The four-factor solution was subsequently replicated by Hyler and Lyons (1988).

A number of other studies have also produced three-factor solutions (e.g., Dowson & Berrios, 1991; Hamburger & Hastings, 1986; Morey, Waugh, & Blashfield, 1985; Pilkonis & Frank, 1988; Retzlaff & Gibertini, 1987; Strack, 1987; Strack, Lorr, Campbell, & Lamnin, 1992; Torgersen & Alnaes, 1989; Widiger et al., 1987; Zimmerman & Coryell, 1990), but they typically failed to support the three *DSM-III-R* clusters. For example, consider the three-factor solution of Dowson and Berrios (1991): Factor 1 comprised paranoid, schizoid, schizotypal, avoidant, and self-defeating; Factor 2 comprised antisocial, borderline, passive-aggressive, and sadistic; and Factor 3 comprised histrionic, narcissistic, dependent, and compulsive. There is a resemblance to the *DSM-III-R* clusters but also notable exceptions (e.g., avoidant PD was grouped with the odd or eccentric cluster, passive-aggressive PD was grouped with the dramatic or emotional cluster, and the third factor consisted of an even mix of dramatic or emotional and anxious or fearful PDs). The inadequacy of the three-cluster arrangement is also evident conceptually. The narcissistic and antisocial PDs are not captured well by the constructs of dramatic, emotional, or erratic, nor is the passive-aggressive PD captured well by the constructs of anxious or fearful. There is clearly more to the antisocial PD than being dramatic, emotional, or erratic, and the schizoid personality is more anhedonic than odd or eccentric.

A limitation of many factor analytic studies of PD dimensions is their reliance on subjective judgment for interpreting the factor solutions. For example, it is striking that both Hyler and Lyons (1988) and Kass et al. (1985) obtained four-factor solutions yet concluded that their findings supported a three-dimensional model defined by the *DSM-III* cluster arrangements. They dismissed the fourth factor as an uninterpretable methodological artifact. Had they used more objective procedures (e.g., split their samples into random halves and compared the obtained factor solutions via factor congruence; Everett, 1983), they might have come to a different conclusion. The fourth factor contrasted the compulsive (and narcissistic) PD with the borderline and antisocial PDs in Kass et al.'s study, and it was confined largely to the compulsive PD in Hyler and Lyons's study. This factor has since been interpreted as representing conscientiousness in factor analyses by Schroeder, Wormworth, and Livesley (1992), Widiger et al. (1991), and Wiggins and Pincus (1989). Even when dimensions have been interpreted in a similar manner (e.g., the dimensions of social involvement in the multidimensional scaling studies of Blashfield, Sprock, Pinkston, & Hodgin, 1985, and Widiger et al., 1987), the solutions have at times failed to be consistent (e.g., the social involvement dimensions correlated −.28; Widiger et al., 1991). It would be useful in future studies to include marker variables to help interpret the factors rather than relying solely on subjective impressions.

Analysis of PD Symptoms

Some investigators have analyzed PD symptoms rather than the *DSM* diagnostic criterial sets. Because of the complexity and heterogeneity of the PD constructs, this approach may prove to be more successful. For example, Clark (1990) identified a set of 167 PD symptoms, with 68 from the *DSM-II* (APA, 1968) and *DSM-III* (APA, 1980) descriptions of the PDs, 41 from *DSM-III* descriptions of other clinical syndromes (because many had been associated with and interpreted as PDs), 17 from Cleckley's (1941) description of psychopathy, and 41 from two or more of these three sources. The symptoms were then sorted by 29 judges according to similarity and meaning, and a factor analysis of the co-occurrence matrix yielded 23 factors, including (for example) suspiciousness, grandiose egocentrism, emotional coldness, anger and aggression, anhedonia, social isolation, eccentric thought, high energy, impulsivity, self-centered exploitation, hypersensitivity, pessimism, suicide proneness, and insincerity.

Livesley and Jackson (1986) identified trait descriptions for PDs through a content analysis of the *DSM-III*, the personality disorder section of the ninth edition of the *International Classification of Diseases* (World Health Organization, 1977), and various review articles. The list was reduced to 100 on the basis of ratings obtained from 938 psychiatrists regarding the prototypicality for each trait with respect to the 11 *DSM-III* PDs (additional scales were subsequently developed to accommodate the *DSM-III-R* additions). The 100 items were then administered to 158 patients with a primary diagnosis of a PD and to 274 subjects obtained from the community, each of whom rated themselves on a 1 to 5 scale. Factor analyses of the correlations among the 100 scales yielded 15 factors, including (for example) affective reactivity, social apprehensiveness, stimulus seeking, diffidence, intimacy problems, interpersonal disesteem, cognitive distortion, and obsessionality (Livesley et al., 1992).

Harkness (1992) obtained a pool of 136 PD items, with 120 taken from the *DSM-III-R* PD criteria (11 accepted and 2 proposed) and 16 from Cleckley's (1941) description of psychopathy. These items were translated into lay terms and then sorted with respect to similarity by 55 subjects drawn from volunteers from a local Department of Veterans Affairs medical center and from university undergraduates. A factor analysis of the resulting co-occurrence matrix yielded 39 principal components or "topics" (e.g., engages repeatedly in illegal antisocial activities, generally shows little emotion or emotional responsiveness to others, and is suspicious and distrusting of others' motives without reason).

Even though Harkness's (1992) methods differed from those of Clark (1990) and Livesley et al. (1986, 1992) and, more important, Harkness was exploring more specific traits in the hierarchy, all three analyses resulted in quite comparable findings. Nineteen of Clark's 23 symptom clusters were identified in Harkness's set of 39 factors, and 14 of Livesley's 15 factors were common to Clark's 23 symptom clusters and Harkness's 39 factors. Another way of expressing the agreement is to note that 14 components were common to all three sets and that 37 of Harkness's 39 components were found in either Clark's or Livesley et al.'s sets. Clark and Livesley (in press) recently collaborated in an effort to assess the convergence and divergence of their respective 23- and 18-scale models. Livesley had focused on prototypical traits and behaviors for the PDs, whereas Clark had focused more directly on the criterial symptomatology. Nevertheless, they identified substantial convergence and little divergence in their respective models, and the divergence reflected largely minor variations in emphasis and degree of specificity (e.g., narcissism versus grandiose egocentrism).

Dimensional Models of Personality and the PDs

In the past several years, there has been renewed interest in applying dimensional models of personality structure from mainstream personality research to the Axis II personality disorders. There have been a variety of structural models to consider, such as the interpersonal circumplex and the FFM. The crucial question has been which model to choose.

Cloninger (1987) proposed a three-dimensional model, consisting of harm avoidance, reward dependence, and novelty seeking. Cloninger, Przybeck, and Svrakic (1991) administered the Tridimensional Personality Questionnaire (TPQ), a self-report measure of the three dimensions, to a national sample of 1,019 community subjects. Internal consistency and factor analyses supported the three-dimensional structure, although the findings were problematic for reward dependence. Svrakic, Przybeck, and Cloninger (1991) subsequently suggested a four-dimensional model, with the additional construct of persistence extracted from reward dependence. Cloninger (1993) has since proposed adding three character dimensions (self-directedness, cooperativeness, and self-transcendence) to the four temperaments of reward dependence, harm avoidance, novelty seeking, and persistence. It is not clear conceptually or empirically, however, whether the three character dimensions are independent of the four temperament dimensions or are derived from them. Cannon, Clark, Leeka, and Keefe (1993) factor analyzed the TPQ in a sample of 303 male alcoholic inpatients and suggested that a five-factor solution was more compelling (consisting of subjective distress, detachment, disinhibition, relaxed confidence, and orderliness or persistence).

A number of studies have demonstrated the insufficiency of the two-dimensional, interpersonal circumplex model in accounting for PD symptomatology (Romney & Bynner, 1989; Sim & Romney, 1990; Soldz, Budman, Demby, & Merry, 1993; Wiggins & Pincus, 1989). Romney and Bynner submitted the factor-analytic solutions of Hyler and Lyons (1988), Kass et al. (1985), and Livesley and Jackson (1986) to structural equation modeling to assess the goodness of fit to a circumplex model. They concluded that interpersonal dimensions of personality are substantially involved in five of the PDs (paranoid, schizoid, dependent, histrionic, and narcissistic) but that additional dimensions are necessary to adequately account for the borderline, compulsive, passive-aggressive, schizotypal, and antisocial PDs.

Wiggins and Pincus (1989) administered Morey et al.'s (1985) PD scales from the Minnesota Multiphasic Personality Inventory, Strack's (1987) Personality Adjective Check List, and a revision of the Interpersonal Adjective Scales (IASR-B5) to 581 college students. They found that "only slightly more than half of the personality disorder categories had interpretable projections on the interpersonal circumplex" (p. 308; i.e., the histrionic, dependent schizoid, antisocial, and narcissistic PDs). They then assessed the PD scales in the context of the FFM (consisting of the dimensions of neuroticism, extraversion, openness, conscientiousness, and agreeableness) and concluded that the PDs "are readily interpretable [within] the 'Big Five' factors" (Wiggins & Pincus, 1989, p. 314).

Soldz et al. (1993) cross-validated Wiggins and Pincus's (1989) findings, using a semistructured interview (the Personality Disorder Examination [PDE]; Loranger, 1988) and the revised Millon Clinical Multiaxial Inventory (MCMI-II; Millon, 1987) to assess the PDs, the Inventory of Interpersonal Problems (Horowitz, Rosenberg, Bauer, Ureno, & Villasenor, 1988) to assess the interpersonal circumplex dimensions, and the 50-Bipolar Self-Rating Scales (50-BSRS; Goldberg, 1992) to assess the FFM dimensions. The subjects were 102 patients referred to a study on group psychotherapy for PDs (from which, however, those with a paranoid, schizotypal, schizoid, or antisocial diagnosis were excluded). The findings are somewhat limited by the exclusion criteria, but Soldz et al. did conclude that "our results appear to lend strong support to the position that the Big Five personality factors can adequately represent the distinctions among the personality disorders" (Soldz et al., 1993, p. 51).

Schroeder et al. (1992) factor analyzed the Dimensional Assessment of Personality Pathology—Basic Questionnaire (DAPP-BQ) with the NEO Personality Inventory (NEO-PI;

Costa & McCrae, 1985) in a sample of 300 subjects. The DAPP–BQ assesses the 15 factors identified by Livesley et al. (1992). Two scales, Self-Harm and Cognitive Distortion, had to be excluded because of low endorsement rates. A joint factor analysis of the NEO–PI and the DAPP–BQ yielded an "interpretable five factor solution: four of these were defined by a Big Five factor; . . . the Neuroticism factor demonstrated the strongest relationships, whereas Openness to Experience showed only modest relationships" (Schroeder et al., 1992, p. 47). Schroeder et al. concluded that "personality disorders are not characterized by functioning that differs in quality from normal functioning" (p. 52) and that "the domain of personality pathology can be explained reasonably well within the five factor model" (p. 52).

Tellegen and Waller (in press) argued that the lexical analyses of Norman and others (from which the FFM was derived) were inadequate because many evaluative terms were excluded that would have represented extreme, maladaptive variants. Their analyses with these terms appeared to yield a seven-factor model, with five of the seven factors corresponding to the FFM (although openness was redefined as low conventionality) and two additional factors of positive valence (e.g., excellence vs. ordinary) and negative valence (e.g., evil vs. decent). Tellegen (1993) suggested that this seven-factor model provides a more adequate representation of the *DSM–III–R* PDs. For example, Tellegen and Waller's conventionality dimension may have more clinical relevance than openness to experience, contrasting as it does being strange, weird, odd, and peculiar (as well as curious, creative, and imaginative) with being conventional, conservative, and old-fashioned (and perhaps thereby including the cognitive and perceptual aberrations of schizotypia that are not currently represented well by the FFM; Costa & McCrae, 1992a). Widiger and Trull (1992), however, suggested that the positive and negative valence dimensions are readily understood as extreme variants of the FFM domains (e.g., cruel, deceitful, vicious, evil, treacherous, and nasty are readily seen as extreme variants of antagonism rather than as negative valence). In addition, Goldberg's (1990) numerous factor analyses included many of the evaluative terms cited by Tellegen and Waller, and his results consistently supported the FFM. In addition, a joint factor analysis by West (1993) of the NEO–PI–R with scales developed by Tellegen and Waller to assess their seven dimensions on data from 451 university students empirically confirmed Widiger and Trull's rational analysis. Five factors had eigenvalues greater than one. Each factor was defined by one of the NEO–PI–R scales, with negative valence loading with antagonism (positive valence, however, loaded with extraversion).

Explaining Personality Disorders in Terms of the Five-Factor Model

The FFM has the most compelling empirical support as the dimensional model of normal personality functioning (Digman, 1990; Goldberg, 1993; John, 1990; McCrae & Costa, 1990; Wiggins & Pincus, 1992). It therefore provides an obvious starting point from which to integrate the conceptions of personality and personality disorder (Costa & McCrae, 1992a; Grove & Tellegen, 1991).

Table 1 presents correlations between the FFM dimensions (assessed by the NEO–PI or the 50–BSRS) and the schizoid, avoidant, and borderline PDs (assessed by five different measures), obtained from five independent studies (Costa & McCrae, 1990; Soldz et al., 1993; Trull, 1992; West, 1993; Wiggins & Pincus, 1989). It is evident from Table 1 that the FFM is helpful in explaining the similarities and differences among these three personality disorders. For example, the comorbidity and differentiation of the schizoid and avoidant PDs has been controversial (Livesley, West, & Tanney, 1985). From the perspective of the FFM, their overlap and comorbidity are understood as reflecting a shared variance with introversion. The avoidant PD, however, is also characterized by excessive neuroticism, which involves such facets as trait anxiety, self-consciousness, and vulnerability (Costa & McCrae, 1992b). From the perspective of the FFM, one should have difficulty differentiating the schizoid and avoidant PDs because introverted persons will vary in their degree of neuroticism. Prototypical (or pure) cases may be readily distinguished (i.e., persons who are low on neuroticism and high on introversion would be clearly schizoid, and persons high on neuroticism and high on introversion would be clearly avoidant, assuming the absence of any complicating elevations on other FFM dimensions), but most actual cases will not be prototypical. Rather than force an arbitrary categorical distinction on the boundary cases or provide both diagnoses to the same patient, a more informative and precise approach would be to describe the extent to which a patient is elevated on introversion and neuroticism.

From the perspective of the FFM, borderline PD involves primarily excessive neuroticism and antagonism (Widiger, Trull, Clarkin, Sanderson, & Costa, in press). Antagonism provides the oppositional, argumentative, and manipulative tendencies that are important to understanding the disorder. As suggested in Table 1, however, the predominant relationship may be with neuroticism. Neuroticism captures much of the borderline pathology, particularly the facets of angry hostility, impulsivity, and depression (Wiggins & Pincus, 1989).

Borderline personality is the most prevalent PD diagnosis, yet it is also one of the most controversial. The borderline diagnosis has been prevalent to the point of being excessive, with a degree of comorbidity with other PDs that leads to questions about its validity (Widiger & Trull, 1993). Conceptualizing borderline personality disorder as extreme neuroticism, however, addresses both its prevalence and comorbidity. Neuroticism "contrasts adjustment or emotional stability with maladjustment" (Costa & McCrae, 1992b, p. 14). Persons who are vulnerable to stress or who tend to be anxious, distressed, sad, depressed, or impulsive will be elevated on neuroticism. This is not to say that the other dimensions of personality are not associated with dysfunction or that a low score on neuroticism presumes an absence of dysfunction (these issues are discussed further later) but that the general tendency to experience negative affects, such as fear, sadness, embarrassment, anger, and guilt, is the core of the neuroticism or negative affectivity domain (Watson & Clark, 1984). It is not surprising, then, to find that neuroticism is an almost ubiquitously elevated trait within clinical populations (Eysenck & Eysenck, 1985) and that most of the PDs involve some degree of neuroticism. There are few persons in treatment for a PD who would not display some degree of neu-

Table 1

Correlations of the Schizoid, Avoidant, and Borderline Personality Disorders With the Five-Factor Model of Personality

Measure and study	Subjects	Factor				
		N	E	O	A	C
		Schizoid				
MMPI						
Costa & McCrae (1990)	274 community volunteers	.16**	−.62***	.06	−.12*	.14*
Trull (1992)	54 patients	.00	−.72***	−.27*	−.19	.02
Wiggins & Pincus (1989)	550+ students	.14**	−.67***	−.14**	−.17**	.01
West (1993)	457 students	.12	−.51***	−.11	−.21***	−.07
MCMI-I						
Costa & McCrae (1990)	207 community volunteers	.04	−.64***	−.08	−.04	−.07
MCMI-II						
Costa & McCrae (1990)	62 community volunteers	−.14	−.49***	.04	.10	.14
Soldz, Budman, Demby, & Merry (1993)	102 patients	.26**	−.69***	−.32**	−.19	.08
PDQ-R						
Trull (1992)	54 patients	−.17	−.34*	−.45**	−.34*	.02
West (1993)	457 students	.20***	−.39***	−.06	−.21***	−.15
SIDPR						
Trull (1992)	54 patients	.05	−.47***	−.37**	−.34*	.07
PDE						
Soldz et al. (1993)	102 patients	.15	−.28**	−.14	−.05	.15
		Avoidant				
MMPI						
Costa & McCrae (1990)	274 community volunteers	.52***	−.54***	−.03	−.02	−.02
Trull (1992)	54 patients	.55***	−.63***	−.27*	−.16	−.19
Wiggins & Pincus (1989)	550+ students	.64***	−.58***	−.13**	−.06	−.13**
West (1993)	457 students	.50***	−.51***	−.15	−.12	−.06
MCMI-I						
Costa & McCrae (1990)	207 community volunteers	.44***	−.53***	−.11	.03	−.07
MCMI-II						
Costa & McCrae (1990)	62 community volunteers	.36**	−.32**	−.11	.05	.03
Soldz et al. (1993)	102 patients	.54***	−.59***	−.30**	−.23*	−.08
PDQ-R						
Trull (1992)	54 patients	.36**	−.39**	−.20	−.20	−.21
West (1993)	457 students	.43***	−.41***	−.13	−.17	−.07
SIDPR						
Trull (1992)	54 patients	.25	−.36**	−.15	−.19	.03
PDE						
Soldz et al. (1993)	102 patients	.23*	−.57***	−.39***	−.17	.03
		Borderline				
MMPI						
Costa & McCrae (1990)	274 community volunteers	.47***	.19**	.09	−.21***	−.32***
Trull (1992)	54 patients	.61***	.13	.18	−.45**	−.24
Wiggins & Pincus (1989)	550+ students	.66***	.00	.13**	−.21***	−.20***
West (1993)	457 students	.43***	.09	.02	−.21***	−.15
MCMI-I						
Costa & McCrae (1990)	207 community volunteers	.52***	−.22**	−.10	.14*	−.10
MCMI-II						
Costa & McCrae (1990)	62 community volunteers	.46***	−.09	−.16	−.22	−.22
Soldz et al. (1993)	102 patients	.56***	.04	−.02	−.26**	−.34***
PDQ-R						
Trull (1992)	54 patients	.60***	.19	.28*	−.39**	−.17
West (1993)	457 students	.49***	−.20***	−.01	−.34***	−.22***
SIDPR						
Trull (1992)	54 patients	.48***	.04	−.08	−.46***	−.31*
PDE						
Soldz et al. (1993)	102 patients	.42***	.06	.20*	−.13	−.10

Note. N = neuroticism; E = extraversion; O = openness to experience; A = agreeableness; C = conscientiousness; MMPI = Minnesota Multiphasic Personality Inventory; MCMI-I = Millon Clinical Multiaxial Inventory (original version); MCMI-II = Millon Clinical Multiaxial Inventory (revised version); PDQ-R = Personality Diagnostic Questionnaire—Revised; SIDPR = Structured Interview for *DSM-III-R* Personality—Revised; PDE = Personality Disorder Examination.

*$p < .05$. **$p < .01$. ***$p < .001$.

roticism, including those persons with PDs that are not defined at least in part by high neuroticism (e.g., schizoid PD and psychopathy). It may be the presence of neuroticism that impels the psychopathic or schizoid person to seek treatment (Widiger & Trull, 1992). Hence, a PD that is defined largely by neuroticism (e.g., the angry hostility, impulsivity, anxiety, depression, and vulnerability of the person with borderline PD) is likely to be extremely prevalent and to usually be comorbid with other PD diagnoses.

Conceptualizing borderline PD as extreme neuroticism is also consistent with Kernberg's (1984) psychoanalytic formulation of borderline personality organization. Borderline personality organization and neuroticism refer to a level of personality functioning that cuts across the *DSM-III-R* diagnostic categories. Kernberg would use a more inferential means by which to assess a patient's characteristic level of personality organization (considering a degree of identity diffusion, reliance on primitive defenses, and reality testing), but there is likely to be a substantial correlation between FFM neuroticism and level of borderline personality organization. The nonspecific manifestations of borderline personality functioning identified by Kernberg (e.g., anxiety tolerance, impulse control, and vulnerability to stress) are consistent with the facets of neuroticism identified by Costa and McCrae (1992b).

Understanding the *DSM-III-R* PDs from the perspective of the FFM is helpful in explaining their excessive comorbidity. For example, comorbidity ought to occur among the narcissistic, antisocial, passive-aggressive, paranoid, and borderline PDs in part because they all involve facets of antagonism. Differentiation is to some extent possible because each of these PDs involves primarily different facets of antagonism. Narcissism can be characterized in particular by low modesty (arrogance and conceit), paranoid PD by low trust (suspiciousness), antisocial PD by low altruism (exploitation) and low tendermindedness (low empathy), and passive-aggressive PD by low compliance (oppositionalism; Widiger et al., in press).

Only one study to date, however, has provided data at the facet level (Wiggins & Pincus, 1989). Exploring the facets of each dimension is important for future research, particularly if one wishes to differentiate among the PDs. Harkness (1992) emphasized this point in his discussion of the factor analysis of PD symptoms. For certain purposes, description at lower levels of the trait hierarchy (e.g., hypersensitivity and pessimism from Clark, 1990) will be more clinically useful than description at the broader higher order or domain level. This is a point on which we are in full agreement with Clark (1990), Harkness (1992), and Livesley et al. (1992). The 15-39 dimensions identified by these researchers are at the same level as and correspond closely to the facets of the FFM.

Differentiating among the *DSM-III-R* PDs will often require a facet level of analysis. As indicated in the preceding paragraphs, the broad dimension of antagonism versus agreeableness from the FFM includes such lower level facets as low trust (suspiciousness), low altruism (exploitation), low compliance (oppositionality and aggression), low modesty (arrogance), low straightforwardness (manipulativeness and scheming), and low tendermindedness (toughness, cruelty, and harshness), which represent the antisocial, narcissistic, and paranoid PD traits identified by Clark (1990), Harkness (1992), and Livesley et al. (1993). Harkness (1991) assessed the convergence of his 39 dimensions with the FFM and concluded that "there is strong resemblance" (p. 258) to the FFM. Clark and Livesley (in press) compared their 23- and 18-dimensional models (respectively) to the FFM and concluded that "measures developed independently to assess these two sets of identified trait dimensions show strongly convergent correlational patterns with measures of the five factor model . . . these data thus provide further support for the notion that the personality trait dimensional structure defined by the five factor model is very robust and will emerge reliably as long as a broad range of personality traits are assessed" (Clark & Livesley, in press, ms. pp. 22-23).

However, it is important to emphasize that an analysis at the facet level will not resolve the ambiguity of the categorical diagnoses. It simply explains why the ambiguity and comorbidity occur. There will be cases that are largely narcissistic and not antisocial (and vice versa), but for many cases it may be more informative to describe the extent to which the person is arrogant, exploitative, and cruel rather than to arbitrarily force a categorical distinction between the constructs of an antisocial and narcissistic PD.

Conceptual Issues in Relating Normal and Abnormal Personality

A formulation of the *DSM-III-R* PDs as maladaptive variants of normal personality traits raises many interesting and provocative questions regarding how or when personality should be considered to be disordered. We consider here three conceptual issues that should be addressed in future research: (a) normative maladaptivity, (b) maladaptivity as an extreme variant of normal traits, and (c) situational maladaptivity.

Normative Maladaptivity

The *DSM-III-R* states that "it is only when personality traits are inflexible and maladaptive and cause either significant functional impairment or subjective distress that they constitute Personality Disorders" (APA, 1987, p. 335), but it is not at all clear when a clinically significant level of inflexibility, maladaptivity, impairment, or distress occurs. The thresholds for diagnosis in the *DSM-III-R* do not themselves identify the point at which personality traits become maladaptive. For example, the decision to require four of seven features to make a diagnosis of avoidant PD was based simply on the rationale that three or fewer features would not be sufficiently close enough to the prototypical case to warrant a diagnosis (Widiger, 1993a). Persons with fewer than four features (e.g., a person who "has no close friends or confidants," who "is unwilling to get involved with people unless certain of being liked," or who "is easily hurt by criticism or disapproval"; APA, 1987, p. 353) do appear to have clinically significant maladaptive avoidant traits.

Data on the prevalence of PD symptomatology within the normal population is quite limited (Weissman, 1993). Nestadt and his colleagues have documented in a series of studies the substantial prevalence of compulsive, histrionic, and antisocial personality traits within an urban community population (Nestadt et al., 1990, 1991; Nestadt, Romanoski, Samuels, Folstein, & McHugh, 1992). For example, whereas only 1.7% of the eastern Baltimore population was estimated to meet the *DSM-III* criteria for compulsive personality disorder, 8% were assessed to be maladaptively perfectionistic, 12% were assessed as obsessively stubborn, 4% displayed severe emotional constriction, and 4% were excessively devoted to their work (Nestadt et al., 1991). Nestadt et al. concluded that the *DSM-III* thresholds for diagnosis grossly underestimated the rate of maladaptive personality traits within the general population.

The *DSM-III-R* includes a diagnosis for persons who fail to meet the arbitrary thresholds for any one of the 11 (or 10 in the *DSM-IV*) officially recognized PDs. This diagnosis of *personality disorder not otherwise specified* has never been a focus of empirical study but perhaps should be. When it has been considered, it is typically the most prevalent PD diagnosis, occurring with more frequency than even borderline PD (e.g., Kass et al., 1985; Loranger, 1990; Morey, 1988; Zimmerman & Coryell, 1989). Its prevalence suggests that the boundary between normal and abnormal personality bears little relationship to the presence versus absence of an officially recognized *DSM-III-R* PD diagnosis.

One of the more highly replicated and validated dimensions of normal personality is neuroticism (Costa & McCrae, 1992b; Eysenck & Eysenck, 1985), characterized by Watson and Clark (1984) as *negative affectivity*. Most persons who meet the *DSM-III-R* criteria for a PD may be characterized by a relatively high degree of neuroticism (Soldz et al., 1993; Trull, 1992; Wiggins & Pincus, 1989). However, persons who are at the normative level of neuroticism are not without neuroticism. Average neuroticism involves some degree of vulnerability, self-consciousness, and dysphoria (Costa & McCrae, 1992b). It is only those persons who score very low on neuroticism who "are usually calm, even-tempered, and relaxed, and are able to face stressful situations without becoming upset or rattled" (Costa & McCrae, 1992b, p. 15). Normal neuroticism is not normal in the sense of being healthy or without maladaptivity; it is normal only in the statistical (normative) sense of representing the common or average level of maladaptivity. It would be of interest in future research to determine whether the average person lacks any clinically significant maladaptive personality traits.

Maladaptivity as Extreme Variants of Normal Traits

To the extent that PDs represent extreme variants of normal personality traits, it should be possible to diagnose a PD solely on the basis of a cutoff point on a scale that assesses the full range of the respective traits. This would provide a possible integration of the *DSM-III-R* categorical PD diagnoses with a dimensional model of personality traits. It would in fact be of interest in future research to assess the extent to which purer groups of subjects would be obtained with diagnoses based on extreme elevations of the FFM in comparison with *DSM-III-R* PD diagnoses. One of the limitations of the *DSM-III-R* has been the excessive heterogeneity and overlap among the diagnostic groups (Widiger, 1992, 1993a). A categorical model based on the FFM dimensions, which were derived empirically for maximal independence (Digman, 1990), might be more successful in obtaining relatively pure cases. Some of the *DSM-III-R* PD diagnoses appear to be confined largely to just one of the FFM domains (e.g., schizoid PD as extreme introversion), but most appear to involve complex profiles (e.g., avoidant PD involves various facets of introversion and neuroticism).

However, it must also be emphasized that pure cases of one particular pole of the FFM (e.g., a person who is extremely introverted and is not elevated on any facet of neuroticism, openness, conscientiousness, or agreeableness) are likely to be infrequent. Most persons (including patients) will be elevated on more than one factor (Costa & McCrae, 1992b). In addition, although maladaptivity does appear to be related to the extent to which one is introverted, extraverted, agreeable, or antagonistic (as indicated by the correlations presented in Table 1), there are a number of qualifications to the proposition that the extent to which one is introverted or antagonistic indicates the extent to which one is maladaptively introverted or antagonistic. For example, each dimension of personality will not have the same degree of implications for maladaptivity. The same degree of neuroticism (negative emotionality), extraversion (positive emotionality), or conscientiousness (constraint) is unlikely to be associated with the same degree of maladaptivity. Negative emotionality may be more closely associated with maladaptivity than positive emotionality, as negatively emotionality (neuroticism) includes a person's characteristic level of dysphoria (Watson & Clark, 1984).

The lack of equivalence in the implications for degree of maladaptivity is not problematic for the hypothesis that personality disorders represent maladaptive variants of normal personality traits. There is also variability in the degree of maladaptivity across dimensions within models that are confined largely to maladaptive traits. Suicide proneness (from Clark, 1990) implies much more impairment, distress, and maladaptivity than does high energy or insincerity. Likewise, a categorical diagnosis of borderline PD is associated with a much greater degree of dysfunction than is a diagnosis of compulsive PD (Nakao et al., 1992).

It could be problematic for a personality-trait model of PDs if one of the fundamental dimensions of personality had no consequential implications for maladaptive functioning. This concern has been raised for the FFM dimension of openness to experience. As a basic dimension of personality, openness should play a fundamental role in shaping the expression of maladaptive personality traits. However, the relevance of openness to the diagnosis of a PD has been questioned by Clark and Livesley (in press) and Harkness (1992). Widiger et al. (in press) suggested that schizotypal PD may involve in part a maladaptively extreme openness to ideas. This hypothesis was verified by Wiggins and Pincus (1989). Similarly, a very high openness to fantasy may suggest a maladaptive degree of absorption in imagination, escapist daydreaming, and excessive absorption in fantasies that could contribute to paraphilic disorders, as suggested in the study by Wise, Fagan, Schmidt, Ponticas, and Costa (1991). On the other hand, the relationship of openness to PD pathology has been marginal in studies by Clark and Livesley (in press), Harkness (1992), Schroeder et al. (1992), and Widiger et al. (1991). Extremely open persons may be receptive to unusual or aberrant ideas and perceptions that are evident in schizotypic persons, but the ideation of schizotypic persons may reflect an inability to reject these ideas rather than a flexible openness to them. Schizotypic persons may in fact be closed to new ideas (particularly to those that question their aberrant ideation) and hence impelled to believe in unusual, aberrant ideas to which a truly open person would simply be receptive. The NEO-PI Openness scale was derived in part from research on self-actualization and personal growth and on Coan's (1974) work on mental health in particular. Whereas increased levels of agreeableness suggest an increase in the inflexibility of agreeableness across situations (e.g., extreme altruism and self-sacrifice that is debilitating to one's own optimal functioning), a greater degree of openness (or intellect, as this dimension is interpreted by Goldberg, 1990) might suggest an increase in the flexibility of thinking.

The relationship of openness to maladaptivity might be more unipolar than bipolar. High levels of neuroticism are more suggestive of maladaptivity than low levels. As indicated previously, a low level of neuroticism suggests a lack of vulnerability to stress, self-consciousness, anxiety, or dysphoria (Costa & McCrae, 1992b; Watson & Clark, 1984). Extremely low neuroticism can suggest an inability to experience adaptive levels of anxiety, self-consciousness, or guilt, which might be seen in persons who are given PD diagnoses of psychopathy or narcissism (Widiger et al., in press), but it is a high level of neuroticism that will be important in most cases of personality dysfunction. This may also be the case with openness to experience. For example, the person who is maladaptively low in openness is likely to be cognitively rigid and inflexible (Costa & McCrae, 1992b). Very low openness to feelings suggests the related construct of alexithymia, which involves the pathological inability to symbolize and express inner feelings.

Our earlier point regarding the appropriate level of the trait hierarchy is also relevant here. Researchers or clinicians working at the domain level can miss important aspects of openness or closedness that will differentiate among various PDs. For example, persons with avoidant PD may be average in overall openness (i.e., average in ideas, aesthetics, feelings, and values) but may have especially low scores only in opennesss to actions. Indeed, the phobic avoidance of novel activities (APA, 1987) is a hallmark symptom of pathologically low openness to actions. The *DSM-III-R* associated features for paranoid PD explicitly acknowledged a low openness to aesthetics: "People with Paranoid Personality Disorder are often interested in mechanical devices, electronics, and automation. They are generally uninterested in art or aesthetics" (APA, 1987, p. 338). Thus, researchers and clinicians may not be appropriately assessing relevant adaptive and maladaptive traits by operating at the broad, global domain level. A more detailed review of current evidence linking specific facets of openness to various personality processes and disorders is provided by Costa and Widiger (in press).

Situational Maladaptivity

The maladaptivity and adaptivity of a personality trait may also vary across situations. The same level of tough-minded antagonism can be adaptive within the context of some situations (e.g., for success within a career as a soldier or police officer) and maladaptive within others (e.g., for success as a pastoral counselor or therapist). Excessive conscientiousness may be maladaptive in social relationships (workaholism) while being largely adaptive for occupational success. Conceptualizing the *DSM-III-R* PDs from the perspective of a normal model of personality emphasizes that any particular trait can have adaptive as well as maladaptive consequences and that the maladaptivity of a trait should be assessed within the social and occupational context in which the person is functioning. This has not been recognized within the *DSM-III-R* PD taxonomy, with one notable exception. The *DSM-III-R* criteria for self-defeating PD has an exclusion criterion that "the behaviors . . . do not occur exclusively in response to, or in anticipation of, being physically, sexually, or psychologically abused" (APA, 1987, p. 374) because the submissive, deferential, and acquiescent behavior could be in response to an ongoing abusive relationship (Walker, 1987). The same point, however, could be raised with respect to the other PDs. Adaptive correlates of the histrionic, compulsive, antisocial (psychopathic), and narcissistic PDs have been noted by a variety of researchers (e.g., Leaf et al., 1990; Sutker, Bugg, & West, 1993).

Because persons below any particular level of a trait dimension may display maladaptivity and persons above any particular level may have some degree of adaptivity, it can be misleading to classify persons as simply disordered versus not disordered. A more informative approach would be to describe the personality of the subject with respect to the basic dimensions of personality and then assess the adaptivity and maladaptivity of that subject's traits relative to the social and environmental context within which that person must function. One could inquire about impairments in functioning that are likely to be associated with particular elevations (e.g., assess for maladaptive gullibility, submissiveness, and acquiescence given an elevation on agreeableness) as well as adaptive strengths that are likely to be associated with particular elevations (e.g., an openness to ideas that will contribute to a receptivity to treatment). A systematic assessment of the areas of dysfunction that commonly result from maladaptive personality traits would also be useful. We are currently developing specific impairment scales (modeled after Axes IV and V of the *DSM-III-R* and *DSM-IV*) to assess maladaptive and adaptive functioning with respect to (a) the social domain, (b) the work domain, and (c) well-being. Each of these areas are differentiated even further. For example, the social domain might include separate scales for (a) family of origin, (b) spouse or lover (i.e., sexual relationships), (c) friends, (d) children, and (e) society (e.g., legal difficulties). (Relationships with coworkers are covered within the work domain.)

Categorical distinctions along the impairment scales may at times be necessary for certain social and clinical decisions (e.g., decisions regarding hospitalization, disability, insurance coverage, or a particular form of therapy). The approach we are recommending not only would be compatible with these decisions but also could provide a more individualized and decision-specific assessment because each clinical situation may emphasize different domains of dysfunction (e.g., legal difficulty, physical well-being, financial condition, or parenting) or a different threshold within a particular domain (e.g., a threshold of impairment that warrants hospitalization may be lower than the threshold that warrants a disability claim).

Methodological Issues in Relating Normal and Abnormal Personality

Many issues and problems in the assessment of personality traits and disorders are beyond the scope of this review. We discuss here three issues that pertain directly to the study of the relationship between normal personality traits and personality disorders: (a) subject sampling, (b) the use of self-report inventories versus semistructured interviews, and (c) the construction of assessment instruments.

Subject Sampling

Wiggins, Phillips, and Trapnell (1989) explored the relationship between scale elevations on a measure of interpersonal traits and correlates of maladaptivity. They noted the general assumption that "vector length [elevation] of a subject's profile is assumed to provide an index of the intensity, flexibility, and adaptiveness of that characteristic pattern" (Wiggins et al., 1989, p. 298). However, they also predicted and confirmed that "one would not expect vector length to be related to measures of interpersonal problems in a random sample of unclassified subjects" (Wiggins et al., 1989, p. 298). For example, it is evident that introversion should correlate positively with schizoid personality traits and negatively with histrionic personality traits. Therefore, in a sample of persons characterized equally by schizoid and histrionic traits, introversion may fail to correlate with maladaptivity, as the maladaptivity of both poles would cancel out in any assessment of an overall association. Wiggins et al. indeed found that interpersonal trait scales failed to correlate with measures of interpersonal maladaptivity across all subjects but that when the analyses were confined to those who shared the traits, the association of the trait scales with maladaptivity was confirmed.

This methodological point may seem trivial because it is unlikely that one would obtain a sample of persons confined to and equally representative of opposing traits or disorders. However, variations on this issue will often occur that will be very difficult to detect because most PD studies involve ill-defined and heterogeneous mixtures of opposing PD symptomatology.

For example, Klein et al. (in press) compared Wisconsin Personality Disorder Inventory (WISPI) scores obtained from 852 community subjects with those obtained from 368 patients. There were no differences between the groups on the histrionic and narcissistic scales. At first glance, this finding might question the validity of the histrionic and narcissistic WISPI scales because Klein et al. apparently failed to distinguish between normal and personality-disordered subjects who appeared to have histrionic and narcissistic pathology. However, patients' scores on the avoidant and dependent scales were among the highest elevations observed. Avoidant and dependent patients are likely to be characterized by excessive introversion and agreeableness, whereas histrionic and narcissistic patients are likely to be characterized by excessive extraversion and antagonism (Widiger et al., in press). The avoidant and dependent subjects who were predominant in their sample may then appear less histrionic and narcissistic than normal subjects (although the avoidant, dependent, histrionic, and narcissistic WISPI scales would still obtain significant positive intercorrelations because of shared neuroticism). This may not fully explain Klein et al.'s anomaly, but comparable results have also occurred in other studies that compared patients and normal subjects without adequately considering the personality traits (or personality disorders) that were likely to predominate within the patient group.

Interviews Versus Inventories

An issue that pervades PD research is the questionable reliability and validity of the assessment instruments. A thorough discussion is beyond the scope of this review (recent overviews are provided by Perry, 1992, and Widiger & Sanderson, in press-a). One issue worth considering here is the use of self-report inventories versus semistructured interviews. Semistructured interviews are at times said to be the preferred method of assessment in PD research (Perry, 1992). It is atypical for the National Institute of Mental Health to fund a PD study that confines its assessment to self-report inventories, but it is typical for major studies to be confined to or to rely primarily on the results provided by a semistructured interview. However, the dimensional models of personality are assessed primarily with self-report inventories.

This disparity parallels to some extent professional tradition. Categorical diagnoses via clinical interviews have been the norm within psychiatry (and medicine in general), whereas dimensional classifications via self-report inventories have been the norm within trait psychology. However, it would be misleading to suggest that the disparity in methodology reflects simply a professional tradition or bias. One of the original and still popular self-report inventories for assessing the *DSM-III-R* PDs is co-authored by psychiatrists (the revised Personality Diagnostic Questionnaire [PDQ-R]; Hyler & Rieder, 1987), and two of the semistructured interviews are authored by psychologists (Loranger, 1988; Widiger & Sanderson, in press-b).

Semistructured interviews are preferred in large part because they allow the judgments of the researcher to influence the assessment. This is somewhat ironic, given that semistructured interviews are preferred over clinical interviews precisely for their curtailment of inference and judgment. Most semistructured interviews emphasize the need to avoid relying on the opinions and attributions of the subject (who may be characterized in part by a distorted self-image) and the need to ask for actual examples and incidents to allow the interviewer to assess whether the trait is indeed present. It is probably unrealistic to assess a complex construct, such as the dependency PD criterion of being unable to make everyday decisions without an excessive amount of advice or reassurance, by simply asking a person to respond true versus false to the PDQ-R item "I would rather make my own decisions than rely on the advice of others" (Hyler & Rieder, 1987).

Self-report inventory assessments have been shown to be particularly problematic when the subject is acutely depressed, anxious, or psychotic (Widiger, 1993b). Interviewers can be more successful in disentangling a mood, anxiety, or psychotic disorder from a personality disorder (Loranger et al., 1991). However, mood state distortions may not be so problematic within outpatient settings (Trull, 1993), and resilience to the distortions of mood states is not inherent to a semistructured interview. The validity of a semistructured interview assessment depends substantially on the training, care, and dependability of the interviewers. Loranger et al. (1991) reported little to no effects of mood states in their administration of the PDE, but it could be somewhat misleading to then conclude an "ability of a particular semistructured interview, the PDE, to circumvent trait-state artifacts" (Loranger et al., 1991, p. 727). One can easily administer and score the PDE in an unreliable fashion. The results from any particular administration of the PDE could reflect simply artifactual mood states (O'Boyle & Self, 1990). Interrater reliability should be established and documented in every administration of a semistructured interview rather than assumed to be present on the basis of prior success.

In addition, interviewers in any particular study may obtain good to excellent interrater reliability in their administration and scoring of the PDE, but this provides no guarantee that their administration and scoring is consistent with that provided in another research site in which comparable levels of interrater reliability were also obtained. Despite the interrater reliability that has been obtained with various semistructured interviews, there may be little agreement in their assessments (Skodol, Oldham, Rosnick, Kellman, & Hyler, 1991). This weak convergent validity reflects not only variation in the content of the interviews but also a variability across sites (and across time within a site) in how any particular interview is being administered and scored. One will likely obtain more intersite reliability with findings provided by self-report inventories than with findings provided by semistructured interviews (see, e.g., Table 1). The findings from the MCMI-II may be distorted by subjects' depressed mood, but one can be more confident in the stability of this distortion in the MCMI-II than in the ability of the PDE to be resilient to this distortion. However, in the spirit of using multiple methods of measurement, future research on the relationship of normal personality traits to personality disorders would benefit from the development of a semistructured interview for assessment of normal as well as abnormal traits (Widiger & Trull, 1992). Additional use of peers, spouses, and other informants should also be encouraged (Costa & McCrae, 1992a; Zimmerman, Pfohl, Coryell, Stangl, & Corenthal, 1988).

Instrument Item Analysis

An additional methodological issue is illustrated by the inconsistent findings that have been obtained for the association of conscientiousness with the compulsive PD (Costa & McCrae, 1990; Soldz et al., 1993; Trull, 1992). Conscientiousness involves the tendency to be thorough, organized, precise, methodical, ambitious, determined, deliberate, and ordered (Costa & McCrae, 1992b). A person who is excessively conscientious would likely display a "perfectionism that interferes with task completion," a "preoccupation with details, rules, lists, order, organization, or schedules," and an "excessive devotion to work and productivity" (APA, 1987, p. 356). One of the *DSM-III-R* compulsive PD criteria explicitly refers to an "overconscientiousness" (APA, 1987, p. 356). However, the only studies that have confirmed this prediction have been those that have used the MCMI or the MCMI-II (Costa & McCrae, 1990; Soldz et al., 1993), and the MCMI and MCMI-II compulsiveness scales have themselves obtained low to negative correlations with the compulsiveness scales from other instruments (e.g., McCann, 1992; Morey & LeVine, 1988; Soldz, Budman, Demby, & Merry, in press).

The MCMI-II contains a number of items that suggest adaptive conscientiousness (e.g., "I always make sure that my work is well planned and organized," "If a person wants something done that calls for real patience, they should ask me," and "I keep very close track of my money so I am prepared if a need comes up") and only a few items that suggest a conscientiousness that is so excessive that it is maladaptive (e.g., "My wish to get things done just perfectly often slows down my work"; Millon, 1987). Other PD instruments, such as the PDQ-R (Hyler & Rieder, 1987), are confined largely to maladaptively excessive conscientiousness (e.g., "I waste time trying to make things too perfect" and "I often get lost in the details and lose sight of the 'big picture' "; Hyler & Rieder, 1987). The NEO-PI-R conscientiousness scale (Costa & McCrae, 1992b), on the other hand, is confined largely to adaptive conscientiousness (e.g., "I strive for excellence in everything I do," "I think things through before coming to a decision," and "I try to perform all the tasks assigned to me conscientiously"), with only a few items that suggest maladaptively extreme conscientiousness (e.g., "I tend to be somewhat fastidious or exacting" and "I'm something of a 'workaholic' "). It is not surprising that a person who would describe him- or herself on the NEO-PI-R as being "a productive person who always gets the job done" and "efficient and effective at my work" (Costa & McCrae, 1992b) would not describe him- or herself as being overconscientious, unable to complete a project because his or her own strict standards are not met, and being preoccupied with order and organization to the extent that the major point of the activity is lost. The NEO-PI-R was constructed primarily for the assessment of the normal (adaptive) range of personality functioning, and it may not provide adequate coverage of the extreme, maladaptive variants of each of the factors.

Clark (1993b; Clark, Vorheis, & McEwen, in press) and Tellegen (1993) made a similar point with respect to the NEO-PI-R coverage of impulsivity and antagonism. Impulsivity on the NEO-PI-R is confined largely to a dyscontrol that would be evident within the normal population (e.g., "I have trouble resisting my cravings"; "When I am having my favorite foods, I tend to eat too much"; and "Sometimes I do things on impulse that I later regret"; Costa & McCrae, 1992b). The impulsivity that would be seen in antisocial or borderline persons (e.g., spouse abuse, larceny, wanderlust, drug abuse, reckless driving, and self-mutilation) is not specifically represented.

Clark (1993b; Clark et al., in press) reported more success in accounting for PD symptomatology with the Schedule for Nonadaptive and Adaptive Personality (SNAP; Clark, 1993a) than with the NEO-PI (Costa & McCrae, 1985). However, the SNAP was constructed to include the range of functioning represented by the *DSM-III-R* PDs, including such items as "I find that different odors have different colors," "I admit that I sometimes take pleasure in hurting someone physically," "I put my work ahead of being with family and friends," "My friendships often seem to swing between being really close and really far apart," "I have a violent temper," and "I have tried to commit suicide" (Clark, 1993a). It is not surprising that a scale that includes items that explicitly represent the *DSM-III-R* criteria for the various PDs would correlate more highly with these disorders than a scale that was confined largely to the domain of normal personality functioning.

In summary, the association that is obtained between a normal personality trait and a personality disorder may reflect in part the extent to which the measure of the normal trait includes maladaptive variants and the measure of the personality disorder includes adaptive variants. In addition, to the extent that the domains covered by the respective measures overlap, the association that is obtained may reflect the fact that the scales are actually assessing the same construct. One is then no longer assessing the association of a normal trait with a maladaptive trait but rather the concurrent validity of two measures of the same construct. The positive findings that have been obtained with the NEO-PI (e.g., in Table 1) are informative in part because the NEO-PI was constructed independently of any knowledge or concerns regarding the *DSM-III-R* PD constructs. In any case, future studies should be cognizant of the extent to which the findings are impelled or constrained by the instruments that are being used to assess the respective constructs.

Conclusions and Recommendations

There is considerable need for research on the definition of PD and its apparent distinction from normal personality functioning. A variety of taxometric studies have failed to document any clear distinction among the PDs or between the PDs and normal personality traits. Just as every person who meets the *DSM-III-R* criteria for a PD may find that their personality traits are adaptive within some situations, most persons who fail to meet the criteria for any one of the *DSM-III-R* PDs may still have some degree of maladaptivity that is secondary to their personality. Future research should address the fundamental question of whether ostensibly normal persons do in fact lack maladaptive personality traits.

There is little doubt that the personality traits described in the *DSM-III-R* are maladaptive, but there are as yet no data to indicate the point at which a trait becomes sufficiently inflexible, intense, impairing, or distressful that a diagnosis of a PD becomes warranted. It would be useful in future studies to identify explicitly the manner in which any particular PD or trait is maladaptive (and adaptive), whether it is the expression of the trait across most situations (inflexibility) or the intensity of the expression within any particular situation (or both). It would also be useful to assess the specific locus of the maladaptivity, whether it involves primarily social dysfunction, occupational dysfunction, personal distress, or some combination thereof.

There is little need for additional exploratory factor analyses whose purpose it is to generate new dimensional models for the PDs. What is needed instead are studies whose purpose it is to separate the wheat from the chaff. The more informative studies will be those that contrast alternative models (e.g., Clark & Livesley, in press; Schroeder et al., 1992; Wiggins & Pincus, 1989) or apply confirmatory analyses of the goodness of fit of an existing model (e.g., Moldin, Rice, Erlenmeyer-Kimling, & Squires-Wheeler, 1993; Soldz et al., 1993; Wiggins & Pincus, 1989). The FFM will likely generate the most empirical interest (Costa & McCrae, 1992a; Widiger & Trull, 1992). However, the research to date has also suggested some concern and caution regarding the adequacy of the model, particularly the importance of openness to experience and the placement of schizotypal cognitive and perceptual aberrations (Costa & McCrae, 1992a; Clark & Livesley, in press; Schroeder et al., 1992). It is not clear whether these findings reflect inadequacies of the FFM (Benjamin, 1993; Tellegen & Waller, in press), limitations of existing measures (Clark, 1993b), or limitations of current conceptions of PDs (Widiger & Trull, 1992). Disentangling the contribution of construct and method variance has always been problematic (Cronbach & Meehl, 1955), and it will be no less important in research on the association, overlap, and differentiation of personality and PDs. There will continue to be as much need for research on the assessment of maladaptive personality traits (e.g., interviews vs. inventories) as there is a need for research on the maladaptive traits themselves.

References

Akiskal, H. S., & Akiskal, K. (1992). Cyclothymic, hyperthymic, and depressive temperaments as subaffective variants of mood disorders. In A. Tasman & M. B. Riba (Eds.), *Review of psychiatry* (Vol. 11, pp. 43–62). Washington, DC: American Psychiatric Press.

American Psychiatric Association. (1968). *Diagnostic and statistical manual of mental disorders* (2nd ed.). Washington, DC: Author.

American Psychiatric Association. (1980). *Diagnostic and statistical manual of mental disorders* (3rd ed.). Washington, DC: Author.

American Psychiatric Association. (1987). *Diagnostic and statistical manual of mental disorders* (3rd ed., rev.). Washington, DC: Author.

Benjamin, L. S. (1993). Dimensional, categorical, or hybrid analyses of personality: A response to Widiger's proposal. *Psychological Inquiry, 4*, 91–94.

Blashfield, R., Sprock, J., Pinkston, K., & Hodgin, J. (1985). Exemplar prototypes of personality disorder diagnoses. *Comprehensive Psychiatry, 26*, 11–21.

Cannon, D. S., Clark, L. A., Leeka, J. K., & Keefe, C. K. (1993). A reanalysis of the Tridimensional Personality Questionnaire (TPQ) and its relation to Cloninger's Type 2 alcoholism. *Psychological Assessment, 5*, 62–66.

Clark, L. A. (1990). Toward a consensual set of symptom clusters for assessment of personality disorder. In J. Butcher & C. Spielberger (Eds.), *Advances in personality assessment* (Vol. 8, pp. 243–266). Hillsdale, NJ: Erlbaum.

Clark, L. A. (1993a). *Manual for the Schedule for Nonadaptive and Adaptive Personality (SNAP)*. Minneapolis: University of Minnesota Press.

Clark, L. A. (1993b). Personality disorder diagnosis: Limitations of the five-factor model. *Psychological Inquiry, 4*, 100–103.

Clark, L. A., & Livesley, W. J. (in press). Two approaches to identifying the dimensions of personality disorder: Convergence on the five-factor model. In P. T. Costa, Jr., & T. A. Widiger (Eds.), *Personality disorders and the five-factor model of personality*. Washington, DC: American Psychological Association.

Clark, L. A., Vorheis, L., & McEwen, J. L. (in press). Personality disorder symptomatology from the five-factor perspective. In P. T. Costa, Jr., & T. A. Widiger (Eds.), *Personality disorders and the five-factor model of personality*. Washington, DC: American Psychological Association.

Cleckley, H. M. (1941). *The mask of sanity*. St. Louis, MO: Mosby.

Cloninger, C. R. (1987). A systematic method for the clinical description and classification of personality variants. *Archives of General Psychiatry, 44*, 573–588.

Cloninger, C. R. (1993, March). *A general biosocial model of personality and psychopathology*. Presidential address presented at the 83rd Annual Meeting of the American Psychopathological Assocation, New York, NY.

Cloninger, C. R., Przybeck, T. R., & Svrakic, D. M. (1991). The Tridimensional Personality Questionnaire: U.S. normative data. *Psychological Reports, 69,* 1047–1057.

Coan, R. W. (1974). *The optimal personality.* New York: Columbia University Press.

Cooper, A. M. (1993). Psychotherapeutic approaches to masochism. *Journal of Psychotherapy Practice and Research, 2,* 1–13.

Costa, P. T., Jr., & McCrae, R. R. (1985). *The NEO Personality Inventory* [Manual]. Odessa, FL: Psychological Assessment Resources.

Costa, P. T., Jr., & McCrae, R. R. (1990). Personality disorders and the five-factor model of personality. *Journal of Personality Disorders, 4,* 362–371.

Costa, P. T., Jr., & McCrae, R. R. (1992a). The five-factor model of personality and its relevance to personality disorders. *Journal of Personality Disorders, 6,* 343–359.

Costa, P. T., Jr., & McCrae, R. R. (1992b). *Revised NEO Personality Inventory (NEO-PI-R) and NEO Five-Factor Inventory (NEO-FFI)* [Professional manual]. Odessa, FL: Psychological Assessment Resources.

Costa, P. T., Jr., & Widiger, T. A. (in press). Summary and unresolved issues. In P. T. Costa, Jr., & T. A. Widiger (Eds.), *Personality disorders and the five-factor model of personality.* Washington, DC: American Psychological Association.

Cronbach, L. J., & Meehl, P. E. (1955). Construct validity in psychological tests. *Psychological Bulletin, 52,* 281–302.

Digman, J. M. (1990). Personality structure: Emergence of the five-factor model. *Annual Review of Psychology, 41,* 417–440.

Dowson, J. H., & Berrios, G. E. (1991). Factor structure of *DSM-III-R* personality disorders shown by self-report questionnaire: Implications for classifying and assessing personality disorders. *Acta Psychiatrica Scandinavica, 84,* 555–560.

Everett, J. E. (1983). Factor comparability as a means of determining the number of factors and their rotation. *Multidimensional Behavioral Research, 18,* 197–218.

Eysenck, H. J., & Eysenck, M. W. (1985). *Personality and individual differences: A natural science approach.* New York: Plenum Press.

Frances, A. J., & Widiger, T. A. (1986). The classification of personality disorders: An overview of problems and solutions. In A. J. Frances & R. E. Hales (Eds.), *Psychiatry update* (Vol. 5, pp. 240–278). Washington, DC: American Psychiatric Press.

Goldberg, L. R. (1990). An alternative "description of personality": The Big-Five factor structure. *Journal of Personality and Social Psychology, 59,* 1216–1229.

Goldberg, L. R. (1992). The development of markers of the Big-Five factor structure. *Psychological Assessment, 4,* 26–42.

Goldberg, L. R. (1993). The structure of phenotypic personality traits. *American Psychologist, 48,* 26–34.

Grove, W. M., & Tellegen, A. (1991). Problems in the classification of personality disorders. *Journal of Personality Disorders, 5,* 31–41.

Hamburger, L. K., & Hastings, J. E. (1986). Personality correlates of men who abuse their partners: A cross-validation study. *Journal of Family Violence, 1,* 323–341.

Hamlin, W. T. (1990). *The chains of psychological slavery: The mental illness of racism.* Baltimore: ICFP.

Harkness, A. R. (1991, April). *Personality disorders' hierarchical structure: The Big Five is one slice.* Paper presented at the 12th Annual Meeting of the Southwestern Psychological Association, New Orleans, LA.

Harkness, A. R. (1992). Fundamental topics in the personality disorders: Candidate trait dimensions from lower regions of the hierarchy. *Psychological Assessment, 4,* 251–259.

Horowitz, L. M., Rosenberg, S. E., Bauer, B. A., Ureno, G., & Villasenor, V. S. (1988). Inventory of Interpersonal Problems: Psychometric properties and clinical applications. *Journal of Consulting and Clinical Psychology, 56,* 885–892.

Hurt, S. W., Clarkin, J. F., Widiger, T. A., Fyer, M. R., Sullivan, T., Stone, M. H., & Frances, A. (1990). Evaluation of *DSM-III* decision rules for case detection using joint conditional probability structures. *Journal of Personality Disorders, 4,* 121–130.

Hyler, S. E., & Lyons, M. (1988). Factor analysis of the *DSM-III* personality disorder clusters: A replication. *Comprehensive Psychiatry, 29,* 304–308.

Hyler, S. E., Lyons, M., Rieder, R. O., Young, L., Williams, J. B. W., & Spitzer, R. L. (1990). The factor structure of self-report *DSM-III* Axis II symptoms and their relationship to clinicians' ratings. *American Journal of Psychiatry, 147,* 751–757.

Hyler, S. E., & Rieder, R. O. (1987). *Personality Diagnostic Questionnaire—Revised (PDQ-R).* Unpublished test, New York State Psychiatric Institute, New York.

John, O. P. (1990). The "Big Five" factor taxonomy: Dimensions of personality in the natural language and in questionnaires. In L. A. Pervin (Ed.), *Handbook of personality: Theory and research* (pp. 66–100). New York: Guilford Press.

Kass, F., Skodol, A. E., Charles, E., Spitzer, R. L., & Williams, J. B. W. (1985). Scaled ratings of *DSM-III* personality disorders. *American Journal of Psychiatry, 142,* 627–630.

Kernberg, O. F. (1984). *Severe personality disorders.* New Haven, CT: Yale University Press.

Klein, M. H., Benjamin, L. S., Rosenfeld, R., Treece, C., Husted, J., & Greist, J. H. (in press). The Wisconsin Personality Disorders Inventory: I. Development, reliability, and validity. *Journal of Personality Disorders.*

Leaf, R. C., DiGiuseppe, R., Ellis, A., Mass, R., Backx, W., Wolfe, J., & Alington, D. E. (1990). "Healthy" correlates of MCMI Scales 4, 5, 6, and 7. *Journal of Personality Disorders, 4,* 312–328.

Livesley, W. J., & Jackson, D. N. (1986). The internal consistency and factorial structure of behaviors judged to be associated with *DSM-III* personality disorders. *American Journal of Psychiatry, 143,* 1473–1474.

Livesley, W. J., Jackson, D. N., & Schroeder, M. L. (1990). Dependent personality disorder and attachment problems. *Journal of Personality Disorders 4,* 131–140.

Livesley, W. J., Jackson, D. N., & Schroeder, M. L. (1992). Factorial structure of traits delineating personality disorders in clinical and general population samples. *Journal of Abnormal Psychology, 101,* 432–440.

Livesley, W. J., West, M., & Tanney, A. (1985). Historical comment on the *DSM-III* schizoid and avoidant personality disorders. *American Journal of Psychiatry, 142,* 1344–1347.

Loranger, A. W. (1988). *Personality Disorder Examination (PDE)* [Manual]. Yonkers, NY: DV Communications.

Loranger, A. W. (1990). The impact of *DSM-III* on diagnostic practice in a university hospital. *Archives of General Psychiatry, 47,* 672–675.

Loranger, A. W., Lenzenweger, M. F., Gartner, A. F., Susman, V. L., Herzig, J., Zammit, G. K., Gartner, J. D., Abrams, R. C., & Young, R. C. (1991). Trait–state artifacts and the diagnosis of personality disorders. *Archives of General Psychiatry, 48,* 720–728.

McCann, J. T. (1992). A comparison of two measures for obsessive-compulsive personality disorder. *Journal of Personality Disorders, 6,* 18–23.

McCrae, R. R., & Costa, P. T., Jr. (1990). *Personality in adulthood.* New York: Guilford Press.

Millon, T. (1987). *Manual for the MCMI-II* (2nd ed.). Minneapolis, MN: National Computer Systems.

Moldin, S. O., Rice, J. P., Erlenmeyer-Kimling, L., & Squires-Wheeler, E. (1993). *Latent structure of DSM-III-R* Axis II psychopathology in a normal sample. Manuscript submitted for publication.

Morey, L. C. (1988). Personality disorders in *DSM-III* and *DSM-III-R*: Convergence, coverage, and internal consistency. *American Journal of Psychiatry, 145*, 573–577.

Morey, L. C., & LeVine, D. J. (1988). A multitrait-multimethod examination of Minnesota Multiphasic Personality Inventory (MMPI) and Millon Clinical Multiaxial Inventory (MCMI). *Journal of Psychopathology and Behavioral Assessment, 10*, 333–344.

Morey, L. C., Waugh, M. H., & Blashfield, R. K. (1985). MMPI scales for *DSM-III* personality disorders: Their derivation and correlates. *Journal of Personality Assessment, 49*, 245–251.

Nakao, K., Gunderson, J. G., Phillips, K. A., Tanaka, N., Yorifuji, K., Takaishi, J., & Nishimura, T. (1992). Functional impairment in personality disorders. *Journal of Personality Disorders, 6*, 24–33.

Nestadt, G., Romanoski, A. J., Brown, C. H., Chahal, R., Merchant, A., Folstein, M. F., Gruenberg, E. M., & McHugh, P. R. (1991). *DSM-III* compulsive personality disorder: An epidemiologic survey. *Psychological Medicine, 21*, 461–471.

Nestadt, G., Romanoski, A. J., Chahal, R., Merchant, A., Folstein, M. F., Gruenberg, E. M., & McHugh, P. R. (1990). An epidemiological study of histrionic personality disorder. *Psychological Medicine, 20*, 413–422.

Nestadt, G., Romanoski, A. J., Samuels, J. F., Folstein, M. F., & McHugh, P. R. (1992). The relationship between personality and *DSM-III* Axis I disorders in the population: Results from an epidemiological survey. *American Journal of Psychiatry, 149*, 1228–1233.

O'Boyle, M., & Self, D. (1990). A comparison of two interviews for *DSM-III-R* personality disorders. *Psychiatry Research, 32*, 85–92.

Perry, J. C. (1992). Problems and considerations in the valid assessment of personality disorders. *American Journal of Psychiatry, 149*, 1645–1653.

Pilkonis, P. A., & Frank, E. (1988). The implications of *DSM-III* personality disorders for patients with major depression. *Journal of Affective Disorders, 7*, 309–318.

Retzlaff, P. D., & Gibertini, M. (1987). Factor structure of the MCMI basic personality scales and common-item artifact. *Journal of Personality Assessment, 51*, 588–594.

Romney, D. M., & Bynner, J. M. (1989). Evaluation of a circumplex model of *DSM-III* personality disorders. *Journal of Research in Personality, 23*, 525–538.

Schroeder, M. L., Wormworth, J. A., & Livesley, W. J. (1992). Dimensions of personality disorder and their relationships to the Big Five dimensions of personality. *Psychological Assessment, 4*, 47–53.

Shea, M. T. (1992). Some characteristics of the Axis II criteria sets and their implications for assessment of personality disorders. *Journal of Personality Disorders, 6*, 377–381.

Sim, J. P., & Romney, D. M. (1990). The relationship between a circumplex model of interpersonal behaviors and personality disorders. *Journal of Personality Disorders, 4*, 329–341.

Skodol, A. E., Oldham, J. M., Rosnick, L., Kellman, H. D., & Hyler, S. E. (1991). Diagnosis of *DSM-III-R* personality disorders: A comparison of two structured interviews. *International Journal of Methods in Psychiatric Research, 1*, 13–26.

Soldz, S., Budman, S., Demby, A., & Merry, J. (1993). Representation of personality disorders in circumplex and five-factor space: Explorations with a clinical sample. *Psychological Assessment, 5*, 41–52.

Soldz, S., Budman, S., Demby, A., & Merry, J. (in press). Diagnostic agreement between the Personality Disorder Examination and the MCMI-II. *Journal of Personality Assessment.*

Strack, S. (1987). Development and validation of an adjective check list to assess the Millon personality types in a normal population. *Journal of Personality Assessment, 51*, 572–587.

Strack, S., Lorr, M., Campbell, L., & Lamnin, A. (1992). Personality disorder and clinical syndrome factors of MCMI-II scales. *Journal of Personality Assessment, 6*, 40–52.

Sutker, P. B., Bugg, F., & West, J. A. (1993). Antisocial personality disorder. In P. B. Sutker & H. E. Adams (Eds.), *Comprehensive handbook of psychopathology* (2nd ed., pp. 337–370). New York: Plenum Press.

Svrakic, D. M., Przybeck, T. R., & Cloninger, C. R. (1991). Further contribution to the conceptual validity of the unified biosocial theory of personality: U.S. and Yugoslav data. *Comprehensive Psychiatry, 32*, 195–209.

Tellegen, A. (1993). Folk concepts and psychological concepts of personality and personality disorder. *Psychological Inquiry, 4*, 122–130.

Tellegen, A., & Waller, N. G. (in press). Exploring personality through test construction: Development of the Multidimensional Personality Questionnaire. In S. R. Briggs & J. M. Cheek (Eds.), *Personality measures: Development and evaluation.* Greenwich, CT: JAI Press.

Torgersen, S., & Alnaes, R. (1989). Localizing *DSM-III* personality disorders in a three-dimensional structural space. *Journal of Personality Disorders, 3*, 274–281.

Trull, T. J. (1992). *DSM-III-R* personality disorders and the five-factor model of personality: An empirical comparison. *Journal of Abnormal Psychology, 101*, 553–560.

Trull, T. J. (1993). Temporal stability and validity of two personality disorder inventories. *Psychological Assessment, 5*, 11–18.

Walker, L. (1987). Inadequacies of the masochistic personality disorder diagnosis for women. *Journal of Personality Disorders, 1*, 183–189.

Watson, D., & Clark, L. A. (1984). Negative affectivity: The disposition to experience aversive emotional states. *Psychological Bulletin, 96*, 465–490.

Weissman, M. M. (1993). The epidemiology of personality disorders: A 1990 update. *Journal of Personality Disorders, 7*, 44–62.

West, K. (1993). *The placement of cognitive and perceptual aberrations within the five-factor model.* Unpublished manuscript, University of Kentucky, Lexington.

Widiger, T. A. (1992). Categorical versus dimensional classification: Implications from and for research. *Journal of Personality Disorders, 6*, 287–300.

Widiger, T. A. (1993a). The *DSM-III-R* categorical personality disorder diagnoses: A critique and an alternative. *Psychological Inquiry, 4*, 75–90.

Widiger, T. A. (1993b). Personality and depression: Assessment issues. In M. H. Klein, D. J. Kupfer, & M. T. Shea (Eds.), *Personality and depression: A current view* (pp. 77–118). New York: Guilford Press.

Widiger, T. A., Frances, A. J., Harris, M., Jacobsberg, L. B., Fyer, M., & Manning, D. (1991). Comorbidity among Axis II disorders. In J. M. Oldham (Ed.), *Personality disorders: New perspectives on diagnostic validity* (pp. 163–194). Washington, DC: American Psychiatric Press.

Widiger, T. A., & Sanderson, C. J. (in press-a). Effective procedures for assessing personality disorders. In J. N. Butcher (Ed.), *Practical considerations in clinical personality assessment.* New York: Oxford University Press.

Widiger, T. A., & Sanderson, C. J. (in press-b). Towards a dimensional model of personality disorder in *DSM-IV* and *DSM-V*. In W. J. Livesley (Ed.), *DSM-IV personality disorders.* New York: Guilford Press.

Widiger, T. A., & Trull, T. J. (1992). Personality and psychopathology: An application of the five-factor model. *Journal of Personality, 60*, 363–393.

Widiger, T. A., & Trull, T. J. (1993). Borderline and narcissistic personality disorders. In P. B. Sutker & H. E. Adams (Eds.), *Comprehensive handbook of psychopathology* (2nd ed., pp. 371–394). New York: Plenum Press.

Widiger, T. A., Trull, T. J., Clarkin, J. F., Sanderson, C., & Costa, P. T., Jr. (in press). A description of the *DSM-III-R* and *DSM-IV* personality disorders with the five-factor model of personality. In P. T. Costa, Jr., & T. A. Widiger (Eds.), *Personality disorders and the five-factor model of personality.* Washington, DC: American Psychological Association.

Widiger, T. A., Trull, T. J., Hurt, S. W., Clarkin, J., & Frances, A. J.

(1987). A multidimensional scaling of the *DSM-III* personality disorders. *Archives of General Psychiatry, 44,* 557–563.

Wiggins, J. S., Phillips, N., & Trapnell, P. (1989). Circular reasoning about interpersonal behavior: Evidence concerning some untested assumptions underlying diagnostic classification. *Journal of Personality and Social Psychology, 56,* 296–305.

Wiggins, J. S., & Pincus, A. L. (1989). Conceptions of personality disorders and dimensions of personality. *Psychological Assessment: A Journal of Consulting and Clinical Psychology, 1,* 305–316.

Wiggins, J. S., & Pincus, A. L. (1992). Personality: Structure and assessment. *Annual Review of Psychology, 43,* 473–504.

Wise, T. N., Fagan, P. J., Schmidt, C. W., Ponticas, Y., & Costa, P. T., Jr. (1991). Personality and sexual functioning of transvestitic fetishists and other paraphilics. *Journal of Nervous and Mental Disease, 179,* 694–698.

World Health Organization. (1977). *International classification of diseases* (9th ed.). Geneva, Switzerland: Author.

Zimmerman, M., & Coryell, W. H. (1989). *DSM-III* personality disorder diagnoses in a nonpatient sample. *Archives of General Psychiatry, 46.*

Zimmerman, M., & Coryell, W. H. (1990). *DSM-III* personality disorder dimensions. *Journal of Nervous and Mental Disease, 178,* 686–692.

Zimmerman, M., Pfohl, B., Coryell, W., Stangl, D., & Corenthal, C. (1988). Diagnosing personality disorder in depressed patients. A comparison of patient and informant interviews. *Archives of General Psychiatry, 45,* 733–737.

Received March 27, 1993
Revision received August 6, 1993
Accepted August 6, 1993 ■

ORIGINAL ARTICLE

The Prevalence of Personality Disorders in a Community Sample

Svenn Torgersen, PhD; Einar Kringlen, MD; Victoria Cramer, PhD

Background: To our knowledge, no previous studies of personality disorders (PDs) in a large representative sample of the common population have been conducted.

Methods: A representative sample of 2053 individuals between the ages of 18 and 65 years in Oslo, the capital of Norway, was studied from 1994 to 1997. Information about PDs was obtained by means of the Structured Interview for *DSM-III-R* Personality Disorders, in conjunction with an interview recording demographic data. The subjects were interviewed primarily at home, but in some instances, also at the clinic.

Results: The prevalence of PDs was 13.4% (SE, 0.7). The prevalence rates (SEs) for specific PDs, irrespective of whether a person had 1 or more PD, were: paranoid, 2.4% (0.3); schizoid, 1.7% (1.6); schizotypal, 0.6% (0.2); antisocial, 0.7% (0.2); sadistic, 0.2% (0.1); borderline, 0.7% (0.2); histrionic, 2.0% (0.3); narcissistic, 0.8; (0.2); avoidant, 5.0% (0.5); dependent, 1.5% (0.3); obsessive-compulsive: 2.0% (0.3); passive-aggressive, 1.7% (0.3); self-defeating, 0.8%, (0.2). The prevalence of PDs was highest among subjects with only a high school education or less, and living without a partner in the center of the city.

Conclusions: Personality disorders were found to be prevalent, with avoidant, schizoid, and paranoid PDs more common, and borderline PD less common than what is usually reported. Personality disorders tend to be more frequent among single individuals from the lower socioeconomic classes in the center of the city. It is impossible to determine what is cause and what is consequence from a cross-sectional study.

Arch Gen Psychiatry. 2001;58:590-596

IN CONTRAST to symptom disorders, few epidemiological studies of personality disorders (PDs) have been conducted to establish their prevalence. As the structured Diagnostic Interview Schedule (DIS)[1] contains questions pertaining to the antisocial PD, it has been studied in epidemiological studies of symptom disorders.[2-6] An attempt has also been made to arrive at estimates of the prevalence of obsessive-compulsive[3] and histrionic[7] PDs in such studies. One study has tried to estimate the frequency of borderline PD using the DIS.[8]

As to studies of the whole realm of PDs, **Table 1** presents an overview of the prevalence of these disorders. The studies show a wide variation of prevalences of all as well as of the specific PDs. The prevalence of any PD varies between 5.9 and 22.5, with a median prevalence of 11.1 and a pooled prevalence of 12.47.

The main limitation of the previous studies is that the samples are not representative of the population at large.

The samples are also small, varying from 133 to 799 individuals, with a median of 302 individuals. Two studies have simply applied clinical interviews,[9,15] thus obtaining the most deviant prevalence. Two studies have applied self-report questionnaires.[11,14] Only 6 of the studies have used structured interviews.[10,12,13,16-18]

The present study was an attempt to examine a relatively representative, large sample from the common population. We sought to establish the prevalence of the specific PDs and study the demographic correlates. From earlier studies, especially clinical samples, our hypotheses were that women are more likely to have a borderline, histrionic, or dependent PD, while men are more likely to have an antisocial, schizoid, or obsessive-compulsive PD. We expected more PDs among younger individuals, especially higher frequencies of antisocial and borderline PDs. As is the case with other psychiatric disorders, we believe that PDs are more common among those with lower socioeconomic status. We chose education as the best measure because low income is so easily a direct consequence of psychiatric disabilities. Our hypothesis was that there are more PDs among those living in the inner city and those living alone. In Norway, as in Scandinavia generally, many couples live together in stable relationships without being married. So we must apply the variable "living alone, living together with a partner," rather than "being married, not being married."

From Center of Research in Clinical Psychology, Department of Psychology (Dr Torgersen), and the Department of Psychiatry, Oslo University, Oslo, Norway (Dr Kringlen); and Diakonhjemmet Hospital, Oslo (Drs Kringlen and Cramer).

METHODS

SAMPLE

Our point of departure was the National Register of Oslo containing the names and addresses of all citizens in Oslo. The group aged 18 to 65 years encompassed 308237 individuals. From this population, a sample of 3590 individuals was drawn by chance according to a computer program in the national register. The **Figure** shows the reduction in the sample of 3590 individuals for various reasons.

Four of the individuals were deceased, 345 had moved from Oslo, and 548 were not found at the given address. It is possible that these individuals were not located either because they had provided an incorrect address to the authorities, or because they had moved to another residence inside or outside of Oslo without informing the authorities of their new address. As a result, one fourth of the sample could not be traced.

Of those who were contacted, 51 were either too medically ill, hospitalized in a medical hospital, or too physically disabled or sensory disabled to participate in an interview. Thirty-three persons, 5 of whom were hospitalized in a psychiatric ward, were too emotionally ill to be interviewed. A few others were taken in at a refugee reception center. Eighty-seven others were unable to be interviewed because they were unable to speak a Scandinavian language or English, French, German, or one of the other foreign languages used by the interviewers (including Asian languages). Altogether, close to 7% of those traced could not be interviewed for the above-named reasons.

Of those remaining, 18% refused to be interviewed, or they postponed the interview for too long. All in all, 2066 of a total sample of 3590 were interviewed. However, among these, it was not possible to establish PD diagnoses for 13 because of inadequate information. Consequently, the total sample amounted to 2053 subjects.

In contrast to most studies, we did not select households, but started with a fixed list of potential subjects. Consequently, we know something about those who did not participate. More women than men participated (62.7% and 52.7%, respectively). Those aged 40 years or older were included more frequently than younger individuals (60.8% compared with 55.0%). More subjects living in the town periphery were included than individuals in the center of the city (60.5% and 49.0%, respectively). The center of the city was defined as the 5 regions that meet in the heart of the city, thus constituting the downtown core of the city. All differences are statistically significant with a χ^2 test ($P<.001$). Combined, men aged 40 years or older living in the center of the city participated least often (42.5%), and women aged 40 or older living on the outskirts of the city participated most often (68.7%). The reason for the lower rate of participation in the different demographic groups was not refusal or illness, but incorrect address and relocation without a new correct address.

INSTRUMENTS

The Structured Interview for *DSM-III-R* (SIDP-R) Personality Disorders[19] was applied to assess PDs in the subjects. The interviewers, mainly experienced nurses, but also medical students and experienced interviewers, were trained by using live patient interviews and videos of patient interviews throughout a period of several weeks. All interviews were conducted face-to-face, mostly at home, but some took place at the psychiatric clinic. The SIDP-R consists of 160 questions grouped under 16 thematic sections, such as "relationships," "emotions," and "reactions to stressful situations." At the end of each section is a listing of relevant *DSM-III-R* criteria rated from 0 to 2, with brief descriptions guiding the ratings. Level 0 corresponds with "not present," and levels 1 and 2, with "present to a moderate degree" and "present to a severe degree," respectively. A rating of 1 or 2 indicates criterion fulfilled.

The instructions for the SIDP-R specify a "five-year rule" which means that behavior typical of the past 5 years was the basis for the ratings. If an individual's personality changed dramatically during the past few years, the personality that dominated most of the time during the last 5 years was considered typical. The PD diagnoses were made without reference to the exclusion criteria, eg, schizophrenia for schizotypal PD.

The reliability was assessed by means of a rater listening to 40 audiotaped interviews. The κ value for any PD was 0.84. The number of persons with a specific PD was too small for making any κ calculation. Instead, intraclass correlations for the scaled PDs were calculated. The intraclass correlation for schizoid PD was 0.78; 0.71 for paranoid; 0.92 for schizotypal; 0.78 for obsessive-compulsive; 0.78 for histrionic; 0.82 for dependent; 0.95 for antisocial; 0.83 for avoidant; 0.89 for borderline; 0.95 for passive-aggressive; 0.87 for sadistic; and 0.85 for self-defeating PD. The median intraclass correlation was thus 0.83.

STATISTICAL PROCEDURE

The prevalence rates were weighted, taking into account the slight, although statistically significant, differences between the interviewed sample and the population at large.

The relationship between PDs and demographic associations was calculated by means of a logistic regression analysis, in which the discrete demographic variables (sex, age group, educational level, living in the center/periphery of the city, living alone/with a partner, married/not married) were independent variables, and each of the PDs were dependent variables. In this way, odds ratios with confidence intervals were calculated taking into account possible correlations between the demographic variables. Multiple regression analysis was also performed. The independent demographic variables were treated as semicontinuous where possible, and the dependent variables were PD scales created by assigning number of criteria fulfilled for the respective PDs.

The α level is 5% if not otherwise stated.

RESULTS

The unweighted prevalence rate of any PD in the present sample was 13.1% in general, 14.6% among women, and 13.7% among men (**Table 2**). The weighted prevalence is slightly higher at 13.4% (Table 2). Generally, there was very little difference between the unweighted and weighted percentages because our sample was fairly representative of the population at large. The most prevalent PD was avoidant PD (5.0%), followed by paranoid

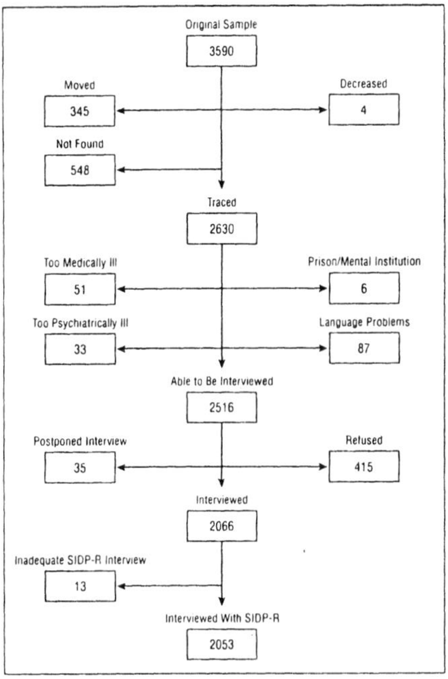

Reduction in the sample size from the original sample to the interviewed sample. SIDP-R indicates Structured Interview for DSM-III-R *Personality Disorders.*

(2.2% and 2.4%, unweighted and weighted, respectively), histrionic, and obsessive-compulsive (both 1.9%-2.0%). The rarest disorders were sadistic (0.2%), schizotypal (0.6%), antisocial (0.6%-0.7%), and borderline PDs (0.7%). The fearful cluster is very common (9.2%-9.4%), while the other 2 clusters are only one third as prevalent. Statistically, antisocial, passive aggressive, and obsessive-compulsive PDs are significantly more common among men. Also, schizoid PD is twice as common among men, but this is not statistically significant. Borderline, histrionic, dependent, and self-defeating PDs are twice as common among women as among men; however, the differences are not statistically significant.

The mean number of PD diagnoses among those with a PD was 1.48. Seventy-one percent of those with PD had only 1, 18.6% had 2, 5.2% had 3, 3.3% had 4, 1.1% had 5, 0.4% had 6, and 0.4% had 7 diagnoses.

Table 3 presents the increased risk of different PDs in various demographic groups. As logistic regression is applied, the possible correlations between the different demographic variables are taken into account.

It is observed that although the prevalence of PDs in general and the prevalence of the different clusters are the same in men and women, there is a sex difference in terms of the specific type of disorders. Men are more often schizoid and passive-aggressive, while women are more often histrionic and dependent.

Personality disorders are diagnosed most frequently in those older than 49 years, which is particularly so for the eccentric cluster.

Those with a high school education or less are more likely to have a PD, especially of the eccentric type. This is in particular the case for paranoid and avoidant PDs. Interestingly, obsessive-compulsive PD is more frequent in subjects with higher education (ie, a college/university education) compared with those with less education.

Living in the center of the city is related to having a PD. Again, this relationship is most often observed for the eccentric cluster, in particular paranoid and schizotypal PDs. Histrionic and passive-aggressive PDs are also relatively more prevalent in the center of the city.

Living without a partner is related to having a PD and to having eccentric and dramatic PDs. In addition, living without a partner is related to the paranoid, schizoid, antisocial, borderline, and self-defeating PDs.

Table 4 presents the statistically significant standardized β weight's from multiple regression analyses in which PD scales are applied by adding the criteria. Age and education are treated as continuous variables. The Enter method was applied. All results from the logistic regression analyses are confirmed, with the exception of the relationship between PDs generally and younger age, more individuals with passive-aggressive PD in the city center, and more women with histrionic PD.

In addition, a number of other relationships appeared in the multiple regression analysis. Antisocial, sadistic, narcissistic, obsessive-compulsive, eccentric, and dramatic traits were related to being male, while self-defeating traits were related to being female. Antisocial, sadistic, borderline, passive-aggressive, and dramatic traits are correlated with younger age. Schizoid, schizotypal, antisocial, sadistic, borderline, dependent, self-defeating, dramatic, and fearful traits are related to less education. Schizoid, borderline, narcissistic, obsessive-compulsive, self-defeating, and dramatic traits are more often observed in the center of the city. Schizoid and obsessive-compulsive traits are more often found among those not married. Schizotypal, histrionic, narcissistic, dependent, passive-aggressive, and fearful traits are more often found among those living without a partner.

COMMENT

Having more than 1 PD diagnosis is common. Our mean number of 1.48 diagnoses among those with a PD is slightly lower than what is observed in clinical populations.[20,21]

The observed prevalence of any PDs in the present study is almost exactly the same as the prevalence in the pooled data from earlier studies (Table 1). The prevalence of avoidant, paranoid, and schizoid PDs is considerably higher in this study compared with previous ones (Table 1), whereas the rate of borderline PD is relatively low. Only the Swedish[14] and German[13] studies show a somewhat similar pattern, with a high prevalence of paranoid and avoidant PDs. It is not clear whether these observations reflect an improved sampling by our study, or national character traits that may be shared with other Scandinavians and Northern Europeans. Studies of patient populations in Norway have demonstrated a high

Table 1. The Prevalence (Percentage) of Personality Disorders in 10 Community Studies*

	Study, y										Totals	
	Drake et al,[8] 1998	Zimmerman et al,[10] 1989	Reich et al,[11] 1989	Black et al,[12] 1992	Maier et al,[13] 1992	Bodlund et al,[14] 1993	Samuels et al,[15] 1994	Moldin et al,[16] 1994	Klein et al,[17] 1995	Lenzenweger et al,[18] 1997	Median	Pooled
No. of participants	369	799	235	247	452	133	762	303	258	229	3786	3786
Location	Boston, Mass	Iowa	Iowa	Iowa	Mainz, Germany	Umeå, Sweden	Baltimore, Md	New York, NY	New York	New York		
Instrument	Clin Int *DSM-III*	SIDP *DSM-III*	PDQ *DSM-III*	SIPO *DSM-III*	SCID-II *DSM-III-R*	SCID-screen *DSM-III-R*	Clin Int *DSM-III*	PDE *DSM-III-R*	PDE *DSM-III-R*	PDE *DSM-III-R*		
Personality disorder												
Paranoid	1.1	0.9	0.9	1.6	1.8	4.5	0.0	0.0	1.7	0.4	0.90 (0.0-4.5)	0.95
Schizoid	4.1	0.9	0.9	0.0	0.4	0.8	0.0	0.0	0.9	0.4	0.60 (0.0-4.1)	0.79
Schizotypal	2.4	2.9	5.1	3.2	0.7	0.0	0.1	0.7	0.0	0.0	0.70 (0.0-5.6)	1.53
Antisocial	0.8	3.3	0.4	0.8	0.2	0.8	1.5	2.6	2.2	0.8	0.80 (0.2-3.3)	1.61
Borderline	0.5	1.6	0.4	3.2	1.1	3.8	0.4	2.0	1.7	0.0	1.35 (0.0-4.6)	1.24
Histrionic	3.8	3.0	2.1	3.2	1.3	4.5	2.1	0.3	1.7	1.9	2.10 (0.3-4.5)	2.72
Narcissistic	3.5	0.0	0.4	0.0	0.0	5.3	0.0	0.0	3.9	1.2	0.20 (0.0-5.3)	0.87
Avoidant	1.6	1.3	0.0	2.0	1.1	3.8	0.0	0.7	5.2	0.4	1.20 (0.0-5.2)	1.22
Dependent	10.3	1.8	5.1	1.6	1.5	0.8	0.1	1.0	0.4	0.4	1.25 (0.4-10.3)	2.22
Obsessive-compulsive	0.5	2.0	6.4	9.3	2.2	4.5	1.7	0.7	2.6	0.0	2.10 (0.0-9.3)	2.32
Passive-aggressive	7.8	3.3	0.0	10.5	1.8	0.0	0.1	1.7	1.7	0.0	1.70 (0.0-10.5)	2.59
Self-defeating	...	...	...	...	...	0.8	...	...	...	0.0	0.4 (0.0-0.8)	0.26
Sadistic	...	... ...	...	...	...	...	...	...	...	0.0	0.0	0.0
Any PD	22.5	17.9	11.1	22.5	10.0	18.8	5.9	7.3	14.8	6.7	14.50 (5.9-22.5)	13.50

Clin Int indicates the clinical interview for DSM-III, SIDP, *Structured Interview for* DSM-III *Personality Disorder (PD);* PDQ, *Personality Diagnostic Questionnaire;* SCID-II, *Structured Clinical Interview for* DSM-III *Axis II Personality Disorders;* PDE, *Personality Disorder Examination for* DSM-III-R; *ellipses, not applicable.*

Table 2. Total Unweighted and Weighted Prevalences of Personality Disorders (Percentages) for Men and Women

	Women (n = 1142)		Men (n = 911)		Unweighted Total (n = 2053)		
Personality Disorder	No.	% ± SE	No.	% ± SE	No.	% ± SE	Weighted, %
Paranoid	25	2.2 ± 0.4	21	2.3 ± 0.5	46	2.2 ± 0.3	2.4
Schizoid	12	1.1 ± 0.3	20	2.2 ± 0.5	32	1.6 ± 0.2	1.7
Schizotypal	7	0.6 ± 0.2	5	0.5 ± 0.2	12	0.6 ± 0.2	0.6
Eccentric	40	3.5 ± 0.5	40	4.4 ± 0.7	80	3.9 ± 0.4	4.1
Antisocial	0	0.0	12	1.3 ± 0.4†	12	0.6 ± 0.2	0.7
Sadistic*	3	0.3 ± 0.2	1	0.1 ± 0.1	4	0.2 ± 0.1	0.2
Borderline	10	0.9 ± 0.3	4	0.4 ± 0.2	14	0.7 ± 0.2	0.7
Histrionic	28	2.5 ± 0.5	11	1.2 ± 0.4	39	1.9 ± 0.3	2.0
Narcissistic	9	0.8 ± 0.3	8	0.9 ± 0.3	17	0.8 ± 0.2	0.8
Dramatic	36	3.2 ± 0.5	26	2.9 ± 0.6	62	3.0 ± 0.4	3.1
Avoidant	57	5.0 ± 0.6	45	4.9 ± 0.7	102	5.0 ± 0.5	5.0
Dependent	23	2.0 ± 0.4	8	0.9 ± 0.3	31	1.5 ± 0.3	1.5
Obsessive-compulsive	15	1.3 ± 0.3	24	2.6 ± 0.5‡	39	1.9 ± 0.3	2.0
Passive-aggressive	10	0.9 ± 0.3	22	2.2 ± 0.5§	32	1.6 ± 0.3	1.7
Self-defeating*	13	1.1 ± 0.3	4	0.4 ± 0.2	17	0.8 ± 0.2	0.8
Fearful	101	8.8 ± 0.8	88	9.7 ± 1.0	189	9.2 ± 0.6	9.4
Any personality disorder	144	12.6 ± 1.0	125	13.7 ± 1.1	269	13.1 ± 0.7	13.4

Diagnostic categories needing further study were subsumed under the cluster they correlate most strongly with.
†*Statistically significant sex differences <.05 with χ^2 test.*
‡*Statistically significant sex differences <.01 with χ^2 test.*
§*Statistically significant sex differences <.001 with χ^2 test.*

Table 3. Demographic Associations With Personality Disorders*

Disorder	Sex: Male	Sex: Female	Age, y: 18-29	Age, y: 30-39	Age, y: 40-49	Age, y: 50-65
Paranoid (n = 46)	1.00 ...	0.84 (0.46-1.54)	0.84 (0.61-1.15)	0.79 (0.35-1.80)	0.89 (0.59-1.34)	1.00 ...
Schizoid (n = 32)	1.00† ...	0.40† (0.19-0.85)	0.45† (0.29-0.68)	0.63 (0.39-1.01)	0.27† 0.09-0.86)	1.00 ...
Schizotypal (n = 12)	1.00 ...	1.09 (0.33-3.58)	0.43† (0.20-0.94)	0.80 (0.38-1.68)	0.47 (0.09-2.51)	1.00 ...
Sadistic (n = 4)	1.00 ...	0.27 (0.03-2.67)	1.35 (0.50-3.70)	0.95 (0.22-4.10)	0.00 ...	1.00 ...
Antisocial (n = 12)	1.00 ...	0.00 ...	0.97 (0.49-1.94)	1.29 (0.51-3.30)	0.00 ...	1.00 ...
Borderline (n = 14)	1.00 ...	2.00 (0.62-6.44)	0.94 (0.48-1.84)	1.77 (0.76-4.12)	0.47 (0.04-5.31)	1.00 ...
Histrionic (n = 39)	1.00 ...	2.10† (1.03-4.27)	1.06 (0.74-1.53)	1.35 (0.84-2.18)	0.76 (0.23-2.43)	1.00 ...
Narcissistic (n = 17)	1.00 ...	0.52 (0.19-1.39)	0.59 (0.27-1.28)	1.40 (0.73-2.66)	1.17 (0.29-4.78)	1.00 ...
Avoidant (n = 102)	1.00 ...	0.99 (0.66-1.48)	0.84 (0.68-1.04)	0.81 (0.60-1.09)	0.81 (0.46-1.45)	1.00 ...
Dependent (n = 31)	1.00 ...	2.30† (1.02-5.20)	0.92 (0.63-1.36)	0.97 (0.56-1.68)	0.59 (0.17-2.08)	1.00 ...
Obsessive-compulsive (n = 39)	1.00 ...	0.57 (0.29-1.10)	0.64† (0.45-0.92)	0.54 (0.33-0.87)†	0.54 (0.23-1.26)	1.00 ...
Passive-aggressive (n = 32)	1.00 ...	0.30† (0.14-0.67)	0.93 (0.65-1.35)	0.93 (0.57-1.53)	0.37 (0.10-1.38)	1.00 ...
Self-defeating (n = 17)	1.00 ...	2.15 (0.69-6.73)	1.14 (0.63-2.05)	1.43 (0.66-3.10)	1.77 (0.41-7.66)	1.00 ...
Eccentric (n = 80)	1.00 ...	0.70 (0.44-1.11)	0.64† (0.50-0.83)	0.79 (0.58-1.08)	0.43† (0.22-0.88)	1.00 ...
Dramatic (n = 62)	1.00 ...	1.01 (0.63-1.64)	1.07 (0.82-1.40)	1.35 (0.95-1.94)	0.72 0.30-1.72)	1.00 ...
Fearful (n = 189)	1.00 ...	0.88† (0.65-1.20)	0.83 (0.70-0.98)	0.81 (0.65-1.01)	0.72 (0.46-1.12)	1.00 ...
Any disorder	1.00 ...	0.86† (0.66-1.12)	0.85 (0.74-0.98)	0.84 (0.69-1.01)	0.60† (0.40-0.89)	1.00 ...

*All the values are expressed as odds ratio (95% confidence interval). Ellipses indicate not applicable.
†$P<.05$.

prevalence of avoidant and paranoid PDs when compared with, for instance, American studies.[22,23]

According to a Norwegian twin study,[24] avoidant, paranoid, and schizoid PDs seem to be less genetically influenced than other PDs. It may be that some cultural factors are responsible for the development of these disorders in Norway, with the consequence that they seem to be both more prevalent and more environmentally determined.

Our finding that schizoid, antisocial, narcissistic and obsessive-compulsive PDs and/or traits are more often observed among men, and histrionic, avoidant, and dependent features are more often found among women has also been reported in earlier studies.[10,25] As in the present study, these researchers did not find that borderline PD was related to the sex of the subject. Most clinical studies do. In fact, we found that borderline PD was twice as frequent among women; however, the low number of subjects with borderline PD made it very difficult to reach statistical significance. Furthermore, it is possible that being female and having borderline features interact to make the person more likely to seek treatment.

Earlier studies[10,25] have also observed that those with antisocial, borderline, and passive-aggressive traits were younger, and those with schizoid features were older. No other study has found that schizotypal, avoidant, and obsessive-compulsive PDs and traits are more frequent in older age.

No other epidemiological study has investigated whether those with PDs or PD traits more often live alone. In Norway, this is significant because many couples live together in stable relationships without being married; however, if one considers marital status (single, married, divorced, separated, widowed), one may make a comparison with previous studies. Earlier studies have shown that those with borderline PD were more often single, those with antisocial PD were more often divorced, those with passive-aggressive PD were more often not married, and those with a PD were more often separated at the time of the interview.[10] The present study showed that those with these PDs and traits more often lived without a partner.

Educational level has seldom been related to the prevalence of PDs. Reich et al[11] found no demographic connection to PDs in general. Nor did Nestad et al[7] find any demographic correlations to histrionic PD.

No other study of PDs has investigated the difference between those living in the city center as opposed

Education		Area		Married		Cohabitant	
≤High School	>High School	City Center	Periphery	Yes	No	Yes	No
2.39†	1.00	3.81†	1.00	1.00	0.52	1.00	2.10†
(1.28-4.47)	...	(2.07-7.00)	...	...	(0.23-1.19)	...	(1.06-4.13)
1.75	1.00	1.72	1.00	1.00	2.23	1.00	3.25†
(0.83-3.66)	...	(0.80-3.69)	...	...	(0.86-5.77)	...	(1.38-7.64)
3.36	1.00	3.44†	1.00	1.00	1.51	1.00	3.26
(0.95-11.89)	...	(1.05-11.28)	...	...	(0.36-6.40)	...	(0.85-12.57)
0.45	1.00	0.98	1.00	1.00	0.54	1.00	2.07
(0.04-4.67)	...	(0.10-9.65)	...	...	(0.03-9.66)	...	(0.18-23.69)
1.40	1.00	0.52	1.00	1.00	1.15	1.00	8.39†
(0.42-4.69)	...	(0.11-2.45)	...	...	(0.18-7.31)	...	(1.40-50.25)
1.18	1.00	0.46	1.00	1.00	1.16	1.00	3.48†
(0.39-3.58)	...	(0.10-2.10)	...	...	(0.31-4.37)	...	(1.01-11.92)
1.07	1.00	3.33†	1.00	1.00	0.89	1.00	1.23
(0.54-2.11)	...	(1.74-6.41)	...	...	(0.39-2.00)	...	(0.59-2.56)
1.83	1.00	1.98	1.00	1.00	0.52	1.00	2.13
(0.68-4.92)	...	(0.71-5.54)	...	...	(0.19-13.9)	...	(0.72-6.29)
1.61†	1.00	1.45	1.00	1.00	1.34	1.00	1.26
(1.06-2.44)	...	(0.92-2.28)	...	...	(0.77-2.30)	...	(0.79-2.00)
1.72	1.00	1.79	1.00	1.00	1.56	1.00	1.84
(0.81-3.63)	...	(0.83-3.83)	...	...	(0.59-4.10)	...	(0.81-4.18)
0.39†	1.00	1.35	1.00	1.00	1.99	1.00	0.93
(0.18-0.88)	...	(0.65-2.78)	...	...	(0.84-4.75)	...	(0.43-2.02)
1.12	1.00	2.28†	1.00	1.00	0.97	1.00	1.73
(0.53-2.36)	...	(1.10-4.72)	...	...	(0.37-2.59)	...	(0.74-4.01)
1.50	1.00	1.03	1.00	1.00	0.33	1.00	8.57†
(0.55-4.12)	...	(0.33-3.27)	...	...	(0.09-1.22)	...	(2.58-28.43)
2.26†	1.00	2.60†	1.00	1.00	1.06	1.00	2.40†
(1.40-3.66)	...	(1.84-4.76)	...	...	(0.57-1.96)	...	(1.41-4.07)
1.09	1.00	1.66	1.00	1.00	0.84	1.00	2.13†
(0.66-1.81)	...	(0.99-2.77)	...	...	(0.45-1.58)	...	(1.23-3.70)
1.27	1.00	1.54†	1.00	1.00	1.28	1.00	1.37
(0.93-1.74)	...	(1.09-2.16)	...	...	(0.85-1.93)	...	(0.97-1.94)
1.38†	1.00	1.81†	1.00	1.00	1.07	1.00	1.51†
(1.06-1.81)	...	(1.36-2.42)	...	...	(0.75-1.53)	...	(1.12-2.05)

Table 4. Statistically Significant Demographic Associations to Personality Disorders Based on Multiple Regression Analysis, Standardized β Weights, and Multiple Regression Correlations

Personality Disorder	β Weights*						
	Sex	Age	Education	City Center	Married	Cohabitant	*R*
Paranoid	...	...	−.07	.08	...	−.07	.13
Schizoid	−.11	.17	−.07	.09	−.08	−.09	.23
Schizotypal	...	.09	−.10	.10	...	−.10	.19
Antisocial	−.18	−.08	−.10	...	...	−.05	.24
Sadistic	−.11	−.10	−.05	...	...	...	.15
Borderline	...	−.09	−.09	.05	...	−.12	.21
Histrionic	...	...	...	.10	...	−.05	.14
Narcissistic	−.06	...	...	.09	...	−.07	.13
Avoidant	...	.07	−.09	...	...	...	.12
Dependent	.11	...	−.07	...	...	−.07	.16
Obsessive-compulsive	−.10	.00	.06	.07	−.06	...	.16
Passive-aggressive	−.12	−.11	...	...	...	−.06	.19
Self-defeating	.10	...	−.05	.06	...	−.18	.22
Eccentric	−.05	.12	−.10	.12	...	−.11	.22
Dramatic	−.06	−.08	−.06	.10	...	−.10	.21
Fearful	...	...	−.05	.05	...	−.09	.13
Total criteria	...	...	−.08	.09	...	−.11	.19

Ellipses indicate not applicable.

to living on the outskirts. Lewis and Booth,[26] however, found that greater London had a higher prevalence of psychiatric morbidity than average. The same authors[27] found the highest General Health Questionnaire scores in those living in built-up urban areas. A somewhat lower score was observed among those in urban areas with "access to gardens or open spaces." The lowest score was found among those living in country areas. Sex, age, marital status, and social class were all controlled for in the study.

The fact that more psychiatric disorders are found in the center of cities has been known since the 1930s.[28] The reason for this is not easy to determine. Two hypotheses have been popular. The drift hypothesis states that those with emotional problems drift to the center, maybe to live anonymously; and the stress hypothesis maintains that there is more emotional hardship in the city center.[29] Which hypothesis is more correct has not yet been decided. Our results cannot be explained by socioeconomic status. The city center has both poorer and more prosperous areas, as has the periphery. Furthermore, we controlled for demographic variables. The population density is higher in the city center. There are 6292 people per square kilometer living in the center of the city, compared with 2912 people per square kilometer living in the periphery. In fact, 5 of 6 of the most densely populated areas in the city (which consists of a total of 25 areas) lie in the center. Anomie as a consequence of population density has been a popular explanation.[29]

Our study has several limitations. Although our sample is more representative than earlier studies of PDs, we did not succeed in obtaining exactly the same proportion of the population in all demographic strata. However, we controlled for the sampling bias and obtained slightly higher prevalence rates.

In conclusion, PDs are relatively prevalent. Nearly 1 in 7 individuals in the Oslo catchment area was identified as meeting criteria for such a disorder. Age, education, area of living, and life situation seem to correlate with PDs and traits.

Whether the demographic associations are causes or consequences, and to what extent there are cohort effects taking place, can only be answered by future, prospective longitudinal studies of large community samples.

Accepted for publication January 23, 2000.

This study was supported by a grant from the Norwegian Council for Mental Health, Oslo, and the Foundation for Health and Rehabilitation, Oslo.

Corresponding author and reprints: Svenn Torgersen, PhD, Department of Psychology, Oslo University, PO Box 1039, Blindern, N-0315 Oslo, Norway (e-mail: Svenn.Torgersen@psykologi.uio.no).

REFERENCES

1. Robins LN, Helzer JE, Croughan J, Ratcliff KS. National Institute of Mental Health Diagnostic Interview Schedule: its history, characteristics, and validity. *Arch Gen Psychiatry.* 1982;39:381-389.
2. Robins LN, Helzer JE, Weissman MM, Orvaschel H, Gruenberg E, Burke JD, Regier DA. Lifetime prevalence of specific psychiatric disorders in three sites. *Arch Gen Psychiatry.* 1984;41:949-958.
3. Nestadt G, Romanoski AJ, Samuels JF, Folstein MF, McHugh PR. The relationship between personality and DSM-III Axis I disorder in the population: results from an epidemiological survey. *Am J Psychiatry.* 1992;149:1228-1233.
4. Wells JE, Bushnell JA, Hornblow AR, Joyce PR, Oakley-Browne MA. Christchurch psychiatric epidemiology study, I: methodology and lifetime prevalence for specific psychiatric disorders. *Aust N Z J Psychiatry.* 1989;23:315-326.
5. Oakley-Browne MA, Joyce PR, Wells JE, Bushnell JA, Hornblow AR. Christchurch psychiatric epidemiology study, II: six month and other period prevalences of specific psychiatric disorders. *Aust N Z J Psychiatry.* 1989;23:327-340.
6. Hwu H-G, Yih E-K, Chang L-Y. Prevalence of psychiatric disorders in Taiwan defined by the Chinese Diagnostic Interview Schedule. *Acta Psychiatr Scand.* 1989;79:136-147.
7. Nestadt G, Romanoski AJ, Chagal R, Merchant A, Folstein MF, Gruenberg EM, McHugh PR. An epidemiological study of histrionic personality disorder. *Psychol Med.* 1990;20:413-422.
8. Swartz M, Blazer D, George L, Winfield I. Estimating the prevalence of borderline personality disorder in the community. *J Personal Disord.* 1990;4:257-272.
9. Drake RE, Adler DA, Vaillant GE. Antecedents of personality disorders in a community sample of men. *J Personal Disord.* 1988;2:60-68.
10. Zimmerman M, Coryell W. *DSM-III* personality disorder diagnoses in a nonpatient sample: demographic correlates and comorbidity. *Arch Gen Psychiatry.* 1989;46:682-689.
11. Reich J, Yates W, Nduaguba M. Prevalences of *DSM-III* personality disorders in the community. *Soc Psychiatry Psychiatr Epidemiol.* 1989;24:12-16.
12. Black DW, Noyes Jr R, Pfohl B, Goldstein RB, Blum N. Personality disorder in obsessive-compulsive volunteers, well comparison subjects, and their first-degree relatives. *Am J Psychiatry.* 1993;150:1226-1232.
13. Maier W, Lichtermann D, Klingler T, Heun R, Hallmayer J. Prevalences of personality disorders (*DSM-III-R*) in the community. *J Personal Disord.* 1992;6:187-196.
14. Bodlund O, Ekselius L, Lindström E. Personality traits and disorders among psychiatric outpatients and normal subjects on the basis of the SCID screen questionnaire. *Nord Psykiatr Tidsskr.* 1993;47:425-433.
15. Samuels JF, Nestadt G, Romanoski AJ, Folstein MF, McHugh PR. DSM-III personality disorders in the community. *Am J Psychiatry.* 1994;151:1055-1062.
16. Moldin SO, Rice JP, Erlenmeyer-Kimling L, Squires-Wheeler E. Latent structure of *DSM-III-R* Axis II psychopathology in a normal sample. *J Abnorm Psychol.* 1994;103:259-266.
17. Klein DN, Riso LP, Donaldson SK, Schwartz JE, Anderson RL, Ouimette PC, Lizardi H, Aronson TA. Family study of early-onset dysthymia: mood and personality disorders in relatives of outpatients with dysthymia and episodic major depressive and normal controls. *Arch Gen Psychiatry.* 1995;52:487-496.
18. Lenzenweger MF, Loranger AW, Korfine L, Neff C. Detecting personality disorders in a nonclinical population: application of a 2-stage procedure for case identification. *Arch Gen Psychiatry.* 1997; 54:345-351.
19. Pfohl B, Blum N, Zimmerman M, Stangl D. *Structured Interview for DSM-III-R Personality Disorders (SIDP-R).* Iowa City, Iowa: Department of Psychiatry, University of Iowa; 1989.
20. Stuart S, Pfohl B, Battaglia M, Bellodi L, Grove W, Cadoret R. The cooccurences of *DSM-III-R* personality disorders. *J Personal Disord.* 1998;12:302-315.
21. Alnæs R, Torgersen S. *DSM-III* symptom disorders (Axis I) and personality disorders (Axis II) in an outpatient population. *Acta Psychiatr Scand.* 1988;78:348-355.
22. Mehlum L, Friis S, Irion T, Karterud S, Vaglum P, Vaglum S. Personality disorders 2-5 years after treatment: a prospective follow-up study. *Acta Psychiatr Scand.* 1991;84:72-77.
23. Hoffarth A, Martinsen EW. The effect of personality disorders and anxious depressive comorbidity on outcome in patients with a unipolar depression and with panic disorder and agoraphobia. *J Personal Disord.* 1993;7:304-311.
24. Torgersen S, Lygren S, Øien PA, Skre I, Onstad S, Edvardsen J, Tambs K, Kringlen E. A twin study of personality disorders. *Compr Psychiatry.* 2000;41:416-425.
25. Zimmerman M, Coryell NH. Diagnosing personality disorders in the community: a comparison of self-report and interview measures. *Arch Gen Psychiatry.* 1990;47:527-531.
26. Lewis G, Booth M. Regional differences in mental health in Great Britain. *J Epidemiol Community Health.* 1992;46:608-611.
27. Lewis G, Booth M. Are cities bad for your mental health? *Psychol Med.* 1994;24:913-915.
28. Faris REL, Dunham HW. *Mental Disorders in Urban Areas: An Ecological Study of Schizophrenia and Other Psychoses.* Chicago, Ill: Chicago University Press; 1939.
29. Opler MK. *Culture and Social Psychiatry.* New York, NY: Atherton Press; 1967.

Articles

Sources of Human Psychological Differences: The Minnesota Study of Twins Reared Apart

THOMAS J. BOUCHARD, JR.,* DAVID T. LYKKEN, MATTHEW MCGUE, NANCY L. SEGAL, AUKE TELLEGEN

Since 1979, a continuing study of monozygotic and dizygotic twins, separated in infancy and reared apart, has subjected more than 100 sets of reared-apart twins or triplets to a week of intensive psychological and physiological assessment. Like the prior, smaller studies of monozygotic twins reared apart, about 70% of the variance in IQ was found to be associated with genetic variation. On multiple measures of personality and temperament, occupational and leisure-time interests, and social attitudes, monozygotic twins reared apart are about as similar as are monozygotic twins reared together. These findings extend and support those from numerous other twin, family, and adoption studies. It is a plausible hypothesis that genetic differences affect psychological differences largely indirectly, by influencing the effective environment of the developing child. This evidence for the strong heritability of most psychological traits, sensibly construed, does not detract from the value or importance of parenting, education, and other propaedeutic interventions.

MONOZYGOTIC AND DIZYGOTIC TWINS WHO WERE SEPArated early in life and reared apart (MZA and DZA twin pairs) are a fascinating experiment of nature. They also provide the simplest and most powerful method for disentangling the influence of environmental and genetic factors on human characteristics. The rarity of twins reared apart explains why only three previous studies of modest scope are available in the literature (*1–4*).

More than 100 sets of reared-apart twins or triplets from across the United States and the United Kingdom have participated in the Minnesota Study of Twins Reared Apart since it began in 1979. Participants have also come from Australia, Canada, China, New Zealand, Sweden, and West Germany. The study of these reared-apart twins has led to two general and seemingly remarkable conclusions concerning the sources of the psychological differences—behavioral variation—between people: (i) genetic factors exert a pronounced and pervasive influence on behavioral variability, and (ii) the effect of being reared in the same home is negligible for many psychological traits. These conclusions will not come as revelations to the many behavioral geneticists who have observed similar results and drawn similar conclusions (*5*). This study and the broader behavioral genetic literature, nevertheless, challenge prevailing psychological theories on the origins of individual differences in ability, personality, interests, and social attitudes (*6*). Here we summarize our procedures and review our results and interpretations of them.

Participants complete approximately 50 hours of medical and psychological assessment. Two or more test instruments are used in each major domain of psychological assessment to ensure adequate coverage (for example, four personality trait inventories, three occupational interest inventories, and two mental ability batteries). A systematic assessment of aspects of the twins' rearing environments that might have had causal roles in their psychological development is also carried out. Separate examiners administer the IQ test, life history interview, psychiatric interview, and sexual life history interview. A comprehensive mental ability battery is administered as a group test. The twins also complete questionnaires independently, under the constant supervision of a staff member.

Reared-apart twins have been ascertained in several ways, such as: (i) friends, relatives, or the reunited twins themselves, having learned of the project, contact the Minnesota Center for Twin and Adoption Research (MICTAR); (ii) members of the adoption movement, social workers, and other professionals who encounter reared-apart twins serve as intermediaries; (iii) twins who are, or become aware of, a separated co-twin solicit assistance from the MICTAR staff in locating this individual. Selection on the basis of similarity is minimized by vigorously recruiting all reared-apart twins, regardless of known or presumed zygosity and similarity. We have been unable to recruit to the study six pairs of twins reared apart whom we believe to be monozygotic.

Zygosity diagnosis is based on extensive serological comparisons, fingerprint ridge count, and anthropometric measurements. The probability of misclassification is less than 0.001 (*7*). Where appropriate, our data are corrected for age and sex effects (*8*). Due to space limitations and the smaller size of the DZA sample (30 sets), in this article we focus on the MZA data (56 sets). The results reported here are, for the most part, based on previously reported findings, so that the sample sizes do not include the most recently assessed pairs and vary depending on when in the course of this ongoing study the analyses were conducted.

As shown in Table 1, the sample consists of adult twins, separated very early in life, reared apart during their formative years, and reunited as adults. Circumstances of adoption were sometimes

T. J. Bouchard, Jr., and M. McGue are in the Department of Psychology and the Institute of Human Genetics, University of Minnesota, Minneapolis, MN 55455. D. T. Lykken, N. L. Segal, and A. Tellegen are in the Department of Psychology, University of Minnesota, Minneapolis, MN 55455.

*To whom reprint requests should be addressed.

Table 1. Means, standard deviations (SD), and ranges for age, measures of contact, IQ, and parental educational level for MZA twins. Two MZA male triplet sets were each entered as one set. Data are based on the first 56 sets of MZAs recruited, although the sample size varies slightly from measure to measure, as data are not always available or relevant (for example, rearing mother died very early in twins' life or twins could not be tested with an English language WAIS).

Statistic	Age (years)	Time together prior to separation (months)	Time apart to first reunion (years)	Total contact time (weeks)	IQ (WAIS)	Rearing father's education level (years)	Rearing mother's education level (years)
Mean	41.0	5.1	30.0	112.5	108.1	10.7	10.3
SD	12.0	8.5	14.3	230.7	10.8	4.5	3.7
Range	19.0–68.0	0–48.7	0.5–64.7	1–1233	79–133	0–20	0–19

informal, and the adoptive parents, in comparison to parents who volunteer to participate in most adoption studies, have a lower level of education (mean equals 2 years of high school), and are quite heterogeneous in educational attainment and socioeconomic status (SES). Because our sample includes no subjects with IQs in the retardate range (≤70), the mean IQ is higher and the standard deviation lower than for the general population.

Components of Phenotypic Variance

If genetic and environmental factors are uncorrelated and combine additively (points we return to later), the total observed variance, V_t, of a trait within a population can be expressed as

$$V_t = V_g + V_e + V_m \qquad (1)$$

where V_g is variance due to genetic differences among people, V_e is variance due to environmental or experiential factors, and V_m is variance due to measurement error and unsystematic temporal fluctuations. For measures of psychological traits, V_m ranges from approximately 10% (of V_t) for the most reliably measured and stable of traits (for example, IQ) to as high as 50 to 60% for traits that are less reliable or that show considerable secular instability (for example, some social attitudes). The environmental component, V_e, can be divided into variance due to experiences that are shared, V_{es}, and experiences that are unshared, V_{eu}. Shared events may be experienced differently by two siblings (for example, a roller coaster ride or a family vacation), in which case they contribute to the V_{eu} component. If the total variance, V_t, is set at unity, the correlation between MZ twins, R_{mz}, equals $V_g + V_{es}$. The heritability of a trait equals V_g; the heritability of the stable component of a trait (for example, the mean value around which one's aggressiveness varies) equals $V_g/(V_t - V_m)$. V_t and V_m can be estimated from studies of singletons, but V_g is more elusive: for monozygotic twins reared together (MZT), some of the within-pair correlation might be due to effects of shared experience, V_{es}. The power of the MZA design is that for twins reared apart from early infancy and randomly placed for adoption, V_{es} is negligible, so that V_g can be directly estimated from the MZA correlation.

Similarity in the IQ of MZA Twins

The study of IQ is paradigmatic of human behavior genetic research. There are more than 100 relevant twin, adoptee, and family studies of IQ, and IQ has been at the center of the nature-nurture debate (*9*). The analysis of IQ is also paradigmatic of the approach taken by this study. It illustrates our use of replicated measures, evaluation of rearing environmental effects, and analysis of environmental similarity. We obtain three independent measures of IQ: (i) the Wechsler Adult Intelligence Scale (WAIS); (ii) a Raven, Mill-Hill composite; and (iii) the first principal component (PC) of two multiple abilities batteries.

The WAIS consists of a set of six verbal and five performance subtests that are individually administered, requiring about 1.5 hours, and that yield an age-corrected estimate of IQ (*10*). To avoid examiner bias, we administer the WAIS simultaneously to the twins in different rooms by professional psychometrists. The Raven Progressive Matrices (Standard Set) is a widely used nonverbal measure of problem-solving ability often paired with the Mill-Hill Vocabulary Test, a multiple-choice word knowledge test (*11*). In this study, the Raven and Mill-Hill are both administered and scored by computer. The two age- and sex-corrected scores are transformed to have a mean equal to 50 and a standard deviation of 10. The sum of these transformed scores (which intercorrelate about 0.57) provides a separate estimate of IQ. The first major ability battery included in our assessment is an expanded version of the battery used in the Hawaii Family Study of Cognition (*12*). The second major ability battery is the Comprehensive Ability Battery (*13*). Detailed results from analysis of both tests are reported elsewhere (*14*).

In each of the three prior studies of MZA twins, two independent estimates of intelligence were obtained. The sample sizes and intraclass correlations for all four studies are compared in Table 2. The table illustrates the remarkable consistency of the MZA correlations on IQ across measurement instrument, country of origin, and time period. These correlations vary within a narrow range (0.64 to 0.74) and suggest, under the assumption of no environmental similarity, that genetic factors account for approximately 70% of the variance in IQ.

This estimate of the broad heritability of IQ is higher than the recent estimates (0.47 to 0.58) based on a review of the literature that includes all kinship pairings (*9*, *15*). Virtually the entire literature on IQ similarity in twins and siblings is limited, however, to studies of children and adolescents. It has been demonstrated (*16*) that heritability of cognitive ability increases with age. A heritability estimate of approximately 70% from these four studies of mainly middle-aged adults is not inconsistent with the previous literature.

Do Environmental Similarities in Rearing Environments Explain MZA IQ Similarity?

Such marked behavioral similarities between reared-apart MZ twins raise the question of correlated placement: were the twins' adoptive homes selected to be similar in trait-relevant features which, in turn, induced psychological similarity? If so, given that the total variance equals 1.0, then V_{es} will equal at least $R_{ff} \times r^2_{fi}$, where R_{ff} is the within-pair correlation for a given feature, *f*, of the adoptive homes (the placement coefficient), and r_{fi} is the product-

Table 2. Sample sizes and intraclass correlations (± standard error) for all IQ measures and weighted averages for four studies of MZA twins.

Study and test used (primary/secondary/tertiary)	*n* for each test	Primary test	Secondary test	Tertiary test	Mean of multiple test (*43*)
Newman *et al.* (*1*) (Stanford-Binet/Otis)	19/19	0.68 ± 0.12	0.74 ± 0.10		0.71
Juel-Nielsen (*1*) (Wechsler-Bellevue/Raven)	12/12	0.64 ± 0.17	0.73 ± 0.13		0.69
Shields (*1*) (Mill-Hill/Dominoes)	38/37	0.74 ± 0.07	0.76 ± 0.07		0.75
Bouchard *et al.* (*42*) (WAIS/Raven, Mill-Hill/ first principal component)	48/42/43	0.69 ± 0.07	0.78 ± 0.07	0.78 ± 0.07	0.75

moment correlation between the feature and the trait in question, *t*.

A checklist of available household facilities (for example, power tools, sailboat, telescope, unabridged dictionary, and original artwork) provides an index of the cultural and intellectual resources in the adoptive home (*17*). Each twin completes the Moos Family Environment Scale (FES), a widely used instrument with scales describing the individual's retrospective impression of treatment and rearing provided by the adoptive parents during childhood and adolescence (*18*). The age- and sex-corrected placement coefficients for these and other measures are shown in Table 3, together with the correlations between twins' IQ and the environmental measure (r_{fi}) and the total estimated contribution to MZA twin similarity. The maximum contribution to MZA trait correlations that could be explained by measured similarity of the adoptive rearing environments on a single variable is about 0.03 (*19*). The absence of any significant effect due to SES or other environmental measures on the IQ scores of these adult adopted twins is consistent with the findings of other investigators (*20*). Rearing SES effects on IQ in adoption studies have been found for young children but not in adult samples (*21*), suggesting that although parents may be able to affect their children's rate of cognitive skill acquisition, they may have relatively little influence on the ultimate level attained.

Table 3. Placement coefficients for environmental variables, correlations between IQ and the environmental variables, and estimates of the contribution of placement to twin similarity in WAIS IQ.

Placement variable	MZA similarity (R_{ff})	Correlation between IQ and placement variable (r_{fi})	Contribution of placement to the MZA correlation ($R_{ff} \times r^2_{fi}$)
SES indicators			
Father's education	0.134	0.100	0.001
Mother's education	0.412	−0.001	0.000
Father's SES	0.267	0.174	0.008
Physical facilities			
Material possessions	0.402	0.279**	0.032
Scientific/technical	0.151	−0.090	0.001
Cultural	−0.085	−0.279**	−0.007
Mechanical	0.303	0.077	0.002
Relevant FES scales			
Achievement	0.11	−0.103	0.001
Intellectual orientation	0.27	0.106	0.003

**r_{fi} significantly different from zero at $P < 0.01$.

Has Pre- and Post-Reunion Contact Contributed to MZA Twin Similarity in IQ?

MZA twins share prenatal and perinatal environments, but except for effects of actual trauma, such as fetal alcohol syndrome, there is little evidence that early shared environment significantly contributes to the variance of psychological traits. Twins are especially vulnerable to prenatal and perinatal trauma, but these effects are most likely to decrease, rather than increase, within-pair similarity (*22*). There is evidence that twins who maintain closer contact with each other later in life tend to be more similar in some respects than twins who engage in infrequent contact (*23*). It appears, however, that it is the similarity that leads to increased contact, rather than the other way around (*24*). MZA twins in this study vary widely in the amount of contact they have had prior to assessment. All twin pairs spent their formative years apart. Some had their first adult reunion at the time of assessment, whereas others met as much as 20 years earlier and had experienced varying degrees of contact. A small number of the pairs actually met at intervals during childhood. As shown in Table 1, total contact time for the MZA twins ranges from 1 to 1233 weeks. In the one case of 1233 weeks of contact, the twins met as teenagers and lived near each other until assessment when they were adults. Since they met on a regular basis, most of this time was coded as contact time. Degree of social contact between two members of a reared-apart twin pair accounts for virtually none of their similarity. The correlations with the within-pair absolute WAIS IQ difference are 0.06 ± 0.15 for time together prior to separation, 0.08 ± 0.15 for time apart to first reunion, −0.14 ± 0.15 for total contact time, and 0.17 ± 0.15 for percentage of lifetime spent apart (*25*).

The absolute within-pair difference in WAIS IQ of co-twins as a function of degree of contact are plotted in Fig. 1. Also shown are the expected absolute IQ differences between randomly paired individuals and between two testings of the same individual (*26*). Although the MZA average difference approximates the absolute difference expected between two testings of a single individual, we do observe a wide range of differences. It is not that we have found no evidence of environmental influence; in individual cases environmental factors have been highly significant (for example, the 29 IQ point difference in Fig. 1). Rather, we find little support for the types of environmental influences on which psychologists have traditionally focused (*27*).

Similarity of MZA Twins on a Variety of Dimensions

Table 4 (*28*) gives the MZA correlations, most previously published, on variables ranging from anthropometry and psychophysiology, to aptitudes, personality and temperament, leisure-time and vocational interests, to social attitudes. Correlations for MZT twins and retest stability coefficients are also provided for comparison. Stable, reliably measured variables like fingerprint ridge count and stature show the highest correlations. Brain wave spectra are highly reproducible (29) and are strongly correlated in both MZA and MZT twins. Most other psychophysiological variables (for example, blood pressure and electrodermal response) vary considerably across time so that the retest correlations between repeated measurements on the same persons range from 0.5 to 0.8 (30). These retest correlations set the upper limit of similarity that might be found between MZ co-twins. The retest stability of aptitude measures, such as IQ, is rather better, ranging from 0.8 to 0.9 (10), whereas stability of personality and interest measures ranges from 0.6 to 0.7.

With these upper limits in mind, the findings in Table 4 demonstrate remarkable similarity between MZA twins. In terms of standardized tests and measures, the MZA twin similarities are often nearly equal to those for MZT twins (last column) and constitute a substantial portion of the reliable variance (column 5) of each trait.

The Minimal Effect of Being Reared Together

Some of the MZA twins have had considerable contact as adults, but all of them were reared apart throughout the formative periods of childhood and adolescence. If being reared together enhances similarity in twins, within-pair correlations for MZA twins are expected to be smaller than those for MZT twins. For example, the mean MZT correlation for IQ, based on 34 studies of primarily children or adolescents, is 0.86 (9) as compared to 0.72 for all, primarily adult, MZA twins. If the mean MZT correlation were maintained into adulthood, its difference from the MZA correlation would suggest that common rearing increases the similarity of IQ in twins (and siblings). However, the MZT correlation apparently declines with age (for example, as a result of the accumulation of nonshared environmental effects) (16), in which event the small MZT-MZA correlation difference would suggest little influence of common rearing on adult IQ. In any case, a significant contribution of shared environment is found for the personality trait of social closeness (31), and possibly religious interests and values (32).

As illustrated in Table 4, however, adult MZ twins are about equally similar on most physiological and psychological traits, regardless of rearing status. This finding and the failure to find

Table 4. Interclass correlations (R), sample sizes, and MZA/MZT ratio for monozygotic twins reared apart and together for nine classes of variables. NA, not available.

Variables (reference)	Minnesota MZAs		MZTs		Reliability*	R_{MZA}/R_{MZT}
	R	Pairs (no.)	R	Pairs (no.)		
Anthropometric variables (28)						
Fingerprint ridge count	0.97	54	0.96	274	0.99	1.01
Height	0.86	56	0.93	274	0.98	0.925
Weight	0.73	56	0.83	274	NA	0.880
Electroencephalographic (brainwave) variables (28)						
Amount of 8- to 12-Hz (alpha) activity	0.80	35	0.81	42	NA	0.987
Midfrequency of alpha activity	0.80	35	0.82	42	NA	0.975
Psychophysiologic variables (29)						
Systolic blood pressure	0.64	56	0.70	34	0.70	0.914
Heart rate	0.49	49	0.54	160	0.58–0.80	0.907
Electrodermal response (EDR) amplitude†						
Males	0.82	20	0.70	17	NA	1.17
Females	0.30	23	0.54	19	NA	0.555
Trials to habituation EDR	0.43	43	0.42	36	NA	1.02
Information processing ability factors (17)						
Speed of response	0.56	40	0.73	50	NA	0.767
Acquisition speed	0.20	40	NA	NA	NA	NA
Speed of spatial processing	0.36	40	NA	NA	NA	NA
Mental ability—general factor (44)						
WAIS IQ–full scale	0.69	48	0.88	40	0.90	0.784
WAIS IQ–verbal	0.64	48	0.88	40	0.84	0.727
WAIS IQ–performance	0.71	48	0.79	40	0.86	0.899
Raven, Mill-Hill composite	0.78	42	0.76	37	NA	1.03
First principal component of special mental abilities	0.78	43	NA	NA	NA	NA
Special mental abilities (14)						
Mean of 15 Hawaii-battery scales	0.45	45	NA	NA	0.80	NA
Mean of 13 Comprehensive Ability Battery scales	0.48	41	NA	NA	0.78	NA
Personality variables (31)						
Mean of 11 Multidimensional Personality Questionnaire (MPQ) scales	0.50	44	0.49	217	0.88	1.02
Mean of 18 California Psychological Inventory (CPI) scales	0.48	38	0.49	99	0.65	0.979
Psychological interests (45)						
Mean of 23 Strong Campbell Interest Inventory scales (SCII)	0.39	52	0.48	116‡	0.82	0.813
Mean of 34 Jackson Vocational Interest Survey scales (JVIS)	0.43	45	NA	NA	0.84	NA
Mean of 17 Minnesota Occupational Interest scales	0.40	40	0.49	376	0.75	0.816
Social attitudes (32)						
Mean of 2 religiosity scales	0.49	31	0.51	458	0.80	0.961
Mean of 14 nonreligious social attitude items	0.34	42	0.28	421	0.48	1.21
MPQ traditionalism scale	0.53	44	0.50	217	0.49	1.06

*The correlation between two testings of the same individual. These estimates of the stable component of the observed trait variance also estimate the upper limit for R_{MZ}. †The marked difference in EDR amplitude between males and females is discussed in Lykken *et al.* (29). ‡This value is for 116 studies, not pairs.

significant r_{fi} effects for cognitive abilities (*17*) or personality (*31*), together with findings from numerous studies of MZT and DZT twins, sibs, and foster sibs, implies that common rearing enhances familial resemblance during adulthood only slightly and on relatively few behavioral dimensions. This conclusion is given detailed discussion by Plomin and Daniels (*5*).

Why Are MZA Twins So Similar?

It is well known to naturalists and to animal breeders that there are wide and heritable differences in behavior within other species, but there is a curious reluctance among some scientists (*33*) to acknowledge the contribution of genetic variation to psychological differences within the human species. Our findings support and extend those from many family, twin, and adoption studies (*15*), a broad consilience of findings leading to the following generalization: For almost every behavioral trait so far investigated, from reaction time to religiosity, an important fraction of the variation among people turns out to be associated with genetic variation. This fact need no longer be subject to debate (*34*); rather, it is time instead to consider its implications. We suggest the following:

1) *General intelligence or IQ is strongly affected by genetic factors.* The IQs of the adult MZA twins assessed with various instruments in four independent studies correlate about 0.70, indicating that about 70% of the observed variation in IQ in this population can be attributed to genetic variation. Since only a few of these MZA twins were reared in real poverty or by illiterate parents and none were retarded, this heritability estimate should not be extrapolated to the extremes of environmental disadvantage still encountered in society. Moreover, these findings do not imply that traits like IQ cannot be enhanced. Flynn (*35*), in a survey covering 14 countries, has shown that the average IQ test score has significantly increased in recent years. This increase may be limited to that part of the population with low IQs (*36*). The present findings, therefore, do not define or limit what might be conceivably achieved in an optimal environment. They do indicate that, in the current environments of the broad middle-class, in industrialized societies, two-thirds of the observed variance of IQ can be traced to genetic variation.

2) *The institutions and practices of modern Western society do not greatly constrain the development of individual differences in psychological traits.* The heritability of a psychological trait reveals as much about the culture as it does about human nature. Heritability must increase as V_e, the variance affected by the environment, decreases. Where the culture's influence is relatively homogeneous and efficacious, V_e will decrease and heritability will increase; most American boys, for example, have similar opportunities to play baseball, so that one expects heritability of baseball skill in American young men to be high. Where culture is efficacious, but heterogeneous, V_e (and total phenotypic variance) will increase; thus, one would expect the heritability of specific linguistic or religious behaviors in the United States or in the Soviet Union to be low. Individuals in Western societies are heterogeneous with respect to personality traits, interests, and attitudes, yet the heritabilities of these traits are relatively high. We infer that the diverse cultural agents of our society, in particular most parents, are less effective in imprinting their distinctive stamp on the children developing within their spheres of influence—or are less inclined to do so—than has been supposed.

Psychologists have been surprised by the evidence that being reared by the same parents in the same physical environment does not, on average, make siblings more alike as adults than they would have been if reared separately in adoptive homes. It is obvious that parents can produce shared effects if they grossly deprive or mistreat

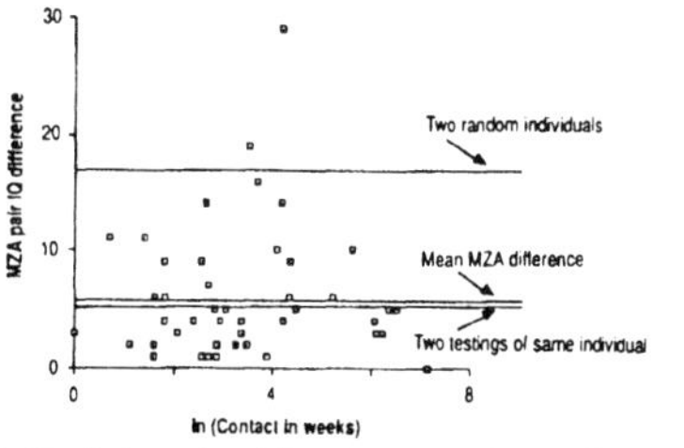

Fig. 1. The absolute value of the MZA within-pair IQ difference as a function of the natural logarithm of pair contact in weeks. The horizontal lines are the expected absolute IQ difference between two randomly selected individuals, the observed average MZA absolute difference, and the expected IQ difference between two testings of the same individual.

all their children. It seems reasonable that charismatic, dedicated parents, determined to make all their children share certain personal qualities, interests, or values, may sometimes succeed. Our findings, and those of others (*37*), do not imply that parenting is without lasting effects. The remarkable similarity in MZA twins in social attitudes (for example, traditionalism and religiosity) does not show that parents cannot influence those traits, but simply that this does not tend to happen in most families.

3) *MZA twins are so similar in psychological traits because their identical genomes make it probable that their effective environments are similar.* Specific mechanisms by which genetic differences in human behavior are expressed in phenotypic differences are largely unknown. It is a plausible conjecture that a key mechanism by which the genes affect the mind is indirect, and that genetic differences have an important role in determining the effective psychological environment of the developing child (*38*).

Infants with different temperaments elicit different parenting responses. Toddlers who are active and adventurous undergo different experiences than their more sedentary or timid siblings. In addition, children and adolescents seek out environments that they find congenial. These are forms of gene-environment covariance, C_{ge}. Moreover, different individuals pay different attention to or respond differently to the same objective experience, or both. These are forms of gene-environment interaction, V_{ge}. From infancy onwards, genetic individuality helps to steer the developing organism through the multitude of possible experiences and choices. That is, Eq. 1 must be elaborated to include these indirect and modifiable ways in which the genome exerts its influence

$$V_t = V_g + V_e + C_{ge} + V_{ge} + V_m \qquad (2)$$

The proximal cause of most psychological variance probably involves learning through experience, just as radical environmentalists have always believed. The effective experiences, however, to an important extent are self-selected, and that selection is guided by the steady pressure of the genome (a more distal cause). We agree with Martin *et al.* (*39*) who see "humans as exploring organisms whose innate abilities and predispositions help them select what is relevant and adaptive from the range of opportunities and stimuli presented in the environment. The effects of mobility and learning, therefore, augment rather than eradicate the effects of the genotype on behavior" (p. 4368).

If this view is correct, the developmental experiences of MZ twins are more similar than those of DZ twins, again as environmentalist critics of twin research have contended. However, even MZA twins tend to elicit, select, seek out, or create very similar effective environments and, to that extent, the impact of these experiences is counted as a genetic influence. Finally, if the genome impresses itself on the psyche largely by influencing the character, selection, and impact of experiences during development—if the correct formula is nature via nurture—then intervention is not precluded even for highly heritable traits, but should be the more effective when tailored to each specific child's talents and inclinations.

Relevance to Evolutionary Psychology and Sociobiology

This research focuses on individual differences, but like other animals we share certain species-specific tendencies by virtue of our being human. Whereas behavioral geneticists study variations within a species, evolutionary psychologists or sociobiologists attempt to delineate species-typical proclivities or instincts and to understand the relevant evolutionary developments that took place in the Pleistocene epoch and were adaptive in the lives of tribal hunter-gatherers. The genes sing a prehistoric song that today should sometimes be resisted but which it would be foolish to ignore.

At the interface of behavioral genetics and sociobiology is the question of the origin and function, if any, of the within-species variability we have been discussing. One view is that it represents evolutionary debris (*40*), unimportant to fitness and perhaps not expressed in prehistoric environments. Another view is that variability has an adaptive function and has been selected for. Whether sociobiologists can make evolutionary sense of the varieties of human genetic variation we have discussed here remains to be seen (*41*).

Whatever the ancient origins and functions of genetic variability, its repercussions in contemporary society are pervasive and important. A human species whose members did not vary genetically with respect to significant cognitive and motivational attributes, and who were uniformly average by current standards, would have created a very different society than the one we know. Modern society not only augments the influence of genotype on behavioral variability, as we have suggested, but permits this variability to reciprocally contribute to the rapid pace of cultural change. If genetic variation was evolutionary debris at the end of the Pleistocene, it is now a salient and essential feature of the human condition.

REFERENCES AND NOTES

1. H. H. Newman, F. N. Freeman, K. J. Holzinger, *Twins: A Study of Heredity and Environment* (Univ. of Chicago Press, Chicago, 1937); N. Juel-Nielson, *Acta Psychiatr. Neurol. Scand. Suppl.* **183**, (1965); J. Shields, *Monozygotic Twins: Brought up Apart and Brought up Together* (Oxford Univ. Press, London, 1962). There are two other ongoing studies of twins reared apart, one in Sweden (*2*) and one in Finland (*3*). The questionable study by Burt (*4*) has been omitted.
2. N. Pedersen, G. E. McClearn, R. Plomin, L. Friberg, *Behav. Genet.* **15**, 407 (1985); R. Plomin, P. Lichtenstein, N. L. Pedersen, G. E. McClearn, J. R. Nesselroade, *Psychol. Aging* **5**, 25 (1990).
3. H. Langainvainio, J. Kaprio, M. Koskenvuo, J. Lonnqvist, *Acta Genet. Med. Gemellol.* **33**, 259 (1984).
4. L. Hearnshaw, *Cyril Burt: Psychologist* (Hodder & Stoughton, London, 1979), but see R. B. Joynson, *The Burt Affair* (Routledge, London, 1990).
5. R. Plomin and D. Daniels, *Behav. Brain Sci.* **10**, 1 (1987); L. J. Eaves, H. J. Eysenck, N. G. Martin, *Genes Culture and Personality: An Empirical Approach* (Academic Press, New York, 1989).
6. T. J. Bouchard, Jr., in *The Chemical and Biological Bases of Individuality*, S. Fox, Ed. (Plenum, New York, 1984), p. 147; N. L. Segal, W. M. Grove, T. J. Bouchard, Jr., in *Genetic Issues in Psychosocial Epidemiology*, M. Tsuang, K. Kendler, M. Lyons, Eds. (Rutgers Univ. Press, New Brunswick, NJ, in press).
7. D. T. Lykken, *Behav. Genet.* **8**, 437 (1978).
8. M. McGue and T. J. Bouchard, Jr., *ibid.* **14**, 325 (1984).
9. T. J. Bouchard, Jr., and M. McGue, *Science* **212**, 1055 (1981).
10. J. D. Matarazzo, *Wechsler's Measurement and Appraisal of Adult Intelligence* (Williams and Wilkins, Baltimore, ed. 5, 1972).
11. J. Raven, *Manual for Raven's Progressive Matrices and Vocabulary Scales* (Lewis, London, 1986).
12. J. C. DeFries *et al.*, *Behav. Genet.* **9**, 23 (1979).
13. A. R. Hakstian and R. B. Cattell, *J. Educ. Psychol.* **70**, 657 (1978).
14. T. J. Bouchard, Jr., N. L. Segal, D. T. Lykken, *Acta Genet. Med. Gemellol.* **39**, 193 (1990).
15. J. C. Loehlin, *Am. Psychol.* **44**, 1285 (1989); R. Plomin and J. C. Loehlin, *Behav. Genet.* **19**, 331 (1989).
16. K. McCartney, M. J. Harris, F. Bernieri, *Psychol. Bull.* **107**, 26 (1990).
17. M. McGue and T. J. Bouchard, Jr., in *Advances in the Psychology of Human Intelligence*, R. J. Sternberg, Ed. (Erlbaum, New York, 1989), vol. 5, p. 7. This checklist yields four relatively independent scales: scientific or technical, cultural, mechanical, and material possessions.
18. R. H. Moos and B. S. Moos, *Manual: Family Environment Scale* (Consulting Psychologists Press, Palo Alto, CA, 1986).
19. Formally, this is the maximum linear contribution; nonlinear effects are, of course, possible. For these data, however, investigation of higher-ordered relationships (quadratic and cubic) showed no associations that did not exist at the linear level, and there was no discernible nonlinearity detected in visual inspection of the scatterplots.
20. T. J. Bouchard, Jr., *Intelligence* **7**, 175 (1983).
21. C. Capron and M. Duyme [*Nature* **340**, 552 (1989)] have shown an SES effect in an adoption study of young children; S. Scarr and R. Weinberg [*Amer. Sociol. Rev.* **43**, 674 (1978)] did not find an SES effect in a study of young adult adoptees.
22. B. Price, *Am. J. Hum. Genet.* **2**, 293 (1950).
23. R. J. Rose and J. Kaprio, *Behav. Genet.* **18**, 309 (1988).
24. D. T. Lykken, T. J. Bouchard, Jr., M. McGue, A. Tellegen, *Behav. Genet.*, in press.
25. As in our earlier analysis, nonlinear relationships were tested for and found not to exist. Additionally, deletion of a single outlier (IQ difference of 29 points) did not appreciably change the correlation estimates.
26. Expected difference (D) can be expressed as a function of the correlation (r) and standard deviation as $D = 1.13\,\sigma\sqrt{1 - r}$ [R. Plomin and J. C. DeFries, *Intelligence* **4**, 15 (1980)].
27. K. R. White, *Psychol. Bull.* **86**, 461 (1982).
28. D. T. Lykken, T. J. Bouchard, Jr., M. McGue, A. Tellegen, *Acta Genet. Med. Gemellol.* **39**, 35 (1990); and (*6*).
29. H. H. Stassen, D. T. Lykken, G. Bomben, *Eur. Arch. Psychiatry Neurol. Sci.* **237**, 244 (1988).
30. Systolic blood pressure from Minnesota twin studies. Heart rate from B. Hanson *et al.*, *Am. J. Cardiol.* **63**, 606 (1989). Electrodermal and habituation data from D. T. Lykken, W. G. Iacono, K. Haroian, M. McGue, T. J. Bouchard, Jr., *Psychophysiology* **25**, 4 (1988). Reliability data from K. Matthews, C. Rakczky, C. Stoney, S. Manuck, *ibid.* **24**, 464 (1987); M. Llabre *et al.*, *ibid.* **25**, 97 (1988).
31. MPQ data from A. Tellegen *et al.*, *J. Pers. Soc. Psychol.* **54**, 1031 (1988); CPI data from T. J. Bouchard, Jr., and M. McGue, *J. Pers.* **58**, 263 (1990). Reliability data from test manuals.
32. MZA and MZT Religiosity data from N. G. Waller, B. A. Kojetin, T. J. Bouchard, Jr., D. T. Lykken, A. Tellegen, *Psychol. Sci.* **1**, 138 (1990). Reliability of religious leisure time interests and religious occupational interests and mean of 14 nonreligious social attitude items from Minnesota twin study data base (*28*). Reliability of other scales from test manuals. For a general discussion of the reliability of traits such as those measured in this study, see K. C. H. Parker, R. K. Hanson, J. Hunsley [*Psychol. Bull.* **103**, 367 (1988)] and J. J. Conley [*Pers. Individ. Differ.* **5**, 11 (1984)].
33. R. C. Lewontin, S. Rose, L. J. Kamin, *Not in Our Genes; Biology, Ideology, and Human Nature* (Pantheon, New York, 1984).
34. S. Scarr, *Behav. Genet.* **17**, 219 (1987).
35. J. R. Flynn, *Psychol. Bull.* **101**, 171 (1987).
36. R. Lynn, *Pers. Individ. Differ.* **11**, 273 (1990); T. W. Teasedale and D. R. Owen, *Intelligence* **13**, 255 (1989).
37. R. Wilson, *Child Dev.* **54**, 298 (1983).
38. K. J. Hayes, *Psychol. Rep.* **10**, 299 (1962); C. J. Lumsden and E. O. Wilson, *Genes, Mind and Culture* (Harvard Univ. Press, Cambridge, MA, 1981); S. Scarr and K. McCartney, *Child Dev.* **54**, 424 (1983).
39. N. G. Martin *et al.*, *Proc. Nat. Acad. Sci. U.S.A.* **83**, 4364 (1986).
40. M. W. Feldman and R. C. Lewontin, *Science* **190**, 1163 (1975); D. Symonds, *The Evolution of Human Sexuality* (Oxford Univ. Press, New York, 1979).
41. D. M. Buss, *J. Pers.* **58**, 1 (1990).
42. T. J. Bouchard, Jr., D. T. Lykken, M. McGue, N. L. Segal, A. Tellegen, this article.
43. The MZA correlation of 0.771 reported by the late Sir Cyril Burt and questioned for its authenticity after his death (*4*) falls within the range of findings reviewed here.
44. WAIS data for MZTs from K. Tambs, J. M. Sundet, P. Magnus, *Intelligence* **8**, 283 (1984). Reliabilities from (*10*). Raven, Mill-Hill, and composite data from Minnesota twin studies (*6, 42*).
45. MZA data on SCII and JVIS from D. Moloney, unpublished thesis (University of Minnesota, Minneapolis, 1990). Minnesota Occupational Interest Scale data from N. Waller, D. T. Lykken, A. Tellegen, in *Wise Counsel: Essays in Honor of Lloyd Lofquist*, R. Dawis and D. Lubinski, Eds. (Univ. of Minnesota Press, Minneapolis, in press). SCII MZT data from Nichols [*Homo* **29**, 158 (1978)]. Reliability data from test manuals.

46. We thank our colleagues E. D. Eckert, L. L. Heston, and I. I. Gottesman for their help on the medical and psychiatric portions of the study and H. Polesky, director, for the blood testing. This research has been supported by grants from The Pioneer Fund, The Seaver Institute, The University of Minnesota Graduate School, The Koch Charitable Foundation, The Spencer Foundation, The National Science Foundation (BNS-7926654), The National Institute of Mental Health (MH37860), The National Institute on Aging (AG06886), and the Harcourt Brace Jovanovich Publishing Company.

Twin Research (1999) 2, 62–80

http://www.stockton-press.co.uk/tr

Comparing the biological and cultural inheritance of personality and social attitudes in the Virginia 30 000 study of twins and their relatives

Lindon Eaves[1], Andrew Heath[2], Nicholas Martin[3], Hermine Maes[1], Michael Neale[1], Kenneth Kendler[1], Katherine Kirk[3] and Linda Corey[1]

[1]*Virginia Institute for Psychiatric and Behavioral Genetics, Virginia Commonwealth University, Richmond, Virginia*
[2]*Department of Psychiatry, Washington University, St Louis, USA*
[3]*Queensland Institute of Medical Research and Joint Genetics Program, University of Queensland, Brisbane, Australia*

Measures of four dimensions of personality (Psychoticism, Extraversion, Neuroticism, and Lie scores) and six aspects of social attitudes (to sex, taxation, militarism, politics, religion and a general conservatism scale) were obtained by mailed questionnaire from 29 691 US subjects including adult twins (n = 14 761) their parents (n = 2360), their spouses (n = 4391), siblings (n = 3184) and adult children (n = 4800). After correction for the average effects of age, sex and source of sample, familial correlations were computed for 80 distinct biological and social relationships. The data allow for the estimation of the additive and non-additive effects of genes, assortative mating, vertical cultural inheritance and other non-parental effects of the shared environment on differences in personality and social attitudes. The interaction of genetic and environmental effects with sex may also be analyzed. Model-fitting analyses show that personality and social attitude measures differ markedly in major features of family resemblance. Additive and dominant genetic effects contribute to differences in both personality and attitudes, but the effects of the family environment, including vertical cultural transmission from parent to child, are much more marked for social attitudes than for personality. There is substantial assortative mating for social attitudes and almost none for personality. The causes of family resemblance depend significantly on sex for almost every variable studied. These findings clarify and extend the more tentative findings derived from previous twin, family and adoption studies.

Keywords: personality, attitudes, cultural transmission, assortative mating, twins, behavior genetics, heritability, sex differences

Introduction

Four primary sources of data have been exploited in separate studies of the inheritance of personality: twins reared together,[1–5] twins reared apart,[6–9] nuclear families[10,11] and adoption studies.[12–15] These studies concur in showing a small to moderate contribution of genetic factors to variation in the major dimensions of personality. They also appear to show virtually no effect of the shared family environment on the correlations between relatives. Indeed, even when attempts have been made to measure particular environmental factors[1,4,16] their contribution to personality differences has been pitifully small.

Such studies, however, have left unanswered a number of important questions. It has been claimed that the different kinds of data yield different estimates of heritability – those from twin studies being greater than those from adoption and nuclear family studies.[12,13] Whether such differences could be attributed to genetic non-additivity, the interaction of genetic effects with age, or to methods of ascertainment or choice of measures cannot be decided with certainty given the available data. Furthermore, although twin studies have been large enough to suggest sex differences in the expression of genes and environment on personality, the studies of other types of relationship have typically been too small to confirm or refute this basic finding. Also, it is not clear whether the results for personality can be generalized to other non-cognitive behavioral domains, notably social attitudes. Several large studies of twins reared together[5] have suggested that family resemblance is greater for social attitudes than personality and that there are indications from twin data of a large effect of the shared family environment and assortative mating. However, the weight of this claim is based on twin studies and these leave open the issue of whether the claim that attitudes are transmitted different from personality can be borne out by studies of other kinds of relationships.

Correspondence: Dr Lindon Eaves, Department of Human Genetics, PO Box 980003, Richmond, Virginia 23298-0003, USA.

Experience with computer simulation studies,[17,18] and with the outcome of actual data analyses suggested that a large study of an extremely broad range of different relationships was necessary if we were to have a reasonable hope of analyzing the inheritance of complex traits with any degree of subtlety. A study was needed which could not just detect the effects of genes or the shared environment, but allow us to resolve different kinds of gene action such as additive and non-additive gene action. Such a study must also provide for the resolution of the different sources of non-genetic family resemblance including the environmental impact of mothers and fathers on their children and those environmental effects originating independently of the parental phenotype which are, nevertheless, shared by siblings and twins. Within this basic requirement it is also necessary that the study permits analysis of the contribution of assortative mating to variation and family resemblance and allows for the interaction of all the major sources of variation with sex differences. For example, the design should permit separation of the effects of sex-limited gene expression from the differential social interactions which may occur between mothers and fathers and their male and female offspring.

The Virginia 30 000

The series of simulation studies[18] had indicated that, although the full adoption study involving adoptees with both their adopting and biological parents were more powerful for the purpose of detecting the effects of the parental environment, the difficulty of securing large enough samples vitiated the theoretical advantage, especially when the sexes were likely to differ in the contribution and type of genetic and environmental effects. Furthermore, given we cannot know in advance that the parental environment is not the only salient determinant of individual differences, and given the need for large samples in order to resolve subtle genetic and environmental effects, the study of the extended kinships of adult identical and non-identical twins, with their parents, siblings, spouses and adult children, had many advantages. Indeed, it provides a powerful basis for the resolution of additive and non-additive genetic effects, alternative models of assortative mating[19] and a wide variety of components of the shared family environment including the environmental effects of the maternal and paternal phenotype and the additional environmental correlation induced between siblings ('sibling environment') and members of a twin pair ('twin environment').

The Virginia 30 000 study was designed to exploit this strategy in a comprehensive examination of the causes of individual differences in attitudes, personality, habits, life styles, life events, physical characteristics, social support and psychosocial variables known to affect risk to physical and mental health.

Figure 1 gives an idealized pedigree sought for the Virginia 30 000. In practice, very few three-generation pedigrees were ascertained. Most families comprised either twins with their collateral relatives and parents, or twins and their collateral relatives and children. Ascertainment was in two stages. Names and addresses of Virginia-born twins were supplied by the Virginia Twin Registry under the supervision of Dr Linda Corey. In addition, a nationwide sample of volunteer twins aged 50+ was recruited through publicity provided by the American Association of Retired Persons ('AARP'). Truett *et al*[20] describe some of the properties of the sample. Twins were mailed a 16-page 'Health and Life-styles Questionnaire for Twins' (HLQ-T) developed for the study. At the end of the questionnaire twins were asked to supply names, addresses and telephone numbers of their parents, spouses, siblings and children who were then asked to complete versions of the HLQ identical to the twin versions as far as the measures of personality and attitudes were concerned. These questionnaires were designed for the parents of twins (HLQ-P) and other relatives of twins, including their spouses (HLQ-R).

Zygosity of the twins was established on the basis of two questions dealing with perceived similarity (Table 1). Any pair of twins who agree that they were frequently mistaken for each other and describe themselves as identical may be classified as monozygotic with a high degree of confidence. The validity of this approach to zygosity diagnosis has been generally accepted for large-scale studies as providing correct zygosity diagnoses in about 95% of cases. In cases where the zygosity algorithm identified inconsistent or uncertain responses, the twins were classified as unknown and used only for those

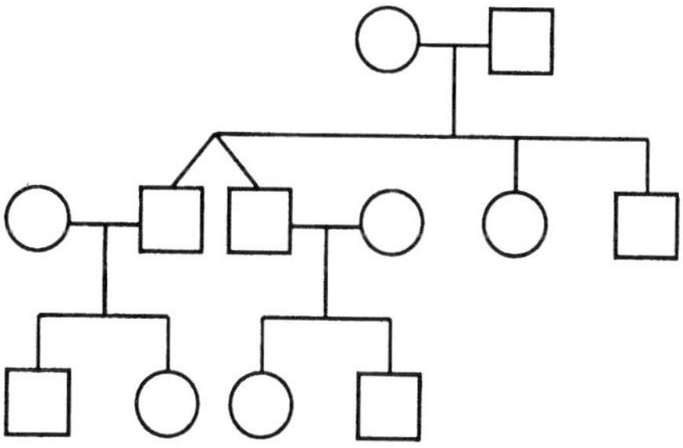

Figure 1 Idealised pedigree for Virginia 30 000 study: a three-generational pedigree including twins and their parents, children, siblings and spouses

Table 1 Items used in questionnaire zygosity diagnosis

1. As children, were you and your twin mistaken by people who knew you?
   (1)___Frequently
   (2)___Sometimes
   (3)___Rarely

2. Non-identical twins are no more alike than ordinary brothers and sisters. Identical twins, on the other hand, have such a strong resemblance to each other in stature, coloring, facial features, etc., that people often mistake one for the other, or say they are 'as alike as two peas in a pod'.

   Having read the above statement, do you think you are:
   (1)___An identical twin
   (2)___A non-identical twin?

correlations in which the zygosity of twins was expected to make no difference (eg spousal correlations, parent–offspring and sibling correlations).

The final sample comprised 29 691 individuals. Table 2 summarizes the composition of the sample by sex and relationship to the twins. A few other relationships (eg half-siblings, adoptees) are also represented in the sample but their numbers are generally too small to have a significant impact on the analysis and these individuals are not included in these numbers.

In subsequent computations of the correlations between relatives, three-generational relationships (eg grandparent/grandchild), were omitted because sample sizes were small. However, all the unique combinations of relatives with respect to the sex of both parents and children were kept separate for the purposes of computing the correlations between relatives since, under a full model for the effects of sex on familial transmission, subtle differences may be introduced as a function of the sex of both the parents and children contributing genetic and environmental effects to a particular relationship. For example, if the impact of maternal effects depends on the sex of the offspring, then unlike-sex cousins related through unlike-sex dizygotic twin parents produce two distinct correlations, one involving the male offspring of the *female* twin as parent and one

Table 2 Sample sizes of twins and the principal adult relatives of twins in the Virginia 30 000 study

	Males	*Females*	*Total*
Twins	5 325	9 436	14 761
Parents of twins	913	1 447	2 360
Spouses of twins	2 515	1 876	4 391
Children of twins	1 890	2 910	4 800
Siblings of twins	1 260	1 924	3 184
Other	67	128	195
Total	11 970	17 721	29 691

with the *male* twin as the parent of the male offspring. When such distinctions are made, we have so far identified *80* distinct biological and social relationships, excluding those across three generations, in the extended kinships derived from monozygotic male, monozygotic female, dizygotic male, dizygotic female and unlike-sex dizygotic twin pairs.

Table 3 lists all the relationships distinguished in this analysis, together with an acronym for each correlation which is used to identify the correlations in subsequent tables. It is important to note that within each of the major categories of relationship tabulated, apart from nuclear families, there are two main sub-categories. Although the graphical structure of kinships based on MZ and DZ twins is the same, relationships within MZ kinships are biologically different from relationships within DZ kinships. Thus, the table distinguish relationships involving MZ twins from those involving DZs and siblings. For example, the spouses of MZ twins ('SPMZ') are expected to correlate differently from the spouses of DZ twins ('SPDZ') if genetic factors influence the choice of mate.[19,21,22] Similarly, avuncular relationships between a nephew or niece and the MZ co-twin of a father or mother ('PatMav' and 'MatMav') are expected to involve a higher genetic correlation (equal to that between parents and offspring) than the conventional avuncular relationships involving a DZ co-twin or a sibling of a parent (eg 'PatSav' and 'MatDav').

Measurement of personality and attitudes

The HLQ included, with the authors' permission, the short form (54 items) of the Eysenck Personality Questionnaire.[23] The short EPQ is scored for the three principal dimensions of Eysenck's personality theory: Psychoticism, Extraversion and Neuroticism (P,E and N). A fourth scale may also be scored, measuring the tendency of the subjects to 'fake good' – the 'Lie-scale' (L). The authors' scales were used to obtain scores for P,E,N and L. The E,N and L scales are represented by 12 items each and the P scale by 13 items. The items comprising the scales are reproduced in Table 4. In order to minimize the impact of occasional missing values scores were imputed for those subjects who had ten or more valid responses to a given scale.

Social attitudes were assessed by a 28-item inventory modeled on the Wilson-Patterson Conservatism scale. The items were chosen after review of the loadings on the first principal component of the

Table 3 Key to relationships in Virginia 30 000

Group and Acronym	*Description*
Nuclear families	
Spouses	Spouses
Sibs: MM	Male–male sibling pairs
Sibs: FF	Female–female siblings
Sibs: MF	Male–female siblings
Fath–Son	Father–son
Fath–Dau	Father–daughter
Moth–Son	Mother–son
Moth–Dau	Mother–daughter
Twins	
DZ: MM	Dizygotic male–male
DZ: FF	Dizygotic female–female
DZ: MF	Dizygotic male–female
MZ: MM	Monozygotic male
MZ: FF	Monozygotic female
Avuncular	
PatSavMM	Nephew with father's brother
PatSavMF	Niece with father's brother
MatSavFM	Nephew with mother's sister
MatSavFF	Niece with mother's sister
PatSavFM	Nephew with father's sister
PatSavFF	Niece with father's sister
MatSavMM	Nephew with mother's brother
MatSavMF	Niece with mother's brother
PatDavMM	Nephew with father's DZ brother
PatDavMF	Niece with father's DZ brother
MatDavFM	Nephew with mother's DZ sister
MatDavFF	Niece with mother's DZ sister
PatDavFM	Nephew with father's DZ sister
PatDavFF	Niece with father's DZ sister
MatDavMM	Nephew with mother's DZ bother
MatDavMF	Niece with mother's DZ brother
PatMavMM	Nephew with father's MZ twin
PatMavMF	Niece with father's MZ twin
MatMavFM	Nephew with mother's MZ twin
MatMavFF	Niece with mother's MZ twin
Siblings-in-law	
SibInlMF	Wife with husband's brother
SibInlFM	Husband with wife's sister
SibInlMM	Husband with wife's brother
SibInlFF	Wife with husband's sister
DZInlMF	Wife with husband's DZ male cotwin
DZInlFM	Husband with wife's DZ female cotwin
DZInlMM	Husband with wife's DZ male cotwin
DZInlFF	Wife with husband's DZ female cotwin

Group and Acronym	*Description*	
MZInlMF	Wife with husband's MZ male cotwin	
MZInlFM	Husband with wife's MZ female cotwin	
Parent-in-Law		
Fa–DIL	Father with daughter-in-law	
Fa–SIL	Father with son-in-law	
Mo–DIL	Mother with daughter-in-law	
Mo–SIL	Mother with son-in-law	
Spouses of uncles and aunts		
SPaDavFM	Male with wife of father's DZ twin	
SPaDavFF	Female with wife of father's DZ twin	
SMaDavMM	Male with husband of mother's DZ	
SMaDavMF	Female with husband of mother's DZ	
SPaDavMM	Male with husband of father's DZ	
SPaDavMF	Female with husband of father's DZ	
SMaDavFM	Male with wife of mother's DZ	
SMaDavFF	Female with wife of mother's DZ	
SPaMavFM	Male with wife of father's MZ twin	
SPaMavFF	Female with wife of father's MZ	
SMaMavMM	Male with husband of mother's MZ	
SMaMavMF	Female with husband of mother's MZ	
Spouses of twins		
SPDZM	Wives of DZ male twins	
SPDZF	Husbands of DZ female twins	
SPDZMF	Spouses of DZ male–female twins	
SPMZM	Wives of male MZ twins	
SPMZF	Husbands of female MZ twins	
Cousins	Sex of cousins	Parents' relation
MZMCsMM	Male–male	MZ male
MZMCsFF	Female–female	MZ male
MZMCsMF	Male–female	MZ male
MZFCsMM	Male–male	MZ female
MZFCsFF	Female–female	MZ female
MZFCsMF	Male–female	MZ female
DZMCsMM	Male–male	DZ male
DZMCsFF	Female–female	DZ male
DZMCsMF	Male–female	DZ male
DZFCsMM	Male–male	DZ female
DZFCsFF	Female–female	DZ female
DZFCsMF	Male–female	DZ female
DZMFCsMM	Male–male	DZ male–female
DZMFCsFF	Female–female	DZ male–female
DZMFCsMF	Male–female	DZ male–female
DZMFCsFM	Female–male	DZ male–female

items of the full scale used in an earlier study of Australian twins.[5] Some supplementary items were added to reflect issues (eg segregation, busing, moral majority) deemed newsworthy in the US at the time the survey was constructed. The items are listed in Table 5. Each may be answered 'Yes', 'Uncertain', 'No' (scored 1,2,3) to indicate agreement or otherwise with the topic.

The eigenvalues of the inter-item correlations for the attitude items suggested that a general 'conservative–liberalism' factor is a substantial, but not exhaustive, component of the social attitudes sampled in our brief inventory. A conservatism scale (Con) was thus constructed using all of the items keyed according to whether they had a positive or negative loading on the first general factor (Table 5). More detailed preliminary factor analysis of the attitude items confirmed that five (oblique) factors were clearly defined. On the basis of the factor pattern, we constructed scales (see Table 5) to reflect these main dimensions of the attitude responses: sexual permissiveness (Sex); economic liberalism

Table 4 Items from Eysenck Personality Questionnaire

	Scale	Scoring
1. Does your mood often go up and down?	N	+
2. Do you take much notice of what people think?	P	–
3. Are you a talkative person?	E	+
4. If you say you will do something, do you always keep your promise?	L	+
5. Do you ever feel 'just miserable' for no reason?	N	+
6. Would being in debt worry you?	P	+
7. Are you rather lively?	E	+
8. Were you every greedy by helping yourself to more than your share?	L	–
9. Do you stop to think things over before doing anything?	P	–
10. Are you an irritable person?	N	+
11. Would you take drugs which may have strange or dangerous effects?	P	+
12. Do you enjoy meeting new people?	E	+
13. Have you ever blamed someone for what was really your fault?	L	–
14. Are your feelings easily hurt?	N	+
15. Do you prefer to go your own way rather than act by the rules?	P	+
16. Can you usually let yourself go and enjoy yourself at a lively party?	E	+
17. Are *all* your habits good and desirable ones?	L	+
18. Have people said that you sometimes act too rashly?	E	+
19. Do you often feel 'fed-up'?	N	+
20. Do good manners and cleanliness matter much to you?	P	–
21. Do you usually take the initiative in making new friends?	E	+
22. Have you ever taken anything that belonged to someone else?	L	–
23. Would you call yourself a nervous person?	N	+
24. Do you think marriage is old-fashioned and should be done away with?	P	+
25. Can you easily put some life into a rather dull party?	E	+
26. Have you ever broken or lost something belonging to someone else?	L	–
27. Do you often make decisions on the spur of the moment?	E	+
28. Are you a worrier?	N	+
29. Do you enjoy co-operating with others?	P	–
30. Do you tend to keep in the background on social occasions?	E	–
31. Does it worry you if you know there are mistakes in your work?	P	–
32. Have you ever said anything bad or nasty about anyone?	L	–
33. Would you call yourself tense or 'high-strung'?	N	+
34. Do you think people spend too much time safeguarding their future with savings and insurances?	P	+
35. Do you like mixing with people?	E	+
36. Do you often take on more activities than you have time for?	E	+
37. As a child, were you ever 'fresh' towards your parents?	L	–
38. Do you worry too long after an embarrassing experience?	N	+
39. Do you try not to be rude to people?	P	–
40. Do you like plenty of bustle and excitement around you?	E	+
41. Have you ever cheated at a game?	L	–
42. Do you suffer from 'nerves'?	N	+
43. Would you like other people to be afraid of you?	P	+
44. Have you ever taken advantage of someone?	L	–
45. Do you like doing things in which you have to act quickly?	E	+
46. Are you mostly quiet when you are with other people?	E	–
47. Do you often feel lonely?	N	+
48. Is it better to follow society's rules than go your own way?	P	–
49. Do other people think of you as being very lively?	E	+
50. Do you always practice what you preach?	L	+
51. Are you often troubled about feelings of guilt?	N	+
52. Do you sometimes put off until tomorrow what you ought to do today?	L	–
53. Can you get a party going?	E	+
54. Would you call yourself happy-go-lucky?	E	+

Table 5 Key to social attitude items

Item	*Conservatism*	*Primary*
1. Death penalty	+	Mil
2. Astrology	–	Sex
3. X-rated movies	–	Sex
4. Modern art	–	Sex
5. Women's liberation	–	Sex
6. Foreign aid	–	Tax
7. Federal housing	–	Tax
8. Democrats	–	Pol
9. Military drill	+	Mil
10. The draft	+	Mil
11. Abortion	–	Sex
12. Property tax	–	Tax
13. Gay rights	–	Sex
14. Liberals	–	Sex
15. Immigration	–	Tax
16. Capitalism	+	Tax
17. Segregation	+	Rel
18. Moral majority	+	Rel
19. Pacificism	–	Mil(–) Rel(–)
20. Censorship	+	Rel
21. Nuclear power	+	Mil
22. Living together	–	Sex
23. Republicans	+	Pol(–)
24. Divorce	–	
25. School prayer	+	Rel
26. Unions	–	
27. Socialism	–	
28. Busing	+	

Note: Subjects are asked to indicate agreement or otherwise by circling 'Yes' or 'No' as appropriate, or to indicate uncertainty by circling '?'. In the above key a '+' indicates 'Yes' is the keyed direction of response.

(Tax); militarism (Mil); political preference for democrats or republicans (Pol); religious fundamentalism (Rel).

Data summary

In order to remove specific extraneous causes of variation and correlation between relatives that might interfere with the analysis of other genetic and environmental effects, the subjects' scores for each scale were examined for their regression on dummy variables coded for sex, whether or not the subject was a twin, and the source of ascertainment (the Virginia Twin Registry *vs* the AARP registry). Interactions between these effects were specified as the regressions on products of the dummy variables. The linear and quadratic effects of age, and the interactions of these components with the dummy variables and *their* interactions were also included in the regression model. The SAS regression procedure was used for this part of the analysis and the residuals from the regression model were then normalized using the 'BLOM' method incorporated in the SAS 'RANK' procedure.

In an ideal world, the correlations between relatives for the extended pedigrees should be computed by the method of maximum likelihood.[5,24] With 80 distinct relationships, however, securing ML estimates of the correlations is prohibitive with current algorithms since, in addition to the 80 correlations of primary concern, it would be necessary also to estimate a large number of others (eg three-generational correlations) which are based on numbers too small to provide estimates of any practical value. We chose an acceptable but not ideal alternative. All possible pairs of individuals contributing to a given relationship were identified and a pooled correlation for that group of individuals was computed. Although simulation studies have shown such estimates to be unbiased, the repeated use of the same individual in computing a correlation leads to estimates that are less precise than might be assumed as they have been based on samples of independent pairs.[25] One consequence of the false assumption of independence among the estimated correlations is that tests of goodness of fit tend to be more likely to be rejected than should be the case.

We present the correlations between relatives for the normalized residuals for personality in Table 6 and for social attitudes in Table 7.

In order to simplify preliminary perusal of the patterns of family resemblance, the correlations were pooled across sexes. Also, correlations which involved the DZ twin relationship were pooled with those involving the sibling relationship. Note that these correlations are frequently heterogeneous, given the very large sample sizes, and they are pooled for the purposes of preliminary inspection only. Subsequent model-fitting analyses are based on the entire set of 80 correlations and allow for the various possible sources of heterogeneity. The pooled correlations for personality are summarized in Table 8. Those for attitudes are given in Table 9.

The summary correlations for personality (Table 8) are all quite small, the only exception being those for MZ twins. Even here, however, that for the 'P' scale is only 0.29. Thus, over 50% of the variation in personality as measured by the short EPQ is due to non-familial factors such as errors of measurement and within-family environmental factors. In no case does the DZ correlation exceed half of the MZ correlation, suggesting that shared environmental effects are likely to be small. Generally, the sibling and parent offspring correlations are about equal. The avuncular correlations involving MZ co-twins of parents ('MZ avuncular') are close to the parent–offspring correlation for E,N and L and higher than the conventional avuncular correlations involving siblings and DZ co-twins of parents ('avuncular'). These correlations point to a small additive genetic contribution to family resemblance accounting for

Table 6 Correlations between relatives for Eysenck Personality Questionnaire scales

Relation	*n(Pr)*	*Correlation*			
		Psychoticism (P)	*Extraversion (E)*	*Neuroticism (N)*	*Lie (L)*
Nuclear family					
Spouses	4815	0.094	0.017	0.092	0.187
Sibs: MM	1514	0.128	0.139	0.109	0.122
Sibs: FF	3551	0.087	0.196	0.172	0.184
Sibs: MF	4304	0.078	0.131	0.137	0.129
Fath–Son	2218	0.047	0.154	0.134	0.105
Fath–Dau	3033	0.055	0.123	0.127	0.154
Moth–Son	3034	0.078	0.155	0.148	0.150
Moth–Dau	4542	0.087	0.162	0.157	0.173
Twins					
DZ: MM	556	0.170	0.153	0.178	0.271
DZ: FF	1141	0.098	0.120	0.224	0.255
DZ: MF	1295	0.104	0.108	0.097	0.158
MZ: MM	766	0.218	0.480	0.353	0.445
MZ: FF	1799	0.321	0.520	0.410	0.473
Avuncular					
PatSavMM	94	−0.055	0.003	0.062	0.094
PatSavMF	156	−0.052	0.069	−0.028	0.060
MatSavFM	388	0.016	0.163	0.145	0.058
MatSavFF	537	0.009	0.167	0.032	0.107
PatSavFM	130	−0.030	−0.058	0.081	0.245
PatSavFF	192	−0.017	−0.067	0.188	0.024
MatSavMM	234	−0.034	0.025	0.098	−0.005
MatSavMF	291	0.025	0.091	−0.005	0.066
PatDavMM	104	−0.014	0.134	0.118	0.067
PatDavMF	140	0.010	0.087	0.094	0.074
MatDavFM	331	0.127	0.106	0.107	0.103
MatDavFF	511	−0.040	0.174	0.183	0.151
PatDavFM	114	−0.069	0.121	−0.012	0.106
PatDavFF	180	0.028	−0.023	0.089	0.019
MatDavMM	152	−0.006	0.063	0.141	−0.021
MatDavMF	199	0.024	0.082	0.042	0.037
PatMavMM	216	−0.013	0.073	−0.016	0.059
PatMavMF	327	−0.018	0.172	0.034	0.158
MatMavFM	645	0.033	0.121	0.190	0.119
MatMavFF	1006	0.070	0.144	0.118	0.200
Cousins					
MZMCsMM	41	0.366	−0.198	−0.027	0.236
MZMCsFF	93	−0.051	0.205	0.102	−0.073
MZMCsMF	103	0.040	0.164	0.114	0.080
MZFCsMM	153	0.018	0.028	0.097	−0.033
MZFCsFF	341	0.000	0.102	0.096	0.100
MZFCsMF	453	0.005	0.091	0.044	0.121
DZMCsMM	17	−0.066	−0.231	−0.197	0.364
DZMCsFF	40	0.415	−0.228	−0.046	0.220
DZMCsMF	49	−0.134	−0.032	0.042	−0.165
DZFCsMM	52	0.160	0.145	−0.068	−0105
DZFCsFF	139	0.122	0.201	0.243	0.177
DZFCsMF	158	0.038	0.156	0.189	0.090
DZMFCsMM	38	0.090	0.023	0.250	0.010
DZMFCsFF	72	−0.004	0.179	0.238	−0.095
DZMFCsMF	50	−0.124	−0.182	0.330	0.057
DZMFCsFM	70	−0.249	−0.027	0.154	−0.131
Siblings-in-law					
SibInlMF	350	−0.049	−0.032	0.070	0.057
SibInlFM	732	0.039	0.078	0.056	0.055
SibInlMM	431	0.097	0.066	0.092	0.104
SibInlFF	463	0.094	0.101	0.047	0.064
DZInlMF	405	0.003	−0.048	−0.039	0.156
DZInlFM	594	−0.013	0.049	−0.002	0.043
DZInlMM	361	0.074	0.055	−0.062	0.032
DZInlFF	450	0.008	−0.032	−0.017	0.056
MZInlMF	602	0.038	0.117	0.064	0.066
MZInlFM	1132	0.075	−0.018	0.066	0.074
Parent-in-Law					
Fa–DIL	215	−0.008	0.028	0.085	0.109
Fa–SIL	210	0.067	−0.006	0.002	0.181
Mo–DIL	302	0.045	0.115	0.053	0.068
Mo–SIL	348	0.023	−0.050	−0.047	0.014
Affine avuncular					
SPaDavFM	55	−0.172	0.054	−0.076	0.003
SPaDavFF	77	0.117	−0.147	−0.075	0.133
SMaDavMM	124	−0.050	0.092	0.084	0.079
SMaDavMF	172	−0.003	0.016	0.213	−0.073
SPaDavMM	35	−0.407	−0.036	−0.417	−0.288
SPaDavMF	67	−0.190	0.063	0.033	−0.010
SMaDavFM	69	−0.006	0.101	0.304	0.047
SMaDavFF	95	−0.010	0.013	−0.128	−0.082
SPaMavFM	129	−0.061	0.076	−0.146	0.080
SPaMavFF	212	0.012	0.042	0.105	0.082
SMaMavMM	340	−0.022	0.064	0.051	0.015
SMaMavMF	501	0.053	0.069	0.009	0.124
Twins' spouses					
SPDZM	101	0.200	0.057	0.005	0.048
SPDZF	124	0.059	−0.032	0.098	−0.043
SPDZMF	169	0.050	−0.072	−0.022	0.140
SPMZM	180	0.065	0.040	−0.045	0.089
SPMZF	296	0.030	−0.014	0.018	0.116

Table 7 Correlations between relatives for Social Attitude Scales

Relation	*Social Attitudes*						*Conservatism*	
	n(pr)	*Sex*	*Tax*	*Mil*	*Pol*	*Rel*	*n(pr)*	*Con*
Nuclear family								
Spouses	4692	0.567	0.360	0.413	0.522	0.452	4915	0.619
Sibs: MM	1523	0.328	0.257	0.206	0.234	0.312	1551	0.341
Sibs: FF	3497	0.355	0.256	0.197	0.233	0.330	3643	0.405
Sibs: MF	4262	0.305	0.229	0.193	0.231	0.248	4395	0.328
Fath–Son	2164	0.359	0.284	0.261	0.303	0.318	2247	0.410
Fath–Dau	2988	0.338	0.236	0.212	0.278	0.312	3095	0.396
Moth–Son	3020	0.311	0.238	0.237	0.275	0.300	3138	0.369
Moth–Dau	4466	0.401	0.273	0.254	0.290	0.306	4667	0.456
Twins								
DZ: MM	556	0.377	0.299	0.245	0.308	0.224	579	0.379
DZ: FF	1080	0.435	0.317	0.247	0.341	0.310	1142	0.432
DZ: MF	1239	0.290	0.201	0.218	0.299	0.236	1312	0.319
MZ: MM	765	0.531	0.473	0.478	0.442	0.472	790	0.593
MZ: FF	1739	0.602	0.484	0.384	0.455	0.499	1839	0.637
Avuncular								
PatSavMM	100	0.314	0.298	0.275	0.115	0.263	100	0.334
PatSavMF	153	0.229	0.188	–0.042	0.014	0.261	156	0.324
MatSavFM	388	0.238	0.203	–0.058	0.049	0.219	405	0.200
MatSavFF	520	0.189	0.131	0.063	0.027	0.241	547	0.226
PatSavFM	128	0.324	0.078	0.182	–0.226	0.133	133	0.264
PatSavFF	189	0.211	–0.039	–0.026	0.064	0.034	200	0.112
MatSavMM	226	0.101	0.071	0.121	0.142	0.254	235	0.175
MatSavMF	281	0.047	0.142	0.075	0.071	0.189	297	0.166
PatDavFM	109	0.034	0.124	0.143	0.091	0.164	110	0.107
PatDavMF	143	0.103	0.039	–0.012	–0.047	0.035	144	0.108
MatDavMM	323	0.190	0.032	0.012	0.143	0.206	332	0.200
MatDavFF	489	0.190	0.106	0.081	0.076	0.302	516	0.250
PatDavFM	109	0.186	0.125	0.142	0.395	0.094	114	0.282
PatDavMF	171	0.210	0.235	0.212	0.217	0.122	180	0.314
MatDavFM	151	0.015	0.055	0.241	0.146	0.209	154	0.185
MatDavMF	201	0.115	0.147	0.002	0.036	0.217	206	0.225
PatMavMM	219	0.393	0.234	0.259	0.059	0.294	221	0.428
PatMavMF	333	0.329	0.096	0.085	0.135	0.283	341	0.315
MatMavFM	637	0.323	0.161	0.166	0.054	0.249	661	0.367
MatMavFF	994	0.337	0.229	0.146	0.179	0.251	1035	0.318
Cousins								
MZMCsMM	39	0.273	–0.046	0.175	0.383	0.063	40	0.564
MZMCsFF	95	0.243	0.170	0.226	0.206	0.093	95	0.265
MZMCsMF	107	0.281	–0.068	0.037	0.092	0.042	107	0.264
MZFCsMM	156	0.247	0.033	0.068	0.035	0.212	158	0.239
MZFCsFF	335	0.272	0.178	0.037	0.095	0.205	339	0.287
MZFCsMF	454	0.247	0.131	0.081	0.094	0.381	459	0.309
DZMCsMM	19	0.216	0.532	0.020	0.187	0.203	19	0.091
DZMCsFF	42	0.146	–0.131	0.158	–0.011	0.058	42	0.339
DZMCsMF	52	0.032	–0.030	0.335	–0.019	0.009	52	0.173
DZFCsMM	52	–0.274	–0.018	0.150	0.136	–0.073	53	–0.117
DZFCsFF	137	0.173	0.259	0.134	0.128	0.330	141	0.275
DZFCsMF	153	0.191	0.155	0.050	0.067	0.156	163	0.240
DZMFCsMM	39	–0.043	0.007	0.520	0.427	0.186	39	0.242
DZMFCsFF	69	0.123	0.114	0.267	0.253	0.242	70	0.227
DZMFCsMF	50	0.190	0.014	0.062	0.046	–0.047	52	0.066
DZMFCsFM	69	0.102	0.056	0.141	0.440	–0.017	70	0.112
Siblings-in-law								
SibInlMF	364	0.380	0.322	0.128	0.160	0.265	371	0.386
SibInlFM	710	0.268	0.175	0.103	0.100	0.176	745	0.219
SibInlMM	428	0.229	0.144	0.154	0.145	0.163	443	0.222
SibInlFF	472	0.169	0.131	0.172	0.187	0.127	486	0.175
DZInlMF	402	0.211	0.131	0.096	0.182	0.211	417	0.263
DZInlFM	586	0.328	0.160	0.116	0.190	0.238	618	0.310
DZInlMM	350	0.167	0.173	0.238	0.153	0.201	363	0.202
DZInlFF	434	0.203	0.196	0.205	0.223	0.207	455	0.290
MZInlMF	594	0.405	0.235	0.255	0.303	0.432	625	0.490
MZInlFM	1098	0.343	0.166	0.164	0.241	0.303	1153	0.409
Parent-in-Law								
Fa–DIL	198	0.287	0.152	0.117	0.217	0.226	208	0.312
Fa–SIL	206	0.289	0.215	0.180	0.173	0.172	211	0.219
Mo DIL	293	0.227	0.213	0.113	0.049	0.262	311	0.250
Mo–SIL	345	0.196	0.122	0.159	0.104	0.292	360	0.308
Affine avuncular								
SPaDavFM	57	–0.063	0.065	–0.083	–0.215	–0.116	57	–0.048
SPaDavFF	80	0.102	–0.019	–0.028	–0.097	–0.009	82	0.159
SMaDavMM	120	0.062	0.113	–0.100	0.235	0.267	128	0.158
SMaDavMF	164	0.152	0.090	–0.175	0.017	0.172	179	0.166
SPaDavMM	38	–0.110	–0.052	0.258	0.241	0.115	38	0.015
SPaDavMF	67	0.000	0.092	0.150	0.121	0.052	70	0.066
SMaDavFM	69	0.200	0.213	0.270	0.149	0.167	71	0.230
SMaDavFF	96	–0.071	0.107	0.159	0.018	0.295	99	0.195
SPaMavFM	129	0.305	0.086	0.199	0.088	0.198	134	0.366
SPaMavFF	213	0.348	0.095	0.083	0.184	0.223	224	0.276
SMaMavMM	341	0.166	0.138	0.072	0.028	0.167	353	0.239
SMaMavMF	494	0.238	0.169	0.052	0.139	0.182	511	0.222
Twins' spouses								
SPDZM	103	0.154	0.082	0.057	0.163	0.109	104	0.212
SPDZF	120	0.373	0.201	0.241	0.271	0.251	129	0.325
SPDZMF	169	0.106	–0.069	0.204	0.161	0.288	172	0.185
SPMZM	175	0.426	0.128	0.270	0.374	0.355	188	0.378
SPMZF	289	0.214	0.181	0.065	0.214	0.213	304	0.267

Note: Sex: sexual permissiveness; Tax: economic liberalism; Mil: militarism; Pol: political preference; Rel: religious fundamentalism; Con: general conservatism factor

Table 8 Summary correlations between relatives (pooled across sexes) for EPQ measures

Relation	*n(Pr)*	*Correlation*			
		Psychoticism (P)	*Extraversion (E)*	*Neuroticism (N)*	*Lie (L)*
Spouses	4815	0.094	0.017	0.092	0.187
Sibs	9369	0.089	0.157	0.146	0.149
DZ twins	2992	0.114	0.121	0.161	0.216
MZ twins	2565	0.291	0.508	0.394	0.465
Parents	12827	0.070	0.150	0.144	0.151
Avuncular	3753	0.003	0.097	0.092	0.080
MZ avuncular	2194	0.038	0.135	0.114	0.157
MZ cousins	1184	0.016	0.092	0.074	0.081
DZ cousins	685	0.030	0.074	0.166	0.041
Sib-in-law	3786	0.032	0.036	0.021	0.069
MZ-in-law	1734	0.062	0.029	0.065	0.071
Parent-in-law	1075	0.032	0.021	0.017	0.081
Affine avuncular	694	−0.051	0.025	0.065	−0.011
MZ affine avuncular	1182	0.012	0.064	0.022	0.080
Spouses of DZ	394	0.091	−0.026	0.023	0.059
Spouses of MZ	476	0.043	0.006	−0.006	0.106

Table 9 Summary correlations between relatives (pooled across sexes) for social attitude measures

Relation	*Social Attitudes*						*Conservatism*	
	n(pr)	*Sex*	*Tax*	*Mil*	*Pol*	*Rel*	*n(pr)*	*Con*
Spouses	4692	0.567	0.360	0.413	0.522	0.452	4915	0.619
Sibs	9282	0.328	0.244	0.197	0.232	0.290	9589	0.360
DZ twins	2875	0.363	0.264	0.234	0.317	0.262	3033	0.374
MZ twins	2504	0.581	0.481	0.414	0.451	0.491	2692	0.624
Parents	12638	0.358	0.258	0.241	0.286	0.308	13147	0.414
Avuncular	3681	0.172	0.119	0.067	0.076	0.206	3829	0.216
MZ avuncular	2183	0.337	0.190	0.154	0.124	0.260	2258	0.343
MZ cousins	1186	0.258	0.112	0.077	0.105	0.250	1198	0.296
DZ cousins	682	0.110	0.112	0.164	0.156	0.140	701	0.193
Sib-in-law	3746	0.250	0.176	0.146	0.164	0.197	3898	0.257
MZ-in-law	1692	0.365	0.190	0.196	0.263	0.350	1778	0.439
Parent-in-law	1042	0.241	0.172	0.142	0.124	0.248	1090	0.276
Affine avuncular	691	0.065	0.087	0.128	0.059	0.148	724	0.140
MZ affine avuncular	1177	0.245	0.138	0.080	0.110	0.187	1222	0.253
Spouses of DZ	392	0.203	0.054	0.178	0.196	0.231	405	0.238
Spouses of MZ	464	0.297	0.161	0.144	0.276	0.268	492	0.310

no more than 25–30% of the total variance. The fact that the MZ correlations for E and N somewhat exceed these values may be due to non-additive genetic effects or a special MZ twin environment. The fact that other relationships involving MZ twins, especially those for social attitudes (see below) are also inflated seems to point to a very pervasive effect of monozygosity on other biological and non-biological relationship. Obviously a genetic model has a built-in capability to predict and explain these findings. It is less clear that the often-touted 'special MZ twin environment' has these capabilities.

The spousal correlations, and all correlations by marriage are uniformly small, although with these sample sizes very small correlations are statistically significant. The spousal correlation for the 'Lie' scale is twice that of any of the other EPQ scales and even that is too small to have biologically or socially significant impact of genetic and environmental correlations between relatives. Thus, in general, the effects of assortment on personality are fairly trivial.

All these findings are consistent with other studies of personality, including adoption studies and studies of separated twins[5,13–15,26] and the larger studies of twins (see Eaves *et al*[5] for a summary of these studies).

The correlations for social attitudes (Table 9) extend to other relationships those characteristics of the transmission of social attitudes, as distinct from personality, that we have come to recognize on the basis of earlier studies of twins especially.[5] The correlations for conservatism ('C') are typical and represent the general trend found in the primary attitude scales. Family resemblance is generally greater. Correlations for first degree relatives are twice those for personality and there is a very striking correlation between spouses which has a pervasive impact on all the other relationships by marriage ('In-laws', avuncular correlations by marriage, spouses of twins). The potential impact of mate selection on the transmission of, and variation in, attitudes clearly cannot be ignored. The other striking feature of the attitude data is that all the correlations involving monozygotic twins exceed the corresponding correlations involving DZ twins or siblings. This is true for biological relationships and for relationships by marriage. Thus, the avuncular correlations involving an MZ co-twin as uncle/aunt (genetically a parent–offspring relationship) are generally greater than the corresponding conventional avuncular correlations involving aunts and uncles who are siblings or DZ twins of the parents. Similarly, the correlations between cousins related through MZ twin parents (genetically half-siblings[27]) exceed those for conventional cousins related through DZ twin parents. Thus the data are consistent with previous studies in lending support to the counter-intuitive notion that genetic factors account for some of the variation in social attitudes in western, Caucasian culture.

A model for family resemblance in extended twin kinships

The preliminary examination of the pooled correlations suggests the main features that might emerge from a more rigorous analysis but does not capture the subtleties that are apparent in the full tables of correlations, not does it yield a more thorough quantitative resolution of the effects of biological and cultural transmission which, *a priori*, are expected to be correlated in kinships based on nuclear families alone. Furthermore, many of the correlations pooled to generate the summary tables are significantly heterogeneous, suggesting that sex differences may interact with the causes of family resemblance.

Figure 2 presents a tractable path model for family resemblance which can be extended to include all the relationships in the kinships of twins listed above in Table 3. It is not the only possible model and others may be developed which feature other nuances of the mate selection process or non-genetic inheritance.[19]

Basic parameters of the model

The model is discussed in detail by Truett *et al*[20] who illustrate its application to the analysis of biological and cultural inheritance to twin-kinship data on frequency of church attendance. Ignoring, for the moment, the provision for sex differences in genetic and environmental effects, the model allows for the a series of basic genetic and social influences on variation. These are denoted in the path diagram (Figure 2) by lower case letters as follows:

1. additive genetic effects, *h*;
2. genetic dominance, *d*;
3. path from environment to phenotype, *e*;
4. path from parental phenotype to offspring environment, *w*;
5. phenotypic correlation between mates, μ;
6. path from residual sibling shared environment to phenotype, *s*;
7. path from additional twin shared environment to phenotype, *t*;
8. the correlation between genotype and environment, ρ.

The model assumes initially that assortative mating, if present, is based on the measured phenotype, P ('primary phenotypic assortative mating'[19]). Similarly, it is assumed that vertical cultural transmission from parent to offspring is based on the measured phenotype of the parents rather than on some latent or correlated variable ('P to E' vertical cultural inheritance). The effects of the sibling and twin shared environments are assumed to contribute to variation among individuals regardless of relationship. However, the sibling environment is perfectly correlated in sibling and twin pairs, and the twin environment is perfectly correlated in twin pairs. Thus, the model assumes that twins and siblings will differ in *correlation* as a result of how they are influenced by their shared environment but not in their *variance*. That is, twins and siblings are assumed to sample the same marginal distribution of environmental effects as other individuals but they differ in the environmental correlation. The *genotype–environment correlation*, ρ, occurs when the parental phenotype, which contributes to the offspring's environment through parent–offspring transmission, is partly genetic in origin. This results in a correlation between the offspring's environment and genes. The process of transmission and assortment is assumed to be in equilibrium, and thus, ρ is constant between generations. That is, ρ_{parent} is constrained to be equal to ρ_{child}. Since models are fitted to correlations, the scale of measurement has unit variance; therefore, we impose the further constraint that the sum of all sources of variation is unity.

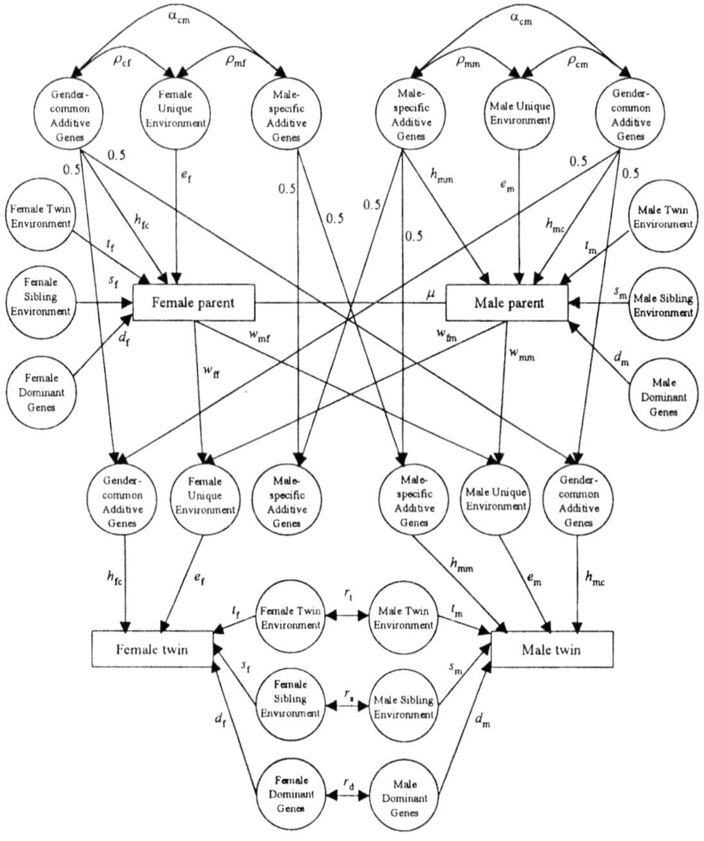

Figure 2 Path model for family resemblance including all 80 possible relationships in the kinships of twins as listed in Table 3 (after[20])

Assortment and cultural transmission based on a latent variable

The measured trait may not correlate perfectly with the trait for which mate selection and cultural transmission are actually occurring. Morton[28] argued for a model of 'social homogamy' in which assortment and cultural transmission are based on a correlated latent variable to which genes make no contribution. Another mechanism of assortment (proposed by Heath and Eaves[19]) presents a model for mixed homogamy in which mate selection is based on both the social background of the spouses and the phenotype of the mate. We have used 'phenotypic assortment plus error'[29] in which the actual measurement is considered a more or less unreliable index of the latent score on which assortment is based. In this model, all expected correlations were multiplied by the square of the path from 'true' (or latent) score to 'observed' score (the reliability [rel]). When there is significant assortative mating or cultural inheritance, there is sufficient information to estimate rel without repeated measurements.

Allowing for sex differences in model parameters

One of the principal advantages of a study involving large samples of relatives is the provision of an opportunity to test a variety of models of sex-dependent etiology and transmission. For the simple case of randomly mating populations, a model for sex differences in gene action was specified by Eaves[30] which allowed for the same genes to have different magnitudes of effect on males and females. This model allows for estimation of separate genetic variances for males and females and a correlation between gene effects in males and females. The genetic correlation between the sexes will be unity if the effects of all autosomal loci on one sex are constant multiples of their effects on the other sex. In this case, we speak of 'scalar sex limitation of the gene effects'. Analogous definitions maybe given for the 'sex-limited' effects of the shared environment. If the magnitudes of the loci or, by analogy, 'environmental effects' on one sex are not constant multiples of their effects on the other sex, then we speak of non-scalar sex limitation of genetic (or environmental) effects.

The present model extends the analysis of sex-dependent effects to the more difficult case of combined assortative mating and cultural inheritance. In the path diagram (Figure 2) we employ the following notation for the effects of dominance, sibling environment and special twin environment: d_m, s_m, and t_m in males respectively, and d_f, s_f and t_f for their counterparts in females; and r_d, r_s and r_t for the correlations across sexes of the dominant, sibling environmental and twin environmental effects.

Since vertical cultural transmission is assumed under this model to be based on the parental phenotype for the trait under investigation the question of 'non-scalar' vertical cultural transmission does not apply. However, the cultural impact of mothers may differ from that of fathers, and may further depend on the sex of the offspring. In the model for sex differences, therefore, we require *four* cultural parameters: $> w_{mm}$; w_{mf}; w_{fm}; w_{ff}. The first subscript denotes the sex (m = male) of the offspring and the second denotes the sex of the parent.

Specification of sex-limited additive genetic effects is more difficult when there is assortative mating which induces correlations between loci that would otherwise be independent, see, for example, Fisher.[31] We have adopted one of several, formally equivalent, ways of parameterizing the additive sex-limited effects. Recognizing that the additive genetic variances in the two sexes and the genetic covariance between them require three free parameters for their complete specification, we assume that one set of genes explains *all* the genetic variance in females, and the genetic covariance between the sexes. The paths from this 'common' set of genes to the male and female phenotypes are denoted by h_{mc} and h_{fc}, respectively. A second set of genes has effects which are specific only to males and the path from these genes to the male phenotype is specified by h_{mm}. Although the 'male-specific' genes are not expressed in females, they are still present in females and correlated, through phenotypic assortment, with the 'common genes'. We denote the induced correlation between the two sets of additive genetic effects by α_{cm}.

The joint effects of assortment and vertical cultural transmission induce *four* genotype–environment correlations: two between the 'common' additive genetic effects and the environments of males and females, ρ_{cm} and ρ_{cf}, respectively; two between the 'male-specific' additive genetic effects and the environments of males and females, ρ_{mm} and ρ_{mf}, respectively. These genotype–environment correlations are estimated as constrained parameters when fitting the model (ie they are functions of other parameters). Separate parameters are required to specify the path from male environment to phenotype (e_m) and female environment to phenotype (e_f). Under the simple model for 'phenotypic assortment with error', the paths from true score to observed score, rel_m and rel_f, may differ between males and females.

Since the total phenotypic variance is standardized to unity in both sexes, two further constraints are required to enforce these conditions. Thus, seven constraints are imposed on parameter values under the full model. The full model for sex-limited effects is given for pairs of unlike-sex DZ twins in Figure 2.

Fitting the model

The method of iterative constrained diagonal weighted least squares was used to fit the full (non-linear) model to the 80 correlations for each personality and social attitude variable in turn. The model is fitted to the z-transforms of the raw correlations to improve the approximation to normality.[32] Truett *et al*[26] give further details of the model fitting method. The expected correlations between relatives may be derived algebraically from the path model. These are extremely complex and are not reproduced here. However, copies of the FORTAN program, which incorporates annotated code for the algebraic expectations for the correlations between relatives and expressions for derived estimates of variance components (see following), are available from the first author by electronic mail. The Numerical Algorithms Group's FORTRAN subroutine E04UEF was used for constrained numerical minimization of the residual sum of squares.[33]

The full model, involving 19 free parameters, was fitted first. The weighted residual sum of squares for 80 − 19 = 61 d.f. is employed as a guide to the overall goodness of fit of the model. The false assumption of independence in the observed correlations is likely to result in our rejecting the model too often if we treat this statistic uncritically as χ^2. However, comparisons of alternative models based on examination of changes in χ^2 associated with reductions in the full model are less open to such biases.[34]

In order to test the significance of combinations of effects having particular theoretical importance, a series of reduced models was fitted in every case and the increase in the residual sum of squares noted as a guide to the deterioration in fit associated with deleting specific effects from the model. Reduced models were fitted to test the following specific hypotheses:

1) that all genetic and environmental effects were homogenous over sexes;
2) that there were no *genetic* effects ($h = 0$, $d = 0$ in both sexes);
3) that there were no *non-additive (dominant) genetic effects* ($d = 0$ in both sexes);
4) that there were no effects of the *shared environment* of any kind ($s = t = w = 0$ in both sexes). In the presence of significant shared environmental effects a further test was conducted:
5) that there was no *vertical cultural inheritance* ($w = 0$ in both sexes).

These tests do not exhaust all the possibilities. However, in view of the danger of capitalizing on chance with multiple tests it is more appropriate to restrict testing to a few major effects of *a priori* importance.

Results

Tables 10 and 11 present the weighted least squares estimates of the parameters of the full model for the correlations for personality and attitudes respectively. The models for personality involve two fewer parameters than those for social attitudes because the virtual absence of assortative mating and vertical cultural inheritance meant there was no need to test whether these effects were based on a latent variable. That is, $r_m = r_f = 1$ for all the models of personality. Two χ^2 statistics are also tabulated testing for approximate goodness of fit of the model and testing for heterogeneity of the model parameters across sexes.

Tables 12 and 13 summarize, for personality and social attitude measures respectively, the estimated contributions of the various effects included in the 'full' model to variation in males and females. The formulae used to compute these components of variance from the parameters of the path model are given by Truett *et al.*[20]

Discussion

Before considering the positive findings, it is essential to note what possible causes of variation are not considered in the current model. There are three main exclusions. First, although we correct for population linear and quadratic trends in response with age, we do not consider the implications of the interaction between age, cohort effects or generational differences and individual genetic and environmental differences. Modeling these effects requires different approaches from those used here[5,35,36] and remains a goal for future data analysis. One consequence of these effects is the decay of family resemblance with increasing age differences between relatives. As a result, analyses of family resemblance which ignore these effects may find increased non-additivity (because parent–offspring correlations are reduced relative to siblings who are more similar in age but share same additive genetic similarity and 'twin environment effects' because MZ and DZ twins are being measured at more comparable stages of gene expression than siblings who have larger age differences within pairs. Second, although we allow for an increased environmental correlation for MZ and DZ twins, we do not specify any extra 'special MZ' shared environment. If such environmental effects are important they will increase the MZ correlation relative to the DZ correlation and inflate the estimate of non-additive genetic effects in our model. Finally, although we model social interactions between parents and children ('vertical cultural inheritance') we assume that any additional environment correlation between siblings and twins is not due to the social interaction between the siblings and twin themselves ('sibling effects';[37] or 'imitation and contrast effects'[38]). The extra environmental correlation of siblings and twins is assumed to arrive from residual shared environmental influences external to the pair and the family. These may include the effects of peers, schooling etc as long as these are not caused by the phenotypes of the parents or the measured behavior of their children. Such 'sibling' effects will produce differences in the dispersions of traits in families of different density and, again, require different models

Table 10 Results of model-fitting to personality correlations

Parameter		*Estimate*			
		P	E	N	L
Genetic	h_{fc}	0.136	0.525	0.566	0.617
	h_{mc}	0.101	0.413	0.391	0.446
	h_{mm}	0	0	0	0
	d_f	0.520	0.477	0.209	0.188
	d_m	0.268	0.508	0.337	0.295
	r_d	1.000	0.306	1.000	−0.287
Assortment	μ	0.099	0.003	0.098	0.194
	α_{cm}	0	0	0	0
Cultural transmission	w_{ff}	0.090	0.029	−0.017	−0.045
	w_{mf}	0.078	0.055	0.043	−0.003
	w_{fm}	0.046	0.002	−0.005	−0.018
	w_{mm}	0.036	0.070	0.043	−0.022
Other shared environment	s_f	0.087	0	0.059	0
	s_m	0.310	0	0	0.041
	r_s	1.000	–	–	–
	t_f	0.123	0.018	0.223	0.262
	t_m	0.195	0.120	0.251	0.400
	r_t	1.000	−1.000	−0.790	0.272
Unique environment	e_f	0.829	0.700	0.767	0.730
	e_m	0.884	0.734	0.810	0.746
Genotype–environment correlations	r_{ef}	0.010	0.008	0.023	−0.020
	r_{em}	0.008	0.031	0	−0.007
	r_{mf}	0	0	0	0
	r_{mm}	0	0	0	0
Tests of significance					
Goodness-of-fit	χ^2_{63}	66.85	94.01	88.96	66.46
Sex heterogeneity	χ^2_{11}	15.58	29.59	24.31	34.35
Genetic effects	χ^2_{6}	614.01	1834.83	?	91.71
Dominance	χ^2_{3}	239.45	503.77	361.80	?
Family environment	χ^2_{10}	16.07	3.53	8.46	8.37

Note: '?' denotes instances where numerical difficulties precluded computation of reliable parameter estimates

from those we have presented here, (for instance, Zajonc and Markus[39]).

Such warnings having been sounded, we note that the data from these large samples of more heterogeneous relationships allow us to test the claims based on other studies of fewer kinds of relationship, including the very large twin studies of personality and attitudes that have been reported.[5]

With the exception of psychoticism and political preference, the results show consistent evidence of heterogeneity in the parameter values across sexes. The fact that the sex-specific additive genetic effect on males is always zero suggests that the cause of heterogeneity in the additive genetic effects over sexes is epigenetic, ie the same genes are having effects of differing magnitudes in males and females. Although the sexes differ in the *magnitudes* of the expressed additive genetic effects, there is no suggestion that the traits are under the control of different genes in these data. When we turn to epigenetic effects, however, including genetic non-additivity, we see almost every conceivable variety of sex dependence. The same genes seem to be involved in non-additive interactions for psychoticism and extraversion (r_d = 1) whilst distinct genetic effects may interact in males and females to create differences in extraversion and lie scores (r_d < 1). We note that the sibling and twin environments generally play a larger role in the development of female attitudes than is the case for males (see estimates of twin and sibling environmental variance components in Table 13).

The results confirm the now commonplace finding of the inheritance of personality and attitudes that by far the most consistent effects on individual differences are those of the unique, within family, environment ('residual' in Tables 12 and 13). In our cross-sectional study, these effects include both long-term environmental influences and short term fluctuations. Previous studies[5] suggest strongly the short-term influences outweigh long-term effects in creating the within-family environment.

Table 11 Results of model-fitting to correlations in social attitudes

Parameter		*Estimate*					
		Sex	*Tax*	*Mil*	*Pol*	*Rel*	*Con*
Genetic	h_{fc}	0.720	0.557	0.266	0.261	0.649	0.580
	h_{mc}	0.703	0.368	0.441	0.090	1	0.867
	h_{mm}	0	0	0	0	0	0
	d_f	0	0.354	0.424	0.328	0.393	0.360
	d_m	0.382	0.547	0.561	0.512	0.315	0.297
	r_d	–	0.486	1	1	0.456	–0.002
Assortment	μ	0.706	0.546	0.593	0.633	0.750	0.720
	α_{cm}	0	0	0	0	0	0
Cultural transmission	w_{ff}	0.020	0.208	0.258	0.164	0.181	0.172
	w_{mf}	–0.339	0.008	0.119	0.135	–0.271	–0.368
	w_{fm}	–0.028	0.066	0.119	0.267	–0.062	0.026
	w_{mm}	0.375	0.445	0.338	0.426	–0.200	0.208
Other shared environment	s_f	0.223	0.238	0.228	0.251	0.322	0.233
	s_m	0.256	0.328	0.118	0.289	0	0
	r_s	0.406	0.796	1	1	–	–
	t_f	0.315	0.271	0.272	0.355	0.106	0.210
	t_m	0.080	0.038	0.277	0.274	0.015	0.036
	r_t	–1	–0.934	1	1	1	1
Unique environment	e_f	0.521	0.597	0.581	0.746	0.386	0.493
	e_m	0.580	0.595	0.755	0.775	0.506	0.592
Genotype–environment correlations	r_{ef}	–0.005	0.122	0.133	0.086	0.079	0.124
	r_{cm}	0.022	0.228	0.169	0.110	–0.322	–0.094
	r_{mf}	0	0	0	0	0	0
	r_{mm}	0	0	0	0	0	0
Latent variable	r_f	0.948	0.838	0.867	0.958	0.801	0.979
	r_m	0.848	0.790	0.801	0.862	0.749	0.878
Tests of significance							
Goodness-of-fit	χ^2_{61}	84.76	84.53	90.72	110.05	90.03	62.51
Sex heterogeneity	χ^2_{12}	66.43	22.07	96.27	19.22	141.13	65.46
Genetic effects	χ^2_6	107.52	96.23	116.29	102.29	212.83	233.89
Dominance	χ^2_3	?	4.32	12.73	11.42	76.39	195.36
Family environment	χ^2_{10}	28.03	16.47	22.87	63.38	13.01	25.25
Vertical cultural inheritance	χ^2_4	12.38	6.64	16.34	33.99	5.91	16.24

Note: '?' denotes instances where numerical difficulties precluded computation of reliable parameter estimates

Our new data confirm the earlier claims based on a variety of relationships, that the shared environment plays only a small and non-significant role in the creation of personality differences in adults. There are noticeable contributions of the 'twin' environment (t) to neuroticism and lie scores but the direct environmental impact (w) of parental personality on children is virtually non-existent.

Previous twin studies of social attitudes have shown that the correlations for DZ twins are significantly greater than one half of the correlations for MZ twins, pointing to the importance of either the shared environment, or the genetic consequences of assortative mating, or both. The new results allow us to be clearer about the confounded role of assortment and the shared environment. It is clear that, for all the social attitude measures, the high degree of marital resemblance can account for some of the apparent excess DZ correlation in terms of the increased genetic resemblance of family members arising from the fact that like spouses bring together alleles of similar effect ('assortment', Table 13). These effects are absent in the personality scales (Table 12). However, for many attitude factors, the total effects of the shared environment equal or exceed those of assortment. We also see that vertical cultural inheritance within the family – the direct impact of parental attitudes on offspring attitudes[40] – is a significant factor in parent offspring similarity in attitudes. The path coefficients (w) in Table 11 show values ranging from –0.368 for the impact of maternal conservatism on the environment of her sons, to +0.445 for the impact of paternal attitudes to taxation for welfare of others on the environment of their sons. In this respect, the proportions of variance attributed to the cultural impact of parents on

Table 12 Estimated contributions (%) of principal sources of variation to differences in personality among males and females based on parameter estimates from most general path model

Component	*Proportion of variance(%)*							
	P		E		N		L	
	Male	*Female*	*Male*	*Female*	*Male*	*Female*	*Male*	*Female*
Genetic								
Additive	1.0	1.8	16.9	27.4	14.9	31.3	18.8	36.2
Assortment	0	0	0.1	0.2	0.3	0.7	1.0	2.0
Dominance	7.2	27.0	25.8	22.8	11.3	4.4	8.7	3.5
Total	8.2	28.8	42.8	50.4	26.6	36.4	28.6	41.7
Environmental								
Maternal	0.5	0.6	0.2	0	0.1	0	0	0.1
Paternal	0.1	0.2	0.3	0	0.1	0	0	0
Sibling	9.6	0.8	0	0	0	0.4	0	0
Twin	3.8	1.5	1.4	0	6.3	5.0	16.0	6.9
Residual	77.6	67.9	53.4	49.0	65.4	58.8	55.7	53.1
Total parental	0.6	0.8	0.5	0	0.3	0	0	0.1
Total shared	14.0	3.0	1.9	0	6.5	5.4	16.2	7.0
Total	91.7	71.0	55.3	49.0	71.9	64.1	71.9	60.2
G–E covariance	0.1	0.2	1.9	0.6	1.5	–0.5	–0.5	–1.9

Table 13 Estimated contributions (%) of principal sources of variation to differences in social attitudes among males and females based on parameter estimates from most general path model

Component	*Proportion of variance(%)*											
	Sexual		*Taxes*		*Military*		*Political*		*Religious*		*Conservatism*	
	M	*F*	*M*	*F*	*M*	*F*	*M*	*F*	*M*	*F*	*M*	*F*
Genetic												
Additive	35.5	46.6	7.0	18.0	11.0	4.7	0.6	6.2	30.7	14.8	35.5	19.8
Assortment	12.9	16.9	1.5	3.8	1.5	0.6	0	0.2	25.4	12.3	22.2	12.4
Dominance	10.5	0	18.7	8.8	20.2	13.5	19.5	9.9	5.6	9.9	6.7	12.5
Total	46.0	46.6	27.2	30.6	32.7	18.8	20.1	16.1	61.6	37.0	64.5	44.7
Environmental												
Maternal	0.5	0	0.6	1.3	0.8	3.6	2.3	3.0	1.0	0.4	1.5	0.1
Paternal	1.0	0	4.9	0.3	3.0	1.4	9.0	5.5	0.7	0	0	0
Sibling	4.7	4.5	6.7	4.0	0.9	3.9	6.2	5.8	0	6.7	0	5.2
Twin	0.5	8.9	0.1	5.1	3.3	5.6	5.6	11.6	0	0.7	0.1	4.2
Residual	45.5	40.4	58.2	53.2	53.7	62.7	55.7	54.9	50.6	40.3	40.1	36.6
Total parental	1.5	0	5.5	1.6	3.8	5.0	11.3	8.5	1.7	0.4	1.5	0.1
Total shared	6.7	13.4	12.3	10.6	8.0	14.5	23.1	25.8	1.7	7.8	1.6	10.6
Total	52.2	53.8	66.5	63.8	61.7	77.2	78.8	80.7	52.3	59.7	41.7	47.2
G–E covariance	1.2	–0.4	6.3	5.7	5.6	4.0	1.1	3.2	–13.9	3.3	–6.2	8.1

their children are misleadingly small because quite large parent–offspring paths are squared when computing the contributions to variation in the next generation. Furthermore, negative paternal effects may tend to cancel out positive maternal effects and vice versa when there is substantial assortative mating. Although the specific parameters of vertical cultural inheritance should probably be treated with some sensitivity to the possible role of sampling error, we note that the coefficients for like-sex relationships are usually somewhat higher than those for unlike-sex parent–offspring pairs. This finding is consistent with the view that children model on their like-sex parent. In data on ordinary nuclear families alone, such effects are confounded with those of sex-limited gene expression. An extreme example of this tendency in our data is provided by the marked opposition between the roles of mothers and fathers in creating the attitudes of sons on sexual issues (Table 11). The path from mothers' attitudes to sons' environments is estimated as –0.339. That from fathers' attitudes to sons' environments is +0.375. The opposite signs of these effects result in an apparent contribution of the paternal environment (Table 13) of only 1.5% although, if the finding is replicated, the process would seem to be very important for understanding the process of socialization in the development of sexual values.

The total contribution of genetic factors to differences in personality and attitudes is significant and pervasive. We note that the total estimated contribution of genetic variability to social attitudes is not much different from their effects on personality. We confirm the findings of previous twin studies that the effect of genetic factors in creating variation for social attitudes, as distinct from personality, may be exaggerated by the genetic consequences of assortative mating. The estimated contributions of 'assortment' to genetic variation are larger for attitudes (Table 13) than personality (Table 12).

Non-additive genetic effects also appear to play a significant role in the creation of the personality and attitude variables measured in our study. Although these are parameterized as 'dominance' in the model, other epistatic interactions between loci will tend to be confounded with the additive and dominance effects. Epistasis of the duplicate type, in which the phenotype is buffered against change by the evolution of multiple loci having parallel functions, is especially likely to inflate the estimate of dominant genetic effects.[41]

Taken as a whole, the data from the Virginia 30 000 show remarkable consistency with the earlier twin, family and adoption studies as far as personality as concerned and allow a far more detailed analysis of the transmission of social attitudes than has been possible in the past.[42,43] We note the same apparent inconsistencies between the findings for personality that had been noted before between studies using different instruments and separate populations. It is clear from our data that this result is not a matter of the population sampled or the choice of measurement but that it resides in a large effect of genetic non-additivity. In our model these effects contribute to the large estimate of the dominance parameter because the correlations between parents and siblings are much lower than those between MZ twins. Another possibility is that some of the genetic non-additivity is due to the interaction of genetic differences with age. Such effects would produce a lot of apparent dominance in our model, because parents are measured at different ages from children and twins. They would also tend to inflate the twin correlation relative to the sibling correlation. The overall effect of additive genetic effects, and thus the narrow heritability, is small for most of the personality dimensions.

One of the truly remarkable findings to emerge from behavior genetics over the past 20 years in the replication and consistency of findings about the transmission of personality and social attitudes in different studies using different approaches and methods of analysis. Even if investigators may differ in the models they use to interpret their data, it is still little short of astonishing that the actual correlations between relatives show such consistency between studies, not merely in their relative magnitudes for a given variable but also for the differential patterns of family resemblance seen between measures in different domains. This does not mean that the last word has been said on the subject. Understanding the origin of the apparently large non-additive genetic component will require more detailed analysis of the effects of age on family resemblance. We still do not understand the adaptive significance of assortment for social attitudes in contrast to the essentially random mating we see persistently for personality. We have little idea about the developmental role of genetic differences in shaping the environment to which individuals are subjected. Such effects all serve to enhance the expression of genetic differences which might be small at the outset and may still provide a foundation for behavioral rather that medicinal intervention in certain kinds of behavioral disorder. Finally, we do not yet know certainly whether the absence of shared environmental effects on adult personality is simply a feature of adult adaptation or whether it characterizes personality measures throughout development. Such findings will be crucial for how personality is viewed biologically.

Our results underscore the striking differences between the inheritance of personality and social attitudes. What appeared as an excess correlation among DZ twins reared together in previous twin studies of social attitudes has now been resolved into a number of different possible factors. Some of the additional variation between DZ twin pairs may indeed be the genetic consequences of assortative mating as implied by the model of Martin *et al*,[43] but our data show that this is not the whole story because the vertical cultural inheritance of attitudes from parents to children cannot be discounted, neither can the extra-familial environmental effects shared by siblings and twins. The Virginia 30 000 data confirm the repeated findings of other twin studies that genetic factors cannot be ignored in the creation of social attitude differences. The consistent difference between attitudes and personality may point to different roles in human adaptation. The absence of any assortment and vertical cultural inheritance for personality may indicate that personality is the manifestation of phylogenetically early properties of the nervous system that predate the evolution of the *human* brain. The fact that researchers have proposed animal models for personality[44] is consistent with this view. On the other hand, it is impossible to conceive of attitudes without a culture depending on learning and social interaction for its maintenance and requiring, therefore, those aspects of the brain which are most fully differentiated in humans. In evolving systems to deal with life in society humans have not left behind their genetic diversity. Individual differences at the genetic level, as well as differences in personal history and family environment, still bias for good or ill the choices and prejudices of individuals in society.

The significant contribution of genetic factors to social attitudes means that virtually no measurable aspect of human behavioral variation is so far removed from the impact of events at the genetic level as to be considered in complete isolation from the emerging theory and knowledge in genetics and sociobiology. It is as naive to suppose that there is a simple link between events at the DNA level and complex behavioral outcomes such as social attitudes, as it is to suppose that culture has completely immunized humans from the effects of their genes. We conceive of an ontogenetic process in which small initial genetic differences in behavior and preference are augmented over time by the incorporation into the phenotype of environmental information, correlated with the genotype, in a continual process of sifting and evaluation. Much of the apparent genetic variation in normal human behavior may ultimately turn out to be of this type. It will require far greater ingenuity to understand the processes of developmental feedback and gene-environment correlation which create such 'extended phenotypes'[45] than it has taken so far to quantify the complex contributions of genes and environment to adult behavioral outcomes.

Acknowledgements

Data collection was supported by USDHHS grants AA06781, MH40828 and a gift from RJR Nabisco. Theory and data analysis were supported by USDHHS grants GM30250, AG04954 and HL48148, and by a grant from the John M Templeton Foundation.

References

1 Loehlin JC, Nichols RC. Heredity, environment, and personality: a study of 850 sets of twins. University of Texas Press: Austin, 1976.
2 Floderus-Myrhed B, Pedersen N, Rasmuson I. Assessment of heritability for personality, based on a short-form of the Eysenck Personality Inventory: a study of 12,898 twin pairs. *Behav Genet* 1980; **10**: 153–162.
3 Martin NG, Jardine R. Eysenck's contribution to behavior genetics. In: Modgil S, Modgil C (eds). *Hans Eysenck: Consensus and Controversy.* Falmer Press: Philadelphia, 1986, pp 13–47.
4 Rose RJ, Koskenvuo M, Kaprio J, Sarna S, Langinvainio H. Shared genes, shared experiences, and similarity of personality: data from 14,288 adult Finnish co-twins. *J Pers Soc Psychol* 1988; **54**: 161–171.
5 Eaves LJ, Eysenck HJ, Martin NG. Genes, culture and personality: an empirical approach. Oxford University Press: London, 1989.
6 Shields J. *Monozygotic Twins: Brought up Apart and Brought up Together.* Oxford University Press: London, 1996.
7 Langinvainio H, Kaprio J, Koskenvuo M, Lonnqvist J. Finnish twins reared apart. III: Personality factors. *Acta Genet Med Gemellol (Roma)* 1984; **33**: 259–264.
8 Tellegen A, Lykken DT, Bouchard TJ Jr, Wilcox KJ, Segal NL, Rich S. Personality similarity in twins reared apart and together. *J Pers Soc Psychol* 1988; **54**: 1031–1039.
9 Pedersen NL, Plomin R, McClearn GE, Friberg L. Neuroticism, extraversion, and related traits in adult twins reared apart and reared together. *J Pers Soc Psychol* 1988; **55**: 950–957.
10 Ahern FM, Johnson RC, Wilson JR, McClearn GE, Vandenberg SG. Family resemblances in personality. *Behav Genet* 1982; **12**: 261–280.
11 Buss DM. Marital assortment for personality dispositions: assessment with three different data sources. *Behav Genet* 1984; **14**: 111–123.
12 Scarr S, Webber PL, Weinberg RA, Wittig MA. Personality resemblance among adolescents and their parents in biologically related and adoptive families. *J Pers Soc Psychol* 1981; **40**: 885–898.
13 Loehlin JC, Horn JM, Willerman L. Personality resemblance in adoptive families. *Behav Genet* 1981; **11**: 309–330.
14 Loehlin JC, Willerman L, Horn JM. Personality resemblances between unwed mothers and their adopted-away offspring. *J Pers Soc Psychol* 1982; **42**: 1089– 1099.
15 Loehlin JC, Willerman L, Horn JM. Personality resemblances in adoptive families when the children are late-adolescent or adult. *J Pers Soc Psychol* 1985; **48**: 376–392.
16 Rose RJ, Kaprio J. Frequency of social contact and intrapair resemblance of adult monozygotic cotwins – or does shared experience influence personality after all? *Behav Genet* 1988; **18**: 309–328.
17 Eaves LJ. Computer simulation of sample size and experimental design in human psychogenetics. *Psychol Bull* 1972; **77**: 144–152.
18 Heath AC, Kendler KS, Eaves LJ, Markell D. The resolution of cultural and biological inheritance: informativeness of different relationships. *Behav Genet* 1985; **15**: 439–465.
19 Heath AC, Eaves LJ. Resolving the effects of phenotype and social background on mate selection. *Behav Genet* 1985; **15**: 15–30.
20 Truett KR, Eaves LJ, Walters EE, Heath AC, Hewitt JK, Meyer JM, Silberg J, Neale MC, Martin NG, Kendler KS. A model system for analysis of family resemblance in extended kinships of twins. *Behav Genet* 1994; **24**: 35–49.
21 Eaves LJ. The use of twins in the analysis of assortative mating. *Heredity* 1979; **43**: 399–409.
22 Eaves LJ, Heath AC. Sex-limitation and 'asymmetric' assortative mating. *Twin Research 3: Intelligence, Personality and Development* 1981; 73–86.
23 Eysenck HJ, Eysenck SBG. *Personality Questionnaire (junior and adult).* Hodder and Stoughton Educational: Chigwell Press: Essex, 1975.
24 Lange K, Westlake J, Spence MA. Extensions to pedigree analysis. III. Variance components by the scoring method. *Ann Hum Genet* 1976; **39**: 485–491.
25 McGue M, Wette R, Rao DC. Evaluation of path analysis through computer simulation: effect of incorrectly assuming independent distribution of familial correlations. *Genet Epidemiol* 1984; **1**: 255–269.

26 Bouchard TJ Jr, Lykken DT, McGue M, Segal N, Tellegen A. Sources of human psychological differences: the Minnesota study of twins reared apart. *Science* 1990; **250**: 223–228.
27 Corey LA, Nance WE. The monozygotic half-sib model: a tool for epidemiologic research. *Prog Clin Biol Res* 1978; **24** Pt A: 201–209.
28 Morton NE. Analysis of family resemblance I. Introduction. *Am J Hum Genet* 1974; **26**: 318–330.
29 Heath AC. Human quantitative genetics: Some issues and applications. Unpublished doctoral dissertation, University of Oxford, Oxford, 1983.
30 Eaves LJ. Inferring the causes of human variation. *J Roy Stat Soc, Series A* 1977; **140**: 324–355.
31 Fisher RA. The correlation between relatives on the supposition of Mendelian inheritance. *Trans Roy Soc (Edinburgh)* 1918; **52**: 399–433.
32 Rao DC, Morton NE, Elston RC, Yee S. Causal analysis of academic performance. *Behav Genet* 1977; **7**: 147–159.
33 Numerical Algorithms Group. *NAG Fortran Library Manual, Mark 17.* Numerical Algorithms Group Ltd: Oxford, 1995.
34 Rao DC, McGue M, Wette R, Glueck CJ. Path analysis in genetic epidemiology. In: Chakravarti A (ed.). *Human Population Genetics: the Pittsburgh Symposium.* Van Nostrand Reinhold: New York, 1984, pp 35–81.
35 Eaves LJ, Long J, Heath AC. A theory of developmental change in quantitative phenotypes applied to cognitive development. *Behav Genet* 1986; **16**: 143–162.
36 Tambs K, Moum T. Low genetic effect and age-specific family effect for symptoms of anxiety and depression in nuclear families, halfsibs and twins. *J Affective Disorders* 1993; **27**: 183–195.
37 Eaves LJ. A model for sibling effects in man. *Heredity*; **36**: 205–214.
38 Carey G. Sibling imitation and contrast effects. *Behav Genet* 1986; **16**: 319–341.
39 Zajonc RB, Markus GB. Birth order and intellectual development. *Psychol Rev* 1975; **82**: 74–88.
40 Cavalli-Sforza LL, Feldman MW. Cultural versus biological inheritance: phenotypic transmission from parents to children. (A theory of the effect of parental phenotypes on children's phenotypes). *Am J Hum Genet* 1973; **25**: 618–637.
41 Eaves LJ. Dominance alone is not enough. *Behav Genet* 1988; **18**: 27–33.
42 Cavalli-Sforza LL, Feldman MW. *Cultural Transmission and Evolution: a Quantitative Approach.* Princeton University: Princeton, 1981.
43 Martin NG, Eaves LJ, Heath AC, Jardine R, Feingold LM, Eysenck HJ. Transmission of social attitudes. *Proc Natl Acad Sci USA* 1986; **83**: 4364–4368.
44 Gray JA. The psychophysiological basis of introversion-extraversion. *Behav Res Ther* 1970; **8**: 249–266.
45 Dawkins R. *The Extended Phenotype: the Gene as the Unit of Selection.* Oxford University Press: Oxford, 1982.

J. Child Psychol. Psychiat. Vol. 38, No. 8, pp. 943–963, 1997
Cambridge University Press

0021-9630/97 $15.00 + 0.00

Genetics and Developmental Psychopathology: 1. Phenotypic Assessment in the Virginia Twin Study of Adolescent Behavioral Development

John K. Hewitt
University of Colorado, Boulder, U.S.A.

Judith L. Silberg
Virginia Commonwealth University, Richmond, U.S.A.

Michael Rutter and Emily Simonoff
Institute of Psychiatry, London, U.K.

Joanne M. Meyer and Hermine Maes
Virginia Commonwealth University, Richmond, U.S.A.

Andrew Pickles
Institute of Psychiatry, London, U.K.

Michael C. Neale
Virginia Commonwealth University, Richmond, U.S.A.

Rolf Loeber
University of Pittsburgh, U.S.A.

Marilyn T. Erickson and Kenneth S. Kendler
Virginia Commonwealth University, Richmond, U.S.A.

Andrew C. Heath
Washington University School of Medicine, St Louis, U.S.A.

Kim R. Truett
Virginia Commonwealth University, Richmond, U.S.A.

Chandra A. Reynolds
University of Colorado, Boulder, U.S.A.

Lindon J. Eaves
Virginia Commonwealth University, Richmond, U.S.A.

We introduce an overlapping cohort sequential longitudinal study of behavioral development and psychopathology in a representative sample of 1412 pairs of twins aged 8 through 16 years. Multiple phenotypic assessments involve a full psychiatric interview with each child and each parent, and supplementary parental, teacher, and child interview material and questionnaires. For the first wave of assessments, the numbers of reported DSM-III-R symptoms of Major Depressive Disorder (MDD), Separation Anxiety Disorder (SAD), Overanxious Disorder (OAD), Oppositional Defiant Disorder (ODD), Conduct Disorder (CD), and Attention Deficit Hyperactivity Disorder (ADHD), assessed through interviews, confirm patterns of age and sex trends found in other epidemiological samples, but underscore their dependence on whether the child or the parent is the informant. Correlations across domains for symptoms reported by the same informant are often as large as correlations across informants for the same domain of symptoms. Factor analyses of these symptom counts, taking account of informant view and unreliability of assessment, show the high degree of correlation between SAD and OAD, between MDD and OAD, and between CD and ODD. ADHD symptoms are relatively independent of the other domains, but show moderate correlations with CD, ODD, and MDD. Factorially derived dimensional questionnaire scales, based on child, parental, and teacher reports, show patterns of relationship to symptom counts consistent with both convergent and discriminant validity as indices of liability to clinical symptoms. Across informants, questionnaire scales provide as good a prediction of symptoms as do clinical interviews. Multitrait-multimethod confirmatory factor analysis reveals the patterns of relationship between symptoms of psychiatric disorder in children taking due account of informant and unique sources of variance. Gender differences are consistent within the correlated clusters of ODD/CD and MDD/SAD/OAD, although there are disorder-specific age trends. There are large informant-specific influences on the reporting of symptoms in clinical interviews. Dimensional questionnaire scales provide a useful source of additional information. In subsequent analyses of genetic and environmental etiology of childhood psychopathology we must expect that results may differ by informant and method of assessment. Multivariate and developmental analyses that explore the sources of these differences will shed new light on the

---

Requests for reprints to: Professor John K. Hewitt, Institute for Behavioral Genetics, University of Colorado, Campus Box 447, Boulder, Colorado CO 80309-01447, U.S.A.

relationship between genetic and environmentally influenced vulnerability and the manifestation of psychopathology in specific circumstances.

Keywords: Depression, anxiety, conduct disorder, attention deficit disorder, adolescence, twins.

Abbreviations: ADHD: attention deficit hyperactivity disorder; CAPA: Child and Adolescent Psychiatric Assessment; CD; conduct disorder; DZ; dizygotic; MDD: major depressive disorder; MFQ: Mood and Feelings Questionnaire; MZ: monozygotic; NFI: Normed Fit Index; OAD: overanxious disorder; ODD: oppositional defiant disorder; SAD: separation anxiety disorder; TLI: Tucker Lewis Index; VTSABD: Virginia Twin Study of Adolescent Behavioral Development.

Introduction

In the absence of knowledge of the genetic contributions to psychopathology and to behavioral development in general, our understanding of childhood and adolescent mental health is incomplete. For some rare conditions, such as autism, genetics may provide the *only* route to understanding (Rutter, Bailey, Bolton, & Le Couteur, 1993), while for the more common psychiatric disorders genetic predisposition may combine with environmental risks in a complex manner. Recognizing the need for basic genetic epidemiological information about developmental psychopathology, we initiated a longitudinal study of a representative sample of identical and nonidentical twins from the ages of 8 through 16. This paper introduces the study and its rationale, and summarizes the overall pattern of phenotypic variation assessed by interviews with children and their parents, and questionnaires completed by the children, their parents, and their teachers.

Genetics and Epidemiology

Community surveys of children and adolescents have suggested that as many as one in five or one in six children present a diagnosable psychiatric condition (Brandenburg, Friedman, & Silver, 1990; Costello, 1989; Verhulst & Koot, 1992), although some epidemiological studies have reported rather lower proportions of children with diagnosable disorders (Rutter, Tizard, Yule, Graham, & Whitmore, 1976). Common problems are attention deficits and/or hyperactivity, oppositional and conduct disorders, separation anxiety and other anxieties, simple phobias, and, somewhat less frequently, depression (Bird et al., 1988; McGee et al., 1990; Offord et al., 1987; Verhulst, Berden, & Sanders-Woudstra, 1985). There are also food-related and alcohol- and drug-related social and psychological problems. Age and sex differences in prevalence rates are apparent for many of the common problems and there is comorbidity or overlap between the various disorders to a more marked extent than for adult psychopathology. These general observations are fairly robust across the available epidemiological surveys, but details of the picture will depend on the informant (e.g. child, parent, or teacher) (Achenbach, McConaughy, & Howell, 1987) and on the method of assessment (e.g. checklist, structured interviews, or semi-structured interviews) (Verhulst & Koot 1992). Studies of community samples have also brought into focus the question of what the relationship is between the normal range of occurrence of troublesome behavior and the manifestation of a clinical disorder (Eaves, Silberg, Hewitt, Meyer, et al., 1993; Eaves, Silberg, Hewitt, Rutter, et al., 1993; Eaves et al., 1997; Fergusson & Horwood, 1995; Offord, 1995; Plomin, 1996; Rutter, 1988; Verhulst et al., 1992).

The data on familial aggregation from community or population-based samples of children are limited, although there is a series of studies pointing to familial aggregation of behavioral and emotional problems (Szatmari, Boyle, & Offord, 1993; Thapar & McGuffin, 1994, 1995), to familial aggregation, and probably genetic determination, for hyperactivity and attention deficit disorders (Faraone & Biederman, 1994; Goodman & Stevenson, 1989; Stevenson, 1992; Thapar, Hervas, & McGuffin, 1995), and to familial aggregation, and probably both genetic and shared family environmental influence, for externalizing behavior problems assessed by parental checklists (Eaves, Silberg, Hewitt, Rutter, et al. 1993; Hewitt, Silberg, Neale, Eaves, & Erickson, 1992; Silberg et al., 1994). The evidence for genetic influences on psychiatric disorder in childhood has been reviewed by Rutter et al. (1990), who concluded that genetic vulnerability is likely to play an important role in autism, some forms of chronic tics and Tourette's syndrome, and early-onset affective disorders; for other disorders the situation was less clear. Thus there is a need for a comprehensive study of the role of genetic and environmental variation in determining the vulnerability of children to common psychiatric disorders. In a subsequent paper of this series, we report extensive further evidence of genetic influences on symptoms of childhood psychopathology in a community sample (Eaves et al., 1997).

Developmental Issues

Comparatively few psychiatric conditions are present from birth onwards and we have yet to explain the timing of the emergence of psychiatric problems (e.g. the increase in the frequency of depressive feelings and depressive disorders after puberty [Rutter, 1979]). Early experiences such as parental loss may increase the risk of adult problems (Brown & Harris, 1978; Kendler, Neale, Kessler, Heath, & Eaves, 1992a), but we have yet to understand the continuities between early events and later adult psychopathology (Rutter, 1986). There are predictive relationships between earlier and later behavioral problems, such as hyperactivity or oppositional disorder in childhood and conduct disorder in adolescence, but it is not known whether this represents heterotypic continuity, i.e. the changing manifestation of the same underlying psychopathology, whether the earlier disorder creates a *de novo* risk for the later, or whether there is simply a correlation between the risk factors for the disorders (Rutter, 1991; Sampson & Laub, 1993; Silberg et al., in press). To explore possibilities of this kind we needed to carry out a study that would be informative not only about genetic and environmental variation, but also about developmental stability and change.

Comorbidity

Understanding the mechanisms underlying comorbidity presents a particular challenge within the study of developmental psychopathology, not least because of the high levels of comorbidity (Caron & Rutter, 1991). The mechanisms by which this comorbidity arises may differ among comorbid associations (Rutter, Simonoff, & Silberg, 1993). In some situations, disorders may be pleiotropic manifestations of the same underlying genetic disposition; in other cases, comorbid disorders result from a common environmental risk factor. In a third type, associated disorders are manifestations of correlated genetic and environmental risks; Rutter, Simonoff, et al. (1993) and Downey and Coyne (1990) have proposed such a mechanism for the comorbidity of depression and conduct disorder "where both are related to parental depression but possibly through different mechanisms—with genetic factors [perhaps] being more important for depression, and family discord an environmental risk factor for conduct disorder" (Rutter, Simonoff, et al., 1993, p. 448). To be able to explore such possibilities our study had to be both multivariate in its phenotypic assessments and able to provide assessments of environmental risk factors, including parental characteristics.

Phenotype Definition

As Rutter et al. (1990) have noted, genetic research raised issues not only about the causes of comorbidity, but also about phenotype definition and the dimensional versus categorical conceptualization of psychopathology (Fergusson & Horwood, 1995). Genetic studies have suggested that phenotypically distinct disorders, such as generalized anxiety disorder and major depressive disorder, may be highly genetically correlated or may represent the manifestation of a single pathway of genetic vulnerability (Kendler, Neale, Kessler, Heath, & Eaves, 1992d). Moreover, genetic vulnerability might be better thought of as a continuously distributed dimension, perhaps polygenic, rather than in terms of distinct classes. In the case of anxiety and depression, an index of the genetic liability might be provided by a dimensional assessment of the personality trait of neuroticism (Jardine, Martin, & Henderson, 1984; Eaves, Eysenck, & Martin, 1989). Since little is known about the validity of dimensions versus categories, we needed to avoid prejudgement and to include both clinical assessments (based on an essentially categorical approach to disorder) and dimensional assessments. In practice, clinical assessments are more usually based on psychiatric interviews and dimensional assessments are more usually provided by questionnaires.

The data collected in the Virginia Twin Study of Adolescent Behavioral Development (VTSABD) will provide an initial empirical base from which to explore all of these issues in detail. In this paper we introduce the study, focusing on the phenotypic properties of our key assessments. In our accompanying introductory paper we present genetic and environmental analyses of the causes of individual differences in the major domains of disorder (Eaves et al., 1997).

The Design and Assessment Protocol

The VTSABD employs a sequential cohort design in which monozygotic (MZ) and dizygotic (DZ) twin pairs from 8 years through 16 years of age, and their parents, are recruited and then followed longitudinally. In some cases the twins had reached age 17 by the time an interview took place, and these have been grouped together with the 16-year-olds throughout this report. As the study progresses older pairs may graduate from the study and new 8-year-olds may be recruited. Among the many strengths of this design is that approximately equal numbers of pairs are available for study at any age within the target range, at any time from the beginning of the study onwards. The cross-sectional analyses reported in this first paper therefore span the full age range, with approximately equal amounts of information across that range.

Parent and Child Interviews

Child and Adolescent Psychiatric Assessment. The core of our measurements is the Child and Adolescent Psychiatric Assessment (CAPA) semi-structured investigator-based interview (Angold et al., 1995). This is an investigator, rather than respondent, based instrument designed to be conducted in a conversational mode appropriate to the assessment of children. It provides detailed accounts of behavioral and psychological symptomatology relevant to the common areas of childhood and adolescent disorder. The VTSABD version includes: depression, suicide, and self-injurious behavior, hyperactivity and attention deficit, oppositional and conduct disorders, separation anxiety, anxious affect and worries, school performance and behavior, food-related behavior, sleep problems, and tobacco, alcohol, and drug use. In addition, the impact of problems on social and personal functioning (i.e. impairment) is assessed, as is family structure and function, peer relationships, and children's pubertal stage.

In each area of behavior, the presence of symptoms of clinical intensity determined during the 3-month period prior to the interview and, if present, the frequency of occurrence, duration, and earliest age of onset of the symptoms is also recorded. Operational definitions of symptom intensity usually reflect the intrusiveness of the symptoms together with their controllability and a minimum duration or frequency of the feeling or behavior.

The coverage of symptoms was designed to be sufficiently comprehensive to permit application of either DSM–III–R or ICD–10 research diagnostic criteria and can also accommodate many of the changes in DSM–IV. Given the current state of uncertainty about the appropriateness of diagnostic schemes for psychiatric disorders in children and adolescents, our goal was to keep open the possibility of working directly with the reported symptoms and behavior or applying any of the proposed diagnostic schemes.

The CAPA is available as an interview with the child and as an interview with the parent about the child. The child and parent versions we have used differ in that hyperactivity and attention problems are assessed only in the parent interview. We interviewed both twins individually and both parents (where available) about each twin, giving us, in the majority of cases, three independent interviews about each child. In interviewing the parents, we also gain a detailed early developmental and health history of the twins and obtain zygosity information.

Parental psychiatric assessment. Using interview materials developed for Kendler's study of adult twins (Kendler, Neale, Kessler, Heath, & Eaves, 1992b, c) based on the SCID; (Spitzer, Williams, & Gibson, 1987) we assess lifetime episodes of Generalized Anxiety Disorder, Major Depression, Alcohol Abuse and Alcoholism, Phobias and Panic Disorder in the parents and, using parallel material developed by two of us (ES and MR), evidence for Antisocial Personality. On the second visit to families we obtain demographic information paralleling as closely as possible the U.S. census.

Parent, Teacher, and Self-report Questionnaires

The twins and their parents also complete questionnaires under the supervision of the field workers in the home. For the children, dimensional assessments of clinically relevant domains include: Reynolds and Richmond's scale for manifest anxiety (Reynolds & Richmond, 1978); the Recent Mood and Feelings Questionnaire (MFQ) (Costello & Angold, 1988), a 33-item questionnaire assessing depressed feelings and moods; an adapted version of the Olweus self-report questionnaire assessing delinquent and aggressive behavior (Olweus, 1989); a modified version of Ollendick's assessment of specific fears (Ollendick, King, & Frary, 1989); and the EASI temperament scale (Buss & Plomin, 1975). To assess environmental risk factors we used a modified Life Events Checklist (Johnson, 1986; Johnson & McCutcheon, 1980) assessing both shared and individual events over the last 12 months; a modified version of the Sibling Inventory of Differential Experiences (SIDE) (Daniels & Plomin, 1985); and Olsson's Family Adaptability and Togetherness questionnaire (Olsson, Sprenkle, & Russel, 1979). A subset of these questionnaires (the first four listed) are read to children 11 years or younger or who are 12 years or older but do not reach 6th grade reading on the Slosson Oral Reading Test (Slosson, 1963) administered at the beginning of the session (along with the recording of heights and weights and the taking of a set of standardized photographs).

To obtain multiple informants, the parents rate each of their twins on all of questionnaire scales listed above, along with the Rutter "A(2)" Scale Parent Questionnaire (Fergusson & Horwood, 1987; Graham & Stevenson, 1985; Rutter, Cox, Tupling, Berger, & Yule, 1975; Rutter, Tizard, & Whitmore, 1970; Schachar, Rutter, & Smith, 1981). They also complete a version of the Dyadic Adjustment Scale assessing marital relations (Spanier, 1976). In addition the Rutter "B(2)" Scale Teacher Questionnaire, augmented by 10 items from the Connors scales (Connors, 1969), has been completed and returned in over 90% of cases.

Home Visit Protocol

The complex array of assessment information to be gathered from each family places burdens on both the family and the field workers, and raises concerns about the independence of interview assessments, the possibility of order effects on assessment of the twins, the possibility of interviewer bias, and so on. To ameliorate these possible problems we adhere to a protocol involving independent interviewers, randomized assignments, and supervised privacy for questionnaires.

Essential aspects of this protocol bear on the question of artifactual correlations. First, members of a twin pair were interviewed simultaneously by different interviewers, randomly assigned, in separate rooms or places around the home. This means three important possible artifacts were eliminated: the zygosity perceived by the field workers cannot influence the similarity of these assessments; there was no possibility of collusion or discussion among the twins affecting the assessments (once the home visit was under way); any effects of interviewer style or other possible interviewer-associated effects cannot contribute to the similarity of the twins' interviews or questionnaire responses.

Second, the parents were interviewed, each by a separate interviewer, about each of their twins by conducting the entire CAPA for one twin before repeating the interview for the co-twin. Which twin was reported on first in this procedure was determined by random assignment at the time that all other aspects of the family assignments were being arranged by computer program. These aspects of the protocol increase the likelihood that parents can make absolute rather than comparative judgements about the individual twins and ensure that any possible order of interview effects are random with respect to individual twins.

However, organizational constraints mean that in most cases the parental interviewer had earlier interviewed one (but certainly not both) of the twins, and this prior knowledge might influence the parental interview about this twin. The random assignment of interviewers to interviewees means that such effects can be explored and taken into account (Simonoff et al., 1995).

Third, all twins 11 and under, or 12 and over but without at least a 6th-grade reading ability, were read their questionnaire material by the interviewer and, with some exceptions, for all family members the field workers were on hand to respond to questions about the content or format of the questionnaire. This reduced the possibility of reading or conceptual difficulties interfering with

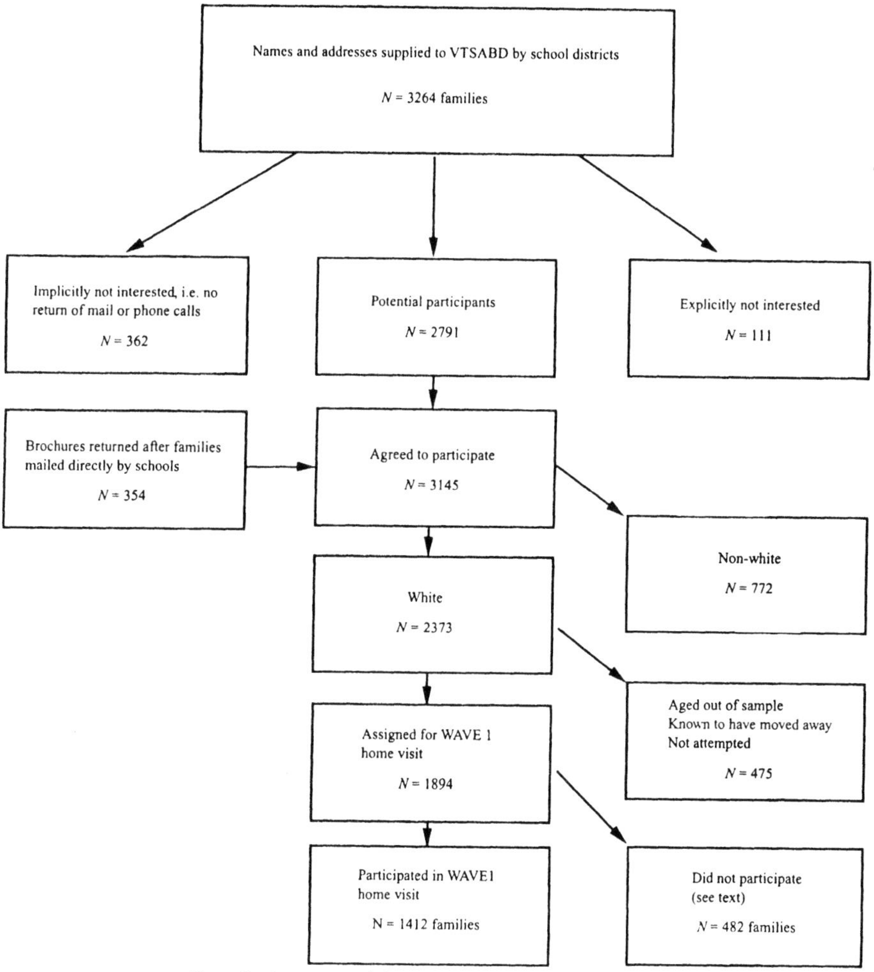

Figure 1. A summary of the ascertainment scheme for the VTSABD.

the accuracy of the questionnaire responses. Materials were presented in a controlled sequence, using standard introductory scripts, and any significant departures from established protocols by fieldworkers (in response to particular circumstances encountered in the field for example) had to be approved in advance by the project manager.

The target level of qualification for field workers was a Master's degree in Social Work or an equivalent professional degree, or extensive experience of psychiatric interviewing. Training consisted of 3 weeks of residential instruction, interspersed with practice interviews, both under observation and in the field. All interviews are audiotaped and all components of each assessment are reviewed by senior monitors. Regular field meetings are conducted with small groups of interviewers to avoid drift in use of the interview or other aspects of the protocol. About once a year, a full residential meeting, including all the field workers and the appropriate members of the investigating team, is held for the purpose of refresher training, protocol review, and to ensure continued standardized implementation of the protocol.

Subjects and Data Collection

Ascertainment and Sample Composition

The ascertainment process is schematized in Fig. 1. In the school year 1987/88 we identified all putative twin pairs known

Table 1
The Numbers of Pairs Participating by Age, Sex, and Zygosity at First Family Interview

Age (years)	Zygosity type: MZ Male	MZ Female	DZ Male	DZ Female	DZ Opposite sex	Unknown	Total
8	26	39	14	13	23	4	119
9	32	59	32	33	40	7	203
10	28	48	24	18	36	4	158
11	35	36	20	23	45	8	167
12	45	38	17	31	29	5	165
13	40	47	20	23	28	7	165
14	27	33	25	14	22	7	128
15	33	42	12	16	30	4	137
16+	34	47	20	16	42	11	170
Total	300	389	184	187	295	57	1412
Per cent	21.2	27.5	13.0	13.2	20.9	4.0	100.0

to the public school system of the Commonwealth of Virginia. In the subsequent year we canvassed all private schools in the Commonwealth. When field work began in 1990, this exercise had yielded a target population of 3264 twin pairs born between 1974 and 1982, with initially valid addresses. Of these, 2791 (86%) responded to a brief request for information either by mail (after one, two, or three contacts) or by telephone (following extensive efforts to locate and to make contact with our target families), 111 refused to participate (3%), and 362 failed to return our brochure and could not be contacted by telephone (11%). This yielded an 86% participation rate from the target families. In some cases the school districts had made the initial contact with families on our behalf, yielding an additional 354 families. The subsequent study was restricted by design to Caucasian families who represented 75%, i.e. 2373, of the 3145 families according to our initial information. Support for comparable assessments of ethnic minority families has been sought.

Following this, 1894 eligible families, who continued to meet the age and residence requirements for inclusion in the study, were assigned to field workers for the first time for contact and interview from March 1990 through March 1992. Of these, 1412 families (75%) have participated in the home visit, 189 families (10%) have refused to participate at any level, 137 (7%) declined the home interview but agreed to participate in questionnaire studies, 84 (5%) were unable to be contacted or located, and 72 families (4%) continue to defer full interview participation. Of the 1412 families visited at home, 1408 were successfully interviewed and in 4 cases only questionnaires could be obtained. Of the 1408 families successfully interviewed, 1108 (79%) were interviewed after the first assignment to a field worker, the remainder after additional assignments. In some cases as many as 10 appointments have been made before actually securing the home interview. Because we know from previous epidemiological studies of psychopathology that such families may differ in important behavioral characteristics (Cox, Rutter, Yule, & Quinton, 1977; Farrington, Gallagher, Morley, St. Ledger, & West, 1990; Verhulst, Koot, & Berden, 1990), we expended every practical effort to gain the participation of these families. Second visits to families have begun and attrition at initial follow-up is currently 20% of initially interviewed families, although we expect this to be reduced as we continue our efforts to include these families at least at some level of participation. In this paper we are concerned only with the Wave 1 assessments.

Sample Characteristics

Table 1 shows the composition by age, sex, and zygosity for the 1412 Wave 1 families. Details of zygosity determination are given in the subsequent paper in this series (Eaves et al., 1997). We note that we have a small excess of female twins ($p < .01$) and some undersampling of opposite-sex DZ twins ($p < .05$). The ratio of MZ to DZ twins is different from that observed early in this century, when MZs represented only about one third of all twins (Bulmer, 1970). However, the DZ twinning rate has declined markedly during the second half of this century in developed nations (Doherty & Lancaster, 1986; Hurr, McGue, & Iacono, 1995; MacGillivray, 1981) and, in Virginia, a recent estimate for MZ twins as a proportion of all live twin births was .43 (Mosteller, Townsend, Corey, & Nance, 1981) while in Minnesota this estimate averaged .45 for the birth years 1974 to 1982 in a 98% Caucasian population (Hurr et al., 1995). MZ twins, and particularly MZ female twins, may therefore have been oversampled to a modest degree in our study.

Statistical Analyses and Results

Age- and Sex-specific Levels of Symptomatology

In Table 2 we characterize the prevalence of DSM-III-R symptoms for the major common disorders, paying particular attention to the trends across ages and the differences between boys and girls. The VTSABD provides us with a number of ways of looking at the prevalence rates for symptomatology, utilizing the multiple informant and multimethod data. Here, we present symptoms occurring during the last 3 months prior to interview and reported by the children themselves, their mothers, and their fathers. In each case we report symptom counts based on the CAPA interviews for

Table 2
Mean DSM-III-R Symptom Counts and Sample Size by Age Group, Gender, and Informant

			Age group								
			8–10 years			11–13 years			14–16 years		
Disorder	Gender of child	Informant	Mean	*SD*[a]	*N*	Mean	*SD*[a]	*N*	Mean	*SD*[a]	*N*
ADHD	Male	Mother	0.88	2.40	376	0.82	2.22	435	0.83	2.22	368
		Father	0.76	1.95	324	0.64	1.81	354	0.63	1.88	279
	Female	Mother	0.70	1.93	483	0.61	1.88	460	0.32	1.17	406
		Father	0.59	1.75	398	0.51	1.62	372	0.19	0.85	300
CD	Male	Child	0.30	0.69	406	0.41	0.80	441	0.68	1.19	380
		Mother	0.35	0.67	382	0.29	0.60	437	0.31	0.67	370
		Father	0.29	0.58	326	0.23	0.56	358	0.29	0.70	283
	Female	Child	0.19	0.52	513	0.24	0.65	491	0.37	0.78	418
		Mother	0.27	0.59	488	0.26	0.56	461	0.24	0.62	408
		Father	0.25	0.55	404	0.16	0.49	377	0.16	0.56	308
ODD	Male	Child	0.50	0.96	403	0.67	1.17	434	0.68	1.24	373
		Mother	0.54	1.09	383	0.55	1.01	432	0.61	1.27	370
		Father	0.51	1.05	319	0.39	1.03	356	0.35	1.10	282
	Female	Child	0.37	0.87	504	0.46	0.94	478	0.46	0.99	411
		Mother	0.56	1.12	480	0.64	1.22	455	0.44	1.04	396
		Father	0.44	0.91	398	0.39	0.95	365	0.28	0.81	303
MDD	Male	Child	0.17	0.48	387	0.18	0.65	420	0.36	1.05	351
		Mother	0.21	0.65	359	0.16	0.65	401	0.27	0.82	341
		Father	0.07	0.30	312	0.12	0.49	334	0.12	0.44	264
	Female	Child	0.22	0.64	487	0.27	0.79	456	0.45	1.10	390
		Mother	0.19	0.52	446	0.26	0.68	431	0.32	0.88	373
		Father	0.11	0.40	383	0.12	0.50	347	0.15	0.62	285
SAD	Male	Child	0.48	1.17	359	0.36	0.95	405	0.19	0.79	342
		Mother	0.12	0.55	355	0.09	0.52	397	0.03	0.19	349
		Father	0.08	0.41	294	0.06	0.31	332	0.05	0.26	262
	Female	Child	0.63	1.39	457	0.34	1.00	444	0.34	0.87	376
		Mother	0.23	0.75	443	0.20	0.64	441	0.12	0.49	383
		Father	0.12	0.55	378	0.09	0.42	351	0.07	0.42	281
OAD	Male	Child	0.42	0.94	394	0.76	1.32	426	0.99	1.42	371
		Mother	0.50	1.09	373	0.57	1.13	421	0.75	1.32	361
		Father	0.21	0.67	315	0.38	0.97	343	0.66	1.27	275
	Female	Child	0.58	1.16	502	0.76	1.31	475	1.42	1.67	411
		Mother	0.59	1.23	472	0.83	1.43	451	0.94	1.52	395
		Father	0.34	0.90	389	0.48	1.01	357	0.66	1.35	298

[a] Standard deviations (*SD*) are computed within each year of age and pooled across ages within the 3-year age group

Depression (DSM-III-R Major Depressive Episode; maximum of 9 symptoms), Separation Anxiety Disorder (9 symptoms), and Overanxious Disorder (7 symptoms), and maternal reports for Oppositional Defiant Disorder (9 symptoms), Conduct Disorder (12 symptoms, omitting forced sexual activity), and for Hyperactivity (Attention Deficit Hyperactivity Disorder; 14 symptoms).

Table 3 summarizes the patterns of significant age trends and sex differences observed for symptoms of each disorder as reported by each of the three informants: the child, the mother, and the father. Mean symptom scores for boys and girls at each year of age were regressed on the children's age, sex, and their interaction using weighted least squares. In the absence of a significant interaction, this term was dropped from the model. This procedure provides best linear unbiased estimators on the assumption of homoscedasticity of individual differences within age and sex groups, and approximate best linear estimators otherwise. The significance of each parameter was tested against its standard error derived from the residual sum of squares for departure from the model.

Examination of Tables 2 and 3 reveals strong evidence that symptoms are, as expected, more frequent for boys than for girls, for ADHD reported by mothers ($p = .004$) or fathers ($p = .036$) and for CD ($p < .001$) and for ODD ($p < .001$) reported by the children themselves during interview. The evidence from parental reports is less reliable, although the observed trends are consistent. For

Table 3
Summary of Significant Age and Sex Effects on Reported Number of Symptoms

Domain	Informant	Sex	Age	Sex*Age
ADHD	Mother	Boys > Girls**, $p = .004$	Decreases, $p = .111$	Girls decrease*, $p = .037$
	Father	Boys > Girls*, $p = .036$	Decreases, $p = .086$	
CD	Child	Boys > Girls***, $p < .001$	Increases***, $p < .001$	Boys increase more*, $p = .016$
	Mother	Boys > Girls*, $p = .051$	No trend	
	Father	Boys > Girls**, $p = .010$	No trend	
ODD	Child	Boys > Girls***, $p < .001$	Increases*, $p = .017$	
	Mother	No trend	No trend	
	Father	Boys > Girls, $p = .117$	Decreases***, $p < .001$	
MDD	Child	Girls > Boys*, $p = .034$	Increases***, $p < .001$	
	Mother	Girls > Boys, $p = .071$	Increases**, $p = .006$	
	Father	No trend	No trend	
SAD	Child	Girls > boys*, $p = .048$	Decreases***, $p < .001$	
	Mother	Girls > boys***, $p < .001$	Decreases***, $p < .001$	
	Father	Girls > boys, $p = .082$	Decreases*, $p = .048$	
OAD	Child	Girls > boys**, $p = .007$	Increases***, $p < .001$	
	Mother	Girls > boys**, $p = .007$	Increases***, $p < .001$	
	Father	Girls > boys, $p = .171$	Increases***, $p < .001$	

*$p < .05$; **$p < .01$; ***$p < .001$.

MDD ($p = .034$), SAD ($p = .048$), and OAD ($p = .007$) girls report more symptoms than boys; their parents tend to confirm this, although the sex difference is not always significant.

Perhaps somewhat unexpectedly, the evidence for a decrease in symptoms of ADHD in adolescence was not significant overall ($p = .111$, mothers; $p = .086$, fathers), although there was a significant interaction in the maternal reports caused by a decrease in numbers of symptoms with age for girls only. For both CD and ODD, older children reported significantly more symptoms than did younger children, and for CD this age effect was significantly greater for boys than for girls. Parental reports either showed no age trend or, in the case of fathers' reports of symptoms of ODD, a significant decline over our age range. Symptoms of MDD increase significantly with age judged by the children's own reports ($p = .001$) or that of their mothers ($p = .001$). For fathers, the average levels of MDD symptoms reported were both lower than for other informants and equivocal regarding age trends or gender differences. For SAD there is a decline in the number of symptoms with age, whereas for OAD there is a reported increase, and these trends are consistent across informants.

Correlations among Reported Symptoms: Psychiatric Interviews with Multiple Informants

Table 4 presents the correlations for the DSM-III-R symptom counts reported by children (except in the case of ADHD), their mothers, and their fathers, based on the CAPA interviews for the same six disorders. In the table we have highlighted correlations across informants for the same symptoms (dark shading), correlations across disorders for the same informant (light shading), and then we have indicated by the grid pattern the remaining correlations across informants and disorders. Because of the significant, and substantial, age trends and the presence of marked non-normality in the distributions of symptom counts, we have applied an age correction and normalizing transformation to the raw data prior to computation of the reported correlations. Specifically, we have used SAS transformation procedures (SAS Institute Inc., 1990) to rank normalize the symptom counts and then to standardize the distributions to constant mean and variance within age and sex groups. This procedure preserves the cross-sectional pattern of correlations for each sex, independent of age, and removes correlations that would otherwise result from the age trends in mean symptom counts. However, the initial analyses presented here do not address the possibility that the patterns of relationship between the disorders may change with age.

Three characteristics of these correlations deserve comment: first, across the entire matrix, the correlations are small although generally positive. Second, correlations across informants (inter-informant agreement) are typically quite low and range from .05 to .35. In keeping with other findings (Achenbach et al., 1987; Simonoff et al., 1995; Verhulst & Koot, 1992) correlations between mothers and fathers tend to be higher than correlations between parents and children. Third, correlations across disorders for symptoms reported by the same informant, ranging from .02 to .49, are in many cases as high as those across informants for the same disorder. This pattern is especially clear for closely related disorders such as CD and ODD or SAD and OAD, where the correlations across disorders reported by the informant are highest.

Table 4
Phenotypic Intercorrelation Matrix (Pearson ~ × 100) for DSM–III–R Sympton Counts from Child and Parental Interviews. Males are above the Diagonal, Females below.

Disorder	Informant	ADHD		CD			ODD			MDD			SAD			OAD		
		M	F	C	M	F	C	M	F	C	M	F	C	M	F	C	M	F
ADHD	Mother	-	[illegible]	10	17	12	10	25	12	02	27	14	02	10	07	03	12	02
	Father	[illegible]	-	07	12	16	07	17	25	04	18	24	05	07	06	01	-02	13
CD	Child	13	05	-	24	20	41	16	15	19	12	09	10	02	02	09	01	04
	Mother	23	10	23	-	[illegible]	24	45	21	07	26	00	05	02	03	03	04	-03
	Father	13	18	[illegible]	24	-	13	21	47	06	22	16	06	08	16	06	14	14
ODD	Child	07	09	36	18	15	-	[illegible]	20	24	15	08	14	04	05	20	05	08
	Mother	25	12	11	49	15	15	-	50	13	32	14	10	07	03	09	16	04
	Father	13	25	11	19	43	[illegible]	20	-	09	28	23	03	06	08	04	08	20
MDD	Child	12	-02	18	08	12	26	08	09	-	[illegible]	[illegible]	25	13	07	32	12	12
	Mother	25	13	14	18	14	13	30	15	[illegible]	-	[illegible]	04	19	12	07	25	15
	Father	05	17	-01	05	09	03	07	12	[illegible]	[illegible]	-	06	05	17	04	12	29
SAD	Child	01	02	13	04	09	13	02	10	23	09	05	-	[illegible]	[illegible]	37	08	07
	Mother	10	08	03	14	16	08	19	13	08	29	07	[illegible]	-	[illegible]	11	24	07
	Father	05	08	04	06	11	03	05	18	09	13	17	[illegible]	[illegible]	-	07	16	27
QAD	Child	02	03	15	06	08	19	04	10	21	12	05	36	04	01	-	[illegible]	[illegible]
	Mother	20	09	07	19	08	09	24	09	11	35	12	11	39	12	[illegible]	-	[illegible]
	Father	09	11	10	12	09	09	13	18	08	18	29	01	14	26	[illegible]	[illegible]	-

Sample sizes range from 792 to 1185 for boys, and from 904 to 1390 for girls.
[a]Raw scores were rank normalized and then standardized within age and sex groups, prior to computation of correlations using pairwise deletion of subjects with missing data.
M = Mother, F = Father, C = Child.

The relatively low correlations across disorders and across informants suggests that analyses of the etiology of symptoms will need to be interpreted in the light of symptom-specific and informant-specific variance, including errors of assessment, situational factors, and informant biases or views (Simonoff et al., 1995). This will be the case both for analyses of the genetic and environmental causes of differences between children for specific disorders, and in terms of the interrelationships of, or comorbidity between, disorders. Depending on the study design and the structure of the analysis, if we do not take these factors into account we will underestimate the role of systematic (genetic or environmental) influences on the etiology of individual differences and comorbidity in some cases, but may also overestimate the role of the shared family environment (Hewitt, Silbert, Neale, Eaves, & Erickson, 1992) where assessments are based on a single parental informant, or suggest spurious patterns of comorbidity where any single informant is used.

Multitrait-Multimethod Factor Analysis

The systematic design and implementation of our protocol provides an opportunity to examine the underlying structure of symptom correlations through a confirmatory factor analysis that takes informant effects into account (Kenny & Kashy, 1992). Figure 2 sets out the structure of our assessments for the six disorders based on interviews with the three informants for the model corresponding to Campbell and Fiske's (1959) original conceptualization of the multitrait–multimethod matrix. We assume that each informant assesses the child's behavior from his or her own viewpoint, resulting in correlations across disorders rated by the same informant; we allow for the viewpoint of the child and the parents to be correlated. We assume that assessments by the three informants reflect some common behavior of the child being described in each of the disorders, and we allow for any pattern of correlations among the disorders. Not shown in the figure are influences unique to each disorder rated by each informant. This factor model can be fit by maximum likelihood using the program Mx (Neale, 1994). Estimates of unique variance will include both systematic (i.e. reliable) unique effects together with unreliability variance, which could be substantial. Angold and Costello (1995) have reported test–retest intraclass correlations (mean interval = 5 days, different interviewers) for child-reported CAPA symptom counts ranging from .37 for ODD in an outpatient sample to .91 for MDD in an inpatient group. For their combined patient group, reliability correlations were .60, .50, .88, .63, and .80 for CD, ODD, MDD, SAD, and OAD respectively, suggesting that in some cases as much as half of the symptom count variance could be unreliable.

All our analyses were based on the pairwise correlations, computed for all cases where both variables were scored, and so the sample sizes range from 792 to 1185 for boys and from 904 to 1390 for girls and the reported correlation matrices are not constrained to be positive definite (i.e. they may have negative eigenvalues). In addition, for these phenotypic analyses the subjects, being twins, do not represent independent observations, and so the effective sample size may be less than the observed number of individual children. Finally, we computed fit statistics based on the smallest observed N for the correlations in the matrix, i.e. 792 for boys and 904 for girls. (Use of average N or maximum N would increase the reported chi-square values proportionately, i.e. by a multiple of 1.22 for both boys and girls for the average N and by multiples of 1.50 and 1.54 for boys and girls respectively for the maximum N). Thus any fit statistics we computed could be used only as guides to interpreting the adequacy of the factor models and comparisons among alternative models.

Before estimating the factor loadings and correlations for this model, we explored the evidence for sex differences in the pattern of correlations. An omnibus test for the heterogeneity of the 17 × 17 correlation matrices gave $\chi^2 = 211.03$ for 136 df. Although this suggests some heterogeneity, we note that with sample sizes over 500, very small discrepancies between observed and expected correlations become statistically significant (Hayduk, 1987). Against a null model, the assumption of homogenous correlations matrices gave a Formed Fit Index (NFI) of .950, a Tucker Lewis Index (TLI) of .962. Fitting the factor model separately for boys ($\chi^2 = 195.5$, $df = 86$) and girls ($\chi^2 = 218.0$, $df = 86$) provided some improvement in fit over constraining all factor loadings and intercorrelation to be equal for boys and girls ($\chi^2 = 490.0$, $df = 220$). However, the joint model provided an adequate account according to a suggested criterion of chi-square/$df < 3$ (Hayduk, 1987) with NFI = .883 and TFI = .915. Where there were differences between the models for boys and girls, these were in the relative magnitudes of loadings on the disorder and informant factors and did not fall into a predicative pattern. Thus, rather than attempting to interpret gender differences that may not be robust, we focus on the overall features of the factor model that are common to boys and girls. In Table 5 we give the factor loadings and intercorrelations for the model diagrammed in Fig. 2 and fit jointly to boys and girls.

Here we see first that more than half of the variance is unique to a particular informant for a particular disorder in most cases. Next, the informant factors contribute substantially to variance in the symptom counts. Third, as would be expected, correlations between informant factors are higher for parents than for parents with their children.

In as much as symptoms can be agreed upon by different reporters, we are able to consider the intercorrelations among the disorders. The highest correlations are between CD and ODD, and between SAD and OAD. In the latter case, this is true in spite of the markedly different age trends for the two types of symptoms. With cross-sectional data we are unable to test the hypothesis that SAD in early childhood is predictive of OAD in adolescence, but this is clearly a possibility. MDD correlates moderately with SAD and more strongly with OAD, as might be expected given their similar developmental trajectories. Neither SAD nor OAD correlate substantially with CD, ODD, or ADHD, with the possible exception of a modest correlation between OAD and ODD. Finally, ADHD has

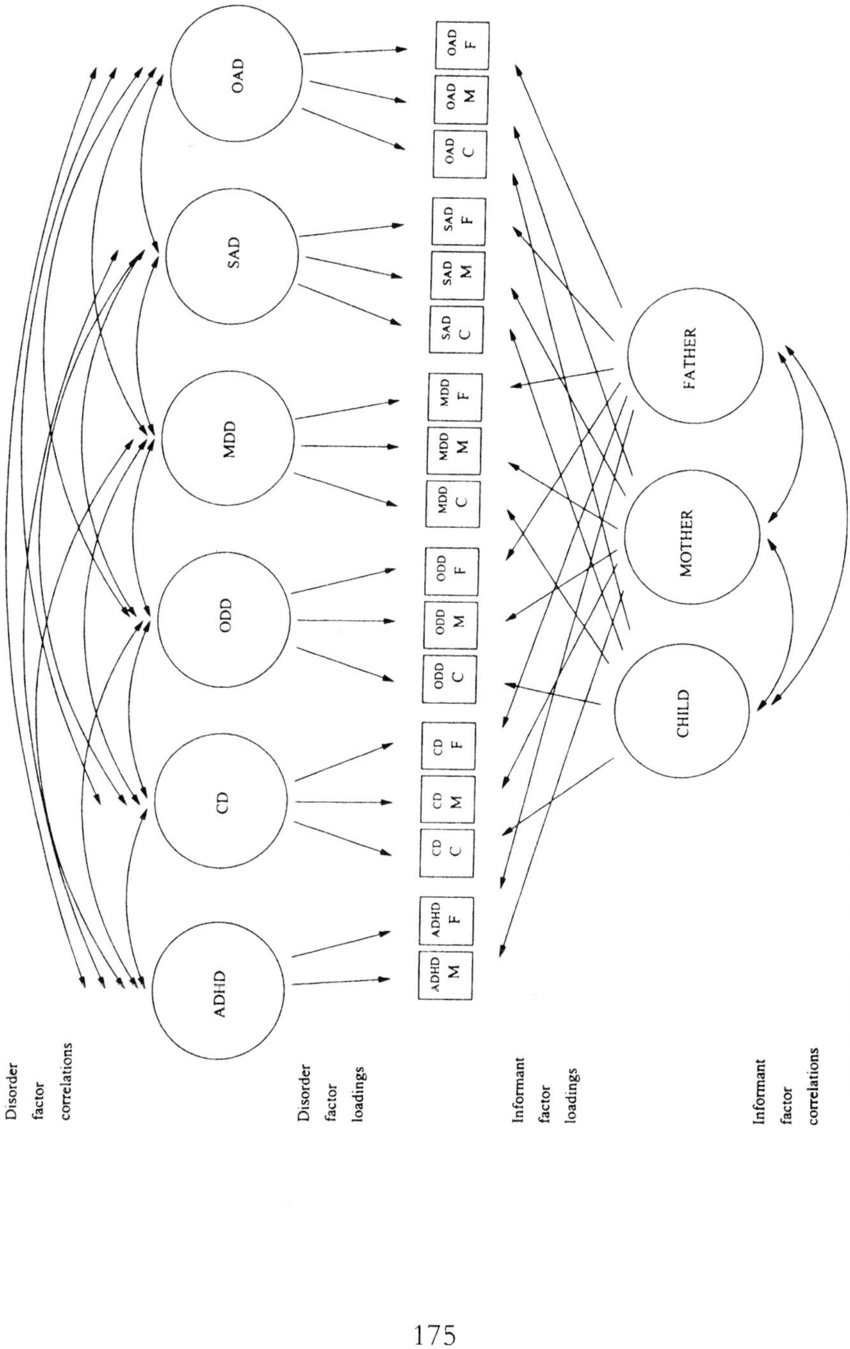

Figure 2. Multitrait–multimethod confirmatory factor model for 17 interview assessments of symptoms of 6 disorders reported by 3 informants.

Table 5
Factor Loadings (× 100), Factor Correlations (× 100), and Components of Variance (percentages)

		Disorder factor loading						Informant factor loading			Components of variance[a] (squared loadings)		
Disorder	Informant	ADHD	CD	ODD	MDD	SAD	OAD	C	M	F	Disorder	Informant	Unique
ADHD	Mother	62							33		39	11	50
	Father	49								32	24	10	66
CD	Child		67					23			45	5	50
	Mother		32						52		10	27	62
	Father		26							58	7	33	60
ODD	Child			61				30			37	9	53
	Mother			23					70		5	48	46
	Father			22						70	5	49	46
MDD	Child				31			45			10	20	71
	Mother				56				40		13	16	53
	Father				40					22	16	5	79
SAD	Child					16		52			2	27	70
	Mother					46			22		21	5	74
	Father					39				21	15	4	81
OAD	Child						14	59			2	34	64
	Mother						45		26		20	7	73
	Father						39			24	15	6	79
Factor correlations:	ADHD	100						C	100				
	CD	20	100					M	16	100			
	ODD	21	75	100				F	16	44	100		
	MDD	34	25	37	100								
	SAD	10	7	12	51	100							
	OAD	15	11	22	74	90	100						

[a]Components sum to 100 except for rounding error.
C = Child, M = Mother, F = Father.

Table 6
Summary of Factorially Derived Questionnaire Scales

Scale description	Scale label	Target disorders	Source and (number) of items[a]	Informants[b]
Hyperactivity	ADHD	ADHD	Rutter (3)	M, F
			Rutter (3) & Connors (4)	T
Impulsivity	IMPULS	ADHD	EASI (7)	C, M, F
Planning	PLANNG	ADHD	EASI (5)	C, M, F
Conduct problems	CONDUCT1	CD, ODD	Rutter (8)	M, F
			Rutter (7) & Connors (1)	T
Conduct problems	CONDUCT2	CD, ODD	Olweus (28)	C, M, F
Oppositional behavior	OPPOSN	ODD	Olweus (4)	C, M, F
Social *un*desirability	SOCDES	CD, ODD	R & R lie scale (9)	C, M, F
Anxiety, neuroticism	ANXIETY	SAD, OAD	R & R (14) & EASI (8)	C, M, F
Depressed mood	DEPRES	MDD	R & R (3) & MFQ (17)	C, M, F
Psychomotor retardation	RET	MDD	R & R (1) & MFQ (7)	C, M, F

[a]Rutter = Rutter A(2) parental[11–14] or B(2) teacher questionnaire; Connors = Connors scale (1990); EASI = EASI Temperament scale[35]; Olweus = Olweus antisocial and delinquent behavior scale[33]; R & R = Reynolds and Richmond "What I think and feel" measure of manifest anxiety[31]; MFQ = Recent Mood and Feelings Questionnaire[32].
[b]Informants: C = Child, M = Mother, F = Father, T = Teacher.

modest correlations with CD, ODD, and MDD. Perhaps it is worth remarking that even after we have taken account of informant biases as best we can, correlations among symptoms of all disorders remain uniformly positive albeit small in some instances.

An Overview of 30 Factorially Derived Questionnaire Scales

To complement the assessment of clinical symptoms by CAPA interview, dimensional assessments by questionnaire are included in the VTSABD protocol. Guided by exploratory phenotypic factor analyses of the questionnaire data, we constructed a total of 30 questionnaire scales, reported by the children themselves, their mothers, fathers, or teachers. Principal components analyses were first performed in SAS (SAS Institute Inc., 1990) on the product-moment correlations (or phi coefficients) among items. The Kaiser-Guttman rule (number of eigenvalues of the original correlation matrix greater than unity) was used to determine the number of factors to retain initially. Oblique PROMAX rotation, following VARIMAX prerotation, was employed. Factors that were consistent across raters were identified by inspection and, within those factors, items that showed highly variable (inconsistent) loadings were dropped. With the exception of four items of the Olweus questionnaire that form an oppositional behaviour scale (OPPOSN), scales were defined where the highest loading items were the same for children, mothers, and fathers, or, in the case of teachers and parents, were clearly equivalent. Table 6 summarizes the content of these scales, their item sources, and the informant. Tables 7 and 8 summarize the observed phenotypic correlations between these scales (and the Slosson Oral Reading Test) and their related DSM-III-R symptom counts, after all scores were rank normalized by age and sex.

Questionnaire Scales Related to ADHD

Questionnaire scales assessing hyperactivity, impulsivity, and planning (high scores indicate lack of planning or persistence with tasks) were related primarily to ADHD although for both boys and girls these scales had several significant and substantial (> 0.2) loadings on CD and ODD and, for boys, on MDD. The hyperactivity scale is based on the same three items from the Rutter A(2) parent questionnaire used by Goodman and Stevenson (1989). The behaviours described in the questionnaire are: "Very restless, has difficulty staying seated for long," "Squirmy, fidgety child," and "Cannot settle to anything for more than a few moments." Response options are: "Doesn't apply," "Applies somewhat," and "Certainly applies." This short scale has very high validity judged against the interview assessment of clinical symptoms. For questionnaire scale and clinical interview with the same informant, the validity correlations range from .42 to .54. Across informants (mother with father or vice versa), the correlations of questionnaire with symptom count range from .32 to .37, i.e. as high as the .35 correlation between symptom counts based on mothers' and the fathers' interviews. The pattern of correlations of the questionnaire scale with symptom counts across disorders very closely parallels the comorbidity correlations for ADHD symptom counts, providing further evidence of both convergent and discriminant validity for the questionnaire scale.

The teachers' hyperactivity questionnaire assessments and the parental impulsivity and planning questionnaire scales are less strongly related to parental interview ADHD symptom counts, although here again the questionnaire scales show a similar pattern of relationship to symptom counts across the six disorders. Where we have children's self-assessments for impulsivity and planning, these show little relationship to clinical assessments with the exception of those for ODD based on the child interview.

Questionnaire Scales Related to CD and ODD

We defined three scales that a priori would be expected to relate to the externalizing disorder cluster of CD and ODD. CONDUCT1 summed eight items from the parental and teacher Rutter questionnaires (augmented with a Connors item) relating to: bullying, fighting, destroying property, lying, stealing, truancy, disobedience, and temper tantrums (parental scale) or disturbing other children (teacher scale). These last two items were included because they loaded on the same factor as the more obviously CD-related items. CONDUCT2 included the 28 items loading highest on the first general factor from the 35 items of our adapted version of the Olweus self-report questionnaire assessing delinquent and aggressive behavior. Responses were scored 1 for any reported example of the behavior and 0 otherwise. OPPOSN comprises the four items of the Olweus questionnaire concerning "yelling or screaming at" or "hitting or slapping" either the mother or father. These items were the only four contributing to our derived questionnaire scales where the pattern of factor loadings was inconsistent between children's reports and parental reports; for parental reports these items loaded on the general factor defining CONDUCT2, whereas in children they did not. SOCDES summed the eight social desirability items from Reynolds and Richmond's "What I think and feel" measure of manifest anxiety and reversed the score to provide a measure of *un*desirability.

CONDUCT1 and CONDUCT2 have similar patterns of correlations with symptom counts, both having the highest correlations with CD and ODD and lower correlations with both ADHD and MDD; once again, these closely follow the patterns observed for the symptom counts themselves. Across parental informants, these questionnaire scales provided as good a prediction of symptom counts as did the interviews, and the same was true for children's self-reported CONDUCT2 with parental symptom counts, except in the case of boys' CONDUCT2 with parental CD. Correlations between OPPOSN and the symptom counts showed a similar pattern but with weaker relationships in general and a tendency towards higher correlations with ODD than with CD. Unlike CONDUCT2, children's self-reported OPPOSN did not correlate with ADHD for either boys or girls; this observation, and the lower correlations generally for OPPOSN compared to CONDUCT2, may well result from the much shorter scale (4 items vs. 28 items). SOCDES was only weakly related to symptom counts but is included here because, being based on the absence of egregiously "good" behaviors rather than the presence of undesirable behaviors, it provides a different perspective on externalizing behavior problems. Although the associations with symptom counts are weak, their pattern suggests both modest convergent and discriminant validity as an indicator of externalizing disorder symptoms.

Table 7
Significant ($p < .05$) Correlations (Pearson × 100) between Boys' Questionnaire Scales and DSM-III-R Symptom Counts Based on CAPA Interviews

		Disorder																
		ADHD		CD			ODD			MDD			SAD			OAD		
Scale	Informant	M	F	C	M	F	C	M	F	C	M	F	C	M	F	C	M	F
READING	C	−15	−15	−07	−09	−08							−12					
ADHD	M	54	36	11	22	17	11	28	18		25	13	09	10			11	
	F	37	52	18	17	21	10	19	20		19	20	09		07			12
	T	29	26	13	20	17	17	19	22	08	21	14	09	09		07		
IMPULS	C			17			22			14			17	12		15		
	M	35	31	16	24	21	16	32	25	10	23	08	11	10	09		13	
	F	25	28	16	12	18	12	18	26	12	15	13	12	09	10		13	09
PLANNG	C	11		20								10				−10		
	M	23	15	09	09	11	10	14	09		11	09						−07
	F	20	21	08	08	15	11	12	18		12	10						
CONDUCT1	M	33	21	23	43	33	20	40	33	10	32	12	07	12	11		16	
	F	24	27	24	32	39	15	29	39		17	15	08	13			09	11
	T	23	22	15	17	13	18	18	23	12	14	14		09		08		
CONDUCT2	C	15	15	40	18	13	31	19	15	18	13	07		09		10	06	
	M	24	19	22	29	29	17	29	28	07	21	12		09			10	08
	F	19	16	23	30	31	17	24	32	10	14	15	08				08	
OPPOSN	C			19		11	13	09	12	14	11	10			08	09	11	09
	M	13	09	10	18	16	11	25	22	07	17	09		07	12	13		13
	F	12	15	11	12	15	12	16	30	09	15	12		08		10		
SOC DES	C			17			17	07		09				−06				
	M	13	09	10	20	21	12	21	20		10	07						
	F	11	06	08	16	14	09	10	21									07
ANXIETY	C		11	10			17			25	10		27	15	11	37		15
	M	23	16	09	16	18	10	22	18	10	32	17	13	19	16	12	29	19
	F	17	23			17		09	21	14	19	25	11	15	19	10	20	29
DEPRES	C	12	10	23	13	10	26	14	09	33	21	20	27	11	07	23	07	07
	M	30	13	12	22	27	14	28	24	15	44	23	07	15	20	12	26	21
	F	20	23	11	11	18	09	15	25	14	25	37	09	13	19	07	12	27
RET	C	10	11	19	10		20	06	07	21	13	13	20			20		07
	M	26	19	11	23	19	08	21	13		28	11		07	13		17	10
	F	20	25	09	10	17	09	16	23	10	16	18		11	09		10	16

[a] C = Child, M = Mother, F = Father, T = Teacher.

Table 8
Significant (p < .05) Correlations (Pearson × 100) for Girls' Questionnaire Scales and DSM–III–R Symptom Counts Based on CAPA Interviews

		Disorder																
		ADHD		CD			ODD			MDD			SAD			OAD		
Scale	Informant[a]	M	F	C	M	F	C	M	F	C	M	F	C	M	F	C	M	F
READING	C	−16	−12		−08	−14			−09		−07		−10				−06	
ADHD	M	47	37	13	23	24	11	30	22	12	16		06	13	11	08	17	15
	F	32	42	10	18	23	16	19	26		13	15	13	12	07		11	15
	T	21	21	10	19	14	12	16	13	11	11	10	06	10	07			09
IMPULS	C	11		19	09	10	26	13	14	16	13		11		09	19	09	14
	M	29	25	10	29	22	13	37	18	07	20			14	08		18	14
	F	23	28	13	19	20	15	18	29	06	14	09		10	12		12	17
PLANNG	C	11		10	11	13	10	08	10									
	M	22	17	08	15	14	08	11	16		08						−06	
	F	13	17	11	16	16	05	11	12		14							
CONDUCT1	M	25	22	21	40	28	19	44	28	12	26	11		15	09	06	21	16
	F	18	22	16	30	36	20	27	40	10	23	15	09	14	16	07	14	18
	T	13		14	22	18	16	16	16	11	13	10		10			06	08
CONDUCT2	C	13		36	23	19	27	12	12	17	11		11		07	12	08	08
	M	20	11	19	34	29	15	23	17	07	15			16	11	07	14	12
	F	18	15	20	25	31	15	17	27	08	14	07	07	10	12	08	13	14
OPPOSN	C			20	13	08	20	08	11	11	10					10	08	08
	M	15	11	11	22	19	10	24	18		18	08		13	07	06	14	12
	F	07	11	11	13	13		11	19		07				10			10
SOC DES	C			20	07		21	10		07						07		
	M	07	07	09	20	15	11	24	18		10		−06				07	
	F		06	14	18	18	08	11	22		10							
ANXIETY	C			09			20	10		37	21	10	33		09	32	17	11
	M	18	11		15	08		24	10	11	35	17	09	24	17	12	39	25
	F	07	18		10	14	07	15	23	09	22	26	13	21	17	11	24	32
DEPRES	C	11		17	17	13	30	14	12	40	24	14	26	09	07	25	14	12
	M	21	11	13	23	12	15	33	17	18	43	17	07	21	15	11	31	26
	F	12	14	08	17	18	14	18	25	13	31	30	08	17	21	11	24	32
RET	C	11		23	16	14	27	10	15	27	15	06	26	09	13	22	11	12
	M	22	14	09	16	16	07	19	14	15	22			15	09	07	22	13
	F	18	16	14	17	19	11	17	19	12	18	13	08	18	16		14	16

[a] C = Child, M = Mother, F = Father, T = Teacher.

Questionnaire Scales Related to Anxiety and Depression

Our questionnaire scale for anxiety and neuroticism (ANXIETY) incorporates 14 items from Reynolds and Richmond's manifest anxiety scale and 8 neuroticism items from the EASI temperament scale. Within informants, this scale is correlated most substantially with OAD and about equally, though a little less, with SAD and MDD. There are also some significant, though generally lower, correlations between ANXIETY and ADHD and ODD and, somewhat lower still, with CD. These findings are consistent with those of Perrin and Last (1992) who found that Reynolds and Richmond's manifest anxiety scale did not discriminate between clinically anxious boys and those with a diagnosis of ADHD, although both groups had significantly higher anxiety scale scores than nonpsychiatric controls. In adults, neuroticism scale scores are an index of a generalized genetic risk for self-reported symptoms of anxiety and depression (Eaves et al., 1989). However, few empirical data are available to assess the extent to which the vulnerability to psychiatric disturbance, indexed by neuroticism, might be still more general.

Our DEPRES scale, drawing on 17 items from the Recent Mood and Feelings questionnaire and 3 from the manifest anxiety scale, chosen on the basis of their loading on the same phenotypic factor, correlates most substantially with MDD but, like ANXIETY, has significant correlations with ADHD, ODD, and to a lesser extent, CD, as well as SAD and OAD. A shorter scale, RET, assessed items primarily describing psychomotor retardation – "felt so tired [...] just sat around and did nothing," "moving and walking more slowly than usual," "felt like talking less than usual"—but also indications of more general psychosomatic unease: "ate more than usual," "worried about aches and pains," "didn't sleep as well as usual [...]," "hard [...] to keep [...] mind on school work." The correlations of this scale with symptom counts were low to modest across the six categories of disorder.

Reading

The Slosson Oral Reading Test was included in our protocol primarily to provide an index of the ability of children to read their own questionnaire material—children 11 years or younger or 12 years or older who do not reach 6th-grade reading ability were read their questionnaires by the interviewers. However, this short 5-minute test is highly reliable and has highly heritable individual differences (Eaves et al., 1997; Reynolds et al., 1996), has strong relationships to indices of school success or failure (Reynolds et al., in preparation), and a pattern of familial correlations that is typical of individual tests of general intelligence. We report the correlations of READING with symptom counts to show that the correlations are nonsignificant or small (and negative) with all our symptom counts. The most substantial correlations are with ADHD, a result consistent with the commonly found comorbidity of ADHD and reading problems (Gilger, Pennington, & DeFries, 1992; Stevenson, Pennington, Gilger, DeFries, & Gillis, 1993). There are also weak correlations (though significant in our large samples), replicated in boys and girls, with SAD based on children's interviews and with CD based on parental interviews. In all these cases, poor READING is associated weakly with higher symptom levels.

Discussion

No one study can answer all the questions we would like to ask about the genetic and environmental influences that affect the development of behavior problems and psychopathology in childhood and adolescence. However, in designing the VTSABD our goal was that it should not only be informative about the genetic epidemiology of the common disorders of childhood but should also permit the study of developmental continuity and change throughout childhood and adolescence, the causes of the extensive comorbidity among childhood disorders, and the role of environmental risk factors as well as genetic vulnerability. Because there is still considerable uncertainty about the definition of psychiatric disorders in childhood, and about the best way to assess behavior problems or symptoms of disorder, we chose to use both dimensional questionnaire assessments as well as the assessment of clinical symptoms based on psychiatric interviews. We also systematically involved the children themselves, their mothers, their fathers, and their teachers as informants about the children's behavior. The resulting longitudinal overlapping cohort study of a statewide representative sample of 1412 pairs of twins will provide a wealth of new empirical information about genetics, development, environmental risks, and phenotype definition. In this initial report we have described the characteristics of the phenotypic assessments of the children: these assessments will provide the target variables for subsequent genetic and environmental analyses (Eaves et al., 1997).

Symptom Counts and Disorders

It is an unresolved question whether a boundary between normal and abnormal behavior in childhood can be determined in a way that meaningfully distinguishes between phenomenologically or etiologically distinct categories. As Offord (1995, p. 285) noted, using CD as an example,

> many children have a few antisocial symptoms, and as the symptom count increases, the number of affected children decreases. The issue then becomes where does one set the threshold that separates children into 2 categories... If the variability among symptom counts is low and the symptoms are grouped around the existing threshold, then changing the threshold slightly will have a noticeable effect on the prevalence of disorder (Robins, 1985).

The arbitrary quality of the thresholds implied by diagnostic definitions is underscored by changes in numbers of symptoms required for diagnosis, such as the change from one (in DSM-III) to three symptoms (in DSM-III-R) required for CD (Offord, 1995), or in the severity, duration, impairing consequences, and pervasiveness of symptoms, such as the DSM-IV requirement that for a diagnosis of ADHD some impairment from symptoms be present in two or more settings. Despite the difficulty of defining the boundary between abnormal and normal, the question of whether the more extreme clinical syndromes may have a distinct genetic or environmental etiology remains to be addressed; in the context of the VTSABD, analytical approaches to this question, based on latent class analysis, are being developed (Eaves, Silberg, Hewitt, Rutter, et al., 1993; Eaves, Silberg, Hewitt, Meyer, et al., 1993).

Here, our data presentation focuses on symptom counts for six common disorders of childhood defined in DSM-III-R and the intercorrelations of these symptom counts with each other and with dimensional questionnaire scales. In reporting symptom counts, rather than diagnosed disorders, we are recognizing that the relatively low prevalence of disorders in a nonclinical sample such as ours will considerably lower the statistical power of analyses of variation and covariation based only on diagnosed cases and, potentially, obscure the correlational relationships, both across disorders or risk factors and among family members, evident from the variation in numbers of symptoms. Thus our overview of the genetic and environmental variation revealed in the VTSABD (Eaves et al., 1997) will be based on the symptom counts and scale scores described here rather than on diagnosed disorders. Rates of DSM-III-R defined disorders in the VTSABD are reported and discussed by Simonoff et al. (in press) who show that the age, gender, and informant influences for rates of disorder closely parallel the trends reported here for symptom counts.

Gender, Age, and Informant Effects

Girls reported more symptoms of MDD, SAD, and OAD; boys reported more symptoms of CD and ODD. Parents describe more ADHD and CD symptoms in their sons than their daughters and mothers report more anxiety symptoms for their daughters. These gender differences are consistent with other community-based epidemiological studies (e.g. Angold, 1988; Bird et al., 1988; Offord et al., 1987). The self-reported numbers of symptoms of CD, ODD, MDD, and OAD increase during adolescence, and those for SAD decrease. For girls, maternal reports of ADHD symptoms are lower in adolescence. Again, none of these findings is unexpected, although the gender by age interaction for ADHD is slightly different from that found by Offord et al. (1987), who reported significantly higher rates in young boys and no age effect in girls.

An important observation is the extent to which the detailed picture of symptom prevalence depends on the informant. Adolescent boys report twice as many symptoms of CD as are reported by their parents, a finding consistent with the previously reported higher prevalence of youth-identified compared with parent-identified CD (Offord, Boyle, Fleming, et al., 1989). Similarly, higher rates of reporting by children are found for SAD at all ages and, less consistently, for OAD and, in boys, for MDD in the mid-teens when these symptoms, and their associated disorders, begin to increase in frequency.

Informant Agreement and Disagreement

Low levels of agreement among informants are a consistent finding in child psychiatric epidemiology (Angold et al., 1987; Boyle et al., 1993; Edelbrock, Costello, Dulcan, Conover, & Kala, 1986; Simonoff et al., 1995), and the VTSAB is no exception. We find low levels of correlation among informants reporting on the same symptoms in the same children. Correlations between symptom numbers reported by mothers and fathers range from a high of .35 for ADHD to a low of .2 or less for the anxiety symptoms. Correlations between children and parents range from a high of around .2 for the externalizing symptoms (CD and ODD) to a low of around .1 for the anxiety disorders. Kappa coefficients based on clinical diagnoses are similarly low (Simonoff et al., in press).

The multitrait–multimethod factor analysis indicated that the largest component of variance for symptom counts is, in most cases, unique to the specific informant for the specific disorder being assessed, that a large component of variance is common to the range of psychopathology but specific to a given informant, and that, with some exceptions among the externalizing disorders, the component of variance attributable to symptoms that mothers, fathers, and children can agree on is smaller than the informant-specific variance.

Although such low levels of agreement among informants might be troubling, evidence that informant-specific variance is not accounted for simply by unreliability can be inferred from the genetic analyses reported by Eaves et al. (1997); they find that monozygotic twin correlations (which provide lower bound estimates of reliability) for symptom counts are as high as .6 for externalizing disorders and .4 for internalizing disorders. Similarly, test–retest reliability studies of the CAPA interview give kappa coefficients of .55 or greater for diagnoses assessed several days apart (Angold & Costello, 1995). Given that the reports have at least moderate reliability, we may interpret the low correlations to suggest that different informants may provide nonredundant information from their different perspectives on the child's behaviour and their different opportunities to interact with the child. The VTSABD will provide us with additional opportunities to determine the validity of information from specific informants as we explore the differential correlates and predictive validity of the individual assessments and of alternative algorithms for combining information across informants. However, for now, we must anticipate that assessments based on interviews with parents or with the children themselves may reflect different patterns of genetic and environmental influence.

Comorbidity

Beyond the issue of inter-informant agreement and disagreement, the multitrait–multimethod factor analysis provides a method for examining comorbidity among symptom clusters that neither overestimates the level of comorbidity based on individual informants, nor underestimates comorbidity as the result of instability or unreliability of assessments. In fact, the multitrait–

multimethod factor analysis provided confirmatory evidence that, when informant-specific effects (and any associated biases) have been taken into consideration, there are high levels of correlation among different clusters of the symptoms that are agreed upon by parents and children. Thus, for example, even though SAD and OAD have distinct time courses—symptoms of the former being more prevalent in younger children and those of the latter in older children—their interfactor correlations are high enough to suggest the hypothesis that the same individuals may be vulnerable to SAD in early childhood and OAD in later childhood, and possibly to GAD as adults. Similarly, high correlations are found for symptoms of OAD and MDD and between symptoms of ODD and CD. There are also moderate correlations between the externalizing disorders and MDD, and between ADHD and CD, ODD, and MDD. The correlations between the externalizing disorders and the anxiety disorders are lower, with the exception of ODD and OAD.

This pattern of correlations is suggestive of the high levels of comorbidity found in other community surveys (Anderson, Williams, McGee, & Silva, 1987; Bird et al., 1988, 1993; Offord, Boyle, & Racine, 1989). Although the correlation between ADHD and CD in our analysis is somewhat lower than we might have predicted (Szatmari, Boyle, & Offord, 1989), this follows in part from the fact that ADHD was assessed only by parental informants, whereas in all the other domains the children as well as the parents provided information. Thus the correlations between ADHD and other domains will reflect the difference between a shared *parental* view of ADHD and a shared *family* view of the other domains. The correlations between the internalizing symptoms are consistent with the overlap found among these disorders (Kovacs, Feinberg, Crouse-Novak, Paulauskas, & Finkel stein, 1984; Strauss, Last, Hersen, & Kazdin, 1988). Perhaps what is most interesting is that, when we consider information that children and parents agree upon, the symptoms of the externalizing disorders are so clearly distinguished from symptoms of internalizing disorders. Although we must await the appropriate multivariate genetic analyses to interpret these results fully, we might predict that the VTSABD will confirm at least two broad vulnerability factors for symptoms of the common disorders of childhood.

Questionnaire Measures

In addition to symptoms assessed through clinical interview, we have presented data obtained through questionnaires that were designed to obtain dimensional information relevant to the development of risk for disorder. The scales we have extracted from our questionnaire battery were based on phenotypic factor analyses carried out separately for the different informants. These analyses were carried out for the questionnaire items only, without including the symptom counts, so that any subsequent correlations observed between questionnaire scale and symptom counts do not capitalize on chance associations. With one exception (the four-item OPPOSN scale), the items that loaded on each of the derived scales were the same for parents and children, suggesting that the scales will be assessing the same underlying constructs.

To assess the relationship between our derived questionnaire scales and the interview-based symptom assessments, we examined the correlations between the questionnaire scales and the symptom counts. What is evident from Tables 7 and 8 is that the questionnaire scales perform extremely well as predictors of symptom counts based on the interviews. For the same informant, the correlation between the relevant scale and the symptom count is often .4 and sometimes greater. Although these values are modest, they are in all cases higher than the correlations between any two informants for symptom count of the same disorder. Moreover, across informants, questionnaire assessments are as good a predictor of assessed symptoms as are the interview-based symptom counts themselves. Finally, examination of Tables 7 and 8 reveals that not only do the questionnaire scales exhibit a high degree of convergent validity, they also show discriminant validity in their pattern of correlations with symptom counts for externalizing and internalizing disorders.

At a practical level, these results suggest that questionnaire assessments may perform well as screening instruments for several of the clinical disorders we are targeting. This may be true for the three-item ADHD scale (Goodman & Stevenson, 1989) in relation to ADHD, for our CONDUCT1 or CONDUCT2 scales in relation to CD and ODD, and our DEPRES or ANXIETY scales in relation to MDD, SAD, and OAD. It is less clear whether questionnaire scales can differentiate among the correlated disorders (i.e. between CD and ODD, or between MDD, SAD, and OAD), although it is also unclear to what extent disorders within those clusters can or should be differentiated in terms of individual vulnerability (Offord, 1995).

Conclusion

The inclusion of questionnaire measures alongside clinical interviews has enabled us to establish the convergent and discriminant validity of the questionnaires as indices of dimensional variation in vulnerability to symptoms of disorder. Perhaps most importantly, this means that in our developmental analyses, we will have useful indices of vulnerability that, though not yet manifest as a clinical disorder, may be predictive of disorder at later ages. Such measures may reveal evidence of the risk factors that operate in the early stages of the development of a disorder, before their influence could be detected using clinical information alone.

Conversely, because we have clinical assessments from psychiatric interviews, we will be able to assess quite directly whether the development and etiology of quantitatively assessed individual differences properly characterizes the development and etiology of clinical disorders. As Cantwell and Rutter (1994) have emphasized, dimensional and categorical conceptualizations of disorders are not mutually exclusive and each may have its advantages and disadvantages. It is our intention that, by inclusion of phenotypic assessments of both kinds, the VTSABD will provide empirical data that will help us to determine what these advantages and disadvantages are in each specific case.

Although the next step in this endeavor is the characterization of the genetic and environmental contributions to variation in our phenotypic assessments (Eaves et al., 1997), the full power of the VTSABD comes from the multivariate and developmental analyses that will now be possible. Combining conventional quantitative genetic and environmental models with analyses that incorporate measurements of the environment, and examining our data from both dimensional and categorical perspectives, we will be able to use the VTSABD to learn more about the developmental pathways from genetic vulnerability and environmental risks to the manifestation of psychopathology in childhood and adolescence.

Acknowledgements—Supported by grant MH45268, and a grant from the Carman Trust, and Junior Faculty Research Awards from the John D. and Catherine T. MacArthur Foundation to Joanne M. Meyer and Judith L. Silberg.

References

Achenbach, T. M., McConaughy, S. H., & Howell, C. T. (1987). Child/adolescent behavioral and emotional problems: Implications of cross-informant correlations for situational specificity. *Psychological Bulletin, 101*, 213–232.

Anderson, J. C., Williams, S., McGee, R., & Silva, P. A. (1987). DSM-III disorders in preadolescent children. Prevalence in a large sample from the general population. *Archives of General Psychiatry, 44*, 69–76.

Angold, A. (1988). Childhood and adolescent depression: I. Epidemiological and aetiological aspects. *British Journal of Psychiatry, 152*, 601–617.

Angold, A., & Costello, E. J. (1995). A test–retest reliability study of child-reported psychiatric symptoms and diagnoses using the Child and Adolescent Psychiatric Assessment (CAPA–C). *Psychological Medicine, 25*, 755–762.

Angold, A., Prendergast, M., Cox, A., Harrington, R., Simonoff, E. S., & Rutter, M. (1995). The Child and Adolescent Psychiatric Assessment (CAPA). *Psychological Medicine, 25*, 739–753.

Angold, A., Weissman, M. M., John, K., Merikangas, K. R., Prusoff, B. A., Gammon, G. D., & Warner, V. (1987). Parent and child reports of depressive symptoms in children at low and high risk of depression. *Journal of Child Psychology and Psychiatry, 28*, 901–915.

Bird, H., Canino, G., Rubio-Stipec, M., Gould, M. S., Ribera, J., Sesman, M., Woodbury, M., Huertas-Goldman, S., Pagan, A., Sanchez-Lacay, A., & Moscoso, M. (1993). Estimates of the prevalence of childhood maladjustment in a community survey in Puerto Rico: The use of combined measures. *Archives of General Psychiatry, 45*, 1120–1126.

Boyle, M. H., Offord, D. R., Racine, Y., Sanford, M., Szatmari, P., Fleming, J. E., & Price-Munn, N. (1993). Evaluation of the diagnostic interview for children and adolescents for use in general population samples. *Journal of Abnormal Child Psychology, 21*, 663–681.

Brandenburg, N. A., Friedman, R. M. S., & Silver, S. E. (1990). The epidemiology of childhood psychiatric disorders: Prevalence findings from recent studies. *Journal of the American Academy of Child and Adolescent Psychiatry, 29*, 76–83.

Brown, G. W., & Harris, T. (1978). *Social origins of depression.* London: Tavistock.

Bulmer, M. G. (1970). *The biology of twinning in man.* Oxford: Clarendon Press.

Buss, A. H., & Plomin, R. (1975). *A temperament theory of personality development.* New York: Wiley.

Campbell, D. T., & Fiske, D. W. (1959). Convergent and discriminant validation by the multitrait–multimethod matrix. *Psychological Bulletin, 56*, 81–105.

Cantwell, D. P., & Rutter, M. (1994). Classification: Conceptual issues and substantive findings. In M. Rutter, E. Taylor, & L. Hersov (Eds.), *Child and adolescent psychiatry* (3rd edn.). Oxford: Blackwell Scientific Publications.

Caron, R. J., & Rutter, M. (1991). Comorbidity in child psychopathology: Concepts, issues and research strategies. *Journal of Child Psychology and Psychiatry, 32*, 1063–1080.

Connors, C. K. (1969). A teacher rating scale for use in drug studies with children. *American Journal of Psychiatry, 126*, 884–888.

Costello, E. J. (1989). Developments in child psychiatric epidemiology. *Journal of the American Academy of Child and Adolescent Psychiatry, 28*, 836–841.

Costello, E. J., & Angold, A. (1988). Scales to assess child and adolescent depression: Checklists, screens and nets. *Journal of the American Academy of Child and Adolescent Psychiatry, 27*, 726–737.

Cox, A., Rutter, M., Yule, W., & Quinton, D. (1977). Bias resulting from missing information: Some epidemiological findings. *British Journal of Preventative Social Medicine, 31*, 131–136.

Daniels, D., & Plomin, R. (1985). Differential experience of siblings reared in the same family. *Developmental Psychology, 21*, 747–760.

Doherty, J. D., & Lancaster, P. A. (1986). The secular trend of twinning in Australia 1853–1982. *Acta Geneticae Medicae et Gemellologiae, 35*, 61–76.

Downey, G., & Coyne, J. C. (1990). Children of depressed parents: Integrative review. *Psychological Bulletin, 108*, 50–76.

Eaves, L. J., Eysenck, H. J., & Martin, N. G. (1989). *Genes, culture and personality.* New York: Academic Press.

Eaves, L. J., Silberg, J. L., Hewitt, J. K., Meyer, J. M., Rutter, M., Simonoff, E. S., Neale, M. C., & Pickles, A. (1993). Genes, personality and psychopathology: A latent class analysis of liability to symptoms of attention-deficit disorder in twins. In R. Plomin & G. E. McClearn (Eds), *Nature, nurture and psychology* (pp. 285–303). Washington, DC: APA Books.

Eaves, L. J., Silberg, J. L., Hewitt, J. K., Rutter, M., Meyer, J. M., Neale, M. C., & Pickles, A. (1993). Analyzing twin resemblance in multi-symptom data: Genetic applications of a latent class model for symptoms of conduct disorder in juvenile boys. *Behavior Genetics, 23*, 5–19.

Eaves, L. J., Silberg, J. L., Meyer, J. M., Maes, H. H., Simonoff, E. S., Neale, M. C., Pickles, A., Reynolds, C., Erickson, M., Heath, A. C., Loeber, R., Rutter, M., Truett, K. R., & Hewitt, J. K. (1997). Genetics and developmental psychopathology: 2. The main effects of genes and environment on behavioral problems in the Virginia Twin Study of Adolescent Behavioral Development. *Journal of Child and Adolescent Psychiatry, 38*, 965–980.

Edelbrock, C., Costello, E. J., Dulcan, M. K., Conover, N. C., & Kala, R. (1986). Parent–child agreement on child psychiatric symptoms assessed via structured interview. *Journal of Child Psychology and Psychiatry, 27*, 181–190.

Faraone, S., & Biederman, J. (1994). Is attention deficit disorder familial? *Harvard Review of Psychiatry, 1*, 271–287.

Farrington, D. P., Gallagher, B., Morley, L., St. Ledger, R. J., & West, D. J. (1990). Minimizing attrition in longitudinal research: Methods of tracing and securing cooperation in a

24-year follow-up study. In D. Magnusson & L. R. Bergman (Eds.), *Data quality in longitudinal research* (pp. 122–147). Cambridge: Cambridge University Press.

Fergusson, D. M., & Horwood, L. J. (1987). Trait and method components of ratings of conduct disorder—Part I. Maternal and teacher evaluations of conduct disorder in young children. *Journal of Child Psychology and Psychiatry, 28*, 249–272.

Fergusson, D. M., & Horwood, L. J. (1995). Predictive validity of categorically and dimensionally scored measures of disruptive childhood behaviors. *Journal of American Academy of Child and Adolescent Psychiatry, 34*, 477–485.

Gilger, J. W., Pennington, B. F., & DeFries, J. C. (1992). A twin study of the etiology of comorbidity: Attention-deficit Hyperactivity Disorder and Dyslexia. *Journal of the American Academy of Child and Adolescent Psychiatry, 31*, 343–348.

Goodman, R., & Stevenson, J. (1989). A twin study of hyperactivity. II. The aetiological role of genes, family relationships and perinatal adversity. *Journal of Psychology and Psychiatry, 30*, 691–709.

Graham, P. J., & Stevenson, J. (1985). A twin study of genetic influences on behavioral deviance. *Journal of the American Academy of Child Psychiatry, 24*, 33–41.

Hayduk, L. A. (1987). *Structural equation modeling with LISREL. Essentials and advances*. Baltimore, MD: The Johns Hopkins University Press.

Hewitt, J. K., Silberg, J. L., Neale, M. C., Eaves, L. J., & Erickson, M. (1992). The analysis of parental ratings of children's behavior using LISREL. *Behavior Genetics, 22*, 293–318.

Hurr, Y., McGue, M., & Iacono, W. G. (1995). Unequal rate of monozygotic and like-sex dizygotic twin birth: Evidence for the Minnesota Twin Family Study. *Behavior Genetics, 25*, 337–340.

Jardine, R., Martin, N. G., & Henderson, A. S. (1984). Genetic variation between neuroticism and the symptoms of anxiety and depression. *Genetic Epidemiology*, 89–107.

Johnson, J. H. (1986). *Life events as stressors in childhood and adolescence*. Beverly Hills, CA: SAGE.

Johnson, J. H., & McCutcheon, S. (1980). Assessing life stress in older children and adolescents: Development of the Life Events checklist. In I. G. Garason & C. D. Spielberger (Eds.), *Stress and anxiety*. Washington, DC: Hemisphere.

Kendler, K. S., Neale, M. C., Kessler, R. C., Heath, A. C., & Eaves, L. J. (1992a). Childhood parental loss and adult psychopathology in women: A twin study perspective. *Archives of General Psychiatry, 49*, 109–116.

Kendler, K. S., Neale, M. C., Kessler, R. C., Heath, A. C., & Eaves, L. J. (1992b). A population based twin study of major depression in women: Varying definitions of illness. *Archives of General Psychiatry, 49*, 257–266.

Kendler, K. S., Neale, M. C., Kessler, R. C., Heath, A. C., & Evans, L. J. (1992c). Generalized anxiety disorder in women: A population based twin study. *Archives of General Psychiatry, 49*, 267–272.

Kendler, K. S., Neale, M. C., Kessler, R. C., Heath, A. C., & Eaves, L. J. (1992d). Major depression and generalized anxiety disorder: Same genes, (partly) different environments? *Archives of General Psychiatry, 49*, 716–722.

Kenny, D. A., & Kashy, D. A. (1992). Analysis of multitrait–multimethod matrix by confirmatory factor analysis. *Psychological Bulletin, 112*, 165–172.

Kovacs, M., Feinberg, T. L., Crouse-Novak, M. A., Paulauskas, S. L., & Finkelstein, R. (1984). Depressive disorders in childhood. I. A longitudinal prospective study of characteristics and recovery. *Archives of General Psychiatry, 41*, 229–237.

MacGillivray, I. (1981). The probable explanation for the falling twinning rate in Scotland. *Progress in Clinical and Biological Research, 69a*, 15–19.

McGee, R., Feehan, M., Williams, S., Partridge, F., Silva, P. A., & Kelly, J. (1990). DSM–III disorders in a large sample of adolescents. *Journal of the American Academy of Child and Adolescent Psychiatry, 29*, 611–619.

Mosteller, M., Townsend, J. I., Corey, L. A., & Nance, W. (1981). Twinning rates in Virginia: Secular trends and the effects of maternal age and parity. *Progress in Clinical and Biological Research, 69a*, 57–69.

Neale, M. C. (1994). *Mx: A package for statistical modelling*. Genetics and Human Development Technical Report. Richmond, VA: Medical College of Virginia.

Offord, D. R. (1995). Child psychiatric epidemiology: Current status and future prospects. *Canadian Journal of Psychiatry, 40*, 284–288.

Offord, D. R., Boyle, M. H., Fleming, J. E., Blum, H. M., & Grant, N. I. (1989). Ontario Child Health Study. Summary of selected results. *Canadian Journal of Psychiatry, 34*, 483–491.

Offord, D. R., Boyle, M. H., & Racine, Y. (1989). Ontario Health Study: Correlates of disorder. *Journal of the American Academy of Child and Adolescent Psychiatry, 28*, 856–860.

Offord, D. R., Boyle, M. H., Szatmari, P., Rae-Grant, N. I., Links, P. S., Cadman, D. T., Byles, J. A., Crawford, J. W., Monroe Blum, H., Byrne, C., Thomas, H., & Woodward, C. A. (1987). Ontario Child Health Study: Six-month prevalence of disorder and rates of service utilization. *Archives of General Psychiatry, 44*, 832–836.

Ollendick, T., King, N., & Fray, R. B. (1989). Fears in children and adolescents. Reliability and general liability across gender, age and nationality. *Behaviour Research and Therapy, 27*, 19–26.

Olsson, D. H., Sprenkle, D. H., & Russel, C. S. (1979). Circumplex models of marital and family systems. I. Cohesion and adaptability dimension, family types and clinical adaptations. *Family Processes, 18*, 3–28.

Olweus, D. (1989). Prevalence and incidence in the study of anti-social behavior: Definitions and measurements. In M. W. Klein (Ed.), *Cross-national research in self-reported crime and delinquency*. Dordrecht, The Netherlands: Kluwer.

Perrin, S., & Last, C. G. (1992). Do childhood anxiety measures measure anxiety? *Journal of Abnormal Child Psychology, 20*, 567–578.

Plomin, R. (1996). Genetic risk and psychosocial disorders: Links between the normal and abnormal. In M. Rutter & P. Casaer (Eds.), *Biological risk factors for psychosocial disorders* (pp. 101–138). Cambridge: Cambridge University Press.

Reynolds, C. A., Hewitt, J. K., Erickson, M., Silberg, J. L., Rutter, M., Simonoff, E. S., Meyer, J. M., & Eaves, L. J. (1996). The genetics of children's oral reading performance. *Journal of Child Psychology and Psychiatry, 37*, 425–434.

Reynolds, C. A., Hewitt, J. K., Erickson, M., Silberg, J. L., Rutter, M., Simonoff, E. S., Meyer, J. M., & Eaves, L. J. (in preparation). *Sources of variation contributing to the receipt of school based interventions*. Manuscript in preparation.

Reynolds, C. R., & Richmond, B. O. (1978). What I think and feel: A revised measure of children's manifest anxiety. *Journal of Abnormal Child Psychology, 27*, 726–737.

Rutter, M. (1979). *Changing youth in a changing society*. London: Nuffield Provincial Hospitals Trust.

Rutter, M. (1986). The developmental psychopathology of depression: Issues and perspectives. In M. Rutter, C. E. Izard, & P. B. Read (Eds.), *Depression in young people: Developmental and clinical perspectives* (pp. 3–30). New York: Guilford Press.

Rutter, M. (1988). Epidemiological approaches to developmental psychopathology. *Archives of General Psychiatry, 45*, 486–500.

Rutter, M. (1991). Childhood experiences and adult psychosocial functioning. In G. R. Bock & J. Whelan (Eds.), *The childhood environment and adult disease* (pp. 189–200). Chichester, U.K.: Wiley.

Rutter, M., Bailey, A., Bolton, P., & Le Couteur, A. (1993). Autism: Syndrome definition and possible genetic mechanisms. In R. Plomin & G. E. McClearn (Eds.), *Nature, nurture and psychology* (pp. 269–284). Washington, DC: APA Books.

Rutter, M., Cox, A., Tupling, C., Berger, M., & Yule, W. (1975). Attainment and adjustment in two geographical areas. *British Journal of Psychiatry, 126*, 493–509.

Rutter, M., Macdonald, H., Le Couteur, A., Harrington, R., Bolton, P., & Bailey, A. (1990). Genetic factors in child psychiatric disorders. II. Empirical findings. *Journal of Child Psychology and Psychiatry, 31*, 39–83.

Rutter, M., Simonoff, E. S., & Silberg, J. L. (1993). Whither behavior genetics? A developmental psychopathology perspective. In R. Plomin & G. E. McClearn (Eds.), *Nature, nurture and psychology* (pp. 433–456). Washington, DC: APA Books.

Rutter, M., Tizard, J., & Whitmore, K. (1970). *Education, health and behaviour*. London: Longman.

Rutter, M., Tizard, J. R., Yule, W., Graham, P., & Whitmore, K. (1976). Research report: Isle of Wight Studies 1964–1974. *Psychological Medicine, 6*, 313–332.

Sampson, R. J., & Laub, J. H. (1993). Crime and deviance in the life course. *Annual Review of Sociology, 18*, 63–84.

SAS Institute Inc. (1990). *SAS procedures guide, version 66*. Cary, NC: SAS Institute Inc.

Schachar, R., Rutter, M., & Smith, A. (1981). The characteristics of situationally and pervasively hyperactive children: Implications for syndrome definition. *Journal of Child Psychology and Psychiatry, 22*, 375–392.

Silberg, J. L., Erickson, M. T., Eaves, L. J., Meyer, J. M., Rutter, M., & Hewitt, J. K. (1994). The contribution of genetic and environmental factors to maternal ratings of behavioral and emotional problems in children and adolescents. *Journal of Consulting and Clinical Psychology, 62*, 510–521.

Silberg, J. L., Rutter, M., Meyer, J. M., Simonoff, E. S., Hewitt, J. K., Loeber, R., Pickles, A., Maes, H. H., & Eaves, L. J. (in press). Genetic and environmental influences on the co-variation between hyperactivity and conduct disturbance in juvenile twins. *Journal of Child Psychology and Psychiatry*.

Simonoff, E. S., Pickles, A., Hewitt, J. K., Silberg, J. L., Rutter, M., Loeber, R., Meyer, J. M., Neale, M. C., & Evans, L. J. (1995). Multiple raters of disruptive child behavior: Using a genetic strategy to examine shared views and bias. *Behavior Genetics, 25*, 311–326.

Simonoff, E. S., Pickles, A., Meyer, J. M., Silberg, J. L., Maes, H. H., Loeber, R., Rutter, M., Hewitt, J. K., & Eaves, L. J. (in press). Epidemiology of child psychopathology in the Virginia Twin Study of Adolescent Behavioral Development: Age, gender, and informant influences on the rates of disorder. *Archives of General Psychiatry*.

Slosson, R. L. (1963). *Slosson Oral Reading Test (SORT)*. East Aurora, NY: Slosson Educational Publications.

Spanier, G. B. (1976). Measuring dyadic adjustment: New scales for assessing the quality of marriage and other dyads. *Journal of Marriage and Family, 38*, 15–28.

Spitzer, R. L., Williams, J. B., & Gibson, M. (1987). *Structured clinical interview for DSM-III-R*. New York: Biometrics Research Department, New York State Psychiatric Institute.

Stevenson, J. (1992). Evidence for a genetic etiology in hyperactivity in children. *Behavior Genetics, 22*, 337–344.

Stevenson, J., Pennington, B. F., Gilger, J. W., DeFries, J. C., & Gillis, J. J. (1993). Hyperactivity and spelling disability: Testing for shared aetiology. *Journal of Child Psychology and Psychiatry, 34*, 1137–1152.

Strauss, C. C., Last, C. H., Hersen, M., & Kazdin, A. E. (1988). Association between anxiety and depression in children and adolescents with anxiety disorders. *Journal of Abnormal Child Psychology, 16*, 57–68.

Szatmari, P., Boyle, M. H., & Offord, D. R. (1989). ADDH and conduct disorder: Degree of diagnostic overlap and differences among correlates. *Journal of the American Academy of Child and Adolescent Psychiatry, 228*, 865–872.

Szatmari, P., Boyle, M. H., & Offord, D. R. (1993). Familial aggregation of emotional behavioral problems of childhood in the general population. *American Journal of Psychiatry, 15*, 1398–1403.

Thapar, A., Hervas, A., & McGuffin, P. (1995). Childhood hyperactivity scores are highly heritable and show sibling competition effects: Twin study evidence. *Behavior Genetics, 25*, 537–544.

Thapar, A., & McGuffin, P. (1994). A twin study of depressive symptoms in childhood. *A British Journal of Psychiatry, 165*, 259–265.

Thapar, A., & McGuffin, P. (1995). Are anxiety symptoms in childhood heritable? *Journal of Child Psychology and Psychiatry, 36*, 439–447.

Verhulst, F. C., Berden, G. F., & Sanders-Woudstra, J. A. R. (1985). Mental health in Dutch children: II. The prevalence of psychiatric disorder and relationship between measures. *Acta Psychiatrica Scandinavica, 72*, 1–45.

Verhulst, F. C., & Koot, H. M. (1992). *Child psychiatric epidemiology: Concepts, methods and findings*. Newbury Park, CA: Sage Publications.

Verhulst, F. C., Koot, H. M., & Berden, G. F. (1990). Four year follow-up of an epidemiological sample. *Journal of the American Academy of Child and Adolescent Psychiatry, 29*, 440–448.

Accepted manuscript received 6 May 1997

ORIGINAL ARTICLE

Childhood Maltreatment Increases Risk for Personality Disorders During Early Adulthood

Jeffrey G. Johnson, PhD; Patricia Cohen, PhD; Jocelyn Brown, MD; Elizabeth M. Smailes, MA; David P. Bernstein, PhD

Background: Data from a community-based longitudinal study were used to investigate whether childhood abuse and neglect increases risk for personality disorders (PDs) during early adulthood.

Methods: Psychosocial and psychiatric interviews were administered to a representative community sample of 639 youths and their mothers from 2 counties in the state of New York in 1975, 1983, 1985 to 1986, and 1991 to 1993. Evidence of childhood physical abuse, sexual abuse, and neglect was obtained from New York State records and from offspring self-reports in 1991 to 1993 when they were young adults. Offspring PDs were assessed in 1991 to 1993.

Results: Persons with documented childhood abuse or neglect were more than 4 times as likely as those who were not abused or neglected to be diagnosed with PDs during early adulthood after age, parental education, and parental psychiatric disorders were controlled statistically. Childhood physical abuse, sexual abuse, and neglect were each associated with elevated PD symptom levels during early adulthood after other types of childhood maltreatment were controlled statistically. Of the 12 categories of *DSM-IV* PD symptoms, 10 were associated with childhood abuse or neglect. Different types of childhood maltreatment were associated with symptoms of specific PDs during early adulthood.

Conclusions: Persons in the community who have experienced childhood abuse or neglect are considerably more likely than those who were not abused or neglected to have PDs and elevated PD symptom levels during early adulthood. Childhood abuse and neglect may contribute to the onset of some PDs.

Arch Gen Psychiatry. 1999;56:600-606

RESEARCH[1-12] HAS indicated that many patients with personality disorders (PDs) report histories of childhood abuse or neglect. These findings, and studies[13,14] indicating that PDs are more prevalent among persons who experienced child abuse than among matched comparison groups, have suggested that childhood abuse and neglect may play an important role in the onset of PDs.[15,16] Most

See also page 607

of this evidence, however, is based on retrospective reports by psychiatric patients.[17,18] Although research[19-22] has supported the validity of retrospective reports of childhood maltreatment, to infer from retrospective data[17,18,23,24] alone that childhood maltreatment increases risk for the onset of PDs is problematic. Until prospective research demonstrates that persons with documented childhood maltreatment are at increased risk for PDs independent of other risk factors, it cannot be established that childhood maltreatment plays a role in the onset of PDs.[18]

Two longitudinal studies[25,26] have supported the hypothesis that childhood maltreatment increases risk for PDs. Family instability and lack of parental affection and supervision during adolescence were found[25] to predict dependent and passive-aggressive PDs among men. Physical and sexual abuse were not assessed, however, and not all PDs were investigated. Childhood maltreatment has been reported to predict increased risk for antisocial PD during early adulthood.[26] Neither the association between different types of maltreatment and risk for antisocial PD nor the association between childhood maltreatment and other PDs was investigated. Therefore, many questions about the effects of childhood maltreatment on the risk for PDs remain unanswered. We report findings from a community-based longitudinal study to investigate whether childhood maltreatment increases the risk for *DSM-IV*[27] PDs during early adulthood independent of the effects

From Columbia University and the New York State Psychiatric Institute, New York (Drs Johnson, Cohen, Brown, and Ms Smailes), and Fordham University, Bronx, NY (Dr Bernstein).

SUBJECTS AND METHODS

PARTICIPANTS AND PROCEDURE

Six hundred thirty-nine families with children between the ages of 1 and 11 years from 2 counties in northern New York State were representatively sampled and interviewed in 1975[28] and reinterviewed in 1991 to 1993. These face-to-face interviews, also conducted in 1983 and 1985 to 1986, were administered by extensively trained and supervised lay interviewers.[29] At each assessment, written informed consent was obtained from all participants after the study procedures were fully explained. The 639 families in the present study were a subsample of 776 families interviewed in 1983 for whom data regarding childhood maltreatment were available from retrospective self-reports by the young adult participants in 1991 to 1993 and from the New York State Central Registry for Child Abuse and Neglect (NYSCR). Childhood maltreatment data were not available for 137 families who no longer lived in New York. These families did not differ from the rest of the sample with regard to socioeconomic status, urban vs rural status, or ethnicity, but there was a higher proportion of male offspring and the mothers were less well educated. The 1983 sample was representative of the regional population in a range of demographic variables, according to US census data.[29] Demographic characteristics of the sample are presented in **Table 1**. Further information regarding the study methodology is available from previous reports.[28,29]

ASSESSMENT OF PERSONALITY DISORDERS

Interview items used to assess early adulthood PDs in 1991 to 1993 were drawn from the parent and youth versions of the Diagnostic Interview Schedule for Children,[30] the Personality Diagnostic Questionnaire,[31] and the Disorganizing Poverty Interview.[28] Items were originally selected by consensus among 1 psychiatrist and 2 clinical psychologists based on correspondence with *DSM-III-R* diagnostic criteria.[32] Following the publication of *DSM-IV*,[27] items from the study protocol were added or deleted to maximize correspondence with *DSM-IV* diagnostic criteria, most notably to assess depressive PD in *DSM-IV* appendix B. One hundred fifty-two items were available to assess 88 (93.6%) of the 94 *DSM-IV* PD diagnostic criteria. For dependent, histrionic, narcissistic, obsessive-compulsive, and paranoid PDs, items were available for the assessment of 78% to 89% of the diagnostic criteria. For the other 7 PDs, all criteria were assessed. The Cronbach α inter-item reliability coefficients for clusters A, B, and C PD symptoms were .66, .72, and .68, respectively. For overall PD symptoms, the α was .87.

Personality disorder diagnoses were assigned to persons who met *DSM-IV* diagnostic criteria, as reported by the youth or mother. The use of multiple informants has been found[33,34] to increase the reliability and validity of psychiatric diagnoses. Evidence[32] supports the reliability and validity of the protocol items and computer algorithms used to assess PD symptoms (J.G.J.; P.C.; Andrew E. Skodol, MD; John M. Oldham, MD; Stephanie Kasen, PhD; Judith Brook, PhD; unpublished data, 1999). Adolescent *DSM-IV* PD symptoms predicted early adulthood Axis I disorders and suicidality, and PD symptom stability when the participants were adolescents was similar to the stability of PD symptoms among adults in the community (J.G.J.; P.C.; Andrew E. Skodol, MD; John M. Oldham, MD; Stephanie Kasen, PhD; Judith Brook, PhD; unpublished data, 1999).

ASSESSMENT OF CHILDHOOD MALTREATMENT

Official data regarding childhood maltreatment was obtained from the NYSCR. Cases referred to state agencies, investigated by childhood protective services, and confirmed as verified cases of abuse or neglect are retained in the NYSCR. The verification of physical abuse required evidence of injury. The verification of sexual abuse required evidence of sexual penetration or a judgment that the youth experienced unwanted sexual contact. The verification of neglect required evidence of educational, emotional, physical, or supervisory neglect. The NYSCR staff ascertained whether confirmed cases of childhood maltreatment were present. Information about the type of abuse was abstracted by one of us (J.B.) under the supervision of NYSCR staff. To ensure confidentiality, participants were identified only by numbers, and data were entered by persons who had no access to information that revealed participants' identities.

Continued on next page

of offspring age and sex, difficult childhood temperament, parental education, and parental psychiatric disorders.

RESULTS

DESCRIPTIVE STATISTICS

In the 639 families, there were 31 (4.9%) documented cases of childhood maltreatment, including 15 cases (2.3%) of physical abuse, 4 cases (0.6%) of sexual abuse, and 23 cases (3.6%) of neglect. Twenty patients (3.1%) had 1 type of maltreatment, and 11 patients (1.8%) had 2 kinds of maltreatment. Fifty-eight persons (9.1%) self-reported childhood maltreatment, including 34 cases (5.3%) of physical abuse, 21 cases (3.3%) of sexual abuse, and 17 cases (2.7%) of neglect. Forty-six persons (7.2%) had 1 type of maltreatment, and 12 persons (1.9%) had 2 or 3 types of maltreatment. There was little overlap between documented and self-reported cases of childhood maltreatment. Only 8 cases of childhood abuse or neglect were identified from both NYSCR records and self-reports, yielding a κ coefficient of 0.11. There were 81 (12.7%) documented or self-reported cases of childhood maltreatment, including 44 cases (6.9%) of physical abuse, 22 cases (3.4%) of sexual abuse, and 39 cases (6.1%) of neglect. Fifty-nine persons (9.2%) had 1 type of maltreatment, and 22 persons (3.4%) had 2 or 3 types of maltreatment. Eighty-six youths (13.5%) were diagnosed as having PDs in 1991 to 1993.

EFFECTS OF CHILDHOOD PHYSICAL ABUSE ON PD SYMPTOM LEVELS DURING EARLY ADULTHOOD

Documented physical abuse was associated with elevated symptom levels of antisocial, borderline, dependent, depressive, passive-aggressive, schizoid, and total PDs after offspring

Self-reports of childhood maltreatment were obtained from the offspring in 1991 to 1993. Participants were asked whether, before age 18 years, they experienced the following events: anyone they lived with had ever hurt them physically so that they were still injured or bruised the next day, could not go to school as a result, or needed medical attention; they had been left overnight without an adult caretaker before age 10 years; and any older person who was not a boyfriend or girlfriend had ever touched them sexually or forced them to touch the older person sexually.

ASSESSMENT OF PARENTAL EDUCATION AND PSYCHIATRIC DISORDERS AND CHILDHOOD TEMPERAMENT

Parental education and psychiatric disorders were assessed as dichotomous variables. Maternal and paternal education was assessed during the maternal interviews in 1975, 1983, and 1985 to 1986. Low parental education was identified in 28.0% of the families, for whom the mean number of years of parental education was less than 12. Parental psychiatric disorders were assessed using 4 instruments administered during the maternal interview: current maternal emotional problems were assessed in 1983 and 1985 to 1986 using the Hopkins Symptom Checklist-90[35] anxiety, depression, and interpersonal difficulty subscales; parental alcohol and drug abuse between 1975 and 1985 to 1986 was assessed in 1983 and 1985 to 1986; the lifetime parental history of "trouble with the police" was assessed in 1975, 1983, and 1985 to 1986; and the lifetime parental history of psychiatric disorders was assessed in 1983 and 1985 to 1986, with items assessing whether or not the parents had ever been treated for a mental disorder. Parental psychiatric disorders were considered present if significant emotional problems, substance abuse, or trouble with the police was present in either parent in 1975, 1983, or 1985 to 1986 or if, in 1985 to 1986, either parent had ever been treated for a mental disorder. Using these procedures, the lifetime prevalence of parental psychiatric disorders was 38.0%. If the mother could not provide information regarding the father's education or psychiatric disorders, only information regarding the mother was used.

Nine dimensions of childhood temperament[29] were assessed during the 1975 maternal interviews: clumsiness-distractibility, nonpersistence-noncompliance, anger, aggression to peers, problem behavior, temper tantrums, hyperactivity, crying-demanding, and moodiness. If a child experienced severe problems in 1 or more of these domains, the child was identified as having a difficult temperament. Difficult childhood temperament has been found, in this sample, to predict behavior problems,[36] PDs,[37] and Axis I psychiatric disorders during adolescence[38] and drug use during early adulthood.[39]

STATISTICAL ANALYSES

Data analyses were conducted in 5 phases. First, analyses of contingency tables, correlational analyses, and *t* tests were computed to investigate whether risk factors identified by previous research[40,41] predicted childhood maltreatment and early adulthood PD symptom levels (ie, the number of PD diagnostic criteria that were met). Second, analyses of covariance (ANCOVAs) were conducted to investigate whether documented childhood abuse and neglect were associated with elevated early adulthood PD symptoms after offspring age, parental education, and parental psychiatric disorders were controlled. Third, logistic regression analyses were conducted to investigate whether documented childhood maltreatment was significantly associated with the risk for early adulthood PDs after controlling for offspring age, parental education, and parental psychiatric disorders. Fourth, ANCOVAs were computed to investigate whether documented or self-reported childhood maltreatment was significantly associated with elevated symptom levels of early adulthood PD after controlling for the covariates that were associated with both early adulthood PD symptom levels and other types of childhood maltreatment. Fifth, ANCOVAs were computed to investigate whether specific types of PD symptoms remained significantly associated with documented or self-reported childhood abuse or neglect after controlling for other types of PD symptoms that were significantly associated with childhood abuse or neglect. All statistical analyses were conducted using a comparison group that included individuals who did not experience childhood abuse or neglect.

age, parental education, and parental psychiatric disorders were controlled statistically (**Table 2**). Antisocial and depressive PD symptoms remained significantly associated with documented physical abuse after symptoms of other PDs were controlled statistically. Evidence of physical abuse, obtained from either NYSCR records or retrospective self-reports, was associated with elevated symptom levels of antisocial ($F_{1,599}$ = 10.62; $P<.005$), borderline ($F_{1,599}$ = 16.44; $P<.005$), passive-aggressive ($F_{1,599}$ = 6.06; $P<.05$), schizotypal ($F_{1,599}$ = 8.13; $P<.005$), and total PDs ($F_{1,599}$ = 6.95; $P<.01$) after controlling for offspring age, parental education, parental psychiatric disorders, sexual abuse, and neglect.

EFFECTS OF CHILDHOOD SEXUAL ABUSE ON PD SYMPTOM LEVELS DURING EARLY ADULTHOOD

Documented sexual abuse was associated with elevated symptom levels of borderline PD after offspring age and parental psychiatric disorders were controlled statistically ($F_{1,577}$ = 5.77; $P<.02$). Evidence of sexual abuse, obtained from either NYSCR records or retrospective self-reports, was associated with elevated symptom levels of borderline ($F_{1,577}$ = 31.09; $P<.005$), histrionic ($F_{1,577}$ = 11.50; $P<.005$), depressive ($F_{1,577}$ = 9.85; $P<.005$), and total PDs ($F_{1,577}$ = 11.02; $P<.005$) after controlling for offspring sex, parental education, parental psychiatric disorders, physical abuse, and neglect.

EFFECTS OF CHILDHOOD NEGLECT ON PD SYMPTOM LEVELS DURING EARLY ADULTHOOD

Documented childhood neglect was associated with elevated symptom levels of antisocial, avoidant, borderline, dependent, narcissistic, paranoid, passive-aggressive, schizotypal, and total PD after controlling for offspring age, parental education, and parental psychi-

Table 1. Demographic Characteristics of the 639 Sample Offspring

Characteristic	Variable
Age, mean (SD) [range], y	
1975	6.4 (2.6) [1-10]
1991-1993	22.3 (2.6) [18-28]
Sex, No. (%)	
Male	334 (52.3)
Female	305 (47.7)
Ethnicity, No. (%)	
White	575 (90.0)
African American	58 (9.1)
Other	6 (0.9)
Residence, No. (%)	
Rural communities and small towns	341 (53.4)
Large towns	51 (8.0)
Central cities	78 (12.2)
Suburban communities	169 (26.4)
Education, No. (%)	
<12 y	57 (8.9)

Table 2. Documented Childhood Physical Abuse and Personality Disorder (PD) Symptoms* During Young Adulthood

PD Symptoms	PD Criteria Among Those Not Abused or Neglected (n = 608)	PD Criteria Among Victims of Physical Abuse (n = 15)	$F_{1,621}$†
Paranoid	0.73 (0.89)	1.60 (1.45)	3.47
Schizoid	0.75 (0.87)	1.67 (1.23)	6.65‡
Schizotypal	0.95 (1.05)	1.47 (1.41)	0.10
Any cluster A PD	2.43 (2.10)	4.73 (3.13)	4.32§‖
Antisocial	1.18 (1.11)	2.20 (1.57)	5.66‡§
Borderline	0.97 (1.15)	2.00 (1.51)	3.94‡
Histrionic	1.40 (1.21)	2.00 (1.13)	1.51
Narcissistic	0.86 (1.06)	1.87 (1.60)	4.42‡
Any cluster B PD	4.41 (3.20)	8.07 (4.60)	7.62¶
Avoidant	0.72 (0.97)	1.33 (1.45)	1.87
Dependent	1.04 (1.22)	2.27 (1.53)	8.67‖
Obsessive-compulsive	0.88 (0.88)	1.13 (1.19)	0.33
Any cluster C PD	2.63 (2.25)	4.73 (3.26)	4.87‡
Depressive	0.72 (1.04)	1.53 (1.64)	7.07§¶
Passive-aggressive	0.82 (1.00)	1.47 (1.30)	3.92‡
Any PD	9.83 (6.45)	18.33 (10.35)	10.50‖

*Data are given as the mean (SD) number of DSM-IV PD criteria met at assessment interviews conducted during early adulthood.

†Results of analyses of covariance, controlling for offspring age, parental psychiatric disorders, and parental education.

‡$P<.05$.

§Association remained statistically significant after controlling for co-occurring PD symptoms.

‖$P<.005$.

¶$P<.01$.

atric disorders (**Table 3**). Supplemental analyses indicated that symptoms of antisocial, avoidant, borderline, narcissistic, and passive-aggressive PD remained significantly associated with documented neglect after co-occurring PD symptoms were controlled statistically. Evidence of neglect, obtained from either NYSCR records or retrospective self-reports, was associated with elevated symptom levels of antisocial ($F_{1,594}$ = 7.41; $P<.05$), avoidant ($F_{1,594}$ = 5.71; $P<.05$), borderline ($F_{1,594}$ = 17.90; $P<.005$), dependent ($F_{1,594}$ = 7.91; $P<.01$), narcissistic ($F_{1,594}$ = 7.30; $P<.005$), passive-aggressive ($F_{1,594}$ = 10.92; $P<.005$), schizotypal ($F_{1,594}$ = 11.33; $P<.005$), and total PDs ($F_{1,594}$ = 15.27; $P<.005$) after offspring age, parental education, parental psychiatric disorders, physical abuse, and sexual abuse were controlled.

EFFECTS OF ANY CHILDHOOD ABUSE OR NEGLECT ON RISK FOR PD DURING EARLY ADULTHOOD

Documented childhood maltreatment was associated with increased risk for antisocial, borderline, dependent, depressive, narcissistic, paranoid, and passive-aggressive PDs after controlling for offspring age, parental education, and parental psychiatric disorders (**Table 4**). Antisocial, borderline, narcissistic, and passive-aggressive PD symptoms remained significantly associated with documented childhood maltreatment after controlling for symptoms of other PDs. Evidence of childhood abuse or neglect, obtained from either NYSCR records or retrospective self-reports, was associated with elevated symptom levels of antisocial ($F_{1,637}$ = 16.26; $P<.005$), avoidant ($F_{1,637}$ = 4.97; $P<.05$), borderline ($F_{1,637}$ = 53.96; $P<.005$), dependent ($F_{1,637}$ = 13.59; $P<.005$), depressive ($F_{1,637}$ = 9.89; $P<.005$), histrionic ($F_{1,637}$ = 8.66; $P<.005$), narcissistic ($F_{1,637}$ = 9.74; $P<.005$), passive-aggressive ($F_{1,637}$ = 9.19; $P<.005$), schizotypal ($F_{1,637}$ = 26.44; $P<.005$), and total PDs ($F_{1,637}$ = 31.65; $P<.005$) after offspring age, parental education, parental psychiatric disorders, and difficult childhood temperament were controlled statistically.

As the **Figure** indicates, persons who experienced childhood maltreatment were at an elevated risk for *DSM-IV* cluster B, cluster C, and appendix B PDs during early adulthood. When the effects of co-occurring PDs were controlled statistically, however, only cluster B (adjusted odds ratio = 7.94; 95% confidence interval, 1.33-14.82) and *DSM-IV* appendix B (adjusted odds ratio = 4.43; 95% confidence interval, 1.45-13.87) PDs were independently associated with childhood abuse or neglect.

COMMENT

The major finding of the present study is that persons with documented childhood abuse and neglect in a representative community sample were more than 4 times as likely as those who had not been abused or neglected to have PDs during early adulthood. This finding is particularly meaningful because childhood maltreatment predicted early adulthood PDs even after the effects of difficult childhood temperament, parental education, and parental psychiatric disorders were controlled statistically. The present findings are consistent with previous findings[1-13,18,25,42-45] suggesting that childhood physical abuse, sexual abuse, and neglect play an important role in the onset of some PDs.

These findings are also of interest because they are consistent with prior findings[1-12] indicating that patients with PDs are more likely than persons without PD

Table 3. Documented Childhood Neglect and Personality Disorder (PD) Symptoms* During Young Adulthood

PD Symptoms	PD Criteria Among Those Not Abused or Neglected (n = 608)	PD Criteria Among Victims of Neglect (n = 23)	$F_{1,625}$†
Paranoid	0.73 (0.89)	1.65 (1.47)	10.69‡
Schizoid	0.75 (0.87)	1.30 (1.10)	3.07
Schizotypal	0.95 (1.05)	1.87 (1.36)	7.60§
Any cluster A PD	2.43 (2.10)	4.83 (2.89)	12.87‖¶
Antisocial	1.18 (1.11)	2.22 (1.88)	10.19‡‖
Borderline	0.97 (1.15)	2.48 (1.86)	23.10‖¶
Histrionic	1.40 (1.21)	2.04 (1.55)	3.32
Narcissistic	0.86 (1.06)	2.00 (1.81)	12.05‖¶
Any cluster B PD	4.41 (3.20)	8.74 (5.90)	22.10‖¶
Avoidant	0.72 (0.97)	1.52 (1.38)	9.48‡‖
Dependent	1.04 (1.22)	2.26 (1.51)	14.62‖¶
Obsessive-compulsive	0.88 (0.88)	1.17 (1.03)	1.82
Any cluster C PD	2.63 (2.25)	4.96 (3.02)	15.51¶
Depressive	0.72 (1.04)	1.17 (1.56)	3.29
Passive-aggressive	0.82 (1.00)	1.83 (1.64)	15.69‖¶
Any PD	9.83 (6.45)	19.30 (11.08)	27.33¶

*Data are given as the mean (SD) number of DSM-IV PD criteria met at assessment interviews conducted during early adulthood.

†Results of analyses of covariance, controlling for offspring age, parental psychiatric disorders, and parental education.

‡$P<.005$.

§$P<.01$.

‖Association remained statistically significant after controlling for co-occurring PD symptoms.

¶$P<.001$.

Table 4. Documented Childhood Abuse or Neglect and Risk for Personality Disorders (PDs) During Young Adulthood

	Prevalence of PD, No. (%)		
PD Diagnosis	Among Those Not Abused or Neglected (n = 608)	Among Victims of Abuse or Neglect (n = 31)	Adjusted Odds Ratio (95% CI)*
Paranoid	5 (0.8)	3 (9.7)	6.59 (1.20-36.03)
Schizoid	6 (1.0)	1 (3.2)	0.84 (0.08-8.44)
Schizotypal	4 (0.7)	1 (3.2)	2.48 (0.22-28.23)
Any cluster A PD	14 (2.3)	4 (12.9)	2.22 (0.59-8.27)
Antisocial	13 (2.1)	4 (12.9)	4.97† (1.33-18.49)
Borderline	7 (1.2)	4 (12.9)	7.73† (1.78-33.48)
Histrionic	9 (1.5)	1 (3.2)	2.65 (0.28-25.06)
Narcissistic	2 (0.3)	3 (9.7)	18.21† (2.19-150.93)
Any cluster B PD	29 (4.8)	11 (35.5)	8.91† (3.53-22.62)
Avoidant	11 (1.8)	3 (9.7)	4.35 (1.00-18.92)
Dependent	12 (2.0)	3 (9.7)	6.35-(1.43-28.21)
Obsessive-compulsive	4 (0.7)	0 (0.0)	...
Any cluster C PD	25 (4.1)	6 (19.4)	4.36† (1.50-12.63)
Depressive	7 (1.2)	2 (6.5)	7.19 (1.17-43.95)
Passive-aggressive	10 (1.6)	4 (12.9)	5.54† (1.30-23.58)
Any appendix B PD	17 (2.8)	6 (19.4)	6.83 (2.19-21.26)
Any PD	69 (11.3)	17 (54.8)	6.38 (2.83-14.32)

*Controlling for age, parental education, and parental psychiatric disorders. Odds ratios are considered statistically significant if the number 1.0 falls outside the 95% confidence interval (CI). Ellipses indicate not computed.

†Association remained statistically significant after controlling for co-occurring PDs.

to report histories of childhood maltreatment. Because concerns have been raised[17,18,23,24] that patients' reports of childhood maltreatment may be due in part to biased memory or reporting, inferring from only retrospective findings that childhood maltreatment plays a role in the onset of PDs has been problematic. Our findings and previous longitudinal research[25,26] indicate that the tendency of many patients with PDs to report childhood maltreatment is not merely an artifact of biased memory or reporting. Childhood maltreatment is indeed much more likely to have occurred among young adults with PDs than among young adults without PDs.

Childhood physical abuse, sexual abuse, and neglect may also be associated with elevations in different types of PD symptoms. After symptoms of other PDs were accounted for, documented physical abuse was associated with elevated antisocial and depressive PD symptoms, sexual abuse was associated with elevated borderline PD symptoms, and neglect was associated with elevated symptoms of antisocial, avoidant, borderline, narcissistic, and passive-aggressive PDs. These findings, and previous research[9,25,46] indicating that childhood physical abuse, sexual abuse, and neglect may be differentially associated with PDs, suggest that it is important that researchers investigate specific etiologic models for each of the different PDs.

Although childhood neglect is more frequently reported than childhood physical or sexual abuse,[47] more research[48-50] has investigated physical and sexual abuse than neglect. Thus, although childhood physical and sexual abuse have been hypothesized to play an etiologic role in PDs,[18,42] childhood neglect has not played a prominent role in etiologic theories. Nonetheless, the present findings and previous research indicating that childhood neglect is associated with an increased risk for PDs, attachment difficulties, antisocial behavior, and other interpersonal and psychological problems[39,51-55] suggest that future theoretical work regarding the onset of PDs should examine the deleterious effects of childhood neglect.

Although the association between self-reported childhood maltreatment and PDs has received considerable investigation, few hypotheses[56,57] have been developed regarding the mechanisms of this association. Childhood maltreatment may independently increase the risk for PDs; maladaptive parenting, rather than childhood maltreatment, may increase the risk for PDs; childhood maltreatment may increase the risk for PDs among persons with biological diatheses for psychiatric disorders; and/or childhood maltreatment may be an indicator of preexisting PDs. Childhood abuse and neglect may increase the risk for PDs independent of childhood and parental psychiatric disorders. Many questions about the association between childhood maltreatment and PDs will not be answered definitively until further research is conducted.

Because the prevalence of specific PDs and specific types of documented childhood maltreatment was low,

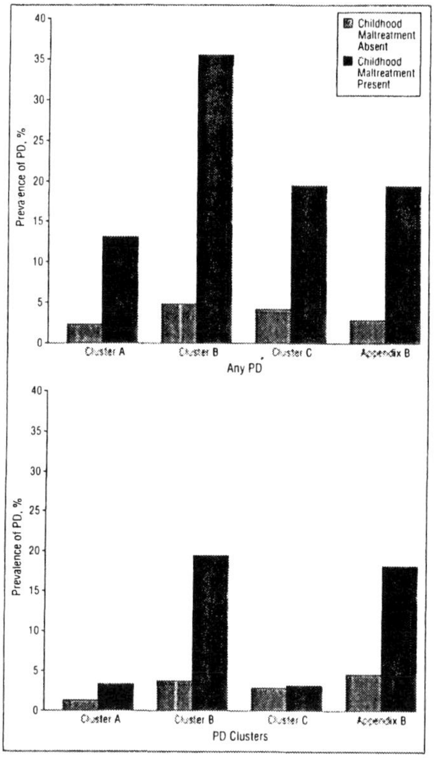

Overall (top) and unique (bottom) associations between documented childhood maltreatment and risk for early adulthood personality disorders (PDs).

it was necessary to investigate associations between documented childhood maltreatment and PD symptoms, rather than PD diagnoses. There was sufficient power, however, to permit investigation of the association between any documented childhood maltreatment and the risk for PDs during early adulthood. Furthermore, supplementing documented evidence of childhood maltreatment with self-reports of childhood abuse and neglect permitted investigation regarding unique associations between different types of childhood maltreatment and different types of PD symptoms.

Because we conducted numerous statistical analyses, some significant associations may have been due to chance. Although numerous findings support the reliability and validity of the items and algorithms used to assess PDs, it is possible that different findings would have been obtained if a structured clinical interview such as the Structured Clinical Interview for *DSM-IV*[58] had been administered. Because a few PD diagnostic criteria were not assessed, more statistically significant associations might have been obtained if all PD criteria had been assessed. A strength of the present study is that we investigated whether childhood maltreatment predicted PD symptoms after controlling for parental psychiatric disorders. Diagnostic interviews were not administered to the parents, however, and parental sociopathy was assessed using a measure of parental trouble with the police, although the present findings were not affected when this item was not included in the analyses. In addition, data regarding paternal education and psychiatric disorders were obtained from the mothers, and data were not available regarding interrater reliability.

Despite these limitations, our study has numerous methodological strengths, including a representative sample, a longitudinal design, the use of official records of childhood abuse and neglect and retrospective self-report data, the assessment of all *DSM-IV* PDs using data from both offspring and their mothers, and the use of statistical procedures to control for offspring age and sex, difficult childhood temperament, parental education, and parental psychiatric disorders. Thus, the present findings contribute to an increased understanding of the association between childhood maltreatment and early adulthood PD symptoms.

Accepted for publication January 14, 1999.

This study was supported by grant MH-36971 from the National Institute of Mental Health, Rockville, Md (Dr Cohen).

Corresponding author: Jeffrey G. Johnson, PhD, Box 60, New York State Psychiatric Institute, 1051 Riverside Dr, New York, NY 10032.

REFERENCES

1. Brodsky BS, Cloitre M, Dulit RA. Relationship of dissociation to self-mutilation and childhood abuse in borderline personality disorder. *Am J Psychiatry.* 1995; 152:1788-1792.
2. Goldman SJ, D'Angelo EJ, DeMaso DR, Mezzacappa E. Physical and sexual abuse histories among children with borderline personality disorder. *Am J Psychiatry.* 1992;149:1723-1726.
3. Herman JL, Perry JC, van der Kolk BA. Childhood trauma in borderline personality disorder. *Am J Psychiatry.* 1989;146:490-495.
4. Ogata SN, Silk KR, Goodrich S, Lohr NE, Westen D, Hill EM. Childhood sexual and physical abuse in adult patients with borderline personality disorder. *Am J Psychiatry.* 1990;147:1008-1013.
5. Weaver TL, Clum GA. Early family environments and traumatic experiences associated with borderline personality disorder. *J Consult Clin Psychol.* 1993;61: 1068-1075.
6. Brown GR, Anderson B. Psychiatric morbidity in adult inpatients with childhood histories of sexual and physical abuse. *Am J Psychiatry.* 1991;148:55-61.
7. Paris J, Zweig-Frank H, Guzder J. Psychological risk factors for borderline personality disorder in female patients. *Compr Psychiatry.* 1994;35:301-305.
8. Paris J, Zweig-Frank H, Guzder J. Risk factors for borderline personality disorder in male outpatients. *J Nerv Ment Dis.* 1994;182:375-380.
9. Norden KA, Klein DN, Donaldson SK, Pepper CM, Klein LM. Reports of the early home environment in *DSM-III-R* personality disorders. *J Personal Disord.* 1995; 9:213-223.
10. Shearer SL, Peters CP, Quaytman MS, Ogden RL. Frequency and correlates of childhood sexual and physical abuse histories in adult female borderline inpatients. *Am J Psychiatry.* 1990;147:214-216.
11. Raczek SW. Childhood abuse and personality disorders. *J Personal Disord.* 1992; 6:109-116.
12. Windle M, Windle RC, Scheidt DM, Miller GB. Physical and sexual abuse and associated mental disorders among alcoholic inpatients. *Am J Psychiatry.* 1995; 152:1322-1328.
13. Pribor EF, Dinwiddie SH. Psychiatric correlates of incest in childhood. *Am J Psychiatry.* 1992;149:52-56.
14. Silverman AB, Reinherz HZ, Giaconia RM. The long-term sequelae of child and

adolescent abuse: a longitudinal community study. *Child Abuse Negl.* 1996;20: 709-723.
15. Kroll J. *PTSD/Borderlines in Therapy.* New York, NY: WW Norton & Co Inc; 1993.
16. Herman J. *Trauma and Recovery.* New York, NY: Basic Books Inc Publishers; 1992.
17. Maughan B, Rutter M. Retrospective reporting of childhood adversity: issues in assessing long-term recall. *J Personal Disord.* 1997;11:19-33.
18. Paris J. Childhood trauma as an etiological factor in the personality disorders. *J Personal Disord.* 1997;11:34-49.
19. Bifulco A, Brown GW, Lillie A, Jarvis J. Memories of childhood neglect and abuse: corroboration in a series of sisters. *J Child Psychol Psychiatry.* 1997;38: 365-374.
20. Brewin CR, Andrews B, Gotlib IH. Psychopathology and early experience: a reappraisal of retrospective reports. *Psychol Bull.* 1993;113:82-98.
21. Herman JL, Schatzow E. Recovery and verification of memories of childhood sexual trauma. *Psychoanal Psychol.* 1987;4:11-14.
22. Robins LN, Schoenberg SP, Holmes SJ, Ratcliff KS, Benham A, Works J. Early home environment and retrospective recall: a test for concordance between siblings with and without psychiatric disorders. *Am J Orthopsychiatry.* 1985;55: 27-41.
23. Widom CS. Does violence beget violence? a critical examination of the literature. *Psychol Bull.* 1989;106:3-28.
24. Loftus EF. The reality of repressed memories. *Am Psychol.* 1993;48:518-537.
25. Drake RE, Adler DA, Vaillant GE. Antecedents of personality disorders in a community sample of men. *J Personal Disord.* 1988;2:60-68.
26. Luntz BK, Widom CS. Antisocial personality disorder in abused and neglected children grown up. *Am J Psychiatry.* 1994;151:670-674.
27. American Psychiatric Association. *Diagnostic and Statistical Manual of Mental Disorders, Fourth Edition.* Washington, DC: American Psychiatric Association; 1994.
28. Kogan LS, Smith J, Jenkins S. Ecological validity of indicator data as predictors of survey findings. *J Soc Serv Res.* 1977;1:117-132.
29. Cohen P, Cohen J. *Adolescent Life Values and Mental Health.* Mahwah, NJ: Lawrence Erlbaum Assoc Inc Publishers; 1996.
30. Costello EJ, Edelbrock CS, Duncan MK, Kalas R. *Testing of the NIMH Diagnostic Interview Schedule for Children (DISC) in a Clinical Population: Final Report to the Center for Epidemiological Studies, National Institute of Mental Health.* Pittsburgh, Pa: University of Pittsburgh; 1984.
31. Hyler SE, Reider R, Williams JBW, Spitzer RL, Hendler J, Lyons M. The Personality Diagnostic Questionnaire: development and preliminary results. *J Personal Disord.* 1988;2:229-237.
32. Bernstein DP, Cohen P, Velez CN, Schwab-Stone M, Siever LJ, Shinsato L. Prevalence and stability of the *DSM-III-R* personality disorders in a community-based survey of adolescents. *Am J Psychiatry.* 1993;150:1237-1243.
33. Bird HR, Gould MS, Staghezza B. Aggregating data from multiple informants in child psychiatry epidemiological research. *J Am Acad Child Adolesc Psychiatry.* 1992;31:78-85.
34. Piacentini J, Cohen P, Cohen J. Combining discrepant diagnostic information from multiple sources: are complex algorithms better than simple ones? *J Abnorm Psychol.* 1992;20:51-63.
35. Derogatis LR, Lipman RS, Rickels K, Uhlenhuth EH, Covi L. The Hopkins Symptom Checklist (HSCL): a self-report symptom inventory. *Behav Sci.* 1974;19: 1-15.
36. Cohen P, Brook JS. Family factors related to the persistence of psychopathology in childhood and adolescence. *Psychiatry.* 1987;50:332-345.
37. Kasen S, Cohen P, Brook JS, Hartmark C. A multiple-risk interaction model: effects of temperament and divorce on psychiatric disorders in children. *J Abnorm Child Psychol.* 1996;24:121-150.
38. Bernstein DP, Cohen P, Skodal A, Bezirganian S, Brook JS. Childhood antecedents of adolescent personality disorders. *Am J Psychiatry.* 1996;153:907-913.
39. Brook JS, Whiteman M, Finch SJ, Cohen P. Young adult drug use and delinquency: childhood antecedents and adolescent mediators. *J Am Acad Child Adolesc Psychiatry.* 1996;35:1584-1592.
40. Brown J, Cohen P, Johnson JG, Salzinger S. A longitudinal analysis of risk factors for child maltreatment: findings of a 17-year prospective study of officially recorded and self-reported child abuse and neglect. *Child Abuse Negl.* 1998;22: 1065-1078.
41. Johnson JG, Cohen P, Dohrenwend BP, Link BG, Brook JS. A longitudinal investigation of social causation and social selection processes involved in the association between socioeconomic status and psychiatric disorders. *J Abnorm Psychol.* In press.
42. Laporte L, Guttman H. Traumatic childhood experiences as risk factors for borderline and other personality disorders. *J Personal Disord.* 1996;10:247-259.
43. Oldham JM, Skodol AE, Gallagher PE, Kroll ME. Relationship of borderline symptoms to histories of abuse and neglect: a pilot study. *Psychiatr Q.* 1996;67:287-295.
44. Steiger H, Jabalpurwala S, Champagne J. Axis II comorbidity and developmental adversity in bulimia nervosa. *J Nerv Ment Dis.* 1996;184:555-560.
45. Weine SM, Becker DF, Levy KN, Edell WS, McGlashan TH. Childhood trauma histories in adolescent inpatients. *J Trauma Stress.* 1997;10:291-298.
46. Bernstein DP, Stein JA, Handelsman L. Predicting personality pathology among adult patients with substance use disorders: effects of childhood maltreatment. *Addict Behav.* 1998;23:855-868.
47. National Center on Child Abuse and Neglect. *Child Maltreatment, 1993.* Washington, DC: US Dept of Health and Human Services; 1995.
48. Ruegg R, Frances A. New research in personality disorders. *J Personal Disord.* 1995;9:1-48.
49. Wolock T, Horowitz B. Child maltreatment as a social problem: the neglect of neglect. *Am J Orthopsychiatry.* 1984;15:223-238.
50. Straus MA, Kinard EM, Williams LM. The neglect scale. Paper presented at: 4th International Conference on Family Violence Research; July 23, 1995; Durham, NC.
51. Dubo ED, Zanarini MC, Lewis RE, Williams AA. Childhood antecedents of self-destructiveness in borderline personality disorder. *Can J Psychiatry.* 1997;42: 63-69.
52. Widom CS. The cycle of violence. *Science.* 1989;244:160-166.
53. Gauthier L, Stollak G, Messé L, Aronoff J. Recall of childhood neglect and physical abuse as differential predictors of current psychological functioning. *Child Abuse Negl.* 1996;20:549-559.
54. Robins LN. *Deviant Children Grow Up: A Sociological and Psychiatric Study of Sociopathic Personality.* Baltimore, Md: Williams & Wilkins; 1966.
55. Bowlby J. *Attachment and Loss.* 2nd ed. New York, NY: Basic Books Inc Publishers; 1982.
56. van der Kolk BA, Fisler RE. Childhood abuse and neglect and loss of self-regulation. *Bull Menninger Clin.* 1994;58:145-168.
57. Dodge KA, Bates JE, Pettit GS. Mechanisms in the cycle of violence. *Science.* 1990;250:1678-1683.
58. First MB, Gibbon M, Spitzer RL, Williams JBW, Benjamin L. *Users Guide for the Structured Clinical Interview for DSM-IV Axis II Personality Disorders (SCID-II).* New York: New York State Psychiatric Institute; 1996.

Behavior Genetics, Vol. 23, No. 1, 1993

A Test of the Equal-Environment Assumption In Twin Studies of Psychiatric Illness

Kenneth S. Kendler,[1,2,5] Michael C. Neale,[2] Ronald C. Kessler,[3] Andrew C. Heath,[4] and Lindon J. Eaves[1,2]

Received 30 April 1992—Final 3 June 1992

The traditional twin method is predicated on the equal-environment assumption (EEA)—that monozygotic (MZ) and dizygotic (DZ) twins are equally correlated in their exposure to environmental events of etiologic importance for the trait under study. In 1968, Scarr proposed a test of the EEA which examines the impact of phenotypic similarity in twins of perceived versus true zygosity. We apply this test for the EEA to five common psychiatric disorders (major depression, generalized anxiety disorder, phobia, bulimia, and alcoholism), as assessed by personal interview, in 1030 female–female twin pairs from the Virginia Twin Registry with known zygosity. We use a newly developed model-fitting approach which treats perceived zygosity as a form of specified familial environment. In 158 of the 1030 pairs (15.3%), one or both twins disagreed with the project-assigned zygosity. Model fitting provided no evidence for a significant influence of perceived zygosity on twin resemblance for any of the five disorders. Although limited in power, these results support the validity of the EEA in twin studies of psychiatric disorders.

KEY WORDS: Twin studies; equal-environment assumption; psychiatric disorders; depression; alcoholism; anxiety disorders.

INTRODUCTION

The traditional twin method, as well as more recent biometrical models for twin analysis, are predicated on the equal-environment assumption (EEA)—that monozygotic (MZ) and dizygotic (DZ) twins are equally correlated for their exposure to environmental influences that are of etiologic relevance to the trait under study. If the EEA is not correct, then the excess resemblance of MZ over DZ twins, which is usually attributed to genetic factors, could in part be explained by environmental effects.

Four major methods have been designed to test the validity of the EEA in twin studies (Kendler, 1983). The first method to test the EEA assumes that resemblance in twins is influenced by the similarity of their treatment by the social environment, which in turn reflects their degree of physical resemblance. If this is the case, then, controlling for zygosity, physical similarity of twin pairs should correlate with trait similarity. We are aware of three studies using this method, two examining the normative traits of intelligence and personality (Plomin *et al.*, 1976; Matheny *et al.*, 1976) and one examing schizophrenia (Kendler, 1983). None of these studies suggested that twin resemblance was substantially influenced by physical similarity.

The second method involves direct observation of twins in a social or family setting in which the behavior of other individuals is divided into

[1] Department of Psychiatry, Medical College of Virginia/Virginia Commonwealth University, Richmond, Virginia 23298.
[2] Department of Human Genetics, Medical College of Virginia/Virginia Commonwealth University, Richmond, Virginia 23298.
[3] Institute for Social Research, University of Michigan, Ann Arbor, Michign 48109.
[4] Department of Psychiatry, Washington University School of Medicine, St. Louis, Missouri 63130.
[5] To whom correspondence should be addressed at Box 710 MCV Station, Richmond, Virginia 23298-0710.

0001-8244/93/0100-0021$07.00/0

those which are self-initiated and those which occur in response to behavior of the twins. In the one application of this method known to us, Lytton (1977) studied very young twins and their parents and found that the excess resemblance in the parental treatment of MZ vs. DZ twins was entirely attributable to parental behavior which was *in response* to twin behavior.

The third method rests on observations that certain measurable features of the childhood and adult environments of MZ twins are more similar than for DZ twins. For example, MZ twins report that they more frequently shared playmates, shared the same room, and were dressed alike as children than same-sex DZ twins (Loehlin and Nichols, 1976; Kendler *et al.*, 1986, 1992c). Furthermore, as adults MZ twins are in more frequent contact than same-sex DZ twins and more frequently cohabit (Kendler *et al.*, 1986, 1992c; Rose *et al.*, 1990). If these environmental experiences influence twin similarity, then this might represent a violation of the EEA and should be detectable by correlating, separately within each zygosity group, the degree of resemblance to the degree of similarity of environment in childhood or adulthood. Loehlin and Nichols (1976) were unable to find significant correlations between childhood environmental similarity and similarity for personality or intellectual ability in adolescents. Kendler and colleagues were unable to find any consistent relationship between childhood or adult environmental similarity and twin resemblance for self-report symptoms of anxiety and depression (Kendler *et al.*, 1986) or clinically diagnosed major depression (Kendler *et al.*, 1992c), phobia (Kendler *et al.*, 1992a), generalized anxiety disorder (Kendler *et al.*, 1992b), or alcoholism (Kendler *et al.*, 1992d). A similar pattern of results has been reported for personality and symptoms of anxiety and depression (Morris-Yates *et al.*, 1990), social attitudes (Martin *et al.*, 1986), and alcohol consumption (Heath *et al.*, 1989). In contrast, Clifford *et al.* (1984) found that the similarity of adult environment did influence self-report psychiatric symptoms and Kaprio *et al.*, (1990) found the same pattern of effects on alcohol intake and personality. The limitation of this method, as Lykken *et al.* (1990) have pointed out, is that a correlation between frequency of adult contact and phenotypic similarity in twin pairs need not be a causal one. Degree of phenotypic similarity could also influence frequency of contact.

The fourth method, initially proposed by Scarr (1968), involves a comparison of trait similarity in twins as a function of both "real" zygosity, as assessed by the investigators, and "perceived" zygosity, as reported by the twins or their parents. If their families, their social environment, or the twins themselves expect MZ twins to be more similar than DZ twins, and this expectation influences trait similarity in the twins, then perceived zygosity should influence twin similarity. This method for testing the EEA has one distinct advantage over the preceding approaches. While all three previous methods require the investigator to assess only one potential source of trait similarity in twins (physical appearance, dressing alike as children, actions of parent in a lab situation, etc.), this method provides a global test for *all* potential environmental influences that are dependent on zygosity associated attitudes and expectations. Studies using this method, which requires that a certain proportion of twins be misinformed about their zygosity, have examined traits such as intelligence, attitudes, hyperactivity, and personality and have found little evidence that perceived zygosity influences twin resemblance (Scarr, 1968; Munsinger and Douglass, 1976; Matheny, 1979; Scarr and Carter-Saltzman, 1979; Goodman and Stevenson, 1989).

In this report, we apply, for the first time to our knowledge, an assessment of the impact of perceived zygosity on twin resemblance for psychiatric disorders as diagnosed by personal structured psychiatric interview in a large population-based sample of female–female twin pairs.

METHODS

Sample and Diagnostic Methods

As detailed elsewhere (Kendler *et al.*, 1992c), as part of a longitudinal study of the genetic and environmental risk factors for common psychiatric disorders in women, we personally interviewed 2163 female twins from the population-based Virginia Twin Register, where both members had previously returned mailed questionnaires. This sample included both members of 1033 pairs and 97 individual twins, whose mean age (±SD) was 30.1 + 7.6. The refusal rate during the personal interview phase of this project was 8%. All twins were interviewed by an individual with a master's degree in social work and/or at least 2 years' clinical experience, blind to the psychopathologic status of the cotwin. Eighty-nine percent of the interviews were conducted face to face, usually in the twin's residence, and 11% by phone.

The interview included, in modified form, sections of the Structured Clinical Interview for DSM-III-R (Sptizer *et al.*, 1987) for major depression, generalized anxiety disorder, bulimia nervosa, and alcohol dependence. Phobias were assessed by an adaption of the Phobic Disorders section of the Diagnostic Interview Schedule (DIS) Version III-A (Robins and Helzer, 1985), which in turn was based on the DSM-III criteria (American Psychiatric Association, 1980). The diagnoses of major depression, bulimia and generalized anxiety disorder were based on a blind review by K.S.K., using DSM-III-R criteria (American Psychiatric Association, 1987), of the interview protocols. Because of the relative rarity of bulimia, in the analyses of this diagnosis only, we included "possible" cases that appeared to be clinically affected but did not meet full diagnostic criteria (Kendler *et al.*, 1991). We have previously shown that from both an epidemiologic and a genetic perspective, possible and definite cases of bulimia appear to share all the same risk factors (Kendler *et al.*, 1991). Phobia was defined as the presence of 1 of 17 specific fears which the respondent considered to be irrational and which, in the interviewer's judgment, produced objective behavioral interference with the respondent's life. To maximize our statistical power for the study of "alcoholism," we chose the broad criteria of alcohol dependence as defined by DSM-III-R (American Psychiatric Association, 1987) or "problem drinking," in which the respondent admits to having had, or being considered by others as having, a significant "drinking" problem not limited to single isolated incidents. A multiple-threshold model indicates that in these data, problem drinking reflects a milder disturbance on the same liability dimension that influences alcohol dependence (Kendler *et al.*, 1992d). We have reanalyzed the data using the standard DSM-III-R definition of alcohol dependence, and they do not differ qualitatively from those reported here.

Zygosity Determination

All zygosity information from the 1033 pairs where both members were interviewed was reviewed by two experienced twin researchers blind to information about their psychiatric status. Information reviewed included responses to questions about physical similarity, frequency of confusion as children by parents, teachers, and strangers, and whether, as children, the twin and her cotwin were as alike as "two peas in a pod" or only of "normal family likeness." Furthermore, in over 80% of the pairs, frontal photographs were available for both members. On the basis of this review, twin pairs were classified into five groups: definitely MZ, definitely DZ, probably MZ, probably DZ, and zygosity uncertain. Disagreement between the two raters was resolved by consensus. We attempted to obtain blood samples from both members of the pairs in the final three categories and were successful in 119 of the 186 pairs so classified. Zygosity was determined by the examination of DNA polymorphisms, using 8 highly informative probes, which, if all identical, produced a probability of monozygosity of 0.9997 (Spence *et al.*, 1988). Final zygosity determination, which used blood samples where available and a definite or probable zygosity diagnosis otherwise, yielded 590 MZ twin pairs, 440 DZ twin pairs, and 3 pairs classified as uncertain. DNA methods validated our zygosity diagnosis in 87 of 105 (83%) twin pairs in the "probable" category. DNA- or previously obtained blood group-based zygosity diagnoses confirmed our assignment in 26 of 26 pairs in the "definite" category. In our analyses here, we focus on the 1030 twin pairs of known zygosity.

All twins were also asked whether, in their opinion, they were definitely identical, probably identical, probably fraternal, definitely fraternal, or not sure what kind of twin they were. We then asked them, "On what do you base your opinion?" to which the interviewers coded five non-mutually exclusive responses: (i) physical appearance, (ii) parents told at birth because of number of placentas, (iii) parents told at birth—other reasons or reasons unknown, (iv) told by doctor—no blood tests, and (v) blood tests.

Method of Analysis

As outlined in Figure 1, one of us (MCN) has developed, using the software package Mx (Neale, 1991), a method of testing for the presence of violations of the EEA by including in the standard twin model a "specified" form of familial environment. In the present study, this specified environment was indexed by self-report zygosity and reflected the impact on twin similarity of the expectations of the twins themselves, their families, and their more extended social environment (e.g., teachers, friends). On this hypothetical scale of self-report zygosity, we assigned twins who both considered themselves to be identical a score of 1.0, pairs who both considered themselves to be fraternal a score of 0, and all other pairs (e.g., twins who disagreed about their zygosity or where one or both members of the pair responded that they did not know their own zygosity) as 0.50. The model for any given disorder was then fit directly to six 2 × 2 contingency tables cross-classifying the affection status of twin 1 and twin 2, three each for MZ and DZ twins, each divided into pairs with a score of 0, 0.5, and 1 on our scale of specified familial environment.

The full model for these analyses, as shown in Figure 1, includes the standard estimates of *A*, additive genetic effects, and *E*, individual specific environment. In addition, estimates were available for the specified common or family environment (C_S) (i.e., the effect of perceived zygosity) and the remaining or residual common environment (C_R).

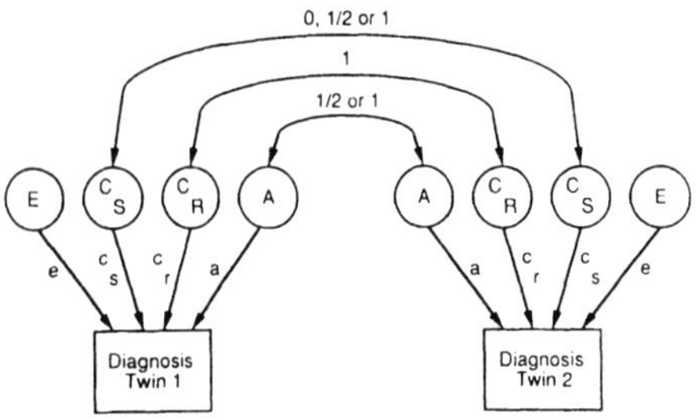

Fig. 1. A path diagram of the model used for analyzing the impact of perceived zygosity on twin resemblance for psychiatric disorders. Four sources of variation in liability to the diagnosed disorder are considered: additive genetic effects (*A*), specified common or familial environment (C_S), residual common environment (C_R), and individual-specific environment (*E*). The path coefficients associated with these sources of variation are, respectively, *a*, c_s, c_r, and *e*. Specified family environment here reflects the effects of "perceived zygosity"—the expectations from the twins themselves, their families, and their social environment that twins considered to be MZ will be similar. This specified family environment is assumed to have a correlation of (i) unity in twins who agree that their zygosity is MZ, (ii) zero in twins who agree that their zygosity is DZ, and (iii) one-half in those who disagree or are uncertain about their zygosity. Residual common environment is, by definition, assumed to be perfectly correlated in all twin pairs. Additive genetic effects are assumed to be perfectly correlated in MZ twins are correlated one-half in DZ twins.

The proportions of variance in liability due to these four sets of factors are termed a^2, e^2, c_s^2, and c_r^2, respectively. The model assumes that being considered MZ twins results in an excess twin similarity in liability by an amount equal to c_s^2. Disagreeing or being of uncertain zygosity contributes $\frac{1}{2}c_s^2$ to twin similarity. The model assumes that being considered a DZ twin makes no additional contribution to twin similarity. Since we have previously demonstrated that additive genetic effects were prominent for all these disorders (Kendler *et al.*, 1991, 1992a–d), we considered two tests for the validity of the EEA. First, we compared the fit of the full or AC_SC_RE model to that of the AC_RE model. Second, we compared the fit of the AC_sE model to that of the *AE* model. The fit of these models was evaluated by Akaike's information criterion (AIC) (1987), which equals chi-square minus twice the degrees of freedom. The better the overall balance of goodness of fit and parsimony, the more *negative* is the AIC.

RESULTS

The relationship between the assigned zygosity and the self-report zygosity in the 1030 pairs of evaluated twins is shown in Table I. In 477 of the 590 twins (80.9%) classified as MZ, both twins agreed that they were definitely or probably identical. In 395 of the 440 (89.8%) twins classified as DZ, both twins agreed that they were definitely or probably fraternal. Of interest, while in 10.9% of the pairs classified as MZ, both twins considered themselves fraternal, in only 0.7% of pairs classified as DZ, did both pairs consider themselves identical.

In the 2060 members of the complete twin pairs of known zygosity, the lifetime prevalence of the disorders considered here is as follows: major depression, 31.4%; generalized anxiety disorder, 23.6%; phobia, 30.5%; bulimia, 5.7%; and broadly

Table I. Perceived Versus Assigned Zygosity in 1030 Personally Evaluated Female–Female Twin Pairs

	Assigned zygosity			
	MZ		DZ	
Perceived zygosity	*N*	%	*N*	%
Agree identical	477	80.9	3	0.7
Disagree on zygosity	29	4.9	17	3.9
One or both zygosity unknown	20	3.4	25	5.7
Agree fraternal	64	10.9	395	89.8

defined "alcoholism," 17.3%. The formal evaluations of the EEA assumption for these disorders are shown in Table II. For all disorders, the fit of the AC_RE model, as assessed by the AIC, was superior to that of the full or AC_SC_RE model. In fact, for all disorders except major depression, the deterioration in fit with setting C_S to zero was less than 0.05 χ^2 unit. A very similar pattern of results was obtained when comparing the fit of the AC_SE model to that of the AE model. For all the disorders, the best fit by AIC was provided by the AE model.

DISCUSSION

This report represents, to our knowledge, the first application to psychiatric disorders of a test for the EEA initially proposed by Scarr (1968) of comparing phenotypic similarity as a function of perceived versus "true" zygosity. In a population-based sample of female–female adult twin pairs, self-reported zygosity in both members of the twin pair agreed with assigned zygosity in about 85% of pairs. This is a somewhat higher rate than in most previous reports (Loehlin and Nichols, 1976; Scarr, 1968; Scarr and Carter-Saltzman, 1979; Matheny, 1979; Munsinger and Douglass, 1976). However, these studies examined younger twins and often asked the parents of the twins rather than the twins themselves. Adult twins may be more accurate in their assessment of their own zygosity than are twins in adolescence or childhood or their parents.

Consistent with some (Matheny, 1979; Lytton, 1977), but not other (Scarr, 1968; Munsinger and Douglass, 1976), reports the disagreements between self-reported and assigned zygosity were not symmetrical in this sample; many more MZ twins considered themselves to be DZ than vice versa. In an attempt to understand this finding, we compared the reasons given for belief about zygosity in MZ twins where both considered themselves DZ vs. twins who were, in our judgment, both correct in considering themselves either MZ or DZ (Table III). Compared to either MZ or DZ twins who were correct about their zygosity, MZ twins who believed that they were DZ were much *less* likely to base their opinion on physical appearance but *more* likely to base their opinion on what their parents were

Table II. Model-Fitting Results for Major Depression, Generalized Anxiety Disorder, Phobia, Bulimia, and Alcoholism, Including Perceived Zygosity as a Form of Specified Family Environment[a]

	Fit of the model (χ^2 units)				Parameter estimates of best-fit model by AIC	
Disorder	AC_SC_RE (df = 14)	AC_RE (df = 15)	AC_SE (df = 15)	AE (df = 16)	a^2	e^2
Major depression						
χ^2	20.25	22.42	20.78	22.42[b]	0.43	0.57
AIC	−7.44	7.59	−9.22	−9.59		
Generalized anxiety disorder						
χ^2	21.32	21.32	21.32	21.32[b]	0.34	0.66
AIC	−6.68	−8.68	−8.68	−10.68		
Phobia						
χ^2	5.68	5.68	5.68	5.68[b]	0.28	0.72
AIC	−22.32	−24.32	−24.32	−26.32		
Bulimia						
χ^2	12.82	12.83	13.05	13.05[b]	0.52	0.49
AIC	−15.18	−17.17	−16.95	−18.95		
Alcoholism						
χ^2	6.03	6.07	6.03	6.07[b]	0.61	0.39
AIC	−21.97	−23.93	−23.97	−25.93		

[a] The models fitted imposed an equal threshold constraint, estimating a single threshold for all six tables.
[b] Best-fit model by AIC (Akaike, 1987).

Table III. Reasons Given for Belief About Zygosity in Twin Pairs Where Both Correctly Felt They Were MZ, Both Mistakenly Felt They Were DZ When They Were Really MZ, and Both Correctly Felt They Were DZ

	True/perceived zygosity					
	MZ/MZ (n = 954)		MZ/DZ (n = 128)		DZ/DZ (n = 790)	
Reason(s) for belief about zygosity[a]	n	%	n	%	n	%
Physical appearance	862	90.4***	56	43.8	745	94.3***
Parents told at birth						
Total	598	62.7**	97	75.8	324	41.0***
Because of number of placentas	230	24.1*	44	34.4	126	15.9***
Told by Doctor	165	17.3	20	15.6	80	10.1
Blood test	63	6.6**	1	0.8	13	1.6
Other	208	21.8	22	17.2	122	15.4

[a] Adds up to more than 100% because answers were not mutually exclusive.
* $p < .05$, by χ^2, df = 1, vs. pairs with true zygosity of MZ and perceived zygosity of DZ.
** $p < .01$, by χ^2, df = 1, vs. pairs with true zygosity of MZ and perceived zygosity of DZ.
*** $p < .001$ by χ^2, df = 1, vs. pairs with true zygosity of MZ and perceived zygosity of DZ.

told at their birth. These results support the hypothesis that the asymmetry in mistaken zygosity beliefs in twins derives, in part, from mothers of dichorionic MZ twins being mistakenly told at birth, because of separate placentas, that their children were DZ.

We applied structural equation modeling to five relatively common major psychiatric disorders in this sample, estimating separately the impact on twin similarity of "self-report" zygosity as a form of specified common environment. For all five disorders, model fitting provided no evidence for a significant effect of perceived zygosity on twin resemblance. More generally, these results suggest that the social and personal expectations associated with being considered an identical or fraternal twin pair have little effect on twin resemblance for common psychiatric disorders and are therefore unlikely to be major biases in twin studies of psychiatric illness. Our results are further supported by previous analyses which suggest that, when controlling for zygosity in the disorders examined, twin resemblance is generally unrelated to either childhood environmental similarity or frequency of adult contact (Kendler *et al.*, 1991, 1992a–d).

The results of this report should be interpreted in the context of two potentially significant methodologic limitations. First, because of the relatively small number of twins whose perceived zygosity disagreed with their assigned zygosity, our statistical power to detect a phenotypic effect of perceived zygosity is modest. However, for four of the five disorders, the estimate of $c_S{}^2$ in the full model was zero or very close to zero, suggesting that the failure to find significant evidence for self-report zygosity may not be a result of small sample size. However, modest effects of self-report zygosity on twin resemblance for psychiatric disorders would probably go undetected in our analyses. Therefore, our results can most properly be considered as evidence against the hypothesis that a large proportion of the excess similarity of MZ over DZ twins for psychiatric disorders results from the expectation of greater resemblance in MZ twins by the twins themselves or their environment.

Second, only a limited number of our zygosity diagnoses were made using blood-group or DNA polymorphisms. With a twin sample this large, we were forced, for the sake of economy, to use an algorithm which obtained blood samples only in twin pairs where zygosity could not be confidently assigned after a review of traditional zygosity questions and personal photographs. Since our validation attempts for this method suggested that our error rate was very low, it is unlikely that the small number of errors made in zygosity assignment substantially biased our estimates of the impact of perceived zygosity on twin similarity.

ACKNOWLEDGEMENTS

This work was supported by Grants MH-40828 and AA-09095 from the United States National Institutes of Health. The Virginia Twin Registry, established and maintained by W. Nance M.D., Ph.D., and L. Corey, Ph.D., is supported by United States National Institutes of Health Grants HD-26746 and NS-25630. Leroy Thacker, M.S., assisted in the data analysis.

REFERENCES

Akaike, H. (1987). Factor analysis and AIC. *Psychometrika* **52**:317–332.

American Psychiatric Association (1980). *Diagnostic and Statistical Manual of Mental Disorders, 3rd ed.*, American Psychiatric Association, Washington, DC.

American Psychiatric Association (1987). *Diagnostic and Statistical Manual of Mental Disorders, rev. 3rd ed.*, American Psychiatric Association, Washington, DC.

Clifford, C. A., Hopper, J. L., Fulker, D., and Murray, R. M. (1984). A genetic and environmental analysis of a twin family study of alcohol use, anxiety, and depression. *Genet. Epidemiol.* **1**:63–79.

Goodman, R., and Stevenson, J. (1989). A twin study of hyperactivity. II. The aetiological role of genes, family relationships and perinatal adversity. *J. Child. Psychol. Psychiat.* **30**:691–709.

Heath, A. C., Jardine, R., and Martin, N. G. (1989). Interactive effects of genotype and social environment on alcohol consumption in female twins. *J. Stud. Alcohol* **60**:38–48.

Kaprio, J., Koskenvuo, M., and Rose, R. J. (1990). Change in cohabitation and intrapair similarity of monozygotic (MZ) cotwins for alcohol use, extraversion, and neuroticism. *Behav. Genet.* **20**:265–276.

Kendler, K. S. (1983). Overview: A current perspective on twin studies of schizophrenia. *Am. J. Psychiat.* **140**:1413–1425.

Kendler, K. S., Heath, A. C., Martin, N. G., and Eaves, L. J. (1986). Symptoms of anxiety and depression in a volunteer twin population: The etiologic role of genetic and environmental factors. *Arch. Gen. Psychiat.* **43**:213–221.

Kendler, K. S., MacLean, C. J., Neale, M. C., Kessler, R. C., Heath, A. C., and Eaves, L. J. (1991). The genetic epidemiology of bulimia nervosa. *Am. J. Psychiat.* **148**:1627–1637.

Kendler, K. S., Neale, M. C., Kessler, R. C., Heath, A. C., and Eaves, L. J. (1992a). The genetic epidemiology of phobias in women: the inter-relationship of agoraphobia, social phobia, situational phobia and simple phobia. *Arch. Gen. Psychiat.* **49**:273–281.

Kendler, K. S., Neale, M. C., Kessler, R. C., Heath, A. C., and Eaves, L. J. (1992b). Generalized anxiety disorder in women: a population based twin study. *Arch. Gen. Psychiat.* **49**:267–272.

Kendler, K. S., Neale, M. C., Kessler, R. C., Heath, A. C., and Eaves, L. J. (1992c). A population based twin study of major depression in women: The impact of varying definitions of illness. *Arch. Gen. Psychiat.* **49**:257–266.

Kendler, K. S., Heath, A. C., Neale, M. C., Kessler, R. C., and Eaves, L. J. (1992d). A population-based twin study of alcoholism in women *JAMA* **268**:1877–1882.

Loehlin, J. C., and Nichols, R. C. (1976). *Heredity, Environment and Personality: A Study of 850 Sets of Twins*, University of Texas Press, Austin.

Lykken, D. T., McGue, M., Bouchard, T. J., and Tellegen, A. (1990). Does contact lead to similarity or similarity to contact? *Behav. Genet.* **20**:547–561.

Lytton, H. (1977). Do parents create, or respond to, differences in twins? *Dev. Psychol.* **13**:456–459.

Martin, N. G., Eaves, L. J., Heath, A. C., Jardine, R., Feingold, L., and Eysenck, H. J. (1986). Transmission of social attitudes. *Proc. Natl. Acad. Sci.* **83**:4364–4368.

Matheny, A. P., Jr. (1979). Appraisal of parental bias in twin studies: Ascribed zygosity and IQ differences in twins. *Acta Genet. Med. Gemmellol.* **28**: 155–160.

Matheny, A.P., Jr., Wilson, R. S., and Dolan, A. B. (1976). Relations between twins' similarity of appearance and behavioral similarity: Testing an assumption. *Behav. Genet.* **6**:343–351.

Morris-Yates, A., Andrews, G., Howie, P., and Henderson, S. (1990). Twins: A test of the equal environments assumption. *Acta Psychiat. Scand.* **81**:322–326.

Munsinger, J., and Douglass, A., II (1976). The syntactic abilities of identical twins, fraternal twins, and their siblings. *Child Dev.* **47**:40–50.

Neale, M. C. (1991). *Statistical Modelling with Mx*, Department of Human Genetics, Medical College of Virginia, Virginia Commonwealth University, Richmond.

Plomin, R., Willerman, L., and Loehlin, J. C. (1976). Resemblance in appearance and the equal environments assumption in twin studies of personality traits. *Behav. Genet.* **6**:43–52.

Robins, L. N., and Helzer, J. E. (1985). *Diagnostic Interview Schedule (DIS): Version III-A*, Washington University School of Medicine, St. Louis, MO.

Rose, R. J., Kaprio, J., Williams, C. J., Viken, R., and Obremski, K. (1990). Social contact and sibling similarity: facts, issues, and red herrings. *Behav. Genet.* **20**:763–778.

Scarr, S. (1968). Environmental bias in twin studies. *Eugen. Q.* **15**:34–40.

Scarr, S., and Carter-Saltzman, L. (1979). Twin method: Defense of a critical assumption. *Behav. Genet.* **9**:527–542.

Spence, J. E., Corey, L. A., Nance, W. E., Marazita, M. L., Kendler, K. S., and Schieken, R. M. (1988). Molecular analysis of twin zygosity using VNTR DNA probes. *Am. J. Hum. Genet.* **43(3)**:A159.

Spitzer, R. L., Williams, J. B., and Gibson, M. (1987). *Structured Clinical Interview for DSM-III-R*, Biometrics Research Department, New York State Psychiatric Institute, New York.

Edited by N. G. Martin

Annu. Rev. Psychol. 2000. 51:1–27

PARENTING AND ITS EFFECTS ON CHILDREN: On Reading and Misreading Behavior Genetics

Eleanor E. Maccoby
Department of Psychology, Stanford University, Building 420, Jordan Hall, Stanford, California 94305-2130; e-mail: maccoby@psych.stanford.edu

■ **Abstract** There is clear evidence that parents can and do influence children. There is equally clear evidence that children's genetic makeup affects their own behavioral characteristics, and also influences the way they are treated by their parents. Twin and adoption studies provide a sound basis for estimating the strength of genetic effects, although heritability estimates for a given trait vary widely across samples, and no one estimate can be considered definitive. This chapter argues that knowing only the strength of genetic factors, however, is not a sufficient basis for estimating environmental ones and indeed, that attempts to do so can systematically underestimate parenting effects. Children's genetic predispositions and their parents' childrearing regimes are seen to be closely interwoven, and the ways in which they function jointly to affect children's development are explored.

CONTENTS

INTRODUCTION

What are the forces that affect when and how children will change as they grow older? Can development be seen as a progressive process whereby children move toward a specifiable outcome or end state that we can call maturity? What conditions

0084-6570/00/0201-0001$12.00

determine differences among children in their rates of development or their ultimate outcomes? These questions have been at the heart of much of the work in developmental psychology since the inception of the field. In pursuing the answers, the broad forces of nature and nurture, and the interplay between them, have been of central concern. It has long been clear that there are powerful maturational time-tables governing developmental change: e.g. the progression in infancy from sitting to crawling to standing to walking, or in the acquisition of language, the transition from rudimentary one-word utterances through intermediate phrases to the production of full, well-formed sentences. However, it has been equally obvious that children are learning many things through their daily experiences in interacting with the physical and social world, and that what is learned is not encoded in the genes. Some of the experiences children have are random—not planned or organized by any outside agency—but some occur according to what might be called a socialization time table. It is here that parenting has its place.

All societies prescribe certain characteristics that their members are expected to possess and certain things people must not do, if they are to function adequately as members of their society. Some of these prescriptions and proscriptions are nearly universal across cultures. such as the requirement for parents, or specified parent surrogates, to provide nurturance and protection for children. Other standards and values vary greatly from one cultural setting to another. In all societies, training of children occurs, and social controls are in place to ensure that children are socialized—that is, brought up in such a way that each new generation acquires the prescribed patterns of beliefs and behaviors. Of course, cultures do change, either slowly or rapidly, so that the cross-generational transmission is by no means absolute. A new generation may need to adapt to conditions that the parent generation did not face. And transmission of values, even when they continue to be appropriate for succeeding generations, is not always successful. Some children in every cohort may be seen to be inadequately socialized by the criteria that the society applies.

Not all socialization occurs in childhood. People are socialized into the customs and standards of an occupational culture when they take up an entry-level job. Socialization and resocialization occur when adults enter into new life roles (e.g. marriage, parenthood). In considering the role of parents, however, we are mainly concerned with childhood socialization. Some of the socialization that occurs throughout childhood is in a sense anticipatory, in that it functions to prepare children for adaptation to a fairly wide range of life roles and the various contexts children will encounter as they grow older. But childhood socialization also concerns the training of children in modes of behavior that are acceptable for the stage of childhood they currently occupy. Societies set different standards for people at different stages of their life cycle, and there are requirements that loom especially large in childhood. These include requirements for children to comply with adult demands, to avoid irritating adults or disrupting their activities, to accept age-appropriate responsibility, and to function as a pleasant, cooperative family member.

In modern societies, there are least three major contexts in which childhood socialization takes place: families, peer groups, and out-of-home contexts such as school classrooms or day-care centers in which the daily experiences of children are structured and overseen by adults. The enormous body of literature on childhood socialization has strongly emphasized the role of parents. This emphasis has a long and deep tradition. The idea that "as the twig is bent, so grows the tree" can be traced at least as far back as Greek and Biblical times—(probably earlier), and in most societies parents are the ones assigned primary responsibility for "bending" the children in desirable directions, by supervising, teaching, and disciplining them as they grow up. Early childhood in particular has long been thought to be a period in the life cycle when humans are especially plastic—a time when children are especially open to social influences on characteristics they will carry with them long after they have left their family of origin. Things thought to be especially vulnerable to influence in the first 5–7 years of children's lives include the language they speak, their food preferences, their religious beliefs, and certain enduring personality traits.

In the twentieth century, assumptions about the importance of within-family childhood socialization have been part of the fabric of mainstream psychological theories. From roughly the 1920s through the 1960s, behaviorist learning theories held sway, emphasizing the "blank slate" status of infants and the power of adults to teach young children, for good or ill, what they must learn. Parents, of course, were seen as the most available teachers, and the ones responsible for carrying out the training of their children. The physiological drive states (hunger, fatigue) with which children are innately endowed were not ignored in the learning theories of the time, so there was some blending of nature and nurture, but the major emphasis was on the control of learning processes exercised by environmental inputs. Psychoanalytic theories of this period emphasized the importance of early in-family experience in determining subsequent inner conflicts, defense mechanisms, and internalization of values. In more recent decades, as the cognitive revolution took hold and learning theory (as it related to socialization) was reformulated as cognitive social learning theory, the active role of children as participants in their own socialization was increasingly stressed. Currently, there is increasing emphasis on the role of parents' and children's mutual perceptions and understandings about each other's dispositions and intentions as determiners of their influence upon one another. But none of these theoretical shifts has greatly affected the underlying assumption that parents have a powerful impact on the characteristics children develop and the directions their lives take. The child development research literature has continued to include a wide range of studies on such things as (*a*) familial risk factors (i.e. aspects of family functioning that are related to the subsequent development of externalizing or internalizing disorders in children); (*b*) social conditions that affect such parenting practices as how well parents are able to monitor their children, or how warm and responsive they are; and (*c*) parenting behaviors as mediators of the connection between societal risk factors (e.g. poverty or dangerous neighborhoods) and children's adjustment.

In recent decades, there has been a countervailing ground swell of research and theorizing about nature—the genetic endowment of parents and children—as exerting a powerful influence on the characteristics that children develop. Of course, for many decades, elementary psychology textbooks have carried tables comparing identical and fraternal twins with respect to their degree of similarity on IQ or other traits. Studies of adopted children were also widely reported many years ago, and inferences were routinely drawn from both twin and adoption studies concerning the importance of genetic factors in development. Still, for many years, thinking remained largely compartmentalized, and readers continued to believe in both the importance of genetic factors and the importance of socialization factors as though they were in no way incompatible. In recent years, however, there has been more sophisticated work in behavior genetics, and there are insistent voices claiming that the findings from this work are indeed incompatible with many widely-held views about the power of within-family socialization.

These messages from behavior genetics have been picked up and synthesized with other misgivings about the weaknesses of socialization research into a more broad-based attack on traditional assumptions concerning parenting and its effects. Rowe's book, *The Limits of Family Influence* (1994), stated the case strongly, and Harris's more popular book *The Nurture Assumption* (1998) attracted a flurry of media attention to the issues. These authors have drawn together the findings from some well-known studies of parenting effects and findings from behavior genetics to make the following claims:

1. The connections that studies have found between the way parents deal with their children and how the children turn out are actually quite weak and have proved difficult to replicate. When parent "effects" are found, they tend to be effects on the way children behave at home and the relationships they develop with their parents. There is little carry-over from at-home experiences to the way children function in out-of-home contexts
2. When studies do establish connections between parenting and children's attributes, these are correlational findings. An example is Baumrind's early finding—now widely replicated—that the children of parents who are both responsive and firm tend to be more competent and cooperative than children of parents who are either authoritarian or permissive (Baumrind & Black 1967). Such findings have traditionally been interpreted as showing that authoritative parenting has beneficial effects on children, ignoring the possibility that the causal connection may run the other way—i.e. that competent, cooperative children may make it easier for their parents to be firm and responsive. In fact, the critics argue, parent behavior is substantially driven by the behavior of children, and much if not most of the parent/child correlation can be accounted for by the child's genetic predispositions.
3. Parental influence has been emphasized at the expense of sources of influence that in fact have great—or perhaps greater—importance in shaping children's development. Two kinds of influence which critics argue have been underemphasized are genetic predispositions and the influence of peers.

In the popular media, these critiques have been condensed into the oversimplified message "Parents don't matter" or "matter very little"—news bites that, on their face, have little relation to reality as it is experienced daily in family life. Often, reports in the popular media do not reflect what the cited authors actually said. For example, late in her book, Harris (1998) says she believes parents can foster the development of specific talents (e.g. by providing music lessons) and can influence such things as children's leisure time activities, their food preferences, their religious beliefs and practices, and the acquisition of knowledge and skills and preferences that will contribute to their ultimate choice of a profession. Yet, the burden of her book is to down-play such influences and stress the respects in which parents are not influential. Rowe says: " . . . parents in most working to professional-class families may have little influence on what traits their children may eventually develop as adults." (1994:7). His use of the word "may" does not greatly soften the import of his message. He goes on to say that he doubts whether any undesirable trait displayed by a child can be significantly modified by anything a parent does. Scarr (1992) expresses a similarly skeptical view about the possible effects of interventions. Such views, of course, when picked up and simplified in the popular press, can have serious implications for public policies concerning whether to invest in remedial or supportive programs for children and families.

These critiques constitute serious efforts to present a point of view that is clearly different from the traditional emphasis on the importance of parenting. They cite large bodies of data and have attracted the support of highly reputable psychologists. They deserve to be taken seriously. Nonetheless, I believe that they are out of date with respect to both the genetic studies and the parenting-effects studies they cite, and that they seriously misinterpret the pertinent body of research.

I turn first to the question of how strong the connections are between what parents do with their children and how the children turn out. I then turn to issues of genetic factors, in particular the ways in which these factors may determine or limit how we can interpret parenting effects.

HOW STRONG IS THE CONNECTION BETWEEN PARENT AND CHILD BEHAVIORS?

As noted above, critics charge that interpreters of traditional socialization studies have exaggerated the importance of parenting in children's lives—that in fact, the effect sizes reported in many widely-cited studies are really quite small. Indeed, reviews of research done before the mid-1980s did show weak correlations between parenting processes and children's characteristics (e.g. Maccoby & Martin 1983). Since then, many studies have come up with more robust findings, no doubt reflecting improvements in the ways in which parent and child characteristics are assessed. Leading researchers no longer rely on a single measure, such as a parent or child interview or a parent or child self-report scale, as a measure of parent or child attributes. Instead information is obtained from multiple sources—from parents, children, teachers, school records, sometimes from children's peers and police records as well—and importantly, from direct observation of parent-child interactions and of children in out-of-home settings. When several measures such as these are aggregated, associations between parent attributes and children's behavior can be quite substantial. Parenting variables have typically accounted for 20% to 50% of the variance in child outcomes (Conger & Elder 1994, Reiss et al 1995). Exceptionally robust connections are reported in the recent large-scale study of adolescents in never-divorced and step-families, Hetherington and colleagues (Hetherington et al 1999). Using composite scores for both parenting styles and children's attributes, report a concurrent coefficient of 0.76 between mothers' "authoritative parenting" and adolescents' "social responsibility" (the coefficient for fathers is 0.49). Parental negativity has very strong connections for both parents with adolescents' depression and internalizing behavior.[1] Patterson and colleagues have also found substantial correlations between parental characteristics (e.g. disciplinary practices and monitoring) and children's antisocial behavior (Patterson & Forgatch 1995). They are able to show connections between parental behaviors and the children's negative, coercive behavior both at home and in out-of-home contexts.

Concurrent correlations are usually considerably larger than predictive ones. Longitudinal studies present the opportunity to examine the connections, if any, between child-rearing styles at one point in time and subsequent attributes of the child. The strength of the connections that have been found depends on many things, such as what "packages" or clusters of parent and child variables are considered, the way they are measured, the length of time between predictive and outcome measures, and whether background variables are statistically controlled. A few examples will illustrate the range of findings. Kochanska 1997b:94 has been able to show that aspects of early parenting account for a significant but moderate (Beta coefficient 0.29, F 9.96) portion of the variance in young children's self-regulation and internalization assessed a year later. Pettit and colleagues (1997:908) found some—but fewer and weaker—predictive relationships between parenting as assessed at the beginning of the kindergarten year and children's adjustment and academic performance seven years later, in the sixth grade. Strong predictive power of family interaction processes over much longer spans of time have been found in longitudinal studies of antisocial behavior (see Loeber & Dishion 1983). In current socialization studies, simple first-order correlations between parenting characteristics and child outcomes are seldom relied on. Indeed, sometimes they are not even reported. Instead, multivariate analyses are used to investigate such questions as whether a given aspect of parenting has different effects on different kinds of children or in families living in different circumstances; or whether different aspects of parenting have independent, addi-

[1]The coefficient connecting mothers' negative/conflictual behavior with children's externalizing behavior was 0.82; for fathers this coefficient was 0.79. These coefficients are path coefficients in structural models in which two aspects of parenting (authoritative parenting parental negativity/conflict) are considered simultaneously along with measures of sibling relationships. Scores derived from videotapes of parent-child interactions were a contributing element (though a minor one) in the composite scores of both parenting characteristics and child outcomes.

tive effects, whether they are interchangeable, or whether they interact so that the effects of one depend on the level of another.

In longitudinal work, the initial level of a child's characteristic at time 1 is sometimes statistically controlled to determine whether a time-l parent attribute is associated with subsequent *change* change in the child's behavior. As an example, Patterson & Bank (1989) studied families when their sons were in grade school, and again when the boys were adolescents. They found that changes in parenting during these years were strongly related to the chances of a boy's being arrested for delinquent activities in adolescence, even after the boy's anti-social tendencies at grade-school age were controlled. We see, then, that a variety of questions are being asked in current and recent research—questions to which simple parent/child correlations, either concurrent or time-lagged, will not provide answers.

A word should be said, too, about how large a correlation between some aspect of parenting and a child outcome is required for the relationship to be considered important or meaningful. Along with the rest of the psychological discipline, developmental psychologists are currently turning away from reporting the outcomes of studies primarily (or only) in terms of significance levels (p values) that indicate degree of departure from the null hypothesis. Instead, results are beginning to be reported in terms of effect sizes. For purposes of policy decisions in the medical arena, correlations as small as 0.03 between the use of a medication and reduction of disease have been considered strong enough to justify FDA approval of the drug (Rosenthal 1999). The importance of a medical intervention can be estimated in terms of such outcomes as the number of heart attacks averted or the number of people for whom a debilitating, chronic disease can be arrested or reversed. In the past, correlations in the 0.20s or 0.30s between aspects of family functioning and children's outcomes have often been dismissed as inconsequential. But when translated into the number of children who are at risk, for example, for failing in school or becoming delinquent or seriously depressed, predictive coefficients of this magnitude can be seen as by no means trivial. From the standpoint of social policy, the issue becomes one of how much importance a society attaches to social/behavioral outcomes, as compared with medical ones. This is obviously a matter of values, not statistics.

Studies continue to vary considerably with respect to the size of first-order correlations between parent and child characteristics. Clearly, a given parent behavior may have different effects on different children, depending on such things as age, sex, temperament, and distinctive prior experiences. If such differential effects exist, aggregating data across a whole sample of children will wash out parent/child effects—effects that might be quite robust within sub-groups of children. (See section on interactions, below.) It is not possible to arrive at any general rule as to when dividing by subgroups will increase or decrease a parent-child correlation. That will depend on the researcher's theoretical and empirical skill in identifying what the pertinent groupings might be. The use of more sophisticated statistical methods has contributed significantly to the ability of present-day researchers to identify parenting effects within the matrix of other factors with which they often co-vary.

Not only have methods of assessment been improved, but current socialization research includes a broader array of parenting attributes and focuses on a set of parenting processes that were not so clearly delineated in times past. One aspect of parental skill that has emerged in several recent studies as related to children's well-being is household organization; another concerns the ability of some parents to develop a reciprocal form of interaction with their children (e.g. shared positive affect, mutual responsivity). Studies of the predictive power of parent-child reciprocation in early childhood have yielded quite robust parenting effects (See Kochanska & Thompson 1997 for a review of this work). These examples illustrate the ways in which the field of family-impact studies has been growing in conceptual as well as methodological strength. Nevertheless we must be reconciled to the fact that there are important aspects of parenting that will never be revealed in studies that, by necessity, try to encapsulate parental characteristics into measurable clusters or traits. There are the memorable little socialization moments when the members of a parent/child dyad are, for some reason, especially attuned to one another—when the child, perhaps by virtue of having encountered a new and salient issue, is ready to both explain and listen. At such a moment, the parent may do or say something that makes a deep impression and can have a lasting influence. Conversely, a broken promise or a revealed deception may break the prevailing relationship of trust between the two, changing the nature of the influence that is possible between them. Such moments are unique to a dyad and may not be captured in socialization studies, even though our awareness of them is highlighted in biographies, autobiographies, and fiction.

I do not want to claim too much for the strength of parental influence in children's lives. Critics are right in pointing out that we have overemphasized these influences at the expense of other kinds of environmental influences. To what extent early childhood is a time of especially great plasticity, during which environmental inputs will be more likely to have a lasting influence than inputs later in life is an open question. Probably the answer will vary, depending on what domain of children's development we are talking about. (See for example, Neville's finding [Neville 1995] that the openness to influence by early experience differs between the semantic and syntactic language systems). Because parents are usually the ones who spend the most time with young children over extended periods of time, these questions of changing plasticity do matter in our efforts to understand the parental realm of influence. Still, parents are never the only source of influence on children, and as children grow older, they are more and more subject to the influence of peers, of schools and teachers, and of television. Also, there are the random events—a serious illness or accident, an unexpected success, a residential move, an environmental catastrophe—that can alter the trajectory of a child's life in ways that have little to do with parenting.

Of course, when we do see robust correlations between parent and child attributes, the question of the direction of effects arises at once. In making their argument that we may be seeing child-to-parent effects rather than the reverse, critics have relied heavily on the findings of behavior genetics[2], especially on studies of twins and adopted children. They have also relied on these findings to urge that nonparental aspects of a child's environment have greater weight than parental inputs in determining how a child will develop.

THE CHALLENGE FROM BEHAVIOR GENETICS

Some of the major findings of behavior genetics are powerful and require students of socialization to rethink some of their assumptions. Many of these findings are well known, and I do not summarize them in any detail here, but focus on the main lines of argument that bear on the issue of parenting effects.

The Focus on Variation

Behavior geneticists seek to understand the sources of variation in some human trait or characteristic. Their approach is to be distinguished from that of evolutionary psychologists, who seek to understand the genetic underpinnings of characteristics that are relatively uniform across a species.

There are important effects of both genes and environment that are overlooked in studies that focus on the variation of a characteristic within a given population. A human characteristic such as being born with two eyes is entirely genetic, yet its heritability would be computed as zero in a twin or adoption study since it is a characteristic that does not vary within the population studied. Similarly, there may be an environmental factor that affects the mean level of a characteristic—raising or lowering all scores to a similar degree—without greatly disturbing the rank-order of individuals on the characteristic. Thus, adoption studies have found that the correlation of adopted children's IQs with those of their biological parents can remain substantial, while at the same time the average IQ of the adopted children is higher than that of their natural parents, as though children receive an IQ bonus from being adopted into relatively stable, middle-class homes, while nevertheless continuing to differ from each other according to their genetic endowment. In a study of French children adopted at about the age of 5, it was found that the amount of increase in their IQs (assessed again in adolescence) was considerably greater for children adopted into affluent, well-educated families than for those adopted into underprivileged homes (Duyme et al 1999).

Secular trends illustrate the same point. The "Flynn effect" (Flynn 1987, 1999)—the substantial, monotonic rise in mean IQ scores over many decades in

[2]The term "behavior genetics" is a commonly used term for twin studies, adoption studies, and epidemiological studies of family resemblance. Currently, since molecular geneticists also study certain "behavioral" phenotypes in their relation to genes, the term quantitative genetics is sometimes used to distinguish studies that rely on statistical genetic analyses of family resemblance rather than on molecular gene identifiers. However the term "behavior genetics" is used here because it is more familiar to readers.

Western industrialized countries—is well known. There has been a substantial rise in the rates of smoking among American women in the last several decades, and the rates of drinking alcohol dropped during prohibition. These changes, of course, have occurred during periods of time that are much too short to reflect any genetic changes and they have occurred despite the fact that heritability estimates for IQ, drinking, and smoking have remained quite stable over the same time periods during which the average levels were changing. A similar phenomenon is seen in some migration studies, in which second-generation immigrants are on average quite different from their foreign-born grandparents, even on highly heritable traits such as height (Angoff 1988) or obesity (Price at all 1993, Ravussin et al 1994). The implication of these phenomena for parenting effects is this: There may have been secular changes in parenting—triggered perhaps by such things as changes in family structure or overall economic level—that have had widespread effects on children without affecting heritability estimates for the outcome characteristics being affected.

These powerful environmental effects are missed in the estimates of E (environment) derived from behavior genetics studies of twins and adopted children. Another way of putting this point is to note that high heritability of a trait does not imply that it is not also subject to the influence of environmental factors, or that it cannot be changed by alterations in environmental conditions. It is for this reason that, when comparing group means (by race, sex, or socioeconomic status) it is not legitimate to interpret any group differences in terms of estimates of genetic or environmental effects derived from quantitative behavior genetic studies.

Experimental Interventions with Parents If large-scale environmental events can change mean levels of a characteristic without greatly changing the rank-order of individuals, it follows that experimental interventions might do the same. It is difficult to change actual parenting practices through parent-training programs, and then to document that program-induced changes in parenting change the mean levels of children's characteristics. Such programs must be longitudinal, of course, and must have an untreated control group for comparison. Studies that intervene with the parents but do not simultaneously treat the children, and that have random assignment of families to treatment or control groups, are understandably rare, but several have clearly shown that when treatment is able to change parental behavior toward children in specified ways, the behavior of children changes correspondingly (e.g. Patterson & Forgatch 1995, Van den Boom 1994, Forehand et al 1980). Dishion et al (1992) were able to show that it was indeed the reduction of parent-to-child coercive behavior, brought about by a parent-training intervention with a randomly assigned experimental group, that produced declining levels of antisocial behavior in a group of aggressive children. An intervention program that changes the mean of a group of parents (and consequently, of their children's behavior as well) may or may not change the initial rank order of the children. Researchers commonly find that some parents are influenced more than others by an intervention, and some children are affected more than others by improvements in parental disciplinary or monitoring practices. These differential effects might either increase or decrease the range of outcome scores in the treatment group, depending on whether it was the initially better-functioning or poorly-functioning families who were most affected by the intervention. However, expanding or shrinking the range of outcome scores does not necessarily change the initial rank-order. The point here is that changes in a mean can be independent of any changes in rank order. Thus, changes in a mean can clearly demonstrate an environmental effect, quite apart from any correlational information (based on rank orders of individuals) that might be used to compute genetic or environmental effects in a genetic analysis. The environmental effects revealed by the mean change would go undetected in a correlational analysis.

The Claim for Substantial Genetic Effects

In traditional behavior genetic research, data from studies of twins and adopted children are used to compute heritability estimates (h^2), which are interpreted as estimates of the proportion of variance accounted for by genetic factors. Many such studies have yielded substantial heritability estimates. Identical twins have been found to be more similar to each other than are same-sex fraternal twins with respect to a wide range of characteristics, including susceptibility to certain diseases, intelligence, temperament, and a number of personality characteristics. The inference is that this must be due to their greater genetic similarity, because the important aspects of their environments—parenting received, neighborhood, presence of a same-age, same-sex sibling—are presumably equally similar for the two kinds of twin pairs. Adopted children have been found to be more similar to their biological parents than to their adoptive parents with respect to a selected set of characteristics for which researchers have been able to obtain measures from both biological and adoptive parents.

In a general sense, the behavior geneticists have made their case. Children's genetic endowments do clearly affect how individuals will develop—in comparison to other children—to a much greater extent than was thought to be the case during the years of the ascendancy of reinforcement learning theories and psychodynamic theories (the middle decades of the twentieth century.)

How substantial is this genetic contribution? Critics have argued that estimates derived from twin studies systematically overestimate the genetic contribution to a trait because identical twins in fact have more similar environments than do same-sex fraternal twins. Identical twins (compared with fraternals) are treated more similarly by their parents, spend more time together (and hence constitute a greater proportion of each other's social environment), and more often share the same friends (Dunn & Plomin 1986, Plomin et al 1988, Reiss et al 1999, Rowe 1983). Probably, the greater similarity in the environments of identical twins is not sufficiently strong to negate the findings on genetic effects, but it does weaken them. Very likely, it helps to account for the fact that heritability estimates are usually larger in twin studies than in adoption studies.

Of course, the genetic contribution might be expected to be greater for some human attributes than others. It appears to be more substantial for measures of intellectual abilities than for social or personality attributes. However, it is difficult to establish a reliable, generalizable estimate for any given trait. For one thing, estimates vary depending on the source of information for measuring a trait. When children's characteristics are assessed through parents' ratings, heritability estimates are often considerably higher than when assessments are derived from behavioral observations of the children, from children's self-reports, or from teacher ratings. It appears that parents see their children as more different from one another than other sources of information find them to be (a contrast effect). In a recent review of studies of the heritability of aggressive behavior, Cadoret and colleagues (Cadoret et al 1997) report a very wide range of heritability coefficients, (from near zero to over 0.70), with the higher figures coming from studies using parent report measures, and the lower ones from observational studies. Miles & Carey (1997), in a meta-analysis of 24 twin and adoption studies, report substantially greater values for h^2 based on parent reports than for those based on adolescent self-reports.

Especially important is the fact that the size of a heritability coefficient depends greatly on the range of both genetic and environmental factors in the population being studied (G. Patterson, under review). Estimates of the heritability of a given trait can change considerably when a new estimate is based on a culturally different population, or especially when a new estimate includes families from a wider range of subcultures and socioeconomic levels.

All this means that while the fact of a genetic contribution to human variability is not in doubt, the size of this contribution is indeterminate for any given trait. More specifically, the size of a heritability estimate cannot be generalized from the specific population—in its specific environment—assessed with the specific set of measures used in a given study.

Estimating the Size of Environmental Effects

In twin and adoption studies, estimates of the power of environmental factors are derived by adopting the additive assumption, i.e. by assuming that that the sources of variation in a trait can be separated into independent genetic (G) and environmental (E) components that together (along with error variance) add to 100% of the variance to be accounted for. On the basis of this assumption, the heritability coefficient can be subtracted from 100% to yield an estimate of the environmental contribution to variance. Estimating E in this way can be done without utilizing any direct measures of environmental factors. Obviously, if the estimates of h^2 are indeterminate, so are the estimates of E derived by subtracting h^2 from 100%.

The validity of the additive assumption has been widely challenged (Feldman & Lewontin 1975, Gottlieb 1995, Block 1995, Rose 1995, Turkheimer 1998) A number of these critiques have appeared in connection with the controversy over Hernstein & Murray's book *The Bell Curve* (1994), but they are equally pertinent to the current debate over parenting effects. If one adopts the additive assumption, it follows that when h^2 is large, the effects of all environmental factors—including parenting—must be correspondingly small. A major counter-argument has been that in fact, everything that human beings are or do must be a joint function of both their genes and their life experiences. The pathway between genes and phenotypes is a long one, with G and E being interwoven all along the way (see Elman et al 1996). The effects of genes depend on environmental triggers or enabling conditions, and the effects of different environments depend on the genetic characteristics of the individuals encountering an environment. When genes and environment act jointly, this can emerge empirically in behavior genetics studies in the form of either G × E correlations or G × E interactions. In estimating environmental effects, much depends on how these joint processes are handled (or not handled). Both kinds of coaction are considered below, but the main point here is that neither G × E covariances nor interactions fit into an additive model

Shared and Unshared Environmental Effects

In twin and adoption studies, once an overall estimate of E has been derived by subtracting h^2 from 100%, E can be further subdivided into two environmental components: Es (shared environment) and Eus (unshared environment). Once again, this can be done without utilizing direct measures of either. If fraternal twins are quite similar—more similar than would be expected from their shared genetics alone—or if adopted children are more similar to the parents or siblings in their adopted families than they are to adults or children in other households, this would imply an effect of their rearing environment, including of course the parents' child-rearing methods. Es is estimated from sibling similarities, and any variance still unexplained after the effects of G and Es have been accounted for are attributed to unshared environment or error of measurement.

An especially surprising finding emerging from the body of behavior genetics work has been that the effects of nonshared environment appear to be much greater than those of shared environment (see Plomin & Daniels 1987 and Plomin et al 1994). Recent estimates of nonshared environmental effects are much reduced when measurement error is taken into account (Rutter et al 1999). And a number of studies of social behavior or pathology have found substantial shared-environment effects. Nevertheless, shared environmental effects consistently emerge as small, and indeed are often reported as being close to zero (Plomin & Bergeman 1991). Adopted children do not appear to resemble their adoptive siblings or parents any more closely than they resemble children growing up in different households. Also,in many respects fraternal twins—or ordinary siblings, for that matter—do not greatly resemble each other or their parents.

Critics have urged that it is not valid to estimate environmental effects, either shared or unshared, without measuring them (Goodman 1991, Hoffman 1991, Rose 1995, Stoolmiller 1999, Patterson 1975). Recent work has involved designs in which both genetic and environmental factors have been directly assessed. For example, a group of leading behavior geneticists and leading students of parent-child interaction collaborated in a study comparing children of different degrees of genetic relatedness (twins, full siblings, half siblings, step siblings), in which parental child-rearing inputs were assessed through observations of parent-child interactions, as well as through parent and child reports (Reiss 1997, Reiss et al 1999, Hetherington et al 1999).

Relying on the additive assumption, these investigators have partitioned the variance in child adjustment outcomes into the three components: G, Es, and Eus, reporting substantial contributions from genetics. Effects of shared environment are variable, making clear contributions to some outcomes but not others; in general, though, they are considerably smaller than the substantial contributions from unshared environment. Unfortunately the design of this study confounds genetic similarities and family structures: the group in which siblings are most genetically unlike (stepsiblings) is also the group in which the two siblings receive the most discordant parenting (Hetherington et al 1999). It should be noted, too, that the range of environmental variation is restricted in this study. Thus, many of the reported findings of this important study are difficult to interpret.

The inference of behavior geneticists' claims concerning shared and unshared environments might be that children are not greatly affected by the characteristics of the household in which they are growing up. The weak shared-environment effects have been interpreted to mean that such factors as the parents' income or education, parental pathology, the level of harmony or conflict between the parents, or the neighborhood where the family lives must have little impact on how well the child will do in school, how socially competent the children will be, and so forth (Plomin et al 1994, Scarr & Grajek 1982).

These findings on weak shared-environment effects are startling, considering how consistently studies of parenting effects have found substantial relationships between these family characteristics and child outcomes. As an example, McLoyd (1998) made a strong case for the mediating role of parenting in the deleterious effects of poverty. In McLoyd's analysis, it emerges that the great stresses on impoverished parents—stresses stemming from the day-to-day struggle to find the resources to pay for food and rent, and the stresses of trying to cope with living in crowded housing and deteriorated, dangerous neighborhoods—bring about a weakening of parenting skills and a disorganization of family life. It is the deterioration of parenting, McLoyd found, that in its turn is responsible for many of the adjustment difficulties of children growing up in impoverished families. (See also Conger et al 1994 and Pettit et al 1997 for findings supporting this conclusion.)

It is difficult to reconcile findings such as these with the claim that the aspects of family environments that are shared by siblings do not affect their development. An obvious possibility is that while the family environment does have an effect on each child, its effects are different for different children. There probably was an unspoken assumption, in traditional socialization work, that the effects of shared environments would be to make siblings similar to one another. What the behavior geneticists are telling us is that any influences of familial circumstances—such as parental illness or health, economic prosperity or adversity, good or poor parenting—often function to make siblings different rather than similar. It is possible that a dysfunctional family environment may have effects on both members of a sibling pair, but that the effects are not such as to make siblings more alike, but indeed might function to make them more different. We know from Elder's work on effects of the Great Depression (Elder 1974) that when a father loses his job, the effects on the child will depend on the age and sex of the child at the time that this stressful event occurs. Even for same-sex twins, we can imagine that if they were adolescents at the time, one might react to a father's job loss by going out to get an after-school job to help support the family while the other might distance himself from the family and spend more time "hanging out" with friends. Both children would be affected by the change in the family environment, but differently.

Any familial or parental factors that serve to make siblings different rather than similar to one another are assigned, in behavior genetics, to the unshared rather than the shared environmental component when computing environmental effects. Behavior geneticists have never said that estimates of unshared environments did not include parent effects, but they argue that if parenting does have effects it must take one of two forms: parents must be treating different children in their families differently (or providing different environments for them), or different children in the same family who are exposed to similar parenting must react to the same parental inputs differently.

A considerable body of recent work has focussed on the question, What is it that makes siblings different from one another? (see Hetherington et al 1994). In these studies evidence is presented that siblings tend to join different peer groups and that siblings have considerably different experiences within the context of the sibling relationship itself. The question of how differently they are treated by their parents remains open. Studies done during a single time period often show that two siblings are treated differently by their parents (see summary by Brody & Stoneman 1994) However, in a longitudinal study Dunn found that parents were fairly consistent in how they treated children at a specific age. That is, a second child, when reaching the age of four, is treated in a similar way to the way his/her older sibling was treated at that age, even though the older sibling may now be receiving different treatment. Thus, over the span of the "growing up" years, different children in the same family received comparable treatment. This fact, of course, would be missed in any study that did not look for it longitudinally; the extent of differential treatment is likely to be overestimated in cross-sectional studies (except in the case of twins). Whether or not children actually are treated differently over the whole span of childhood, there is reason to believe that children's perceptions of how differently they are treated may be of considerable importance in children's development, so concurrent differences are important in their own right (Dunn & McGuire 1994).

In general, the exploration of siblings' unshared environments has been a productive and instructive enterprise. We now know that the environments of children growing up in the same family can indeed be different. But this does not solve the problem of how to interpret aspects of the environment that are truly shared, such as a parental illness, family income, parents' education, or the neighborhood where the family lives—factors that have an impact even when they function to make siblings different rather than alike. As noted above, behavior geneticists tend to conclude that, since it is clear that these aspects of environment are truly shared, they must not be having an effect because Es effects are negligible. As Plomin and colleagues say, "So often, we have assumed that the key influences on children's development are shared: their parents' personality and childhood experiences, the quality of their parents' marriage relationship, children's educational background, the neighborhood in which they grow up, and their parents' attitude to school or to discipline. Yet to the extent that these influences are shared, they cannot account for the differences we observe in children's outcomes" (Plomin et al 1994:23).

On the contrary, it seems plausible that these shared factors may indeed have powerful effects that do not show up in computations of shared environmental effects because of the requirement that only an environmental factor that makes siblings more similar can be called "shared." A behavior geneticists might say about the effect of a shared environmental factor that makes siblings different, "Oh, but we are calling those unshared effects." But to call an environmental input unshared even though it is experienced by all children in a family (e.g. a father's job-loss, a mother's depression, a move to a better neighborhood) is an unfortunate distortion of the simple meaning of the word "shared." We could see this as only a trivial matter of terminology choice, but it can lead to serious misunderstandings of behavior geneticists' findings. By definition, they have ruled out the possibility that a truly shared aspect of the environment could have a significant effect on at least one child, when the effects on different children are not the same.

When we deal with a shared environmental factor that impacts different children in the family differently, it could be argued—and behavior geneticists do so argue—that the effect stems from the fact that some children are more genetically vulnerable to an environmental event than others. In the usual computations of heritability, such an effect would then be assigned to the G component of the equation, rather than to the environmental one. Surely, it is equally plausible that both G and E are important here. Risk factors, such as poverty, a father's unemployment, or a mother's depression, are indeed environmental conditions that are shared by all the children in a family. In large population studies they will rightly emerge as having a negative impact on children, even though some children are more vulnerable to them than others. In the extreme case, we could imagine that in every two-child family, one of the children would show the deleterious effects of poverty and the other would not (perhaps because of genetic differences between them). Across many families, there would be a very powerful effect of poverty and it would be rightly identified as a strong risk factor, even though the shared environment effect would be computed at zero. The obvious danger here is that low estimates for Es can be interpreted as meaning that family environmental conditions that children share do not have an impact on their development, whereas in fact the opposite can be true, and often is.

The findings from behavior genetics on shared and unshared environments have profound implications for the way we think about child-rearing practices and their effects. For one thing, they focus attention on sibling differences. This is something that traditional research on child-rearing—almost always involving only one child per family—did not deal with. It should be noted that there is nothing about the findings of these traditional studies that is invalidated by their having studied only one child. The connections identified between the parental inputs to this child and the child's characteristics can be reliable, replicable ones, even though if we had studied a different parent-child pair in the same family we might have gotten a different constellation of parenting and outcomes. The picture emerging from aggregating data across a set of one-child cases is valid as well, though the findings are surely attenuated by the within-family sibling variation. Still, we get a less differentiated picture than the one that emerges from the study of siblings. Family systems theorists have alerted us to "niche-picking" by different children in a family—the effort of children to find distinctive roles. Evolutionary theorists have argued that there is natural competition among siblings for parental attention and other resources provided by parents. In short, there is reason to believe that there are forces motivating children to differentiate themselves from their siblings, and these may counterbalance, or transform, the effects of parental inputs that might otherwise function to make them the same. Of course, some of the differentiation between siblings can come directly from differential treatment by the parents, or it can stem from differential reactions by different children to the same parental inputs.

INTERPRETING PARENT-CHILD COVARIANCE

As noted above, quantitative geneticists have raised serious questions concerning the direction of effects when parental behaviors and child characteristics are found to be correlated. They point out that parent-child correlations could stem from genetic predispositions shared by parents and children that are directly transmitted from one generation to the next. In addition, evocative covariance occurs when children with different genetic predispositions elicit correspondingly different reactions from their parents. Thus, when a child is predisposed to be resistive or distractible and does not pay attention to the parent, the parent reacts by becoming more authoritarian, whereas a cooperative child will evoke a different reaction. (See Ge et al 1996, which shows clearly how the parenting by adoptive parents is affected by the predispositions of their adopted children.) Active covariance occurs when children select from a range of potential environmental influences only certain features with which to engage—certain TV programs, certain friends, certain sports—presumably on the basis of their own predispositions. Although children do not have the freedom to choose their parents, they do have some power to select which aspects of parental inputs they will attend to. Children with different genetic predispositions no doubt react differently to the same parental input, depending either on what they attend to, how they interpret their parents' actions, or what behavioral predisposition of their own has been triggered. In twin and adoption studies, all these forms of covariance between parent and child are thought to imply that genetics—either the child's own or the genes shared with parents—are driving the parental behaviors. For these reasons, it has seemed reasonable, in behavior genetic analyses, to assign parent-child covariances to the genetic component in the G + E = 100% equation.

I would argue that to assign parent-child covariance to G systematically underestimates the strength of parenting effects. It does so by ignoring the feed-back loop whereby parents, in reacting to a given child's distinctive input, reciprocate with counter influences of their own.

The fact that parents respond differently to children with different predispositions is not in doubt, and it has been one of the contributions of behavior genetics to bring this fact into the foreground of our thinking. Socialization researchers, too, have for some time been centrally aware of this issue and in the past several decades have by no means ignored the problem of direction of effects. A great deal of effort has been devoted to examining the processes whereby parents and children influence one another. The predominant modern viewpoint among students of socialization is an interactionist one, in which it is assumed that in any ongoing relationship, each member of an interacting pair is a significant feature of the other's environment to which each must adapt. In addition, it has become clear that the developmental level of a child is a powerful determiner of what kind of socialization inputs a parent will provide and what kind of receptiveness, resistance, or negotiation the child will bring to a parent-child encounter. We cannot expect to find generalizations about the nature and effects of specific parent/child interactions that will span all the ages and stages of a child's development.

From an interactionist perspective, the idea that in a long-standing relationship such as the one between a parent and child, the child would be influencing the parent but the parent would not be influencing the child is absurd. While it is entirely reasonable to assign the child's part in parent-child covariance (i.e. evocative effects) to the genetic component, it is not reasonable to assign the reciprocal parent contribution to the child's genetics. The parent's response is surely a function not only of the child's initiative but also of the parent's genetics, learned modes of behavior, perceptions of the child's needs and characteristics, and socialization objectives. And, just as surely, the parent's response to the child's initiatives is a central element in the child's environment. Thus, to assign the whole of parent-child covariance to G is surely to overestimate G and underestimate E.

A recent study from the Rutter-Plomin research group in London (O'Connor et al 1998) beautifully identifies the contributions of correlated G and E factors to developmental outcomes. Using longitudinal data from the Colorado Adoption Study, these researchers identified two groups of adoptees: one at genetic risk for anti-social behavior (i.e. a history of anti-social behavior in the biological mother) and the other not at risk. At several points during the adoptees' childhood, both the children's characteristics and the adoptive parents' child-rearing methods were assessed. Findings were that children carrying a genetic risk for antisocial behavior were more likely to receive negative socialization inputs from their adoptive parents—an evocative effect. But parental negative behavior made an independent contribution to children's externalizing, over and above the children's genetic predispositions.

This study illustrates what an interactionist perspective would lead us to expect: Parent-child covariance reflects the reciprocal effects of both parent and child inputs to a relationship. The issue here is not to compare G and E effects to see which is stronger. Instead, it is to explore how they intersect or how one mediates the effect of the other. Such issues remain largely unexplored. The relative strength of each contribution is difficult to assess and is almost entirely unknown in the large body of research literature on within-family socialization. The study by O'Connor et al illustrates the futility of efforts to compartmentalize the variance in children's characteristics into separate G and E components without getting independent measures of each. What this study shows is that G and E operate jointly to produce an outcome.

THE INTERACTION OF GENETIC AND ENVIRONMENTAL FACTORS

Interactions are found when a given environment has different effects on an organism, depending on the organism's genetic traits. Interactions are also seen when organisms with a given set of genetic traits react in one way under one set of environmental conditions, but another way under different environmental conditions. Plant biologists are able to point to dramatic examples, such as when there are two genetic strains of a grain, and strain 1 grows taller than strain 2 at high altitudes and shorter than strain 2 at low altitudes.

G × E Interactions in Animal Studies

A careful review of animal studies that looked for G × E interactions (Plomin 1986) reported that though interactions were sometimes found, they were not consistent within or across studies and accounted for only a small portion of variance. Since that review, some progress has been made in the difficult enterprise of mapping the complex processes that intervene between genotype and phenotype, and recently there has been some success in uncovering interactions with respect to these better-defined processes. In several mammalian species, it is now known that there are genetic factors underlying variation in "reactivity," that is, in the tendency to become emotionally aroused and fearful. Different levels of reactivity in rats are associated with both neuroendocrine and behavioral functioning (Caldji et al 1998, Liu et al 1997). Reactive animals appear jittery and hesitate to explore novel environments. In Rhesus monkeys, a gene has been isolated one of whose alleles is associated with the emergence of a reactive temperament (Suomi 1999). It has been found that young animals carrying the "reactive" allele are particularly vulnerable to variations in early rearing experience. If they are subjected to maternal deprivation during their first six months (reared with peers but no adult females) their neuroendocrine functioning is affected and they display a variety of pathological symptoms into adulthood, including incompetence in social interactions, low status in peer groups, and incompetence in mothering their own offspring (Suomi 1997). By contrast, young animals who do not carry the genetic risk factor are much less affected by maternal deprivation. In current work, genetically reactive newborn monkeys are being cross-fostered to non-reactive mothers, and preliminary observations indicate that calm mothering does indeed buffer them from the development of strongly reactive behavior. Cross-fostering work with rodents is also showing the positive effects of rearing genetically at-risk infants by a nurturant mother (Anisman et al 1998).We see here that the effects of a genetic predisposition are strongly seen under one set of environmental (rearing) conditions but not another.

G × E Interactions in Adoption Studies

Of course it is not possible to carry out systematic experiments of this sort with humans, but quantitative genetic studies can be used to test for G × E interactions. However, in such studies it is no longer possible to bypass measures of the environment and estimate E effects only as a residual after G effects have been estimated and subtracted out. Instead, there must be direct measures of both G and E. In most twin studies, the environments of twin pairs are too homogeneous to permit good estimates of G × E interactions, and there are difficulties in interpreting the differences between identical and fraternal twins in interaction terms. As Plomin said, " . . . it is difficult if not impossible to use the twin design to estimate the overall contribution of genotype-environment interaction to phenotypic variance" (Plomin 1986:96).[3] Since that time, there have been some innovations in utilizing twin studies to study interactions. One method is to use one twin's characteristic as an index to the co-twin's genetic risk; when the two are not highly concordant for the trait, their respective environments can then be examined for clues as to the origins of their non-genetic differences. Another method is simply to compare the heritability estimates found in two different environments.

In studies of adopted children, adoptive families vary with respect to the kind of environments they provide (though the range of environmental variation is usually consistently narrower than in unselected populations), and interactions can be effectively studied. In a large-scale study of adopted children in Finland (Tienari et al 1994), children with a schizophrenic biological parent were contrasted with adopted children who did not carry this genetic risk factor. It was found that the at-risk children were more likely to develop a range of psychiatric problems, but only if they were adopted into dysfunctional adoptive families. A study of adopted children whose biological parents did or did not have a history of criminality (Bohman 1996) yielded similar results: Among adoptees who carried a risk factor from their biological parents, those who had been adopted into dysfunctional homes were over three times more likely to become petty criminals than those whose adoptive parents had provided a stable, supportive environment.

These findings from adoption studies are consistent with studies of cross-generational transmission of psychiatric disorders (Ge et al 1996, Downey & Walker 1992). These studies point to a mediating role of parenting: Children whose parents suffer from a psychiatric disorder are usually no more likely than children with normal parents to develop psychiatric disorders, unless the children are exposed directly

[3]In studies of twins reared apart more variation in environments is of course usually present but the Ns for such studies are small and environmental information fragmentary.

to harsh parenting and/or an otherwise dysfunctional family environment by the parents who are rearing them.

Taken together, these studies indicate that genetic risks may or may not become manifest, depending on the quality of the parenting children receive. In other words, whatever genetic risks a child carries can require an environmental trigger to emerge into phenotypic expression. Well-functioning parents can buffer children against the emergence of negative genetic potentials.

Studies of Interactions with Temperament

It is possible to approximate the study of G × E interactions even when no direct information on children's genetics is available. Since several dimensions of temperament are known to have a significant genetic component,[4] researchers have identified children with different temperaments, and studied how they differ in the way they interact with their parents and in the impact parental inputs have on them. Children's temperamental characteristics appear to set the stage for the kind of bi-directional processes that will emerge between them and their parents (Collins et al 1999). Evidence has been emerging that a given parental practice can have different effects on children with different temperaments. Kochanska (1995, 1997a) studied the development of conscience in young children. She reported that for shy, temperamentally fearful children, parental power-assertion does not appear to promote conscience development—gentler techniques are called for. But with bold assertive children, effective parenting involves firmness, along with maternal responsiveness and the formation of a close emotional bond with the child. In a similar way, it has been found that for children who are initially difficult, impulsive, and/or resistive, parental firmness and restrictiveness are more important ingredients in preventing the subsequent development of externalizing behavior than is the case for children with easier temperaments (Bates et al 1998). Other studies finding interactions between children's temperament and parenting effects are those by Belsky et al (1997) and Deater-Deckard & Dodge (1997).

In Plomin's (1986) review of the studies on G × E interactions in children that were available at that time, significant interactions were found to be quite rare. It is possible at this time to be more positive—though guardedly so—concerning the prevalence and power of these interactions. They may be more prevalent with respect to personality dimensions and psychopathology than they are with respect to cognitive dimensions, but they obviously cannot be detected by using the traditional additive approach to partitioning variance between G and E. Indeed, the presence of interactions constitutes strong evidence against the validity of this approach. In molecular genetics, it is axiomatic that interactions are the rule, not the exception and that efforts to partition variance into the two traditional components are counterproductive.

[4]Temperament is currently defined as " . . . constitutionally based individual differences in reactivity and self-regulation . . . " (Rothbart & Ahadi 1994:54).

OVERVIEW

Behavior genetics studies have made substantial contributions to our understanding of the factors that underlie the variation among children in their intellectual and personality characteristics. Studies of twins and adopted children have shown beyond reasonable doubt that a wide range of children's attributes are influenced substantially by the genes they inherit from their biological parents. These studies first began to appear in the 1930s, and work done since that time has continued to confirm the power of genetic factors. The precise magnitude of the genetic contribution to a given trait, however, has proved to be difficult to establish: Heritability estimates vary widely, and indeed there is no reason to expect that there exists any one valid number for any given trait. Instead, heritability inevitably depends on the range of variation within a given sample being studied, and on the socio-cultural milieu in which the studied population lives. No single estimate can ever be taken as definitive.

I have argued that when genetic factors are strong, this does not mean that environmental ones, including parenting, must be weak. The relation between the two is not a zero-sum game, and the additive assumption is untenable. There are environmental factors that can affect a group or population without greatly rearranging the rank order of individuals within that group. In such a case, estimates of heritability can remain high while at the same time powerful environmental forces are at work. For this reason, it is not legitimate to extrapolate G or E estimates derived from a behavior genetic analysis to differences between groups (e.g. between races, social classes, or genders) that differ in their environmental milieu.

Experimental interventions have been designed to change children's behavior by means of changing the child-rearing practices of their parents. These intervention programs have amply demonstrated that parenting does have direct effects on how children behave, both inside and outside the home. When families are randomly assigned to an intervention group, the children show a reduction in problem behaviors by comparison with an untreated control group, and these effects are clearly independent of any genetic contribution to the outcome behavior being studied. Equally important is the presence of interactions between genes and environment, such that an environmental trigger is needed to evoke a genetic predisposition. Included here would be instances in which competent, supportive parenting protects a child from developing a dysfunction for which he or she is genetically predisposed. Such interactions have been largely ignored in traditional behavior genetic studies. What I argue here is that while the contribution of genetic factors to children's characteristics has been solidly documented in behavior genetics work, the contribution of environmental factors as derived from these studies has not.

A crucially important contribution of behavior genetics has been to draw our attention to the unlikeness of siblings. While we may have been marginally aware of sibling disparities, the traditional studies of childhood socialization included only one child per family, and there was an implicit assumption that parents treated their various children much alike and that the effects of what they did would be similar for all their children. We must now seriously reexamine these assumptions. We now know that the correlations between siblings with respect to many of their characteristics are very low—indeed, sometimes lower than their genetic relatedness would predict. Is the unlikeness of siblings due to their being treated differently by their parents? To some extent, yes, though findings are not consistent across studies. What the behavior geneticists have shown is that the genetic predispositions of different children often drive the responses of parents, determining to some degree the kind of parenting a child will receive. Understandably then, behavior geneticists have assigned correlations between parent and child behaviors to the child's genetics, but I argue that this is a mistake, in that it ignores the return feed-back loop whereby a parent, whose behavior has been triggered by the child, responds with actions which in their turn influence the child. To ignore this reciprocal influence is to seriously underestimate parenting effects.

The unlikeness of siblings continues to be something we do not fully understand. It has been interpreted to mean that aspects of environment which siblings share—amount of inter-parental conflict, good or poor neighborhoods, poverty or affluence, level of parental education or the "cultural" level of the home environment, household organization or disorganization, the amount of good humor characterizing the family atmosphere—all these things must have very little influence on children's development. This interpretation flies in the face of the large body of research on risk factors, which repeatedly finds strong relationships between these aspects of family functioning and children's outcomes. I argue that the risk-factor findings are indeed valid, but that they need not have the same effects on all children in a family nor function to make siblings more alike. It begins to seem likely that there are strong factors pushing siblings toward differentiation from one another, including perhaps competition for parental attention or other resources, "niche picking," counteridentification, and differential perceptions of the sibling relationship on the part of the participants in it. Such factors could function as counter forces, working against parental inputs that might otherwise make siblings more alike. But this is speculation. Much remains to be learned about this complex matter.

Many factors other than parents' actions influence how children grow and develop. As children grow beyond the preschool years, they are exposed more and more to other adult socialization agents (teachers, coaches) and, of course, to individual friends and larger peer groups. Within the matrix of factors that affect children's development, it is clear that parenting effects are real, though they often combine with genetic effects in influencing an outcome. Along with many other students of these phenomena, I urge that we give up the effort to partition the causal factors influencing children's development into two separate "nature" and "nurture" components, and that we abstain from asking ourselves which is more important. The two are inextricably interwoven all along the pathway from birth to maturity. So be it. Let us not underestimate either, but concentrate on the ways in which they function jointly.

ACKNOWLEDGMENTS

During the time I have been working on this chapter, I have also been participating with four colleagues in writing a closely related paper. These colleagues are W Andrew Collins, E Mavis Hetherington, Lawrence Steinberg, and Marc Bornstein. I gratefully acknowledge their help in searching out references and the clarifying value of our discussions. Others who have been helpful in providing materials for this chapter are Michael Rutter, Andrew Heath, Gerald Patterson, Stephen Suomi, Rich Weinberg, Megan Gunnar, John Flavell, Grazyna Kochanska, Robert Cairns, and Tom Dishion.

Visit the Annual Reviews home page at www.AnnualReviews.org.

LITERATURE CITED

Angoff WH. 1988. The nature-nurture debate, aptitudes and group differences. *Am. Psychol.* 43:713–20

Anisman H, Zaharia MD, Meaney MJ, Merali Z. 1998. Do early-life events permanently alter behavioral and hormonal responses to stressors. *Int. J.Dev. Neurosci.* 16:149–64

Bates J, Pettit G, Dodge K, Ridge B. 1998. Interaction of temperamental resistance to control and restrictive parenting in the development of externalizing behavior. *Dev. Psychol.* 34:982–95

Baumrind D, Black AE. 1967. Socialization practices associated with dimensions of competence in preschool boys and girls. *Child Dev.* 38:291–327

Belsky J, Hsieh K, Crnic K. 1997. Mothering, fathering and infant negativity as predictors of boys' externalizing problems and inhibition. *Dev. Psychopathol.* 10:301–19

Block N. 1995. How heretability misleads about race. *Cognition* 56:99–128

Bohman M. 1996. Predispositions to criminality: Swedish adoption studies in retrospect. In *Genetics of Criminal and Anti-Social Behavior, Ciba Found. Symp. 194,* ed. GR Bock, JA Goode, pp. 99–114. Chickester/New York: Wiley. 283 pp.

Brody G, Stoneman Z. 1994. Sibling relationships and their association with parental differential treatment. See Hetherington et al 1994, pp. 129–42

Cadoret RJ, Leve LD, Devor E. 1997. Genetics of aggressive and violent behavior. *Psychol. Clin. N. Am.* 20:301–22

Caldji C, Tannenbaum B, Sharma S, Francis D, Plotsky PM, Meaney MJ. 1998. Maternal care during infancy regulates the development of neural systems mediating the expression of fearfulness in the rat. *Proc. Nat. Acad. Sci.* 95:5335–40

Collins WA, Maccoby EE, Steinberg L, Hetherington EM, Bornstein M. 1999. Contemporary research on parenting: the case for nature *and* nurture. *Am. Psychol.* In press

Conger RD, Elder GH. 1994. *Families in Troubled Times: Adapting to Change in Rural America.* Hawthorne, NY: Aldine

Conger RD, Ge X, Elder GH, Lorenz FO, Simons R. 1994. Economic stress, coercive family process, and developmental problems of adolescents. *Child Dev.* 65:541–61

Deater-Deckard K, Dodge K. 1997. Spare the rod, spoil the authors: emerging themes in research on parenting. *Psychol. Inq.* 8:230–35

Dishion TJ, Patterson GR, Kavanagh K. 1992. An experimental test of the coercion model: linking theory, measurement, and intervention. In *The Interaction of Theory and Practice: Experimental Studies of Interventions,* ed. J McCord, R Trembly, pp. 253–82. New York: Guilford. 29 pp.

Downey G, Walker E. 1992. Distinguishing family-level and child-level influences on the development of depression and aggression. *Dev. Psychopathol.* 4:81–96

Dunn J, McGuire S. 1994. Young children's nonshared experiences: a summary of studies in Cambridge and Colorado. See Hetherington et al 1994, pp. 111–28

Dunn J, Plomin R. 1986. Determinants of maternal behavior toward three-year-old siblings. *Br. J. Dev. Psychol.* 57:348–56

Duyme M, Dumaret AC, Stanislaw T. 1999. How can we boost IQs of "dull" children?: a late adoption study. *Proc. Nat. Acad. Sci.* In press

Elder GH. 1974. *Children of the Great Depression.* Chicago: Univ. Chicago Press. 400 pp.

Elman JL, Bates EA, Johnson MH, Karmiloff-Smith A, Parisi D, Plunkett K. 1996. *Rethinking Innateness: A Connectionist Perspective on Development.* Cambridge, MA: MIT Press

Feldman MW, Lewontin RC. 1975. The heritability hangup. *Science* 190:1163–68

Flynn JR. 1999. Searching for justice: the discovery of IQ gains over time. *Am. Psychol.* 54:5–20

Flynn JR. 1987. Massive IQ gains in 14 nations: what IQ tests really measure. *Psychol. Bull.* 101:171–91

Forehand R, Wells KC, Griest DL. 1980. An examination of the social validity of a parent training program. *Behav. Ther.* 11:488–502

Ge X, Conger R, Cadoret R, Neiderhiser J, Yates W, et al. 1996. The developmental interface between nature and nurture: a mutual influence model of child antisocial behavior and parent behavior. *Dev. Psychol.* 32:574–89

Goodman R. 1991. Growing together and growing apart: the non-genetic forces on children in the same family. In *The New Genetics of Mental Illness,* ed. R McGuffin, R Murray, pp. 212–24. Oxford: Oxford Univ. Press

Gottlieb G. 1995. Some conceptual deficiencies in "developmental" behavior genetics. *Hum. Dev.* 38:131–41

Harris JR. 1998. *The Nurture Assumption: Why Children Turn Out the Way They Do.* New York: Free Press. 462 pp.

Herrnstein RJ, Murray C. 1994. *The Bell Curve: Intelligence and Class Structure in American Life.* New York: Free Press

Hetherington EM, Reiss D, Plomin R, eds. 1994. *Separate Social Worlds of Siblings.* Hillsdale, NJ: Erlbaum. 232 pp.

Hetherington EM, Henderson SH, Reiss D. 1999. *Adolescent Siblings in Stepfamilies: Family Functioning and Adolescent Adjustment.* Monog. Soc. Res. Child Dev. In press

Hoffman LW. 1991. The influence of the family environment on personality: accounting for sibling differences. *Psychol. Bull.* 110:187–203

Kochanska G. 1995. Children's temperment, mothers' discipline, and security of attachment: multiple pathways to emerging internalization. *Child Dev.* 66:597–615

Kochanska G. 1997a. Multiple pathways to conscience for children with different temperaments: from toddlerhood to age five. *Dev. Psychol.* 33:228–40

Kochanska G. 1997b. Mutually responsive orientation between mothers and their young children: implications for early socialization. *Child Dev.* 68:908–23

Kochanska G, Thompson RA. 1997. The emergence and development of conscience in toddlerhood and early childhood. In *Parenting and Children's Internalization of Values,* ed. JE Grusec, L Kuczunski pp. 53–77. New York: Wiley

Liu D, Diorio J, Tannenbaum B. Cladji C. Francis D, et al. 1997. Maternal care, hippocampal glucocorticoid receptors and hypothalamic-pituitary-adrenal responses to stress. *Science* 277:1659–62

Loeber R, Dishion TJ. 1983. Early predictors of male delinquency: a review. *Psychol. Bull.* 94:68–99

Maccoby EE, Martin JA. 1983. Socialization in the context of the family: parent-child inter action. In *Handbook of Child Psychology,* Vol. 4, ed. PH Messen, EM Herrington, 4:1–102. New York: Wiley. 4th ed. pp.1–102

McLoyd VC. 1998. Socioeconomic disadvantage and child development. *Am. Psychol.* 53:185–204

Miles D, Carey G. 1997. Genetic and environmental architecture of human aggression. *J. Pers. Soc. Psychol.* 72:207–17

Neville HJ. 1996. Developmental specificity in neurocognitive development in humans. In *The Cognitive Neurosciences*, ed. M Gazzaniga, pp. 219–31 Cambridge, MA: MIT Press

O'Connor TG, Deater-Deckard K, Fulker D, Rutter M, Plomin R. 1998. Genotype-environment correlations in late childhood and early adolescence: antisocial behavioral problems and coercive parenting. *Dev. Psychol.* 34:970–81

Patterson GR. 1975. Multiple evaluations of a parent-training program. In *Applications of Behavior Modification*, ed. T Thompson, W Dockens, pp. 299–322. New York: Academic

Patterson GR, Bank LI. 1989. Some amplifying mechanisms for pathologic processes in families. In *Systems and Development: The Minnesota Symposium on Child Psychology*, ed. MR Gunnar, E. Thelen pp. 167–209. Hillsdale, NJ

Patterson GR, Forgatch M. 1995. Predicting future clinical adjustment from treatment outcome and process variables. *Psychol. Assess.* 7:275–85

Pettit GS, Bates JE, Dodge KA. 1997. Supportive parenting, ecological context, and children's adjustment: a seven-year longitudinal study. *Child Dev.* 68:908–23

Plomin R. 1986. *Development, Genetics, and Psychology*. Hillsdale, NJ: Erlbaum. 372 pp.

Plomin R, Bergman CS. 1991. The nature of nurture: genetic influences on "environmental" measures. *Behav. Brain Sci.* 14:1–15

Plomin R, Chipuer HM, Neiderhiser JM. 1994. Behavioral genetic evidence for the importance of nonshared environment. See Hetherington et al 1994, pp. 1–31

Plomin R, Daniels D. 1987. Why are children in the same family so different from each other? *Behav. Brain Sci.* 10:1–16

Plomin R, DeFries J, Fulker D. 1988. *Nature and Nurture During Infancy and Early Childhood*. Pacific Grove, CA: Brooks-Cole

Price RA, Charles MA, Pettit DJ, Knowler WC. 1993. Obesity in Pima Indians: large increases in post- World War II birth cohorts. *Am. J. Phys. Anthropol.* 92:473–79

Ravussin E, Bennett PH, Valencia ME, Schulz LO, Esparaz J. 1994. Effects of a traditional lifestyle on obesity in Pima Indians. *Diabetes Care* 17:1067–74

Reiss D. 1997. Mechanisms linking genetic and social influences in adolescent development: beginning a collaborative search. *Curr. Dir. Psychol. Sci.* 6:100–6

Reiss D, Hetherington EM, Plomin R, Howe GW, Simmens SJ, et al. 1995. Genetic questions for environmental studies: differential parenting and psychopathology in adolescence. *Arch. Gen. Psychol.* 52:925–36

Reiss D, Neiderhiser J, Hetherington EM, Plomin R. 1999 *The Relationship Code: Deciphering Genetic and Social Patterns in Adolescent Development*. Cambridge, MA: Harvard Univ. Press. In press

Rose R. 1995. Genes and human behavior. *Annu. Rev. Psychol.* 46:625–54

Rosenthal R. 1999. *Discussion on effect sizes at symposium on, "Does Child Care Quality matter?"* Presented at Biennial Meet. Soc. Res. Child Dev., April, Albuquerque, NM

Rothbart M, Ahadi S. 1994. Temperament and the development of personality. *J. Abnorm. Psychol.* 103:55–66

Rowe D. 1994. *The Limits of Family Influence: Genes, Experience, and Behavior.* New York: Guilford

Rowe D. 1983. A biometrical analysis of perceptions of family environment: a study of twin and singleton sibling kinship. *Child Dev.* 54:416–23

Rutter M, Silberg J, O'Connor T, Simonoff E. 1999. Genetics and child psychiatry: I. Advances in quantitative and molecular genetics. *Child Psychol. Psychol.* 40:3–18.

Scarr S. 1992. Developmental theories for the 1990's: development and individual differences. *Child Dev.* 63:1–19

Scarr S, Grajek S. 1982. Similarities and differences among siblings. In *Sibling Relationships: Their Nature and Significance Across the Lifespan*, ed. ME Lamb, B Sutton-Smith, pp. 357–82. Hillsdale, NJ: Erlbaum

Stoolmiller M. 1999. Implications of the restricted range of family environments for estimates of heritability and nonshared environment in behavior genetic adoption studies. *Psychol. Bull.* In press

Suomi SJ. 1999. A biobehavioral perspective on developmental psychopathology: excessive aggression and serotonergic dysfunction in monkeys. In *Handbook of Developmental Psychopathology*, ed. AJ Samaroff, M Lewis, S Miller. New York: Plenum. In press

Suomi SJ. 1997. Long-term effects of different early rearing experiences on social, emotional and physiological development in non-human primates. In *Neurodevelopmental Models of Adult Psychopathology*, ed. MS Kesheven, RM Murra, pp. 104–16. Cambridge: Cambridge Univ. Press

Tienari P, Wynne LC, Moring J, Lahti I, Naarala M, et al. 1994. The Finnish adoptive family study of schizophrenia: implications for family research. *Br. J. Psychiatry* 23(Suppl. 164):20–26

Turkheimer E. 1998. Heritability and biological explanation. *Psychol. Rev.* 105:1–10

Van den Boom DC. 1994. The influence of temperament and mothering on attachment and exploration: an experimental manipulation of sensitive responsiveness among lower-class mothers with irritable infants. *Child Dev.* 65:1457–77

The Role of Inheritance in Behavior

ROBERT PLOMIN

Inheritance plays a major role in behavior as shown by selection and strain studies for animal behavior and by twin and adoption studies for human behavior. Unlike simple Mendelian characteristics, genetic variance for behavioral dimensions and disorders rarely accounts for more than half of the phenotypic variance, and multiple genes with small effects appear to be involved rather than one or two major genes. Genetic research on behavior will be transformed by techniques of molecular biology that can be used to identify DNA sequences responsible for behavioral variation. However, the importance of nongenetic factors and the multigenetic control of behavior require new strategies to detect DNA markers that account for small amounts of behavioral variation.

BEHAVIOR IS A NEW FRONTIER FOR MOLECULAR BIOLOGY. IT is the most complex phenotype that can be studied because behavior reflects the functioning of the whole organism and because it is dynamic and changes in response to the environment. Indeed, behavior is in the vanguard of evolution for these very reasons. Genetic analysis of behavioral dimensions and disorders is especially difficult for three additional reasons. First, unlike characteristics that Mendel studied in the edible pea such as smooth versus wrinkled seeds, most behaviors and behavioral problems are not distributed in "either/or" dichotomies—we are not either smooth or wrinkled, psychologically. Second, unlike classic Mendelian disorders such as Huntington's disease that are caused by a single gene with little effect from other genes or environmental background, most behavioral traits appear to be influenced by many genes, each

The author is professor of human development in the Center for Developmental and Health Genetics, College of Health and Human Development, Pennsylvania State University, University Park, PA 16802.

with small effects. Finally, behavior is substantially influenced by nongenetic factors.

In this article, I will provide an overview of the results of quantitative genetic research on behavior with a focus on the multigenetic control of behavior and the magnitude of genetic influence and, second, will consider the implications of these findings for the application of molecular biology techniques to the investigation of behavior. But the question must be asked at the outset, why should scientists bother with behavior if it is so complex? The answer lies in the importance of behavior per se rather than in its usefulness for revealing how genes work. Some of society's most pressing problems, such as drug abuse, mental illness, and mental retardation, are behavioral problems. Behavior is also key in health as well as illness, in abilities as well as disabilities, and in the personal pluses of life, such as sense of well-being and the ability to love and work.

Although the effects of major genes and chromosomal abnormalities on behavior are sometimes studied, most genetic research on behavior employs the theory and methods of quantitative genetics. Quantitative genetics identifies genetic influence even when many genes and substantial environmental variation are involved. This theory emerged in the early 1900s as a resolution to the problem of how Mendelian laws of inheritance could be applied to quantitatively distributed complex characteristics, such as behavior. The essence of quantitative genetic theory is that Mendel's laws of discrete inheritance also apply to such complex characteristics if we assume that many genes, each with small effect, combine to produce observable differences among individuals in a population. Quantitative genetics also applies to behavioral differences among individuals dichotomized into affected and unaffected categories, as is typical in research on behavioral disorders.

Quantitative genetic research determines the sum of heritable genetic influence on behavior, regardless of the complexity of genetic modes of action or the number of genes involved. However, quantitative genetics does not tell us which genes are responsible for genetic influence. An exciting direction for genetic research on behavior is the identification of genes responsible for genetic variance on behavior, the theme of the second half of this article. In the first half of the article, I review results of quantitative genetic research on animal and human behavior. I hope to provide an overview that will be useful for researchers outside the field who might be interested in the role of inheritance in behavior. For details concerning the methods and results of animal and human behavioral genetic research, see (*1*).

Animal Behavior

Applied behavioral genetics began thousands of years ago when animals were bred for their behavior as much as for their morphology. The results of such artificial selection can be seen most dramatically in differences in behavior as well as physique among dog breeds, differences that testify to the great range of genetic variability within a species and its effect on behavior. Selection studies in the laboratory still provide the most convincing demonstrations of genetic influence on behavior. The results of two selection studies in mice, the favorite mammalian organism of behavioral geneticists, are depicted in Fig. 1. In one of the longest mammalian selection studies of behavior, replicated high and low lines were selected for activity in a brightly lit open field, an aversive situation thought to assess emotional reactivity (*2*). After 30 generations of selection, a 30-fold difference exists between the activity of the high and low lines, and there is no overlap between them. Similar results have been found for most mouse behaviors subjected to selection in the laboratory, such as alcohol sensitivity (*3*), preference, and withdrawal; various types of learning; exploratory behavior; nest building; and aggressiveness. Many behaviors of rats and *Drosophila* have also responded to selective breeding (*1*).

In addition to providing dramatic evidence of the existence of genetic influence on behavior, two other implications can be drawn from the results of these selection studies. The first concerns the magnitude of the genetic effect as measured by statistical tests. Heritability is a descriptive statistic that estimates the extent to which observed variability is due to genetic variability. In selection studies, heritability estimates derived from the magnitude of the response to selection are nearly always less than 50%. Even though genetic influence of this magnitude can result in major differences between selected lines after just a few generations of selection, most behavioral variability is not genetic in origin.

The second implication of these results is that many genes appear to affect behavior. Despite intense selection pressure, the response to selection continues unabated during the course of most selection studies of behavior. For example, in the study of open-field activity in Fig. 1, although the low-active lines have reached the bottom limit of zero activity scores, the high lines show no sign of reaching a selection limit, even after 30 generations of selection. If only one or two major genes were responsible for genetic effects on these behaviors, the relevant alleles would be sorted into the high and low lines in a few generations. The steady divergence of selected lines provides the best available evidence that many genes affect behavior.

Other genetic methods used to investigate animal behavior are family studies and studies of inbred strains. Family studies assess the sine qua non of transmissible genetic influence, the resemblance between genetically related individuals. They also provide test

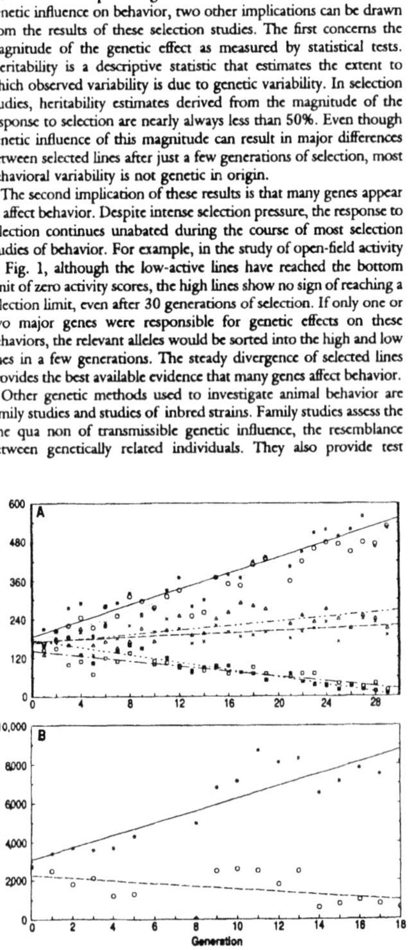

Fig. 1. Two selection studies of mouse behavior. (**A**) Mean open-field activity scores during two 3-min test periods for six lines of mice: two selected for high open-field activity [H1 (•) and H2 (O)], two selected for low open-field activity [L1 (⊠) and L2 (□)], and two randomly mated within line to serve as controls [C1 (X) and C2 (Δ)]. Data reported by (*2*). (**B**) Sleep time (loss of righting response after ethanol injection) for two lines of mice: one selected for long sleep times (•) and one selected for short sleep times (O). Data reported in (*3*).

crosses that can be used to explore hypotheses of single-locus transmission. Hundreds of single-locus mutations have been found that result in neurological defects. For example, there is a gene responsible for head shaking and rapid circling in "waltzer" mice. However, normal behavioral variability has not shown the effects of one major gene.

Inbred strains are created by mating brother to sister for at least 20 generations. This severe inbreeding eliminates heterozygosity and results in animals that are virtually identical genetically. Behavioral differences between inbred strains reared under the same laboratory conditions can be ascribed to genetic differences. Similar to the results of selection studies, comparisons among inbred strains point to significant genetic influence on most behaviors that have been examined (*1*). Also in line with selection studies, estimates of the magnitude of genetic influence from comparisons among inbred strains indicate that, although substantial, genetic factors do not explain the majority of the variance in behavioral characteristics. Crosses and backcrosses between inbred strains and their progeny have been used to find patterns of inheritance consistent with single-gene transmission, but this approach in fact has little power to discriminate single-gene from multiple-gene transmission.

A powerful strategy to uncover major-gene effects in animal behavior is the recombinant inbred (RI) strain method (*4*). RI strains are different inbred strains that were derived from separate brother-sister pairs from the same genetically segregating F_2 generation (crosses among hybrid offspring of two inbred strains). They are called RI strains because parts of chromosomes from the parental strains have recombined in the F_2 generation from which the RI strains were derived. If a single gene is responsible for a behavior that differs between the two parental strains, half of the RI strains should be like one parent and half like the other. In other words, there should be no intermediate phenotypes if just one locus is involved, because each RI strain will be homozygous for the allele of either one or the other parental strain. Behaviors studied in RI strains show no single-gene effects; a few, but only a few, major-gene effects have been suggested (*1*).

Human Behavior

For human behavior, no quantitative genetic methods as powerful as selection or inbred strain studies exist. Human behavioral genetic research relies on family, adoption, and twin designs. As in studies of nonhuman animals, family studies assess the extent of resemblance for genetically related individuals, although they cannot disentangle possible environmental sources of resemblance. That is the point of adoption studies. Genetically related individuals adopted apart give evidence of the extent to which familial resemblance is due to hereditary resemblance. Twin studies are like natural experiments in which the resemblance of identical twins, whose genetic identity can be expressed as genetic relatedness of 1.0, is compared to the resemblance of fraternal twins, first-degree relatives whose coefficient of genetic relatedness is 0.50. If heredity affects a behavior, identical twins should be more similar for the behavior than fraternal twins. As in studies of nonhuman animals, family, adoption, and twin studies can be used to estimate the magnitude of genetic influence as well as its statistical significance. For example, for height, an exemplar of a complex quantitative trait, correlations for first-degree relatives are 0.45, where reared together or adopted apart, and identical and fraternal twin correlations are 0.90 and 0.45, respectively. These results suggest that heritability, the proportion of phenotypic variance that can be accounted for by genetic factors, is 90% for height.

Below I review results of family, twin, and adoption research on the role of inheritance in human behavior, emphasizing the focal areas of cognitive abilities and disabilities, personality, and psychopathology.

Cognitive abilities and disabilities. One of the most studied traits in human behavioral genetics is general cognitive ability (IQ). In more than 30 twin studies involving more than 10,000 pairs of twins, identical and fraternal twin correlations averaged 0.85 and 0.60, respectively (*5*). The IQ correlation for first-degree relatives living together is about 0.40; for adopted-apart first-degree relatives, the correlation is about 0.20; and for adoptive parents and their adopted children, the correlation is about 0.20. These results, and model-fitting analyses that incorporate all of the data on IQ, are consistent with heritabilities of about 50% (*6*). The error surrounding this estimate may be as high as 20%, so we can only say with confidence that the heritability of IQ scores is between 30 and 70%. Nonetheless, even if the heritability of IQ scores is at the bottom of this range, it is a remarkable finding. To account for 30% of the variance of anything as complex as IQ scores is a remarkable achievement.

One direction for research on IQ is to trace the unfolding of genetic influence during development (*7*). For example, for 15 years, my colleagues and I have been engaged in a prospective longitudinal adoption study of over 200 adoptive and 200 matched nonadoptive families in which adopted and nonadopted children are studied yearly (*8*). For IQ, model-fitting analyses indicate that heritability increases steadily from infancy to the early school years (*9*) and also suggest that genetic effects on IQ during childhood are highly correlated with genetic effects on IQ in adulthood (*10*).

Specific cognitive abilities such as verbal ability and spatial ability show as much genetic influence as IQ; some types of memory ability appear to be less influenced by heredity than other specific cognitive abilities (*11*). Measures of academic achievement also show genetic influence, and recent multivariate research suggests that genetic effects on academic achievement tests correlate highly with genetic effects on cognitive abilities (*12*). Surprisingly, there are no twin or adoption studies of mental retardation.

There is no evidence for major-gene effects on normal variation in general or specific cognitive abilities. For example, earlier reports of sex linkage for spatial ability have not been confirmed (*13*). Common cognitive problems such as reading disability have yielded no clear major-gene effects. For example, a 1983 report of chromosome 15 linkage for reading disability (*14*) is in doubt—only 1 in 21 families now shows a near significant lod score (logarithm of the likelihood ratio for linkage) (*15*). However, as in mouse research, many rare genes have been identified that drastically disrupt normal cognitive development. Of the more than 4000 single-gene effects cataloged for human beings, more than a hundred include lowered IQ scores as a clinical symptom (*16*). Although these recessive alleles may have devasting effects for homozygous individuals, they are rare and thus can account for only a minuscule portion of IQ variance in the population. For example, the fragile X marker, which appears to be a source of the excess of mild mental retardation in males (*17*), cannot account for much IQ variance in the population because its incidence is less than 1 in 1000 and many males with the fragile X marker do not show lowered IQ (*18*).

Personality. Twin and adoption studies that use personality questionnaires typically yield heritability estimates in the range of 20 to 50%. For example, identical and fraternal twin correlations are on average about 0.50 and 0.30, respectively. Activity level, emotional reactivity (neuroticism), and sociability-shyness (extraversion) have accumulated the best evidence for significant genetic influence (*19*). For example, four twin studies in four countries involving over 30,000 pairs of twins yield heritability estimates of about 50% for neuroticism and extraversion (*20*). Adoption studies of first-degree relatives suggest lower estimates of heritability for these traits than do twin studies—about 30% rather than 50%. This may be due to nonadditive genetic variance (especially higher order interaction among loci, called epistasis), which covaries completely for identical twins but contributes little to the resemblance of first-degree relatives (*21*).

For the past decade, my colleagues and I have conducted a large-scale behavioral genetic study in the last half of the life-span: a Swedish study of hundreds of pairs of identical and fraternal twins reared apart and matched twins reared together. The results of this study support the hypothesis of nonadditive genetic variance for personality and also suggest that heritability of these traits may be somewhat lower, about 30%, later in life (*22*). As in the case of cognitive abilities, there is no evidence for major-gene effects on personality.

Psychopathology. A third major domain of behavioral genetic research is psychopathology. In the past, most research focused on schizophrenia; attention has now turned to the affective disorders, which include major depressive disorder and manic-depressive disorder.

In 14 studies involving over 18,000 first-degree relatives of schizophrenics, their risk was 8%, eight times greater than the base rate in the population (*23*). Twin and adoption studies suggest that familial resemblance for schizophrenia is due to heredity rather than to shared family environment. For example, the most recent twin study involves all male twins who were veterans of World War II (*24*). Twin concordances were 30.9% for 164 pairs of identical twins and 6.5% for 268 pairs of fraternal twins. Adoption studies of schizophrenia support the twin findings of genetic influence (*23*). Although these data suggest that inheritance plays a major role in schizophrenia, the same data also indicate that nongenetic factors are of critical importance as well. A risk of 30% for an identical co-twin of a schizophrenic far exceeds the population risk of 1%, but it is a long way from the 100% concordance expected if schizophrenia were entirely a transmissible genetic disorder. There is no way to explain such substantial discordance for identical twins for schizophrenia as currently diagnosed other than by nongenetic factors.

Genetic effects on schizophrenia appear to be independent of genetic effects on the affective disorders. Furthermore, unipolar depression may be distinct genetically from bipolar manic-depressive disorder (*25*). The most recent family study of unipolar depression involved 235 probands with major depressive disorder and their 826 first-degree relatives (*26*). Major depression was diagnosed for 13% of the male relatives and for 30% of the female relatives, which exceeds the base rate in the population. The familial risk for bipolar illness is lower, 6% in eight studies of 3000 first-degree relatives of bipolar probands, with no gender differences in risk, as compared with a risk of 1% in a control sample (*27*). Twin results for affective disorders suggest greater genetic influence than for schizophrenia, but adoption studies indicate less genetic influence (*28*). In the most recent adoption study, affective disorders were diagnosed in only 5.2% of biological relatives of affectively ill adoptees, although this risk was greater than the risk of 2.3% found in the biological relatives of unaffected adoptees (*29*).

Psychopathology was the first behavioral domain for which major-gene linkages were reported with restriction fragment length polymorphisms (RFLP) markers. In 1987, bipolar manic-depressive disorder was reported to be linked to a dominant gene on the short arm of chromosome 11 in an Amish pedigree of 81 individuals, 19 of whom were affected (*30*). However, the Amish results have essentially been withdrawn (*31*): Follow-up work on the original Amish pedigree yielded two new diagnoses of manic-depressive disorder, which reduced the evidence for linkage to nonsignificance, and an extension of the original pedigree also failed to replicate the original result. Manic-depression may be linked to the X chromosome in some families, despite the frequent occurrence of father-son transmission, which rules out a major X-linked gene for manic-depressive illness in the population (*32*).

For schizophrenia, linkage to a dominant gene on chromosome 5 was reported in 1988 for five Icelandic and two English families with a high incidence of schizophrenia (*33*). Several failures to replicate the linkage have been reported (*34*), and as yet no positive replication has appeared.

Molecular Biology and Behavior

This overview of behavioral genetic research suggests that genetic influence is nearly ubiquitous for both animal and human behavior. However, these same data lead to two additional conclusions with important implications for the application of molecular biology techniques to the investigation of behavior: Genetic influence on behavior appears to involve multiple genes rather than one or two major genes, and nongenetic sources of variance are at least as important as genetic factors. This suggests the need for molecular biology strategies that can detect DNA markers that account for small amounts of behavioral variation.

If this view is correct, current linkage studies—including the large-pedigree approach as well as the affected-sib-pair method (*35*)—will not succeed in identifying linkage because they can only detect major-gene effects in which one gene is largely responsible for a behavioral disorder. Linkage is a powerful strategy for identifying the chromosomal location of a disorder caused by a single gene that has its effect regardless of environmental or genetic background, as in Huntington's disease (*36*). However, replicated linkages have not been demonstrated for human behavior, despite claims for linkages in manic depression and schizophrenia. Attention has shifted to the possibility that certain families may have their own unique major gene responsible for a disorder (genetic heterogeneity). In this view, multiple-gene influence is seen in the population because of the concatenation of different major genes in different families. Failure to find major-gene effects on complex characteristics in plants and animals and the absence of major-gene linkages to date for human behavioral variation does not prove that linkages will not be found. Only a small portion of the genome and only a few families have been examined for such linkages. Linkages may be found during the coming decades because closely spaced markers are available for nearly all human chromosomes; however, this will also make it possible to exclude linkage for behavior. I predict that such exclusions will eventually provide the best evidence that human behavior and behavioral disorders are not due to major genes. This should not be interpreted to mean that genes do not affect human behavior; it only demonstrates that genetic influence on behavior is not due to major-gene effects.

An alternative hypothesis is that genetic influence on behavior is not due to a major gene in the population or in a family. That is, for each individual, many genes make small contributions toward behavioral variability and vulnerability. Nonetheless, some rare major-gene effects may be found in some families, just as hundreds of rare single-gene mutations have been found that cause neurological defects in mice and more than a hundred rare alleles are known for human beings that drastically lower IQ scores in affected individuals. This suggests an important principle: Although any one of many genes can disrupt behavioral development, the normal range of behavioral variation is orchestrated by a system of many genes, each with small effects.

Rare alleles that disrupt behavioral development are probably just the most easily noticed tip of the iceberg of genetic variability. It seems reasonable to expect that many more alleles nudge development up or down and do not show such striking single-gene effects on a few individuals. It is not the case that we are identical genetically with the exception of major mutational flaws: Many loci are polymorphic and many of these are likely to contribute to variability in behaviors as complex as cognitive abilities and in behavioral disorders as complex as schizophrenia.

Applications of molecular biology techniques to the study of behavior are unlikely to succeed if they need to assume that a major gene is largely responsible for genetic variation. Behavior is not too complex for molecular biology; strategies are needed to identify genes that account for a small amount of variance.

If this quantitative genetic view of behavior is correct, we need to find many tiny needles in the haystack. Research in plant genetics suggests that a very large number of genes with very small effects are responsible for genetic influence on complex characteristics. For example, the results of a study of associations between 20 electrophoretic genetic markers and 82 quantitative traits in maize (37) can be summarized as follows: (i) Significant associations were found for each of the 82 quantitative traits; (ii) the maximum variance of any quantitative trait explained by a single marker was 16%; (iii) more than half of the significant associations accounted for less than 1% of the trait variance; (iv) only 5% of the marker loci accounted for more than 5% of the variance; and (v) in concert, the genetic markers predicted between 8 and 37% of the variance of a subset of 25 relatively independent traits, which is most of the genetic variance for these traits.

Such association studies may be useful in finding the needles in the haystack because sample sizes can be increased to provide sufficient power to detect associations that account for small amounts of variance. Association, usually called *linkage disequilibrium*, refers to covariation between allelic variation in a marker and phenotypic variation among individuals in a population. The use of genetic markers to study associations with complex traits is not new (38); the first association between genetic markers and quantitative traits was found more than 60 years ago (39). Many associations were reported even before the widespread use of RFLP markers (40). However, this approach is greatly enhanced by the increase in available markers that permits quantitative trait loci (QTL) interval mapping—appraisal of associations with many closely spaced RFLPs simultaneously by the use of the interval between markers rather than the markers themselves (41). With this method, six QTL were identified that together accounted for 58% of the variance of fruit mass in a backcross between a domestic tomato and a wild green-fruited tomato.

Research of this type uses crosses between inbred strains because their chromosomes have segregated as units broken up only slightly by recombination. As a result, a genetic marker indexes a region of millions of base pairs. In contrast, in outbred populations including humans, many generations of recombination have eliminated linkages between alleles on the same chromosome so that the range of a marker is limited to a very small stretch of DNA not broken up by recombination, probably no more than a few hundred thousand base pairs. For this reason, trying to find associations between markers and human behavior is very much like trying to find needles in a haystack. Nonetheless, a blood marker (HLA A9) has been found that appears to be associated with paranoid schizophrenia (42). Perhaps because the marker accounts for only a small portion of variance, linkage studies have not yet found evidence for linkage between the marker and schizophrenia.

Instead of using random RFLPs to look painstakingly through the human genome, a more efficient initial strategy may be to screen candidate genes with known function, especially genes suspected to be involved in neurological processes, for their individual and joint contributions to behavior (43). For example, an association has recently been found between alcoholism and alleles of the aldehyde dehydrogenase locus (44). However, association studies of common disorders such as heart disease and diabetes indicate that this approach is not a panacea.

Although association studies using very large samples might begin to uncover some QTL, success in identifying all of the many genes responsible for genetic variance for a particular behavior is likely to depend on the development of new techniques. It may not be overly optimistic to expect such developments given the pace of advances in molecular biology (45). For example, it may be possible to use new modifications of subtractive hybridization (46) to identify genes that differ between groups or even between individuals, yielding a set of trait-relevant DNA sequences that could be used as markers in association studies. The human genome project is another example. One of the many benefits of the project will be the identification of more markers and genes that might play a role in genetic variation in behavior. In addition, the human genome project will no doubt foster technological spin-offs such as sequence-tagged sites which, with new developments in polymerase chain reaction techniques and automated sequencing equipment, make it possible to produce genetic markers from published sequence data without obtaining the DNA itself (47).

Conclusions

Just 15 years ago, the idea of genetic influence on complex human behavior was anathema to many behavioral scientists. Now, however, the role of inheritance in behavior has become widely accepted, even for sensitive domains such as IQ (48). Indeed, acceptance of genetic influence has begun to outstrip the data in some cases, such as alcoholism (49). For most domains of behavior, too few twin and adoption studies have been conducted to answer the basic question of whether genetic influence is significant. Only for a handful of behaviors is it possible to estimate effect size with reasonable certainty, estimates that one might expect to be prerequisite to exploring the relative importance of individual genes. More quantitative genetic research is needed, too, because such research can go well beyond the basic question of the relative importance of nature and nurture. For example, new developments include multivariate analyses of the genetic covariance among behaviors or between biology and behavior, consideration of age-to-age change as well as continuity of genetic effects as they unfold during development, and exploration of the interface with the environment (1).

An equally important conclusion from behavioral genetic research must be emphasized: Nongenetic sources of variance are important because genetic variance rarely accounts for as much as half of the variance of behavioral traits. That is, evidence for significant genetic influence is often implicitly interpreted as if heritability were 100%, whereas heritabilities for behavior seldom exceed 50%. Another conclusion with far reaching implications for molecular biology is the absence of evidence that genetic influence on behavior is primarily due to one or two major genes. It seems more reasonable to hypothesize that many genes each with small effect are involved.

If it is the case that behavioral variation involves many genes and much environmental influence, linkage analyses are unlikely to succeed in the population or even in a single family if they can only detect major-gene effects. New strategies are required that can isolate DNA markers associated with small amounts of variance. Quantitative genetic research will be important in this endeavor in order to assess the extent to which genetic variance accounts for phenotypic variance and the extent to which individual genes account for genetic variance.

In conclusion, the use of molecular biology techniques will revolutionize behavioral genetics, and the quantitative genetic perspective of behavioral genetics will transform our use of these techniques as we continue to explore the role of inheritance in the most complex of phenotypes, behavior.

REFERENCES AND NOTES

1. R. Plomin, J. C. DeFries, G. E. McClearn, *Behavioral Genetics* (Freeman, New York, 1990).
2. J. C. DeFries, J. C. Gervais, E. A. Thomas, *Behav. Genet.* **8**, 3 (1978).
3. G. E. McClearn, in *Aspects of Genetics in Paediatrics*, D. Barltrop, Ed. (Fellowship of Postdoctorate Medicine, London, 1976), pp. 31–39.
4. D. W. Bailey, *Transplantation* **11**, 325 (1971).
5. T. J. Bouchard, Jr., and M. McGue, *Science* **212**, 1055 (1981).
6. H. M. Chipuer, M. Rovine, R. Plomin, *Intelligence*, in press.
7. R. Plomin, *Development, Genetics, and Psychology* (Erlbaum, Hillsdale, NJ, 1986).
8. ______, J. C. DeFries, D. W. Fulker, *Nature and Nurture During Infancy and Early Childhood* (Cambridge Univ. Press, New York, 1988).
9. D. W. Fulker, J. C. DeFries, R. Plomin, *Nature* **336**, 767 (1988).
10. J. C. DeFries, R. Plomin, M. C. LaBuda, *Dev. Psychol.* **23**, 4 (1987).
11. R. Plomin, in *Advances in the Psychology of Human Intelligence*, R. Sternberg, Ed. (Erlbaum, Hillsdale, NJ, 1988), pp. 1–33.
12. L. A. Thompson, D. K. Detterman, R. Plomin, *J. Ed. Psychol.*, in press.
13. J. C. DeFries *et al.*, *Behav. Genet.* 9, 23 (1979).
14. S. D. Smith, W. J. Kimberling, B. F. Pennington, H. A. Lubs, *Science* **219**, 1345 (1983).
15. S. D. Smith, W. J. Kimberling, Y. Y. Shugart, P. S. Ing, B. F. Pennington, *Am. J. Hum. Genet.* **45**, A65 (1989).
16. V. A. McKusick, *Mendelian Inheritance in Man* (Johns Hopkins Univ. Press, Baltimore, MD, 8th ed., 1988).
17. R. L. Nussbaum and D. H. Ledbetter, *Annu. Rev. Genet.* **20**, 109 (1986).
18. D. M. Barnes, *Science* **243**, 171 (1989).
19. A. H. Buss and R. Plomin, *Temperament: Early Developing Personality Traits* (Erlbaum, Hillsdale, NJ, 1984); L. J. Eaves, H. J. Eysenck, N. G. Martin, *Genes, Culture and Personality* (Academic Press, New York, 1989).
20. J. C. Loehlin, *Am. Psychol.* **44**, 1285 (1989).
21. R. Plomin, H. M. Chipuer, J. C. Loehlin, in *Handbook of Personality Theory and Research*, L. A. Pervin, Ed. (Guilford, New York, in press).
22. N. L. Pedersen, R. Plomin, G. E. McClearn, L. Friberg, *J. Pers. Soc. Psychol.* **55**, 950 (1988); R. Plomin, N. L. Pedersen, G. E. McClearn, J. R. Nesselroade, C. S. Bergeman, *Psychol. Aging* **3**, 43 (1988).
23. I. I. Gottesman and J. Shields, *Schizophrenia: The Epigenetic Puzzle* (Cambridge Univ. Press, Cambridge, 1982).
24. K. Kendler and C. D. Robinette, *Am. J. Psychiatry* **140**, 1551 (1983).
25. S. G. Vandenberg, S. M. Singer, D. L. Pauls, *The Heredity of Behavioral Disorders in Adults and Children* (Plenum, New York, 1986).
26. T. Reich *et al.*, *J. Psychiatry Res.* **21**, 613 (1987).
27. J. P. Rice *et al.*, *Arch. Gen. Psychiatry* **44**, **441** (1987).
28. J. C. Loehlin, L. Willerman, J. M. Horn, *Annu. Rev. Psychol.* **39**, 101 (1988).
29. P. H. Wender *et al.*, *Arch. Gen. Psychiatry* **43**, 923 (1986).
30. J. A. Egeland, D. S. Gerhard, D. L. Pauls, J. N. Sussex, K. K. Kidd, *Nature* **325**, 783 (1987).
31. J. R. Kelsoe *et al.*, *ibid.* **342**, 238 (1989).
32. M. Baron, N. Risch, R. Hamburger, B. Mandel, S. Kushner, *ibid.* **326**, 289 (1987).
33. R. Sherrington *et al.*, *ibid.* **336**, 164 (1988).
34. J. L. Kennedy *et al.*, *ibid.*, p. 167; D. St. Clair *et al.*, *ibid.* **339**, 305 (1989); S. D. Detera-Wadleigh *et al.*, *ibid.* **340**, 391 (1989); compare W. F. Byerley, *ibid.*, p. 340.
35. D. E. Weeks and K. Lange, *Am. J. Hum. Genet.* **42**, 315 (1988).
36. J. F. Gusella *et al.*, *Nature* **306**, 234 (1983).
37. M. D. Edwards, C. W. Stuber, J. F. Wendel, *Geneticae* **116**, 113 (1987).
38. H. W. Kloepfer, *Ann. Eugenics* **13**, 35 (1946).
39. K. Sax, *Genetics* **8**, 552 (1923).
40. J. N. Thompson, Jr., and J. M. Thoday, *Quantitative Genetic Variation* (Academic Press, New York, 1979).
41. A. H. Paterson *et al.*, *Nature* **335**, 721 (1988).
42. P. McGuffin and E. Sturt, *Hum. Hered.* **36**, 65 (1986).
43. E. Boerwinkle, R. Chakraborty, C. F. Sing, *Ann. Hum. Genet.* **50**, 181 (1986).
44. D. W. Crabb, H. J. Edenberg, W. F. Bosron, T-K. Li, *J. Clin. Invest.* **83**, 314 (1989).
45. U. Landegren, R. Kaiser, C. T. Caskey, L. Hood, *Science* **242**, 229 (1988).
46. G. H. Travis and J. G. Sutcliffe, *Proc. Natl. Acad. Sci. U.S.A.* **85**, 1696 (1988).
47. M. Olson, L. Hood, C. Cantor, D. Botstein, *Science* **245**, 1434 (1989).
48. M. Snyderman and S. Rothman, *The IQ Controversy, the Media and Public Policy* (Transaction Books, New Brunswick, NJ, 1988).
49. J. S. Searles, *J. Abnormal Psychol.* 97, 153 (1988).

50. I thank J. C. DeFries, G. Gora-Maslak, and G. E. McClearn for their suggestions. Support for the Colorado Adoption Project (J. C. DeFries, D. W. Fulker, and R. Plomin, coinvestigators) was provided by the NIH (HD 10333, HD 18426, MH 43899) and the NSF (BNS 8806589). Research support for the Swedish Adoption/Twin Study of Aging (G. E. McClearn, J. R. Nesselroade, N. Pedersen, and R. Plomin, coinvestigators) was provided by the NIH (AG 04563) and the MacArthur Foundation Research Network on Successful Aging.

"Don't worry about it. It's probably just another one of those sociological experiments."

Journal of Personality and Social Psychology
1988, Vol. 54, No. 6, 1031-1039

0022-3514/88/$00.75

Personality Similarity in Twins Reared Apart and Together

Auke Tellegen
University of Minnesota

David T. Lykken
Departments of Psychology and Psychiatry
University of Minnesota

Thomas J. Bouchard, Jr., Kimerly J. Wilcox, and Nancy L. Segal
University of Minnesota

Stephen Rich
Department of Pathology and Laboratory Medicine and Institute of Human Genetics
University of Minnesota

We administered the Multidimensional Personality Questionnaire (MPQ) to 217 monozygotic and 114 dizygotic reared-together adult twin pairs and 44 monozygotic and 27 dizygotic reared-apart adult twin pairs. A four-parameter biometric model (incorporating genetic, additive versus nonadditive, shared family-environment, and unshared environment components) and five reduced models were fitted through maximum-likelihood techniques to data obtained with the 11 primary MPQ scales and its 3 higher order scales. Solely environmental models did not fit any of the scales. Although the other reduced models, including the simple additive model, did fit many of the scales, only the full model provided a satisfactory fit for all scales. Heritabilities estimated by the full model ranged from .39 to .58. Consistent with previous reports, but contrary to widely held beliefs, the overall contribution of a common family-environment component was small and negligible for all but 2 of the 14 personality measures. Evidence of significant nonadditive genetic effects, possibly emergenic (epistatic) in nature, was obtained for 3 of the measures.

Until recently, almost all knowledge regarding environmental and genetic causal influences on stable personality traits has come from studies of twins reared together. The findings have been both remarkable and puzzling. On the genetic side, regardless of the trait studied, the intraclass correlation for fraternal, or dizygotic (DZ), twins has approached .25; that for identical, or monozygotic (MZ), twins has approached .50 (Goldsmith, 1983; Nichols, 1978). Application of the simplest genetic model, the Falconer (1960) formula for heritability, [$h^2 = 2(R_{MZ} - R_{DZ})$], to those results yields a heritability of about .50. This leaves 50% of the variance to systematic environmental influences, measurement error, and temporal instability.

Particularly puzzling, and contrary to what many psychologists would predict, is the finding that almost none of the environmental variance is due to sharing a common family environment. Loehlin and Nichols (1976) reached this conclusion on the basis of personality data collected on a large National Merit Scholarship twin sample. Eaves and Young (1981) carried out an informative additional analysis of Extraversion–Introversion and Neuroticism scores from the same twin sample, using a biometric model similar to the one to be reported in this article. They fitted three models to the data. The first model allowed for unshared environment effects and additive gene effects. The second allowed for two environmental effects: shared family-environment effects and unshared environment effects, but no genetic effects. The third specified the joint effect of all three. The results were straightforward: The second model, which only specified environmental parameters, did not fit the data for either sex or for the two sexes considered jointly. The first model, which assumes no common family-environment effect, fit all three cases and was as capable of fitting both sexes simultaneously (with identical parameter estimates) as it was of fitting the results of each sex separately. Adding the common family-environment effect did not improve the fit of the third model over the first. These results essentially confirmed Loehlin and Nichols's (1976) earlier analysis.

Loehlin and Nichols (1976) carried out many additional analyses of their data. In particular, they attempted to identify the effects of systematic within-family variations. Because identical twins share all of their genes, any differences between them must be environmental in origin. By relating within-pair zygosity-group differences in experiences to personality differences, they could answer questions such as, "Do identical twins who were dressed alike turn out to be more similar in personality than identical twins who were not?" The results were essentially negative. Greater similarity in the twins' experiences could ac-

This research has been supported by grants from the University of Minnesota Graduate School, the Koch Charitable Foundation, the Spencer Foundation, the National Science Foundation (BNS-7926654), the Pioneer Fund, and the Harcourt Brace Jovanovich Publishing Company.

We thank the following people for the time and effort they have given to testing the twins: Margaret Keyes, Jeff McHenry, Elizabeth Rengel, Susan Resnick, Joy Fisher, Jan Englander, and Ann Riggs. We are indebted to our colleagues and collaborators on the Minnesota Study of Twins Reared Apart project, Elke Eckert and Leonard Heston for their help and advice. We owe special thanks to our colleagues, Greg Carey and Matt McGue, for their valuable biometric advice and assistance. We also thank Jack Darley for his resolute and dedicated support and the Minneapolis War Memorial Blood Bank, Herbert Polesky, Director, for the blood testing.

Correspondence concerning this article should be addressed to Auke Tellegen, Department of Psychology, Elliott Hall, University of Minnesota, 75 East River Road, Minneapolis, Minnesota 55455.

count for only a small fraction of the MZ twins' similarity in personality. Loehlin and Nichols (1976) concluded the following:

> Thus, a consistent—though perplexing—pattern is emerging from the data (and it is not purely idiosyncratic to our study). Environment carries substantial weight in the determination of personality—it appears to account for at least half the variance[1]—but that environment is one for which twin pairs are correlated close to zero. Attempts to treat twins alike do not lead to greater similarity between them. In short, in the personality domain we seem to see environmental effects that operate almost randomly with respect to the sorts of variables that psychologists (and other people) have traditionally deemed important in personality development. (p. 92)

However, adoption data (Scarr, Weber, Weinberg, & Witting, 1981a; 1981b) and nontwin family data (Ahern, Johnson, Wilson, McClearn, & Vandenberg, 1982; Loehlin, Horn, & Willerman, 1981) complicate the picture. Scarr et al. (1981a) found not only modest correlations between nonbiological relatives (.04 between adoptive parent and child and .07 between adoptive siblings), confirming the slight influence of a common family environment on personality, but also low correlations for first-degree biological relatives (.15 between parent and child and .20 between siblings). These latter figures are not unlike those compiled by Loehlin et al. (1981) for first-degree relatives. In addition, Ahern et al. (1982) reported a parent–offspring correlation of about .12 and a sibling correlation of about .10, on the basis of 54 scales. Ahern et al. suggested that the heritability of personality estimated from nontwin family data approaches .20. Scarr et al. (1981a) suggested a figure between .14 and .22.

Price, Vandenberg, Iyer, and Williams (1982) fitted a random effects linear model to six personality measures obtained from the extended families of MZ and DZ twins in the Swedish twin registry. Their analysis incorporated 13 consanguineous relationships (e.g., MZ twin pairs, DZ twin pairs, siblings, and mother–child pairs) and 9 nonconsanguineous relationships (e.g., spouses, siblings-in-law through MZ twins). The analysis yielded estimates of additive variance of nearly zero for four traits and very modest estimates for the remaining two traits (.04 and .07, respectively). Hewitt (1984) has argued, however, that the Price et al. (1982) analysis does not adequately support their conclusions because the data also fit a simple additive model that yields heritability estimates of about .50 (cf. also Heath, Martin, & Eaves, 1984). With the exception of Hewitt's reanalysis, conclusions based on twin data and nontwin family data appear to be at odds. Even Hewitt's critique is not so much a refutation of the Price et al. conclusions as a demonstration that their data fit contrasting models and are not decisive. How are we to proceed given these seeming discrepancies?

First, parent–offspring data have the disadvantage of being collected when subjects are at different ages. If personality traits are expressed differently at different ages (i.e., some personality traits may be age dependent for genetic or environmental reasons), then the parent–offspring data simply do not reflect the same phenomena as the twin data. The sibling data are not subject to this problem to the same degree, and they do show a slightly higher correlation in some studies. Only twin data have the obvious advantage of involving pairs of individuals of identical age, but the twin design has its own problems. Twin methodology depends on the assumption of equal environmental influences on both MZ and DZ twins and unbiased sampling of MZ and DZ twins from the twin population. Although there is considerable evidence to support the assumption of equal trait-relevant environments (Bouchard, 1984), many investigators still find it unpalatable. This is one instance in which the study of twins reared apart can contribute critical new information, a point to which we return shortly.

Second, most previous analyses of personality data have suggested that a simple additive model, reflecting the contribution of an unspecified number of independently segregating genetic factors, explains the data adequately. If genetic effects are entirely additive and there are no shared family-environment effects, then the DZ correlations should be about half the size of the MZ correlations. It has been observed, however, that for some traits the DZ correlations, like nontwin familial correlations, are clearly less than one half the size of MZ correlations (e.g., Lykken, 1982). This suggests nonadditive genetic effects, particularly dominance, or if DZ correlations are very low, epistasis (i.e., interaction between nonallelic genes).

Lykken and his colleagues (Lykken, 1982; Lykken & Bouchard, 1983/84; Lykken, Tellegen, & Iacono, 1982) have suggested that a complex form of epistasis, called *emergenesis*, may account for a significant portion of the discrepancy between twin data and Parent × Offspring and sibling data. Particularly in the case of epistasis, genetic effects could be both substantial and nonfamilial. In those instances, rather than exaggerating "the degree to which personality differences are explained by genetic differences" (Scarr et al., 1981a, pp. 896–897), twin data may tell a truer story, and the data based on nontwins may underestimate the actual impact of genetic factors.

Another striking phenomenon in the personality domain is the apparent lack of differences in heritability among personality variables. Loehlin and Nichols's (1976) findings are a case in point. Their twin personality data involved a well-known instrument, the California Psychological Inventory (CPI; Megargee, 1972), and revealed that the scales of this multimeasure instrument have highly similar heritabilities. The differential heritability of personality variables (or the lack thereof) has subsequently become a subject of some controversy (Carey, Goldsmith, Tellegen, & Gottesman, 1978; Carey & Rice, 1983; Loehlin, 1982; Zonderman, 1982). What on the surface may appear to be lack of differential heritability among psychologically diverse scales may in reality reflect substantial content (and item) overlap and high correlations among scales in inventories such as the CPI (Carey et al., 1978).

Even factor analytically constructed multiscale inventories usually reflect substantial saturation with only a small number of higher order superfactors, particularly Positive Emotionality (extraversion) and Negative Emotionality (neuroticism). Watson and Clark (1984) have discussed the diverse names given to what are essentially Negative Emotionality measures, reflecting the wide scope of that dimension. If, in addition, the superfactors themselves do not differ much in heritability, then only the addition of scales that are not excessively superfactor saturated could lead to evidence of differential heritability. Loehlin

[1] *Environment*, as defined by these authors, presumably also includes measurement error and nonsystematic changes over time.

(1982) has adduced evidence that this is in fact the case. Given all of the problems involving subject samples and choice of measures, it is desirable to cross-check the various findings discussed earlier using a design and instruments that avoid these difficulties.

Our study makes use of a design that has never, to our knowledge, been implemented: the simultaneous use of MZ and DZ twins reared together (MZTs and DZTs, respectively) and reared apart (MZAs and DZAs, respectively). Although several personality findings have been reported on MZAs (cf. Bouchard, 1984, Table 10), we know of no one who has ever reported personality data gathered on all four groups using the same personality inventory. This design circumvents many of the problems discussed earlier. First, the use of twins avoids the problem of testing at different ages. Second, the use of twins reared apart, although possibly subject to other flaws (Bouchard, 1984), relieves us of the assumption of equal environmental similarity for MZ and DZ twins. Because they were placed for adoption at such a young age, placement practices are unlikely to have been different for MZAs and DZAs (cf. Bouchard, 1984). Finally, with respect to the role of a common environment, it is difficult to believe that twins reared apart (even if placed in somewhat similar homes) would have the similarity in trait-relevant environments that are experienced by twins reared together. Under a purely common-environment hypothesis, MZ twins and DZ twins would be expected to show the same degree of within-twin similarity, but twins reared together should exhibit greater similarity than twins reared apart. The biometric model allowed us to test specific hypotheses of this type.

To test the hypothesis of differential heritability of personality variables, we found it necessary to use an instrument composed of relatively independent scales. We used the Multidimensional Personality Questionnaire (MPQ), formerly called the Differential Personality Questionnaire (DPQ), in this study. The MPQ (discussed in more detail in the Method section) was developed using a factor analytic strategy (Tellegen, 1982). Its scales, compared with those in other multiscale inventories, are relatively independent but can still be meaningfully integrated into higher order factor measures. The latter correspond closely to the superfactor scales that were developed by Eysenck and Eysenck (1975) and analyzed by Eaves and Young (1981) and many others. The MPQ thus permitted us to assess differential heritability on lower as well as higher order factor levels.

Method

Samples

The MZ and DZ twins reared together participated in the Minnesota Twin Study between 1970 and 1984. Details of their recruitment are reported in Lykken (1982) and Lykken et al. (1982). The zygosity diagnosis of all twins included in this study was based on analyses of eight blood group systems, four serum proteins, six red blood cell enzymes, fingerprint ridgecount, ponderal index, and cephalic index. Probability of misdiagnosis is less than .001 (Lykken, 1978).

The MZA and DZA twins participated in the Minnesota Study of Twins Reared Apart between 1979 and 1986. Details of their recruitment are reported in Bouchard (1984) and references cited therein. The twins' age at separation ranged from birth to 4.5 years, with a median of 0.2 years. Separation time (number of years from separation to first contact) ranged from 0 to 64 years, with a median of 33.8 years.[2] Zygosity was determined for all reared-apart twins in the same way as for reared-together twins. All twin pairs used in this study were of the same sex, except for 4 opposite-sex DZA twin pairs. Descriptive statistics on the samples are presented in Table 1.

Table 1
Sample Sizes, Percentage Females, and Means and Standard Deviations for Age for MZA, DZA, MZT, and DZT Twins

Descriptive statistics	MZA	DZA	MZT	DZT
Total sample size (sets)	44[a,b]	27[b]	217	114
Percentage females	66.7	75.5	65.0	64.9
Mean age (years)	40.7	41.1	23.5	19.8
SD of age	12.0	11.3	11.1	4.3

Note. MZA = Monozygotic twins reared apart, DZA = dizygotic twins reared apart, MZT = monozygotic twins reared together, and DZT = dizygotic twins reared together.
[a] Two MZA male triplet sets entered as 1 set each. [b] One reared-apart triplet set (two MZA females and one male) entered as 1 MZA pair and 2 DZA pairs.

Personality Inventory

The MPQ is a factor analytically developed self-report instrument. Its scales represent 11 primary personality dimensions and 3 higher order traits; alpha coefficients range from .76 to .89, with a median of .85; 30-day test–retest correlations range from .82 to .92, with a median of .89 (Tellegen, 1982, 1985). Particular care was taken during the development of the MPQ to achieve relatively independent primary scales. Thus, unlike the CPI used in the Loehlin and Nichols (1976) study, we had a number of scales that are not primarily superfactor markers. We did, however, essentially tap these factors at the higher order level.

The higher order MPQ scales are interpreted as self-report dimensions describing basic parameters of emotional and behavioral regulation. Factor 1, Positive Emotionality, is primarily associated with the MPQ Well-Being, Social Potency, Achievement, and Social Closeness scales and has clear "extraverted" features. High scorers on these scales present themselves as being engaged in active, pleasurable, and efficacious transactions with their environment and as being ready to experience the positive emotions congruent with these involvements. Low scorers report few of these pleasurable transactions, a lower degree of self-efficacy, a higher threshold for experiencing positive affect, and a tendency toward depressive, nonpleasurable disengagement. Positive Emotionality is related to Eysenck's Extraversion (E; Eysenck & Eysenck, 1975) and clearly resembles the Norman-Goldberg Surgency dimension (Goldberg, 1981).

Factor 2, Negative Emotionality, is primarily associated with the MPQ Stress-Reaction, Alienation, and Aggression scales. High scorers describe themselves as being unpleasurably engaged, stressed and harassed, and prone to experiencing strong negative emotions such as anxiety and anger. Low scorers convey a less "catastrophizing" picture, a higher threshold for negative affect, greater resiliency under stress (Block, 1964), and a tendency toward phlegmatic, non-unpleasurable disengagement. This dimension shares important features with Eysenck's Neuroticism (N) and Norman–Goldberg's (reversed) Agreeability and (reversed) Emotional Stability factors, particularly the latter.

[2] Separation time was arbitrarily set at zero for twin pairs who were reared in different homes but who had had periodic contact during childhood.

The affective interpretation of higher order MPQ Trait Factors 1 and 2 is supported by their convergent-discriminant relations to the state dimensions of Positive and Negative Affect, respectively (Tellegen, 1982), which dominate measures of current mood (Watson & Tellegen, 1985). The same pattern of relations to Positive and Negative Affect has been reported for Eysenck's Extraversion and Neuroticism scales, respectively (Costa & McCrae, 1980; Warr, Barter, & Brownbridge, 1983).

The third higher order MPQ dimension, Constraint, is most strongly associated with the MPQ Control, Harm Avoidance, and Traditionalism scales. High scorers on these scales describe themselves as being restrained, cautious, avoiding dangerous kinds of excitement and thrills, deferential, and conventional. Low scorers present a picture of impulsiveness, fearless sensation seeking, and rejection of conventional strictures on their behavior. Constraint is most clearly related to Eysenck's (reversed) Psychoticism (P) and the Norman–Goldberg Conscientiousness factor.

A more detailed exposition of this three-dimensional scheme and its conceptual relations, particularly to Eysenck and Eysenck's (1975), Gray's (1973, 1981), and psychodynamic views, has appeared elsewhere (Tellegen, 1985). Depue, Krauss, and Spoont (1987) have presented an entirely consonant interpretation of Positive Emotionality as a "behavioral engagement" dimension and have emphasized its particular relevance to euphoric and depressive diatheses. Watson and Clark (1984) have provided a comprehensive interpretive review of Negative Emotionality, documenting the breadth of its manifestations.

Analytic Procedures

Age- and sex-correction of personality scores. Raw scores on the MPQ were corrected for age, age^2, and Age × Sex using the combined samples of MZT, DZT, MZA, and DZA twins. Scores were then standardized (M = 0, SD = 1). The regression procedures are described in McGue and Bouchard (1984).

Biometric models. Although intraclass correlations are often informative and are presented here, for analytic purposes they can be misleading if MZ and DZ variances differ. Biometric geneticists, following Jinks and Fulker (1970), therefore, prefer analyzing variances over correlations. We also take this approach in this article. The expected values of the between (B) and within (W) mean squares of each twin group are expressed as appropriately weighted sums of the particular environmental and genetic variance components that are incorporated into one's chosen model. The weights (coefficients) are estimated from the observed mean squares. For presentations of biometric approaches, see Eaves (1978, 1982); Eaves, Last, Young, and Martin (1978); Jinks and Fulker (1970); Martin, Eaves, Kearsey, and Davies (1978); Nance and Corey (1976); and Rose et al. (1980).

Our full model decomposes the phenotypic variance of each trait into three main components: genetic, shared family environment, and unshared environment, each estimated as a parameter. The genetic component is further analyzed in terms of an additive subcomponent (reflecting the contribution of an unspecified number of independently segregating genetic factors) and a nonadditive component. Specifically, the model, as developed by G. Carey (personal communication, 1986), exploits the joint availability of twins reared together and apart to estimate an "additivity" parameter. This fourth parameter permits us in principle (albeit with low power, due to the small number of DZAs) to distinguish traits that are primarily additive from ones that are primarily nonadditive. Marked nonadditivity is attributable to epistasis, a genetic effect of particular interest to us, as explained earlier. As for environmental components, the shared family-environment component represents the contribution of those distinctive family characteristics (distinguishing families from one another) that influence individuals reared in the same family in the same way. The unshared environment component reflects, among other things, measurement error and state fluctuations.

Table 2
Biometric Model Specifying Genetic and Environmental Components of Variance of Between (B) and Within (W) Mean Squares of Twins Reared Together and Apart

		Environmental	
Mean square	Genetic	Shared familial	Unshared
B(MZT)	2	2	1
W(MZT)	0	0	1
B(MZA)	2	1	1
W(MZA)	0	1	1
B(DZT)	1 + C	2	1
W(DZT)	1 − C	0	1
B(DZA)	1 + C	1	1
W(DZA)	1 − C	1	1

Note. MZT = Monozygotic twins reared together, MZA = monozygotic twins reared apart, DZT = dizygotic twins reared together, and DZA = dizygotic twins reared apart. C is a parameter ranging between 0 and .5, reflecting degree of additive versus nonadditive genetic control. If C equals .5, the genetic effects are entirely additive; if C approaches 0, the genetic effects are increasingly nonadditive, reflecting an unknown mixture of additive, dominant, and epistatic effects; and if C equals 0, the genetic effects are entirely epistatic.

The full model is displayed in Table 2. The table shows how the B and W mean squares can be expressed in terms of the four parameters mentioned earlier: genetic, additive, shared family environment, and unshared environment. The model can be examined by determining how it specifies expected genetic and environmental twin correlations, as follows.

Using the formula for the intraclass correlation, $R = (B - W)/(B + W)$, we learn from Table 2 that the genetic correlation for MZ twins equals $(2 - 0)/(2 + 0) = 1$, as required (see the Genetic column, rows 1 and 2 or 3 and 4). For DZ twins, if the additivity parameter C is set at its maximum value of .5, the genetic correlation equals $[(1 + .5) - (1 - .5)]/[(1 + .5) + (1 - .5)] = .5$ (see Genetic column, rows 5 and 6 or 7 and 8), in accordance with the theoretical expectation that the additive genetic correlation between DZ cotwins is half that of MZ cotwins. If C is set at its minimum value of 0, then the genetic DZ correlation, computed in the same way, equals $(1 - 1)/(1 + 1) = 0$, showing that complete epistasis eliminates any genetic correlation between DZ cotwins. Turning to environmental correlations, we can see from the appropriate rows in the Shared Familial-Environmental column of Table 2 that for twins reared together and apart, the shared family-environ-, ment correlation equals 1 and 0, respectively. The unshared environment correlation equals 0 by definition, which is the value entailed by the entries in the last column of the table.

The four parameters are estimated and statistically evaluated with the maximum likelihood method described by Martin et al. (1978). Expressed as proportions of the total variance, these estimates are the heritability (in the broad sense, incorporating both the additive and nonadditive components), additivity versus nonadditivity, shared family-"environmentality," and unshared "environmentality" values that, given the model, best fit the data for a given scale.

In addition to the full model shown in Table 2, one can also evaluate simpler (reduced) versions. This is done by assigning a priori values to one or more of the parameters while fitting the remaining ones to the data. In this analysis, six models were investigated: (1) unshared environment effects; (2) shared family-environment and unshared environment effects; (3) additive genetic and unshared environment effects; (4)

Table 3
Intraclass Correlations for 11 Primary Scales and 3 Higher Order Scales for the Multidimensional Personality Questionnaire for Four Kinship Groups

Scale	MZA	DZA	MZT	DZT
Primary				
Well-Being	.48	.18	.58	.23
Social Potency	.56	.27	.65	.08
Achievement	.36	.07	.51	.13
Social Closeness	.29	.30	.57	.24
Stress Reaction	.61	.27	.52	.24
Alienation	.48	.18	.55	.38
Aggression	.46	.06	.43	.14
Control	.50	.03	.41	−.06
Harm Avoidance	.49	.24	.55	.17
Traditionalism	.53	.39	.50	.47
Absorption	.61	.21	.49	.41
Higher order				
Positive Emotionality	.34	−.07	.63	.18
Negative Emotionality	.61	.29	.54	.41
Constraint	.57	.04	.58	.25

Note. MZA = Monozygotic twin pairs reared apart (n = 44), DZA = dizygotic twin pairs reared apart (n = 27), MZT = monozygotic twin pairs reared together (n = 217), and DZT = dizygotic twin pairs reared together (n = 114).

additive genetic, shared family-environment, and unshared environment effects; (5) additive and nonadditive genetic effects, and unshared environment effects; and (6) the complete four-parameter model (additive and nonadditive genetic effects, as well as shared family- and unshared environment effects). For each of the six models, the estimates were made through maximum likelihood techniques and were evaluated by means of appropriate residual chi-square computations. Acceptance of a model required a nonsignificant chi-square.[3]

Results

Descriptive Statistics

We inspected the means and standard deviations of the MPQ raw scores of the four twin groups and found them to be comparable to those of other samples. The scale intercorrelations, computed separately for women and men, were likewise similar to those found in other samples. The results confirm the relative independence of the primary scales and justify our choice of this instrument to evaluate differential heritability of personality variables. Table 3 shows intraclass correlations for the four twin groups. The modest size of the DZA sample is reason for caution in comparing results for this group with the other twin samples. The DZA twins are, however, clearly much less similar than the MZA twins. Additionally, the correlations for the MZA and MZT samples are overall highly similar: The median correlations for the 11 primary MPQ scales are .49 and .52, respectively. This pattern suggests that a purely environmental model will not provide an adequate explanation. The B and W mean squares on which our analyses are based are shown in Table 4.

Biometric Analysis

Of the reduced models, neither Model 1 nor Model 2, the two purely environmental models, came close to fitting the data for any of the 14 scales: The relevant chi-squares were all highly significant and large. The other four models fared substantially better. Model 3, the simple additive model, yielded an adequate fit for 11 of 14 scales, with the exception of the Well-Being, Control, and Positive Emotionality scales. Model 4, which adds the shared family-environment component as a parameter to Model 3, fit all scales except Well-Being and Control. Model 5 adds the nonadditive parameter to Model 3 and fit all scales except Well-Being. Finally, Model 6, the complete four-parameter model, provided a good fit for all 14 scales. The complete set of parameter estimates of Model 6 is presented in Table 5.

As Table 5 shows, the genetic parameter estimates (i.e., the heritabilities) range from .39 to .58, with an average of .48. Given the good fit of the simple additive genetic model (Model 3), it is not surprising that Table 5 does not show many instances of appreciable nonadditivity or shared family environmentality. Nevertheless, for three scales—Social Potency, Control, and Positive Emotionality—the estimates of the C parameter indicate statistically significant nonadditivity and are low enough to be consistent with an emergenic (epistatic) interpretation. We saw already that of these three scales, Control and Positive Emotionality did not fit the simple additive genetic Model 3. The third scale, Social Potency, although accommodated by all four genetic models, fit Models 5 and 6 (which contain the [non]additivity parameter) better than Models 3 and 4. With increased power that can, for example, be attained by increasing the size of the DZA sample, additional evidence of nonadditivity may be forthcoming. Table 5 shows significant familial effects for just two scales, Social Closeness and Positive Emotionality.

Discussion

These results confirm and extend earlier findings and have several implications for current thinking and future research concerning determinants of variation in personality. First, our analyses indicate that, on average, about 50% of measured personality diversity can be attributed to genetic diversity. This re-

[3] It is still customary practice to arrive at conclusions about data by accepting or rejecting null hypotheses on the basis of statistical significance tests. We have also followed this approach. One reason is that null hypothesis testing, given our sample sizes and the power of the analyses, appears to lead to reasonable comparisons of the extent to which the several models adequately represent major features of the data. In addition, we did not wish to deflect attention from our present topic, which is substantive and not methodological. Anticipating future discussions, however, we wish to be on record as viewing null hypothesis testing as inherently flawed. Given large enough samples, one can be sure that even our full model will "significantly" fail to fit the data. All models are simplications and their falsehood can be assumed without conducting significance tests. Psychologists need not spend time deciding the truth or falsehood of their strictly false models. We can do better by attempting to assess the degree to which alternative models of high content fit the data and to evaluate which model or models fit the data best. Although these issues have been widely discussed by structural-modeling specialists (e.g., Bentler & Bonett, 1980; Cudeck & Browne, 1983), they appear not to have been considered in applications of biometric genetic models to psychological data. For critical discussions of significance testing, see also Lykken (1968) and Meehl (1978).

Table 4
Between (B) and Within (W) Mean Squares of Twins Reared Apart and Together for Multidimensional Personality Questionnaire Data

Scale	MZA		DZA		MZT		DZT	
	B	W	B	W	B	W	B	W
Well-Being	1.62	0.56	1.85	1.28	1.52	0.40	1.13	0.71
Social Potency	1.90	0.53	1.10	0.64	1.67	0.35	1.00	0.86
Achievement	1.33	0.61	1.25	1.09	1.58	0.52	1.02	0.78
Social Closeness	1.32	0.71	1.53	0.83	1.46	0.40	1.37	0.84
Stress Reaction	1.95	0.46	1.03	0.59	1.50	0.47	1.16	0.72
Alienation	1.21	0.42	1.36	0.94	1.58	0.46	1.36	0.61
Aggression	1.09	0.40	1.13	1.00	1.49	0.59	1.13	0.85
Control	1.87	0.61	1.08	1.02	1.32	0.55	0.94	1.06
Harm Avoidance	1.25	0.42	0.79	0.49	1.63	0.47	1.25	0.89
Traditionalism	1.66	0.51	1.78	0.78	1.39	0.46	1.55	0.56
Absorption	1.90	0.46	1.25	0.82	1.50	0.51	1.34	0.57
Positive Emotionality	1.29	0.62	0.95	1.09	1.70	0.38	1.11	0.77
Negative Emotionality	1.58	0.37	1.44	0.80	1.50	0.45	1.39	0.58
Constraint	1.43	0.39	0.82	0.76	1.63	0.44	1.28	0.77

Note. MZA = Monozygotic twins reared apart, DZA = dizygotic twins reared apart, MZT = monozygotic twins reared together, and DZT = dizygotic twins reared together.

sult confirms previous findings and represents an extension to a wide range of distinctive personality characteristics. The remaining 50% is technically classified as all environmental and includes the unshared environment effect that, in turn, includes measurement error and nontrait score fluctuations that reflect the influence of transient states on self-report trait measures. If one considers both the internal consistency and stability of personality scales (cf. Conley, 1984), it is not unreasonable to guess that not more than about 70 to 85% of the observed variance represents trait variance. Because the 15 to 30% nontrait variance is presumably confined to the environmental 50% of the observed variance, the environmentally based trait variance may not amount to more than 20 to 35%, compared with the roughly 50% that is genetic in origin. Improving the consistency and stability of a trait scale should increase its measured genetic and trait-relevant environmental components, but not their relative magnitude. It seems reasonable, therefore, to conclude that personality differences are more influenced by genetic diversity than they are by environmental diversity.

Consistent with these observations is the absence of substantial shared family-environment effects in our data. Positive Emotionality and Social Closeness, however, yielded significant estimates of .22 and .19, respectively. These results warrant some partially speculative comment.

Table 5
Estimates of Genetic and Environmental Variance Components From a Biometric Model Applied to Multidimensional Personality Questionnaire Data of Twins Reared Apart and Together

Scale	Variance component			
	Genetic	C parameter	Shared familial	Unshared
Well-Being	.48[a] (.08)	.29 (.16)	.13 (.09)	.40[a] (.04)
Social Potency	.54[a] (.07)	.05[a] (.21)	.10 (.08)	.36[a] (.04)
Achievement	.39[a] (.10)	.13 (.27)	.11 (.11)	.51[a] (.05)
Social Closeness	.40[a] (.08)	.19 (.22)	.19[a] (.09)	.41[a] (.05)
Stress Reaction	.53[a] (.04)	.49 (.17)	.00[b]	.47[a] (.04)
Alienation	.45[a] (.13)	.50[b]	.11 (.12)	.44[a] (.04)
Aggression	.44[a] (.05)	.27 (.19)	.00[b]	.56[a] (.05)
Control	.44[a] (.05)	.00[a,b]	.00[b]	.56[a] (.05)
Harm Avoidance	.55[a] (.04)	.31 (.15)	.00[b]	.45[a] (.04)
Traditionalism	.45[a] (.10)	.50[b]	.12 (.10)	.43[a] (.04)
Absorption	.50[a] (.10)	.50[b]	.03 (.10)	.47[a] (.04)
Positive Emotionality	.40[a] (.08)	.00[a,b]	.22[a] (.07)	.38[a] (.04)
Negative Emotionality	.55[a] (.11)	.50[b]	.02 (.11)	.43[a] (.04)
Constraint	.58[a] (.04)	.40 (.14)	.00[b]	.43[a] (.04)

Note. Standard errors are in parentheses.
[a] Significantly different from null value at $p < .05$. [b] Boundary solution; therefore, no standard error computed.

With respect to its environmental origins, Positive Emotionality contrasts with the other two higher order MPQ dimensions, Negative Emotionality and Constraint, which show no shared family environmentality. Of these three, Positive Emotionality (extraversion) is most clearly an affective-interactive dimension. High Positive Emotionality is characterized by active engagement with one's environment, whereas low Positive Emotionality is characterized by weak engagement or disengagement. Because of its inherently interactive-communicative character, it seems plausible that a person's Positive Emotionality trait level is particularly responsive to and reflective of the surrounding social climate, including the prevailing and more or less engaging climate of the rearing environment.

Of the primary scales, only Social Closeness exhibited a significant shared family-environmental component. Although Social Closeness is a secondary marker of Positive Emotionality, it is the main marker of one of the major MPQ dimensions that emerge when four, rather than three, second-order factors are extracted. In the four-factor solution, Positive Emotionality essentially is split into Agentic Positive Emotionality and Communal Positive Emotionality, with Achievement being the salient marker of the former and Social Closeness of the latter. It is interesting to contrast Social Closeness with Social Potency, which is more "agentic" than Social Closeness and does not have a significant shared family-environment component.

Social Closeness and Social Potency represent the basic dimensions (sometimes called affiliation and control, respectively) in interpersonal theory (Kiesler, 1983; Wiggins, 1982). As explained by Kiesler, behavior variations along these two continua differ with respect to the complementary responses that each invites and by which they are sustained. High and low affiliativeness are complemented by similar behaviors (affiliativeness by affiliativeness, nonaffiliativeness by nonaffiliativeness). High and low control, on the other hand, are complemented by their opposites (dominance "pulling" submissiveness and vice versa). Given these dynamics, we would expect that family environments tend to provide more uniform family-interaction norms with respect to affiliativeness than to control. Thus, the communal facet of Positive Emotionality may be particularly responsible for its shared family environmentality.

Our findings suggest more saliently, nonetheless, that the common environment generally plays a very modest role in the determination of many personality traits. This conclusion is now supported by studies using samples of four different types: twins reared together, twins reared apart, adoptive parents and their offspring, and adoptive siblings. It runs counter, however, to the belief, influential among psychologists, that personality similarity is profoundly enhanced by a shared family environment. Mischel (1981) has confronted this issue directly:

> Genes and glands are obviously important, but social learning also has a dramatic role. Imagine the enormous differences that would be found in the personalities of twins with identical genetic endowments if they were raised apart in two different families. . . . Through social learning vast differences develop among people in their reactions to most stimuli they face in daily life. (p. 311)

Although some psychologists (e.g., Feshbach & Weiner, 1986; Liebert & Spiegler, 1987; Singer, 1984) have been impressed by the genetic implications of personality similarities in twins reared together, others attribute much of this resemblance to reciprocal influences, to more similar treatment, and to greater expectations of behavioral similarity accorded by their families to monozygotic twins who look so much alike.

The remarkably similar overall magnitude of the MZA and MZT intraclass correlations deserves special mention in this connection. Slight family-environment effects do indeed entail highly similar MZA and MZT correlations. Although surprising, these results are entirely consistent with reported data on ordinary twins and data from adoption studies.

In our own case, it was unexpected that the Traditionalism scale (measuring endorsement of traditional moral and family values) did not show a systematic familial environmental effect. To find such an effect may, however, require a different model. It is possible, for example, that for some traits, including Traditionalism, the co-twin is a particularly important similarity-inducing component of the common family environment of twins reared together and that this assimilative co-twin influence is potentiated only to the extent that genetically determined, within-pair differences exist to begin with, as among DZ twins but not MZ twins. In that case, one would expect the increase in within-pair similarity of DZTs, relative to DZAs, to be larger than that of MZTs relative to MZAs (as the Traditionalism data may suggest). Although only conjectures at this point, these ideas at least illustrate the need for exploring a wider range of gene–environment models (and for going beyond a study of assortative mating that would also be indicated in a full-fledged analysis of Traditionalism).

In the area of personality development, studies that limit examination to variables such as social class, child-rearing patterns, and other common-environment characteristics of intact biological families cannot be decisive because they confound genetic and environmental factors. In light of studies that have provided pertinent data, it is evident that new designs and theoretical approaches to personality development are needed (Plomin & Daniels, 1987; Rowe & Plomin, 1981; Scarr & McCartney, 1983). Particularly helpful would be research on individual rearing environments that would identify psychologically meaningful components of the unshared environment and separate these from measurement error and other trait-irrelevant variance. On the other hand, only so much meaningful information can be recovered from this source of variation. As indicated earlier, our guess is that 15 to 30% of the observed variance is nontrait variance, all of it concentrated in the unshared environment component. From the last column of Table 5 we can see that unshared environmentality estimates vary around 45%. A ceiling of 45% does not exceed the conjectured 15 to 30% noise baseline by a large margin. A realistic pursuit of meaningful unshared variance components cannot overlook these limits, which may be more restrictive in some areas than in others.

Our results also bear on the question of differential heritability. We find indications of differences in heritability among the various relatively independent traits measured by the MPQ. We are not arguing, then, that given sufficient power no substantial differences in heritability can be found between some personality traits. On the other hand, our data indicate (consistent with other studies) that several diverse personality variables have comparable heritabilities. The same point is illustrated in a study by Rushton, Fulker, Neale, Nias, and Eysenck (1986), who found that measures of altruism and aggression (traits expected a priori to be heavily influenced by socialization processes) both had heritabilities of about .50 and no common family-environment influence.

It should be kept in mind that heritability estimates can vary depending on the genetic model that is being fit to the data. Clarification of the differential-heritability issue will, therefore, partly depend on better understanding of the genetic architecture underlying different personality traits. This leads us to our final major point.

Although most previous analyses of personality data have led to the acceptance of a simple additive genetic model, this view has recently been challenged (Carey & Rice, 1983; Lykken, 1982; Lykken & Bouchard, 1983/84; Lykken et al., 1982). Carey and Rice (1983) concluded that the "genetic and environmental architecture of personality may be complex and trait-specific" (p. 54). The Carey and Rice analysis was carried out on three MPQ scales, Social Potency, Social Closeness, and Control (previously named *impulsivity* and scored in the reverse direction). Our own results also suggest that the simple additive model has to be rejected in some cases. Only the complete four-parameter model accommodated all of the data, and it indicated nonadditivity for three scales: Social Potency, Control, and Positive Emotionality. The nonadditivity patterns encountered in these cases are consistent with an epistatic interpretation and in this sense support the concept of emergenesis discussed in the introduction.

In this study, purely additive genetic models were nevertheless found to fit the data well in many cases. Larger sample sizes, particularly more DZAs, and additional family groups (including offspring of twins) would better enable us to determine the comparative adequacy of additive, nonadditive, and combined additive–nonadditive genetic models; to isolate dominant and epistatic components of the nonadditive genetic variance; and to examine further the effect of systematic environmental influences on MZ and DZ twin similarity through environmental assessments. We hope to expand our data base in these directions.

References

Ahern, F. M., Johnson, R. C., Wilson, J. R., McClearn, G. E., & Vandenberg, S. G. (1982). Family resemblances in personality. *Behavior Genetics, 12,* 261–280.

Bentler, P. M., & Bonett, D. G. (1980). Significance tests and goodness of fit in the analysis of covariance structure. *Psychological Bulletin, 88,* 588–606.

Block, J. (1964). *The challenge of response sets.* New York: Appleton-Century-Crofts.

Bouchard, T. J., Jr. (1984). Twins reared apart and together: What they tell us about human diversity. In S. Fox (Ed.), *The chemical and biological bases of individuality* (pp. 147–184). New York: Plenum Press.

Carey, G., Goldsmith, H. H., Tellegen, A., & Gottesman, I. I. (1978). Genetics and personality inventories: The limits of replication with twin data. *Behavior Genetics, 8,* 299–313.

Carey, G., & Rice, J. (1983). Genetics and personality temperament: Simplicity or complexity? *Behavior Genetics, 13,* 43–63.

Conley, J. J. (1984). The hierarchy of consistency: A review and model of longitudinal findings on adult individual differences in intelligence, personality and self-opinion. *Personality and Individual Differences, 5,* 11–25.

Costa, P. T., & McCrea, R. R. (1980). Influence of extraversion and neuroticism on subjective well-being: Happy and unhappy people. *Journal of Personality and Social Psychology, 38,* 668–678.

Cudeck, R., & Browne, M. W. (1983). Cross-validation of covariance structures. *Multivariate Behavioral Research, 18,* 147–167.

Depue, R. A., Krauss, S., & Spoont, M. R. (1987). A two-dimensional threshold model of seasonal bipolar affective disorder. In D. Magnusson & A. Ohrman (Eds.), *Psychopathology: An interactional perspective* (pp. 95–123). New York: Academic Press.

Eaves, L. J. (1978). Twins as a basis for the causal analysis of human personality. In W. E. Nance, G. Allen, & P. Parisi (Eds.), *Twin research: Psychology and methodology* (pp. 151–174). New York: Alan R. Liss.

Eaves, L. J. (1982). The utility of twins. In V. E. Anderson, W. A. Hauser, J. K. Penry, & C. F. Sing (Eds.), *Genetic basis of the epilepsies* (pp. 249–276). New York: Raven Press.

Eaves, L. J., Last, K. A., Young, P. A., & Martin, N. G. (1978). Model fitting approaches to the analysis of human behavior. *Heredity, 41,* 249–320.

Eaves, L. J., & Young, P. A. (1981). How stable are personality traits? In L. Gedda, P. Parisi, & W. E. Nance (Eds.), *Twin research 3: Part B. Intelligence, personality and development* (pp. 87–97). New York: Alan R. Liss.

Eysenck, H. J., & Eysenck, S. B. G. (1975). *Manual of the Eysenck Personality Questionnaire.* San Diego, CA: Educational and Industrial Testing Service.

Falconer, D. S. (1960). *Introduction to quantitative genetics.* New York: Ronald Press.

Feshbach, S., & Weiner, B. (1986). *Personality* (2nd ed.). Lexington, MA: Heath.

Goldberg, L. R. (1981). Language and individual differences: The search for universals in personality lexicons. In C. Wheeler (Ed.), *Review of personality and social psychology* (Vol. 2, pp. 141–165). Beverly Hills, CA: Sage.

Goldsmith, H. H. (1983). Genetic influences on personality from infancy to adulthood. *Child Development, 54,* 331–335.

Gray, J. A. (1973). Causal theories of personality and how to test them. In J. R. Royce (Ed.), *Multivariate analysis and psychological theory* (pp. 409–463). New York: Academic Press.

Gray, J. A. (1981). A critique of Eysenck's theory of personality. In H. J. Eysenck (Ed.), *A model for personality* (pp. 233–252). Berlin: Springer-Verlag.

Heath, A. C., Martin, N. G., & Eaves, L. J. (1984). Sense and nonsense in genetic epidemiology: A critique of the statistical model of Williams and Iyer. *Acta Geneticae Medicae et Gemellologiae, 33,* 557–563.

Hewitt, J. K. (1984). Normal components of personality variation. *Journal of Personality and Social Psychology, 47,* 671–675.

Jinks, J. L., & Fulker, D. W. (1970). A comparison of the biometrical genetical, MAVA, and classical approaches to the analysis of human behavior. *Psychological Bulletin, 73,* 311–349.

Kiesler, D. J. (1983). The 1982 interpersonal circle: A taxonomy for complementarity in human transactions. *Psychological Review, 90,* 185–214.

Liebert, R. M., & Spiegler, M. D. (1987). *Personality: Strategies and issues* (5th ed.). Homewood, IL: Dorsey Press.

Loehlin, J. C. (1982). Are personality traits differentially heritable? *Behavior Genetics, 12,* 417–428.

Loehlin, J. C., Horn, J. M., & Willerman, L. (1981). Personality resemblance in adoptive families. *Behavior Genetics, 11,* 309–330.

Loehlin, J. C., & Nichols, R. C. (1976). *Heredity, environment and per-*

sonality: A study of 850 sets of twins. Austin: University of Texas Press.

Lykken, D. T. (1968). Statistical significance in psychological research. *Psychological Bulletin, 70,* 151–159.

Lykken, D. T. (1978). The diagnosis of zygosity in twins. *Behavior Genetics, 8,* 437–473.

Lykken, D. T. (1982). Research with twins: The concept of emergenesis. *Psychophysiology, 19,* 361–373.

Lykken, D. T., & Bouchard, T. J., Jr. (1983/84). Genetische Aspekte menschlicher Individualität [Genetic aspects of human individuality]. In H. V. Ditfurth (Ed.), *Mannheimer Forum 1983/84* (pp. 79–117). Hamburg: Hoffman and Campe Verlag.

Lykken, D. T., Tellegen, A., & Iacono, W. G. (1982). EEG spectra in twins: Evidence for a neglected mechanism of genetic determination. *Physiological Psychology, 10,* 60–65.

Martin, N. G., Eaves, L. J., Kearsey, M. J., & Davies, P. (1978). The power of the classical twin study. *Heredity, 40,* 87–116.

McGue, M., & Bouchard, T. J. (1984). Adjustment of twin data for the effects of age and sex. *Behavior Genetics, 14,* 325–343.

Meehl, P. E. (1978). Theoretical risks and tabular risks: Sir Karl, Sir Ronald, and the slow progress of soft psychology. *Journal of Consulting and Clinical Psychology, 46,* 806–834.

Megargee, E. I. (1972). *The California Psychological Inventory handbook.* San Francisco: Jossey-Bass.

Mischel, W. (1981). *Introduction to personality* (3rd ed.). New York: Holt, Rinehart & Winston.

Nance, W. E., & Corey, L. A. (1976). Genetic models for the analysis of data from the families of identical twins. *Genetics, 83,* 811–826.

Nichols, R. C. (1978). Twin studies of ability, personality, and interests. *Homo, 29,* 158–173.

Plomin, R., & Daniels, D. (1987). Why are children in the same family so different from one another? *Behavioral and Brain Sciences, 10,* 1–16.

Price, R. A., Vandenberg, S. G., Iyer, H., & Williams, J. S. (1982). Components of variation in normal personality. *Journal of Personality and Social Psychology, 43,* 328–340.

Rose, R. J., Boughman, J. A., Corey, L. A., Nance, W. E., Christian, J. C., & Kang, K. W. (1980). Data from kinships of monozygotic twins indicate maternal effects on verbal intelligence. *Nature, 283,* 375–377.

Rowe, D. C., & Plomin, R. (1981). The importance of nonshared (E1) environmental influences in behavioral development. *Developmental Psychology, 17,* 517–531.

Rushton, J. P., Fulker, D. W., Neale, M. C., Nias, D. K. B., & Eysenck, H. J. (1986). Altruism and aggression: To what extent are individual differences inherited? *Journal of Personality and Social Psychology, 50,* 1192–1198.

Scarr, S., & McCartney, K. (1983). How people make their own environments: A theory of genotype–environment effects. *Child Development, 54,* 424–435.

Scarr, S., Weber, P. L., Weinberg, R. A., & Wittig, M. A. (1981a). Personality resemblance among adolescents and their parents in biologically related and adoptive families. *Journal of Personality and Social Psychology, 40,* 885–898.

Scarr, S., Weber, P. L., Weinberg, R. A., & Wittig, M. A. (1981b). Personality resemblance among adolescents and their parents in biologically related and adoptive families. In L. Gedda, P. Parisi, & W. E. Nance (Eds.), *Twin Research 3: Part B. Intelligence, personality and development* (pp. 99–120). New York: Alan R. Liss.

Singer, J. L. (1984). *The human personality.* New York: Harcourt Brace Jovanovich.

Tellegen, A. (1982). *Brief manual for the Differential Personality Questionnaire.* Unpublished manuscript, University of Minnesota, Minneapolis.

Tellegen, A. (1985). Structure of mood and personality and their relevance to assessing anxiety, with an emphasis on self-report. In A. H. Tuma & J. D. Maser (Eds.), *Anxiety and the anxiety disorders* (pp. 681–706). Hillsdale, NJ: Erlbaum.

Warr, P., Barter, J., & Brownbridge, G. (1983). On the independence of positive and negative affect. *Journal of Personality and Social Psychology, 44,* 644–651.

Watson, D., & Clark, L. A. (1984). Negative Affectivity: The disposition to experience aversive emotional states. *Psychological Bulletin, 96,* 465–490.

Watson, D., & Tellegen, A. (1985). Toward a consensual structure of mood. *Psychological Bulletin, 98,* 219–235.

Wiggins, J. S. (1982). Circumplex models of interpersonal behavior in clinical psychology. In P. C. Kendall & J. N. Butcher (Eds.), *Handbook of research methods in clinical psychology* (pp. 183–221). New York: Wiley.

Zonderman, A. B. (1982). Differential heritability and consistency: A reanalysis of the NMSQT CPI data. *Behavior Genetics, 12,* 193–208.

Received March 21, 1986
Revision received August 31, 1987
Accepted October 30, 1987 ■

A Twin Study of Personality Disorders

Svenn Torgersen, Sissel Lygren, Per Anders Øien, Ingunn Skre, Sidsel Onstad, Jack Edvardsen, Kristian Tambs, and Einar Kringlen

No twin study has previously investigated the whole range of personality disorders (PDs) recorded by interviews. Based on twin and patient registries, 92 monozygotic (MZ) and 129 dizygotic (DZ) twin pairs were interviewed with the Structured Clinical Interview for DSM-III-R Personality Disorders (SCID-II). Observed prevalence rates from a normal population study of more than 2,000 individuals were used in combination with data from the present study to generate statistics assumed to be valid for a normal twin population, and these statistics were used for structural equation modeling. The best-fitting models had a heritability of .60 for PDs generally, .37 for the eccentric (A) cluster, .60 for the emotional (B) cluster, and .62 for the fearful (C) cluster. Among the specific PDs, the heritability appeared to be .79 for narcissistic, .78 for obsessive-compulsive, .69 for borderline, .67 for histrionic, .61 for schizotypal, .57 for dependent, .54 for self-defeating, .29 for schizoid, .28 for paranoid, and .28 for avoidant PDs. The best-fitting models never included shared-in-families environmental effects. However, a model with only shared familial and unique environmental effects could not be ruled out for dependent PD. Shared familial environmental effects may also influence the development of any PD and borderline PD. Passive-aggressive PD did not seem to be affected by genes or family environment at all. The low occurrence of antisocial PD in the twin sample precluded any model for this disorder. PDs seem to be more strongly influenced by genetic effects than almost any axis I disorder, and more than most broad personality dimensions. However, we observed a large variation in heritability among the different PDs, probably partly because of a moderate sample size and low prevalence of the specific disorders.

DURING THE LAST two decades, we have learned a lot more about the genetic aspects of psychiatric clinical conditions. The final results from the Danish Adoptive Study have demonstrated the genetic influence on the development of schizophrenia and schizophrenia spectrum disorders.[1] The Virginia Twin project has shown that genes are of importance in the etiology of anxiety disorders, depression, bulimia, and alcoholism; even smoking is partially genetically influenced.[2,3]

Correspondingly, the studies of twins reared together and apart suggest that broad, common personality dimensions such as neuroticism, extraversion, conscientiousness, and openness to experience are genetically influenced.[4-8] Thus, one would expect that genes also influence personality disorders (PDs).

Till now, not very much has been known about the contribution of genes to the development of PDs. Most of the evidence is indirect, pertaining to traits or behavior characteristic of PDs rather than the disorders themselves, as classified according to the DSM systems (for a review, see McGuffin and Thapar[9]). There are a few exceptions. Adoptive studies have demonstrated the influence of genes on the development of antisocial PD.[10] Also for schizotypal PD, genes seem to be relevant and a genetic relationship to schizophrenia seems to exist.[1] However, only the eccentric, affect-constricted aspect of schizotypal PD seems to be within the genetic spectrum of schizophrenia.[11-13] A twin study suggests that borderline PD, in contrast to schizotypal PD, is solely environmentally determined.[14]

Regarding the remaining PDs, very little is known. A Canadian twin study has shown that a number of PD traits are genetically influenced.[15] However, these traits, resembling some of the DSM-III/IV PDs, were based on self-report questionnaires, and the correlations between PDs measured by questionnaires and by interview are rather low.[16]

One study has investigated the transmission of avoidant and dependent PDs in families[17] and confirmed that these disorders run in families. However, a family study cannot disentangle the effects of genes from the common familial environmental effects, as these two types of effects will be confounded in such studies.

The aim of the present study is to investigate the contribution of genes and environment to the

---

From the Department of Psychology, Oslo University, Oslo, Norway.

Supported by grants from the Scottish Rite Schizophrenia Research Program, United States, and the National Council of Research and Council of Research in Psychological Disorders, Norway.

Address reprint requests to Svenn Torgersen, Ph.D., Center for Research in Clinical Psychology, Department of Psychology, Oslo University, Postbox 1039-Blindern, N-0315 Oslo, Norway.

0010-440X/00/4106-0004$10.00/0
doi:10.1053/comp.2000.16560

development of different PDs. To our knowledge, this is the first study investigating the whole variety of PDs, assessed by interview.

METHOD

Subjects and Procedure

The twin sample was drawn from different sources. The main part of the sample was ascertained by matching the Norwegian Twin Register with the National Register for Mental Disorder. A smaller number of twins were directly obtained from the inpatient and outpatient clinics of the University Department of Psychiatry, Vinderen, and Modum Bad Hospital. Subsamples of the twins have been described elsewhere.[11,18,19] The criterium for inclusion was that at least one of the twins had been treated for mental disorder. When both twins had been ascertained as a case, the twin pair was entered twice (in eight cases). Only same-sexed twins were studied.

Nineteen percent of the twin pairs were lost because one or both twins refused to participate. All twins included participated voluntarily after informed consent was obtained. The total number of twin pairs analyzed (where eight pairs were counted twice) amounted to 221, with 62% females and 38% males. The mean age was 51 years (range, 19 to 83).

All twins were personally interviewed about their lifetime history of mental disorders. Most often, the same person interviewed both twins in a pair. The interviewers were initially blind to the zygosity of the twins, but in practice, they may have been able to guess quite accurately who were monozygotic and who were not.

Instruments

Twin zygosity was determined by means of a questionnaire, which in a previous study had predicted zygosity correctly in 95% of the cases as compared with 10 genetic blood and serum markers.[20] Ninety-two twin pairs were classified as monozygotic (MZ) and 129 as dizygotic (DZ).

The occurrence of mental disorder was assessed by the Structured Clinical Interview for DSM-III Axis I (SCID-I)[21] and the Structured Clinical Interview for DSM-III-R Axis II (SCID-II).[22]

Twins with a diagnosis of schizophrenia were excluded. It goes without saying that the assessment of PDs in a person with schizophrenia is difficult, if not impossible. In determining the PD, the point of departure is the common way of reacting, independent of axis I disorder, medication, medical illness, or other confounding aspects.

The reliability of the diagnoses was assessed on the basis of ratings by two independent judges listening to the recorded interview made by a third person. The κ between the three raters was .94 for schizophrenic disorder, .68 for paranoid, .74 for schizoid, .79 for schizotypal, 1.00 for antisocial, .76 for borderline, .65 for histrionic, .59 for narcissistic, .68 for avoidant, .68 for dependent, .59 for obsessive-compulsive, .47 for self-defeating, and .32 for passive-aggressive PDs.[11,18]

Statistical Analyses

The PDs were treated in a semicontinuous way. "Definite disorder" was defined as having obtained the required number of criteria for the disorder according to DSM-III-R. "Probable disorder" was defined as meeting the same number of criteria except one or two. Concordance rates were calculated for definite and definite plus probable (broad) disorders for MZ and DZ twins separately.

As a further step, tetrachoric cotwin correlations were computed using the PRELIS computer program.[23] Tetrachoric correlations are based on two by two table statistics. In population-based classic twin studies, such tables show the frequency of cases and noncases among the first and second twin in a pair. The data from the present study are informative with regard to the probability of a twin being affected if his/her cotwin is affected, but not with respect to the probability of a twin being affected if his cotwin is not affected. However, if the prevalence of the disorder in the population is known, the latter probability can be calculated, assuming that the prevalence is equal for twins and singletons. For instance, suppose that the frequency of cases and noncases among cotwins of 20 affected twins has been observed to be 5 and 15, respectively (first row in Fig 1). This distribution is expected to be the same in a population-based twin sample, and in such a sample, the expected frequency is assumed to be identical in the diagonal cells *b* and *c*. Now estimating the frequency in cell *c* to be 15, the frequency in cell *d* (both cotwins not affected) can be estimated if the prevalence among the (twin) population is known to be 5%, for example. The table already includes 10 cases (five among twin 1 and five among twin 2) in cell *a* and 15 cases in cells *b* and *c*, altogether 40 cases. Thus, the expected number of noncases in a corresponding normal population sample is 40 × (95/5) = 760. Cells *b* and *c* already include 30 noncases, and the expected number of twins in cell *d* is 760 − 30 = 730, or 730/2 = 365 pairs.

The calculations rest on the assumption that only a negligible part of the cases in the twin population were recruited to the study. If a large part of the cases in a twin population are ascertained, the chances of finding a positive cotwin will decrease with the "draining" of new cases from the population. In the extreme case in which all cases in the population are identified, the chance for the cotwin of the last identified proband to be a case is zero, simply because there are no cases left. It is likely that at least from some areas in Norway, a nontrivial part of the cases among the twin population were identified. This may have deflated the proportion of positive concordant pairs among MZs and DZs. A likely consequence is

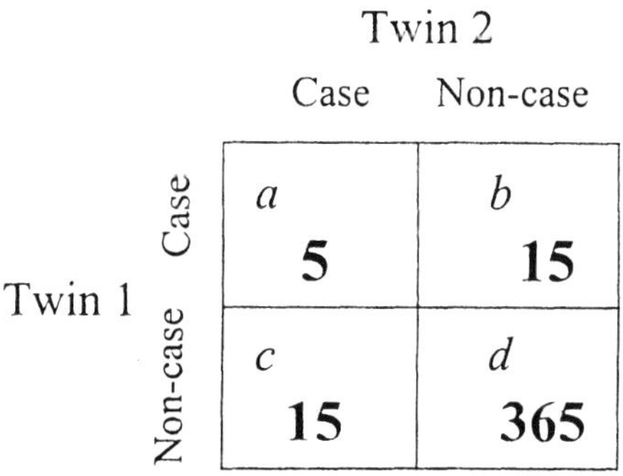

Fig 1. Example of the statistical analyses.

somewhat deflated estimates of environmental effects common to cotwins (the family environment).

Two by two tables were generated for all types of disorders both for MZ and DZ twins and analyzed with structural equation modeling.[24] Data from an unselected community sample including more than 2,000 individuals[25] were used for calculation of the various prevalences in the Norwegian population. Using tetrachoric correlations based on such generated data gave rise to a new problem, namely what is the correct number of pairs to be specified for the model fit procedures? Clearly, our observed data provide much more information than a corresponding number of randomly drawn pairs, because the observed data are "augmented" with a higher proportion of cases than expected in a normal population sample, and the analyses use the information about the prevalence obtained from other sources. On the other hand, the sometimes largely expanded numbers of pairs of the simulated data hardly reflect the real precision of these data. We conservatively chose to specify the numbers of pairs for the model testing as the real numbers of observed pairs, that is, 92 MZ pairs and 129 DZ pairs. Standard errors for the correlations based on these numbers of pairs were computed by the PRELIS program.

The correlations were calculated for broadly defined disorders and for definite disorders if there were any cases with the disorder among the cotwins. The self-defeating PD is included in the fearful cluster C, as it is most strongly correlated with this cluster.

Four different parameters were estimated by means of the LISREL 8 program,[26] each of which explains a proportion of the variance of liability of a certain disorder. The parameters were additive genetic effects (A), nonadditive genetic effects (D), common or shared-in-families environmental effects (C), and unique or not-shared-in-families environmental effects (E). First, the full model including effects of the environment shared by cotwins (ACE) or including nonadditive genetic effect instead of shared environment (ADE) were tested. The choice of one of the two full models depended on whether the DZ correlations were less than half of the MZ correlations. Then, the reduced models AE and CE were tested. The DE model was not tested because a model with only nonadditive genetic effect is not consistent with genetic theory. Finally, a model with only E was tested. The fits of the various models were compared according to Akaike's Information Criterion (AIC),[27] stating that the model with the lowest ($\chi^2 - 2$ df) is the best-fitting model from a parsimonious point of view.

RESULTS

Concordance

Tables 1 and 2 show the occurrence of the disorders among the index twins. In addition, the frequencies of the disorders among cotwins of index twins with (concordance) and without the disorder are compared separately for MZ and DZ pairs. Finally, the frequencies of the disorder among MZ and DZ cotwins of index twins with the disorder are compared. Chi-square (χ^2) tests are used if the numbers are high enough; if not, Fishers's exact test is applied. The first comparison shows whether the concordance of a disorder, based on cotwins of index twins, is higher than by chance and thus a familial transmission is suggested. The second comparison, showing whether the concordance is higher in MZ versus DZ pairs, points to a genetic influence on the development of the disorder.

For the occurrence of any type of PD, the concordance is statistically significant for both MZ

Table 1. Probandwise Concordance Rates for Any PD and for the Eccentric (A), Emotional (B), and Fearful (C) Clusters Definite and Broad (including probable cases lacking one or two criteria)

	Prevalence of Probands With the Disorder		Frequency (%) Among Cotwins of Probands			
			MZ		DZ	
Disorder	MZ	DZ	Without the Disorder	With the Disorder*	Without the Disorder	With the Disorder*
Any PD						
Definite	48.9	58.4	10.6	40.0†	7.7	28.8‡
Broad	79.3	78.4	26.3	68.5§	25.9	60.2‖
Cluster A						
Definite	12.1	19.8	5.0	9.1	4.0	16.0
Broad	38.5	53.2	17.9	40.0¶	13.6	26.9
Cluster B						
Definite	20.7	34.1	1.4	31.6#	3.7	11.9
Broad	39.1	48.0	16.1	50.0**	10.9	33.9††
Cluster C						
Definite	36.3	37.5	8.6	33.3‡‡¶¶	8.8	12.5
Broad	62.6	60.2	20.6	63.2§§	25.5	46.8‖‖

*Probandwise concordance.

Difference between cotwins of probands with and without the disorder: †$\chi^2 = 9.06$, $df = 1$, $P = .0026$, ‡$\chi^2 = 7.16$, $df = 1$, $P = .0074$, §$\chi^2 = 9.47$, $df = 1$, $P = .0021$, ‖$\chi^2 = 8.65$, $df = 1$, $P = .0033$, ¶$\chi^2 = 4.36$, $df = 1$, $P = .0368$, #$\chi^2 = 15.51$, $df = 1$, $P = .0001$, **$\chi^2 = 10.58$, $df = 1$, $P = .0011$, ††$\chi^2 = 8.15$, $df = 1$, $P = .0043$, ‡‡$\chi^2 = 7.24$, $df = 1$, $P = .0071$, §§$\chi^2 = 13.82$, $df = 1$, $P = .0002$, ‖‖$\chi^2 = 5.01$, $df = 1$, $P = .0253$.

Difference between MZ cotwins and DZ cotwins of probands with the disorder: ¶¶$\chi^2 = 3.94$, $df = 1$, $P = .0472$.

Table 2. Probandwise Concordance Rates for Any PD and for the Different PDs, Definite and Broad (including probable cases lacking one or two criteria) In preparation.

	Prevalence of Probands With the Disorder		Frequency (%) Among Cotwins of Probands			
			MZ		DZ	
Disorder	MZ	DZ	Without the Disorder	With the Disorder*	Without the Disorder	With the Disorder*
Paranoid						
Definite	6.6	14.3	2.4	—	3.7	11.1
Broad	30.8	38.1	14.3	28.6	11.5	20.8
Schizoid						
Definite	1.1	3.2	1.1	—	0.5	—
Broad	9.8	16.7	8.4	22.2	1.0	14.3†
Schizotypal						
Definite	8.7	8.3	3.6	—	0.9	8.3
Broad	20.7	28.3	12.3	31.6‡	4.4	11.1
Antisocial						
Definite	—	5.8	1.1	—	—	—
Broad	2.2	7.4	2.3	—	1.8	—
Borderline						
Definite	18.5	23.8	1.3	35.3§‖‖‖	1.0	6.7
Broad	37.0	37.3	1.7	38.2‖¶¶¶	2.5	19.1¶
Histrionic						
Definite	6.6	12.7	3.5	16.7	3.6	18.8#
Broad	15.4	20.6	15.6	50.0**	8.0	30.8††
Narcissistic						
Definite	5.5	6.5	1.2	—	1.7	—
Broad	12.1	17.7	1.3	45.5‡‡###	3.9	9.1
Avoidant						
Definite	23.1	21.1	2.9	28.6§§	5.9	7.4
Broad	38.5	38.3	10.7	37.1‖‖	13.9	22.4
Dependent						
Definite	14.3	18.3	7.7	—	3.9	4.3
Broad	34.1	32.5	16.7	35.5¶¶	4.7	24.4##
Obsessive-compulsive						
Definite	8.8	8.8	2.4	37.5***	5.3	—
Broad	31.9	32.8	14.5	52.2†††****	22.6	24.4
Passive-aggressive						
Definite	3.3	4.8	1.1	—	0.8	—
Broad	11.0	17.6	4.9	10.0	6.8	4.5
Self-defeating						
Definite	11.0	6.5	1.2	20.0‡‡‡	3.5	12.5
Broad	19.8	25.2	4.1	27.8§§§	8.7	12.9

*Probandwise concordance.

Difference between cotwins of probands with and without the disorder: †χ^2 = 6.25, df = 1, P = .0015, ‡Fisher exact, 1-tail, P = .0527, §χ^2 = 18.16, df = 1, P = .0000, ‖χ^2 = 19.41, df = 1, P = .0000, ¶χ^2 = 8.23, df = 1, P = .0433, #Fisher exact, 1-tail, P = .0433, **χ^2 = 6.54, df = 1, P = .0106, ††χ^2 = 7.71, df = 1, P = .0053, ‡‡χ^2 = 23.92, df = 1, P = .0000, §§χ^2 = 10.31, df = 1, P = .0013, ‖‖χ^2 = 7.58, df = 1, P = .0059, ¶¶Fisher exact, 1-tail, P = .0413, ##χ^2 = 8.95, df = 1, P = .0028, ***χ^2 = 11.20, df = 1, P = .0008, †††χ^2 = 14.41, df = 1, P = .0002, ‡‡‡χ^2 = 4.83, df = 1, P = .0280, §§§χ^2 = 7.35, df = 1, P = .0067.

Difference between MZ cotwins and DZ cotwins of probands with the disorder: ‖‖‖χ^2 = 4.43, df = 1, P = .0353, ¶¶¶Fisher exact, 1-tail, P = .0497, ###Fisher exact, 1-tail, P = .0274, ****χ^2 = 5.64, df = 1, P = .0176.

and DZ twins and both probable and definite PD. These results imply that the disorders aggregate in families due to either genetic or environmental transmission. Also, the results for clusters A, B, and C suggest familial transmission, genetic for cluster B, as the difference in concordance between MZ and DZ twins is statistically significant. Regarding the specific PDs, there are indications of familial transmission for all, except paranoid and passive-aggressive disorders. The low prevalence of antisocial PD precludes any further analysis of this disorder in the present sample. There is evidence of genetic effects on borderline, narcissistic, and obsessive-compulsive PDs, because the concordance

Table 3. Tetrachoric Correlations (R_{MZ} and R_{DZ}), Additive (a^2), Nonadditive (d^2), Common Shared-in-Families Environmental (c^2), and Unique Not-Shared-in-Families Environmental (e^2), Variance Estimates, Significance Testing, and AIC, According to Different Genetic Models for Any PD and the Three Clusters of PDs

PD	R_{MZ} SE	R_{DZ} SE	Model	a^2	d^2	c^2	e^2	χ^2	*df*	*P*<	AIC
Any PD	.58 ± .10‡	.36 ± .10‡	ACE	.44	–	.14	.42	–	–	–	–
			AE	.60	–	–	.40	0.74	1	.50	−1.26§
			CE	–	–	.45	.55	5.18	1	.02	3.18
			E	–	–	–	1.00	55.08	2	.001	51.08
Eccentric	.37 ± .14†	.09 ± .11	ADE	.00	.37	–	.63	–	–	–	–
			AE	.33	–	–	.67	1.05	1	.50	−0.95§
			E	–	–	–	1.00	14.63	2	.001	10.63
Emotional	.60 ± .11‡	.31 ± .12†	ACE	.59	–	.01	.40	–	–	–	–
			AE	.60	–	–	.40	0.01	1	.95	−1.99§
			CE	–	–	.43	.57	8.80	1	.01	6.80
			E	–	–	–	1.00	30.37	2	.001	26.37
Fearful	.61 ± .09	.23 ± .11*	ADE	.59	.00	–	.41	–	–	–	–
			AE	.59	–	–	.41	0.90	1	.80	−1.10§
			E	–	–	–	1.00	49.41	2	.001	45.41

*$P < .05$.
†$P < .01$.
‡$P < .001$.
§Best model according to AIC.

rates are significantly higher in MZ versus DZ pairs.

These analyses can only unveil familial and genetic transmission. To estimate the effect of genes and shared environment, we applied structural equation modeling.

Model Testing

Tables 3 to 6 show the tetrachoric correlations in MZ and DZ pairs and the results of the model testing. Antisocial PD is excluded because of its low frequency in the twin sample.

The best-fitting of the full models, either ACE or ADE, is first presented, then the two reduced models, and finally a model with only E, unique, not-shared-in-families environmental variance. The value of AIC is presented for each model. The best model according to this criterion is indicated.

Table 3 shows that the best genetic model for any PD according to AIC is the AE model, with 60% of the variance accounted for by additive genetic factors, and 40% unique environmental variance. All models without a genetic component were rejected.

Also for the eccentric (A), emotional (B), and fearful (C) clusters, models without a genetic component are rejected. The AE model gives the best fitting for each of the clusters, according to AIC.

Table 4 shows that a model without a genetic

Table 4. Tetrachoric Correlations (R_{MZ} and R_{DZ}), Additive (a^2), Nonadditive (d^2), Common Shared-in-Families Environmental (c^2), and Unique Not-Shared-in-Families Environmental (e^2), Variance Estimates, Significance Testing, and AIC, According to Different Genetic Models for the Eccentric PDs

PD	R_{MZ} SE	R_{DZ} SE	Model	a^2	d^2	c^2	e^2	χ^2	*df*	*P*<	AIC
Paranoid	.30 ± .15*	.12 ± .13	ADE	.18	.12	–	.70	–	–	–	–
			AE	.28	–	–	.72	0.10	1	.80	−1.90‡
			E	–	–	–	1.00	10.20	2	.01	6.20
Schizoid	.31 ± .26	.12 ± .12	ADE	.17	.13	–	.69	–	–	–	–
			AE	29	–	–	.71	0.12	1	.80	−1.88‡
			E	–	–	–	1.00	10.86	2	.01	6.86
Schizotypal	.62 ± .14†	.25 ± .14*	ADE	.36	.27	–	.38	–	–	–	–
			AE	.61	–	–	.39	0.65	1	.50	−1.35‡
			E	–	–	–	1.00	52.81	2	.001	48.81

*$P < .05$.
†$P < .001$.
‡Best model according to AIC.

Table 5. Tetrachoric Correlations (R_{MZ} and R_{DZ}), Additive (a^2), Nonadditive (d^2), Common Shared-in-Families Environmental (c^2), and Unique Not-Shared-in-Families Environmental (e^2), Variance Estimates, Significance Testing, and AIC, According to Different Genetic Models for the Emotional PDs

PD	R_{MZ} SE	R_{DZ} SE	Model	a^2	d^2	c^2	e^2	χ^2	*df*	$P<$	AIC
Borderline	.69 ± .08†	.40 ± .10†	ACE	.57	—	.11	.32	—	—	—	—
			AE	.69	—	—	.31	0.55	1	.50	−1.45‡
			CE	—	—	.52	.48	11.74	1	.001	9.74
			E	—	—	—	1.00	79.84	2	.001	75.84
Histrionic	.67 ± .15†	.35 ± .15*	ACE	.63	—	.04	.34	—	—	—	—
			AE	.67	—	—	.33	0.06	1	.90	−1.94‡
			CE	—	—	.48	.52	12.20	1	.001	10.20
			E	—	—	—	1.11	69.95	2	.001	65.95
Narcissistic	.77 ± .11†	.18 ± .19	ADE	.00	.77	—	.23	—	—	—	—‡
			AE	.75	—	—	.25	6.71	1	.01	4.71
			E	—	—	—	1.00	86.69	2	.001	82.69

*$P<.01$.
†$P<.001$.
‡Best model according to AIC.

component was also rejected for the paranoid, schizoid, and schizotypal PDs. The AE models provide the best fit according to AIC, yielding a heritability estimate of .28, .29, and .61, respectively.

A model without a parameter for genetic effects was also rejected for the borderline, histrionic, and narcissistic PDs. The AE model provides a better fit than the full model for the borderline and histrionic PDs, while the reduced models both fit significantly worse than the full model, ADE, for narcissistic PD. The heritability estimates are high, .69 for borderline, .67 for histrionic, and .77 for narcissistic PDs.

A model without a genetic component is rejected for the avoidant, obsessive-compulsive, and self-defeating PDs. For avoidant PD, not even the "full" model fits. This is because the correlation between DZ partners is too low to fit any model. The lower limit for the DZ correlation is one fourth of the MZ partners. A DZ correlation lower than this value is equivalent to imposing a constraint on the data, and the model fit can be tested with 1 *df*. Both reduced models fit worse than the full model

Table 6. Tetrachoric Correlations (R_{MZ} and R_{DZ}), Additive (a^2), Nonadditive (d^2), Common Shared-in-Families Environmental (c^2), and Unique Not-Shared-in-Families Environmental (e^2), Variance Estimates, Significance Testing, and AIC, According to Different Genetic Models for the Fearful PDs

PD	R_{MZ} SE	R_{DZ} SE	Model	a^2	d^2	c^2	e^2	χ^2	*df*	$P<$	AIC
Avoidant	.31 ± .14*	−.03 ± .13	ADE	.00	.28	—	.72	1.46	1§	.30	−0.54‖
			AE	.22	—	—	.78	3.46	1	.10	1.46
			E	—	—	—	1.00	9.03	2	.02	5.03
Dependent	.55 ± .11‡	.37 ± .12‡	ACE	.36	—	.19	.45	—	—	—	—
			AE	.57	—	—	.43	1.33	1	.30	−0.67‖
			CE		—	.44	.56	3.30	1	.10	1.30
			E	—	—	—	1.00	51.23	1	.001	47.23
Obsessive-compulsive	.78 ± .08‡	.31 ± .12†	ADE	.47	.31	—	.22	—	—	—	—
			AE	.77	—	—	.23	1.03	1	.50	−0.97‖
			E	—	—	—	1.00	96.90	2	.001	92.90
Passive-aggressive	−.01 ± .29	−.23 ± .21	ADE	.00	.00	—	1.00	7.02	1§	.01	5.02
			AE	.00	—	—	1.00	7.02	1	.01	5.02
			E	—	—	—	1.00	7.02	2	.05	3.02‖
Self-defeating	.55 ± .14‡	.25 ± .15*	ADE	.47	.07	—	.46	—	—	—	—
			AE	.54	—	—	.46	0.05	1	.90	−1.95‖
			E	—	—	—	1.00	40.61	2	.001	36.61

*$P<.05$.
†$P<.01$.
‡$P<.001$.
§The model is in effect constrained because the DZ correlation is lower than can be explained by any model.
‖Best model according to AIC.

in terms of AIC. The AE model gives the best fit for dependent, obsessive-compulsive, and self-defeating PDs. Even if an AE model, providing a heritability of .57, is the best-fitting for the dependent PD, a CE model cannot be rejected, meaning that the heritability estimate is not significantly different from zero. For the passive-aggressive PD, there are no twin correlations at all, and nonshared, unique environmental effects can explain all of the variance.

For the PD clusters and disorders that are sufficiently frequent to avoid empty cells in the two by two tables (proband or cotwin affected or not), we also fitted models to the data for the definite disorders. The heritability estimates hardly changed at all for "any PD" (.55) or the emotional (.64) or fearful (.53) clusters as compared with those based on "probable disorder" data. As to the eccentric cluster, the best model had a shared environment estimate of .31 and no heredity.

Among the specific PDs, the heritability estimate based on the data on definite borderline personality was .80. For histrionic PD, a CE model gave the best fit, with the effect of shared environment estimated at .52. For the avoidant PD definite cases, an ADE model gave the best fit, with a heritability of .56. Finally, for the definite self-defeating PD, an ACE model with a heritability of .24 and a shared environmental variance estimate of .39 best fit the data.

Due to the low prevalence, estimates for the specific disorders and, to a lesser extent, the eccentric and emotional clusters are rather unreliable. However, the average heritability estimates, for the clusters and among the specific PDs, do not depend much on whether the data on definite cases are included, and vary between .50 and .60. Furthermore, in both instances, the evidence for the heritability of the eccentric cluster is weak compared with the other clusters.

DISCUSSION

Our results from the first twin study that includes all types of PDs except antisocial suggest that PDs generally, the eccentric A cluster, emotional B cluster, and fearful C cluster, as well as all specific disorders except passive-aggressive PD, appear to be genetically influenced. The data do not have sufficient statistical power to precisely disentangle nonadditive (dominance) and additive genetic effect.

However, regarding the dependent PD, a model with only shared and unique environmental effects was not rejected, although a model with genetic effects gave a better fit. The heritability was rather low for the paranoid, schizoid, and avoidant PDs. For the other PDs, the genetic estimates were high.

Our findings demonstrate that almost all PDs are genetically influenced, and confirm the results from a twin study with questionnaire scales measuring personality traits resembling the PDs[15] and twin studies of personality traits in general.[4]

A previous Norwegian twin study also demonstrated genetic influence on schizotypal PD, while borderline PD only appeared to be influenced by shared environment.[14] Perhaps the lack of evidence for the heritability of borderline PD in the previous study was due to the low number of twins.

The influence of heredity on the development of schizotypal features was also observed in a questionnaire study by Kendler and Hewitt.[28] Furthermore, the Danish Adoption Study demonstrated an increased risk of schizotypal PD among the biological relatives of adoptees with schizotypal PD.[1] A previous twin study with a few questionnaire items showed a weak genetic influence on paranoid features.[29]

One may speculate as to whether the weak genetic influence on the avoidant, paranoid, and schizoid PDs may be related to the fact that these disorders are common in Norway compared with other countries.[25,30] A strong cultural effect in the direction of developing these disorders might both increase their frequency and weaken the genetic effects.

Some may wonder about the low tetrachoric correlation for avoidant PD in DZ pairs. However, low correlations between DZ twin partners are very common in studies of personality features. Only seldomly are the DZ correlations half of the MZ correlations or more.[4] The reason may be nonadditive genetic effects, polarization in DZ twin pairs, or a more equal environment for MZ versus DZ partners. However, the fact that the same phenomenon is observed among twins reared apart[5-8] suggests that the two latter explanations are unlikely.

Some previous studies have demonstrated results pointing to genetic effects on personality dimensions, which are similar to borderline PD in one pole and obsessive-compulsive PD in the other pole. Studies of twins reared apart have found genetic influences on impulsivity and "monotony avoidance,"[7] aggression, constraint, and control,[5] as well as conscientiousness.[8] Finally, a specific genetic locus that contributes to the variation in novelty seeking has been identified.[31,32]

The strong influence of genes and the absence of effects of shared environment in borderline PD may seem surprising and in disagreement with popular clinical theories. However, a trend in the results from the full model was compatible with some effect of shared environment, even if this model was not the best according to AIC. Kernberg[33] states that the basic cause of the development of borderline personality organization may be an inherited, extra strong aggressive drive plus an inborn deficiency in the ability to tolerate anxiety. Moreover, Linehan and Koerner[34] maintain that the basis for borderline PD is an inherited biological predisposition to emotional dysregulation. This dysregulation implies an accentuated sensitivity to emotional stimuli, intense reaction to such stimuli, and a slow, delayed return to a more quiet emotional level. In addition, this dysregulation means a lack of ability to suppress inappropriate behavior related to strong positive and negative affects, a lack of ability to comfort oneself when strong affects produce intense physiologic outcomes, problems in turning the attention toward other aspects, and finally difficulties in organizing and coordinating actions to reach important aims. Thus, both theories state that inborn tendencies are important.

Most PDs, especially borderline, self-defeating, avoidant, and dependent PDs, are shown to be related to neuroticism.[35] Studies of twins reared together and apart,[5-7] as well as molecular genetic studies,[36] demonstrate that the genetic influence on neuroticism is perhaps better established than for any other personality dimension.

Study Limitations

The sample was not drawn from the general population, but from patient populations. This fact may have biased the estimates. However, to obtain the same number of twins with PDs through a population study would have required a very large sample. To personally interview such a population-based sample would have been extremely costly. Furthermore, results for anxiety[37] and affective[38,39] disorders from general population studies have yielded data very similar to those from clinical samples.[19,40,41] Finally, our twin data were augmented by data from a population-based Norwegian sample with more than 2,000 persons.

The same interviewers often interviewed both the proband and the cotwin. This may have biased the results somewhat toward inflated genetic or family effects. However, such a possible bias cannot explain that some PDs seem to be mainly due to genes and others again to nonshared environment.

We included definite and probable PDs in our analysis. The data on disorders with sufficiently high prevalence to permit analyses of definite, as well as probable, disorders showed very similar results for probable and definite cases.

The number of cases was low for some types of PDs. This means that the estimates are not very precise, and the power to reject the models is weak. Besides, our "simulation" of two by two tables by using the population-based prevalence data from another study may have added some statistical fluctuation. The somewhat arbitrarily chosen values for the number of pairs for the model-fitting may have contributed, in some cases, to type 1 errors (falsely rejecting more parsimonious models, and hence falsely assigning statistical significance to some of the parameter estimates). More likely, however, the number of pairs are underspecified compared with the real body of information inherited in the data, resulting in type 2 errors (systematic effects are left undetected). Thus, our results should be regarded as preliminary. Probably, the highest genetic estimates are too high and the lowest are too low. However, as both the heritability of "any PD," as well as the average heritability for the specific disorders, narrowly or broadly defined, are about .50 to .60, the results clearly demonstrate substantial genetic effects on PDs in general.

The results seem to suggest only small or no effects of the family environment. However, the power to detect such effects is generally poor in classic twin studies. Besides, calculations of the tetrachoric correlations were based on the assumption that only a small part of the cases from the twin population were included in the study. The violation of this assumption may have caused deflated correlations among MZ pairs, as well as DZ pairs, and thus deflated estimates of effects of the family environment. Although the absence of evidence for effects of the family environment is in agreement with most results from studies of personality traits,[25] our results are not conclusive regarding the existence of such effects on PDs.

Conclusion

This first twin study of the whole realm of PDs except antisocial disorder shows that PDs in general are genetically influenced. Among the PD clusters, genes markedly influence the emotional and fearful clusters, while genetic effects are weaker for the eccentric cluster. Within the emotional cluster, narcissistic, borderline, and histrionic PDs are strongly genetically influenced. Among the fearful PDs, obsessive-compulsive and self-defeating PDs are particularly strongly influenced by genes. Passive-aggressive PD does not seem to be genetically influenced at all. The schizotypal PD from the eccentric cluster is also obviously influenced by genes. Most genetic effects are between .50 and .60 for single disorders, clusters, and PD generally. This number is clearly higher than for most axis I disorders, with the possible exception of schizophrenia and bipolar disorder,[42] and is also higher than for most general personality dimensions.[4-8]

Common, shared-in-families environmental factors such as socioeconomic status and parenting style and cultural variation among families in the sample, etc., seem to be of little importance, except maybe for any PD, borderline PD, and dependent PD. Passive-aggressive PD does not seem to run in families at all. However, the low power to detect effects of shared environment in general, together with the low prevalence of and low reliability for this disorder, makes such a conclusion unsafe. Unique environmental effects are generally about .40 to .50, except for the eccentric cluster or the "Scandinavian" disorders, i.e., paranoid, schizoid, and avoidant PDs, where such effects seem to be high. However, the unique environmental effect estimates are also likely to contain measurement errors, and are thus regularly overestimated.

It is interesting that even if the criteria for DSM-III/IV are drawn from different sources, including adoption studies (schizotypal) and psychodynamic theories (narcissistic), most disorders seem to be relatively strongly genetically influenced.

The present study comprises a relatively large number of definite or probable PDs. Even so, uncertainty related to a moderate number of definite specific PDs and method problems associated with the ascertainment procedure call for a replication of the results from large normal twin population studies.

REFERENCES

1. Kendler KS, Gruenberg AM, Kinney DK. Independent diagnoses of adoptees and relatives as defined by DSM-III in the provincial and national samples of the Danish Adoption Study of Schizophrenia. Arch Gen Psychiatry 1994;51:456-468.

2. Kendler KS, Walters EE, Neale MC, Kessler RC. The structure of the genetic and environmental risk factors for six major psychiatric disorders in women: phobia, generalized anxiety disorder, panic disorder, bulimia, major depression, and alcoholism. Arch Gen Psychiatry 1995;52:374-383.

3. Kendler KS, Neale MC, MacLean CJ, Heath AC, Eaves LJ, Kessler RC. Smoking and major depression: a causal analysis. Arch Gen Psychiatry 1993;50:36-43.

4. Eaves LJ, Eysenck HJ, Martin NG. Genes, cultures and personality: an empirical approach. London, UK: Academic, 1989.

5. Tellegen A, Lykken TD, Bouchard TJ, Wilcox KJ, Segal NL, Rich S. Personality similarity in twins reared apart and together. J Pers Soc Psychol 1988:54:1031-1039.

6. Pedersen NL, McClearn GE, Plomin R, Nesselsroade JR, Berg S, DeFaire U. The Swedish Adoption/Twin Study of Aging: an update. Arch Gen Med 1991;40:7-20.

7. Pedersen NL, Plomin R, McClearn GE, Friberg L. Neuroticism, extraversion and related traits in adult twins reared apart and reared together. J Pers Soc Psychol 1988;55:950-957.

8. Bergeman CS, Chipur HM, Plomin R, Pedersen NL, McClearn GE, Nesselroade JR, et al. Genetic and environmental effects on openness to experience, agreeableness, and conscientiousness: an adoptive/twin study. J Pers 1993;61:159-178.

9. McGuffin P, Thapar A. The genetics of personality disorders. Br J Psychiatry 1992;160:12-23.

10. Cadoret R, Stewart MA. An adoptive study of attention deficit/hyperactivity/aggression and their relationship to adult antisocial personality. Psychiatry 1991;32:73-82.

11. Torgersen S, Skre I, Onstad S, Edvardsen J, Kringlen E. "True" schizotypal personality disorder: a study of co-twins and relatives of schizophrenic probands. Am J Psychiatry 1993;150:1661-1667.

12. Squires-Wheeler E, Skodol A, Bassett A, Erlenmeyer-Kimling L. DSM-III-R schizotypal personality traits in offspring of schizophrenic disorder, affective disorder, and normal control parents. J Psychiatr Res 1989;23:229-239.

13. Lyons MJ, Toomey R, Faaone SV, Tsuang MT. Comparison of schizotypal relatives of schizophrenia versus affective probands. Am J Med Genet 1994;54:279-285.

14. Torgersen S. Genetic and nosological aspects of schizotypal and borderline personality disorders: a twin study. Arch Gen Psychiatry 1984;41:546-554.

15. Jang KL, Livesley WJ, Vernon PA, Jackson DN. Heritability of personality disorder traits: a twin study. Acta Psychiatr Scand 1996;94:438-444.

16. Zimmermann M. Diagnosing personality disorders. A

review of issues and research methods. Arch Gen Psychiatry 1994;51:225-242.

17. Reich JH. Familiality of DSM-III dramatic and anxious personality clusters. Nerv Ment Disord 1989;177:96-100.

18. Onstad S, Skre I, Edvardsen J, Torgersen S, Kringlen E. Mental disorders in first-degree relatives of schizophrenics. Acta Psychiatr Scand 1991;83:463-467.

19. Skre I, Onstad S, Torgersen S, Lygren S, Kringlen E. A twin study of DSM-III-R anxiety disorders. Acta Psychiatr Scand 1993;88:85-92.

20. Torgersen S. The determination of twin zygosity by means of a mailed questionnaire. Acta Genet Med Gemellol (Roma) 1979;28:225-236.

21. Spitzer RL, Williams JBW. Structured Clinical Interview for DSM-III (SCID-I). New York, NY: New York State Psychiatric Institute, Biometrics Research, 1985.

22. Spitzer RL, Williams JBW. Structured Clinical Interview for DSM-III-R Personality Disorders (SCID-II). New York, NY: New York State Psychiatric Institute, Biometrics Research, 1985.

23. Jøreskog K, Sørbom D. PRELIS 2: A Preprocessor for LISREL. Chicago, IL: Scientific Software, 1993.

24. Neale MC, Cardon LR. Methodology for Genetic Studies of Twins and Families. Dordrecht, The Netherlands: Kluwer Academic, 1992.

25. Torgersen S, Kringlen E, Cramer V. The prevalence and demographic associations of personality disorders in the community. Submitted.

26. Jøreskog K, Sørbom D. LISREL 8: A Guide to Program and Applications. Chicago, IL: Scientific Software, 1993.

27. Akaike H. Factor analysis and AIC. Psychometrica 1987;52:317-332.

28. Kendler KS, Hewitt J. The structure of self-report schizotypy in twins. J Pers Disord 1992;6:1-17.

29. Kendler KS, Heath A, Martin NG. A genetic epidemiologic study of self-report suspiciousness. Compr Psychiatry 1987;28:187-196.

30. Alnaes R, Torgersen S. DSM-III symptom disorders (axis I) and personality disorders (axis II) in an outpatient population. Acta Psychiatr Scand 1988;78:348-355.

31. Ebstein RP, Novick O, Umansky R, Priel B, Osher Y, Blaine D, et al. Dopamine D4 receptor (D4DR) exon III polymorphism associated with the human personality trait of novelty seeking. Nat Genet 1996;12:78-80.

32. Benjamin J, Li L, Patterson C, Greenberg BD, Murphy DL, Hamer DH. Population and familial association between the D4 dopamine receptor gene and measures of novelty seeking. Nat Genet 1996;12:81-84.

33. Kernberg O. Severe Personality Disorders: Psychotherapeutic Strategies. New Haven, CT: Yale University Press, 1984.

34. Linehan M, Koerner K. A behavioral theory of borderline personality disorder. In: Paris J (ed): Borderline Personality Disorder: Etiology and Treatment. Washington, DC: American Psychiatric Press, 1993:103-121.

35. Trull TJ. DSM-III-R personality disorders and the five-factor model of personality: an empirical comparison. J Abnorm Psychol 1992;101:553-560.

36. Lesch KP, Bengel D, Petri S, Benjamin J, Muller CR, Hamer DH, et al. Association of anxiety-related traits with a polymorphism in the serotonin transporter gene regulator region. Science 1996;274:1527-1531.

37. Kendler KS, Neale MC, Kessler RL, Heath AC, Eaves LJ. Panic disorder in women: a population-based twin study. Psychol Med 1993;23:397-406.

38. Kendler KS, Neale MC, Kessler RL, Heath AC, Eaves LJ. A population based twin study of major depression in women: the impact of varying definitions of illness. Arch Gen Psychiatry 1992;49:257-266.

39. Lyons MJ, Eisen SA, Goldberg J, True W, Lin N, Meyer JM, et al. A registry-based twin study of depression in men. Arch Gen Psychiatry 1998;55:468-472.

40. Torgersen S. Genetic factors in anxiety disorders. Arch Gen Psychiatry 1983;40:1085-1089.

41. Torgersen S. Genetic factors in moderately severe and mild affective disorders. Arch Gen Psychiatry 1986;43:222-226.

42. Torgersen S. Genetic basis and psychopathology. In: Turner SM, Hersen M (eds): Adult Psychopathology and Diagnosis. New York, NY: Wiley, 1997:58-8.

Psychological Review
1995, Vol. 102, No. 3, 458–489

0033-295X/95/$3.00

Where Is the Child's Environment? A Group Socialization Theory of Development

Judith Rich Harris
Middletown, New Jersey

Do parents have any important long-term effects on the development of their child's personality? This article examines the evidence and concludes that the answer is no. A new theory of development is proposed: that socialization is context-specific and that outside-the-home socialization takes place in the peer groups of childhood and adolescence. Intra- and intergroup processes, not dyadic relationships, are responsible for the transmission of culture and for environmental modification of children's personality characteristics. The universality of children's groups explains why development is not derailed by the wide variations in parental behavior found within and between societies.

In 1983, after many dozens of pages spent reviewing the literature on the effects parents have on children, Eleanor Maccoby and John Martin paused for a critical overview of the field of socialization research. They questioned the size and robustness of the effects they had just summarized; they wondered whether the number of significant correlations was greater than that expected by chance. They cited other research indicating that biological or adoptive siblings do not develop similar personalities as a result of being reared in the same household. This was their conclusion:

> These findings imply strongly that there is very little impact of the physical environment that parents provide for children and very little impact of parental characteristics that must be essentially the same for all children in a family . . . Indeed, the implications are either that parental behaviors have no effect, or that the only effective aspects of parenting must vary greatly from one child to another within the same family. (Maccoby & Martin, 1983, p. 82)

Since 1983, many developmental psychologists have focused on the second of Maccoby and Martin's two possible implications, "that the only effective aspects of parenting must vary greatly from one child to another." The other possibility, "that parental behaviors have no effect," has never been considered as a serious alternative.

This article examines both alternatives. I begin by showing why "must vary greatly from one child to another" cannot explain the results that puzzled Maccoby and Martin. Then I consider the possibility "that parental behaviors have no effect." The conclusion reached is that, within the range of families that have been studied, parental behaviors have no effect on the psychological characteristics their children will have as adults. To explain this outcome, I propose a theory of group socialization (GS theory), based on the findings of behavioral genetics, on sociological views of intra- and intergroup processes, on psychological research showing that learning is highly context-specific, and on evolutionary considerations.

Does the Family Environment Matter?

By the time they are adults, adoptive siblings who were reared in the same home will, on average, bear no resemblance to each other in personality. Biological siblings who were reared in the same home will be somewhat more alike, but still not very similar. Even identical (monozygotic) twins reared in the same home will not be identical in personality. They will not be noticeably more alike than identical twins reared in separate homes (Bouchard, Lykken, McGue, Segal, & Tellegen, 1990; Plomin & Daniels, 1987; Scarr, 1992).

These are some of the findings of the field of developmental behavioral genetics. The data on which they are based consist of correlations between pairs of people who share all, some, or none of their genes, and who did or did not grow up in the same home. Two conclusions—one surprising and the other not—emerged from the analysis of such data. The unsurprising conclusion was that about half of the variance in the measured psychological characteristics was due to differences in heredity. The surprising conclusion involved the other half of the variance: Very little of it could be attributed to differences in the home environments in which the participants in these studies were reared (Loehlin & Nichols, 1976; Plomin, Chipuer, & Neiderhiser, 1994; Plomin & Daniels, 1987; Scarr, 1992).

Behavioral Genetic Methods and Results

Behavioral genetic studies begin by collecting data—for example, scores on personality or intelligence tests—from pairs of people. Ideally, data from two or more types of subject pairs, such as twins and adoptive siblings, are combined in the data analysis. That makes it possible to test different mathematical models, based on slightly different assumptions, to see which provides the best fit for the data. The winning model is then used to divide up the variance calculated from the test scores—

I thank the following people, who do not necessarily agree with the views presented here, for their helpful comments on earlier versions of this work: William A. Corsaro, Judith L. Gibbons, Charles S. Harris, Neil J. Salkind, Sandra Scarr, and Naomi Weisstein.

Correspondence concerning this article should be addressed to Judith Rich Harris, 54 Crawford Road, Middletown, New Jersey 07748. Electronic mail may be sent via Internet to 72073.1211@compuserve.com.

the individual differences among the subjects—into three, or sometimes four, sectors.

The first sector consists of variance that can be attributed to shared genes; this is called *heritability.* Heritability generally accounts for 40% to 50% of the variance in personality characteristics, if the measurements are made in adulthood (McGue, Bouchard, Iacono, & Lykken, 1993; N. L. Pedersen, Plomin, Nesselroade, & McClearn, 1992; Plomin, Owen, & McGuffin, 1994).

The second sector consists of variance that can be attributed to *shared environmental influence*—the home in which a given pair of people were reared. This sector is very small if the measurements are made in adulthood: from 0 to 10% in most studies (Bouchard, 1994; Loehlin, 1992; Plomin & Daniels, 1987). The implication of this finding is that resemblances between siblings are due almost entirely to shared genes. Their shared environment has not made them more alike.

The third sector consists of measurement error, which is around 20% for personality tests (Plomin, 1990). Some analyses do not produce an estimate for this component of the variance, in which case it is included in the last sector, which consists of variance that can be attributed neither to shared genes nor to shared rearing environment (Goldsmith, 1993a). This sector of the variance is usually referred to as *nonshared environmental influence,* but a more accurate label for it is *unexplained environmental variance.* On the average, from 40% to 50% of the variance in adult personality characteristics falls into the unexplained or nonshared sector.

If heredity can account for only about half of the reliable variation among adults, then environmental influences must account for the rest. The challenge is to find the source of these influences. Behavioral genetic studies have demonstrated which aspects of the environment are *not* likely to be important. The aspects that are not likely to be important are all those that are shared by children who grow up in the same home: the parents' personalities and philosophies of child rearing, their presence or absence in the home, the number of books or TV sets or guns the home contains, and so on. In short, almost all of the factors previously associated with the term *environment,* and associated even more closely with the term *nurture,* appear to be ineffective in shaping children's personalities.

Within-Family Environmental Differences

This outcome went against the deeply held beliefs of many developmental psychologists. But, unlike the socialization research that was judged by Maccoby and Martin (1983) to be lacking in robustness, the findings of behavioral genetics are quite reliable. The results are consistent within and between studies and cannot readily be explained away (Scarr, 1993). Children reared in the same home by the same parents do not, on average, turn out to be similar unless they share genes, and even if they share all of their genes, they are not as similar as one might expect. For identical twins reared in the same home, correlations of personality characteristics are seldom above .50, which leaves at least 30% of the variance unexplained by shared genes plus a shared home environment.[1]

Faced with these results, most behavioral geneticists and many socialization theorists turned to Maccoby and Martin's (1983) second alternative, "that the only effective aspects of parenting must vary greatly from one child to another within the same family" (p. 82). The unexplained variance was attributed to *within-family environmental differences* (Daniels & Plomin, 1985; Dunn, 1992; Hoffman, 1991). According to this concept, each child in a family inhabits his or her unique niche in the ecology of the family, and it is within these niches, or *microenvironments* (Braungart, Plomin, DeFries, & Fulker, 1992; Dunn & Plomin, 1990), that the formative aspects of development are presumed to occur.

In the past decade, much attention has been focused on these microenvironments. That they exist is unquestionable; the question is whether they can account for almost half the variance in personality characteristics. The next section summarizes the evidence that has led one behavioral geneticist to admit that the matter "remains largely a mystery" (Bouchard, 1994, p. 1701) and another to conclude that the family environment (macro- and micro-) may, in fact, "exert little influence on personality development over the life course" (Rowe, 1994, p. 1).

Can Within-Family Environmental Differences Explain the Unexplained Variance?

Why does growing up in the same home not make siblings alike? Perhaps because two children growing up in the same home might have very different experiences in that home. In particular, their parents might treat them differently. There are several possible reasons why parents might treat their children differently; McCartney and her colleagues (McCartney, Robeson, Jordan, & Mouradian, 1991) have divided them into *child-driven, relationship-driven, parent-driven,* and *family context* effects.

Child-driven effects. If parents do not treat their children alike, it may be because the children themselves are not alike. Perhaps one child has a more pleasing personality or is more physically attractive than the other. There is good evidence that adults do not behave in the same way to a beautiful child and a homely one (Burns & Farina, 1992; Ritter, Casey, & Langlois, 1991), or to an easy child and a difficult one (Lytton, 1990; Thomas & Chess, 1977), or to a healthy child and an ill one (Quittner & Opipari, 1994). The tendency for a child's behavior or appearance to evoke a particular reaction from parents or other interactive partners is called a *reactive* effect (also known as an *evocative* effect; Scarr & McCartney, 1983). A reactive effect is an example of a *gene–environment correlation* (Plomin, DeFries, & Loehlin, 1977)—a correlation between a genetically influenced characteristic, such as a pretty face or a pleasing disposition, and a particular environmental variable, such as doting parents.

Although gene–environment correlations are often found (Plomin & Bergeman, 1991), they contribute primarily to genetic variance rather than environmental, because their effects are predictable on the basis of the proportion of genes shared. Genetically

[1] A correlation of .50 between twins means that .50 of the variance covaries between them; therefore the correlation accounts for 50% of the variance in that measure (for a detailed explanation, see Plomin, 1990). Allowing 20% for measurement error leaves 30% of the variance unaccounted for.

influenced characteristics tend to be most similar in identical twins, less similar in fraternal (dizygotic) twins and nontwin biological siblings, and uncorrelated in adoptive siblings. The effects of any environmental influences that are evoked by these characteristics should also be most similar for identical twins and least similar for adoptive siblings. This pattern of correlations, identical twins > fraternal twins > adoptive siblings, is identified by behavioral genetic models as genetic variance (McGuire, Neiderhiser, Reiss, Hetherington, & Plomin, 1994). Thus, it is unlikely that reactive effects could account for much of the unexplained environmental variance.

It is possible, however, that reactive effects might act in a way that turns small differences into larger ones, thereby adding a major environmental effect to a minor genetic one and increasing overall variance by making children less alike. For example, children who inherit a tendency to be sociable might elicit more interaction from their parents than introverted children, and this extra interaction might cause them to become still more sociable, producing a positive feedback loop, or what is commonly known as a vicious circle (J. R. Harris & Liebert, 1991).

There is evidence that positive feedback loops do occur in development (Anderson, Lytton, & Romney, 1986; Moffitt, 1993b). However, as Bell (1968; Bell & Chapman, 1986) pointed out, there are also negative feedback loops. A child who is very active is frequently admonished to sit still; a sluggish child may be tempted into games of catch or tag. Negative feedback loops would *reduce* variability and make children more alike. Furthermore, there are reactive effects that could loop in either direction: Timidity in a child, for example, might elicit either parental protectiveness or parental anger. Thus, different characteristics engender different feedback loops—positive, negative, or unpredictable. If these effects were responsible for an important part of the unexplained variance, we would expect that sector of the variance to vary in magnitude according to the characteristic that is being measured: It should be large for characteristics in which the feedback loop is likely to be positive and small for those in which it is likely to be negative. Instead, we find that the portion of the variance attributed to unexplained environmental influence is remarkably uniform for a wide variety of personality characteristics (Plomin & Daniels, 1987; Tellegen et al., 1988).

What about child-driven differences in experiences that are not due to differential treatment by the parents? For example, children tend to experience different illnesses or injuries. However, such differences are likely to average out over the course of childhood, unless there is a tendency for a particular child to suffer repeated illnesses or accidents. In this case, a genetically influenced characteristic is likely to be involved—a biological susceptibility that predisposes the child to illness, or an active and impulsive temperament that makes the child accident-prone (Jaquess & Finney, 1994). Again, identical twins are likely to be most similar and adopted children least similar in this respect, and if there are effects on personality they will fall mostly into the sector of variance attributed to heredity.

A final child-driven mechanism that has been proposed to account for the lack of similarity between reared-together siblings is that different children might experience or interpret environmental events in different ways (Hoffman, 1991; Kagan, 1984). For example, parents might treat two children exactly alike but the children might interpret their parents' behavior differently. In fact, adolescent and adult fraternal twins often give differing descriptions of the emotional climate of their childhood home and of the warmth and expressiveness of their parents (Plomin, McClearn, Pedersen, Nesselroade, & Bergeman, 1988; Rowe, 1981). These conflicting reports, however, could represent either different interpretations of the same parental behavior or accurate reports of differential parental treatment. If it could be shown that they were indeed different interpretations of the same events, this would be evidence of a *gene–environment interaction.* Gene–environment interactions, if they occurred, would contribute to the unexplained variance; but attempts to measure such interactions have so far yielded unpromising results. The few interactions that have been found could account for only a negligible portion of variance (Loehlin, 1992).[2] Moreover, gene–environment interactions cannot explain the personality differences between identical twins.

Relationship-driven effects. These effects involve the fit or match between a parent's characteristics and a child's. For example, perhaps the child's temperament does not match the parent's preferences or expectations (Thomas & Chess, 1977). However, temperament is a genetically influenced trait (Braungart et al., 1992; Goldsmith, 1993b; Robinson, Kagan, Reznick, & Corley, 1992), and therefore the probability of a match or mismatch with parental preferences should be similar for identical twins, less similar for fraternal twins. The presumed effects would be equivalent to a gene–environment correlation—one that is specific to a particular parent. Differences between fraternal twins would be increased to a greater degree than differences between identical twins. To account for the unexplained variance, we need effects that are not correlated with the proportion of genes shared—effects that can explain the differences in personality between identical twins reared in the same home.

Parent-driven effects. Parents might treat their children differently for reasons of their own. A parent might have a particular reason for favoring or rejecting a particular child: for example, because the child was unwanted—its conception was unplanned (David, 1992). However, this hypothesis cannot explain the findings of behavioral genetic studies, which are based largely on data from twins and adopted children. The timing of conception is the same for twins, and adoption seldom occurs by accident.

Another possibility is that a child might be treated in a particular way by a parent, not because of that child's own characteristics, but because of the characteristics of his or her sibling. Schachter and Stone (1985) found that parents who consider their first child to be "difficult" tend to label their second-born

[2] Two kinds of gene–environment interactions may prove to be reliable. In the first, the genotypic trait is biological sex: Males and females may respond differently to the same environmental stimuli. This kind of interaction is irrelevant to the present discussion because the subject pairs in behavioral genetic studies are almost always of the same sex. The second kind of interaction involves children who are biologically at risk (e.g., those with neurological impairments). Such children may be especially vulnerable to the effects of unfavorable environments (Moffitt, 1993b; Wachs, 1992).

"easy," and vice versa. Presumably, the parents would then act differently toward the two children, thereby widening any preexisting differences between them. It is difficult to test this hypothesis directly, because when two siblings are found to have different personalities, and the differences are correlated with differences in parental treatment, there is usually no way of determining which is cause and which is effect (Rodgers, Rowe, & Li, 1994). As Dunn and Plomin (1990) admitted, the cause-or-effect problem "is a notoriously intractable issue" (p. 57).

Family context effects. There is one within-family variable that does provide a way to distinguish parent-driven causes from child-driven effects: birth order. Unlike twin studies, birth-order studies are easy to do; anyone who has a sibling of a different age is eligible to participate. Because there should be no systematic genetic differences between a firstborn and a second-born, any systematic differences found between them can be attributed to the order of their arrival and their different positions in the family constellation. There are clear and reliable differences in the experiences these two children will have. Every firstborn child has been the sole recipient of parental attention for at least a year and has then had to relinquish that position and compete with a rival who was in greater need of attention. Every second-born child has always had a sibling, and this older sibling was for a long time larger, stronger, and more knowledgeable. The firstborn is reared by inexperienced parents who may still be ill at ease in their new role, the second-born by parents who are usually more relaxed and more competent at the job (Kreppner, 1992).

Because the microenvironments of older and younger siblings differ in important and consistent ways, and because large amounts of birth-order data are available, any systematic effects of microenvironmental processes should be readily detectable. The results go against the expectations of professionals and nonprofessionals alike: Birth order has no consistent effects on adult personality (Dunn & Plomin, 1990; Ernst & Angst, 1983). Further evidence of the ineffectiveness of the family microenvironment is provided by comparisons between only children and children with siblings: Having a sibling or not having one also has no consistent effects on personality (Ernst & Angst, 1983; Falbo & Polit, 1986; Falbo & Poston, 1993). Ernst and Angst's conclusion, based on their own study of 7,582 young adults and on a survey of the world literature on birth-order and family-size effects, was that socialization within the family does not appear to play an important role in the formation of adult personality characteristics.[3]

The birth-order findings call into question two other hypotheses about differential within-family environments. The first is that adult personality is shaped in part by the relationship between the siblings themselves (Daniels & Plomin, 1985; Dunn & Plomin, 1990). The relationship between siblings, however, is determined partly by birth order: In most families, the older is the leader and model, the younger is the follower and imitator (Abramovitch, Corter, Pepler, & Stanhope, 1986; Brody, Stoneman, MacKinnon, & MacKinnon, 1985; Zukow, 1989). Sibling relationship effects should therefore be detectable in birth-order data, and they are not.

The final hypothesis is that, even if children are not aware of the absolute amount of attention or affection they get from their parents, they may be keenly aware of how much they get relative to their siblings (Dunn, 1992; Dunn & Plomin, 1990)—what might be called the "Mom always loved you best" syndrome. Here again, the effects of such differential treatment should be detectable in birth-order data. Although a mother behaves in a remarkably consistent fashion to her two children when they are the same age—that is, her behavior toward the second-born at 24 months is similar to her behavior toward the firstborn at 24 months (Dunn, Plomin, & Daniels, 1986)—her behavior does depend on the child's age: A younger child gets more attention than an older one (Brody & Stoneman, 1994; Dunn & McGuire, 1994). Thus, when a mother is taking care of both children at once, she will pay more attention to the younger one. Furthermore, there is evidence that, on average, she will also give more affection to the younger one. Dunn and Plomin (1990) reported that two thirds of the American and British mothers they studied were willing to admit that they loved one child more than the other. Of this group, 80% of American mothers and 86% of British mothers said they felt more affection for the younger child. The fact that a parent-driven birth-order difference of this magnitude has no consistent effects on the development of a child's personality is strong evidence against the efficacy of within-family environmental differences.

Conclusions. It is undoubtedly true that children who grow up in the same home have different experiences, and it is also true that they end up with different personalities, but current behavioral genetic methods do not enable us to distinguish causes from effects. However, data from birth-order studies and from studies of children with and without siblings cast serious doubt on the hypothesis that children's within-family microenvironments play a causal role in the shaping of their personalities. It is time to look elsewhere.

The theory presented in the remainder of this article, group socialization (GS) theory, explains the shaping of adult personality characteristics in terms of the child's experiences outside the parental home. It is important to note that this theory does not imply that children can get along without parents. Children are emotionally attached to their parents (and vice versa), are dependent on them for protection and care, and learn skills within the home that may prove useful outside of it; these facts are not questioned. What GS theory implies is that children would develop into the same sort of adults if we left them in their homes, their schools, their neighborhoods, and their cultural or subcultural groups, but switched all the parents around.

Context-Specific Socialization

One of the important roles of parents is presumed to be the socialization of the child. Socialization is the process by which an infant becomes an acceptable member of his or her society—

[3] Ernst and Angst (1983) searched the literature for every study published between 1946 and 1980 in which birth-order data were reported. They found that many of the studies were flawed; due to the lack of proper controls, birth order was often confounded with other demographic variables, especially socioeconomic class. When the proper controls were used, no birth-order effects were found on personality. Whether there is a birth-order effect on intelligence is still unclear (see Retherford & Sewell, 1991); if there is one, it is very small.

one who behaves appropriately, knows the language, possesses the requisite skills, and holds the prevailing beliefs and attitudes.

It is generally assumed that an important method of socialization in all societies is imitation of the parents by the child. Verbal instruction is less likely to be important, because in many preindustrial societies children are given little or no explicit instruction—they are expected to learn the necessary skills and behaviors by observation (Rogoff, Mistry, Göncü, & Mosier, 1993). Young children do imitate their parents in all societies, but they imitate many other people as well: older siblings (Zukow, 1989), nonfamily adults and children (Maccoby & Jacklin, 1974; Perry & Bussey, 1984), and characters they see on television (deMarrais, Nelson, & Baker, 1994; Lasater & Johnson, 1994). Rowe (1994) has pointed out that it would not make evolutionary sense for children to learn only from their parents; it would mean, for example, that children might fail to pick up useful innovations unless the innovator happened to be their parent. Rowe postulated an innate adaptive mechanism that directs the child to learn from any source, not just parents—a learning mechanism that is "general with respect to informational source" (p. 194).

Within the Home and Outside of It

Children can learn from many sources; yet, at the same time, their learning can be highly context-specific. Much current research points to the context-specificity, situation-specificity, or domain-specificity of learned behavior (Ceci, 1993; Deaux & Major, 1987; Garner, 1990; Greer & Stewart, 1989; Tooby & Cosmides, 1992). Very early learning, in particular, appears to be highly context-specific. Rovee-Collier (1993) performed a series of experiments in which young babies learned to kick one foot in order to make a mobile move. If any detail of the experimental setup was changed—for example, if the liner draped around the playpen was changed from yellow with green squares to green with yellow squares—6-month-old infants would merely gape at the mobile as though they had never seen it before, only a day after training. With the original liner in place, they showed evidence of recall (by kicking a foot) as long as 2 weeks after training. It appears that the infant starts out life with a learning mechanism that can learn from any source but that comes with a warning: What you learn in one context will not necessarily work in another.

What children learn in the context of their home may not, in fact, work in the world outside the home. Western societies demand very different behaviors in the home and outside the home; for example, displays of emotion that are acceptable in the home are unacceptable outside of it (Dencik, 1989; Fine, 1981). A central assumption of GS theory is that socialization is a highly context-dependent form of learning. Children learn separately how to behave at home (or in the presence of their parents) and how to behave when they are not at home. The manner of learning, the reinforcement contingencies, may also be quite different: In the home they may be reprimanded for mistakes and praised when they behave appropriately; out of the home they may be ridiculed for mistakes and ignored when they behave appropriately.

Code Switching

The clearest illustration of context-specific socialization is offered by the child of immigrant parents. If the language[4] used in their home is different from the language of the community, the child will learn the local language in order to communicate with her peers (Baron, 1992). By the time she is in first or second grade she will be a competent speaker of both languages, using one language in her home and the other outside of it. She will switch back and forth between them with ease—a process known as *code switching*—as though her mind contained two separate language modules controlled by the flip of a toggle. Even when two languages are acquired simultaneously, from two different caregivers or in two different contexts, children seldom intermix them unless they hear others doing so (Genesee, 1989; Lanza, 1992).

Language is the most conspicuous marker of the bicultural child's context-dependent socialization, but the assumption made here is that other variations in learned behavior are also selectively associated with the two different contexts; this view is similar to the alternation model of biculturalism proposed by LaFromboise, Coleman, and Gerton (1993). In addition to behavior, patterns of cognitive and emotional responses may be "contextually linked" to each other (Rovee-Collier, 1993, p. 133) and triggered by contextual cues. According to Kolers (1968/1975), "Many bilingual people say that they think differently and respond with different emotions to the same experience in their two languages" (p. 190). Thus, for bilingual children who use one language at home and another outside the home, the home language will be contextually linked to behavioral, cognitive, and emotional responses that occurred at home, the other language to those that occurred outside the home.

Context and Personality

Although the differences between home and outside-the-home behaviors are not as obvious in a child who speaks only one language, this child too will develop contextually linked patterns of behavior, cognitions, and emotions. The observation that individuals adopt different personas, or selves,[5] in different social contexts is not new; William James stated it quite clearly in 1890 (p. 294) and it has been reiterated many times since (e.g., Deaux & Major, 1987; Mischel & Shoda, 1995). It has also been observed that an individual's alternate personalities bear more than a passing resemblance to each other (see Carson, 1989). This resemblance need not be taken as evidence for cross-situational generalization. The alternate personalities are,

[4] Language is used here as a paradigmatic example of a socialized behavior. It is true that language acquisition may differ in some ways from other kinds of learning, because it is a specialized skill for which humans appear to be uniquely adapted (Pinker & Bloom, 1992). However, although language may be acquired in a specialized way, the social motivations that cause a child to use one language (or accent or vocabulary) rather than another are not specific to language.

[5] The term *selves* is often used by theorists who believe that behavior in various contexts is controlled or influenced by mediating variables such as self-esteem or self-concept. Variables of this kind play no special role in GS theory.

in effect, identical twins—they bear the same genes. Genetically determined characteristics such as aspects of temperament will be carried along from one context to another and will affect behavior in every context. Genetically determined characteristics, including physical appearance, will also affect the way others react to the child in every context. Children whose characteristics (e.g., a sociable temperament, an appealing smile) evoke positive responses from their parents are likely to evoke positive responses from other interactive partners as well. Thus, a child's experiences in separate social contexts may not be very different.

An individual's *personality*, as defined here, consists of an innate substratum that, during development, is built upon and modified by environmental influences. More precisely, the personality has two components: a genetic component that accompanies the individual wherever he or she goes, and an environmental component that is context-specific. The term *behavioral system* will be used to refer to the context-specific component of personality. It is defined as follows: a pattern of behavior, including language or accent, that is acquired in a particular social context, and the various cognitions and emotions (e.g., self-esteem) that were experienced in, and are associated with, that context.

Because there are alternate behavioral systems for different contexts, personality is, to some extent, context-specific. Because experiences in different contexts tend to have a certain degree of consistency, the alternate behavioral systems may not be very different and the personality is reasonably stable.

Code Switching in Traditional Societies

The bicultural child, who must learn the customs and languages of two different cultures, is not found exclusively in modern-day mobile societies; in fact, this child's task may be an ancient one. In forager (hunter-gatherer) societies, groups tend to be small and most of the people in them are related to each other. Mates are ordinarily obtained from outside the group, often through barter or warfare (Wilson & Daly, 1992). Because the majority of human societies are patrilocal, it is the woman who is more likely to be a newcomer to the group. She may speak a different dialect or even a different language; her customs may be different from those of the group. In order to survive, her children will have to interact successfully both with their mother and with the other members of their group.

Unlike the child in a contemporary Western society, however, the forager child does not have to learn how to behave in two entirely separate contexts. For forager children there is no clear-cut distinction between the family environment and the outside-the-family environment; there is much overlap and no privacy (Draper & Cashdan, 1988). Privatization of the home is a recent innovation, no more than 400 years old (Hareven, 1985; Rybczynski, 1986). Children in contemporary urbanized societies go back and forth between their privatized homes and the world outside the home—two environments that seldom overlap. They must learn what is expected of them in each environment.

GS theory pertains chiefly to outside-the-home socialization. According to the theory, socialization outside the home is primarily a group process, rather than the result of dyadic interactions between individuals. In the next section I review relevant findings on intra- and intergroup behavior, discuss some theoretical approaches to these findings, and introduce the theory.

Group Processes

Two's company, three's a crowd. For the present purposes, two are a *dyad.* Three or more are a *group* if they are allied with each other in some way or similar to each other along some socially relevant dimension. That the behavior of groups differs in important ways from the behavior of individuals has long been recognized.

The Basic Phenomena of Group Behavior

The phenomena of intra- and intergroup behavior described in this section are robust; they can be observed in natural settings and are readily evoked under laboratory conditions.

In-group favoritism. Members of a group prefer their own group to other groups. This can be demonstrated with breathtaking ease. Tajfel (1970) brought a group of boys, who knew each other from school, into his laboratory. The boys were asked to estimate the number of dots flashed on a screen. Purportedly on the basis of their responses (but in fact randomly), the experimenter divided the boys into two groups: Half the boys were privately informed that they were "overestimators" and the other half that they were "underestimators." Then each boy was asked to specify how monetary rewards should be distributed to the other boys in the laboratory. Although their own reward was not in question, and although they did not know which boys belonged to their group, they gave more rewards to their own group than to the other group. A later experiment (Billig & Tajfel, 1973) showed that it is not necessary to create a fictitious criterion for dividing up the groups; participants can explicitly be told that the group assignments are random and they will still favor their own group.

Out-group hostility. Sometimes the tendency to favor the in-group is accompanied by hostility toward the out-group. Two classic experiments provide vivid demonstrations: the prisoners and guards study (Zimbardo, 1972) and the Robbers Cave study (Sherif, Harvey, White, Hood, & Sherif, 1961). Both studies began with about two dozen carefully screened young male participants, demographically homogeneous, who were randomly divided into two groups. The result was strong, even violent, intergroup hostility. In the case of the 11-year-old boys at the Robbers Cave summer camp, animosity between the "Rattlers" and the "Eagles" was evident even before the groups encountered each other: The first time the Rattlers heard the Eagles playing in the distance, they wanted to "run them off" (Sherif et al., 1961, p. 78).

Between-group contrast. According to Wilder (1986), "Assumptions of differences between groups arise even when there is no justification for those inferences other than the mere existence of those groups. More strikingly, persons act to increase the magnitude of assumed intergroup differences" (p. 50). The persons in question are the members of the groups themselves. In the Robbers Cave experiment, the Eagles decided not to do any more "cussing" because the other group, the Rattlers, "used cuss-words all the time" (Sherif et al., 1961, p. 106).

Within-group assimilation. The group norm adopted by the Rattlers involved being "tough"—not a sissy (Sherif et al., 1961). When a Rattler sustained a minor injury, he did not cry, though crying under such circumstances was permitted among the Eagles. In children's groups, group norms are often enforced by ridiculing nonconformists (Adler, Kless, & Adler, 1992). For older groups, overt "peer pressure" is not usually necessary. No pressure was applied to the college-age participants in Asch's (1952/1987) experiments on group conformity. From the point of view of the subject, all that happened was that the seven other "subjects" in the room—actually confederates of the experimenter—gave perceptual judgments that were unanimous and clearly incorrect. The urge to conform came from within the subject. "Most subjects," noted Asch, "see a disturbance created, not by the majority, but by themselves" (p. 462).

Within-group differentiation. The individuals who make up a group are not identical and interchangeable. Within every group there are differences in social status and dominance (Hartup, 1983). Among the Rattlers and the Eagles, one or two boys in each group were regarded by the others as leaders, though this position could be short-lived and statuses changed over time. The boys differentiated themselves in other ways as well: One Rattler adopted the role of group clown; another was dubbed "Nudie" for having been the first to swim in the nude (Sherif et al., 1961).

Social–Cognitive Theories of Group Processes

Theoretical explanations of group behavior must account for the phenomena described above, including the paradoxical finding that the members of a group become more similar to each other (assimilation) and, over the same period of time, more dissimilar (differentiation). One promising approach is the self-categorization theory proposed by Turner (1987). This theory postulates that people can categorize themselves in various ways and on various levels, ranging all the way from *a unique individual* to *a human being.* The part of this range that is of interest here begins at *a unique individual* and extends through various nested or overlapping group identities such as *a female, an Asian American,* and *a college student.*

According to Turner (1987), there is a continuum between self-categorization as an individual and self-categorization as a member of a group. What causes movement along this continuum, and determines which particular self-categorization is adopted at a given point in time, is the relative salience of the various social categories. The salience of social categories (and therefore a person's self-categorization) is highly situation-specific; it varies over time and in different contexts. It is heightened by a comparison, "where two or more categories appear simultaneously, either actually or symbolically" (p. 120). For example, the social category *adult* is made more salient by the presence of members of the category *child; female* is made more salient by *male.*

When individuals categorize themselves as members of a particular group, they identify with that group and take on its "rules, standards, and beliefs about appropriate conduct and attitudes" (Turner, 1987, p. 1). This is the source of within-group assimilation. Differentiation occurs when people categorize themselves as individuals. But these two processes are not mutually exclusive. Individual identity and group identity are not dichotomous choices—"On the contrary, they will tend to operate simultaneously most of the time" (p. 50). Turner believes that people generally spend most of their time in the middle of the individual identity–group identity continuum, somewhere between "me" and "us."

What drives these processes, according to Turner, is the motive to improve or maintain one's self-esteem. People are motivated to evaluate themselves positively, so someone who has categorized herself as *a female college student* is motivated to evaluate that group in a positive way. Because group evaluations are relative, she is also motivated to compare her own group with another group and to evaluate her own group as different from, and better than, the other. The tendency to see her own group as favorably distinctive results in between-group contrast (which creates differences between two groups or causes preexisting differences to widen) and in-group favoritism (which can, under some circumstances, lead to hostility toward the outgroup). Thus, Turner's theory has something to say about all the major phenomena of inter- and intragroup behavior.

Two other social–cognitive theories that should be mentioned here are Tesser's self-evaluation maintenance theory and Brewer's optimal distinctiveness theory. Tesser's (1988) theory explains what Scarr and Grajek (1982) called "niche picking"—the way people in groups (especially small groups such as families) carve out identities of their own by differentiating themselves only in those areas that are important to them. Brewer's (1991; Brewer & Weber, 1994) theory is based on the idea that people must reconcile their opposing needs for assimilation and differentiation; the members of large, inclusive groups will be more motivated to differentiate themselves than the members of smaller groups.

Group Behavior of Other Primates

The three social–cognitive theories just described were designed to account for the behavioral phenomena of human groups. However, many of the same phenomena have also been observed in nonhuman primates. The experiment of dividing subjects randomly into two groups was approximated in a natural setting by chimpanzees (Goodall, 1986). A troop of chimpanzees that Goodall was observing split up, on their own, into two smaller groups. About a year later, a murderous war broke out between the two groups; eventually, one group succeeded in annihilating the other. As Russell (1993) concluded, "Chimpanzees, like humans, divide the world into 'us' versus 'them' " (p. 111).

Chimpanzees' hostility toward "them" may be related to a general tendency to show fear or aggression toward anything strange. A polio epidemic struck the chimpanzee troop that Goodall (1986) was observing, and a few of the animals became partially paralyzed. According to Goodall, "When the other chimpanzees saw these cripples for the first time, they reacted with extreme fear; as their fear decreased, their behavior [toward the cripples] became increasingly aggressive" (p. 330).

Like humans, chimpanzees inhabit social contexts that involve a delicate balance between "individual identity" and "group identity." Within most nonhuman primate groups there are frequent struggles as individual animals attempt to defend or improve their position in the dominance hierarchy. Interestingly, these within-group struggles for dominance cease abruptly when aggression is redirected toward an outside target, such as the members of another troop (de Waal, 1989; Russell, 1993). In humans, this finding would be attributed to the increased salience of group identity.

Motivational Considerations

For Turner, the motivating force behind group processes is the desire to increase one's self-esteem; for Tesser, it is the need to maintain a positive self-evaluation; for Brewer, it is the search for optimal distinctiveness. Even if we consider only human groups, none of these motives seems adequate to account for the powerful emotions generated by intergroup relations. As Brewer (1991) pointed out, "People die for the sake of group distinctions" (p. 475). How can a desire for self-esteem—a motive that seems insufficient to make a preadolescent boy do his homework—account for the fierce emotions and warlike behavior of the preadolescent boys at the Robbers Cave summer camp?

Cognitive Considerations

A second problem with social-cognitive theories of group processes is that they demand a rather high level of cognitive sophistication. Turner (1987) described his theory as "a cognitive (or social-cognitive) elaboration of the nature of social identity as a higher order level of abstraction in the perception of self and other" (p. 42). There is no question that higher order cognitive processes do play a role in human group behavior; we are unlikely to evoke group affiliation in a chimpanzee by informing it that it is an overestimator. It is also clear that *some* form of cognition must be involved, because a group is a category, and a category is a kind of concept (Fiske & Taylor, 1991). However, a category is a very simple kind of concept. Categorization has been reported in brain-damaged patients with amnesia (Knowlton & Squire, 1993) and even in pigeons (Wasserman, 1993). Logically, for the basic "us versus them" phenomena of group behavior to occur, only two cognitive steps are necessary: (a) categorization that results in at least two categories, and (b) identification of one of the categories with the self. The other phenomena of group behavior—the emotional aspects—do not require cognitive explanations. In short, social-cognitive theories presuppose too much brain power and provide too little emotional power.

Evolutionary Considerations

The ambition of theorists is to account for the greatest possible amount of data with the smallest possible number of assumptions. To postulate only a few simple "laws" and to use them to explain all of human and nonhuman behavior, as Skinner (1938) did in *The Behavior of Organisms*, is an intellectual exercise of great elegance. Unfortunately, "There is scant empirical evidence that the world is actually simple or that simple accounts are more likely than complex ones to be true" (Oreskes, Shrader-Frechette, & Belitz, 1994, p. 645).

Evolutionary psychologists Buss (1991) and Cosmides and Tooby (1992) do not believe that human behavior can be explained in terms of a small number of jack-of-all-trades mechanisms (such as operant conditioning) that serve a wide variety of functions. The human body contains specialized organs to solve particular adaptive problems—the intestines digest food, the lungs oxygenate the blood, and so on. Similarly, there are specialized psychological mechanisms that have evolved to solve particular adaptive problems encountered by our ancestors, and which our ancestors had to solve in order to become our ancestors. Because accommodation to a group lifestyle was critical to their survival, many of these special-purpose mechanisms pertain to group behavior.

Buss (1991) has listed some problems that are likely to have special-purpose psychological mechanisms designed to solve them; included in his list are "participating in cooperating groups," "besting members of one's own sex to gain access to desirable members of the opposite sex," and "initiating dyadic relationships characterized by cooperation and reciprocity" (p. 465). What Buss is saying is that these three different jobs—affiliating with a group, achieving status within the group, and forming successful dyadic relationships—may be carried out by three separate mechanisms that operate independently and respond to different kinds of input. They may make use of different motivational sticks or carrots and follow different developmental trajectories. There is no reason to expect them to be mutually exclusive.

Evolutionary psychology can account for the emotional power of group processes (adaptations that evolved to solve survival or reproductive problems tend to be associated with strong emotions) and for the fact that higher mental processes do not appear to be required (special-purpose devices can carry out specific jobs with a minimum of equipment).

The Assumptions of Group Socialization Theory

Accepting the views of evolutionary psychologists does not mean rejecting social-cognitive theories of group processes. The theories of Turner (1987), Tesser (1988), and Brewer (1991) provide good descriptions of aspects of human group behavior that are not found in chimpanzee groups and that require social-cognitive explanations. Humans can belong simultaneously to many groups and can shift their allegiance from one to the other, without moving an inch, in response to changes in relative salience. They can identify with a group even if it never assembles in one place and even if they have never met all of its members[6]—or, for that matter, *any* of its members.

GS theory is based on a view of human group behavior that regards the phenomena described by Turner, Tesser, and Brewer as elaborations built on a much older and deeper foundation. The foundation consists of four built-in predispositions, or evolutionary adaptations, that humans share with other primates.

[6] That humans do not necessarily have personal acquaintanceship with all the members of their group must have been true for a very long time. Before the battle of Jericho, which took place more than 3,000 years ago, Joshua met a stranger outside the walls of the town. The first question he asked the stranger was, "Are you for us or for our adversaries?" (Joshua 5:13).

The first is group affiliation, the basis of in-group favoritism. The second is fear of, or hostility to, strangers, which joins with in-group favoritism to produce out-group hostility. The third is within-group jockeying for status. Improving one's status within a group brings greater access to scarce resources. The fourth causes us to seek, and enables us to form, close dyadic relationships. I am not referring here to the strategic alliances that are common in primate groups and that tend to be short-lived; I am referring to love. Among nonhuman primates, relationships of this type are seen mainly between mother and offspring.

Table 1 summarizes the assumptions of GS theory. Some of these assumptions—notably the context-specificity of personality development—were discussed earlier. The others will be elucidated in the remainder of this article.

Children's Groups

The first step in human group affiliation is the categorization of people into groups. Although Piaget (1952) believed that the ability to categorize is an achievement of toddlerhood, more recent evidence suggests that it is present in infancy (Eimas & Quinn, 1994; Mandler, 1988, 1992). Indeed, if pigeons can categorize (Wasserman, 1993), it would seem unlikely that human infants are incapable of doing so.

For humans categorizing other humans, the top three cues are age, sex, and race (Fiske, 1992). Children do not appear to make racial distinctions before they are of preschool age (Hirschfeld, 1993; H. W. Stevenson & Stevenson, 1960), but age and sex discriminations are made very early. There is evidence that infants make categorical distinctions between men and women (Leinbach & Fagot, 1993; Walker-Andrews, Bahrick, Raglioni, & Diaz, 1991) and between adults and children (Brooks & Lewis, 1976) before they are a year old. Signs of a preferential attraction to others "like me" (Diamond, LeFurgy, & Blass, 1993) also appear at an early age. Year-old infants are interested in and attracted to other infants—including those they have never met before—at an age when they are wary of strange adults (Brooks & Lewis, 1976; Eckerman & Didow, 1988). By the age of 2, they are beginning to show a preference for children of their own sex (Fagot, 1985).

The young of all primates are strongly attracted to one another. As soon as they are able to move around on their own, infant monkeys leave their mothers in order to play with other young monkeys (Napier & Napier, 1985). Young baboons, rhesus macaques, langurs, and orangutans will leave their own troop in order to play with a young conspecific in another troop if no playmates are available in their own (Fagen, 1993).

In humans, customs of child rearing and patterns of parent–infant interaction vary widely from culture to culture (Leiderman, Tulkin, & Rosenfeld, 1977; Whiting, 1963), but the children's play group is universal. If the number of children in a given locality is small, the play group will consist of children of both sexes and a range of ages; if the number is larger, the children generally divide up into age- and sex-segregated groups (Edwards, 1992; Maccoby, 1990; Schlegel & Barry, 1991). Girls' groups tend to be fragmented—they split up into dyads and triads (Maccoby & Jacklin, 1987)—but these unstable dyads and triads are almost always composed of individuals who belong to the same stable social category, as defined by age, sex, and other locally relevant factors (Hallinan, 1992). It is the social category, or psychological group (Turner, 1987), that is important here. Children can categorize themselves as members of a social category even if it does not assemble in one place.

The mixed-age groups in forager and small village societies generally consist of (or include) siblings, half-siblings, cousins, and younger aunts and uncles (Edwards, 1992). In societies where children are brought together in large numbers for schooling, the groups generally consist of unrelated individuals of the same age. School-age children in urbanized societies spend much of their time, when they are not at home, in groups that are segregated both by age and by sex (Hartup, 1983). The age segregation is sanctioned by the educational system, but the sex segregation is created and maintained by the children themselves, even in the face of adult disapproval. In the lunchroom and, if permitted, in the classroom, they will divide up into separate gender groups; there will be a girls' table and a boys' table, a girls' side of the room and a boys' side (Sadker & Sadker, 1994; Thorne, 1986). If the school is racially or ethnically mixed, the children might also split into separate racial or ethnic groups, but the gender distinction is primary (Schofield, 1981).

In adolescence, sex segregation breaks down; adolescents use different criteria to divide up into smaller groups. The peer groups of adolescence are based on athletic, social, or academic interests and abilities; on distinctions of race, ethnicity, and social class; and on proclivities such as drug use and delinquency (Brown, Mounts, Lamborn, & Steinberg, 1993; Eckert, 1989; Schofield, 1981).

According to GS theory, outside-the-home socialization in urbanized societies takes place in these peer groups—the sex-segregated groups of middle childhood and the cliques or crowds of adolescence. They are composed of individuals who categorize themselves in the same way, and they fit Turner's (1987) definition of a psychological group:

> A psychological group is defined as one that is psychologically significant for the members, to which they relate themselves subjectively for social comparison and the acquisition of norms and values . . . from which they take their rules, standards and beliefs about appropriate conduct and attitudes . . . and which influences their attitudes and behavior. (pp. 1–2)

That is also a good description of socialization.

Cultural Transmission

Plomin and Rende (1991) recommended that we think about environmental effects on development "on an individual-by-individual basis" (p. 180). Corsaro and Eder (1990), in contrast, believe that developmental psychology has been held back by its exclusive focus on the individual; they advocated approaches that "break free from this individualistic emphasis" (p. 217). Asch (1952/1987) made a similar recommendation almost 40 years earlier: "It is correct to urge that we should strive to see persons in their uniqueness. But it is wrong to assume that we can best achieve a correct view of a person by ignoring his group relations" (p. 238).

These two contrasting approaches are depicted in Figure 1. The top diagram (Figure 1A) summarizes Rowe's (1994) view

Table 1
The Assumptions of Group Socialization Theory

Component	Assumption
Context-specific socialization and personality development	1. Children learn separately how to behave at home and how to behave outside the home. 2. Personality consists of an innate core plus acquired, context-specific behavioral systems. 3. As children get older, the outside-the-home behavioral system takes precedence over the inside-the-home system and eventually becomes part of the adult personality.
Source of outside-the-home socialization	1. Primates are predisposed, for evolutionary reasons, to affiliate with and adapt to a group. 2. Humans have the ability to identify with more than one group; the group identification that is salient at any given moment depends on social context. 3. The group that children identify with when they are outside the home is the peer group—a group of others who share socially relevant characteristics such as age, gender, ethnicity, and (in adolescence) abilities and interests. 4. Identification with a group entails taking on the group's attitudes and norms of behavior. This is a within-group process that results in assimilation—the group members become more alike.
Transmission of culture via group processes	1. Parents do not transmit their culture directly to their children. Culture is transmitted from the parents' peer group (and from other cultural sources) to the children's peer group. 2. Children transfer behavior learned at home to the peer group only if it is shared by, and approved by, the majority of members of the peer group. Children who come from atypical homes do not transfer their atypical home behaviors to the peer group. 3. Children's peer groups create their own culture by selecting and rejecting various aspects of the adult culture and by making cultural innovations of their own. During childhood, children move through a series of these child-created cultures.
Between-group processes that widen differences between groups	1. In-group favoritism and out-group hostility derive from adaptive mechanisms acquired through evolution and found in humans and other primates. 2. In humans, in-group favoritism and out-group hostility produce group contrast effects, which widen differences between groups or create differences if there were none to begin with.
Within-group processes that widen differences among individuals	1. Status hierarchies within the group—differences in dominance or social power—exist in all primate groups. Differences in status tend to persist and, in humans, may have lasting effects on personality. 2. Social comparisons within the peer group give children information about their own strengths and weaknesses and result in typecasting of individuals by other members of the group.
Assimilation and differentiation	1. Within-group assimilation and between-group contrast are most likely to occur when group identity is salient. Group identity is most salient when other groups are present. 2. Within-group assimilation and within-group differentiation are not mutually exclusive. Children can become more similar to their peers in some ways (socialization) and, over the same period of time, less similar in other ways.

of cultural transmission. According to Rowe, children can acquire cultural knowledge from many sources—parents, teachers, other children—but the knowledge is transmitted on an individual-to-individual basis. GS theory (Figure 1B) generates a different model of transmission, group-to-group: from the parents' group to the children's group.

The Parents' Peer Group

According to the model shown in Figure 1B, it is not only children who influence each other: Adults influence each other as well. In particular, they influence each other's child rearing methods. Although child rearing is often alleged to be something one learns from one's own parents, a group of women who are members of the same social class, ethnic group, or neighborhood may be more similar to each other in their child-rearing practices than they are to their parents. Child-rearing practices and values vary greatly from one generation to another (Alwin, 1988; Wolfenstein, 1953), and this is true not only in developed societies. In Kenya, Gusii infants are no longer force-fed by blocking their nostrils and forcing them to aspirate millet

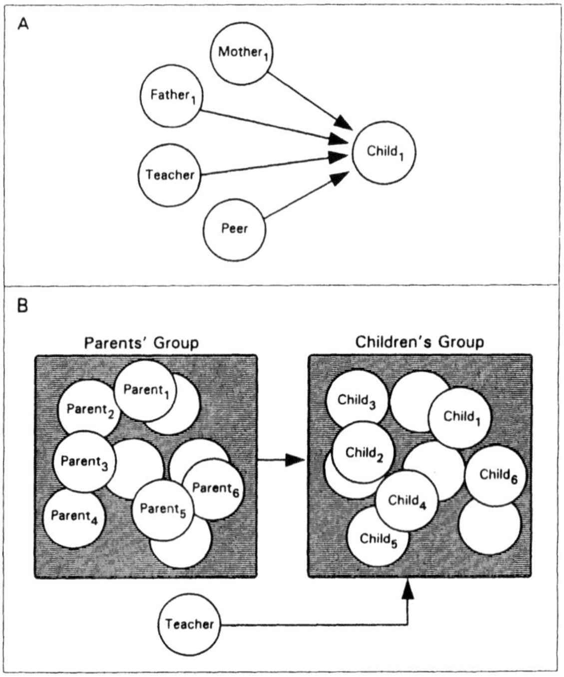

Figure 1. Two views of the transmission of culture from one generation to the next. Matching subscripts designate individuals who belong to the same family. A: The child can acquire cultural knowledge and behavior from many sources; transmission is from individual to individual (Rowe, 1994). B: Transmission is from group to group (group socialization theory).

gruel (LeVine & LeVine, 1988). In Mexico, Yucatec Mayan women who were themselves breast-fed are now bottle-feeding their infants, against the advice of their mothers (Howrigan, 1988). In the United States, the likelihood that a woman will breast-feed her child varies according to her ethnic group and whether or not she has gone to college (Bee, Baranowski, Rassin, Richardson, & Mikrut, 1991).

Peer groups of mothers, also known as maternal support networks, transmit information and social norms for the job of parenting (Salzinger, 1990; see also Riley, 1990). Mothers who do not belong to such networks find parenting more difficult and stressful and are more likely to violate societal norms by physically abusing their children (Melson, Ladd, & Hsu, 1993; Salzinger, 1990). The networks may include relatives and distant friends, but they consist in large part of parents of the same social class who live in the same neighborhoods and whose children go to the same schools or day-care centers. Thus, children of a given social class who live in the same neighborhood and go to the same school are likely to be reared by parents who share common child-rearing methods and values (Corsaro, 1994). The neighborhood and community effects described by Bronfenbrenner (1986) are attributed here to class and local differences in the culture of parenting and to local differences in the peer groups of the children themselves.

The Children's Peer Group

The path of cultural transmission, as shown in Figure 1B, is from the parents' group to the children's group. Most of the children in a given peer group will have parents who also share a peer group; thus, most of the behaviors and attitudes that one child learns at home will also be learned by the other children in the group. According to GS theory, any behaviors or attitudes that are common to the majority of the children in the group are accessible to the group as a whole; the children are not compelled to retain them when they are not at home, but they probably will. For example, if the majority of the children learned to speak English and to eat with a spoon and fork at home, they will probably speak English and eat with a spoon and fork in the school cafeteria. Other social influences common to the group

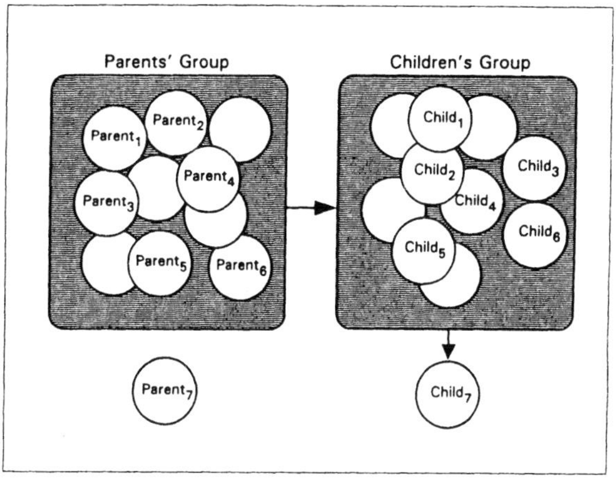

Figure 2. According to group socialization theory, the child whose parents are not members of the parents' group acquires the local language and customs from the children's group. (Matching subscripts designate individuals who belong to the same family.)

are transmitted in the same way: If the majority of children watch a particular television show, they may incorporate it into their play (deMarrais et al., 1994; Lasater & Johnson, 1994); an exceptional teacher can influence the attitudes of an entire classroom of children (E. Pedersen, Faucher, & Eaton, 1978). The results make it appear that culture is passed from the parent, the teacher, or the media to the individual child. However, according to GS theory, the transmission is not direct: Cultural transmission to individual children passes first through the filter of the children's group.

As long as all the children in the peer group come from families that share the same culture and watch the same TV shows, it is difficult to test this hypothesis; there is usually no way of telling whether the children learned their behaviors and attitudes at home or from each other. Consider, however, the child of immigrant parents, whose parents may not speak English, may not use spoons and forks at home, and are not part of the parents' peer group. Their child will pick up the local language and customs from her peers, as illustrated in Figure 2, and will use them when she is not at home. In effect, she has learned them from the parents of her peers.[7]

The most interesting case is when the children in a peer group have no common culture or language. In that case, they must create one. Bickerton (1983) has observed this process in the children of people who immigrated to Hawaii in the late 1800s. The parents' generation, brought to Hawaii to work on the sugar plantations, came from many different countries and had no language in common. To communicate with each other they used a *pidgin*—a rudimentary language that lacks prepositions, articles, verb forms, and standardized word order. Each speaker of a pidgin speaks it a little differently, depending on the native language of that speaker.

Between 1900 and 1920, a new language evolved in Hawaii: a *creole*, based on the pidgin. This was a fully developed language, capable of expressing complex ideas; it was spoken by the children of the immigrants. These children had not learned it from their parents—their parents spoke pidgin or the languages of their homelands. It was developed, according to Bickerton (1983), by the children themselves. The parents' pidgin varied according to their national origin, but the children of a given cohort all spoke the same version of creole. Their national origin was no longer detectable in their speech, even by a linguist. On the other hand, because the creole language evolved over time, there were variations from cohort to cohort. Bickerton was able to trace the development of this language by interviewing middle-aged and older adults, because each cohort continued to use the version they had spoken in their childhood and adolescent peer groups. They had "adopted the common language of their peers as a native language in spite of considerable efforts by their parents to maintain the ancestral tongue" (Bickerton, 1983, p. 119).

Peer Cultures

Though the achievement of the Hawaiian children is remarkable, it is not unique; according to Corsaro (1993), all childhood peer groups create their own culture. Consider a group of children who share a bicultural heritage, such as Native American and Anglo American. They can pick and choose from each

[7] This account does not apply to the immigrant family that lives in an area where there are other families with the same national background. In such areas, children who share a national background often form their own group and maintain their home language and customs.

of their cultures, and the precise blend they settle on will vary from group to group (LaFromboise et al., 1993).

Corsaro (1993) has described childhood socialization as "the production of and movement through a series of peer cultures" (p. 361). Though this series of cultures is capable of adapting to changing times, it is also capable of remaining relatively unchanged while cohort after cohort of children pass through it. Thus, children's games get passed down from generation to generation; Opie and Opie (1969) found British children still playing games that date from Roman times. These traditions are passed on by groups that have a spread of ages; the younger children learn the traditions from the older ones, who forget them, according to Opie and Opie, as soon as they graduate out of the children's group. Nyansongo children in Africa have a private language for describing intimate parts of the body, using words that are forbidden in the presence of adults (LeVine & LeVine, 1963). The words are passed along from older children to younger ones. According to Levine, Resnick, and Higgins (1993), group norms (they are speaking here of adult groups) are "often maintained over several 'generations' during which old members gradually leave the group and new members join. . . . Groups are highly motivated to provide newcomers with the knowledge, ability, and motivation they will need to play the role of full member. . . . Newcomers are typically receptive to these influence attempts" (p. 600).

If the newcomers to a children's group are not particularly receptive, and if no adult intervenes, the influence attempts may be quite forceful. For many generations, upper-class British boys were sent away to boarding schools at the age of eight. Glynn (1970) described his experiences as a newcomer to Eton in the early 1900s:

> A boy's first week at his preparatory school is likely to be the most traumatic experience of his life, one for which he is, at the age of eight, totally unprepared. Until that moment, he has not realized that there are so many people in the world who wish to hit him and hurt him and that they will be given ample opportunity to do so, both by day and by night. (p. 129)

The boys who attended these schools saw very little of their fathers; their first 8 years were spent mainly in the company of nannies and governesses, and for the 10 years after that, paternal contact consisted chiefly of "a lecture each holiday on fortitude, fitness, and trying hard at games" (Glynn, 1970, p. 128). Yet the boys turned out very much like their fathers, including the same upper-class accent. The reason is that their fathers went to the same schools and participated in the same peer culture, which evidently changed very little as generation after generation of boys passed through it. The Duke of Wellington was alluding to this method of socialization when he said, in explanation of his victory at Waterloo, that the character of the British officer was formed "on the playing fields of Eton" (cited in Bartlett, 1955, p. 400).

Between-Group Contrasts

When widening differences are noted between children's groups that differ in gender, race, ethnicity, social class, or academic ability, the blame is usually put on putative socializing agents such as parents or teachers (e.g., Fagot & Hagan, 1991; Minuchin & Shapiro, 1983; Parsons, Adler, & Kaczala, 1982; Sadker & Sadker, 1994; Siegal, 1987; Weinstein, 1991). However, in the Robbers Cave experiment, when the Eagles decided not to do any more "cussing" because the Rattlers "used cusswords all the time" (Sherif et al., 1961, p. 106), no adult was involved in their decision. It is the group members themselves who are responsible for group contrast effects (Wilder, 1986).

Social groups are categories and, like all categories, are based on the perception of within-group similarities and between-group differences (Krueger, 1992). Thus, when group identity is salient, group members perceive themselves to be more similar to each other, and more different from the members of other groups, than they really are. The result is the emergence of contrasting group stereotypes (Wilder, 1986; Williams & Best, 1986). According to Turner (1987), between-group differences are increased or created because "a positive social identity requires that one's own group be favourably different or positively distinctive from relevant comparison groups" (p. 30). An evolutionary view offers an alternative explanation for group contrast effects: They are not driven by a desire for self-esteem, but are a side effect of in-group favoritism and out-group hostility. If we feel favoritism toward our own group and hostility toward another group, for reasons that have more to do with our evolutionary history than with any real differences between the groups, then we are motivated to see the groups as different.

Gender Role Development

Gender is "the most fundamental of human categories" (Banaji & Prentice, 1994, p. 315). The fact that gender differences in behavior are observable in every human culture that has been studied, and that male and female stereotypes are similar across cultures (Williams & Best, 1986), strongly suggests that there is a biological component to these differences (Maccoby & Jacklin, 1974). However, like the sex differences in height and strength, the biologically based differences in behavior are differences between group means; the ranges of the two groups overlap considerably. During middle childhood, according to GS theory, the effects of self-categorization into two dichotomous groups causes these differences to widen and the overlap to decrease. Boys and girls develop contrasting group stereotypes and contrasting peer cultures. Maccoby (1990) has pointed out that behavioral differences between girls and boys are minimal when children are observed individually; the sex differences emerge most clearly when they are playing in sex-segregated groups.

The view that the sex-segregated peer groups of middle childhood play an important part in gender role development, and that parental influence plays no more than a minor part, has been suggested elsewhere (Archer, 1992; Edwards, 1992; Maccoby & Jacklin, 1987; Martin, 1993; Schlegel & Barry, 1991; Serbin, Powlishta, & Gulko, 1993; Tannen, 1990; Thorne, 1986). Indeed, parents in Western societies may be less concerned about gender distinctions than are the children themselves. A meta-analysis turned up no major differences between the ways parents treat their sons and daughters (Lytton & Romney, 1991). Recent efforts to rear children in an androgynous fashion have not reduced their sex-typed behavior or attitudes (Serbin et al., 1993). Children who grow up in homes headed by single mothers (M. R. Stevenson & Black, 1988) or by lesbian or gay couples (Patterson, 1992) are not less sex-typed than children who have two parents of opposite sexes.

Attitudes toward gender roles are part of a culture and can be passed down from the parents' group to the children's group in the manner depicted in Figure 1B. However, in societies where children are able to divide up into sex-segregated groups, sex-typed behavior may appear even though the adults in that culture believe that boys and girls are basically alike. Conversely, in localities where population density is low and there are not enough children for girls and boys to form separate groups, GS theory predicts that sex-typed behavior will be minimized, because the salient social categories will not be *girl* versus *boy*, but rather *child* versus *adult*. Consider Morelli's (1994) description of life among the Efe, a forager people who live in small groups in the Ituri forest of Zaïre:

> Mau, an adolescent forager boy, sits in camp with his brother's 15-month-old daughter draped across his lap, lulled to sleep by the not-so-distant music of a finger piano. Mau reaches over to stir his pot of *sombe* as a group of young boys and girls play "shoot the fruit" using child-sized bows and arrows. The children come dangerously close to Mau's cooking fire, and he utters a disapproving "aa-ooh!". . . As he scans the camp he notices a group of women preparing for a fishing trip, while others lounge, smoking tobacco along with the men. (p. 1)

In contrast, the neighboring Lese, whose farming lifestyle allows for a greater population density, have a highly sex-differentiated society (Morelli, 1994). A similar contrast between foragers and farmers was reported by Draper and Cashdan (1988). They observed that in !Kung nomadic foraging groups, where the number of potential playmates is limited, boys and girls play together and there are few sex differences in their behavior. Among !Kung who have adopted a farming and herding lifestyle and the number of potential playmates is greater, children are more likely to form sex-segregated groups and sex differences are much more pronounced.

Within our own society, GS theory predicts that sex-typed behavior will be minimized at times and in places where the social categories *male* and *female* are not salient because the opposite sex is not present, "either actually or symbolically" (Turner, 1987, p. 120). This prediction seems to hold true, at least for female behavior. Girls and young women who go to all-female high schools and colleges are more likely to retain an interest in, and to excel in, "masculine" subjects such as math and science (Alper, 1993; Sadker & Sadker, 1994). A striking demonstration of the effects of the presence of boys on girls' behavior was reported by C. C. Weisfeld, Weisfeld, and Callaghan (1982). Two groups of preadolescent girls participated in the study: Hopi Indians living on a reservation in Arizona and African Americans attending a middle-class private school in Chicago. The girls were observed as they played dodgeball, a game played by children of both sexes. When no boys were present, the girls played the game in a competitive manner; many of them were quite skillful at it. But when a group of boys was introduced into the game, the girls' behavior changed dramatically. The Hopi girls stood with their legs crossed and their arms folded; they appeared shy and noncompetitive. The African American girls chatted among themselves, nibbled on snacks, and teased the other players. Both groups of girls were completely unaware of the change in their behavior—when they were asked why the boys always won, the girls claimed (erroneously) that the boys cheated. It should be noted that among these preadolescents, ages 11 to 13, the girls were taller and heavier than the boys (C. C. Weisfeld et al., 1982).

Adolescence

From the preschool period through early adolescence, gender-group affiliations are of central concern; age-group issues remain in the background. Although they identify with their own age group, children look up to the age group just ahead of them, both literally and figuratively. Older children are dominant in mixed-age playgroups and, where parents permit it, in mixed-age sibling groups (Edwards, 1992; Whiting & Edwards, 1988). In same-age groups, those who are more advanced in physical maturation tend to have higher status (Savin-Williams, 1979; G. E. Weisfeld & Billings, 1988).

Two changes occur between early and mid-adolescence: Gender ceases to be the primary indicator of group identity, and size ceases to be a useful indicator of age and status. The behavior of adolescents in complex societies (i.e., societies in which they are not able to classify themselves as *adults* as soon as their physical growth is complete) results, according to GS theory, from self-categorization into contrasting groups, *teenagers* versus *adults*.

In Western societies, delinquent acts during adolescence are extremely common, even among individuals who were well-behaved children and who will become law-abiding adults (Moffitt, 1993a). Moffitt concluded that adolescent delinquency "must be a social behavior that allows access to some desirable resource" and suggested "that the resource is mature status, with its consequent power and privilege" (p. 686). GS theory suggests a different explanation: Adolescents are not aspiring to adult status—they are *contrasting* themselves with adults. They adopt characteristic modes of clothing, hairstyles, speech, and behavior so that, even though they are now the same size as adults, no one will have any trouble telling them apart. If they truly aspired to adult status they would not be spraying graffiti on overpasses, going for joyrides in cars they do not own, or shoplifting nail polish from drug stores. They would be doing boring adult things, like figuring out their income tax or doing their laundry.

In-group favoritism is often accompanied by out-group hostility. Although hostility toward other age groups does not emerge in full force until adolescence, signs of it are detectable much earlier. Even for a child barely out of diapers, being called a "baby" is a deadly insult. A mild form of hostility to adults also emerges at an early age: Corsaro (1993) reported that children's resistance to adult rules "is a daily occurrence in the nursery school and is produced in a style that is easily recognizable to members of the peer culture. Such activity is often highly exaggerated (for instance, making faces behind the teacher's back. . .) or is prefaced by 'calls for the attention' of the other children" (p. 360). By late middle childhood, defiance of adult rules becomes more flagrant, especially in boys' groups (Fine, 1988). In their explanation of the children's game Truth or Dare, Opie and Opie (1969) described the dares that might be given to a player:

> He is liable to be instructed to knock at a front door and run away, or to punch a passer-by on the back . . . or to engage in some other provocation of the adult world, for there is a curious feeling in this game of having to respond to the challenge "Are you one of *us*, or one of *them?*" (p. 264).

That, I believe, is the question adolescents are asking when they dare each other to take risks or to defy the rules of the adult world.

Within-Group Processes

Socialization tends to make individuals within a society—or within certain groups in the society, such as males and females—more similar to each other. Behavioral geneticists attempt to account for the ways in which individuals *differ* from each other. GS theory deals both with similarities and with differences; both are attributed to the effects of group processes that work chiefly within, rather than between, groups.

Assimilation

Cooperative interactions between peers begin in toddlerhood. Among the earliest cooperative acts noted by Eckerman and Didow (1988), the most frequent were "acts that imitated the actions of the peer" (p. 65). Imitation of peer models continues all through childhood and adolescence; when they are outside the home, young humans strive to dress, speak, and behave like their same-sex peers (Adler et al., 1992; Reich, 1986). Children's peer groups operate by a "majority rules" rule: If one or two individuals come to the group with behaviors that do not conform to the norms of the majority, they risk rejection by the group unless they modify those behaviors (Bierman, Smoot, & Aumiller, 1993; Coie, 1990).

For those who cannot or will not conform, group sanctions can be harsh. Maccoby and Jacklin (1987) quoted an 11-year-old girl who explained to them what would happen if she should violate one of her group's taboos by voluntarily sitting next to a boy in school: "People would not be my friends. They would scorn me." It would be as bad as "peeing in your pants," she said—"You would be teased for *months*" (p. 245). A psycholinguist (Reich, 1986) described a childhood experience at a Boy Scout Jamboree, where he was mocked by boys from other parts of the country for his Chicago accent: "They would double up with laughter at the appearance of the [ɹ] in the middle of the word. I can still remember practicing hard to change the pronunciation of this and other words that marked my dialect" (p. 306).

Temperament and group behavioral norms. During the course of middle childhood, any children whose behavior is out of step with the behavioral norms of their sex-segregated peer groups will be subjected to pressure to conform to these norms (Adler et al., 1992). Can such group-enforced conformity, practiced in childhood, have long-term effects on personality? Evidence from research on temperament suggests that the answer is yes.

Kagan and his colleagues (Kagan, Reznick, Snidman, Gibbons, & Johnson, 1988; Kagan & Snidman, 1991) have described children who vary along a dimension they call *inhibition*. Highly inhibited children are nervous and fearful of anything new; highly uninhibited children are boisterous and bold. These temperamental differences are detectable early in development, have been linked to neurophysiological factors (Davidson, 1992; Fox, Bell, & Jones, 1992), and show significant heritability (Braungart et al., 1992; Goldsmith, 1993b; Robinson et al., 1992), but, like other heritable characteristics, they can be modified by the environment. A longitudinal study of Swedish children (Kerr, Lambert, Stattin, & Klackenberg-Larsson, 1994) tracked inhibited and uninhibited toddlers from age 18 months through 16 years. There was not much change from 18 months to 6 years, but from 6 to 16, two things happened: Uninhibited children of both sexes calmed down and became more moderate in their behavior, and inhibited males—but not females—became less shy and fearful.

To explain their results, the researchers (Kerr et al., 1994) pointed out that shy, inhibited behavior is acceptable for girls but not for boys; they attributed the gender-specific changes to "culturally shared notions of gender-appropriate behavior" (p. 138), remaining neutral on the question of which social forces were responsible for enforcing these notions. Kagan (1984; Kagan, Arcus, & Snidman, 1993) has hypothesized that parental influence is a major source of the longitudinal changes in inhibited boys. However, if parents were capable of modifying their children's temperaments to conform to their own ideals, the effects should show up in behavioral genetic analyses as shared environmental influence—the influence of the home environment on personality characteristics. The finding that the home environment has little or no effect on adult characteristics such as extraversion, impulsivity, and neuroticism (Bouchard, 1994; Loehlin, 1992) calls Kagan's hypothesis into question. GS theory offers a different interpretation: that timid, anxious behavior is not acceptable in the boys' peer group of middle childhood; that a boy who acts that way will be teased or bullied by his male peers until he learns to master his distress; that similar behavior in a girl is not considered objectionable by her female peers; and that children who are overly boisterous and uninhibited tend to be unpopular regardless of their sex.

"Peer pressure." Adolescent problem behavior is often blamed on "peer pressure," but by adolescence, overt pressure is not usually necessary. According to Lightfoot (1992), "Peer pressure is less a push to conform than a desire to participate in experiences that are seen as relevant, or potentially relevant, to group identity" (p. 235).

The peer groups of middle childhood are based on demographic categories such as sex, age, and social class. This changes in adolescence; most high schools in urbanized societies are large enough to enable adolescents to sort themselves out into groups of like-minded individuals—the "jocks," the "brains," the "burnouts," and so on (Brown & Lohr, 1987; Brown et al., 1993; Eckert, 1989). Because the members of these groups are so similar in behavior and attitudes, the adolescent peer group has been proposed as a possible source of unexplained environmental variance—of environmental influences that siblings do not necessarily share (Daniels & Plomin, 1985; Dunn & McGuire, 1994). However, the uniformity of behavior and attitudes seen among adolescents who belong to the same peer group cannot be attributed entirely to group influences. These adolescents were similar to begin with—the "birds of a feather flock together" phenomenon. Although it is also true that the members of these groups become more similar over time because of mutual influence, most of the similarity predates the formation of the group (Rowe, Woulbroun, & Gulley, 1994). Thus, adolescent peer group influence cannot by itself account for much of the unexplained environmental variance; nor should we expect it to. Group influences on personality occur in childhood as well as adolescence and involve within-group differentiation as well as assimilation.

Differentiation

Assimilation and differentiation are not, according to GS theory, mutually exclusive processes; they are driven by separate adaptive mechanisms. Children can become more similar to their peers in some ways and, over the same period of months or years, less similar in other ways. However, at any given point in time, one or the other of these processes is likely to predominate. Assimilation to the group is most likely to occur when a social category is salient, which is the case when two or more social categories, such as *girls* and *boys*, are present at the same time. When only one group is present, that social category declines in salience (Turner, 1987). The consequence—at least in societies with an individualistic orientation (Miller, 1987)—is that its members become more likely to categorize themselves and each other as distinct individuals, rather than as interchangeable members of a group. Under such circumstances, differences among individuals tend to increase as a result of two phenomena that work on a within-group level: status hierarchies and social comparison.

Status hierarchies. Within every group of children or adolescents there are differences in social status, though they are not always as clear, stable, and transitive as the term *hierarchy* would suggest (Perry & Bussey, 1984). Differences in status involve both dominance (social power) and popularity; the two hierarchies are correlated but are not identical (Pettit, Bakshi, Dodge, & Coie, 1990; Rubin & Coplan, 1992). Of the factors that make children rise or fall in the social hierarchy, many, such as self-confidence and friendliness, have a vicious circle quality (J. R. Harris & Liebert, 1991)—they are both the causes and the effects of social success. Because success leads to more success, and failure to more failure, differences in social skills tend to widen over time; a child who is either at the high or the low end of the social hierarchy is likely to remain there (Coie, 1990; Kennedy, 1990; Rubin & Coplan, 1992).

High or low status in the peer group may leave permanent marks on the personality. Boys who are slow to mature physically tend to be smaller than their peers and to rank low on the dominance hierarchy (Savin-Williams, 1979; G. E. Weisfeld & Billings, 1988). They may eventually grow to above average height; yet, studies have shown that late-maturing boys tend to be less successful, less poised, and more anxious in adulthood than their early-maturing peers (Clausen, 1975; Jones, 1957). Although these effects are usually associated with early or late maturation during adolescence, most late-maturing adolescent boys had been slow to mature in childhood as well; such boys tend to be relatively low in social status all through childhood (G. E. Weisfeld & Billings, 1988).

Girls or boys who are rejected by their peers are, by definition, low on the popularity hierarchy; those who are victimized by their peers are low on the dominance hierarchy (Schwartz, Dodge, & Coie, 1993). Often, these are the same children, and many of them continue to be rejected and victimized year after year (Rubin & Coplan, 1992). As adults, they are at greater risk for a variety of psychopathological problems (Olweus, 1993; Parker & Asher, 1987). There are three possible causal pathways, operating alone or in combination, that may be responsible for the correlation between rejection and later psychopathology: (a) Repeated experiences of rejection during childhood may cause later psychopathology; (b) the lack of normal peer interactions may cause later psychopathology; and (c) certain children may be rejected by their peers because they are already showing subtle signs of psychopathology (Hartup, 1983; Parker & Asher, 1987). These alternatives cannot at present be distinguished. Therefore, the connection between rejection and psychopathology, though consistent with GS theory, cannot be interpreted as supportive evidence.

Social comparison. Children find out what kind of people they are—quick or slow, pretty or plain, leader or follower—by comparing themselves to others. Statements of social comparison (Festinger, 1954) such as "I'm bigger than you!" are heard in the nursery school, but it is not until the elementary school years that children begin in earnest to compare themselves to others (Newman & Ruble, 1988; Stipek, 1992). The others in question are the members of the social group in which they categorize themselves—the group that is "psychologically significant for the members [and] to which they relate themselves subjectively for social comparison" (Turner, 1987, p. 1). Thus, if a child categorizes himself as *a fourth-grade boy,* he will compare himself to the other fourth-grade boys he knows. The comparisons are multidimensional and result in the child's developing an idea of his own capabilities in several different arenas—physical, social, and cognitive (Harter, 1983).

Social comparisons are also made by others, with the result that the members of groups tend to become typecast: "The gang is quick to seize on any idiosyncrasy of appearance, manner, skill, or whatever, and thereafter to treat the child in terms of this trait. The stereotype by which the gang identifies the child is often expressed in his nickname: 'Skinny,' 'Fatso,' 'Four-eyes,' 'Dopey,' 'Professor,' 'Limpy' " (Stone & Church, 1957, p. 207). Stigmatizing labels might also be applied by teachers or other adults: "learning disabled," "hyperactive." Once applied, such labels tend to stick. They become self-fulfilling prophecies—other children expect certain behaviors of the labeled child, their expectations are conveyed by the way they behave toward that child, and the way they behave tends to evoke the behavior they were expecting (M. J. Harris, Milich, Corbitt, Hoover, & Brady, 1992).[8]

When Does Group Influence End?

As adolescents become adults, the peer group declines in importance. They marry, perhaps, and have children; they now belong to a number of groups. Some of these groups—work

[8] GS theory predicts that labeling will have a permanent effect on the personality of the labeled child only if the label is originated by, or known by, the child's peer group. If it is known only by a single individual, such as a teacher, GS theory predicts no long-term effect.

groups, for example—no longer consist solely of people "like me." Group norms of behavior are no longer enforced so stringently; the consequences of being different are not so serious for adults. Perhaps for these reasons, or perhaps because of maturational changes programmed into our genes, group influences seem to have far less impact on adults than on children. Although the ability to acquire new behavioral systems is not lost, adults' accommodations to social contexts seem to be shallow and short-lived, compared with those of children. Adults can learn a new language but they cannot learn to speak it without an accent (Reich, 1986). Personality does not change much during adulthood (McCrae, 1993). The language and personality acquired in childhood and adolescent peer groups persist, with little modification, for the remainder of the life span.

Who Socializes the Child?

In the days when psychoanalytic theory was an influential force in developmental psychology, a child learned how to behave by identifying with his father or her mother. Identification, around age 4 or 5, led to the formation of a superego; good behavior was then enforced by the superego. Fraiberg (1959) used this theory to account for the fact that most children learn family rules and become less likely to violate them as they get older. As an illustration she offered the story of Julia and the eggs:

> Thirty-month-old Julia finds herself alone in the kitchen while her mother is on the telephone. A bowl of eggs is on the table. An urge is experienced by Julia to make scrambled eggs. . . . When Julia's mother returns to the kitchen, she finds her daughter cheerfully plopping eggs on the linoleum and scolding herself sharply for each plop, "NoNoNo. Mustn't dood it. NoNoNo. *Mustn't* dood it!" (Fraiberg, 1959, p. 135)

Fraiberg attributed this lapse to the fact that Julia had not yet acquired a superego, presumably because she had not yet identified with her mother. But notice what Julia was doing: By making "scrambled eggs" and yelling "NoNoNo!" she was behaving exactly like her mother. What Julia must learn is that she is not allowed to behave like her mother. Children in our society spend their early years discovering that they cannot do most of the things they see their parents doing—making messes, telling other people how to behave, and engaging in many other activities that look like fun to those who are not allowed to do them.

Cross-Cultural Considerations

Julia's dilemma is not unique to our society; there are many societies in which the distinction between acceptable adult behavior and acceptable child behavior is greater than in our own. In the Marquesas Islands of Polynesia, children must learn two different sets of rules for social behavior: one for interacting with other children, the other for interacting with parents and other adults. The adult is expected to initiate and control interactions; the child is expected to be restrained and compliant (Martini, 1994). Polynesian children cannot learn the rules of social interaction by observing their parents' behavior. Furthermore, in most traditional societies, parents do not act either as playmates or as teachers to their children. The kind of parental instruction we take for granted in the United States is by no means universal. The Kaluli of Papua, New Guinea do not help children learn language by rephrasing a toddler's poorly formed sentence into proper grammar; they believe it is the responsibility of the child to make the listener understand what she or he wants to say (Snow, 1991). In the Embu District of Kenya, parents and toddlers have few verbal interactions of any sort: "Almost all sustained social interactions and most verbal interchanges of toddlers in this culture involve other children" (McDonald, Sigman, Espinosa, & Neumann, 1994, p. 411).

Fortunately, children can learn things in a variety of ways; even a creature as simple as a honeybee has more than one mechanism for getting to a flower (Gould, 1992). Many kinds of learning do not require the presence of a model, and for those that do, such as language learning, every society provides some kind of a model. In most traditional societies, the models are older children, especially siblings (Zukow, 1989). A common pattern in such societies is that toddlers are given over to the care of an older sister or brother when they are 2 or 2½, and the older sibling—who may be no more than 4 or 5—carries the younger one along to the children's play group. There the toddler might be allowed to participate as a sort of living doll or be left to watch or to whine on the sidelines (Martini, 1994; Whiting & Edwards, 1988). Thus, siblings are a part—often a major part—of the young child's social group. Outside-the-home socialization begins, according to GS theory, in this mixed-age, mixed-sex group. By preadolescence, children in most present-day societies are able to form age- and sex-segregated groups (Edwards, 1992).

Is the Family a Group?

In urbanized societies, school-age children spend most of their time outside the home in age- and sex-segregated groups that do not ordinarily include a sibling. Most of their interactions with their siblings and parents occur within the home. Does the family function like a group? Does the child identify with this group?

In some societies—particularly Asian societies—the answer appears to be yes. Chinese, Japanese, and Indian cultures emphasize the importance of the family group or social group and deemphasize the importance of the individual; independence and autonomy are not considered virtues in a child (Cole, 1992; Guisinger & Blatt, 1994; Miller, 1987; H. W. Stevenson, Chen, & Lee, 1992). In precolonial China, if a man committed a serious crime, his siblings, parents, and children were executed along with him, the idea being that the whole family shared in the responsibility (Heckathorn, 1992).

In contrast, Western culture puts the emphasis on the individual rather than the group (Guisinger & Blatt, 1994; Miller, 1987). Only in certain situations—for example, when they are traveling together in an unfamiliar area—are the members of North American or European families likely to function as a group. When they are at home together, I believe that they function as individuals, each with her own agenda, his own patch of turf to defend. They are not a group because the social category *our family* is not salient. It is not salient because no other social categories are present, either actually or symbolically (Turner, 1987), in the privacy of the contemporary Western home.

Within-Family Effects

When group identity is not salient, differentiation is likely to predominate over assimilation. If siblings see themselves as separate individuals rather than as part of the family group, status hierarchies and social comparisons may increase the differences among them. Dominance hierarchies would tend to make older siblings dominant over younger ones, which happens as a matter of course in most societies and which North American parents try very hard, and not very successfully, to prevent (Whiting & Edwards, 1988). However, there is little or no resemblance between children's relationships with their siblings and their relationships with their peers (Abramovitch et al., 1986; Stocker & Dunn, 1990), which is consistent with the finding that birth order has no reliable effects on personality (Ernst & Angst, 1983; Reiss et al., 1994).

Social comparisons between siblings may have more interesting consequences. Tesser's (1988) self-evaluation maintenance theory predicts that siblings should each develop specialties of their own—areas that they consider important to their self-definition and in which they are willing to compete. If one sibling is an excellent pianist, for example, the other sibling may avoid playing the piano for fear of being bested in the comparison. Note that this "niche-picking" process does not require any parental intervention or labeling; it involves only the two individuals in question. Nor is there need to postulate a special motivator; within-group jockeying for status, found in most human and nonhuman primate groups, is sufficient to do the job.

Within-family social comparisons should also widen personality differences between siblings—a within-family contrast effect. If this effect occurs, it must be small in magnitude. Schachter (1982) asked college students to judge how similar they were to their siblings and found a tendency toward polarization of personality attributes that was significant only between firstborns and secondborns. Loehlin (1992) investigated the possibility that a contrast effect might occur between twins who are reared together; he assumed that if such an effect existed, it would make twins reared together less similar in personality than twins reared apart. He found that twins reared together were somewhat *more* similar than those reared apart[9] and concluded that no contrast effect had occurred. However, twins reared together also share an environment outside the home; they go to the same school and often belong to the same peer group. According to GS theory, the shared outside-the-home environment should make twins reared together more alike than twins reared apart; thus, if they are not more alike, a within-family contrast effect may be reducing their similarity. Notice that this prediction—that inside-the-family effects will make twins more different and outside-the-family effects will make them more alike—is exactly the opposite of the assumption made by behavioral geneticists.

Parental Influence Versus Peer Influence

In a number of studies, researchers have asked children and adolescents questions of the form, "What would you do if your friends wanted you to do something that your parents told you not to do?" (e.g., Berndt, 1979; Bowerman & Kinch, 1969). Depending on the precise wording of the question, the results generally show that parents' influence is high during the early school years and then gradually declines, and that peers' influence is low at first and gradually increases, reaching a peak in early adolescence.

Such experiments are misleading or irrelevant for several reasons. First, the questions are asked by a researcher who is an adult. Given the context-sensitivity of social behavior, the replies might be different if the questioner were a child. Second, replies to questions of the type "What would you do if. . . ?" have low validity, as shown by the lack of correspondence between tests of moral judgment and tests of moral behavior (see Perry & Bussey, 1984). Third, the questions tend to focus on emotionally charged relationships, rather than on behavior; in effect, the child is being asked, "Whom do you love more, your parents or your friends?" Finally, children generally belong to peer groups that share their attitudes and, in many cases, their parents' attitudes. They may know that their friends would not ask them to do something dangerous or illegal.

When researchers observe, rather than ask questions, peer influence is found to be potent, even at ages and in circumstances where parental influence would be expected to have priority. For example, it is well known that preschoolers are loath to eat certain foods, despite much favorable propaganda or forceful urging from their parents. As Birch (1987) discovered, the best way to induce children of this age to eat a disliked food is to put them at a table with a group of children who like it.

Absence of Parents Versus Absence of Peers

No one can question the fact that, without parents, babies and young children are bitterly unhappy (Bowlby, 1969); in fact, an early attachment to a caregiver appears to be a requirement for normal social development (Rutter, 1979), just as early exposure to light and pattern is a requirement for normal development of the visual system (Mitchell, 1980). However, case studies involving deprivation of one kind or another suggest that the absence of peers may have more serious long-term consequences than the absence of parents. Rhesus monkeys reared without peers are more abnormal as adults than those reared without a mother (Harlow & Harlow, 1962/1975). The case of the Jewish children who spent their first 3 years together in a Nazi concentration camp (Freud & Dann, 1951) suggests that the same may be true for humans. The six children had been cared for in the concentration camp by an everchanging series of adults, none of whom survived. When the children arrived in England and came to the attention of Anna Freud, they were found to be completely indifferent—if not hostile—to all adults; they cared only about each other. According to Hartup (1983), these children grew up to become normal adults and at last report were leading "effective lives" (pp. 157–158).

Cases like Victor, the wild boy of Aveyron (Lane, 1976), and Genie, the locked-up girl of California (Curtiss, 1977), do not

[9] Although Loehlin found that identical twins reared together were more similar in personality than those reared apart, other researchers (e.g., Bouchard et al., 1990) have found reared-apart and reared-together identical twins to be equally similar.

have happy endings. Note, though, that these children were deprived not only of normal parent–child relationships but of normal peer relationships as well. There is a case in which two children—twins—were isolated but were locked up together; these children were completely rehabilitated after a few years in which they lived with a foster family and attended school (Koluchová, 1972, 1976).

Dyadic Relationships Versus Group Processes

The view that early relationships with parents are of central importance in personality development is a legacy from psychoanalytic psychology. Among the modern adherents to this view are the attachment theorists (Ainsworth, Blehar, Waters, & Wall, 1978; Bowlby, 1969). According to attachment theory, infants whose mothers care for them in a sensitive, responsive way are likely to become securely attached to their mothers; secure attachments increase the chances of success in later undertakings, especially those that are social in nature. Security of attachment is assessed by observing a child's behavior, generally at age 12 or 13 months, when the mother leaves the child in an unfamiliar laboratory room and then returns a short time later. Children who greet their mothers with unalloyed joy are adjudged securely attached (Ainsworth et al., 1978; Belsky, Rovine & Taylor, 1984; Sroufe, 1985).

There are two major problems that make most socialization research, including the attachment literature, difficult to interpret. First is the nature-or-nurture problem. Behavioral geneticists have pointed out clearly and repeatedly (e.g., Plomin & Daniels, 1987; Scarr, 1993) that most socialization studies lack an essential control: If all the pairs of research participants share 50% of their genes, as do mothers and their biological children, there is no way of factoring out the effects of heredity from those of environment. There is no way of telling whether the observed resemblances between the mothers and their children (in friendliness, nervousness, competence, etc.) are due to heredity, environment, or both.

Second is the cause-or-effect problem. A mother–child relationship, like all dyadic relationships, involves two people who each play a role in the success of the relationship (Hartup & Laursen, 1991; Hinde & Stevenson-Hinde, 1986). Just as some adults are better than others at caring for infants, some infants are better than others at evoking sensitive, responsive parenting. Because infants who are particularly appealing to their mothers are also likely to be appealing to other people, a child who does well in one relationship is likely to do well in others (Jacobson & Wille, 1986).

Thus, it is surprising to discover that the correlations among a child's various relationships are actually quite low. A child who is securely attached to Mother is not necessarily securely attached to Father (Fox, Kimmerly, & Schafer, 1991; Main & Weston, 1981) or to other caregivers (Goossens & van Ijzendoorn, 1990). Efforts to link parent–child relationships with child–peer relationships have had inconsistent results; some studies (Pastor, 1981; Waters, Wippman, & Sroufe, 1979) find a correlation, others do not (Howes, Matheson, & Hamilton, 1994). Sometimes correlations are found that are "counterintuitive" (Youngblade, Park, & Belsky, 1993, p. 564). As mentioned previously, there is also little or no correlation between the nature of children's sibling relationships and their relationships with their peers (Abramovitch et al., 1986; Stocker & Dunn, 1990). These findings are surprising because it is the same child, with the same genes, who participates in all of these relationships.

The most reasonable explanation of why these correlations are so low is that behaviors, emotions, and cognitions acquired in a dyadic relationship are specific to that relationship (Hinde & Stevenson-Hinde, 1986; MacKinnon-Lewis et al., 1994). There may be, as Bowlby (1969) proposed, a "working model" of the mother–child relationship in the child's mind, but if so, it is trotted out only when Mother is around. A child discovers very early in life that learning what to expect from Mother is of limited usefulness for dealing with Father or Sister. A child who has learned through hard experience to avoid the school bully does not avoid all of the other children on the playground (Asendorpf & van Aken, 1994).

Evolutionary considerations discussed earlier led to the view that dyadic relationships and group affiliation are driven by separate adaptive mechanisms. Consistent with this view is the finding that children's group relations are to a large extent independent of their dyadic relationships. Although there are children who get along poorly in every social context, many children who have low status in the group are able to form successful friendships (Bukowski & Hoza, 1989; Parker & Asher, 1993a, 1993b).

According to GS theory, identification with a group, not participation in dyadic relationships, is responsible for environmental modifications of personality characteristics. If two people are a dyad and three are a group, this distinction may appear to be splitting hairs. However, the difference between group processes and dyadic relationships is not just a matter of number. The important point about human groups is that they are social categories. When children categorize themselves as members of a group, they take on its norms of behavior (Turner, 1987). A child who says, "Oh Mom, I can't wear that, the kids will laugh at me," is not worrying about the reaction of her best friend—she is worried about the consequences of violating group norms.

In dyadic relationships, children learn how to behave with Person A, with Person B, and with Person C. In the peer group they learn how to behave in public.

The Transient Effects of the Home Environment

Behavioral genetic data indicate that any transient effect of the home environment on personality fades by adulthood—shared environment accounts for little or no variance in adult characteristics. According to GS theory, the reason the home environment has no lasting effects is that children are predisposed to favor the outside-the-home behavioral system over the one they acquired at home. Children who learn one language at home and a different one outside the home become increasingly reluctant to speak the home language, even at home (Baron, 1992). The language they speak with their peers will become their "native language" when they are adults (Bickerton, 1983).

Some researchers have claimed that the reason the immigrant child drops the home language is that it lacks economic and cultural prestige; it is not valued by the community (Umbel, Pearson, Fernández, & Oller, 1992). Evidence against this view comes from deaf children born to hearing parents during the era when sign language was not valued by the community—in fact, the community tried hard to suppress it. This misguided effort failed. When these children went to schools where, for the first time, they met other deaf children, they picked up sign language in the dormitories. Sign language was brought into the schools by the deaf children of deaf parents, and all the children used it surreptitiously to converse among themselves (Meier, 1991; Newport, 1990). It became their "native language" despite earnest efforts by their teachers to give them a language that had greater economic and cultural prestige.[10]

There are good evolutionary reasons why children might be biologically predisposed to discard what they learned in their first few years of life. First, their parental home is not where they are likely to spend their future. As Erikson (1963) noted about the school-age child, "There is no workable future within the womb of his family" (p. 259). In order to survive and reproduce, children must be able to function successfully in the world outside their home. They must form alliances that go beyond the nuclear family.

Second, children are already similar to their parents for genetic reasons—the 40% or 50% of the variance that is attributable to heritability. If environmental influences added to and increased these similarities, children would be so much like their parents and siblings that the family might lack sufficient variability. This would decrease the number and variety of ecological niches the members of the family could fit into and reduce the likelihood that at least one child would survive.

There is a biological mechanism that reduces the chances of incest: In humans and other animals, the sex drive tends to be dampened by stimuli that are too familiar. Members of the opposite sex who are familiar from infancy and early childhood are generally not regarded as sexually stimulating (Tooby & Cosmides, 1990; Wilson & Daly, 1992). I suggest that a similar mechanism may operate in regard to socialization: When there is a choice, children do not choose what they learned in infancy and early childhood.

Three Views of Personality Development

Figure 3 shows three contrasting models of personality development: a traditional socialization model (Figure 3A, solid lines), a behavioral genetic model (Figure 3A, solid lines plus dashed lines), and the model generated by GS theory (Figure 3B). The arrows in these schematic diagrams represent causal links; all of the links are environmental except for the two marked *Heredity*.

The traditional socialization model is based on the view (no longer as prevalent as it once was) that heredity is important mainly in determining the outward physical characteristics of the child and that parental behavior is a cause and child behavior is an effect. Parent–child relationships are assumed to influence the child's peer relationships, but not vice versa. Mutual influence is acknowledged in peer–peer interactions. Cultural transmission is by way of the parents.

The behavioral genetic model adds a genetic link between parents' personalities and children's personalities. The existence of reactive effects in parent–child interactions is accepted, as is the possibility that children's peer relationships might affect their behavior at home; however, the effect of parent–child relationships on peer relationships is presumed to be stronger than the reverse. The child's personality is still assumed to be influenced primarily by parent–child relationships and by the parents' behavior toward the child, though the possibility of peer effects is now admitted. Culture, which is not ordinarily mentioned in behavioral genetic writings, is presumably passed on by the parents. This figure represents what might be called a "traditional" behavioral genetic view; it does not include that of Rowe (1990, 1994), who at present is alone among behavioral geneticists in concluding that the home environment may not play an important role in development. Rowe's views were depicted earlier, in Figure 1A.

Figure 3B shows the model generated by GS theory. Note that there is no longer a link between the child's behavior inside the home and outside the home—these are two separate behavioral systems—and that parental behavior no longer affects the child's personality. Instead, the child's personality is affected by the behavior of peers toward the child and by the way the child behaves outside the home, which is influenced by peer group norms. Behaviors approved by the peer group (e.g., sex-typed behavior, language) are part of the outside-the-home behavioral system and become a permanent part of the adult personality. Culture is transmitted by way of its effects on peer group norms; there is no path from culture to personality via the parents.

Sources of the Belief in Parental Influence

That parents have important and lasting effects on their offspring is perhaps the least questioned notion in psychology. Why are most psychologists (and nonpsychologists) so convinced that it is true? This section reviews some of the confounding factors that can be mistaken for evidence of effects of the home environment.

Genetic Effects

A recent Cathy cartoon (Guisewite, 1994) shows tubby Cathy sitting between her tubby mother and her tubby father, looking at the family photo album. During the course of the strip, she discovers that it was her father—not, as she previously thought, her mother—who had taught her to reach for cookies or ice cream whenever she was unhappy. Cathy is still wrong: Her father is as innocent (or as guilty) as her mother. They can be blamed only for giving Cathy their DNA. Body weight is not affected by rearing environment; it is largely inherited (Grilo & Pogue-Geile, 1991). Adopted children do not resemble their adoptive parents in fatness or thinness (Stunkard et al., 1986). Yet, the idea that obesity is caused by eating habits learned during childhood is deeply ingrained.

Socialization researchers have typically looked for evidence of parental influence in families consisting of parents and their biological children. In such studies, genetic and environmental

[10] Deaf children who learn sign language in middle childhood never become as proficient in its use as children who are exposed to it from infancy onward (Bebko & McKinnon, 1990; Newport, 1990). Thus, for language, as for vision and attachment, experience early in life appears to be necessary for optimal development.

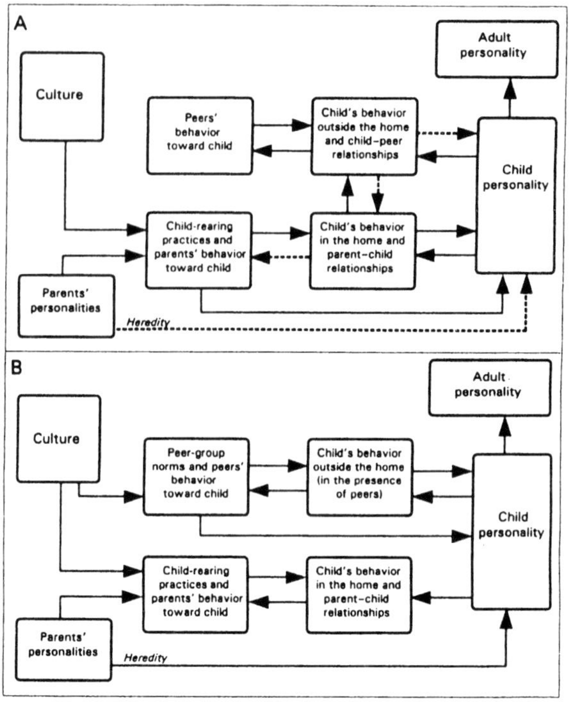

Figure 3. Three views of personality development. All of the arrows in this figure, except for the two labeled *Heredity,* represent environmental effects. A: The models generated by a traditional socialization approach (solid lines) and by a behavioral genetic approach (solid lines plus dashed lines). B: The model generated by group socialization theory.

effects are inevitably confounded (Plomin & Daniels, 1987; Scarr, 1993). Behavioral genetic studies, which include adoptive families and families with twins, have demonstrated that many characteristics thought to be completely environmental in origin have a significant genetic component. Plomin and his colleagues (Plomin, Corley, DeFries, & Fulker, 1990) found a genetic influence on how much television a child watches. Tesser (1993) reported that attitudes such as belief in the death penalty or a liking for jazz are heritable. McGuffin and Katz (1993) found that the number of stress-producing events people experience in their lives is partly determined by genetic factors: Individuals are more likely to experience such events if they have close biological relatives who are always having accidents, losing their jobs, or getting into marital difficulties. Note that the findings of behavioral genetics are not restricted to personality and IQ tests.

Whenever behaviors are "handed down" from one generation to another, the possibility of genetic influences must be considered. For example, the heritability of traits such as aggressiveness (Ghodsian-Carpey & Baker, 1987; van den Oord, Boomsma, & Verhulst, 1994) and impulsivity (Loehlin, 1992) might be partly responsible for the vertical transmission of child abuse (DiLalla & Gottesman, 1991).

Context Effects

When a child who is cooperative and self-confident in other contexts becomes belligerent or anxious in the presence of a parent, it is evident that the parent is influencing the child's behavior. A common, but unwarranted, conclusion drawn from such observations is that the parental influence must be pervasive and long-lasting. The change in behavior does not provide evidence of pervasive parental influence but of the context-specificity of social behavior.

Hoffman (1991) noted that estimates of shared environmental influence vary according to the measurements that are used: The home environment is found to be more important if the measurements are based on observations of behavior (usually made in the participants' homes), less important if they are based on self-report personality inventories (usually administered in the laboratory or classroom). Again, this finding is consistent with the predictions of GS theory. As Council (1993) has pointed out, there is a serious problem with many personality studies: The results may be confounded by context effects, because a positive correlation may be "an artifact of assessing both variables in the same setting" (p. 31). Although Council was referring to two tests given in the same context, his point is equally valid when one measure is a presumed cause and the other a presumed effect. It is unquestionably true that children's behavior in the home will be affected by their experiences in that home. The question is whether these correlations tell us anything about behavior in other contexts. According to GS theory they do not, and behavioral genetic data support that conclusion by showing that the effects of the home environment vanish by adulthood.

Reactive Effects

Behavioral geneticists (e.g., Daniels & Plomin, 1985) have criticized socialization researchers for examining only one child per family. With this procedure, it is impossible to tell whether the parents' treatment of the child is a reaction to the way that particular child behaves or is a behavioral characteristic of the parents and the cause of the child's behavior. Unfortunately, the cause-or-effect problem cannot be solved by looking at two children in a family. If we find that the parents treat the two children differently and that the children behave differently, did the differential treatment cause the different behavior or is it a response to it?

The relationship between a parent and a child is transactional (Hartup & Laursen, 1991; Scarr & McCartney, 1983), which means that the parent's behavior is, in part, a reaction to the child's current and previous behavior and that the child's behavior is, in part, a reaction to the parent's current and previous behavior. Untangling the causes from the effects may be impossible. GS theory holds that dyadic relationships have no long-term effects on personality and thereby evades this particular cause-or-effect problem. However, a similar problem will crop up in testing the theory's predictions, which will be discussed shortly.

Age Effects

According to GS theory, the effects of the home environment are transient; children focus more and more on the world outside their home as they get older. Toddlers and preschoolers are likely to show some effects of home environment even when they are outside the home. By the end of middle childhood, however, it is predicted that children with normal exposure to an outside-the-home environment will have at least two separate behavioral systems—one for use at home, one or more for outside the home (Day, Borkowski, Dietmeyer, Howsepian, & Saenz, 1992; Deaux & Major, 1987; James, 1890, p. 294; Sansone & Berg, 1993).

Parents'-Group-to-Children's-Group Effects

When an Asian American adolescent spends 4 hours a night doing homework, or a Jewish adolescent decides to become a doctor, the usual assumption is that parental influences are at work. Because many Asian American and Jewish parents probably do encourage these attitudes, looking at a single family, or even at a number of families, would only reinforce the impression of parental potency. It is the unusual case—the adolescent whose parents have atypical ideas—that demonstrates the inaccuracy of the impression. GS theory predicts that the children of atypical parents are as likely as their peers to adopt the behaviors and attitudes approved by the majority of the parents. The parental attitudes are not transmitted directly, but by way of the peer group:

> Dr. Snyder's parents suggested that he go to a music conservatory after high school. "I didn't think being a musician was such a good job for a nice Jewish boy," he recalled. Many of his friends wanted to be doctors, and since, he said, "my major goal in life was to be like other boys," he decided to become a doctor too. (Kolata, 1993, p. C8)

Thus, within a particular peer group of adolescents, attitudes toward educational aspirations are likely to be similar; the attitudes of their parents (if they belong to the same social network) will also be similar; but correlations between individual parents and their children should be nonsignificant. Precisely this result was reported in a Mexican American community by Day and her colleagues (Day et al., 1992; see also Kindermann, 1993).

Miscellaneous Effects

Several other minor effects may contribute to the impression that the home environment has had an effect on the way children act outside the home. Children may be tested or observed in a neutral setting, but some aspect of the testing situation—an adult researcher, the nature of the questions, or the absence of peers—may evoke their at-home behavioral system. The questions may pertain to emotional relationships rather than behavior (most children probably do love their parents better than their friends) or to issues that do not come up while children are with their peers. School-age children may not talk about their future career plans with their friends; high school students may eschew discussions of religion and politics.

Finally, retrospective studies in which adults' personality problems are traced to experiences in their childhood home are frequently confounded by memory biases. Depression, for example, predisposes individuals to retrieve unhappy events from their memories (Mathews & MacLeod, 1994). The result is that depressed people report having had more unhappy experiences in childhood than do nondepressed people, which can lead to the unwarranted conclusion that the unhappy childhood experiences caused the depression.

Reinterpreting Previous Research

Two well-established areas of research, on styles of parenting and on the effects of divorce, will be briefly reexamined. Researchers in both areas interpret their findings as evidence for the importance of the home environment on child development.

Styles of Parenting

Baumrind (1971) defined three styles of parenting: authoritarian (bossy parents who do not consider their children's opinions), permissive (wimpy parents who let their children do whatever they want), and authoritative (parents who are firm but warm and who take their children's opinions into account). The children of authoritative parents are found to be more competent, both socially and academically (Baumrind, 1989; Dornbusch, Ritter, Leiderman, Roberts, & Fraleigh, 1987; Lamborn, Mounts, Steinberg, & Dornbusch, 1991).

Maccoby and Martin (1983) pointed out one problem with the style-of-parenting research: The parents could be reacting to their child's behavior, rather than causing it. Because only one child per family was studied, we do not know whether the parents used the observed child-rearing style with all of their children or just with that child. If they used it just with that child, then it would seem that parents tailor their child-rearing styles to the characteristics and behavior of the individual child. On the other hand, if parents use the same child-rearing style for all of their children, why are its effects not visible in behavioral genetic measures of shared environment?

A second problem comes to light when cultural differences in parenting styles are considered. Recent work has demonstrated that the effects of parenting style differ for different subcultural groups. Asian American parents, for example, have the least authoritative and most authoritarian child-rearing style of the subcultural groups that have been studied; yet their children have the highest school achievement (Dornbusch et al., 1987; Steinberg, Dornbusch, & Brown, 1992). These results call Baumrind's conclusions into question and are consistent with a new interpretation of this literature. Different cultural groups have different norms and customs for the job of child rearing, which are transmitted through the parents' peer group. In the United States, most parents' peer groups sanction the style of parenting that Baumrind calls authoritative. What Baumrind was measuring was the ability of middle-class Anglo American parents to rear their children in the style approved by their culture. She found that parents who are competent at this job have biological children who tend to be competent at the jobs children do. Although the precise characteristics that make up the quality called *competence* are difficult to specify, there is no reason to expect them to be less heritable than other personality and intellectual characteristics.

Subcultural groups such as Asian Americans have their own parents' peer groups, and these groups may have different culturally approved styles of child rearing (Chao, 1994). If parents belong to a group that sanctions an authoritarian style of child rearing, or a permissive style, then their ability to rear their children in that style will be a mark of competence. Thus, the correlations reported in the style-of-parenting literature may be due to heritable differences in competence *within* subcultural groups.

The differences *between* subcultural groups can be attributed to group processes. Young people who are members of different subcultural groups are likely to belong to different adolescent peer groups that have different group stereotypes, attitudes, and behavioral norms—differences that are sharpened by contrast effects. Adolescents who belong to a given peer group generally have parents who also share a peer group and who therefore have similar styles of child rearing. Thus, subcultural differences in adolescents' behaviors and attitudes may be associated with, but not caused by, subcultural differences in their parents' child-rearing styles.

The Effects of Divorce

Researchers in this area compare the children of divorced parents with those whose parents are (as yet) not divorced. The conclusion is always the same: On the whole, the children of divorced parents have more behavioral and emotional problems (Hetherington, Stanley-Hagan, & Anderson, 1989; Krantz, 1989). The fact that the adult children of divorced parents have a higher risk of marital failure (Glenn & Kramer, 1987) can be seen as evidence that these effects are long lasting. GS theory generates an explanation of these findings that is different from the traditional one.

Divorce may be inherited. McGue and Lykken (1992) have found that the likelihood that a person will get divorced is heritable. Estimated heritability in their study was around .50; shared environmental influence was not significantly different from zero. What is inherited is not divorce per se, of course, but characteristics such as impulsivity or disagreeableness (Loehlin, 1992) or a tendency toward alcoholism (McGue, 1993) that have a heritable component and that can make divorce more likely.

Children's behavior problems may precede divorce. Many of the behavior problems commonly reported in the children of divorced parents, particularly "acting out" in boys, are visible years before the parents divorce (Block, Block, & Gjerde, 1986; Cherlin et al., 1991). This has been interpreted as evidence that the problems are not caused by the divorce itself, but by the family conflict and "dysfunction" that precedes it. An equally plausible interpretation is that the children's problem behavior may result from personality characteristics that the children inherited from their conflict-prone parents (Frick & Jackson, 1993). Another possible confounding factor is a reactive effect: A child's problem behavior may increase family stress and thereby make divorce more probable.

Divorce often entails a change of residence. McLanahan and Booth (1989) reported that 38% of custodial mothers in one sample moved to a new residence within the first year after a divorce. A change of residence has important effects—usually negative—on children: They lose their peer group and their place in the status hierarchy; they must win acceptance by a new group and establish their status all over again. Vernberg (1990) found that boys whose families had relocated within the past year were at increased risk of being rejected by their peers (this was not true for girls). Another study of the effects of family relocation showed that children whose families had moved frequently were 77% more likely to have multiple behavior problems than children who had moved infrequently or not at all, after all other demographic differences were statistically controlled (Wood, Halfon, Scarlata, Newacheck, & Nessim, 1993).

Divorce often entails a lowering of family financial status. The new neighborhood that children find themselves in after a divorce and relocation may be quite different from the old one; half of all homes headed by single mothers are below the poverty level (McLanahan & Booth, 1989). The change in socioeconomic status means that there may be a change in the norms of the child's peer group. Even if no relocation takes place, the loss of family income can affect children's group relationships by changing their position in the status hierarchy of their current group. Particularly for girls, family income and its consequences—access to luxuries such as expensive clothing, orthodontists, and dermatologists—are important determinants of social status in childhood and adolescent peer groups (Adler et al., 1992).

The children are observed or measured at home. The postdivorce home is different from the predivorce home, and children's at-home behavior will reflect the changes that have occurred there. The data used in the majority of studies of divorced children are collected in the children's home, or in the presence of the children's parents, or consist of replies to questionnaires filled out by the children's parents (who base their replies on the children's behavior at home). When data are collected from neutral, outside-the-home observers, such as the children's teachers, effects become smaller or disappear entirely (Hetherington & Clingempeel, 1992; Neighbors, Forehand, & Armistead, 1992).

The children are observed or measured in childhood. As data on the effects of divorce accumulate, researchers are coming to see parental divorce as something children recover from in time (Hetherington et al., 1989). This view is consistent with the predictions of GS theory. It is also consistent with behavioral genetic data that show little or no effect of shared home environment on adult personality. A parental divorce is, of course, part of the shared home environment.

Directions for Future Research

According to GS theory, experiences in childhood and adolescent peer groups, not experiences at home, account for environmental influences on personality development. The answer to the question "Why are children in the same family so different from one another?" (Plomin & Daniels, 1987) is, because they have different experiences outside the home and because their experiences inside the home do not make them more alike. Testing this assertion appears to be straightforward but it is not. Consider two siblings who have different statuses within their childhood peer groups, who are typecast by their peers in different ways, who belong to different adolescent crowds (one is a brain, the other a burnout), and who turn into adults with very different personalities. Did their peer group experiences cause the differences in personality, or did they have different peer group experiences because they were already different?

In order to test the theory, it is necessary to tease apart three possible influences on personality characteristics: home experiences, peer group experiences, and heredity. Two examples serve as models for the kind of research and analysis that would be useful. The first is an examination of cigarette smoking by adolescents. Rowe (1994) used behavioral genetic data collected by other researchers to show that heredity can account for the fact that parents who smoke tend to have children who smoke. He used data of his own (Rowe, Chassin, Presson, Edwards, & Sherman, 1992) to show that the environmental factor involved in smoking was exposure to peers who smoke. Peer group influences determine whether an adolescent will experiment with tobacco; heredity determines whether he or she will become addicted to nicotine.

The second example is a study by Kindermann (1993) that demonstrates peer group influences on children's motivation to do well in school. Kindermann studied cliques of children within fourth- and fifth-grade classrooms and found that they consisted of children who shared similar attitudes toward schoolwork; these groups are the grade-school equivalents of high school peer groups such as brains and burnouts. In grade school, such groups are unstable in membership—over the course of a school year, Kindermann found, many children changed groups. When they changed groups, their attitude toward schoolwork tended to change to match that of their new group. Neither their intelligence nor the attitudes of their parents would be likely to change over the course of a single school year; therefore, peer group influence is the most plausible explanation for the observed changes in the children's attitudes. Because individual children served as their own controls, the effects of peer group influence can be distinguished from those of other environmental influences and from heredity.

GS theory could also be tested by generating predictions from its specific assumptions. The assumption of the context-specificity of socialization predicts that researchers will be more likely to detect influences of the home environment if their tests or observations are carried out in the home. The corollary of this prediction is that efforts to account for differences in adult personality (measured outside the parental home) by looking for within-family environmental differences (measured within the home) are doomed to failure. Differences in the way a parent acts toward two siblings are likely to be good predictors of the relationships these siblings will have with their parent 20 years from now (Bedford, 1992), but they will not account for the unexplained variance in personality characteristics. Correlations will no doubt be found between adult personality characteristics and differential treatment, but they are uninterpretable: Did Mom love you best because you were nicer than your sibling, or are you nicer because Mom loved you best?

The assumption that children are predisposed to favor behaviors acquired in the peer group over behaviors acquired at home could be tested by looking at those relatively rare occasions when the two contexts overlap. For example, when children bring three or four friends home with them and are playing with them in their parents' house, whose rules of behavior do they follow—their parents' or their peers'? What happens when a 9-year-old boy skins a knee in the presence of both his mother and his peers—does he cry, as he might with his mother, or act "tough," as he would with his peers?

Perhaps the most important effect this article can have on future research is to make investigators more aware of the fact that events taking place outside the family can have a potent effect on children's lives. A recent article on the effects of divorce on siblings (Monahan, Buchanan, Maccoby, & Dornbusch, 1993) reported that siblings who lived in different households after a divorce (one with the mother, the other with the father) differed more in "psychosocial adjustment" than siblings who continued to live in the same household. Of the children who lived in different households, either one or both had shifted residence at least once since their parents' divorce. Moving to a new residence usually means that the child loses the familiar peer group and must adapt to a new one, perhaps with a sizable change in status. It would have been of interest to know whether the psychosocial adjustment of the siblings who moved was worse or better than the siblings who stayed put, but the report does not distinguish between them.

Explaining the Unexplained Variance

The theory described in this article leads to a new interpretation of behavioral genetic data. The reinterpretation involves only the environmental portion of the variance.

Where Are the Shared and Nonshared Environments?

The terms *shared* and *nonshared environment* are defined by behavioral geneticists in terms of the child's postal address: Two children who live in the same home share an environment, two who live in different homes do not. This is not a useful distinction, according to GS theory, because the *effective* environment—the environment that will modify the child's genetic characteristics in ways that can be measured in adulthood—is not in the home, but outside of it. The effective environment may or may not be shared by two children who live in the same house. It is more likely to be shared by two unrelated children of the same age and sex who do not live in the same house but who live in the same neighborhood, go to the same school, and hold similar ranks in the social hierarchy of the same peer group.

Twins are the children who are most likely to share both a home environment and an effective environment. However, even twins who belong to the same peer group may have markedly different social ranks in the group or be typecast by their peers in different ways. With siblings of different ages, in addition to these possible differences in rank and typecasting, there will also be cohort differences, because they will move through the series of child cultures (Corsaro, 1993) at different times. The cohort effect can account for the finding that fraternal twins are generally found to be more alike than nontwin siblings (Plomin & Rende, 1991), even though both pairs share, on average, 50% of their genes.

GS theory predicts that in Western urbanized societies, where people live in privatized homes, within-family processes will tend to make siblings less alike, not more alike. Thus, if siblings show similarities not attributable to shared genes, they are more likely to have acquired those similarities in the environment they share outside the home.

Does the Nonshared Environment Make Siblings Different?

Behavioral geneticists often define the portion of the variance attributed to nonshared environment as environmental influences that make siblings different (e.g., McGuire et al., 1994; Plomin, Owen, & McGuffin, 1994). This is somewhat misleading, because what they are referring to is not a negative correlation, but no correlation at all—randomness. It is what remains of the variance after all the correlations are taken out.

If there is an environment that does make siblings different, it is more likely to be the one that behavioral geneticists call *shared.* The environment that they call *nonshared* does not make siblings different; it simply fails to make them alike—or, to be precise, it fails to make them more alike than children who do not live in the same house.

Sources of Variance

GS theory postulates only one effect, within-group assimilation, that decreases individual differences in personality among children in Western societies. Within-group assimilation also leads to socialization—the transmission of cultural norms. However, socialization has little effect on the measured variance in behavioral genetic studies, because in most cases the participants were all reared in the same culture.

GS theory postulates three major effects and two minor ones (listed in parentheses) that increase individual differences in personality among children in Western societies:

1. Between-group contrasts
2. Within-group differences in status
3. Within-group social comparisons
4. (Within-family differences in status)
5. (Within-family social comparisons and contrasts).

These five effects, minus the effects of within-group assimilation, can account for all environmental variance. The concepts of shared and nonshared environmental influence, as usually defined, are irrelevant; whether a child resides at 42 Oak Street or at 56 Oak Street is a variable that has no long-term consequences.

Conclusions

The answer to the question asked by the title of this article is that children have many environments. Their mission is to learn how to get along in all of them. They are aided by adaptive mechanisms that do not automatically mix together what is learned in different contexts; what is learned in one is used in another only if it proves to be useful in both. Negotiating satisfactory relationships with parents and siblings is an important undertaking of early childhood, but what is learned in the course of it may be of little use outside the home. Outside the home, children may be judged more harshly or less harshly; they must use different strategies to achieve their goals.

According to the theory presented here, children learn how to behave outside the home by becoming members of, and identifying with, a social group. In the preagricultural societies of our ancestors, group socialization would have begun in mixed-age, mixed-sex play groups. In today's urbanized societies, socialization gets its start in the nursery school or day-care center, gathers momentum in the same-age, same-sex peer groups of school-age children, and approaches asymptote in the mixed-sex crowds of adolescents. It is within these groups, according to GS theory, that the psychological characteristics a child is born with become permanently modified by the environment. Two processes, assimilation and differentiation, are responsible for the modifications. Assimilation transmits cultural norms, smooths off rough edges of the personality, and makes children more like their peers. Differentiation exaggerates individual differences and increases variability. Which of these processes will dominate at a given moment depends on contextual variables that cause social categories to become more or less salient.

With these two central hypotheses—that children learn separately how to behave in the home and out of the home, and that out-of-the-home socialization takes place in the peer groups of childhood and adolescence—GS theory can account for a growing body of data showing that the home environment has no lasting effects on psychological characteristics. The shared environment that leaves permanent marks on children's personalities is the environment they share with their peers.

Many psychologists have marveled at the robustness of development; despite vast differences in the way their parents treat them, most children turn out all right. This ceases to be a mystery if we cease to believe that the way their parents treat them (assuming that they do not inflict grievous injury) has important and lasting effects. Children usually turn out all right because the environment that does have important and lasting effects is found with little variation in every society: the children's play group.

There is an African saying, "It takes a village to raise a child." In a village, there are always enough children to form a group.

References

Abramovitch, R., Corter, C., Pepler, D. J., & Stanhope, L. (1986). Sibling and peer interaction: A final follow-up and a comparison. *Child Development, 57,* 217–229.

Adler, P. A., Kless, S. J., & Adler, P. (1992). Socialization to gender roles: Popularity among elementary school boys and girls. *Sociology of Education, 65,* 169–187.

Ainsworth, M. D. S., Blehar, M. C., Waters, E., & Wall, S. (1978). *Patterns of attachment: A psychological study of the Strange Situation.* Hillsdale, NJ: Erlbaum.

Alper, J. (1993, April 16). The pipeline is leaking women all the way along. *Science, 260,* 409–411.

Alwin, D. F. (1988). From obedience to autonomy: Changes in traits desired in children, 1924–1978. *Public Opinion Quarterly, 52,* 33–52.

Anderson, K. E., Lytton, H., & Romney, D. M. (1986). Mothers' interactions with normal and conduct-disordered boys: Who affects whom? *Developmental Psychology, 22,* 604–609.

Archer, J. (1992). Childhood gender roles: Social context and organization. In H. McGurk (Ed.), *Childhood social development: Contemporary perspectives* (pp. 31–61). Hove, England: Erlbaum.

Asch, S. E. (1987). *Social psychology.* Oxford, England: Oxford University Press. (Original work published 1952)

Asendorpf, J. B., & van Aken, M. A. G. (1994). Traits and relationship status: Stranger versus peer group inhibition and test intelligence versus peer group competence as early predictors of later self-esteem. *Child Development, 65,* 1786–1798.

Banaji, M. R., & Prentice, D. A. (1994). The self in social contexts. *Annual Review of Psychology, 45,* 297–332.

Baron, N. S. (1992). *Growing up with language: How children learn to talk.* Reading, MA: Addison-Wesley.

Bartlett, J. (1955). *Familiar quotations* (13th ed.). Boston: Little, Brown.

Baumrind, D. (1971). Current patterns of parental authority. *Developmental Psychology Monograph, 4*(1, Part 2).

Baumrind, D. (1989). Rearing competent children. In W. Damon (Ed.), *Child development today and tomorrow* (pp. 349–378). San Francisco: Jossey-Bass.

Bebko, J. M., & McKinnon, E. E. (1990). The language experience of deaf children: Its relation to spontaneous rehearsal in a memory task. *Child Development, 61,* 1744–1752.

Bedford, V. H. (1992). Memories of parental favoritism and the quality of parent–child ties in adulthood. *Journal of Gerontology: Social Sciences, 47,* S149–S155.

Bee, D. E., Baranowski, T., Rassin, D. K., Richardson, J., & Mikrut, W. (1991). Breast-feeding initiation in a triethnic population. *American Journal of Diseases of Children, 145,* 306–309.

Bell, R. Q. (1968). A reinterpretation of the direction of effects in studies of socialization. *Psychological Review, 75,* 81–95.

Bell, R. Q., & Chapman, M. (1986). Child effects in studies using experimental or brief longitudinal approaches to socialization. *Developmental Psychology, 22,* 595–603.

Belsky, J., Rovine, M., & Taylor, D. G. (1984). The Pennsylvania Infant and Family Development Project: III. The origins of individual differences in infant–mother attachment: Maternal and infant contributions. *Child Development, 55,* 718–728.

Berndt, T. J. (1979). Developmental changes in conformity to peers and parents. *Developmental Psychology, 15,* 606–616.

Bickerton, D. (1983, July). Creole languages. *Scientific American, 249,* 116–122.

Bierman, K. L., Smoot, D. L., & Aumiller, K. (1993). Characteristics of aggressive-rejected, aggressive (nonrejected), and rejected (nonaggressive) boys. *Child Development, 64,* 139–151.

Billig, M., & Tajfel, H. (1973). Social categorization and similarity in intergroup behavior. *European Journal of Social Psychology, 3,* 27–52.

Birch, L. L. (1987). Children's food preferences: Developmental patterns and environmental influences. *Annals of Child Development, 4,* 171–208.

Block, J. H., Block, J., & Gjerde, P. F. (1986). The personality of children prior to divorce: A prospective study. *Child Development, 57,* 827–840.

Bouchard, T. J., Jr. (1994, June 17). Genes, environment, and personality. *Science, 264,* 1700–1701.

Bouchard, T. J., Jr., Lykken, D. T., McGue, M., Segal, N. L., & Tellegen, A. (1990, October 12). Sources of human psychological differences: The Minnesota Study of Twins Reared Apart. *Science, 250,* 223–228.

Bowerman, C. E., & Kinch, J. W. (1969). Changes in family and peer orientation of children between the fourth and tenth grades. In M. Gold & E. Douvan (Eds.), *Adolescent development* (pp. 137–141). Boston: Allyn & Bacon.

Bowlby, J. (1969). *Attachment and loss: Vol. 1. Attachment.* New York: Basic Books.

Braungart, J. M., Plomin, R., DeFries, J. C., & Fulker, D. W. (1992). Genetic influence on tester-rated infant temperament as assessed by Bayley's Infant Behavior Record: Nonadoptive and adoptive siblings and twins. *Developmental Psychology, 28,* 40–47.

Brewer, M. B. (1991). The social self: On being the same and different at the same time. *Personality and Social Psychology Bulletin, 17,* 475–482.

Brewer, M. B., & Weber, J. G. (1994). Self-evaluation effects of interpersonal versus intergroup social comparison. *Journal of Personality and Social Psychology, 66,* 268–275.

Brody, G., & Stoneman, Z. (1994). Sibling relationships and their association with parental differential treatment. In E. M. Hetherington, D. Reiss, & R. Plomin (Eds.), *Separate social worlds of siblings: The impact of nonshared environment on development* (pp. 129–142). Hillsdale, NJ: Erlbaum.

Brody, G. H., Stoneman, Z., MacKinnon, C. E., & MacKinnon, R. (1985). Role relationships and behavior between preschool-aged and school-aged sibling pairs. *Developmental Psychology, 21,* 124–129.

Bronfenbrenner, U. (1986). Ecology of the family as a context for human development: Research perspectives. *Developmental Psychology, 22,* 723–742.

Brooks, J., & Lewis, M. (1976). Infants' responses to strangers: Midget, adult, and child. *Child Development, 47,* 323–332.

Brown, B. B., & Lohr, M. J. (1987). Peer-group affiliation and adolescent self-esteem: An integration of ego-identity and symbolic-interaction theories. *Journal of Personality and Social Psychology, 52,* 47–55.

Brown, B. B., Mounts, N., Lamborn, S. D., & Steinberg, L. (1993). Parenting practices and peer group affiliation in adolescence. *Child Development, 64,* 467–482.

Bukowski, W. M., & Hoza, B. (1989). Popularity and friendship: Issues in theory, measurement, and outcome. In T. J. Berndt & G. W. Ladd (Eds.), *Peer relationships in child development* (pp. 15–45). New York: Wiley.

Burns, G. L., & Farina, A. (1992). The role of physical attractiveness in adjustment. *Genetic, Social, and General Psychology Monographs, 118,* 157–194.

Buss, D. M. (1991). Evolutionary personality psychology. *Annual Review of Psychology, 42,* 459–491.

Carson, R. C. (1989). Personality. *Annual Review of Psychology, 40,* 227–248.

Ceci, S. J. (1993). Contextual trends in intellectual development. *Developmental Review, 13,* 403–435.

Chao, R. K. (1994). Beyond parental control and authoritarian parenting style: Understanding Chinese parenting through the cultural notion of training. *Child Development, 65,* 1111–1119.

Cherlin, A. J., Furstenberg, F. F., Chase-Lansdale, P. L., Kiernan, K. E., Robins, P. K., Morrison, D. R., & Teitler, J. O. (1991, June 7). Longitudinal studies of effects of divorce on children in Great Britain and the United States. *Science, 252,* 1386–1389.

Clausen, J. A. (1975). The social meaning of differential physical and sexual maturation. In S. E. Dragastin & G. H. Elder, Jr. (Eds.), *Adolescence in the life cycle: Psychological change and the social context* (pp. 25–47). New York: Halsted.

Coie, J. D. (1990). Toward a theory of peer rejection. In S. R. Asher & J. D. Coie (Eds.), *Peer rejection in childhood* (pp. 365–401). Cambridge, England: Cambridge University Press.

Cole, M. (1992). Culture in development. In M. H. Bornstein & M. E. Lamb (Eds.), *Developmental psychology: An advanced textbook* (pp. 731–789). Hillsdale, NJ: Erlbaum.

Corsaro, W. A. (1993). Interpretive reproduction in the "*scuola materna*." *European Journal of Psychology of Education, 8,* 357–374.

Corsaro, W. A. (1994). Discussion, debate, and friendship processes: Peer discourse in U.S. and Italian nursery schools. *Sociology of Education, 67,* 1–26.

Corsaro, W. A., & Eder, D. (1990). Children's peer cultures. *Annual Review of Sociology, 16,* 197–220.

Cosmides, L., & Tooby, J. (1992). Cognitive adaptations for social exchange. In J. Barkow, L. Cosmides, & J. Tooby (Eds.), *The adapted mind: Evolutionary psychology and the generation of culture* (pp. 163–228). New York: Oxford University Press.

Council, J. R. (1993). Contextual effects in personality research. *Current Directions in Psychological Science, 2,* 31–34.

Curtiss, S. R. (1977). *Genie: A linguistic study of a modern day "wild child."* New York: Academic Press.

Daniels, D., & Plomin, R. (1985). Differential experience of siblings in the same family. *Developmental Psychology, 21,* 747–760.

David, H. P. (1992). Born unwanted: Long-term developmental effects of denied abortion. *Journal of Social Issues, 48,* 163–181.

Davidson, R. J. (1992). Emotion and affective style: Hemispheric substrates. *Psychological Science, 3,* 39–43.

Day, J. D., Borkowski, J. G., Dietmeyer, D. L., Howsepian, B. A., & Saenz, D. S. (1992). Possible selves and academic achievement. In L. T. Winegar & J. Valsiner (Eds.), *Children's development within social context: Vol. 2. Research and methodology* (pp. 181–201). Hillsdale, NJ: Erlbaum.

Deaux, K., & Major, B. (1987). Putting gender into context: An interactive model of gender-related behavior. *Psychological Review, 94,* 369–389.

deMarrais, K. B., Nelson, P. A., & Baker, J. H. (1994). Meaning in mud: Yup'ik Eskimo girls at play. In J. L. Roopnarine, J. E. Johnson, & F. H. Hooper (Eds.), *Children's play in diverse cultures* (pp. 179–209). Albany: State University of New York Press.

Dencik, L. (1989). Growing up in the post-modern age: On the child's situation in the modern family, and on the position of the family in the modern welfare state. *Acta Sociologica, 32,* 155–180.

de Waal, F. (1989). *Peacemaking among primates.* Cambridge, MA: Harvard University Press.

Diamond, K., LeFurgy, W., & Blass, S. (1993). Attitudes of preschool children toward their peers with disabilities: A year-long investigation in integrated classrooms. *Journal of Genetic Psychology, 154,* 215–221.

DiLalla, L. F., & Gottesman, I. I. (1991). Biological and genetic contributors to violence—Widom's untold tale. *Psychological Bulletin, 109,* 125–129.

Dornbusch, S. M., Ritter, P. L., Leiderman, P. H., Roberts, D. F., & Fraleigh, M. J. (1987). The relation of parenting style to adolescent school performance. *Child Development, 58,* 1244–1257.

Draper, P., & Cashdan, E. (1988). Technological change and child behavior among the !Kung. *Ethnology, 27,* 339–365.

Dunn, J. (1992). Siblings and development. *Current Directions in Psychological Science, 1,* 6–9.

Dunn, J., & McGuire, S. (1994). Young children's nonshared experiences: A summary of studies in Cambridge and Colorado. In E. M. Hetherington, D. Reiss, & R. Plomin (Eds.), *Separate social worlds of siblings: The impact of nonshared environment on development* (pp. 111–128). Hillsdale, NJ: Erlbaum.

Dunn, J., & Plomin, R. (1990). *Separate lives: Why siblings are so different.* New York: Basic Books.

Dunn, J., Plomin, R., & Daniels, D. (1986). Consistency and change in mothers' behavior to two-year-old siblings. *Child Development, 57,* 348–356.

Eckerman, C. O., & Didow, S. M. (1988). Lessons drawn from observing young peers together. *Acta Paediatrica Scandinavica, 77,* 55–70.

Eckert, P. (1989). *Jocks and burnouts: Social categories and identity in the high school.* New York: Teachers College Press.

Edwards, C. P. (1992). Cross-cultural perspectives on family–peer relations. In R. D. Parke & G. W. Ladd (Eds.), *Family–peer relationships: Modes of linkage* (pp. 285–316). Hillsdale, NJ: Erlbaum.

Eimas, P. D., & Quinn, P. C. (1994). Studies on the formation of perceptually based basic-level categories in young infants. *Child Development, 65,* 903–907.

Erikson, E. H. (1963). *Childhood and society* (2nd ed.). New York: Norton.

Ernst, C., & Angst, J. (1983). *Birth order: Its influence on personality.* Berlin, Germany: Springer-Verlag.

Fagen, R. (1993). Primate juveniles and primate play. In M. E. Pereira & L. A. Fairbanks (Eds.), *Juvenile primates* (pp. 182–192). New York: Oxford University Press.

Fagot, B. I. (1985). Beyond the reinforcement principle: Another step toward understanding sex role development. *Developmental Psychology, 21,* 1097–1104.

Fagot, B. I., & Hagan, R. (1991). Observations of parent reactions to sex-stereotyped behaviors: Age and sex effects. *Child Development, 62,* 617–628.

Falbo, T., & Polit, D. F. (1986). Quantitative research of the only child literature: Research evidence and theory development. *Psychological Bulletin, 100,* 176–189.

Falbo, T., & Poston, D. L., Jr. (1993). The academic, personality, and physical outcomes of only children in China. *Child Development, 64,* 18–35.

Festinger, L. (1954). A theory of social comparison processes. *Human Relations, 7,* 117–140.

Fine, G. A. (1981). Friends, impression management, and preadolescent behavior. In S. R. Asher & J. M. Gottman (Eds.), *The development of children's friendships* (pp. 29–52). Cambridge, England: Cambridge University Press.

Fine, G. A. (1988). Good children and dirty play. *Play & Culture, 1,* 43–56.

Fiske, S. T. (1992). Thinking is for doing: Portraits of social cognition from daguerreotype to laserphoto. *Journal of Personality and Social Psychology, 63,* 877–889.

Fiske, S. T., & Taylor, S. E. (1991). *Social cognition.* New York: McGraw Hill.

Fox, N. A., Bell, M. A., & Jones, N. A. (1992). Individual differences in response to stress and cerebral asymmetry. *Developmental Neuropsychology, 8,* 161–184.

Fox, N. A., Kimmerly, N. L., & Schafer, W. D. (1991). Attachment to mother/attachment to father: A meta-analysis. *Child Development, 62,* 210–225.

Fraiberg, S. (1959). *The magic years.* New York: Scribner's.

Freud, A., & Dann, S. (1951). An experiment in group upbringing. *Psychoanalytic Study of the Child, 6,* 127–168.

Frick, P. J., & Jackson, Y. K. (1993). Family functioning and childhood antisocial behavior: Yet another reinterpretation. *Journal of Clinical Child Psychology, 22,* 410–419.

Garner, R. (1990). When children and adults do not use learning strategies: Toward a theory of settings. *Review of Educational Research, 60,* 517–529.

Genesee, F. (1989). Early bilingual development: One language or two? *Journal of Child Language, 16,* 161–179.

Ghodsian-Carpey, J., & Baker, L. A. (1987). Genetic and environmental influences on aggression in 4- to 7-year-old twins. *Aggressive Behavior, 13,* 173–186.

Glenn, N. D., & Kramer, K. B. (1987). The marriages and divorces of the children of divorce. *Journal of Marriage and the Family, 49,* 811–825.

Glynn, A. (1970). *The British: Portrait of a people.* New York: Putnam's Sons.

Goldsmith, H. H. (1993a). Nature–nurture issues in the behavioral genetics context: Overcoming barriers to communication. In R. Plomin & G. E. McClearn (Eds.), *Nature, nurture, and psychology* (pp. 325–339). Washington, DC: American Psychological Association.

Goldsmith, H. H. (1993b). Temperament: Variability in developing emotion systems. In M. Lewis & J. M. Haviland (Eds.), *Handbook of emotions* (pp. 353–364). New York: Guilford Press.

Goodall, J. (1986). *The chimpanzees of Gombe: Patterns of behavior.* Cambridge, MA: Harvard University Press.

Goossens, F. A., & van Ijzendoorn, M. H. (1990). Quality of infants' attachments to professional caregivers: Relation to infant–parent attachment and day-care characteristics. *Child Development, 61,* 550–567.

Gould, J. L. (1992). Interpreting the honeybee's dance. *American Scientist, 80,* 278–279.

Greer, D. L., & Stewart, M. J. (1989). Children's attitude toward play: An investigation of their context specificity and relationship to organized sport experiences. *Journal of Sport & Exercise Psychology, 11,* 336–342.

Grilo, C. M., & Pogue-Geile, M. F. (1991). The nature of environmental influences on weight and obesity: A behavioral genetic analysis. *Psychological Bulletin, 110,* 520–537.

Guisewite, C. (1994, June 19). Cathy. *Asbury Park Press,* Comics Section, p. 1.

Guisinger, S., & Blatt, S. J. (1994). Individuality and relatedness: Evolution of a fundamental dialectic. *American Psychologist, 49,* 104–111.

Hallinan, M. T. (1992). Determinants of students' friendship choices. In E. J. Lawler, B. Markovsky, C. Ridgeway, & H. A. Walker (Eds.), *Advances in group processes* (Vol. 9, pp. 163–183). Greenwich, CT: JAI Press.

Hareven, T. (1985). Historical changes in the family and the life course: Implications for child development. In A. B. Smuts & J. W. Hagen (Eds.), History and research in child development (pp. 8–23). *Monographs of the Society for Research in Child Development, 50*(4–5, Serial No. 211).

Harlow, H. F., & Harlow, M. K. (1975). Social deprivation in monkeys. In R. C. Atkinson (Ed.), *Readings from Scientific American: Psychology in progress* (pp. 225–233). San Francisco: Freeman. (Original work published 1962)

Harris, J. R., & Liebert, R. M. (1991). *The child: A contemporary view of development* (3rd ed.). Englewood Cliffs, NJ: Prentice-Hall.

Harris, M. J., Milich, R., Corbitt, E. M., Hoover, D. W., & Brady, M. (1992). Self-fulfilling effects of stigmatizing information on children's social interactions. *Journal of Personality and Social Psychology, 63,* 41–50.

Harter, S. (1983). Developmental perspectives on the self-system. In P. H. Mussen (Series Ed.) & E. M. Hetherington (Vol. Ed.), *Handbook of child psychology: Vol. 4. Socialization, personality, and social development* (4th ed., pp. 275–385). New York: Wiley.

Hartup, W. W. (1983). Peer relations. In P. H. Mussen (Series Ed.) & E. M. Hetherington (Vol. Ed.), *Handbook of child psychology: Vol. 4. Socialization, personality, and social development* (4th ed., pp. 103–196). New York: Wiley.

Hartup, W. W., & Laursen, B. (1991). Relationships as developmental contexts. In R. Cohen & A. W. Siegel (Eds.), *Context and development* (pp. 253–279). Hillsdale, NJ: Erlbaum.

Heckathorn, D. D. (1992). Collective sanctions and group heterogeneity: Cohesion and polarization in normative systems. In E. J. Lawler, B. Markovsky, C. Ridgeway, & H. A. Walker (Eds.), *Advances in group processes* (Vol. 9, pp. 41–63). Greenwich, CT: JAI Press.

Hetherington, E. M., & Clingempeel, W. G. (with Anderson, E. R., Deal, J. E., Hagan, M. S., Hollier, E. A., & Lindner, M. S.). (1992). Coping with marital transitions: A family systems perspective. *Monographs of the Society for Research in Child Development, 57*(2–3, Serial No. 227).

Hetherington, E. M., Stanley-Hagan, M., & Anderson, E. R. (1989). Marital transitions: A child's perspective. *American Psychologist, 44,* 303–312.

Hinde, R. A., & Stevenson-Hinde, J. (1986). Relating childhood relationships to individual characteristics. In W. W. Hartup & Z. Rubin (Eds.), *Relationships and development* (pp. 27–50). Hillsdale, NJ: Erlbaum.

Hirschfeld, L. A. (1993). Discovering social difference: The role of appearance in the development of racial awareness. *Cognitive Psychology, 25,* 317–350.

Hoffman, L. W. (1991). The influence of the family environment on personality: Accounting for sibling differences. *Psychological Bulletin, 110,* 187–203.

Howes, C., Matheson, C. C., & Hamilton, C. E. (1994). Maternal, teacher, and child care history correlates of children's relationships with peers. *Child Development, 65,* 264–273.

Howrigan, G. A. (1988). Fertility, infant feeding, and change in Yucatán. In R. A. LeVine, P. M. Miller, & M. M. West (Eds.), *Parental behavior in diverse societies* (pp. 37–50). New Directions for Child Development, No. 40. San Francisco: Jossey-Bass.

Jacobson, J. L., & Wille, D. E. (1986). The influence of attachment pattern on developmental changes in peer interaction from the toddler to the preschool period. *Child Development, 57,* 338–347.

James, W. (1890). *The principles of psychology* (Vol. 1). New York: Henry Holt.

Jaquess, D. L., & Finney, J. W. (1994). Previous injuries and behavior problems predict children's injuries. *Journal of Pediatric Psychology, 19,* 79–89.

Jones, M. C. (1957). The later careers of boys who were early or late maturing. *Child Development, 28,* 113–128.

Kagan, J. (1984). *The nature of the child.* New York: Basic Books.

Kagan, J., Arcus, D., & Snidman, N. (1993). The idea of temperament: Where do we go from here? In R. Plomin & G. E. McClearn (Eds.), *Nature, nurture, and psychology* (pp. 197–210). Washington, DC: American Psychological Association.

Kagan, J., Reznick, J. S., Snidman, N., Gibbons, J., & Johnson, M. O. (1988). Childhood derivatives of inhibition and lack of inhibition to the unfamiliar. *Child Development, 59,* 1580–1589.

Kagan, J., & Snidman, N. (1991). Temperamental factors in human development. *American Psychologist, 46,* 856–862.

Kennedy, J. H. (1990). Determinants of peer social status: Contributions of physical appearance, reputation, and behavior. *Journal of Youth and Adolescence, 19,* 233–244.

Kerr, M., Lambert, W. W., Stattin, H., & Klackenberg-Larsson, I. (1994). Stability of inhibition in a Swedish longitudinal sample. *Child Development, 65,* 138–146.

Kindermann, T. A. (1993). Natural peer groups as contexts for individual development: The case of children's motivation in school. *Developmental Psychology, 29,* 970–977.

Knowlton, B. J., & Squire, L. R. (1993, December 10). The learning of categories: Parallel brain systems for item memory and category knowledge. *Science, 262,* 1747–1749.

Kolata, G. (1993, May 25). Brain researcher makes it look easy. *New York Times,* pp. C1, C8.

Kolers, P. A. (1975). Bilingualism and information processing. In R. C. Atkinson (Ed.), *Readings from Scientific American: Psychology in progress* (pp. 188–195). San Francisco: Freeman. (Original work published 1968)

Koluchová, J. (1972). Severe deprivation in twins: A case study. *Journal of Child Psychology and Psychiatry, 13,* 107–114.

Koluchová, J. (1976). The further development of twins after severe and prolonged deprivation: A second report. *Journal of Child Psychology and Psychiatry, 17,* 181–188.

Krantz, S. E. (1989). The impact of divorce on children. In A. S. Skolnick & J. H. Skolnick (Eds.), *Family in transition* (6th ed., pp. 341–363). Glenview, IL: Scott, Foresman.

Kreppner, K. (1992). Development in a developing context: Rethinking the family's role for children's development. In L. T. Winegar & J. Valsiner (Eds.), *Children's development within social context: Vol. 2. Research and methodology* (pp. 161–182). Hillsdale, NJ: Erlbaum.

Krueger, J. (1992). On the overestimation of between-group differences. *European Review of Social Psychology, 3,* 31–56.

LaFromboise, T., Coleman, H. L. K., & Gerton, J. (1993). Psychological impact of biculturalism: Evidence and theory. *Psychological Bulletin, 114,* 395–412.

Lamborn, S., Mounts, N., Steinberg, L., & Dornbusch, S. (1991). Patterns of competence and adjustment among adolescents from authoritative, authoritarian, indulgent, and neglectful homes. *Child Development, 62,* 1049–1065.

Lane, H. (1976). *The wild boy of Aveyron.* Cambridge, MA: Harvard University Press.

Lanza, E. (1992). Can bilingual two-year-olds code-switch? *Journal of Child Language, 19,* 633–658.

Lasater, C., & Johnson, J. E. (1994). Culture, play, and early childhood education. In J. L. Roopnarine, J. E. Johnson, & F. H. Hooper (Eds.), *Children's play in diverse cultures* (pp. 210–228). Albany: State University of New York Press.

Leiderman, P. H., Tulkin, S. R., & Rosenfeld, A. (Eds.). (1977). *Culture and infancy: Variations in the human experience.* New York: Academic Press.

Leinbach, M. D., & Fagot, B. I. (1993). Categorical habituation to male and female faces: Gender schematic processing in infancy. *Infant Behavior and Development, 16,* 317–332.

Levine, J. M., Resnick, L. B., & Higgins, E. T. (1993). Social foundations of cognition. *Annual Review of Psychology, 44,* 585–612.

LeVine, R. A., & LeVine, B. B. (1963). Nyansongo: A Gusii Community in Kenya. In B. B. Whiting (Ed.), *Six cultures: Studies of child rearing* (pp. 15–202). New York: Wiley.

LeVine, R. A., & LeVine, S. E. (1988). Parental strategies among the Gusii of Kenya. In R. A. LeVine, P. M. Miller, & M. M. West (Eds.), *Parental behavior in diverse societies* (pp. 27–35). New Directions for Child Development, No. 40. San Francisco: Jossey-Bass.

Lightfoot, C. (1992). Constructing self and peer culture: A narrative perspective on adolescent risk taking. In L. T. Winegar & J. Valsiner (Eds.), *Children's development within social context: Vol. 2. Research and methodology* (pp. 229–245). Hillsdale, NJ: Erlbaum.

Loehlin, J. C. (1992). *Genes and environment in personality development.* Newbury Park, CA: Sage.

Loehlin, J. C., & Nichols, R. C. (1976). *Heredity, environment, and personality.* Austin: University of Texas Press.

Lytton, H. (1990). Child and parent effects in boys' conduct disorder: A reinterpretation. *Developmental Psychology, 26,* 683–697.

Lytton, H., & Romney, D. M. (1991). Parents' differential socialization of boys and girls: A meta-analysis. *Psychological Bulletin, 109,* 267–296.

Maccoby, E. E. (1990). Gender and relationships: A developmental account. *American Psychologist, 45,* 513–520.

Maccoby, E. E., & Jacklin, C. N. (1974). *The psychology of sex differences.* Stanford, CA: Stanford University Press.

Maccoby, E. E., & Jacklin, C. N. (1987). Gender segregation in childhood. *Advances in Child Development and Behavior, 20,* 239–287.

Maccoby, E. E., & Martin, J. A. (1983). Socialization in the context of the family: Parent–child interaction. In P. H. Mussen (Series Ed.) & E. M. Hetherington (Vol. Ed.), *Handbook of child psychology: Vol. 4. Socialization, personality, and social development* (4th ed., pp. 1–101). New York: Wiley.

MacKinnon-Lewis, C., Volling, B. L., Lamb, M. E., Dechman, K., Rabiner, D., & Curtner, M. E. (1994). A cross-contextual analysis of boys' social competence from family to school. *Developmental Psychology, 30,* 325–333.

Main, M., & Weston, D. R. (1981). The quality of the toddler's relationship to mother and to father: Related to conflict behavior and the readiness to establish new relationships. *Child Development, 52,* 932–940.

Mandler, J. M. (1988). A new perspective on cognitive development in infancy. *American Scientist, 78,* 236–243.

Mandler, J. M. (1992). How to build a baby: II. Conceptual primitives. *Psychological Review, 99,* 587–604.

Martin, C. L. (1993). Theories of sex typing: Moving toward multiple perspectives. In L. A. Serbin, K. K. Powlishta, & J. Gulko, The development of sex typing in middle childhood (pp. 75–85). *Monographs of the Society for Research in Child Development, 58*(2, Serial No. 232).

Martini, M. (1994). Peer interactions in Polynesia: A view from the Marquesas. In J. L. Roopnarine & J. E. Johnson (Eds.), *Children's play in diverse cultures* (pp. 73–103). Albany: State University of New York Press.

Mathews, A., & MacLeod, C. (1994). Cognitive approaches to emotion and emotional disorders. *Annual Review of Psychology, 45,* 25–50.

McCartney, K., Robeson, W. W., Jordan, E., & Mouradian, V. (1991). Mother's language with first- and second-born children: A within-family study. In K. Pillemer & K. McCartney (Eds.), *Parent–child relations throughout life* (pp. 125–142). Hillsdale, NJ: Erlbaum.

McCrae, R. R. (1993). Moderated analyses of longitudinal personality stability. *Journal of Personality and Social Psychology, 65*, 577–585.

McDonald, M. A., Sigman, M., Espinosa, M. P., & Neumann, C. G. (1994). Impact of a temporary food shortage on children and their mothers. *Child Development, 65*, 404–415.

McGue, M. (1993). From proteins to cognitions: The behavioral genetics of alcoholism. In R. Plomin & G. E. McClearn (Eds.), *Nature, nurture, and psychology* (pp. 244–268). Washington, DC: American Psychological Association.

McGue, M., Bouchard, T. J., Jr., Iacono, W. G., & Lykken, D. T. (1993). Behavioral genetics of cognitive ability: A life-span perspective. In R. Plomin & G. E. McClearn (Eds.), *Nature, nurture, and psychology* (pp. 59–76). Washington, DC: American Psychological Association.

McGue, M., & Lykken, D. T. (1992). Genetic influence on risk of divorce. *Psychological Science, 3*, 368–373.

McGuffin, P., & Katz, R. (1993). Genes, adversity, and depression. In R. Plomin & G. E. McClearn (Eds.), *Nature, nurture, and psychology* (pp. 217–230). Washington, DC: American Psychological Association.

McGuire, S., Neiderhiser, J. M., Reiss, D., Hetherington, E. M., & Plomin, R. (1994). Genetic and environmental influences on perceptions of self-worth and competence in adolescence: A study of twins, full siblings, and step-siblings. *Child Development, 65*, 785–799.

McLanahan, S., & Booth, K. (1989). Mother-only families: Problems, prospects, and politics. *Journal of Marriage and the Family, 51*, 557–580.

Meier, R. P. (1991). Language acquisition by deaf children. *American Scientist, 79*, 60–70.

Melson, G. F., Ladd, G. W., & Hsu, H.-C. (1993). Maternal support networks, maternal cognitions, and young children's social and cognitive development. *Child Development, 64*, 1401–1417.

Miller, J. G. (1987). Cultural influences on the development of conceptual differentiation in person description. *British Journal of Developmental Psychology, 5*, 309–319.

Minuchin, P. P., & Shapiro, E. K. (1983). The school as a context for social development. In P. H. Mussen (Series Ed.) & E. M. Hetherington (Vol. Ed.), *Handbook of child psychology: Vol. 4. Socialization, personality, and social development* (4th ed., pp. 197–274). New York: Wiley.

Mischel, W., & Shoda, Y. (1995). A cognitive-affective system theory of personality: Reconceptualizing situations, dispositions, dynamics, and invariance in personality structure. *Psychological Review, 102*, 246–268.

Mitchell, D. E. (1980). The influence of early visual experience on visual perception. In C. S. Harris (Ed.), *Visual coding and adaptability* (pp. 1–50). Hillsdale, NJ: Erlbaum.

Moffitt, T. E. (1993a). Adolescence-limited and life-course-persistent antisocial behavior: A developmental taxonomy. *Psychological Review, 100*, 674–701.

Moffitt, T. E. (1993b). The neuropsychology of conduct disorder. *Development and Psychopathology, 5*, 135–151.

Monahan, S. C., Buchanan, C. M., Maccoby, E. E., & Dornbusch, S. M. (1993). Sibling differences in divorced families. *Child Development, 64*, 152–168.

Morelli, G. A. (1994). *Growing up female in a farmer and forager community.* Manuscript submitted for publication.

Napier, J. R., & Napier, P. H. (1985). *The natural history of the primates.* Cambridge, MA: MIT Press.

Neighbors, B., Forehand, R., & Armistead, L. (1992). Is parental divorce a critical stressor for young adolescents? Grade point average as a case in point. *Adolescence, 27*, 640–645.

Newman, L. S., & Ruble, D. N. (1988). Stability and change in self-understanding: The early elementary school years. *Early Child Development and Care, 40*, 77–99.

Newport, E. L. (1990). Maturational constraints on language learning. *Cognitive Science, 14*, 11–28.

Olweus, D. (1993). Victimization by peers: Antecedents and long-term outcomes. In K. H. Rubin & A. Asendorpf (Eds.), *Social withdrawal, inhibition, and shyness in childhood* (pp. 315–341). Hillsdale, NJ: Erlbaum.

Opie, I., & Opie, P. (1969). *Children's games in street and playground.* London: Oxford University Press.

Oreskes, N., Shrader-Frechette, K., & Belitz, K. (1994, February 4). Verification, validation, and confirmation of numerical models in the earth sciences. *Science, 263*, 641–646.

Parker, J. G., & Asher, S. R. (1987). Peer relations and later personal adjustment: Are low-accepted children at risk? *Psychological Bulletin, 102*, 357–389.

Parker, J. G., & Asher, S. R. (1993a). Beyond group acceptance: Friendship and friendship quality as distinct dimensions of children's peer adjustment. In D. Perlman & W. H. Jones (Eds.), *Advances in personal relationships* (Vol. 4, pp. 261–294). London: Jessica Kingsley Publishers.

Parker, J. G., & Asher, S. R. (1993b). Friendship and friendship quality in middle childhood: Links with peer group acceptance and feelings of loneliness and social dissatisfaction. *Developmental Psychology, 29*, 611–621.

Parsons, J. E., Adler, T. F., & Kaczala, C. M. (1982). Socialization of achievement attitudes and beliefs: Parental influences. *Child Development, 53*, 310–321.

Pastor, D. (1981). The quality of mother–infant attachment and its relationship to toddlers' initial sociability with peers. *Developmental Psychology, 17*, 326–335.

Patterson, C. J. (1992). Children of lesbian and gay parents. *Child Development, 63*, 1025–1042.

Pedersen, E., Faucher, T. A., & Eaton, W. W. (1978). A new perspective on the effects of first-grade teachers on children's subsequent adult status. *Harvard Educational Review, 48*, 1–31.

Pedersen, N. L., Plomin, R., Nesselroade, J. R., & McClearn, G. E. (1992). A quantitative genetic analysis of cognitive abilities during the second half of the life span. *Psychological Science, 3*, 346–353.

Perry, D. G., & Bussey, K. (1984). *Social development.* Englewood Cliffs, NJ: Prentice-Hall.

Pettit, G. S., Bakshi, A., Dodge, K. A., & Coie, J. D. (1990). The emergence of social dominance in young boys' play groups: Developmental differences and behavioral correlates. *Developmental Psychology, 26*, 1017–1025.

Piaget, J. (1952). *The origins of intelligence in children* (M. Cook, Trans.). New York: International Universities Press.

Pinker, S., & Bloom, P. (1992). Natural language and natural selection. In J. Barkow, L. Cosmides, & J. Tooby (Eds.), *The adapted mind: Evolutionary psychology and the generation of culture* (pp. 451–493). New York: Oxford University Press.

Plomin, R. (1990). *Nature and nurture: An introduction to human behavioral genetics.* Pacific Grove, CA: Brooks/Cole.

Plomin, R., & Bergeman, C. S. (1991). The nature of nurture: Genetic influence on "environmental" measures. *Behavioral and Brain Sciences, 14*, 373–427.

Plomin, R., Chipuer, H. M., & Neiderhiser, J. M. (1994). Behavioral genetic evidence for the importance of nonshared environment. In E. M. Hetherington, D. Reiss, & R. Plomin (Eds.), *Separate social worlds of siblings: The impact of nonshared environment on development* (pp. 1–31). Hillsdale, NJ: Erlbaum.

Plomin, R., Corley, R., DeFries, J. C., & Fulker, D. W. (1990). Individual differences in television viewing in early childhood: Nature as well as nurture. *Psychological Science, 1*, 371–377.

Plomin, R., & Daniels, D. (1987). Why are children in the same family so different from one another? *Behavioral and Brain Sciences, 10*, 1–60.

Plomin, R., DeFries, J. C., & Loehlin, J. C. (1977). Genotype–environment interaction and correlation in the analysis of human behavior. *Psychological Bulletin, 84*, 309–322.

Plomin, R., McClearn, G. E., Pedersen, N. L., Nesselroade, J. R., & Bergeman, C. S. (1988). Genetic influence on childhood family environment perceived retrospectively from the last half of the life span. *Developmental Psychology, 24*, 738–745.

Plomin, R., Owen, M. J., & McGuffin, P. (1994, June 17). The genetic basis of complex human behaviors. *Science, 264*, 1733–1739.

Plomin, R., & Rende, R. (1991). Human behavioral genetics. *Annual Review of Psychology, 42*, 161–190.

Quittner, A. L., & Opipari, L. C. (1994). Differential treatment of siblings: Interview and diary analyses comparing two family contexts. *Child Development, 65*, 800–814.

Reich, P. A. (1986). *Language development*. Englewood Cliffs, NJ: Prentice-Hall.

Reiss, D., Plomin, R., Hetherington, E. M., Howe, G. W., Rovine, M., Tryon, A., & Hagan, M. S. (1994). The separate worlds of teenage siblings: An introduction to the study of the nonshared environment and adolescent development. In E. M. Hetherington, D. Reiss, & R. Plomin (Eds.), *Separate social worlds of siblings: The impact of nonshared environment on development* (pp. 63–109). Hillsdale, NJ: Erlbaum.

Retherford, R. D., & Sewell, W. H. (1991). Birth order and intelligence: Further tests of the confluence model. *American Sociological Review, 56*, 141–158.

Riley, D. (1990). Network influences on father involvement in childrearing. In M. Cochran, M. Larner, D. Riley, L. Gunnarsson, & C. R. Henderson, Jr. (Eds.), *Extending families: The social networks of parents and their children* (pp. 131–152). Cambridge, England: Cambridge University Press.

Ritter, J. M., Casey, R. J., & Langlois, J. H. (1991). Adults' responses to infants varying in appearance of age and attractiveness. *Child Development, 62*, 68–82.

Robinson, J. L., Kagan, J., Reznick, J. S., & Corley, R. (1992). The heritability of inhibited and uninhibited behavior: A twin study. *Developmental Psychology, 28*, 1030–1037.

Rodgers, J. L., Rowe, D. C., & Li, C. (1994). Beyond nature versus nurture: DF analysis of nonshared influences on problem behaviors. *Developmental Psychology, 30*, 374–384.

Rogoff, B., Mistry, J., Göncü, A., & Mosier, C. (1993). Guided participation in cultural activity by toddlers and caregivers. *Monographs of the Society for Research in Child Development, 58*(8, Serial No. 236).

Rovee-Collier, C. (1993). The capacity for long-term memory in infancy. *Current Directions in Psychological Science, 2*, 130–135.

Rowe, D. C. (1981). Environmental and genetic influences on dimensions of perceived parenting: A twin study. *Developmental Psychology, 17*, 203–208.

Rowe, D. C. (1990). As the twig is bent? The myth of child-rearing influences on personality development. *Journal of Counseling and Development, 68*, 606–611.

Rowe, D. C. (1994). *The limits of family influence: Genes, experience, and behavior*. New York: Guilford Press.

Rowe, D. C., Chassin, L., Presson, C. C., Edwards, D., & Sherman, S. J. (1992). An "epidemic" model of adolescent cigarette smoking. *Journal of Applied Social Psychology, 22*, 261–285.

Rowe, D. C., Woulbroun, E. J., & Gulley, B. L. (1994). Peers and friends as nonshared environmental influences. In E. M. Hetherington, D. Reiss, & R. Plomin (Eds.), *Separate social worlds of siblings: The impact of nonshared environment on development* (pp. 159–173). Hillsdale, NJ: Erlbaum.

Rubin, K. H., & Coplan, R. J. (1992). Peer relations in childhood. In M. H. Bornstein & M. E. Lamb (Eds.), *Developmental psychology: An advanced textbook* (pp. 519–578). Hillsdale, NJ: Erlbaum.

Russell, R. J. (1993). *The lemurs' legacy: The evolution of power, sex, and love*. New York: Tarcher/Putnam.

Rutter, M. (1979). Maternal deprivation, 1972–1978: New findings, new concepts, new approaches. *Child Development, 50*, 283–305.

Rybczynski, W. (1986). *Home: A short history of an idea*. New York: Penguin.

Sadker, M., & Sadker, D. (1994). *Failing at fairness: How America's schools cheat girls*. New York: Scribner's.

Salzinger, S. (1990). Social networks in child rearing and child development. *Annals of the New York Academy of Science, 602*, 171–188.

Sansone, C., & Berg, C. A. (1993). Adapting to the environment across the life span: Different processes or different inputs? *International Journal of Behavioral Development, 16*, 215–241.

Savin-Williams, R. C. (1979). An ethological study of dominance formation and maintenance in a group of human adolescents. *Child Development, 49*, 534–536.

Scarr, S. (1992). Developmental theories for the 1990s: Development and individual differences. *Child Development, 63*, 1–19.

Scarr, S. (1993). Biological and cultural diversity: The legacy of Darwin for development. *Child Development, 64*, 1333–1353.

Scarr, S., & Grajek, S. (1982). Similarities and differences among siblings. In M. E. Lamb & B. Sutton-Smith (Eds.), *Sibling relationships: Their nature and significance across the lifespan* (pp. 357–381). Hillsdale, NJ: Erlbaum.

Scarr, S., & McCartney, K. (1983). How people make their own environments: A theory of genotype → environment effects. *Child Development, 54*, 424–435.

Schachter, F. F. (1982). Sibling deidentification and split-parent identification: A family tetrad. In M. E. Lamb & B. Sutton-Smith (Eds.), *Sibling relationships: Their nature and significance across the lifespan* (pp. 123–151). Hillsdale, NJ: Erlbaum.

Schachter, F. F., & Stone, R. K. (1985). Difficult sibling, easy sibling: Temperament and the within-family environment. *Child Development, 56*, 1335–1344.

Schlegel, A., & Barry, H., III (1991). *Adolescence: An anthropological inquiry*. New York: Free Press.

Schofield, J. W. (1981). Complementary and conflicting identities: Images and interaction in an interracial school. In S. R. Asher & J. M. Gottman (Eds.), *The development of children's friendships* (pp. 53–90). Cambridge, England: Cambridge University Press.

Schwartz, D., Dodge, K. A., & Coie, J. D. (1993). The emergence of chronic peer victimization in boys' play groups. *Child Development, 64*, 1755–1772.

Serbin, L. A., Powlishta, K. K., & Gulko, J. (1993). The development of sex typing in middle childhood. *Monographs of the Society for Research in Child Development, 58*(2, Serial No. 232).

Sherif, M., Harvey, O. J., White, B. J., Hood, W. R., & Sherif, C. W. (1961). *Intergroup cooperation and competition: The Robbers Cave experiment*. Norman, OK: University Book Exchange.

Siegal, M. (1987). Are sons and daughters treated more differently by fathers than by mothers? *Developmental Review, 7*, 183–209.

Skinner, B. F. (1938). *The behavior of organisms*. New York: Appleton-Century-Crofts.

Snow, C. (1991). A new environmentalism for child language acquisition. *Harvard Graduate School of Education Bulletin, 36*(1), 15–16.

Sroufe, L. A. (1985). Attachment classification from the perspective of infant–caregiver relationships and infant temperament. *Child Development, 56*, 1–14.

Steinberg, L., Dornbusch, S. M., & Brown, B. B. (1992). Ethnic differences in adolescent achievement: An ecological perspective. *American Psychologist, 47,* 723–729.

Stevenson, H. W., Chen, C., & Lee, S. (1992). Chinese families. In J. L. Roopnarine & B. Carter (Eds.), *Parent–child relations in diverse cultures* (pp. 17–33). Norwood, NJ: Ablex.

Stevenson, H. W., & Stevenson, N. G. (1960). Social interaction in an interracial nursery school. *Genetic Psychology Monographs, 61,* 41–75.

Stevenson, M. R., & Black, K. N. (1988). Paternal absence and sex-role development: A meta-analysis. *Child Development, 59,* 793–814.

Stipek, D. (1992). The child at school. In M. H. Bornstein & M. E. Lamb (Eds.), *Developmental psychology: An advanced textbook* (pp. 579–625). Hillsdale, NJ: Erlbaum.

Stocker, C., & Dunn, J. (1990). Sibling relationships in childhood: Links with friendships and peer relationships. *British Journal of Developmental Psychology, 8,* 227–244.

Stone, L. J., & Church, J. (1957). *Childhood and adolescence: A psychology of the growing person.* New York: Random House.

Stunkard, A. J., Sørensen, T. I. A., Hanis, C., Teasdale, T. W., Chakraborty, R., Schull, W. J., & Schulsinger, F. (1986, January 16). An adoption study of human obesity. *New England Journal of Medicine, 314,* 193–198.

Tajfel, H. (1970, November). Experiments in intergroup discrimination. *Scientific American, 223,* 96–102.

Tannen, D. (1990). *You just don't understand: Women and men in conversation.* New York: Ballantine Books.

Tellegen, A., Lykken, D. T., Bouchard, T. J., Jr., Wilcox, K. J., Segal, N. L., & Rich, S. (1988). Personality similarity in twins reared together and apart. *Journal of Personality and Social Psychology, 54,* 1031–1039.

Tesser, A. (1988). Toward a self-evaluation maintenance model of social behavior. In L. Berkowitz (Ed.), *Advances in experimental social psychology* (Vol. 21, pp. 81–227). San Diego, CA: Academic Press.

Tesser, A. (1993). The importance of heritability in psychological research: The case of attitudes. *Psychological Review, 100,* 129–142.

Thomas, A., & Chess, S. (1977). *Temperament and development.* New York: Brunner/Mazel.

Thorne, B. (1986). Girls and boys together . . . but mostly apart: Gender arrangements in elementary school. In W. W. Hartup & Z. Rubin (Eds.), *Relationships and development* (pp. 167–184). Hillsdale, NJ: Erlbaum.

Tooby, J., & Cosmides, L. (1990). The past explains the present: Emotional adaptations and the structure of ancestral environments. *Ethology and Sociobiology, 11,* 375–424.

Tooby, J., & Cosmides, L. (1992). The psychological foundations of culture. In J. Barkow, L. Cosmides, & J. Tooby (Eds.), *The adapted mind: Evolutionary psychology and the generation of culture* (pp. 21–136). New York: Oxford University Press.

Turner, J. C. (with Hogg, M. A., Oakes, P. J., Reicher, S. D., & Wetherell, M. S.). (1987). *Rediscovering the social group: A self-categorization theory.* Oxford, England: Basil Blackwell.

Umbel, V. M., Pearson, B. Z., Fernández, M. C., & Oller, D. K. (1992). Measuring bilingual children's receptive vocabulary. *Child Development, 63,* 1012–1020.

van den Oord, E. J. C. G., Boomsma, D. I., & Verhulst, F. C. (1994). A study of problem behaviors in 10- to 15-year-old biologically related and unrelated international adoptees. *Behavior Genetics, 24,* 193–205.

Vernberg, E. M. (1990). Experiences with peers following relocation during early adolescence. *American Journal of Orthopsychiatry, 60,* 466–472.

Wachs, T. D. (1992). *The nature of nurture.* Newbury Park, CA: Sage.

Walker-Andrews, A. S., Bahrick, L. E., Raglioni, S. S., & Diaz, I. (1991). Infants' bimodal perception of gender. *Ecological Psychology, 3,* 55–75.

Wasserman, E. A. (1993). Comparative cognition: Toward a general understanding of cognition in behavior. *Psychological Science, 4,* 156–161.

Waters, E., Wippman, J., & Sroufe, L. A. (1979). Attachment, positive affect, and competence in the peer group: Two studies in construct validation. *Child Development, 50,* 821–829.

Weinstein, C. S. (1991). The classroom as a social context for learning. *Annual Review of Psychology, 42,* 493–525.

Weisfeld, C. C., Weisfeld, G. E., & Callaghan, J. W. (1982). Female inhibition in mixed-sex competition among young adolescents. *Ethology and Sociobiology, 3,* 29–42.

Weisfeld, G. E., & Billings, R. L. (1988). Observations on adolescence. In K. B. MacDonald (Ed.), *Sociobiological perspectives on human development* (pp. 207–233). New York: Springer-Verlag.

Whiting, B. B. (Ed.). (1963). *Six cultures: Studies of child rearing.* New York: Wiley.

Whiting, B. B., & Edwards, C. P. (1988). *Children of different worlds: The formation of social behavior.* Cambridge, MA: Harvard University Press.

Wilder, D. A. (1986). Cognitive factors affecting the success of intergroup contact. In S. Worchel & W. G. Austin (Eds.), *Intergroup relations* (pp. 49–66). Chicago: Nelson-Hall.

Williams, J. E., & Best, D. L. (1986). Sex stereotypes and intergroup relations. In S. Worchel & W. G. Austin (Eds.), *Intergroup relations* (pp. 244–259). Chicago: Nelson-Hall.

Wilson, M., & Daly, M. (1992). The man who mistook his wife for a chattel. In J. Barkow, L. Cosmides, & J. Tooby (Eds.), *The adapted mind: Evolutionary psychology and the generation of culture* (pp. 289–322). New York: Oxford University Press.

Wolfenstein, M. (1953). Trends in infant care. *American Journal of Orthopsychiatry, 23,* 120–130.

Wood, D., Halfon, N., Scarlata, D., Newacheck, P., & Nessim, S. (1993, September 15). Impact of family relocation on children's growth, development, school function, and behavior. *Journal of the American Medical Association, 270,* 1334–1338.

Youngblade, L. M., Park, K. A., & Belsky, J. (1993). Measurement of young children's close friendship: A comparison of two independent assessment systems and their associations with attachment security. *International Journal of Behavioral Development, 16,* 563–587.

Zimbardo, P. G. (1972). Pathology of imprisonment. *Society, 9,* 4–8.

Zukow, P. G. (1989). Siblings as effective socializing agents: Evidence from Central Mexico. In P. G. Zukow (Ed.), *Sibling interaction across cultures: Theoretical and methodological issues* (pp. 79–104). New York: Springer-Verlag.

Received October 4, 1994
Revision received February 13, 1995
Accepted February 15, 1995 ■

Cognition, 50 (1994) 7–15
0010-0277/94/$07.00

Insensitivity to future consequences following damage to human prefrontal cortex

Antoine Bechara, Antonio R. Damasio*, Hanna Damasio, Steven W. Anderson

Department of Neurology, Division of Behavioral Neurology and Cognitive Neuroscience, University of Iowa College of Medicine, Iowa City, IA 52242, USA

Abstract

Following damage to the ventromedial prefrontal cortex, humans develop a defect in real-life decision-making, which contrasts with otherwise normal intellectual functions. Currently, there is no neuropsychological probe to detect in the laboratory, and the cognitive and neural mechanisms responsible for this defect have resisted explanation. Here, using a novel task which simulates real-life decision-making in the way it factors uncertainty of premises and outcomes, as well as reward and punishment, we find that prefrontal patients, unlike controls, are oblivious to the future consequences of their actions, and seem to be guided by immediate prospects only. This finding offers, for the first time, the possibility of detecting these patients' elusive impairment in the laboratory, measuring it, and investigating its possible causes.

Introduction

Patients with damage to the ventromedial sector of prefrontal cortices develop a severe impairment in real-life decision-making, in spite of otherwise preserved intellect. The impairments are especially marked in the personal and social realms (Damasio, Tranel, & Damasio, 1991). Patient E.V.R. is a prototypical example of this condition. He often decides against his best interest, and is unable to learn

*Corresponding author.
Supported by NINDS PO1 NS19632 and the James S. McDonnell Foundation.

from his mistakes. His decisions repeatedly lead to negative consequences. In striking contrast to this real-life decision-making impairment, E.V.R.'s general intellect and problem-solving abilities in a laboratory setting remain intact. For instance, he produces perfect scores on the Wisconsin Card Sorting Test (Milner, 1963), his performances in paradigms requiring self-ordering (Petrides & Milner, 1982), cognitive estimations (Shallice & Evans, 1978), and judgements of recency and frequency (Milner, Petrides, & Smith, 1985) are flawless; he is not presevera-tive, nor is he impulsive; his knowledge base is intact and so is his short-term and working memory as tested to date; his solution of verbally posed social problems and ethical dilemmas is comparable to that of controls (Saver & Damasio, 1991). The condition has posed a double challenge, since there has been neither a satisfactory account of its physiopathology, nor a laboratory probe to detect and measure an impairment that is so obvious in its ecological niche. Here we describe an experimental neuropsychological task which simulates, in real time, personal real-life decision-making relative to the way it factors uncertainty of premises and outcomes, as well as reward and punishment. We show that, unlike controls, patients with prefrontal damage perform defectively and are seemingly insensitive to the future.

Materials and methods

The subjects sit in front of four decks of cards equal in appearance and size, and are given a $2000 loan of play money (a set of facsimile US bills). The subjects are told that the game requires a long series of card selections, one card at a time, from any of the four decks, until they are told to stop. After turning *each* card, the subjects receive some money (the amount is only announced after the turning, and varies with the deck). After turning *some* cards, the subjects are *both* given money *and* asked to pay a penalty (again the amount is only announced after the card is turned and varies with the deck and the position in the deck according to a schedule unknown to the subjects). The subjects are told that (1) the goal of the task is to maximize profit on the loan of play money, (2) they are free to switch from any deck to another, at any time, and as often as wished, but (3) they are not told ahead of time how many card selections must be made (the task is stopped after a series of 100 card selections). The pre-programmed schedules of reward and punishment are shown on the score cards (Fig. 1). Turning any card from deck A or deck B yields $100; turning any card from deck C or deck D yields $50. However, the ultimate future yield of each deck varies because the penalty amounts are higher in the high-paying decks (A and B), and lower in the low-paying decks (C and D). For example, after turning 10 cards from deck A, the subjects have earned $1000, but they have also encountered 5 unpredicted punishments bringing their total cost to $1250, thus

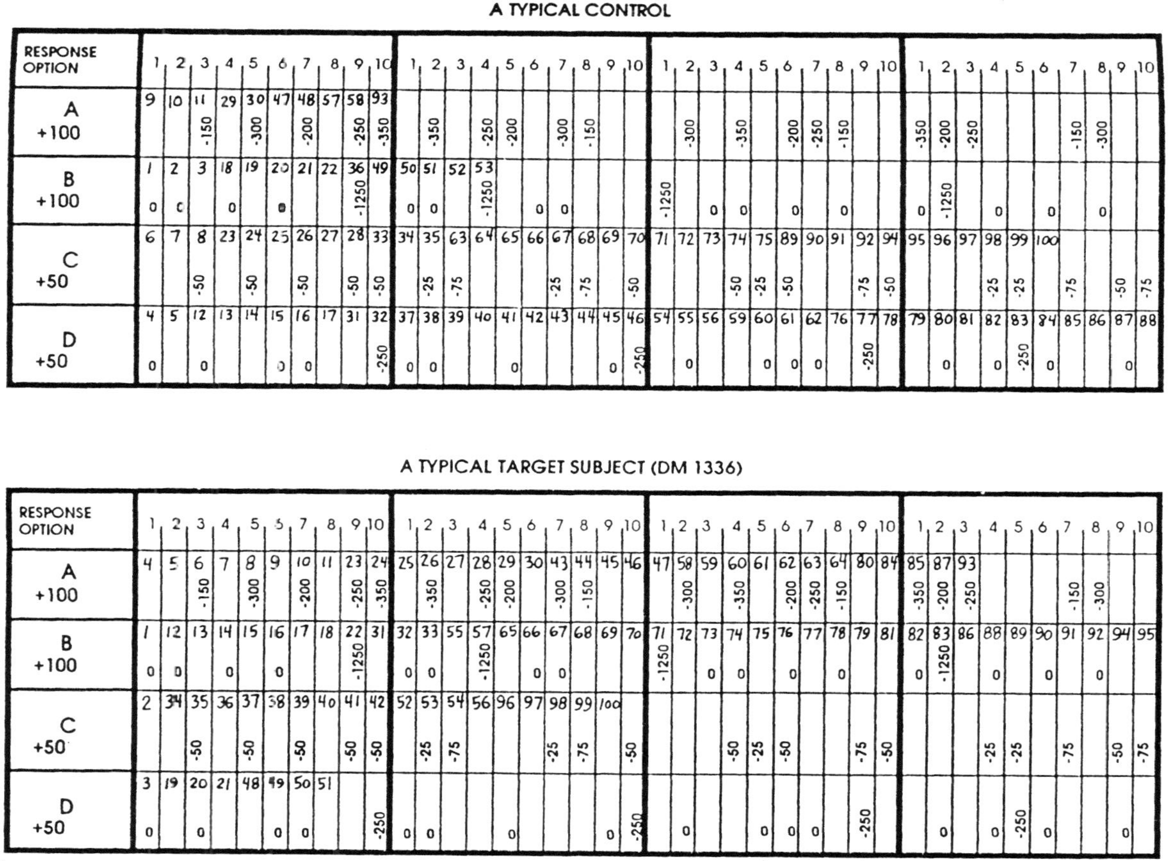

Fig. 1. *The top score card represents that of a typical control subject, and the bottom one that of a typical target subject. The hand-written numbers represent the profiles of card selections from the first to the 100th card. Control subjects select more from decks C and D, whereas target subjects select more from decks A and B.*

incurring a net loss of $250. The same happens on deck B. On the other hand, after turning 10 cards from decks C or D, the subjects earn $500, but the total of their unpredicted punishments is only $250 (i.e. subject nets $250). In summary, decks A and B are equivalent in terms of overall net loss over the trials. The difference is that in deck A, the punishment is more frequent, but of smaller magnitude, whereas in deck B, the punishment is less frequent, but of higher magnitude. Decks C and D are also equivalent in terms of overall net loss. In deck C, the punishment is more frequent and of smaller magnitude, while in deck D the punishment is less frequent but of higher magnitude. Decks A and B are thus "disadvantageous" because they cost the most in the long run, while decks C and D are "advantageous" because they result in an overall gain in the long run.

The performances of a group of normal control subjects (21 women and 23 men) in this task were compared to those of E.V.R. and other frontal lobe subjects (4 men and 2 women). The age range of normal controls was from 20 to 79 years; for E.V.R.-like subjects it was from 43 to 84 years. About half the number of subjects in each group had a high school education, and the other half had a college education. E.V.R.-like subjects were retrieved from the Patient Registry of the Division of Behavioral Neurology and Cognitive Neuroscience. Selection criteria were the documented presence of abnormal decision-making and the existence of lesions in the ventromedial prefrontal region.

To determine whether the defective performance of E.V.R.-like subjects on the task is specific to ventromedial frontal lobe damage, and not merely caused by brain damage in general, we compared the performances of E.V.R.-like subjects and normal controls, to an education matched group of brain-damaged controls. There were 3 women and 6 men, ranging in age from 20 to 71 years. These controls were retrieved from the same Patient Registry and were chosen so as to have lesions in occipital, temporal and dorsolateral frontal regions. Several of the brain-damaged controls had memory defects, as revealed by conventional neuropsychological tests.

Finally, to determine what would happen to the performance if it were repeated over time, we retested the target subjects and a smaller sample of normal controls (4 women and 1 man between the ages of 20 and 55, matched to E.V.R. in level of education) after various time intervals (one month after the first test, 24 h later, and for the fourth time, six months later).

Results

Fig. 2 (left) shows that normal controls make more selections from the good decks (C and D), and avoid the bad decks (A and B). In sharp contrast, E.V.R.-like subjects select fewer from the good decks (C and D), and choose more from the bad decks (A and B). The difference is significant. An analysis of

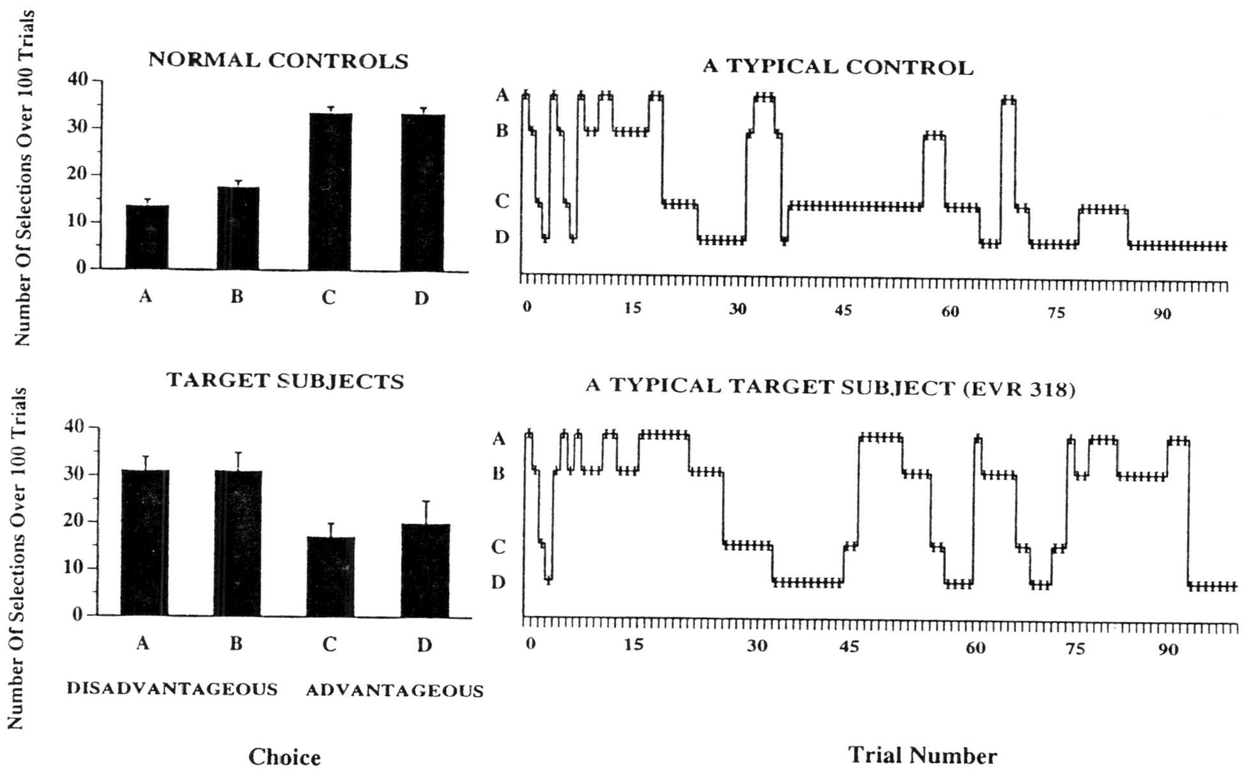

Fig. 2. *(Left panels) Total number of cards selected from each deck (A, B, C or D) by normal controls ($n = 44$) and E.V.R.-like subjects ($n = 7$). Bars represent means ± s.e.m. (Right panels) Profiles of card selections (from the first to the 100th selection) obtained from a typical control and patient E.V.R.*

variance comparing the number of cards from each deck chosen by normal controls and by target subjects revealed a significant interaction of group (controls vs. targets) with choice (A, B, C, D) ($F(3,147) = 42.9$, $p < .001$). Subsequent Newman–Keuls *t*-tests revealed that the number of cards selected by normal controls from deck A or B were significantly *less* than the number of cards selected by target subjects from the same decks ($ps < .001$). On the contrary, the number of cards selected by controls from decks C or D were significantly *higher* than the numbers selected by target subjects ($ps < .001$). Within each group, comparison of the performances among subjects from different age groups, gender and education yielded no statistically significant differences.

Fig. 2 (right) shows that a comparison of card selection profiles revealed that controls initially sampled all decks and repeated selections from the bad decks A and B, probably because they pay more, but eventually switched to more and more selections from the good decks C and D, with only occasional returns to decks A and B. On the other hand, E.V.R. behaves like normal controls only in the first few selections. He does begin by sampling all decks and selecting from decks A and B, and he does make several selections from decks C and D, but then he returns more frequently and more systematically to decks A and B. The other target subjects behave similarly.

Fig. 3 reveals that the performance of brain-damaged controls was no different

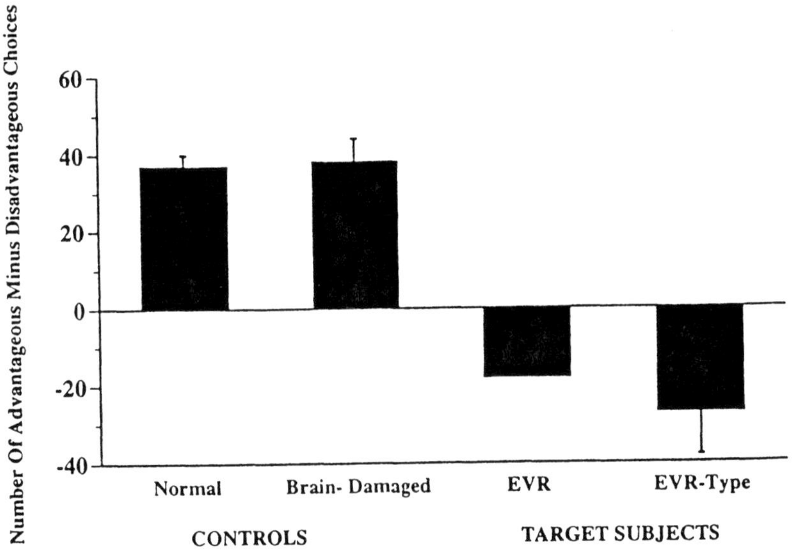

Fig. 3. *Total number of selections from the advantageous decks (C + D) minus the total numbers of selections from the disadvantageous decks (A + B) from a group of normal controls (n = 44), brain-damaged controls (n = 9), E.V.R., and E.V.R.-like subjects (n = 6). Bars represent means ± s.e.m. Positive scores reflect advantageous courses of action, and negative scores reflect disadvantageous courses of action.*

from that of normal controls, and quite the opposite of the performance of the prefrontal subjects. One-way ANOVA on the difference in the total numbers of card selections from the advantageous decks minus the total numbers of selections from the disadvantageous decks obtained from normal and brain-damaged controls did not reveal a significant difference between the two groups ($F(1,52) = 0.1$, $p > .1$), but the difference between the normal and E.V.R.-like groups was highly significant ($F(1,50) = 74.8$, $p < .001$).

As a result of repeated testing, E.V.R.'s performance did not change, one way or the other, when tested one month after the first test, 24 h later, and for the fourth time, six months later. This pattern of impaired performance was also seen in other target subjects. On the contrary, the performance of normal controls improved over time.

Discussion

These results demonstrate that E.V.R. and comparable subjects perform defectively in this task, and that the defect is stable over time. Although the task involves a long series of gains and losses, it is not possible for subjects to perform an exact calculation of the net gains or losses generated from each deck as they play. Indeed, a group of normal control subjects with superior memory and IQ, whom we asked to think aloud while performing the task, and keep track of the magnitudes and frequencies of the various punishments, could not provide calculated figures of the net gains or losses from each deck. The subjects must rely on their ability to develop an estimate of which decks are risky and which are profitable in the long run. Thus, the patients' performance profile is comparable to their real-life inability to decide advantageously, especially in personal and social matters, a domain for which in life, as in the task, an exact calculation of the future outcomes is not possible and choices must be based on approximations. We believe this task offers, for the first time, the possibility of detecting these patients' elusive impairment in the laboratory, measuring it, and investigating its possible causes.

Why do E.V.R.-like subjects make choices that have high immediate reward, but severe delayed punishment? We considered three possibilities: (1) E.V.R.-like subjects are so *sensitive to reward* that the prospect of future (delayed) punishment is outweighed by that of immediate gain; (2) these subjects are *insensitive to punishment*, and thus the prospect of reward always prevails, even if they are not abnormally sensitive to reward; (3) these subjects are generally *insensitive to future consequences*, positive or negative, and thus their behavior is always guided by immediate prospects, whatever they may be. To decide on the merit of these possibilities, we developed a variant of the basic task, in which the schedules of reward and punishment were reversed, so that the punishment is immediate and the reward is delayed. The profiles of target subjects in that task suggest that they were influenced more by *immediate* punishment than by delayed reward (unpublished results). This indicates that neither insensitivity to punishment nor hypersensitivity to reward are appropriate accounts for the defect. A qualitative aspect of the patients' performance also supports the idea that immediate consequences influence the performance significantly. When they are faced with a significant money loss in a given deck, they refrain from picking cards out of that same deck, for a while, just like normals do, though unlike normals they then return to select from that deck after a few additional selections. When we combine the profiles of both basic task and variant tasks, we are left with one reasonable possibility: that these subjects are unresponsive to future consequences, whatever they are, and are thus more controlled by immediate prospects.

How can this "myopia" for the future be explained? Evidence from other studies suggests that these patients possess and can access the requisite knowledge to conjure up options of actions and scenarios of future outcomes just as normal controls do (Saver & Damasio, 1991). Their defect seems to be at the level of acting on such knowledge. There are several plausible accounts to explain such a defect. For instance, it is possible that the representations of future outcomes that these patients evoke are unstable, that is, that they are not held in working memory long enough for attention to enhance them and reasoning strategies to be applied to them. This account invokes a defect along the lines proposed for behavioral domains dependent on dorsolateral prefrontal cortex networks, and which is possibly just as valid in the personal/social domain of decision-making (Goldman-Rakic, 1987). Defects in temporal integration and attention would fall under this account (Fuster, 1989; Posner, 1986). Alternatively, the representations of future outcomes might be stable, but they would not be *marked* with a negative or positive value, and thus could not be easily rejected or accepted. This account invokes the somatic marker hypothesis which posits that the overt or covert processing of somatic states provides the *value mark* for a cognitive scenario (Damasio, 1994; Damasio et al., 1991). We have been attempting to distinguish between these two accounts in a series of subsequent experiments using this task along with psychophysiological measurements. Preliminary results favor the latter account, or a combination of the two accounts. Those results also suggest that the biasing effect of the value mark operates covertly, at least in the early stages of the task.

References

Damasio, A.R. (1994). Descartes' error: Emotion, rationality and the human brain. New York: Putnam (Grosset Books).

Damasio, A.R., Tranel, D., & Damasio, H. (1991). Somatic markers and the guidance of behavior. In H. Levin, H. Eisenberg, & A. Benton (Eds.), *Frontal lobe function and dysfunction* (pp. 217–228). New York: Oxford University Press.

Fuster, J.M. (1989). *The prefrontal cortex* (2nd edn.). New York: Raven Press.

Goldman-Rakic, P.S. (1987). Circuitry of primate prefrontal cortex and regulation of behavior by representational memory. In F. Plum (Ed.), *Handbook of physiology: The nervous system* (Vol. V, pp. 373–401). Bethesda, MD: American Physiological Society.

Milner, B. (1963). Effects of different brain lesions on card sorting. *Archives of Neurology, 9*, 90–100.

Milner, B., Petrides, M., & Smith, M.L. (1985). Frontal lobes and the temporal organization of memory. *Human Neurobiology, 4*, 137–142.

Petrides, M., & Milner, B (1982). Deficits on subject-ordered tasks after frontal and temporal-lobe lesions in man. *Neuropsychologia, 20*, 249–262.

Posner, M.I. (1986). *Chronometric explorations of the mind*. New York: Oxford University Press.

Saver, J.L., & Damasio, A.R. (1991). Preserved access and processing of social knowledge in a patient with acquired sociopathy due to ventromedial frontal damage. *Neuropsychologia, 29*, 1241–1249.

Shallice, T., & Evans, M.E. (1978). The involvement of the frontal lobes in cognitive estimation. *Cortex, 14*, 294–303.

Behavioural Brain Research, 41 (1990) 81–94
Elsevier
BBR 01118

Research Reports

Individuals with sociopathic behavior caused by frontal damage fail to respond autonomically to social stimuli

Antonio R. Damasio, Daniel Tranel and Hanna Damasio

Department of Neurology, Division of Behavioral Neurology & Cognitive Neuroscience, University of Iowa College of Medicine, Iowa City, IA 52242 (U.S.A.)

(Received 8 May 1990)
(Revised version received 26 July 1990)
(Accepted 28 August 1990)

Key words: Sociopathic behavior; Frontal damage; Social stimulus; Decision-making

Following damage to ventromedial frontal cortices, adults with previously normal personalities develop defects in decision-making and planning that are especially revealed in an abnormal social conduct. The defect repeatedly leads to negative personal consequences. The physiopathology of this disorder is an enigma. We propose that the defect is due to an inability to activate somatic states linked to punishment and reward, that were previously experienced in association with specific social situations, and that must be reactivated in connection with anticipated *outcomes* of response options. During the processing that follows the perception of a social event, the experience of certain anticipated outcomes of response options would be marked by the reactivation of an appropriate somatic state. Failure to reactivate pertinent *somatic markers* would deprive the individual of an automatic device to signal ultimately deleterious consequences relative to responses that might nevertheless bring immediate reward (or, alternatively, signal ultimately advantageous outcomes relative to responses that might bring immediate pain). As an example, activation of somatic markers would (1) force attention to future negative consequences, permitting conscious suppression of the responses leading to them and deliberate selection of biologically advantageous responses, and (2) trigger non-conscious inhibition of response states by engagement of subcortical neurotransmitter systems linked to appetitive behaviors. An investigation of this theory in patients with frontal damage reveals that their autonomic responses to socially meaningful stimuli are indeed abnormal, suggesting that such stimuli fail to activate somatic states at the most basic level. On the contrary, elementary unconditioned stimuli (e.g. a loud noise) produce normal autonomic responses.

INTRODUCTION

Following damage to ventromedial frontal cortices, adults with previously normal personalities develop abnormal social conduct and inadequate decision-making and planning that repeatedly lead to negative consequences. The physiopathology of this disorder remains one of the acknowledged enigmas of neuropsychology (e.g. ref. 51). Patient EVR is prototypical of the condition[16], and has appropriately been recognized as a challenge to the elucidation of this problem[22]. By age 35, in 1975, EVR was a successful professional, happily married, and the father of two. He led an impeccable social life, and was a role model to younger siblings. In that year, an orbitofrontal meningioma was diagnosed and, in order to achieve its successful surgical resection, a bilateral excision of orbital and lower mesial cortices was necessary. EVR's basic intelligence and standard

Correspondence: R. Damasio, Department of Neurology, University of Iowa Hospitals & Clinics, Iowa City, Iowa 52242, U.S.A.

memory were not compromised by the ablation. His performances on standardized IQ and memory tests are uniformly in the superior range (WAIS-R Verbal I.Q. = 129 [97th%ile], Performance I.Q. = 135 [99th%ile]; Wechsler Memory Scale M.Q. = 143 [99th%ile]. He passes all formal neuropsychological probes, including the Wisconsin Card Sorting Test[30], the Word Fluency Test[5], and the Category Test[26]. He makes normal cognitive estimations, including judgments of recency and frequency, in paradigms such as those developed by Milner[41] and Shallice[48].

Standing in sharp contrast to this pattern of neuropsychological test performance, EVR's social conduct was profoundly affected by his brain injury. Over a brief period of time, he entered disastrous business ventures (one of which led to predictable bankruptcy), and was divorced twice (the second marriage, which was to a prostitute, only lasted 6 months). He has been unable to hold any paying job since the time of surgery, and his plans for future activity are defective. He now lives in a sheltered environment, unable to support himself and his family. He complies with the core DSM-III diagnostic criteria for 'sociopathic disorder'[2] (e.g. 'inability to sustain consistent work behavior', 'lack of ability to function as a responsible parent', 'inability to maintain enduring attachment to a sexual partner', 'defective planning'), but because these manifestations appeared in adulthood, postsurgically rather than during personality development, we have tentatively termed his condition 'acquired' sociopathy.

EVR's defects cannot be accounted for by conventional impairments of learning or memory. His general fund of information and autobiographical knowledge are normal for material learned before and after the ablation, and he provides accurate accounts of current events. In fact, not even a selective lack of social knowledge can help explain the defect, since EVR is capable of reasoning correctly through subtle hypothetical social problems (e.g. ethical and financial dilemmas), provided the premises are cast verbally. His defects are evident mostly in natural, real-time settings, when the premises are not verbally coded nor simultaneously present.

Theoretical account

(1) Analysis of the defect. The framework for our theoretical account is a model of recall and recognition in which the experience of meaning for entities (e.g. individuals, objects) and events (e.g. the episodes in which they interact), and the selection of appropriate responses to those entities and events, depend on the synchronous activation of separate component representations, based on anatomically discrete records[11,12]. The experience of entities or events in recall always depends on a temporally coherent reconstruction. The model provides an alternative to the traditional notion that entities and events are permanently represented in integrated fashion in cerebral cortex. Within this framework, we have considered two possible and extreme causes for the defect. The first posits that EVR-type patients do not conjure up enough information to define the implications of social situations and consequently cannot act appropriately. In spite of being able to recognize the *manifest* meaning of such situations (e.g. the correct identification of persons in the situation, or their overt actions), they fail to conjure up the situation's *implied* meanings (their future implications from an autobiographical perspective and the courses of action each implication embodies). The second states that although able to conjure up the myriad implications of a social situation (e.g. response options, consequences), EVR-type patients are unable to *mark* those implications with a signal that would automatically distinguish advantageous from pernicious actions, in the perspective of social rules and current contingencies. Because they are deprived of a natural qualifying marker, they must depend instead on a reasoned cost–benefit analysis of numerous and often conflictual options (involving both immediate and future consequences). The adequacy and the speed of response selection are degraded accordingly.

(2) The mechanisms of the defect. The mechanism for cause no. 1 assumes a critical difference between *manifest* and *implied* meaning. Although both levels of meaning call for sustained and synchronous activation of component records so that they can be experienced in a temporally coherent manner, recognition of implied meaning requires a longer time lapse between stimulus and

response. This is because (a) implied meaning is based on a greater number and variety of component records necessary to define the possible consequences and optional responses to a given encounter; and (b) onset of activation of differently located component records is not simultaneous, and the activation of such a large number of sites must be held across a long delay, so that all sites can be attended to and that the activated/attended sites can form a temporally coherent set. Possible physiopathological processes behind this mechanism include defective activation of component records, or defective 'hold' of activated records across the delay necessary for successive attentional shifts and ensuing coherent experience. The available evidence suggests that this mechanism alone might not explain the defects satisfactorily, because EVR remains capable of conjuring up many complex implied meaning scenarios in laboratory paradigms. In other words, under certain circumstances, he is capable of activating multiple pertinent memories, attending to them, and discoursing upon them in a meaningful way. Such evidence in turn suggests that the problem may reside with choosing an advantageous course of action, or with implementing it. We will call this cause no. 2, and we propose that the mechanism behind it is a failure to activate the specific *somatic states*, both visceral and skeletal, that were part of the previous learning of a given social situation. The rationale for the emphasis on somatic states is the role that punishment and reward play in the learning of social knowledge. Punishment and reward modify the parameters of visceral and skeletal function, and those modifications are signaled to somatosensory, higher-order, and limbic association cortices. It is on the basis of such signaling that the consequences of punishment and reward can be experienced consciously as 'feelings' and 'emotions'.

During learning, somatic states, positive or negative, detrivialize and thus appose a *marker* to entities and events. When somatic states are reactivated, we believe that they also detrivialize and mark the appropriately recalled set. They mark unambiguously not only the value of current perceptions, but most importantly, the value of *certain outcomes* to given courses of action, the internal representations of which are experienced after a delay, often after the prompting stimuli are no longer present. Somatic states provide an automated way for the brain to select, consciously *and* not consciously, among response options. On the one hand, it would link a given response option with *both* the pleasure that it may bring immediately, *and* the punishment that it will lead to in the future. By forcing attention on a conflict, a pertinent somatic marker would signal the ultimately deleterious consequences that might arise from a response that might nonetheless bring immediate reward. This would permit conscious suppression of responses that lead to negative consequences and deliberate selection of biologically advantageous ones. But in addition, and perhaps no less importantly, there would be a non-conscious inhibition of excitatory subcortical neurotransmitter systems which mediate appetitive behaviors (or a release of the ones which mediate aversive behaviors). It should be noted that the mechanism operates precisely in the same fashion when the immediate prospect is punishment, and the deferred outcome is reward. It is possible that preventing immediate reward associated with future punishing consequences is the most frequent and basic conflict situation that somatic markers would help resolve. However, the pairing of immediate punishment and deferred reward is also biologically advantageous.

This physiopathologic account rests on the following foundations. First is the notion that somatic states play a privileged role in learning, memory, and behavioral guidance[11,12]. This notion has been intuited from introspection and commented on by other theorists, although, to our knowledge, not in a formal way. Nauta[43] specifically applied this notion to the problem of frontal lobe function, and suggested a relation between affective responses and behavioral alternatives that would be the basis for a conscious choice. As noted above, our account focuses on the somatic state generated to the deferred outcome rather than the alternative at hand or the immediate consequence, and it gives equal weight to the conscious and non-conscious processes related to the somatic state. The second notion pertains to the role of the frontal cortices in the generation of responses that occur after the stimuli that led to them have been removed. This tenet relates to Jacobsen's[31,32] delayed response, which is a cornerstone for Goldman-Rakic's[22] proposal that frontal cortices hold 'on-line' information needed to mount delayed responses, and also critical to Fuster's[21] thesis that frontal cortices are devoted to temporal integration.

To begin to test our formulation empirically, we designed a set of experiments aimed at determining whether EVR-type patients can activate somatic states normally, when confronted with stimuli whose implied meanings are charged with social significance.

MATERIALS AND METHODS

Design

The electrodermal skin conductance response (SCR) was utilized as the dependent measure to assess somatic state activation. The SCR was chosen because: (1) it is a biologically and psychologically relevant index of autonomic neural activity[7,14,15,19], which in turn is the foundation for somatic states (e.g. changes in visceral and circulatory control), thus providing a probe of the system that we hypothesize is malfunctioning in EVR-type patients; and (2) it is reliably elicited by stimuli that have 'signal value', i.e. properties such as affective valence, emotional value, and social relevance (e.g. refs. 6, 47).

Three independent variables were manipulated in these experiments: (1) *subject 'type'*: the contrast between patients with bifrontal lesions (Bifrontals), and patients with lesions outside prefrontal cortices' (Brain-damaged controls) and normal healthy volunteers (Normals); (2) *response condition*: whether the subject was required to produce a verbal response to the stimuli (ACTIVE and PASSIVE); (3) *stimulus valence*: 'socially' charged versus neutral.

Stimulus material and procedure

Stimuli

(1) *Elementary unconditioned* ('orienting'); (2) *Target* pictures; and (3) *Non-target* pictures. The orienting stimuli were a deep breath and hand clap, chosen because they (i) elicit SCRs reliably from normal subjects[20,50] and (ii) provide a contrast to the semantically complex pictorial stimuli. There were 10 target pictures, depicting social disaster, mutilation, and nudity, and their implied meanings were expected to elicit SCRs and be experienced as painful or pleasurable (see refs. 24, 37); there were also 30 non-target pictures, depicting neutral objects. The pictorial stimuli were prepared as color slides, and were randomly ordered.

Procedure

The subject was seated in a comfortable chair, the electrodes were attached, and a 5-min rest period followed. At the end of the rest period, the orienting stimuli were administered. Then, the pictorial stimuli were shown, under two response conditions: (1) PASSIVE: the subject viewed the target and non-target slides, but no verbal or motor response was called for. (2) ACTIVE: this condition immediately followed the PASSIVE condition. The slides were shown in the same order, but this time, the subject was required to give a verbal response to each picture. (Instructions for the ACTIVE condition requested the subject to describe what was being shown in the slide, or to give an impression as to whether the subject liked the picture or not). In both conditions, slides were presented on the internal screen of a Caramate 4000 slide projector, positioned 0.45 m directly in front of the subject. Each slide was shown for 2.0 s, and the screen was blank between slides. Several 'buffer' slides were presented prior to the PASSIVE condition, to allow the subject to habituate to the process of projection. Interstimulus intervals varied slightly, but conformed to the following rules: (1) not shorter than 16 or longer than 25 s; (2) a new stimulus was not presented if the subject was generating or was in the steep recovery limb of an SCR. In the ACTIVE condition, verbal response latencies were not allowed to exceed 4 s.

Following the ACTIVE condition, a short 'debriefing' procedure was implemented. The experimenter engaged the subject in a discussion about the experiment, gave reassurance, and obtained information about the subjects' reactions and recollections regarding the experimental procedures. In particular, the experimenter required the subject to comment on: (1) *stimulus content* (e.g. objects and/or actions featured in the slides); (2) the *feelings* the subject had experienced while viewing the slides; and (3) a *comparison* of the two response conditions referenced to the reactions they experienced in the PASSIVE and ACTIVE conditions. Information from the debriefing was also used to verify systematically that the subjects had paid close attention to the stimuli, particularly during the PASSIVE condition.

Electrodermal recording and scoring

Skin conductance was recorded from the right and left hands, using equipment and techniques described elsewhere[52,53]. For all stimuli, the amplitude of the largest SCR having an onset within 1–5 s after stimulus onset was recorded. This scoring procedure was also applied to the two 'orienting' stimuli. Thus, for each subject, an 'orienting' SCR was calculated by averaging the SCRs to the deep breath and hand clap. Then, for each subject and for each response condition, an average SCR was calculated for the target stimuli and for the non-targets. Following the recommendations of Venables and Christie[56], these averages were based on all target and non-target stimuli, and are, therefore, referred to as 'magnitudes'. The data sets violated several parametric assumptions, thus, statistical analyses were conducted with non-parametric techniques[49]. Because there were no systematic between-hand differences, results were collapsed across hands. Also, we did not find evidence of habituation effects in either of the response conditions.

Subjects

There were 5 subjects (including EVR-318) in the group designated as 'Bifrontal' chosen because they had (1) bilateral lesions in orbital and lower mesial frontal regions (see Fig. 1 and Table I), and (2) severe defects in social conduct, judgment, and planning, acquired in adulthood, after onset of brain damage. Subjects were selected by an independent investigator who was not involved in the psychophysiological experiments. The investigator who conducted the psychophysiological experiments was blind to the neuropsychological and neuroanatomical characteristics of the subjects. The 'Bifrontal' group ranged in age from 24 to 81 years. Three are male, two female, and all are right-handed and at least eighth-grade educated. All had normal IQ scores and memory quotients. All were judged by two independent neuropsychologists to have severe defects in social conduct and planning, which interfered profoundly with effective functioning in the social and interpersonal domains. Subjects

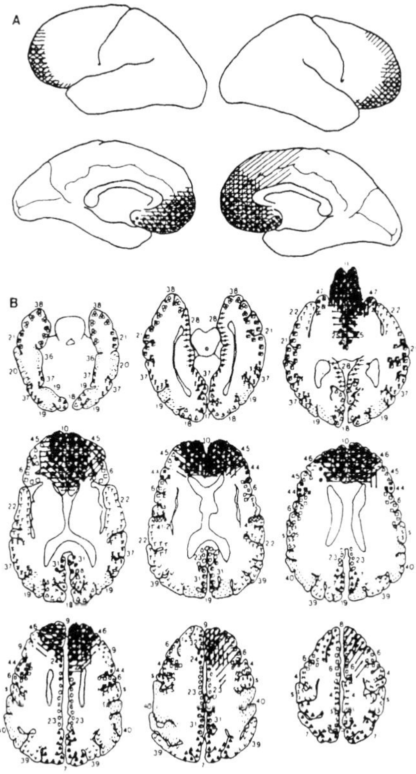

Fig. 1. Composite representation of lesions in the 5 Bifrontal subjects. Note how the maximal overlap of lesions (each denoted by a different symbol) occurs in the ventromedial region. A: lateral and mesial views of both hemispheres. B: templates of horizontal sections.

were characterized with the comprehensive battery of the Benton Neuropsychology Laboratory, and with a neuroanatomical analysis of lesions following a standard method[13].

The 6 'Brain-damaged' controls were selected because they had (1) a focal lesion outside the ventromedial frontal cortices; and (2) no acquired defects in social conduct. They ranged in age from 28 to 76 years. Three were males with right hemisphere lesions; 2 males and 1 female had left hemisphere lesions. All but one were right-handed (one was mixed), and all had at least a high-school education. The Brain-damaged controls had appropriate but circumscribed defects relative to the lesion locus (e.g. the left-hemisphere subjects were aphasic), but none had an impairment of social conduct or intellect. The controls not only represented lesions from both the left and right hemispheres, but also included large lesions (see Fig. 2 and Table I). This permitted us to address the role of factors such as presence, location, and lesion size.

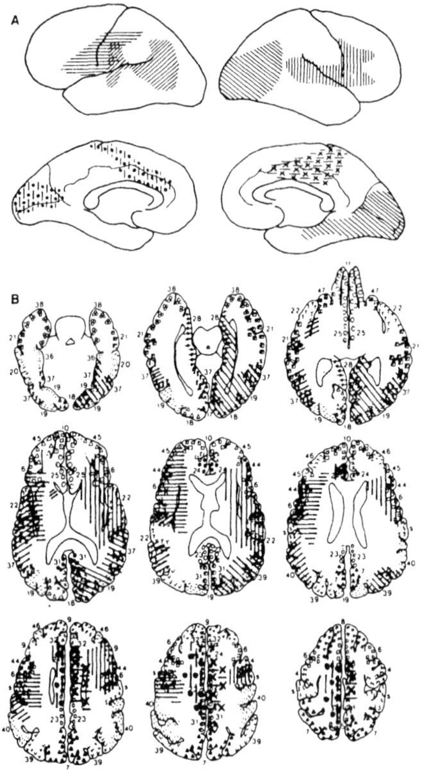

Fig. 2. Composite representation of lesions in the 6 brain-damaged controls (each denoted by a different symbol). Note absence of ventromedial involvement. A: lateral and mesial views of both hemispheres. B: templates of horizontal sections.

We also studied 5 'Normal' controls (no brain injury). This group was similar to the experimental groups in age, education, and gender ratio. The Normal controls were studied with the psychophysiological experiments, so that we would have a basic reference point for the skin conductance data. There were 3 males (right-handed) and 2 females (one right- and one left-handed), with an average age of 48.9 years. All were at least high-school educated.

RESULTS

Control groups

Skin conductance results for the normal and brain-damaged controls are presented in Table II. The orienting responses were similar for the two groups (see below). In the PASSIVE condition, both groups produced much larger SCRs to the target stimuli than to the non-targets, and a similar outcome obtained for the ACTIVE condition. For the Normal group, a Sign Test was significant for both response conditions ($n = 5$, $x = 0$, $P < 0.05$). For the Brain-damaged group, a Wilcoxin Matched-Pairs Signed-Ranks test was significant for both conditions ($T = 0$, $P < 0.05$). The effect occurred in every subject under both response conditions, and was also of substantial magnitude, e.g. the smallest target–non-target difference in a normal control was 0.337 μS. The effect is consistent with previous findings with similar types of stimuli (e.g. refs. 24, 28, 36). The groups did not differ significantly in their responses to the target stimuli, in either response condition (Mann–Whitney U-tests were as follows: PASSIVE condition [$U = 11$, $P = 0.536$]; ACTIVE condition [$U = 13$, $P = 0.792$]. A sample of the polygraph record of

TABLE I

Anatomical distribution of lesions

Ant., anterior; Post., posterior; PreF., prefrontal; PreM., premotor; ++ complete damage; + partial damage.

Subject	Side of lesion	Frontal						Rolandic	Parietal	Insular	Temporal	Occipital
		Orbital		Mesial		Dorsolateral						
		Ant.	Post.	Pre F.	Pre M.	Pre F.	Pre M.					
Bifrontals												
EVR 318	R	+ +		+ +	+	+	+					
	L	+ +		+								
FL 1164	R	+ +	+ +	+ +		+						
	L	+ +	+ +	+ +								
SG 1208	R	+ +	+ +	+ +	+ +	+ +						
	L	+ +		+								
DM 1336	R	+ +	+	+ +		+ +	+					
	L	+ +	+	+ +		+ +	+					
HS 1065	R	+ +	+ +	+ +		+ +	+					
	L	+ +	+ +	+ +		+						
Controls												
JW 1324	R										+ +	+ +
GO 995	L				+			+				+ +
WG 827	R				+ +			+ +				
JP 1172	L						+ +	+ +	+	+ +	+	
MB 1106	R						+ +	+ +	+	+ +	+ +	
NE 1188	L								+ +	+ +	+ +	

TABLE II

Skin conductance magnitudes [in microSiemens (μS); S.D. in parentheses] for normal and brain-damaged controls

	Orienting response	Passive condition		Active condition	
		Target	Non-target	Target	Non-target
Normal controls (n = 5)	0.688	0.802	0.077	0.999	0.150
	(0.208)	(0.327)	(0.066)	(0.384)	(0.027)
Brain-damaged controls (n = 6)	0.520	0.594	0.137	0.949	0.289
	(0.503)	(0.565)	(0.234)	(0.901)	(0.313)

one of the brain-damaged controls (Fig. 3) illustrates the effect, i.e. larger SCRs to the target stimuli, compared to the non-targets, in both the PASSIVE (3A) and ACTIVE (3B) conditions.

Subject EVR-318

(1) Basic experiment

In subject EVR, a strikingly different outcome was observed (Table III). His orienting SCRs

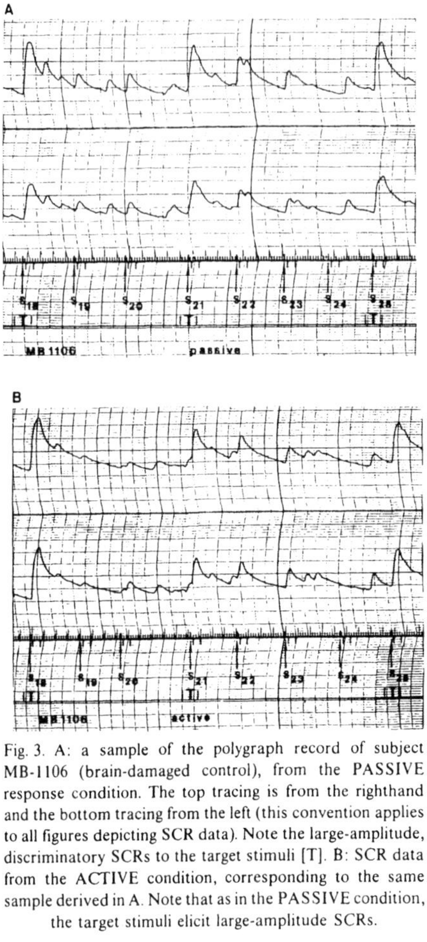

Fig. 3. A: a sample of the polygraph record of subject MB-1106 (brain-damaged control), from the PASSIVE response condition. The top tracing is from the righthand and the bottom tracing from the left (this convention applies to all figures depicting SCR data). Note the large-amplitude, discriminatory SCRs to the target stimuli [T]. B: SCR data from the ACTIVE condition, corresponding to the same sample derived in A. Note that as in the PASSIVE condition, the target stimuli elicit large-amplitude SCRs.

TABLE III

Skin conductance magnitudes (in μS; S.D. in parentheses) for subject EVR-318

Orienting response	*Passive condition*		*Active condition*	
	Target	*Non-target*	*Target*	*Non-target*
0.650	0.003 (0.008)	0.006 (0.023)	0.598 (0.564)	0.012 (0.031)

were normal, but in the PASSIVE condition, he showed a complete failure to produce normal SCRs to the target pictures. This effect is illustrated in Fig. 4A, which depicts a portion of the polygraph record from the PASSIVE condition. In the ACTIVE condition, on the other hand, EVR demonstrated a normal pattern of responding. That is, under the condition in which he provided a verbal comment on the stimuli,, he produced normal, large-amplitude SCRs to the target pictures, clearly discriminating them from the non-targets. Based on Mann–Whitney U-tests, the target–non-target difference was non-significant in the PASSIVE condition ($P > 0.33$), and significant in the ACTIVE condition ($z = -3.87$,

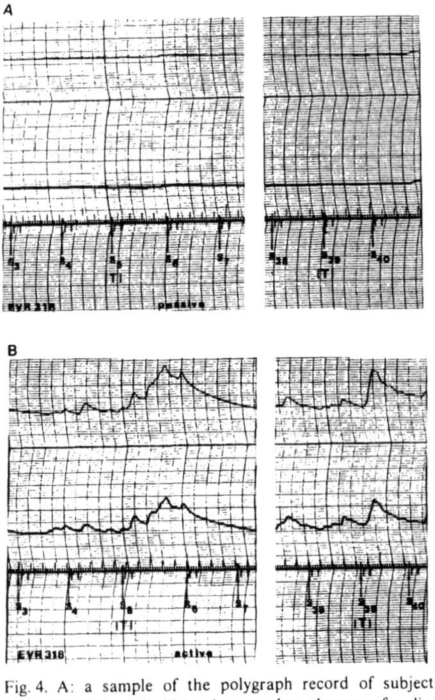

Fig. 4. A: a sample of the polygraph record of subject EVR-318 (Bifrontal). Note the complete absence of a discernible SCR for the two targets [T]. B: SCR data from the ACTIVE condition, corresponding to the same sample described in A. In sharp contrast to the PASSIVE condition, the target stimuli in this condition elicit large-amplitude, discriminatory SCRs.

$P < 0.001$). His average target–non-target difference ($0.586\ \mu S$) in the ACTIVE condition is quite similar to the average difference of the brain-damaged controls ($0.660\ \mu S$). Examples of EVR's SCRs in the ACTIVE condition are illustrated in Fig. 4B.

(2) Follow-up experiments

To establish the reliability of this effect, a follow-up experiment was conducted. Using a new set of stimuli (10 target and 30 non-target pictures, representing the same themes as described previously), we studied EVR with an A-B-A reversal design. The set of 40 pictures was administered first under a PASSIVE response condition, then under an ACTIVE, and then under a PASSIVE again. The administrations were consecutive, and followed the procedures described above.

The results (Table IV) indicate that the skin conductance responses were directly tied to the type of response condition. In the first PASSIVE administration, the SCRs were markedly defective, with no evidence of discriminatory target responses. In the ACTIVE condition, there was excellent discrimination of the targets (the average target–non-target difference was $0.711\ \mu S$). But immediately thereafter, when the condition was PASSIVE again, EVR returned to a severely impaired pattern of response. For the data in Table IV, comparisons were as follows: in the two PASSIVE conditions, the target–non-target difference was non-significant ($P > 0.50$ for both).

TABLE IV

Passive–active–passive reversal experiment

Condition	*SCR magnitudes (in μS) (S.D.)*	
	Target	*Non-target*
Passive	0.000	0.004
	(–)	(0.013)
Active	0.718	0.007
	(0.818)	(0.027)
Passive	0.008	0.031
	(0.018)	(0.092)

In the ACTIVE condition, the target–non-target contrast was significant ($z = -6.28$, $P < 0.001$).

(3) Results of a debriefing interview

After EVR had completed the replication experiments (conducted 3 months after the original study), we conducted a 90-min debriefing interview, in which EVR was questioned about his insights regarding the purpose of the study, and the content and technical characteristics of the stimuli. His responses confirmed the impression we had gathered after each experiment, concerning the careful way in which he attended to the stimuli, and the extent to which he had recognized their manifest meanings and even memorized some stimuli, their serial order, and thoughts that had occurred to him in reaction to the stimuli. But the most important information from the interview came spontaneously from EVR: he noted that he had not experienced the kind of 'feeling' that he thought he ought to have in relation to some stimuli, given their content. EVR seemed to have insight into a lack of 'feeling' that we believe corresponds to the lack of activation of a somatic state appropriate to the stimulus.

(3) Other bifrontal subjects

The SCR results in the other 4 Bifrontal subjects, who are 'EVR-like' in their lesions and acquired social conduct defects, provide further support for the lesion-related specificity of defective skin conductance responding. The data are presented in Table V. The subjects had normal orienting responses. The orienting responses of the Normal, Brain-damaged, and Bifrontal groups were compared with the Kruskal–Wallis one-way analysis of variance by ranks. The outcome was non-significant ($H = 2.082$, df = 2, $0.30 < P < 0.50$). In the PASSIVE condition, however, they failed to produce normal discriminatory SCRs to the target pictures. A sign-test was used to compare target and non-target SCRs in the Bifrontals (PASSIVE condition; EVR was included in the analysis). The outcome was non-significant ($n = 5$, $x = 2$, $P = 0.50$). One subject (SG-1208) showed a significant target–non-target difference ($z = -3.05$, $P < 0.01$, in a Mann–Whitney U-test), but the magnitude of the

TABLE V

Skin conductance magnitudes (in μS; S.D. in parentheses) in other bifrontal subjects

Subjects	*Orienting response*	*Passive*		*Active*	
		Target	*Non-target*	*Target*	*Non-target*
SG-1208	0.788	0.185 (0.211)	0.013 (0.049)	0.335 (0.330)	0.004 (0.014)
FL-1164	0.938	0.088 (0.129)	0.013 (0.034)	0.037 (0.100)	0.004 (0.012)
DM-1336	0.830	0.001 (0.002)	0.006 (0.015)	0.015 (0.046)	0.001 (0.002)
HS-1065	1.543	0.346 (0.179)	0.205 (0.199)	0.630 (0.213)	0.347 (0.203)

average difference (0.172 μS) was smaller than the 0.457 μS and 0.725 μS differences respectively shown by the Brain-damaged and Normal control groups in the PASSIVE condition.

In 3 of the 4 subjects, target SCR discrimination improved in the ACTIVE condition. Taken as a group, the target–non-target comparison in the Bifrontals was significant (n = 5, x = 0, P = 0.031, in a sign-test). One subject (FL-1164) did not improve significantly in the ACTIVE condition.

The defective SCRs exhibited by the Bifrontal subjects in the PASSIVE condition cannot be attributed to lack of attentiveness, limited visual perception, or idiosyncratic mores and values. The experimenter carefully monitored the subjects' behaviors during the procedures in this regard, and the Bifrontals' response protocols from the debriefing procedure were indistinguishable from those of the controls.

DISCUSSION

Defective somatic activation

The finding of defective skin conductance responses to socially significant stimuli suggests that the Bifrontal subjects failed to generate somatic states to the implications of those stimuli, at the most basic level. This defect is probably a correlate of the failure to experience a somatic state appropriate to the consequences of social situations. We propose that in real-life, these subjects are deprived of painful or pleasurable markers relative to the possible negative or positive consequences whose imagetic representation a social stimulus normally conjures up. In all probability covert processing of such signals is also absent.

The possibility that patients with these lesions would simply fail to generate SCRs is denied by the finding that the Bifrontal subjects could generate SCRs to several stimuli, and showed SCR deficiencies only under particular response conditions. The autonomic nervous system can still be activated by elementary unconditioned stimuli, e.g. sounds, air intake. The possibility that the SCR defects were caused by the presence of a brain lesion (irrespective of location), especially a large lesion, can be firmly rejected because the Brain-damaged controls showed normal SCRs even when their lesions were sizable. The defect in SCRs appears specific to brain region, response condition, and stimuli.

Our findings cannot be explained by defects in conventional memory or intelligence. However, the defects might be conceptualized as a domain-circumscribed memory impairment for social knowledge. This would reconcile Mishkin's[42] finding of memory impairments following ablations in the ventromedial region of the frontal lobe in rhesus monkeys, and our contention that damage to the same sector in humans does not lead to conventional amnesia. It might thus resolve a seeming discrepancy between human and non-human primate data.

From a historical perspective, our findings relate to previous work that demonstrated certain psychophysiological defects in patients with frontal lobe damage. Specifically, patients with large frontal lobe tumors showed defects in the vegetative components of the orienting reflex, including pathologically rapid habituation to signal stimuli[38,39]. A comparable result has been demonstrated in monkeys[35]. Unlike those older studies, however, which focused on arousal and the orienting reflex, we have identified particular stimulus–response conditions under which SCRs are abnormal, and particular lesion sites that correlate with those abnormalities. Our findings are not explainable by general defects in arousal or orienting responses.

Neural basis

In normal individuals, the ventromedial frontal cortices receive signals from a large range of neural structures engaged by perception. This includes external information from vision, audition, and even olfaction, and somatic information from concurrent skeletal and visceral states. The signals arrive in the orbital region via multi-stage projections from higher-order association cortices in temporal, parietal, and insular regions. Some projections have intermediate way-stations in other frontal cortices, namely the dorsolateral sector[9,34,44,46]. Furthermore, the ventromedial cortices are the only known source of projections from frontal regions towards central autonomic control structures[43] and those projections have a demonstrated physiological influence on visceral control[25]. The ventromedial cortices also receive and reciprocate projections from the hippocampus and amygdala[1,23,45,54,55]. The ventromedial cortices can thus satisfy two requisites of the mechanism we propose. First, they can form conjunctive records of concurrent signals hailing from external *and* internal stimuli, within neuron ensembles of the type we have proposed elsewhere as convergence zones[11,12]. Second, they can activate somatic effectors. The system would operate as follows. When parts of certain exteroceptive–interoceptive conjunctions are reprocessed, consciously or not, their activation is signaled to ventromedial cortices, which in turn activate somatic effectors in amygdala, hypothalamus, and brainstem nuclei. One might describe this process as an attempt to reconstitute the kind of somatic state that belonged to the conjunction. The re-enacted somatic state can then be signaled to cortical and subcortical somatosensory processing structures, and either be consciously perceived or trigger a covert subcortical process modifying appetitive or aversive behaviors. The type of damage seen in EVR-type patients precludes this chain of events. Further testing of this theory will include the study of patients with damage at the several network components enumerated above. If our interpretation is correct, lesions at those other sites should disrupt the process no less than lesions in ventromedial frontal cortices.

The fact that EVR-type patients continue to generate autonomic responses to elementary and unconditioned environmental stimuli, suggests that a different network must exist to cope with behaviorally relevant stimuli that do not require the complex informational processing that social configurations do. The alternate network would bypass the cerebral cortex altogether and activate autonomic centers (e.g. amygdala) directly from thalamus[10,17]. The dissociation between responses to complex stimuli which require cortical processing and to basic stimuli which do not, might help reconcile the seemingly conflicting views of James[33] and Cannon[8] on the physiology of emotion. Complex social stimuli require the type of process suggested by James, but simpler stimuli which ought to evoke fight-or-flight reactions from the organism, would not.

Acquired structural damage to orbital cortices (or to critical components of the related networks), or abnormal neural development of these structures (see below), would disable the automatic guiding system and call for non-automatic, cost–benefit analysis of many response option/outcome pairs. A non-automatic strategy is inevitably slower, extremely burdensome to working memory, and more prone to error. In all likelihood it requires strong verbal mediation, and that might explain why EVR-type patients and sociopaths can sometimes improve their responses when the approach to the situation is made on purely verbal terms.

Implications for the understanding of sociopathy and obsessive compulsive neurosis

Neither EVR-type patients nor sociopaths respond appropriately to social situations, in spite of adequate intellect, and neither learns from repeated mistakes. Leaving aside the obvious differences in age of onset and in the consequences of their actions for society (EVR-type patients tend to hurt themselves more than others), the similarity does suggest that sociopathy might relate to dysfunction in the network that includes ventromedial frontal cortices. Specifically, these cortices might develop abnormally and not be capable of learning the necessary conjunctions, or else be so weakly activated that their influence on somatic state re-enactment would be minimal.

Some convergent evidence is available. For instance, it is well known that sociopaths fail to demonstrate appropriate levels of anxiety in situations involving punishment or threat of punishment. This failure is evident in observable behavior, and is indexed by measures such as SCRs. Sociopaths show poor SCR conditioning with aversive unconditioned stimuli such as shock, and defective SCRs in anticipation of aversive stimuli[18,27,40]. Even when stimuli are appetitive (e.g., pictures of nudes), sociopaths fail to demonstrate SCR conditioning, and these findings have been interpreted as indicating that the sociopath's inability to avoid punishment is related to a failure to anticipate emotionally the consequences of behavior[29].

Obsessive compulsive neurosis would be due to the very opposite defect. The ventromedial component of the network would form exteroceptive–interoceptive conjunctions readily, abundantly, and excessively. The consequence would be the frequent re-enactment of somatic states relative to stimulus configurations that do not require such processing, resulting in anxiety and excessive response implementation. One might in fact predict that in non-brain-damaged sociopaths studied in emission tomography experiments using emotionally-charged stimuli, ventromedial frontal cortices would be *underactivated*, while neurotic and depressive patients should reveal hyperactivation (there is preliminary support for this hypothesis in the work of Raichle). Acquired and developmental sociopaths may also be contrasted with patients with temporal lobe epilepsy (TLE) and interictal emotional changes. Some TLE patients exhibit hypermoralism, religiosity and excessive rumination over the social consequences of actions[3]. Whereas bifrontal patients exhibit diminished autonomic responses to social stimuli, TLE patients have enhanced autonomic responses to visual stimuli[4].

Finally, it is not implausible that an automatic marker device which would have evolved in nonhuman species for the survival of the individual in simple social settings, would have been co-opted as a mechanism for response selection in complex social domains, and in other knowledge domains. In other words, we believe that some variation of somatic marker provides the signposts that direct our multi-step behaviors and, among many other uses, will make us remember when to remember. This proposal is in general agreement with Shallice's (personal communication) notion that complex multi-step behavior requires some kind of marker device for its implementation.

ACKNOWLEDGEMENTS

We thank Don Fowles for his careful review and advice on SCR procedures, data analysis, and interpretation, and Dr. Saver for a detailed review of the manuscript and several helpful suggestions. Supported by NINDS Program Grant NS 19632.

REFERENCES

1 Amaral, D.G. and Price, J.L., Amygdalo-cortical projections in the monkey (*Macaca fascicularis*), *J. Comp. Neurol.* 230 (1984) 465–496.

2 American Psychiatric Association. *Diagnostic and Statistical Manual of Mental Disorders* (3rd ed.), Author, Washington, DC, 1980.

3 Bear, D.M., Temporal lobe epilepsy: a syndrome of sensory-limbic hyperconnection, *Cortex*, 15 (1979) 357–384.

4 Bear, D., Schenk, L. and Benson, H., Increased autonomic responses to neural and emotional stimuli in patients with temporal lobe epilepsy, *Am. J. Psychiatry*, 138 (1981) 843–845.

5 Benton, A.L., *Multilingual Aphasia Examination*, University of Iowa College of Medicine, Iowa City, IA, 1976.

6 Bernstein, A.S., The orienting response as novelty and significance detector: reply to O'Gorman, *Psychophysiology*, 16 (1979) 263–273.

7 Boucsein, W., *Elektrodermale aktivitat: Grundlagen, methoden und anwendungen*, Springer, New York, 1988.

8 Cannon, W.B., The James-Lange theory of emotions: a critical examination and an alternative theory, *Am. J. Psychol.*, 39 (1927) 106–124.

9 Chavis, D.A. and Pandya, D.N., Further observations on corticofrontal connections in the rhesus monkey, *Brain Res.*, 117 (1976) 369–386.

10 Clugnet, C., LeDoux, J.E., Morrison, S.F. and Reis, D.J., Short latency orthodromic action potentials evoked in amygdala and caudate-putamen by stimulation of the medial geniculate body, *Soc. Neurosci. Abstr.*, 14 (Part II) (1988) 1227.

11 Damasio, A.R., The brain binds entities and events by multiregional activation from convergence zones, *Neural Computation*, 1 (1989) 123–132.

12 Damasio, A.R., Time-locked multiregional retroactivation: a systems-level proposal for the neural substrates of recall and recognition, *Cognition*, 33 (1989) 25–62.

13 Damasio, H. and Damasio, A.R., *Lesion analysis in neuropsychology*. Oxford University Press, New York, 1989.

14 Edelberg, R., The electrodermal system. In N.S. Greenfield and R.A. Sternbach, (Eds.), *Handbook of psychophysiology*. Holt, Rinehart and Winston, New York, 1972, 367–418.

15 Edelberg, R., Mechanisms of electrodermal adaptations for locomotion, manipulation, or defense, *Progr. Physiol. Psychol.*, 5 (1973) 155–209.

16 Eslinger, P.J. and Damasio, A.R., Severe disturbance of higher cognition after bilateral frontal lobe ablation: patient EVR, *Neurology*, 35 (1985) 1731–1741.

17 Farb, C.F., Ruggiero, D.A. and LeDoux, J.E., Projections from the acoustic thalamus terminate in the lateral but not central amygdala, *Soc. Neurosci. Abstr.*, 14 (Part II) (1988) 1227.

18 Fowles, D.C., The three-arousal model: implications of Gray's two-factor learning theory for heart rate, electrodermal activity, and psychopathy. *Psychophysiology*, 17 (1988) 87–104.

19 Fowles, D.C., The eccrine system and electrodermal activity. In M.G.H. Coles, E. Donchin and S.W. Porges (Eds.), *Psychophysiology: Systems, processes and applications*, Guilford, New York, 1986, pp. 51–96.

20 Fowles, D.C. and Schneider, R.E., Electrolyte effects on measurements of palmer skin potential, *Psychophysiology*, 15 (1978) 474–482.

21 Fuster, J.M., *The prefrontal cortex* (2nd ed.), Raven, New York, 1989.

22 Goldman-Rakic, P.S., Circuitry of primate prefrontal cortex and regulation of behavior by representational memory. In F. Plum (Ed.), *Handbook of physiology: Nervous system, Vol. V: Higher Functions of the Brain*, American Physiological Society, Bethesda, MD, 1987, pp. 373–417.

23 Goldman-Rakic, P.S., Selemon, L.D. and Schwartz, M.L., Dual pathways connecting the dorsolateral prefrontal cortex with the hippocampal formation and parahippocampal cortex in the rhesus monkey, *Neuroscience*, 12 (1984) 719–743.

24 Greenwald, M.K., Cook, E.W. and Lang, P.J., Affective judgment and psychophysiological response: dimensional covariation in the evaluation of pictorial stimuli, *J. Psychophysiol.*, (1990) in press.

25 Hall, R.E., Livingston, R.B. and Bloor, C.M., Orbital cortical influences on cardiovascular dynamics and myocardial structure in conscious monkeys, *J. Neurosurg.*, 46 (1977) 638–647.

26 Halstead, W.C., *Brain and intelligence: A Quantitative Study of the Frontal Lobes*, University of Chicago Press, Chicago, 1947.

27 Hare, R.D., Electrodermal and cardiovascular correlates of psychopathy. In R.D. Hare and D. Schalling (Eds.), *Psychopathic Behavior: Approaches to Research*. Wiley, New York, 1970, pp. 107–143.

28 Hare, R.D., Wood, K., Britain, S. and Shadman, J., Autonomic responses to affective visual stimuli. *Psychophysiology*, 7 (1970) 408–417.

29 Hare, R.D. and Quinn, M.J., Psychopathy and autonomic conditioning, *J. Abnormal Psychol.*, 77 (1971) 223–235.

30 Heaton, R.K., *Wisconsin Card Sorting Test. Manual* Psychological Assessment Resources, Odessa, FL., 1981.

31 Jacobsen, C.F., Functions of the frontal association area in primates, *Arch. Neurol. Psychiatry*, 33 (1935) 558–569.

32 Jacobsen, C.F., Studies of cerebral functions in primates: I. The functions of the frontal association areas in monkeys, *Comp. Psychol. Monogr.* 13, (1936) 3–60.

33 James, W., What is an emotion? *Mind*, 9 (1884) 118–205.

34 Jones, E.G. and Powell, T.P.S., An anatomical study of converging sensory pathways within the cerebral cortex of the monkey, *Brain*, 93 (1970) 793–820.

35 Kimble, D.P., Bagshaw, M.H. and Pribram, K.H., The GSR of monkeys during orienting and habituation after selective partial ablations of the cingulate and frontal cortex. *Neuropsychologia*, 3 (1965) 121–128.

36 Klorman, R., Wiesenfeld, A. and Austin, M.L., Autonomic responses to affective visual stimuli, *Psychophysiology*, 12 (1975) 553–560.

37 Lang, P.J. and Greenwald, M.K., *The international affective picture system standardization procedure and initial group results for affective judgments: Technical report 1A*. Gainesville, FL: Center for Research in Psychophysiology, University of Florida, 1988.

38 Luria, A.R., The frontal lobes and the regulation of behavior. In K.H. Pribram and A.R. Luria, (Eds.) *Psychophysiology of the frontal lobes*, Academic Press, New York, 1973, pp. 3–26.

39 Luria, A.R. and Homskaya, E.D., Frontal lobes and the regulation of arousal processes. In D.I. Mostofsky, (Ed.), *Attention: Contemporary theory and analysis*. Appleton-Century-Crofts, New York, 1970; pp. 303–330.

40 Lykken, D.T., A study of anxiety in the sociopathic personality, *J. Abnormal Social Psychol.*, 55 (1957) 6–10.

41 Milner, B. and Petrides, M., Behavioural effects of frontal-lobe lesions in man, *Trends Neurosc.*, 7 (1984) 403–407.
42 Mishkin, M. and Bachevalier, J., Object recognition impaired by ventromedial but not dorsolateral prefrontal cortical lesions in monkeys, *Soc. Neurosci. Abstr.*, 9 (1983) 29.
43 Nauta, W.J.H., The problem of the frontal lobe: a reinterpretation, *J. Psychiatric Res.*, 8 (1971) 167–187.
44 Pandya, D.N. and Kuypers, H.G.J.M., Cortico-cortical connections in the rhesus monkey, *Brain Res.*, 13 (1969) 13–36.
45 Porrino, L.J., Crane, A.M. and Goldman-Rakic, P.S., Direct and indirect pathways from the amygdala to the frontal lobe in rhesus monkeys, *J. Comp. Neurol.*, 198 (1981) 121–136.
46 Potter, H. and Nauta, W.J.H., A note on the problem of olfactory associations of the orbitofrontal cortex in the monkey, *Neuroscience*, 4 (1979) 316–367.
47 Raskin, D.C., Attention and arousal. In W.F. Prokasy and D.C. Raskin (Eds.), *Electrodermal Activity in Psychological Research.* Academic, New York, 1973, pp. 125–155.
48 Shallice, T. and Evans, M.E., The involvement of the frontal lobes in cognitive estimation, *Cortex*, 14 (1978) 294–303.
49 Siegel, S. and Castellan, N.J., *Non-parametric Statistics for the Behavioral Sciences* (2nd ed.), McGraw Hill, New York, 1988.
50 Stern, R.M. and Anschel, C., Deep inspirations as stimuli for responses of the autonomic nervous system, *Psychophysiology*, 6 (1968) 132–141.
51 Stuss, D.T. and Benson, D.F., *The Frontal Lobes*, Raven, New York, 1986.
52 Tranel, D. and Damasio, A.R., Non-conscious face recognition in patients with face agnosia, *Behav. Brain Res.*, 30 (1988) 235–249.
53 Tranel, D. and Damasio, H., Intact electrodermal skin conductance responses in a patient with bilateral amygdala damage, *Neuropsychologia*, 27 (1989) 381–390.
54 Van Hoesen, G.W., Pandya, D.N. and Butters, N., Cortical afferents to the entorhinal cortex of the rhesus monkey, *Science*, 175 (1972) 1471–1473.
55 Van Hoesen, G.W., Pandya, D.N. and Butters, N., Some connections of the entorhinal (area 28) and perirhinal (area 35) cortices of the rhesus monkey: II. Frontal lobe afferents, *Brain Res.*, 95 (1975) 25–38.
56 Venables, P.H. and Christie, M.J., Electrodermal activity. In I. Martin and P.H. Venables (Eds.), *Techniques in psychophysiology.* Wiley, New York, 1980, pp. 3–67.

Dysfunction in the Neural Circuitry of Emotion Regulation—A Possible Prelude to Violence

Richard J. Davidson,* Katherine M. Putnam, Christine L. Larson

Emotion is normally regulated in the human brain by a complex circuit consisting of the orbital frontal cortex, amygdala, anterior cingulate cortex, and several other interconnected regions. There are both genetic and environmental contributions to the structure and function of this circuitry. We posit that impulsive aggression and violence arise as a consequence of faulty emotion regulation. Indeed, the prefrontal cortex receives a major serotonergic projection, which is dysfunctional in individuals who show impulsive violence. Individuals vulnerable to faulty regulation of negative emotion are at risk for violence and aggression. Research on the neural circuitry of emotion regulation suggests new avenues of intervention for such at-risk populations.

The prevalence of violence in our society has stimulated both social and biological scientists to search for the predictors and causes of this often destructive human behavior. Here we focus on the nature of the affective style that might predispose an individual to this aberrant form of behavior. Affective style is a term that refers to consistent individual differences in the various parameters that govern emotional reactivity (*1*). We contend that the propensity for impulsive aggression is associated with a low threshold for activating negative affect (a mixture of emotions and moods that include anger, distress, and agitation) and with a failure to respond appropriately to the anticipated negative consequences of behaving aggressively.

Social psychological research underscores the relation between aggression and emotion. Numerous studies show that negative affect can precipitate and accentuate aggressive behavior (*2, 3*). In this article we feature those forms of aggression that are relatively unplanned and spontaneous, termed impulsive aggression (*4*), which is different from premeditated aggression (*5*). Although most neurobiological studies of aggression and violence typically do not differentiate between premeditated and impulsive aggression, this distinction is likely relevant in understanding their genetic, neurochemical, and functional neuroanatomical bases, and consequently, we have confined our discussion to impulsive aggression, which often culminates in physical violence.

Emotion Regulation: Core Neural Substrates

As reviewed recently (*6, 7*), a circuit that includes several regions of the prefrontal cortex (PFC), the amygdala, hippocampus, hypothalamus, anterior cingulate cortex (ACC) (*8*), insular cortex, ventral striatum, and other interconnected structures has been implicated in various aspects of emotion, affective style, and emotion regulation (Fig. 1). Emotion regulation includes processes that amplify, attenuate, or maintain an emotion. Here we will focus on the associated affective phenomena of anger, general negative affect, and impulsive aggression (*3*).

A variety of evidence indicates that the amygdala is crucial for learning to associate stimuli with primary punishers and rewards (i.e., those events that are intrinsically punishing or rewarding) (*10, 11*). In human neuroimaging studies, the amygdala is activated in response to cues that connote threat (such as facial signs of fear) (*12, 13*), as well as during induced fear (for example, fear conditioning) (*14, 15*) and generalized negative affect (for example, negative affect provoked by watching unpleasant pictures) (*16*). Patients with selective bilateral damage to the amgydala have a specific impairment in the recognition of fearful facial expressions (*17*). The amygdala is more strongly activated by facial expressions of fear than it is by other facial expressions, including anger. For example, increasing intensity of fearful facial expressions is associated with activation of the amygdala. In contrast, increasing intensity of angry facial expressions is associated with increased activation of the orbitofrontal cortex (OFC) and the ACC (*18*). In two neuroimaging studies that have attempted to induce anger specifically (*19, 20*), normal subjects showed increased activation in the OFC and ACC. These activations may normally be part of an automatic regulatory response that controls the intensity of expressed anger. We would expect that in individuals prone to aggression and violence, the increase in OFC and ACC activation usually observed in such conditions would be attenuated.

A large corpus of animal studies has examined the anatomical and neurochemical substrates of fear-potentiated startle reflexes in which modulation of the magnitude of the startle response by concomitant emotion is measured (*21*). This research is now being extended to humans to probe the chronometry and regulation of emotion (*22–26*).

The circuitry underlying this phenomenon has been well characterized in rodents and includes a descending pathway from the central nucleus of the amygdala to the nucleus pontine reticularis in the brain stem that serves as the proximal substrate of the reflex. In rodent studies, the accentuation of the startle response magnitude during fear is produced by the amygdala amplifying the brain stem startle circuit. Lesions of the central nucleus of the amygdala have no effect on baseline startle, but they abolish the fear-potentiation of the startle response (*27*).

In analogous studies in humans, when subjects view unpleasant pictures, there is an increase in the magnitude of the eyeblink reflex (measured from surface electromyographic recording from the orbicularis oculi muscle) in response to a brief burst of noise (*28*). Moreover, the magnitude of the eyeblink reflex to the same stimulus during the viewing of pleasant pictures is smaller than that during the viewing of neutral pictures (*28, 29*).

By triggering a startle response at different times during affective processing, information about the time course of emotion can be gleaned (*23–25, 30*). In one experiment (*25*), normal subjects viewed unpleasant or neutral pictures for 8 s. Four seconds after the picture appeared, a digitized human voice instructed the subject to regulate the emotion they were experiencing in response to the picture. For unpleasant pictures, subjects were asked to suppress, enhance, or maintain their emotional response. Subjects were instructed to continue voluntary regulation of their emotional response even after the picture disappeared. During and after the presentation of the pictures, brief noise bursts were presented to probe the time course of the emotion before and after the instruction to regulate was presented. When subjects were requested to suppress their negative

Laboratory for Affective Neuroscience and W. M. Keck Laboratory for Functional Brain Imaging and Behavior, University of Wisconsin–Madison, Madison, WI 53706, USA.

*To whom correspondence should be addressed. E-mail: rjdavids@facstaff.wisc.edu

affect, they showed significantly diminished startle magnitude during and after unpleasant pictures compared with both the maintain and enhance conditions (Fig. 2). Most important was the fact that subjects varied considerably in their skill at suppressing negative emotion. By inserting startle stimuli before the instruction was presented, we confirmed that this variation in the ability to regulate emotions could not be accounted for by differences in the initial reactivity to the negative stimuli. In more recent work (*26*), we found that baseline levels of regional brain activation inferred from high-density scalp-recorded brain electroencephalography (EEG) (*31*) predicted the ability of subjects to suppress emotions. Those subjects with greater relative left-sided activation in prefrontal scalp regions showed greater startle attenuation in response to the suppression instruction. Although the EEG methods used in this study precluded definitive localization of the sources of these signals, other evidence implicates the OFC in this process. Research with humans who have selective damage to the OFC or ventromedial PFC (*32*), and with nonhuman primates, supports the role of these prefrontal territories in reversal learning [changing emotional behavior in response to a previously rewarded or punished stimulus (*10*)]. Suppressing negative affect in response to a stimulus that previously aroused such emotion can be conceptualized as a form of reversal learning. Patients with lesions in the OFC and those vulnerable to impulsive aggression should be particularly deficient in this task, although they would still show the basic enhancement of startle magnitude in response to negative stimuli.

We have proposed that the mechanism underlying suppression of negative emotion is via an inhibitory connection from regions of the prefrontal cortex, probably the OFC, to the amygdala (*7*). This proposal is based on several lines of evidence. First, data in rodents show that lesions of the PFC interfere with extinction of a classically conditioned aversive response [(*33*), but see (*34*)], implying that the PFC normally inhibits the amygdala and that, when the PFC is lesioned, it releases the amygdala from this inhibition and results in much slower extinction of aversive responses. Second, data from a positron emission tomography (PET) study show reciprocal relations between glucose metabolism in several areas of the frontal cortex (including the OFC) and the amygdala (*35*).

On the basis of this reasoning, we examined by functional magnetic resonance imaging (fMRI) amygdala activation after subjects were instructed to maintain a negative emotion as compared with the subjects' simple passive viewing of unpleasant pictures. We found greater activation of the amygdala after the picture was turned off in the group asked to maintain that emotion as compared with the "passive viewing" condition, as the model would predict (*36*).

The implications of these findings are several: First, individual differences in the capacity to regulate emotion are objectively measurable. Second, individual differences in patterns of prefrontal activation predict ability to perform this task and thus reflect differences in aspects of emotion regulation. Third, individual differences in emotion regulation skills, particularly as they apply to suppression of negative affect, may be especially important in determining vulnerability to aggression and violence.

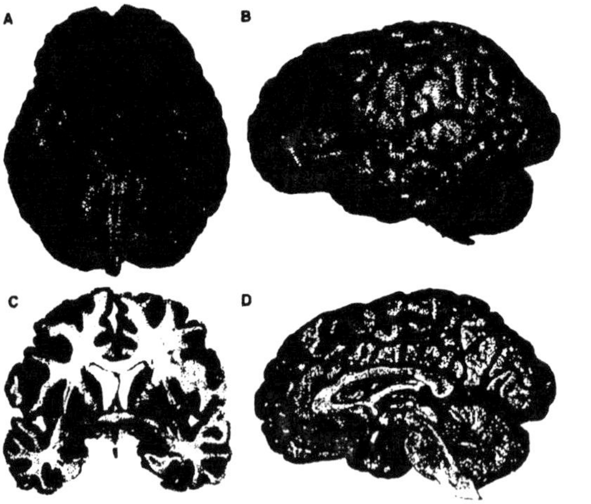

Fig. 1. Key structures in the circuitry underlying emotion regulation. (**A**) Orbital prefrontal cortex in green and the ventromedial prefrontal cortex in red. (**B**) Dorsolateral prefrontal cortex. (**C**) Amygdala. (**D**) Anterior cingulate cortex. Each of these interconnected structures plays a role in different aspects of emotion regulation, and abnormalities in one or more of these regions and/or in the interconnections among them are associated with failures of emotion regulation and also increased propensity for impulsive aggression and violence. [Adapted from (9)]

The Neurobiology of Anger and Aggression

Disruption of the serotonin (5-HT) system has been linked to aggression and violence by a variety of methods. Serotonin has been hypothesized to exert inhibitory control over impulsive aggression (*37*). Cerebrospinal fluid (CSF) level of the 5-HT metabolite 5-hydroxyindoleacetic acid (5-HIAA) is believed to reflect presynaptic serotonergic activity in the brain. Reduced CSF 5-HIAA has been found in aggressive psychiatric patients (*38, 39*); impulsive, violent men (*40, 41*); and victims of suicide by violent means (*42*). Furthermore, 5-HIAA concentration has been found to predict aggression 2 to 3 years in the future in conduct-disordered boys (*43*) and recidivous adults (*44*). Lower CSF 5-HIAA levels have been reported in impulsive violent offenders (*45*) and impulsive fire setters (*46*) than in nonimpulsive violent offenders.

Pharmacological challenge studies provide another indirect method for studying central serotonin function. The prolactin elevation in response to a single dose of a 5-HT agonist has been used to index central 5-HT activity. Lower prolactin responses to a 5-HT agonist have been associated with aggressivity (*38*), antisocial personality disorder (*47*), and suicidal behavior (*38*). Traits of aggression in a large normative community-derived sample were associated with lower prolactin responses to the 5-HT agonist fenfluramine in men (*48*). The synthesis of 5-HT depends on the availability of the amino acid tryptophan. By limiting dietary tryptophan, brain levels of 5-HT can be reduced (*49*). Tryptophan depletion induced by consuming a beverage containing a group of amino acids without tryptophan increased laboratory aggression in normal men (*50, 51*) and both spontaneous and competitive aggression in monkeys (*52*), as compared with increasing tryptophan with a tryptophan-containing beverage.

A polymorphism in the gene that codes for tryptophan hydroxylase (TPH), the rate-limiting enzyme in serotonin biosynthesis, is correlated with indirect measures of central serotonergic function, as well as individual differences in aggressive behavior (*53, 54*). In a study (*54*) with 251 community volunteers, the association between the A218C polymorphism in intron 7 of the TPH gene and interview and self-report measures of aggression and anger-related personality traits was examined. In addition, a fenfluramine challenge was administered to a subsample. Subjects having any TPH A218C U allele scored significantly higher on several measures of aggression, including the tendency to experience unprovoked anger, than individuals homozygous for the alternate A218C L allele. Among the male subjects, prolactin response to fenfluramine was also blunted in those subjects having any U allele compared with the LL homozygotes.

The PFC, an important component of a circuit critical to emotion regulation that has been implicated in aggressive and violent behavior, is a region with a high density of serotonin type 2 receptors (*55*). In a study designed to evaluate the functional impact of a serotonergic challenge on regional cerebral glucose metabolism, Mann and his colleagues (*56*) administered either fenfluramine or a placebo to normal subjects on two separate occasions while cerebral glucose metabolism was measured with PET. Significant drug-induced increases in glucose metabolic rate were found in left hemisphere regions of the PFC, including the inferior and middle frontal gyrus, ventromedial PFC, and anterior cingulate. These regions include those with activation inversely associated with activation in the amygdala (*35*).

The increase in glucose metabolism in PFC and ACC regions in normal subjects in response to fenfluramine is blunted or entirely absent in patients with aggressive impulsive personality disorder (*57, 58*). These findings imply that an important site of serotonergic abnormality in subjects with impulsive aggression is the prefrontal cortex, which likely plays a role in emotion regulation, particularly the regulation of negative affect.

Studies of regional glucose metabolism assessed with PET (unprovoked by pharmacological challenge) also reveal prefrontal abnormalities in individuals prone to impulsive aggression (*59–63*). A study of 41 murderers (*62*) found hypoactivation in prefrontal territories including lateral and medial zones of the PFC, as well as hyperactivation in the right but not the left amygdala, compared with age- and sex-matched controls. In a subsequent reanalysis of these data (*63*), murderers were classified as those who committed planned, predatory murder or those who committed affective and impulsive murder. The affective, impulsive murderers showed reductions in lateral PFC metabolism compared with controls, whereas the predatory group did not. Subcortical regions were averaged together in this report and included the hippocampus, amygdala, thalamus, and midbrain. An increased metabolic rate was observed in these regions in the right hemisphere in the affective, impulsive murderers as compared with the other groups.

Lesions in the OFC and adjacent PFC regions produce syndromes characterized by impulsivity and aggression. Anderson *et al.* (*64*) reported on two individuals, tested in their twenties, who suffered early damage (ages 3 and 15 months) to orbital and lateral sectors of the PFC. Both exhibited a remarkable deficit in moral reasoning; a history of verbal and physical abusiveness; and intermittent, explosive bursts of anger. Blair and Cipolotti (*65*) reported that a 56-year-old man (J.S.), who sustained damage to the OFC bilaterally and some damage to the left amygdala, showed unpredictable, impulsive aggression and violence. J.S. was described by a relative "as being premorbidly a quiet, rather withdrawn person who was never aggressive" (p. 1124). In a series of tasks administered to J.S., a control patient with damage to other sectors of the PFC, and a small group of psychopathic and nonpsychopathic individuals, J.S.'s pattern of affective processing abnormalities was identified. He had deficits in recognition of facial expression, and he was particularly impaired relative to all other groups in the recognition of anger and disgust. J.S. also produced significantly lower skin conductance responses to the anger and disgust expressions compared with the comparison groups. In response to threatening objects such as pointed weapons, J.S. was hyporesponsive compared with other groups. Thus, J.S. exhibited a strikingly specific deficit in the recognition of anger signals and in inferring the emotions of others in situations where anger, disgust, and embarrassment are usual. Facial and other expressive signs of anger function to inhibit the behavior of others in situations where social rules or expectations may be violated.

In other related work, patients with antisocial personality disorder who exhibit a propensity for impulsive aggression exhibit an 11% reduction of overall prefrontal gray matter volume by MRI (*66*). Interictal episodes of impulsive aggression are sometimes observed in patients with temporal lobe epilepsy (TLE). TLE patients who display such episodes of impulsive aggressive (diagnosed as having intermittent explosive disorder) have a highly significant reduction (approximately 17%) in left prefrontal gray matter as compared with TLE patients with no history of aggression or controls (*67*).

Emotion Regulation, Aggression, and Violence: Common Neural Substrates?

Impulsive, affective aggression may be the product of a failure of emotion regulation. Normal individuals are able to voluntarily regulate their negative affect and can also profit from restraint-producing cues in their environment, such as facial and vocal signs of anger or fear, that also serve a regulatory role. We suggest that individuals predisposed to

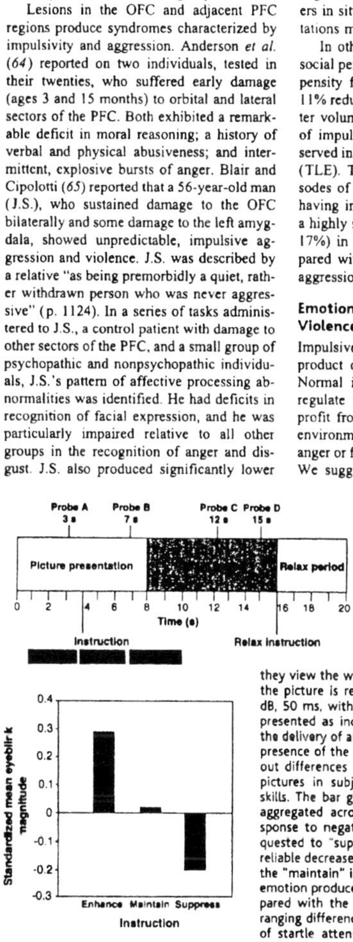

Fig. 2. Experimental paradigm for investigating emotion regulation (*25*). Unpleasant or neutral pictures are presented during the 8-s picture presentation period illustrated in yellow. At 4 s into the picture presentation, an instruction (ENHANCE, MAINTAIN, OR SUPPRESS) is presented. Subjects are instructed to continue to execute the regulatory strategy until they view the word RELAX that is presented 8 s after the picture is removed from sight. Noise bursts (95 dB, 50 ms, with a near instantaneous rise time) are presented as indicated. Probe A is presented before the delivery of any regulation instruction to verify the presence of the intended emotional state and to rule out differences in initial reactivity to the emotional pictures in subjects who differ in their regulatory skills. The bar graph displays data from 43 subjects aggregated across all postinstruction probes in response to negative pictures. When subjects are requested to "suppress" negative emotion, they show reliable decreases in startle magnitude compared with the "maintain" instruction. Instructions to "enhance" emotion produce increases in startle magnitude compared with the other conditions. There were wide-ranging differences among subjects in the magnitude of startle attenuation in response to the SUPRESS instruction.

aggression and violence have an abnormality in the central circuitry responsible for these adaptive behavioral strategies. Four key regions that are components of a circuit underlying emotion regulation are illustrated in Fig. 1. Functional or structural abnormalities in one or more of these regions or in the interconnections among them can increase the propensity for impulsive aggression. The evidence reviewed above suggests that abnormalities in serotonin function in regions of the PFC may be especially important. Other neurotransmitters, neuromodulators, and hormones are also likely involved, including testosterone (*68*), norepinepherine, dopamine and cortiocotropin-releasing hormone (*42*), and cholesterol (*69*), although none of these has received much attention in human studies of aggression and violence.

The role of the amygdala in impulsive aggression is complex (*70*). Individual behaviors that connote threat (e.g., staring eyes, threatening vocalization, lunging posture) are conveyed to the lateral nucleus of the amygdala, which then projects to the basal nuclei, and it is there that information about the social context derived from OFC projections is integrated with the perceptual information (*71, 72*). Behavioral responses can then be initiated via projections from the basal nuclei to various cortical zones, and physiological responses can be produced via projections from the basal nuclei to the central nucleus and then to the hypothalamus and brainstem. Too much or too little activation of the amygdala may give rise to either excessive negative affect or decreased sensitivity to social cues that regulate emotion, respectively.

The evidence we have reviewed indicates that the OFC and the structures with which it is interconnected (including other prefrontal territories, the ACC, and the amygdala) constitute the core elements of a circuit that underlies emotion regulation (Fig. 1). The OFC, through its connections with other zones of the PFC and with the amygdala, plays a crucial role in constraining impulsive outbursts, and the ACC recruits other neural systems, including the PFC, in response to conflict (*8*). In normal individuals, activations in these brain regions that occur during anger arousal and other negative emotions constrain the impulsive expression of emotional behavior. Deficits in this circuit are hypothesized to increase a person's vulnerability to impulsive aggression.

There are many factors that influence the structure and function of this circuitry. Genetic factors clearly play a role as revealed by the association of the polymorphism of the TPH gene with traits of anger and aggressivity (*54*). However, these factors undoubtedly interact with early environmental influences (*73*). Moreover, the very circuitry identified here as playing a crucial role in emotion regulation is dramatically shaped by early social influences (*7*). Interventions that combine pharmacological (*74*) and psychosocial strategies will likely both operate on a common final pathway in the emotion regulatory circuitry of the brain. Novel training procedures based upon experimental paradigms now being used to study the neural substrates of emotion regulation (e.g., suppressing negative emotion) need to be developed and then rigorously evaluated. Nevertheless, the first important step is to recognize that impulsive aggression and violence, irrespective of the distal cause, reflect abnormalities in the emotion regulation circuitry of the brain.

References and Notes

1. R. J. Davidson, in *The Cognitive Neurosciences*, M. S. Gazzaniga, Ed. (MIT Press, Cambridge, MA, 2000), pp.1149–1159.
2. L. Berkowitz, in *Handbook of Cognition and Emotion*, T. Dagleish and M. Power, Eds. (Wiley, Chichester, UK, 1999), pp. 411–428.
3. ———, in *Handbook of Affective Sciences*, R. J. Davidson, K. Scherer, H. H. Goldsmith, Eds. (Oxford Univ. Press, New York, in press).
4. M. Linnoila, D. S. Charney, in *The Neurobiology of Mental Illness*, D. S. Charney, E. J. Nestler, B. S. Bunney, Eds. (Oxford Univ. Press, New York, 1999), pp. 855–871.
5. E. S. Barratt *et al.*, *Psychiatry Res.* **86**, 163 (1999).
6. R. J. Davidson and W. Irwin, *Trends Cognit. Sci.* **3**, 11 (1999).
7. R. J. Davidson, D. C. Jackson, N. H. Kalin, *Psychol. Bull.*, in press.
8. G. Bush, P. Luu, M. I. Posner, *Trends Cognit. Sci.* **4**, 215 (2000).
9. S. J. DeArmond, M. M. Fusco, M. M. Dewey, *Structure of the Human Brain: A Photographic Atlas* (Oxford Univ. Press, New York, 3rd ed., 1989).
10. E. T. Rolls, *The Brain and Emotion* (Oxford Univ. Press, New York, 1999).
11. P. C. Holland and M. Gallagher, *Trends Cognit. Sci.* **3**, 65 (1999).
12. J. S. Morris *et al.*, *Nature* **383**, 812 (1996).
13. P. J. Whalen *et al.*, *J. Neurosci.* **18**, 411 (1998).
14. C. Buchel, J. S. Morris, R. J. Dolan, K. J. Friston, *Neuron* **20**, 947 (1998).
15. K. S. LaBar *et al.*, *Neuron* **20**, 937 (1998).
16. W. Irwin *et al.*, *Neuroreport* **7**, 1765 (1996).
17. R. Adolphs, D. Tranel, H. Damasio, A. Damasio, *Nature* **372**, 613 (1994).
18. R. J. Blair *et al.*, *Brain* **122**, 883 (1999).
19. D. D. Dougherty *et al.*, *Biol. Psychiatry* **46**, 466 (1999).
20. T. A. Kimbrell *et al.*, *Biol. Psychiatry* **46**, 454 (1999).
21. M. Davis, in *The Amygdala*, J. P. Aggleton, Ed. (Wiley-Liss, New York, 1992), pp. 255–306.
22. S. K. Sutton *et al.*, *Psychophysiology* **34**, 217 (1997).
23. J. Globisch, A. O. Hamm, F. Esteves, A. Öhman, *Psychophysiology* **36**, 66 (1999).
24. C. L. Larson, D. Ruffalo, J. Y. Nietert, R. J. Davidson, *Psychophysiology* **37**, 92 (2000).
25. D. C. Jackson, J. R. Malmstadt, C. L. Larson, R. J. Davidson, *Psychophysiology*, in press.
26. D. C. Jackson, C. Burghy, A. Hanna, C. L. Larson, R. J. Davidson, unpublished data.
27. M. Davis, *J. Neuropsychiatry Clin. Neurosci.* **9**, 382 (1997).
28. S. R. Vrana, E. L. Spence, P. J. Lang, *J. Abnorm. Psychol.* **97**, 487 (1988).
29. P. J. Lang, *Am. Psychol.* **50**, 372 (1995).
30. R. J. Davidson, *Cognit. Emotion* **12**, 307 (1998).
31. ———, D. C. Jackson, C. L. Larson, in *Handbook of Psychophysiology*, J. T. Cacioppo, L. Tassinary, G. Bernston, Eds. (Cambridge Univ. Press, New York, 2000), pp. 27–52.
32. A. Bechara, H. Damasio, D. Tranel, A. R. Damasio, *Science* **275**, 1293 (1997).
33. M. A. Morgan, L. M. Romanski, J. E. LeDoux, *Neurosci. Lett.* **163**, 109 (1993).
34. J. C. Gewirtz, W. A. Falls, M. Davis, *Behav. Neurosci.* **111**, 712 (1997).
35. H. C. Abercrombie *et al.*, *Psychophysiology* **33**, 17 (1996).
36. S. M. Schaefer *et al.*, *Neurosci. Abstr.*, in press.
37. J. Volavka, *J. Clin. Psychiatry* **60** (suppl. 12), 43 (1999).
38. E. F. Coccaro, *Br. J. Psychiatry Suppl.* 52 (1989).
39. M. Virkkunen *et al.*, *Arch. Gen. Psychiatry* **51**, 20 (1994).
40. M. Linnoila, J. DeJong, M. Virkkunen, *Psychopharmacol. Bull.* **25**, 404 (1989).
41. A. Roy, B. Adinoff, M. Linnoila, *Psychiatry Res.* **24**, 187 (1988).
42. J. J. Mann, *Nature Med.* **4**, 25 (1998).
43. M. J. Kruesi *et al.*, *Arch. Gen. Psychiatry* **49**, 429 (1992).
44. M. Virkkunen *et al.*, *Arch. Gen. Psychiatry* **46**, 600 (1989).
45. M. Linnoila *et al.*, *Life Sci.* **33**, 2609 (1983).
46. M. Virkkunen, A. Nuutila, F. K. Goodwin, M. Linnoila, *Arch. Gen. Psychiatry* **44**, 241 (1987).
47. H. B. Moss, J. K. Yao, G. L. Panzak, *Biol. Psychiatry* **28**, 325 (1990).
48. S. B. Manuck *et al.*, *Neuropsychopharmacology* **19**, 287 (1998).
49. R. J. Wurtman, F. Hefti, E. Melamed, *Pharmacol. Rev.* **32**, 315 (1980).
50. J. M. Bjork *et al.*, *Psychopharmacology* **142**, 24 (1999).
51. A. J. Cleare and A. J. Bond, *Psychopharmacology* **118**, 72 (1995).
52. B. Chamberlain, F. R. Ervin, R. O. Pihl, S. N. Young, *Pharmacol. Biochem. Behav.* **28**, 503 (1987).
53. D. A. Nielsen *et al.*, *Arch. Gen. Psychiatry* **51**, 34 (1994).
54. S. B. Manuck *et al.*, *Biol. Psychiatry* **45**, 603 (1999).
55. F. Biver *et al.*, *Neurosci. Lett.* **204**, 25 (1996).
56. J. J. Mann *et al.*, *J. Cereb. Blood Flow Metab.* **16**, 418 (1996).
57. L. J. Siever *et al.*, *Neuropsychopharmacology* **20**, 413 (1999).
58. P. H. Soloff *et al.*, *Biol. Psychiatry* **47**, 540 (2000).
59. N. D. Volkow *et al.*, *Psychiatry Res.* **61**, 243 (1995).
60. P. F. Goyer *et al.*, *Neuropsychopharmacology* **10**, 21 (1994).
61. A. Raine *et al.*, *Biol. Psychiatry* **36**, 365 (1994).
62. A. Raine, M. Buchsbaum, L. LaCasse, *Biol. Psychiatry* **42**, 495 (1997).
63. A. Raine *et al.*, *Behav. Sci. Law* **16**, 319 (1998).
64. S. W. Anderson *et al.*, *Nature Neurosci.* **2**, 1032 (1999).
65. R. J. Blair and L. Cipolotti, *Brain* **123**, 1122 (2000).
66. A. Raine *et al.*, *Arch. Gen. Psychiatry* **57**, 119 (2000).
67. F. G. Woermann *et al.*, *J. Neurol. Neurosurg. Psychiatry* **68**, 162 (2000).
68. J. D. Higley *et al.* *Biol. Psychiatry* **40**, 1067 (1996).
69. J. R. Kaplan *et al.*, *Psychosoma. Med.* **56**, 479 (1994).
70. N. J. Emery and D. G. Amaral, in *The Cognitive Neuroscience of Emotion*, R. D. Lane and L. Nadal, Eds. (Oxford Univ. Press, New York, 2000), pp. 156–191.
71. D. Öngür and J. L. Price, *Cereb. Cortex* **10**, 206 (2000).
72. C. Cavada *et al.*, *Cereb. Cortex* **10**, 220 (2000).
73. A. Raine, P. Brennan, S. A. Mednick, *Am. J. Psychiatry* **154**, 1265 (1997).
74. E. F. Coccaro and R. J. Kavoussi, *Arch. Gen. Psychiatry* **54**, 1081 (1997).

75. Supported by NIMH grants MH43454, MH40747, P50-MH52354, and P50-MH61083, by Research Scientist Award K05-MH00875, by a grant from the Research Network on Mind-Body Interaction of the John D. and Catherine T. MacArthur Foundation (R.J.D.), by a National Alliance for Research on Schizophrenia and Depression (NARSAD) Young Investigator Award (K.M.P.), and by NRSA F31-MH12085 (C.L.L.). We thank W. Irwin, D. Jackson, T. Oakes, A. Jahn, J. Lindwall, C. Koepsel, and J. Topolovich for their help with manuscript preparation.

RESEARCH ON DIALECTICAL BEHAVIOR THERAPY FOR PATIENTS WITH BORDERLINE PERSONALITY DISORDER

Kelly Koerner, PhD, and Marsha M. Linehan, PhD

Dialectical behavior therapy (DBT),[29, 30] is a cognitive–behavioral treatment approach originally developed to treat chronically suicidal individuals. DBT has subsequently evolved into treatment for suicidal individuals who meet criteria for borderline personality disorder (BPD) and has been adapted for the treatment of patients with BPD with presenting problems other than suicidal behaviors (e.g., substance abuse). DBT combines basic behavioral procedures of skills training; exposure-based procedures; cognitive modification; contingency management; and problem solving with validation, mindfulness practices, reciprocity, and a focus on the patient–therapist relationship.

DBT is designed to be a comprehensive therapy for BPD patients at all levels of severity and complexity of disorder and is conceptualized as occurring in stages based on severity and complexity of disorder. As a comprehensive treatment, DBT serves five functions: (1) it enhances patient capabilities, (2) it improves patient motivation to change, (3) it ensures that new capabilities generalize to the natural environment, (4) it structures the environment in the ways essential to support patients' and therapists' capabilities, and (5) it enhances therapists' capabilities and motivation to treat patients effectively. In standard DBT, these functions are divided among modes of service delivery (e.g., psychoeducational skills training, individual psychotherapy).

From the Behavioral Technology Transfer Group (KK); and the Department of Psychology, University of Washington (MML), Seattle, Washington

As a treatment conducted according to stage of disorder, the primary focus is on stabilizing patients and achieving behavioral control. In stage 1, DBT addresses specific treatment targets in a hierarchical order of importance: (1) decreasing life-threatening and suicidal behaviors including parasuicide episodes; (2) decreasing behaviors that interfere with treatment, particularly noncompliance and premature dropout; (3) decreasing patterns that have a severe effect on quality of life, including Axis I problems and those that necessitate inpatient psychiatric care; and (4) increasing behavioral skills. Parasuicide is any acute, intentional, self-injurious behavior, with or without intent to die.[25] Subsequent to achieving behavioral control, it becomes possible to work on other important goals, including (5) increasing emotional experiencing and resolving posttraumatic stress responses (stage 2); (6) enhancing self-respect and (7) resolving problems in living (stage 3); and (8) enhancing the capacity for joy (stage 4). Treatment manuals and all research to date focus on severely multidisordered patients who enter treatment at stage 1.

As a manualized treatment, DBT has been rapidly adopted in community mental health settings. Public mental health outpatient services often focus on the needs of schizophrenic and bipolar patients,[43, 44] so DBT has been perceived as a way to improve services by specifically addressing treatment needs of patients diagnosed with BPD. Adequately addressing these needs poses several challenges. BPD is associated with worse outcomes across several Axis I diagnoses,[4, 5, 24, 43] indicating that standard treatments may be less effective with this patient group. Characteristics of suicidal BPD patients (e.g., suicide attempts, threats of suicide attempts, and anger) are among the factors reported by psychotherapists as extreme stressors.[20] In particular, legal and ethical concerns about patient suicide make it difficult to limit hospital use by patients with BPD who are suicidal and self-injurious,[44, 14] contributing to "revolving door" use of involuntary inpatient facilities, which may result in inadvertent iatrogenic effects. The outpatient treatment option of DBT has been discussed as an ethical alternative to involuntary commitment for chronically suicidal patients.[10] Consequently, because of the need of patients and mental health professionals to address these issues, dissemination of DBT proceeded quickly after initial data were published in 1991.

Implementation of DBT in community mental health settings has been described in several articles. For example, the American Psychiatric Association awarded the Community Mental Health Center of Greater Manchester in New Hampshire the 1998 Gold Achievement Award for the excellence of their small, community-based DBT program.[3] Articles have also described adaptations to partial hospital programs[48] and psychiatric inpatient units.[6, 47] Despite the multifaceted combination of treatment strategies in DBT, evidence shows that mental health professionals outside of academic research centers can learn DBT effectively.[19]

Particularly because DBT has been widely adopted as the treatment of choice for chronically suicidal patients with BPD, a critical review of the available evidence for the treatment approach is warranted. This article first reviews the research to date on DBT compared with treatment as usual (TAU) and compared with more rigorous control conditions and turns to the latest findings on DBT applied in new settings and adapted for new treatment populations.

DIALECTICAL BEHAVIOR THERAPY COMPARED WITH TREATMENT AS USUAL

Despite its public health significance, little research is available on the psychosocial treatment of suicidal behavior, and less is available on the treatment of suicidal behavior and other severe dysfunctional behavior among patients meeting criteria for BPD.[36] Therefore, the first criteria of evaluating DBT is to determine the feasibility of the treatment to work for the intended problems compared with TAU. But because by definition a naturalistic TAU control group requires investigators to exert no experimental control over TAU, the lack of experimental control over important variables restricts the conclusions that can be drawn from this design. Nevertheless, the design is sufficiently rigorous to determine whether DBT shows promise as an effective treatment and merits further study.

Linehan et al[31, 34, 35] published post-treatment outcomes and 6-month and 12-month post-treatment follow-up data. This randomized trial was conducted in two cohorts (n = 47), and interpersonal outcome measures were added for the second cohort of this sample (n = 26).[37] Investigators compared outcomes for chronically suicidal women who met criteria for BPD[2, 18] and who had at least two incidents of parasuicide in the past 5 years with one during the past 8 weeks. Subjects were excluded if they met DSM-III criteria for schizophrenia, bipolar disorder, substance dependence, or mental retardation. DBT and TAU subjects were matched on the number of lifetime parasuicides and psychiatric hospitalizations, age, and good versus poor clinical prognosis (with a subthreshold diagnosis on schizophrenia or substance dependence constituting poor prognosis). Participants were randomly assigned to DBT (n = 24) or TAU in the community (n = 23). No significant pretreatment differences were observed between conditions on lifetime parasuicide, psychiatric hospitalizations, Diagnostic Interview for Borderlines (DIB) scores, depression, hopelessness, suicide ideation, reasons for living, age, employment, or marital status.

As hypothesized, those who received DBT showed reduced parasuicidal behavior, better treatment retention, and fewer days of inpatient psychiatric hospitalization. At each assessment point and at year total, the mean number of parasuicide acts among those in TAU was significantly more than with DBT.[31] Those in DBT had less medically severe parasuicide over the year, but no significant difference in proportion of parasuicides that were suicide attempts was found.

Dialectical behavior therapy was also more effective than TAU at limiting treatment dropout. Individuals assigned to DBT were significantly more likely to start treatment (DBT 100%, TAU 73%) and significantly more of those in DBT retained their therapists for the entire year (DBT 83.3%, TAU 42%). Those in DBT had significantly fewer inpatient psychiatric days per patient and a trend for fewer psychiatric admissions, but the proportion of individuals with at least one hospitalization during the treatment year did not differ significantly among groups (DBT 36%, TAU 55%).

After controlling for pretreatment scores, individuals in DBT and TAU improved on measures of depression, (n = 7) suicidal ideation (n = 8), hopelessness (n = 9) and reasons for living post-treatment. No treatment condition × time interactions were observed, nor did either group improve sufficiently to score within the range of unimpaired functioning. TAU and DBT groups did not significantly differ on use of psychotropic medications (no figures or types of medications were reported).

Additional data on interpersonal outcomes were collected from a subsample, the second cohort (n = 26; DBT = 13, TAU = 13) of the full sample (N = 47). Individuals in DBT reported less anger and better self-reported global social adjustment and interviewer-rated global adjustment than those in TAU.[37] Because the TAU group reported higher rates of medication use (antidepressants, neuroleptics, and anxiolytics) during the treatment year, positive results were not likely the result of medication use in the DBT group.

Outcomes for those in DBT were largely maintained during the 6-month and 1-year follow-up period. At 6 months after treatment, those who had received DBT had significantly fewer parasuicide episodes and fewer medically treated episodes, less anger, better self-reported social adjustment, and better employment performance. During the one-year post-treatment follow-up period, the parasuicide repeat rate was significantly lower for the DBT (26%) versus the TAU (60%) group. At 12 months after treatment, however, the DBT and TAU groups did not differ significantly on parasuicide episodes nor on medically treated episodes. At 12 months after treatment, those who had received DBT continued to have significantly fewer days of psychiatric hospitalization, better global adjustment and interviewer-rated social adjustment and employment performance, and showed a trend toward less likelihood of hospitalization.[35] These follow-up data seem to indicate that those who receive DBT improve their level of functioning and maintain these gains relative to TAU over follow-up. DBT seems to produce changes in parasuicide more quickly than TAU, but those in TAU eventually improve to similarly lowered rates of parasuicide by 12 months after treatment.

These data suggest that DBT was more effective than TAU in reducing targeted problem behaviors. However, although TAU is a reasonable first research strategy for treatment development, the lack of experimental control over important variables means competing explanations for these findings are possible. For example, although the DBT and TAU groups received equal amounts of therapy, the two groups differed in type of treatment hours received. Those in DBT reported receiving more group and individual treatment, and those in TAU, more day treatment hours per week. Nonetheless, post hoc analyses found no significant relationships among amount and type of treatment and any dependent variables.[34] Individual treatment hours, outpatient hours, or both did not significantly predict the number of parasuicidal episodes, but stable outpatient treatment (individual or group) may account for effects. Post hoc analyses examined this possibility by comparing those in DBT (n = 20) with those in TAU who had stable individual psychotherapy during the treatment year (n = 9). When number of hours of psychotherapy and of telephone contacts were controlled, those in DBT had fewer parasuicide acts (but not significant differences in medical risk) and fewer days of inpatient psychiatric hospitalization.[36] These analyses seem to indicate that total number of hours, number of hours of individual therapy, number of hours of partial hospitalization, and number of hours of inpatient treatment did not predict any dependent variable in this study.

Two additional randomized clinical trials investigating DBT versus TAU have been conducted and presented in a peer-reviewed setting. Koons et al[23] conducted a small study (n = 20) in a Veterans Administration clinic and reported outcomes after 6 months of weekly comprehensive standard DBT compared with 6 months of usual Veterans Administration treatment. Participants were female veterans who met criteria for BPD but, different from in the study by Linehan et al,[31] were not required to have had a history of parasuicide or a recent parasuicide. This resulted in a sample that was less parasuicidal and less frequently hospitalized than those in the study by Linehan et al.[31] Therapists in the TAU condition described their orientation to individual therapy as cognitive–behavioral. Koons et al[23] found that those in DBT had more reduction in suicidal ideation, depression, hopelessness, and anger than those in TAU after treatment. Those in DBT showed a trend toward significantly fewer psychiatric hospital admissions and inpatient days (however, both groups had low pretreatment frequency of hospitalization). Interestingly, both treatment conditions had good treatment retention, and both groups showed significant decreases in depression, with 60% of those in DBT and 20% of those in TAU showing clinically significant change on the Beck Depression Inventory.[7]

Linehan et al[26] have also reported outcomes from a third randomized clinical trial (n = 28) comparing an adaptation of comprehensive standard DBT for substance abusers dually diagnosed with BPD to TAU. The major modifications to standard DBT were the addition of (1) specific targets relevant to drug use, (2) a set of attachment strategies intended to enhance patients' connection to therapy and the treatment team, (3) a drug-replacement program, (4) three-times-weekly urinalyses, and (5) case management.[28] Subjects meeting criteria for BPD and for polysubstance-use disorder or substance-use disorder for amphetamines, anxiolytics, cocaine, cannabis, hypnotics, opiates, or sedatives were randomly assigned to DBT (n = 12) or TAU (n = 16) for 1 year of treatment. Subjects were assessed at 4, 8, 12, and 16 months. Subjects assigned to DBT had significantly more reductions in drug abuse measured by structured interviews and urinalyses throughout the treatment year and at follow-up than did subjects assigned to TAU. The DBT group had significantly more retention (64% retention in DBT, 27% retention in TAU). No significant differences were found in amount of medical and psychiatric inpatient treatment received during the course of treatment. Although no significant differences were found between the groups during treatment or at 12-month follow-up, those in DBT showed significantly more gains in global and social adjustment and state and trait anger at follow-up compared with those in TAU.

Stanley et al[49] have presented findings on a nonrandomized pilot project comparing standard, comprehensive DBT to a matched group of suicidal patients with BPD. They conducted a small pilot study (n = 30) examining the efficacy of 6 months of treatment, comparing DBT with TAU. The baseline mean number of suicide attempts did not differ among the DBT and TAU groups. No between-group differences in self-reported psychopathology (e.g., assessments of Beck Hopelessness Scale, Hamilton Depression Scale,[42] Beck Depression Inventory, and Global Assessment Scale) were observed, but the investigators found that patients in DBT had greater reductions in self-mutilation acts, suicide ideation, suicidal urges, and urges to self-mutilate than did subjects who received TAU. Neither group had suicide attempts.

Across these studies, each found reductions in the targeted problem areas compared with TAU. In the more severely impaired populations of individuals with BPD, DBT may reduce parasuicidal behavior and substance abuse, increase treatment retention, and improve global functioning. With a less severe population of patients with BPD, DBT seems to produce specific improvements in suicidal ideation, depression and hopelessness, even compared with patients with a TAU condition that also produces clinically significant changes in depression. Available follow-up data seem to indicate that these results may hold up to 1 year after treatment. The studies by Koons et al[23] and Stanley et al[49] suggest that investigators other than the treatment developer can produce good clinical outcomes and that a 6-month treatment may have efficacy. Taken as a group, these findings suggest that effects are likely caused by DBT, but the TAU comparison design does not allow sufficient experimental control to conclude that strongly. Thus, whether DBT is responsible for treatment gains or simply the use of a well-organized psychotherapy remains a question. Data from Koons et al[23] suggest that such may be the case, but their population was also less disordered than in the two randomized clinical trials from Linehan's group. From these studies, the question remains of whether the results are attributable to the efficacy of DBT or to any of a number of competing factors, including: (1) therapist factors (i.e., expertise and training or clinical experience), (2) availability of clinical supervision, (3) hours of individual psychotherapy offered, (4) general factors associated with receiving any psychotherapy, (5) institutional prestige associated with receiving treatment in a university setting for the DBT condition, or (6) other factors associated with design flaws.

RANDOMIZED CLINICAL TRIALS OF DIALECTICAL BEHAVIOR THERAPY VERSUS MORE RIGOROUS CONTROL CONDITIONS

Preliminary findings from two additional randomized clinical trials underway at the University of Washington have been reported.[32, 33] In these studies, Linehan et al[32, 33] evaluated the efficacy of DBT by comparing it with more rigorous control conditions developed specifically to maximize internal validity and to control for effects on clinical outcomes by factors not controlled for in previous DBT studies.

In a replication study[32] treating individuals with BPD and parasuicidal behavior, DBT was compared with a more rigorous control condition—treatment by experts in the community (TBE). TBE therapists were nominated by community mental health leaders (i.e., heads of inpatient psychiatric units; clinical directors of mental health agencies; and training directors of psychiatry, psychology, social work, and nursing) as experts experienced with BPD and suicidal patients (controlling for therapist expertise). TBE therapists were asked to provide the therapy they believed most suited to the patient they were treating, and the content of the treatment they provided was not interfered with or controlled by the research study (controlling for therapist allegiance to treatment provided). Clinical supervision was provided to TBE therapists by a well-respected expert supervisor (therapists were paid to attend, controlling for the availability of clinical supervision). As with the DBT consultation team function, the purpose of supervision was to assist therapists in doing psychotherapy to the best of their abilities, to provide an opportunity for therapists to get support from their peers, and to be on call for therapists in emergencies. The TBE condition was associated with an institution committed to excellence (Seattle Institute for Psychoanalysis, controlling for institutional prestige associated with therapy offered). The study paid (at the same rate of pay) for psychotherapy in both conditions, and subjects were required to pay only a small amount on a sliding fee (controlling for availability of affordable treatment and for hours of individual psychotherapy offered). TBE therapists were matched on treatment-relevant variables (controlling for therapist gender, training, and clinical experience).

Preliminary data analyses from 4-month assessments of this more rigorous replication design[32] showed promising results generally favoring DBT on reduction of suicidal behaviors, greater treatment retention, and decreased use of psychiatric inpatient hospitalization and emergency services.

Thus, with better experimental control, these preliminary results seem to replicate the earlier findings and suggest the efficacy of DBT as a treatment for chronically suicidal individuals.

Linehan et al[33] have also replicated DBT for Substance Abusers (DBT-S) for individuals with BPD and opiate addiction in a second randomized clinical trial with a more rigorous control condition. This is a replication of a pilot trial that compared an adapted version of DBT for substance abusers with TAU. In this "dismantling" study, a component control treatment, DBT-Validation (DBT-V), was used to examine which components of DBT are necessary for change. The rationale for DBT-V is based on the work of Swann as interpreted by Linehan[27] for the treatment of drug abusers. The rationale suggests that emotion dysregulation (and, by extension, BPD) is related to previous experiences in invalidating environments that inhibit individuals' natural responses to situations and teach them to invalidate their own natural responses. This inability to self-validate precipitates extreme emotional arousal and a sense of loss of control when important people invalidate these individuals. Clinical progress requires therapists' use of validation procedures, communicating to patients that they can trust themselves and reinforcing self-verification even when the environment is invalidating. In this control condition, the only focus on patient change concerns patients' attendance at psychotherapy, Narcotics Anonymous meetings, and meetings with sponsors. Preliminary findings from this outcome study provide strong and compelling case for the role of validation in working with substance-dependent women with BPD. All participants were retained for the entire duration of the 12-month treatment program in DBT-V; 64% were retained in DBT. Both treatments performed comparably, as measured by self-report and thrice-weekly urinalyses, in reducing substance abuse over time. By the completion of treatment, 68% of participants in DBT reported abstaining from drug use in the prior month compared with 55% in DBT-V. Rates of abstinence held through 16 months for patients in DBT and increased to 65% abstinent in DBT-V. These preliminary findings from more rigorously controlled studies suggest that the earlier findings of improved outcomes may be robust and that the treatment effects may be the result of DBT and not other factors.

RESULTS FROM EFFECTIVENESS STUDIES: QUASIEXPERIMENTAL DESIGNS AND NONSTANDARD DIALECTICAL BEHAVIOR THERAPY

Several quasiexperimental studies from program evaluations, pilot studies, and preliminary work as part of randomized clinical trials have been presented, expanding the research base on the efficacy of DBT in other settings compared with different controls or extended to different treatment populations. Often, these studies do not investigate comprehensive standard DBT but rather investigate a component of the comprehensive package or a modification of standard components. Consequently, the findings from these studies are limited but suggestive when taken as a group and integrated with more rigorous data.

Three studies have investigated DBT adapted for inpatient settings. Barley et al[6] applied DBT to an inpatient personality disorder psychiatric unit. Participants were 130 patients (79% women) discharged from this unit following a typical length of stay of approximately 100 days. DBT interventions included individual therapy by psychiatrists, group skills training led by a clinical psychologist, DBT homework group led by nurses, an introduction and orientation to DBT for incoming patients and incorporation of DBT into the unit milieu, the privilege system and staff meetings.

The average suicide rates for the 19 months before the introduction of DBT, 10 months while DBT was being introduced, and 14 months when DBT was fully in operation. They found that the parasuicide rate on the unit was lower under full DBT than during either prior period. During the same time, average rates of parasuicide on a general psychiatric unit that followed a traditional approach did not change and were higher than on the DBT unit.

In a second study, Springer et al[47] used a quasi-experimental design to compare outcomes for patients on a brief-stay inpatient personality disorder unit who received treatment from a Creative Coping Group that incorporated a subset of DBT skills or from a TAU festyles and wellness discussion group. Patients in both groups attended an average of six sessions and improved during their hospital stays. Those in the Creative Coping Group were more likely to believe that the lessons learned in the group would help them after discharge, but the investigators note that patients in the Creative Coping Group were significantly more like to "act out" during hospitalization and attribute this to discussing parasuicidal behavior in the group, leading perhaps to a contagion effect. Linehan's Skills Training Manual[30] explicitly cautions that parasuicide should not be discussed in group therapy because of this risk. Because of the significant differences from standard DBT skills group (i.e., modified use of skills modules and discussion of parasuicide in group), these findings are limited but suggest caution when modifying DBT and the importance of evaluating program outcomes.

In a third study of DBT in an inpatient setting, Bohus et al[12] reported pre-post data for an inpatient DBT protocol that included DBT individual psychotherapy, group skills training, and skills coaching provided in the milieu. Study participants were 24 female patients who met criteria for BPD according to DIB-R (8 points) and DSM-IV (at least five criteria) and who had at least two parasuicide acts within the past 2 years. Patients were excluded if they met criteria for schizophrenia, bipolar I disorders, alcohol or drug dependence (current or within the last 6-months), or if suicide attempts or self-injurious behavior occurred only during episodes of major depression or under the influence of alcohol or drugs. Frequency of parasuicide and psychopathology were assessed on admission to the hospital, at discharge, and at 1 month after discharge. The investigators found significantly fewer parasuicidal acts and significant improvements in ratings of depression, dissociation, anxiety, and global stress. The reported effect sizes suggest strong effects and indicate that BPD patients not only do not decompensate but may perhaps show some benefit from a more comprehensive DBT inpatient treatment.

Dialectical behavior therapy can be successfully modified into brief interventions. Evans et al[54] conducted a randomized controlled trial (N

= 34) comparing manual-assisted cognitive–behavioral brief intervention (MACT) with TAU. MACT is a problem-focused psychotherapy (i.e., problem-solving and basic cognitive techniques are taught to manage emotions and prevent relapse) with accompanying brief bibliotherapy. MACT incorporated the behavioral chain analysis of parasuicide episodes and a subset of skills from the DBT distress-tolerance module. Patients were included in the study if they had a recent episode of deliberate self-harm and at least one other episode of parasuicide in the past year and a Cluster B personality disorder. Exposure to MACT ranged from two to six sessions. During the 6-month assessment period, 10 subjects (56% MACT, 71% TAU) engaged in parasuicidal behavior. The rate of parasuicidal acts per month was lower with MACT than TAU (median, 0.17 acts mo versus 0.37 acts mo, respectively). This finding was not statistically significant ($p = 0.11$), which may be the result of a lack of statistical power. A statistically significant difference between conditions was noted on self-report of depression favoring MACT. The observed average cost of care was 46% less with MACT.

One study applying DBT to depressed and suicidal adolescents has been conducted. Miller et al[41] conducted a nonrandomized, controlled pilot study to examine whether DBT for adolescents[40] is more effective than TAU at reducing suicide attempts, reducing psychiatric hospitalization, and increasing treatment completion. Referrals (n = 111) to an adolescent depression and suicide program in the Bronx (78% female, 22% male) who also had made a suicide attempt within the past 16 weeks or had current suicide ideation and who had a diagnosis of BPD or a minimum of three borderline personality features (measured by the Structured Clinical Interview for DSM-IV Axis II Personality Disorders) were included in this study. TAU consisted of 12 weeks of twice-weekly individual and family sessions. DBT for Adolescents (DBT-A) consisted of 12 weeks of twice-weekly individual and multifamily skills training. Modifications to standard DBT included the addition of as-needed family therapy (added onto individual therapy), inclusion of family members in a skills-training group, modifications to the skills, training handouts to make them easier for teens to use, and fewer skills from each module taught. Because of nonrandom assignment, the DBT-A group had lower socioeconomic status, was more ethnically diverse, and was more severely impaired than was the TAU group at pretreatment. They found significant differences in psychiatric hospitalization (DBT-A 0%, TAU 13%) and that those in DBT-A demonstrated significantly increased treatment completion rates (DBT-A 62%, TAU 40%). The researchers found no significant difference in the number of suicide attempts among the groups, but because those in the DBT-A group were diagnosed with more Axis I disorders, were more impulsive, and had more prior hospitalizations, the investigators noted that the fact that they were no more suicidal may represent a treatment effect.

Two studies have reported data from the application of DBT in forensic psychiatric hospitals or the mental health units of criminal justice settings. McCann and Ball[39] used a quasiexperimental design to compare DBT (n = 21) with TAU (n = 14) in primarily male forensic inpatients residing on intermediate-security and medium-security wards, most of whom had committed violent crimes. TAU was defined as "individualized supportive care combining psychotropic medications, individual and group therapy." DBT included DBT individual therapy, skills training and milieu skills coaching, as well as patients' use of chain analysis subsequent to problematic behavior while hospitalized. DBT and TAU patients were compared over a 20-month period. Half of all patients met full criteria for BPD, and the remaining patients met at least three DSM-IV criteria for BPD. Half of the patients met full criteria for antisocial personality disorder. Most patients also carried concommitant Axis I diagnoses, such as schizophrenia or bipolar disorder. DBT patients' depressed or hostile mood, paranoia, and psychotic symptoms significantly decreased during the study period. Similarly, DBT patients had significantly decreased maladaptive interpersonal coping styles (e.g., blaming themselves, blaming others, and avoidance) and increased adaptive coping strategy (e.g., seeking social support). TAU patients did not change significantly on these measures. McCann and Ball also report the effect of DBT on forensic staff (n = 54). DBT staff on the intermediate unit significantly improved on two of three subscales of the Maslach Burnout Inventory[38] and showed a trend in the third in comparison to the TAU staff.

Trupin et al (unpublished observations) compared preoutcomes and postoutcomes of juvenile female offenders residing in the mental health cottage of a correctional facility that incorporated DBT individual psychotherapy, skills training, and milieu coaching with outcomes of juvenile female offenders in a similar cottage receiving TAU programming. The two cottages were not significantly different in percentage with Axis I diagnoses or number of prior offenses, but the percentage of those with extraordinary sentences (more serious crimes) and rates of aggressive and suicidal behavior were significantly higher in the DBT cottage. Behavior problems (i.e., aggression, parasuicide, and class disruption) significantly decreased in the DBT cottage during intervention compared with the comparison cottage and with the 10-month period before intervention. Staff in the DBT cottage used fewer restrictive punitive responses (e.g., room confinement, placing youth on suicide precaution levels, and class suspensions) during the DBT intervention compared with the 10 months before intervention. Following the DBT intervention, youth showed significantly improved transition to and participation in on-campus therapeutic, educational, and vocational services (e.g., keeping a full-time job on campus, completing a GED, completing a drug and alcohol abuse treatment program, and transitioning to an open cottage). No significant difference, however, was found in community risk-assessment scores for those in DBT compared with female offenders in the general population matched for initial risk and severity of mental health symptoms.

Telch et al[50] have reported preliminary pilot data on DBT adapted to treatment of binge-eating disorder. The adaptation was based on the theoretic model that binge eating functions as affect regulation and, therefore, that teaching adaptive emotion-regulation skills eliminates maladaptive emotion-regulation behaviors. Telch et al[50] developed a 20-session group format that modified DBT to binge-eating problems by tailoring the treatment target hierarchy and creating experiential exercises to teach and strengthen skills (e.g., mindful eating exercises). Telch et al[50] also made the treatment distinct from interpersonal psychotherapy (by removing the interpersonal effectiveness module) and distinct from standard cognitive–behavioral therapy for eating disorders (i.e., standard CBT components, e.g., self-monitoring of food intake, prescriptions for normalization of eating, and meal patterning or cognitive restructuring of weight and shape concerns were not included). Data from a small (n = 11) pre–post design are promising; the number of binge episodes and binge days decreased significantly from baseline to post-treatment, and participants also had weight loss. At 3-month and 6-month post-treatment, participants showed strong continued abstinence from binge eating and maintenance of lower weight. Telch et al[50] report having no dropout from treatment and good attendance. Interestingly, Telch et al[50] also report changes in emotion regulation abilities that are independent of changes in emotion experience, suggesting that the treatment may have helped participants became more skillful in responding to negative emotions rather than reducing negative emotions directly.

These preliminary findings suggest that DBT may have promise and warrant further investigation as an inpatient protocol, as a treatment for suicidal behavior in adolescents, and as it is applied within forensic and criminal justice settings. DBT may also be usefully adapted to other disorders in which dysfunctional behaviors regulate emotion, such as binge-eating disorder.

DATA ON MECHANISMS OF CHANGE IN DIALECTICAL BEHAVIOR THERAPY

A few studies provide data regarding mechanisms of change in DBT. Conducted simultaneously with the first randomized clinical trial, Linehan et al[29] investigated the effectiveness of a DBT skills-training group (GST) alone (i.e., without individual psychotherapy, skills coaching, or a therapist consultation team). Suicidal women with BPD (n = 19) were referred by their current and continuing non-DBT individual counselors or psychotherapists for DBT skills training and were randomly assigned to DBT-GST (n = 11) and to the non–DBT-GST treatment control (n = 8). Other than their therapy status, no significant pretreatment differences were found between subjects in this study and those in the first randomized clinical trial. Results suggested that DBT-GST provided with no skills coaching was not effective as an additive treatment to ongoing, non-DBT individual psychotherapy. No significant between-group differences were found on any variable, nor did means or effect sizes suggest that the absence of results was caused by the small sample size.

These null findings suggest that simple expectancies associated with an experimental study are insufficient to produce clinical improvements. Also, although DBT-GST may offer no benefit when added to non-DBT psychotherapy, one cannot conclude that DBT-GST is ineffective or unimportant when offered within the standard DBT format. The integration of individual and GST may be key to the success of standard DBT. Alternatively, therapists' consultation team may play a role in producing treatment outcomes (although the TBE condition included therapist consultation). Component analyses are needed to determine the merit of different components.

Along these lines, the emphasis on ensuring skills generalization may play a role in producing outcomes. Standard DBT uses as-needed telephone coaching or milieu coaching to help generalize the skills learned in therapy and makes these offers of additional help noncontingent on extreme or dysfunctional behavior; patients can contact their therapists before engaging in parasuicide, but not after. Although the mean number of calls per month did not differ significantly between the DBT and TAU groups, the contingency between mean number of parasuicide episodes and mean number of calls to therapists was significantly and positively correlated in the TAU group but not in the DBT group.[34]

Shearin and Linehan[46] reported findings on DBT processes associated with better outcomes in DBT. They predicted that therapists' balancing of treatment strategies (i.e., focus on acceptance with a corresponding focus on change) would be related to outcomes. For example, they hypothesized that suicidal behavior (parasuicide urges and suicidal ideation) would decrease in the weeks following patient ratings of the therapist as simultaneously being accepting (giving autonomy) and endorsing change (being controlling and nurturing), but either alone would not be associated with decreased suicidal behavior. Four therapist–patient dyads completed weekly Structured Analyses of Social Behavior[11] rating scales and weekly diary cards. Graduate clinical psychology students and registered nurses in training served as therapists. Results indicated that reductions in weekly suicidal behaviors were related to the previous weeks rating of their therapists' interactions with them. A dialectical pattern of ratings (high on therapist giving autonomy and exerting control) explained more variance than giving autonomy (i.e., focus on acceptance) or exerting control (i.e., focus on change).

Although preliminary, these studies are suggestive of directions that merit additional research. Certain therapist–patient interactions may be related to subsequent reduction in parasuicide; ensuring generalization of skills training to situations beyond therapy may be important to producing good outcomes; providing this help in a manner that is noncontingent on increased suicidal behavior may differentiate DBT from TAU; and patient experience of therapists as giving autonomy while being controlling and nurturing may each contribute to reduction in parasuicide.

SUMMARY

Research evidence to date indicates that, although DBT was developed for the treatment of patients with suicidal behavior, it can be adapted to treat BPD patients with comorbid substance-abuse disorder and be extended to other patient populations and the treatment of other disorders. Across studies, DBT seems to reduce severe dysfunctional behaviors that are targeted for intervention (e.g., parasuicide, substance abuse, and binge eating), enhance treatment retention, and reduce psychiatric hospitalization. Evidence suggests that additional research is warranted to examine which components of DBT contribute to outcomes. Although preliminary, skills coaching seems to be a crucial ingredient in producing reductions in parasuicidal behavior, and specific strategies (e.g., validation, balance of change, and acceptance interventions) may play an important role in positive behavioral change.

Several investigators are evaluating the efficacy of DBT. For example, Asberg et al at the Karolinska Institute in Sweden have begun a pilot study comparing DBT for women who have made multiple suicide attempts to transference focus psychotherapy, a psychodynamic therapy developed by Kernberg. They have planned a randomized clinical trial to compare DBT and transference focus psychotherapy with TAU in the community. van den Bosch[51] has completed a randomized clinical trial for women who met criteria for BPD and substance abuse comparing DBT-S with TAU. Lynch is conducting a randomized clinical trial examining the efficacy of DBT skills training plus medication versus medication only for the treatment of moderate to severe depression in the elderly. Results from these studies should become available over the next several years, providing further empiric evidence by which to evaluate the efficacy of DBT.

Additional development of DBT seems warranted to improve its efficacy, and additional investigation is needed to establish its effectiveness in public health settings. Analyses from existing data sets of factors that predict treatment response and elements of the treatment that contribute to outcome are needed. Also, longitudinal follow-up studies to determine suicide rates and maintenance of treatment gains are needed. Because DBT has been adopted in a variety of clinical settings, effectiveness studies are needed. Given the difficulty of conducting treatment research with chronically suicidal individuals, perhaps the largest challenge to further treatment development is recruiting young investigators who are willing to conduct research in this area. Nevertheless, in the 6 years since the treatment manuals were published, DBT seems to be a step toward more effective treatment for severely multidisordered patients.

References

1. American Psychiatric Association: Diagnostic and Statistical Manual of Mental Disorders, ed 4. Washington, DC; American Psychiatric Press, 1995
2. American Psychiatric Association: Diagnostic and Statistical Manual of Mental Disorders, ed 3. Washington, DC, American Psychiatric Press, 1980
3. American Psychiatric Association Gold Award: Integrating Dialectical Behavioral Therapy into a community mental health program. Psychiatr Serv 49:1338–1340, 1998
4. Ames-Frankel J, Devlin MJ, Walsh T, et al: Personality disorder diagnoses in patients with bulimia nervosa: Clinical correlates and changes with treatment. J Clin Psychiatry 53:90, 1992
5. Baer L, Jenike MA, Black DW, et al: Effect of axis II diagnoses on treatment outcome with clomipramine in 55 patients with obsessive–compulsive disorder. Arch Gen Psychiatry 49:862, 1992
6. Barley WD, Buie SE, Peterson EW, et al: Development of an inpatient cognitive–behavioral treatment program for borderline personality disorder. J Pers 7:232, 1993
7. Beck AT, Ward CH, Mendelson M, et al: An inventory for measuring depression. Arch Gen Psychiatry 4:561, 1961
8. Beck AT, Kovacs M, Weissman MM: Assessment of suicidal ideation: The scale for suicidal ideation. J Consult Clin Psychol 47:343, 1979
9. Beck AT, Weissman A, Lester D, et al: The measurement of pessimism: The hopelessness scale. J Consult Clin Psychol 42:6, 1974
10. Behnke SH, Saks ER: Therapeutic jurisprudence: Informed consent as a clinical indication for the chronically suicidal patient with borderline personality disorder. Loyola Law Review 31:945, 1998
11. Benjamin LS: Structural Analysis of Social Behavior Psychological Review 81:392, 1974
12. Bohus M, Haaf B, Stiglmayr C, et al: Evaluation of inpatient dialectical-behavioral therapy for borderline personality disorder: A prospective study. Behav Res Ther, in press
13. Coker S, Vize C, Wade T, et al: Patients with bulimia nervosa who fail to engage in cognitive behavior therapy. Int J Eat Disord 13:35, 1993
14. Fine MA, Sansone RA: Dilemmas in the management of suicidal behavior in individuals with borderline personality disorder. Am J Psychother 44:160, 1990
15. First MB, Spitzer RL, Gibbon M, et al: Structured Clinical Interview for Axis I DSM-IV Disorders: Patient Edition (SCID-I/P). New York, Biometrics Research Department, New York State Psychiatric Institute, 1995
16. First MB, Spitzer RL, Gibbons M, et al: User's Guide for the Structured Clinical Interview for DSM-IV Axis II Personality Disorders (SCID-II). New York, Biometrics Research Department, New York State Psychiatric Institute, 1996
17. Geller JL: In again, out again: Preliminary evaluation of a state hospital's worst recidivists. Hospital and Community Psychiatry 37:386, 1986
18. Gunderson JG, Kolb JE, Austin V: The diagnostic interview for borderlines. Am J Psychiatry 138:896, 1981
19. Hawkins KA, Sinha R: Can line clinicians master the conceptual complexities of dialectical behavior therapy? An evaluation of a State Department of Mental Health training program. J Psychiatr Res 32:379–384, 1998
20. Hellman ID, Morrison TL, Abramowitz SI: The stresses of psychotherapeutic work: A replication and extension. J Clin Psychol 42:197, 1986
21. Katz SE, Levendusky PG: Cognitive behavioral approaches to treating borderline and self-mutilating patients. Bull Menninger Clin 54:398, 1990
22. Keller MB, Lavori PW, Friedman B, et al: The longitudinal interval follow-up evaluation: A comprehensive method for assessing outcome in prospective longitudinal studies. Arch Gen Psychiatry, 44:540–548, 1987
23. Koons CR, Robins CJ, Bishop GK, et al: Efficacy of dialectical behavior therapy with borderline women veterans: A randomized controlled trial. Presented at the 32nd Annual Meeting of the Association for the Advancement of Behavior Therapy. Washington, DC, November 1998

24. Kosten RA, Kosten TR, Rounsaville BJ: Personality disorders in opiate addicts show prognostic specificity. J Subst Abuse Treat 6:163, 1989
25. Kreitman N: Parasuicide. London, John Wiley & Sons, 1977
26. Linehan M, Schmidt H, Dimeff L, et al: Dialectical behavior therapy for patients with borderline personality disorder and drug-dependence. Am J Addict, in press
27. Linehan MM: Self-verification and drug abusers: Implications for treatment. Psychol Sci 8:1–3, 1997
28. Linehan MM, Dimeff LA: Dialectical Behavior Therapy Manual of Treatment Interventions for Drug Abusers with Borderline Personality Disorder. Seattle, University of Washington, 1997
29. Linehan MM: Cognitive Behavioral Treatment of Borderline Personality Disorder. New York, Guilford Press, 1993
30. Linehan MM: Skills Training Manual for Treating Borderline Personality Disorder. New York, Guilford Press, 1993
31. Linehan MM, Armstrong HE, Suarez A, et al: Cognitive behavioral treatment of chronically parasuicidal borderline patients. Arch Gen Psychiatry 48:1060, 1991
32. Linehan MM, Comtois KA, Koerner K, et al: University of Washington Study of Dialectical Behavior Therapy: A preliminary report. Presented at the 32nd Annual Meeting of the Association of the Advancement of Behavior Therapy. Washington, DC, November 1998
33. Linehan MM, Dimeff LA, Comtois KA, et al: Dialectical behavior therapy for opiate abusers with borderline personality disorder: Findings to date from two randomized controlled trials. Presented at the 32nd Annual Meeting of the Association for the Advancement of Behavior Therapy. Washington, DC, 1998
34. Linehan MM, Heard HL: Impact of treatment accessibility on clinical course of parasuicidal patients: Reply [letter]. Arch Gen Psychiatry 50:157, 1993
35. Linehan MM, Heard HL, Armstrong HE: Naturalistic follow up of a behavioral treatment for chronically parasuicidal borderline patients. Arch Gen Psychiatry 50:971, 1993
36. Linehan MM, Rizvi SL, Shaw S, et al: Suicide and personality disorders. *In* Hawton K, van Heeringen K (eds): International Handbook of Suicide and Attempted Suicide. Sussex, England, John Wiley & Sons, in press
37. Linehan MM, Tutek DA, Heard HL, et al: Interpersonal outcome of cognitive behavioral treatment for chronically suicidal borderline patients. Am J Psychiatry 151:1771, 1994
38. Maslach C, Jackson SE: Maslach Burnout Inventory Manual, ed 2. Palo Alto, CA, Consulting Psychologists Press, 1986
39. McCann RA, Ball EM: Using dialectical behavior therapy with an inpatient forensic population. Presented at the 1st Annual Meeting of the International Society for the Improvement and Teaching of Dialectical Behavior Therapy. New York, November 1996
40. Miller A, Rathus JH, Linehan MM, et al: Dialectical behavior therapy adapted for suicidal adolescents. J Pract Psychiatry Behav Health 3:78, 1997
41. Miller AL, Rathus JH, Leigh E: Dialectical behavior therapy adapted for suicidal adolsecents. *In* Rathus JH (ed): Dialectical Behavior Therapy: Adaptations for New Modes and New Populations. Presented at the 30th Annual Meeting of the Association for the Advancement of Behavior Therapy. New York, November 1996
42. Miller IW, Bishop SB, Norman WH, et al: The Modified Hamilton Rating Scale for Depression: Reliability and validity. Psychiatry Res 14:131, 1985
43. Phillips KA, Nierenberg AA: The assessment and treatment of refractory depression. J Clin Psychiatry 55:20, 1994
44. Rascati JN: Managed care and the discharge dilemma: Commentary. Psychiatry 53:124, 1990
45. Rissmiller DJ, Steer R, Ranieri WF, et al: Factors complicating cost containment in the treatment of suicidal patients. Hospital and Community Psychiatry 45:782, 1994
46. Shearin EN, Linehan MM: Patient-therapist ratings and relationship to progress in dialectical behavior therapy for borderline personality disorder. Behav Ther 23:730, 1992

47. Springer T, Lohr NE, Buchtel HA, et al: A preliminary report of short-term cognitive behavioral group therapy for inpatients with personality disorders. J Psychother Pract Res 5:57, 1996
48. Simpson EB, Pistorello J, Begin A, et al: Use of dialectical behavior therapy in a partial hospital program for women with borderline personality disorder. Psychiatr Serv 49:669–673, 1998
49. Stanley B, Ivanoff A, Brodsky B, et al: Comparison of DBT and "treatment as usual" in suicidal and self-mutilating behavior. Presented at the 32nd Annual Meeting of the Association for the Advancement of Behavior Therapy. Washington, DC, November 1998
50. Telch CF, Agras WS, Linehan MM: Group dialectical behavior therapy for binge eating disorder: A preliminary uncontrolled trial. In press
51. van den Bosch LMC: A study of the effectiveness of DBT in the treatment of substance and nonsubstance abusing women in Holland. *In* Proceedings of the 33rd Annual Meeting of the Association for the Advancement of Behavior Therapy. Toronto, 1999
52. Weissman MM, Bothwell S: Assessment of social adjustment by patient self-report Arch Gen Psychiatry 33:1111, 1976
53. Zanarini MC, Gunderson JG, Frankenburg FR, et al: The revised diagnostic interview for borderlines: Discriminating borderline personality disorder from other axis II disorders. J Pers 3:10–18, 1989
54. Evans K, Tyrer P, Catalan J, et al: Manual-assisted cognitive-behavioral therapy (MACT): A randomized controlled trial of a brief intervention with bibliotherapy in the treatment of recurrent deliberate self-harm. Psychol Med 29:19, 1999

Address reprint requests to

Kelly Koerner, PhD
Behavioral Technology Transfer Group
4556 University Way NE Suite 222
Seattle, WA 98105

PSYCHOPHARMACOLOGY OF BORDERLINE PERSONALITY DISORDER

Paul H. Soloff, MD

The treatment of personality disorders is one of the last areas in psychiatry to fully embrace a psychobiologic perspective. Although personality is traditionally defined as an integrated structure of biologic temperament and learned character, treatments for personality disorders have historically emphasized the psychodynamic or behavioral correction of maladaptive learning. Temperament was viewed as contributing a biologic basis to the regulation of perception, cognition, affect, and impulse, contributing to the phenomenology of behavior, not to interpersonal meaning. Advances in dimensional modeling of personality, and a growing body of empiric literature on the psychobiology of personality dimensions, have invigorated the search for pharmacologic treatments in personality disordered patients. The neurotransmitter mediation of important dimensions of personality provides a powerful theoretic framework for pharmacologic trials in patients with personality disorders.

This article reviews pharmacologic approaches to the treatment of borderline personality disorder (BPD), which has been the focus of more medication trials than any other Axis II disorder. Medications from every major psychotropic drug family have been employed against aspects of BPD. The background for these studies and quality of existing evidence are reviewed for each drug class. A practical, *symptom specific* approach to pharmacotherapy in the patient with BPD is presented.

From the Department of Psychiatry, Western Psychiatric Institute and Clinic, University of Pittsburgh, Pittsburgh, Pennsylvania

THE PSYCHIATRIC CLINICS OF NORTH AMERICA

VOLUME 23 • NUMBER 1 • MARCH 2000 169

DEFINITIONS: BPD AS A SYNDROMAL DISORDER

BPD is not a disease. It is a syndromal disorder defined by dysregulated temperament and maladaptive character. The symptom domains of BPD may be divided into *cognitive-perceptual* symptoms, *affective dysregulation, impulsive-behavioral dyscontrol,* and *interpersonal psychopathology.* Cognitive-perceptual symptoms in BPD are those stress-related, micropsychotic distortions in thinking, and perception which first gave this syndrome its borderline (e.g., borderline psychotic) appelation. Affective dysregulation and impulsive-behavioral dyscontrol are temperamental vulnerabilities to disinhibition of mood and behavior. Neurotransmitter mediation of perception, cognition, affect, and impulse suggests a role for pharmacotherapy in three of these four domains. Treatments for interpersonal psychopathology, although often facilitated by medication, are properly reserved for psychotherapy.

Research on animal models of learning, and neuropharmacologic challenge studies in man, has established correlations between behavioral patterns of response in animals (or personality traits in man) and specific monoamine neurotransmitter systems in the brain. The dopaminergic system has been implicated in information processing and cognitive-perceptual symptoms in patients with schizotypal personality disorders (SPD),[8] and with dissociative and histrionic traits in impulsive personality disordered patients.[32] In animal studies, dopamine is associated with general behavioral arousal and novelty seeking, which may have parallels in human personality to sensation seeking or some forms of impulsiveness.[7] The noradrenergic system is associated with emotional arousal and reactivity, the serotonergic system with regulation of impulse, and the cholinergic system with decreasing exploration.[49] Although complex interactions between neurotransmitter systems most certainly play a role in modulation of behavior, pharmacologic intervention against dominant monoaminergic systems can modify the final expression of behaviors. Medication can modify expression of personality dimensions in man.

CLINICAL PRESENTATIONS IN BPD

BPD was an early focus for pharmacologic intervention because of the clinical seriousness of the patient's symptomatic presentations, the high morbidity and mortality associated with the disorder. Suicide attempts are reported in as many as 73% of borderline patients admitted to inpatient hospital, with an average of 3.4 ($\pm$2.9) lifetime attempts per patient.[51] Similar rates are reported in outpatient settings.[66] With a completed suicide rate of 3% to 9.5%, BPD is one of the most lethal of psychiatric disorders.[61] Comorbidity with depression, alcohol, and drugs of abuse, are also high, increasing the risk of lethal outcomes.[61] The prominence of impulsive–aggressive behaviors, (often aggravated by alcohol and substance use), places additional burden upon health care providers. It is not surprising that, as each new medication family has been introduced in psychiatry, it has been used to treat the borderline patient.

NEUROLEPTICS

Background

Borderline disorders historically encompassed a spectrum of clinical presentations including both affective and schizotypal subtypes. Terms such as *borderline, pseudoneurotic,* or *pseudopsychopathic schizophrenia,* and *latent* and *larval psychosis* illustrate some of the diagnoses used to define the patient with BPD, "at the psychotic border," (i.e., the patient with BPD characterized by odd-thinking and a vulnerability to brief, stress-related micro-psychotic episodes. Over the many iterations of the diagnostic system, modern BPD came to bear a closer phenomenologic relationship to affective disorders than to the schizophrenias.[62] Stable schizotypal *traits* involving chronic mild thought disorders and negative social symptoms were separated off to become the SPD. *State* symptoms of cognitive-perceptual disturbance, including illusions, ideas of reference, mild paranoid ideation, and even transitory hallucination remained within the definition of BPD (e.g., as "transient, stress-related paranoid ideation or severe dissociative symptoms") and among the criteria for SPD.[2] In BPD, these cognitive-perceptual distortions may actually reflect a dimension of severity of affective dysregulation, and account for extensive (e.g., over 50%) comorbidity between BPD and SPD found in some acute inpatient settings.[56]

The cognitive-perceptual symptoms of patients with BPD (and SPD) may share a common cause in dopaminergic neurotransmission with thought disorders of Axis I psychoses. Dopaminergic stimulation by amphetamine challenge is associated with transient psychotic symptoms in some patients with BPD, suggesting a vulnerability to cognitive-perceptual symptoms.[45]

Studies

Neuroleptic medications are the mainstay of treatments directed against thought disorder. At a time when the borderline diagnoses implied both affective and schizotypal symptoms, neuroleptics were initially directed against the *soft-thought disorders* of the syndrome. However, early case experience with low-dose haloperidol, perphenazine, and thiothixene demonstrated clinical improvements in mood, anxiety, anger, and somatic complaints as well as cognitive disturbances.[3] Two parallel comparison studies of neuroleptics in patients with BPD also reported improvements in both affective and cognitive symptoms. Leone[34] found that loxapine succinate (13.5–14.5 mg/d) or chlorpromazine

(105–120 mg/d) produced improvement in depressed mood, anxiety, hostility, and suspiciousness.[6] Serban and Siegel[46] reported improvement in depression, anxiety, derealization, paranoid ideation, and global functioning with thiothixene (2 mg–40 mg/d) or haloperidol (1.6 mg–4.0 mg/day). Although not placebo-controlled, these parallel drug comparison studies used systematic research ratings to demonstrate significant improvements with low-dose neuroleptics in both affective and cognitive-perceptual symptom domains in criteria-defined patients with BPD.

Double-blind, placebo-controlled trials of thiothixene, trifluoperazine and haloperidol soon followed. Goldberg et al[26] studied a sample of outpatients chosen for meeting DSM-III criteria for either BPD or SPD and having at least one psychotic symptom typical of borderline patients. In this sample, skewed for schizotypal pathology, thiothixene (in mean daily dosages of 8.67 mg), produced significant improvement over placebo in psychotic cluster symptoms, specifically, illusions and ideas of reference, but also in self-rated obsessive–compulsive and phobic anxiety symptoms. The more *severely symptomatic* the patient was at baseline (e.g., on illusions, ideas of reference, obsessive–compulsive, and phobic anxiety symptoms), the better he or she responded to thiothixene. Cowdry and Gardner[14] used low dose trifluoperazine as one of four active drugs in a complex, double-blind, placebo-controlled cross-over study. Patients were defined by DSM–III and Gunderson's Diagnostic Interview for Borderlines (DIB, Scaled Score ≥7) but also had to meet criteria for hysteroid dysphoria (an atypical depressive disorder) and demonstrate evidence of extensive behavioral dyscontrol. This sample was skewed toward affective and impulsive-behavioral symptoms. Patients on trifluoperazine (mean daily dosage of 7.8 mg) showed significant improvement over placebo on physician ratings of depression, anxiety and rejection sensitivity, and significantly decreased suicidality, with a nearly significant trend for less behavioral dyscontrol. Patients who were able to tolerate at least 3 weeks of treatment (7 of 10 starters), showed significant improvement over placebo.

Soloff et al[55, 56, 58] conducted two studies contrasting a low-dose neuroleptic (haloperidol) with an antidepressant (amitriptyline in the first study, phenelzine in the second study) in an effort to pharmacologically dissect the borderline syndrome into affective and schizotypal subtypes by medication response. In the first study, haloperidol (mean daily dosage of 4.8 mg) was contrasted with amitriptyline (mean daily dosage of 149.1 mg) in a 5-week inpatient trial.[56, 58] After 1 week of being medication free, patients had to meet global severity criteria (e.g., GAS <50 and either affective symptom severity or schizotypal symptom severity). This patient sample was skewed toward symptom severity. A midpoint analysis of this study (including some outpatients), showed that haloperidol was significantly superior to placebo (and amitriptyline) on symptom severity, expressed as a statistically derived factor independent of specific content.[58] As in the Goldberg et al[26] study, severity of schizotypal symptoms was a predictor of favorable response. In the final analysis of this study (which excluded all outpatients), haloperidol was found to be significantly superior to placebo on global measures, self and observer rated depression, anger and hostility, schizotypal symptoms, psychoticism, and actual impulsive behaviors on the ward (i.e., a broad spectrum of symptom presentations). Haloperidol was equal to amitriptyline against depressive symptoms in these inpatients with BPD.[56]

A second study by the same group comparing haloperidol to phenelzine failed to replicate the broad spectrum efficacy of haloperidol (mean daily dosage 3.93 mg).[55] However, a comparison of the two study samples was revealing. The second, nonreplicating sample, spent less time in hospital and was found to be significantly less impaired (by GAS), less schizotypal, (by Schizotypal Symptom Inventory), had less psychoticism (by IMPS) and less impulsive ward behavior (Ward Scale) than the first sample. By chance, patients randomized to haloperidol in the second study also were more depressed than patients assigned to phenelzine, with higher scores on the Beck Depression Inventory and Atypical Depression Scale, and had disproportionately more comorbid major despressive disorder (MDD).[55] The differences in sample characteristics and outcomes in the two Soloff[55, 58] studies suggest that low dose neuroleptics have utility primarily against general symptom severity, especially involving psychoticism, schizotypal symptoms, and impulsive behavioral dyscontrol.

Acute treatment studies are brief, lasting 6 to 12 weeks. Is neuroleptic therapy ever indicated in continuation or maintenance therapies of BPD extending months (or years) in duration? Cornelius et al[13] followed the sample described by Soloff et al,[55] on haloperidol, phenelzine or placebo treatment for 16 weeks of double-blind continuation therapy, following the initial 5 weeks of acute treatment. Patients were entered into the continuation phase only if they showed some (even slight) improvement in the acute trial. (Nonresponding patients were not continued in the study.) Continuing on their acute treatment medications and doses, few patients on haloperidol completed the full 22 week trial. Within the first 8 weeks of the continuation, 64.3% of the haloperidol patients terminated treatment. (The 22-week attrition rates were 87.5% for haloperidol, 65.7% for phenelzine, and 58.1% for placebo.) Analysis of end-point data (including all subjects) revealed significant continuing improvement on haloperidol compared to placebo only in the treatment of irritability, with a trend in total hostility. However, patients on haloperidol experienced significant worsening in depressive symptoms over time, which was attributed, in part, to the side effect of akinesia. There was no further improvement in schizotypal symptoms in the longer trial. The improvement in irritability was deemed "modest" in magnitude and "of limited clinical significance."[13]

Continuation therapy with a neuroleptic has been more successful in diminishing suicidal behaviors in chronically parasuicidal patients with personality disorders. Montgomery and Montgomery[40] conducted a double-blind, placebo-controlled trial of depot flupenthixol decanoate, 20 mg once a month, in a 6-month study of parasuicidal patients with BPD and histrionic PD. Patients were recruited following an index suicidal episode and had no comorbid major depression or schizophrenia. For inclusion in the study, patients were required to have a history of two or more prior episodes of suicidal behavior.[40] On flupenthixol decanoate, patients demonstrated significant decreases in suicidal behaviors compared to the placebo group by the fourth month and sustained the difference through 6 months of treatment. The depot strategy minimized the serious problems of patient noncompliance and early study termination. This important study, which has not yet been replicated, strongly supports the continuation of a neuroleptic agent in maintenance treatment of impulsive-behavioral dyscontrol in repeatedly suicidal patients with BPD.

Atypical Neuroleptics

With the advent of the atypical neuroleptics, case reports and open label trials have begun to appear concerning efficacy in BPD. In an open label study, clozapine has been shown to be useful in treating psychotic symptoms in patients with BPD (Psychotic Disorder, not otherwise specified [NOS]), who failed to respond to "three or more standard neuroleptic trials."[20] These 15 patients had recurring delusions or hallucinations that were not typical of schizophrenia, bipolar disorder, or psychotic depression, although 46.7% met criteria for SPD. All had experienced a childhood history of severe and prolonged abuse. Medication trials ranged from 2 to 9 months, with dosages of clozapine from 75 mg to 550 mg (mean daily dosage 253.3 ± 163.7 mg). Improvement was global (e.g., on the Brief Psychiatric Rating Scale [BPRS], Clinical Global Impression [CGI], Global Assessment Scale [GAS]), with significant changes in both positive and negative psychotic symptoms of the BPRS.

Severe chronic self-mutilation in a patient with BPD (refractory to other psychotropic medications) responded rapidly to clozapine 300 mg/day in one extraordinary case noteworthy for the length of acute illness (6.5 years in state hospital), incidents of restraint (226), medical hospitalizations for self injury (39), and total cost of care ($1.25–$1.5 million) prior to institution of clozapine.[5] This patient responded with decreased self-destructive behavior and decreased need for restraints within two weeks of the institution of clozapine, was discharged from hospital 3 months later, and continued doing well at 16-month follow-up. Reports such as this will encourage experimentation with new atypical neuroleptics as they are made available.

Summary

Neuroleptics are the best studied of the psychotropic medications in BPD. The empiric literature supports the use of low-dose neuroleptics for the acute management of global symptom severity in all three symptom domains, with increased specificity in the treatment of schizotypal symptoms and psychoticism, anger and hostility. These indications are often seen on admission to hospital, or acute presentation in the emergency room (ER), where a rapid onset of action and efficacy against global symptom severity are desired. A role for low-dose neuroleptics in continuation and maintenance therapies has yet to be established through multiple controlled treatment trials. The Cornelius study[13] suggests modest use against irritability and hostility, whereas the Montgomery study[40] (noted previously in text) is highly supportive of efficacy against parasuicidal behaviors. Compliance with continuation therapy is the essential condition for a successful trial. Many clinicians, including the author, have used low dose neuroleptics as maintenance prophylaxis against the borderline patients' vulnerability to cognitive-perceptual distortions, disruptive anger, and impulsive–aggression (which frequently motivates suicidal behavior). The clinician must carefully weigh the risks of tardive dyskinesia against the benefits in each patient. If efficacy in BPD is established for the new atypical neuroleptics, concerns with tardive dyskinesia in continuation and maintenance therapies may be lessened.

ANTIDEPRESSANTS

Background

The prominence of depressive moods and affective lability in the core pathology of BPD suggests a role for antidepressant medication. Some authors consider BPD, as currently defined, to be a subaffective disorder, or a temperament related to affective spectrum disorders.[1] Comorbidity with Axis I affective disorders is highly prevalent in BPD, adding further clinical justification to the consideration of antidepressant medications. However, it is often unclear whether the depressed borderline patient has one or two disorders (i.e., where the Axis I disorder ends and the Axis II disorder begins).[52] Characterologic symptoms such as low self-esteem, pessimism, rejection sensitivity, and even chronic suicidal ideation, are exaggerated by the presence of a superimposed major depression, but do not disappear with the resolution of the Axis I disorder. All too often, the clinician views the pre-existing character pathology as a residue of major depression, now termed *refractory*. These so called "refractory" symptoms may lead to ever more aggressive treatment trials, including electroconvulsive therapy (ECT). In the BPD patient with true MDD comorbidity, the clinical dilemma is not when to begin aggressive antidepressant treatment (or ECT), but rather, when to settle for modest gains. This clinical decision requires detailed knowledge of the patient's predepressed (baseline) personality disorder, and an accurate assessment of the neurovegetative symptoms superimposed by the Axis I depression, which is an intercurrent disorder.

When examined systematically for affective disorders, depressed BPD patients may meet diagnostic criteria for major depression, atypical depressive disorder (ADD), or hysteroid dysphoria, an early variant ADD, alone or in combinations. In one systematic study, a majority of BPD patients (64.1%) met criteria for two of these diagnoses and 17.9%

met criteria for all three.[53] Because patients with atypical depression respond preferentially to MAOI antidepressants rather than TCAs, the distinction is clinically important.

Antidepressants have also been directed against impulsive-behavioral symptoms in patients with BPD. Impulsive-aggressive behavior is associated with indices of diminished central serotonergic function in patients with personality disorders, including BPD. Diminished levels of cerebrospinal fluid (CSF) 5–HIAA have been reported in military recruits with BPD who demonstrate high levels of lifetime aggression,[4] in impulsive violent and nonviolent criminal offenders with BPD,[36] and in BPD patients with violent suicide attempts.[63] The neuro-endocrine (prolactin) response to serotonergic agonists (e.g., d,l fenfluramine, m-CPP, buspirone) is diminished in personality disordered patients with impulsive-aggression, especially in BPD.[9] Patients with BPD have decreased metabolic uptake of radio-labeled glucose in areas of frontal cortex on positron emission tomography (PET) scans,[16] and diminished metabolic response to d,1 fenfluramine in areas of the prefrontal cortex, which are associated with regulation of mood and impulse.[50] Taken together, this evidence strongly suggests that diminished central serotonergic regulation, especially in prefrontal cortex, is associated with increased behavioral irritability and disinhibition in BPD, and may predispose to episodes of overt aggression against self and others. Because SSRI antidepressants increase the net transmission of serotonin, also it is reasonable to ask if they have anti-impulsive effects in patients with BPD.

Studies

Affective symptoms of patients recruited primarily for Axis I MDD and characterized by comorbid BPD, respond to tricyclic antidepressants.[60] Results are far less predictable when Axis I MDD is not a primary focus for treatment or a likely cause for the borderline patient's depressive complaints. This point was illustrated in a small, open-label study of amoxapine, an antidepressant with neuroleptic properties, which compared the response of five affective BPD patients (defined by Gunderson's DIB and DSM–III) to five schizotypal BPD patients (meeting DIB, and DSM–III criteria for BPD, and also meeting SPD criteria using Baron's Schedule for Interviewing Borderlines).[28] Axis I was not characterized beyond excluding patients with organic disease or substance abuse. Following a 28-day trial on an average of 200 mg amoxapine per day, there was no significant improvement in depression (HRSD) or global scores (BPRS, CGI) in the five patients with the affective subtype. The schizotypal borderline patients, however, improved significantly in depression, BPRS total and schizophrenic subscale scores, and CGI (on a daily dosage of up to 250 mg amoxapine).[28] This small study suggests that amoxapine may have produced improvement through its neuroleptic properties in global symptom severity, or in depressive and schizotypal symptoms, in the schizotypal borderline patient, but had little antidepressant effect on depressive symptoms in the affective BPD subtype. Randomized, controlled trials of antidepressants in BPD, challange a simple relationship between drug effects in BPD, affective borderline subtype or Axis I affective comorbidity.

In a randomized, double-blind trial comparing amitriptyline (AMI) (average daily dosage 149.1 mg) to low-dose haloperidol and placebo in an inpatient setting, Soloff et al[56] found AMI to be significantly better than placebo on both self- and observed measures of depression, though not different from haloperidol. Surprisingly, response was independent of comorbidity with MDD or BPD subtype diagnosis (e.g., BPD, BPD + SPD, SPD). It was not possible to define an affective BPD subtype through pharmacologic responsiveness (i.e., pharmacologic behavioral dissection). Among patients assigned to AMI in this 5-week trial, 57.7% worsened on a measure of change in hostile depression, and 64% worsened on a measure of change in schizotypal symptoms. Schizotypal features in patients with BPD predicted poor response to AMI. A paradoxical increase was found in suicide threats, paranoid ideation, demanding and assaultive behaviors in 15 AMI nonresponders compared to 14 placebo nonresponders. Treatment failure among the AMI nonresponders was attributable to a paradoxical behavioral toxicity not found among the placebo nonresponders.[57]

Recurrent suicidal behavior in BPD reflects both affective and impulsive-behavioral dysregulation. The Montgomery study[40] (previously described) also conducted a separate 24-week trial of mianserin 30 mg in 58 high-risk, recurrently suicidal patients with DSM–III personality disorders (predominantly borderline and histrionic), who had no comorbid depression, schizophrenia, or organic disease. In this double-blind, placebo-controlled trial, mianserin proved no better than placebo in preventing recurrent suicide attempts. (This was in marked contrast to results reported for the depot neuroleptic flupenthixol decanoate, which reduced suicide attempts after 4 months of treatment compared to placebo.)

Monoamine Oxidase Inhibitors (MAOI)

Studies with MAOI antidepressants in BPD demonstrate a broader spectrum of efficacy (with less toxicity) than the TCAs. Cowdry and Gardner[14] included tranylcypromine in their four drug, placebo-controlled, cross-over study of borderline outpatients. All patients had comorbid hysteroid dysphoria (though no MDD) and an extensive history of behavioral dyscontrol. Patients completing the tranylcypromine trials demonstrated significant improvements in all assessments of mood (including depression, anger, loneliness, and rejection sensitivity), and significant decreases in impulsivity and suicidality compared to placebo trials. There was also a near significant improvement in behavioral dyscontrol compared to placebo ($P = 0.06$), suggesting that tranylcypromine was most useful for mood and impulse symptoms related to mood.

There was a nonsignificant trend ($p = 0.08$) for patients on the MAOI to show more improvement if they had a past history of an affective disorder, though family history of affective disorder was not related to medication response.

Mood symptoms responsive to MAOI antidepressants in the context of BPD include those diagnostic of atypical depression, (e.g., mood reactivity, increased appetite, weight gain, oversleeping, severe fatigue, and rejection sensitivity). Parsons et al[42] demonstrated the superiority of phenelzine over imipramine for the treatment of patients with a primary diagnosis of atypical depressive disorder (e.g., DSMIII–R Major Depression or Dysthymia plus atypical depressive features) who were also comorbid with BPD. However, in a study in which the sample was ascertained for BPD as the primary diagnosis, with atypical depressive features a secondary comorbid condition in some, but not all patients, phenelzine (average daily dosage 60 mg) was not more effective than placebo after 5 weeks of therapy against symptoms of atypical depression, hysteroid dysphoria, or a borderline syndrome index.[55] Phenelzine was superior to placebo against self-rated measures of anger and hostility (BDHI), which are prominent mood disturbances in the patient with BPD. In a continuation phase of this same study, lasting an additional 16 weeks, patients on phenelzine continued to improve modestly in depression (e.g., helplessness) and irritability, while demonstrating more behavioral activation compared to patients on placebo.[13]

SSRI Antidepressants

Case experience and open-label trials with fluoxetine, sertaline, and venlafaxine (not a pure SSRI), indicate efficacy against aggression and irritability[10, 12, 29, 41] and self-mutilation[37] among patients with criteria defined BPD. In these studies, impulsive aggression is assessed as a state variable, measured by observed ward behavior (Ward Scale: [12] by weekly interview (Overt Aggression Scale-Modified: [10]), or, in the case of self-mutilation, by number of episodes per week.[37] An unexpected finding in these open-label reports was that improvement in impulsive behavior appeared early, within the first week of treatment,[10, 41] and disappeared as quickly with discontinuation or noncompliance. Improvement in impulsive–aggression appeared to be independent of effects on depression and anxiety[29] and also independent of comorbid MDD.[37] This separation of effects is consistent with the different time to response for impulsive and affective symptoms. Failure to respond to one SSRI does not predict resistance to all SSRIs. Some patients refractory to fluoxetine 80 mg, have proven responsive to a second trial of sertraline.[39] Similarly, patients who failed to respond to sertraline, paroxetine or fluoxetine previously, have proven responsive to venlafaxine.[38] Higher doses (e.g., to the point of inducing tremor), and longer trials (24 weeks) on sertraline convert half of sertraline nonresponders to responders.[39]

Following these open-label reports, two double-blind, placebo-controlled studies have been reported of SSRI efficacy in criteria defined patients with BPD. Salzman et al[44] conducted a 12-week trial of fluoxetine (20–60 mg/d) in 27 highly functional subjects (not identified as patients) with either BPD or BPD-trait disturbances.[44] The subjects had a mean baseline GAS of 74. One advantage of this mildly symptomatic sample was the absence of other Axis I or Axis II comorbid diagnoses. Exclusion criteria also included recent suicidal behavior, self-mutilation, substance abuse, or current severe aggressive behavior. This strategy severely limits generalizability to more seriously ill patients, but allows for a test of efficacy against subjective mood symptoms unencumbered by over-riding comorbidities. Among 22 subjects completing the study, 13 were randomized to fluoxetine and 9 to placebo. Significant improvements were reported in subjects on fluoxetine compared to placebo in measures of self and observer rated anger (POMS), depression (Ham-D, POMS), and global function (GAS). A large placebo response was noted. Improvement in anger was found to be independent of changes in depressed mood. Improvement in this highly functional sample was modest. No subject improved more than 20% on any measure.

Markovitz[39] studied 17 patients (9 fluoxetine, 8 placebo) for 14 weeks on dosages of fluoxetine ranging from 20 mg to 80 mg daily. The patients studied by Markovitz were noteworthy for a very high incidence of Axis I affective disorder comorbidity (e.g., 10 with MDD, six bipolar), and Axis III somatic complaint. Patients receiving fluoxetine improved significantly more than those on placebo on measures of depression (e.g., Ham-D, BDI), anxiety (Ham-A), and global measures (e.g., SCL-90). Measures of impulsive–aggression were not included in this study. Anecdotally, some patients with somatic complaints, (e.g., premenstrual syndrome and headaches) noted improvement in these somatic presentations on fluoxetine whereas none improved on placebo. Although the general findings agree with case experience, the methods of these two studies significantly limit generalization to other patient groups.

A recent study by Coccaro and Kavoussi[11] focused attention on impulsive-aggression as a dimensional construct (i.e., a serotonergically mediated symptom domain found across personality disorder categories) but especially in BPD and other cluster B personality disorders. They reported a 12-week randomized, double-blind, placebo-controlled trial of fluoxetine (20–60 mg/d) in 40 subjects with criteria defined impulsive–aggression in the context of a DSM–III-R personality disorder. Comorbidity was typical of an outpatient PD sample. Half of patients had a "minor" mood disorder (i.e., dysthymia or depression NOS) whereas MDD and bipolar disorder were excluded. Anxiety disorders, drug and alcohol abuse also were common. By design, the sample was not restricted to BPD (e.g., 13 subjects had BPD, 19 were cluster BPDs). They reported that subjects receiving fluoxetine were significantly improved over placebo on measures of verbal aggression and aggression against objects by week 10 of the 12-week trial, with first trends (i.e., $p = 0.06$) appearing by week 4. Improvement in irritability appeared slightly earlier (week 6), again with an early trend apparent by week 4. Global improvement, favoring fluoxetine, was significant by week 4. As in the open-label trials, these investigators found that there was no statistical interaction between response to fluoxetine against aggression or irritability and presence of current mood or anxiety disorder. Similarly, there was no effect of fluoxetine on alcohol use during the trial and no interaction between changes in alcohol use and improvements in aggression and irritability with fluoxetine.

Summary

Given the prevalence of depression in BPD, the paucity of controlled studies of antidepressants, especially older tricyclic and heterocyclic antidepressants is striking. An important, although puzzling, finding is the apparent independence of antidepressant effects from a comorbid diagnosis of major depression or affective BPD subtype,[55, 56] a past history or family history of affective disorder,[14] or from current depressed mood.[44] The biology of depression in the borderline patient may differ from the biology of classic major depression in the absence of BPD.

Although based on scanty evidence, it appears that tricyclic antidepressants have limited efficacy in BPD as a primary diagnosis. Given the evidence of behavioral toxicity (e.g., for AMI), it would be prudent for clinicians to avoid use of tricyclic antidepressants as first line treatment in this population. MAOI antidepressants should be considered for the atypical depressive pattern of symptoms, (e.g., mood reactivity, hypersomnia, hyperphagia, anergia, and rejection sensitivity) for hostile depressive presentations, and for impulsivity related to mood disturbance. The MAOI antidepressants offer global improvement for multiple presentations of mood pathology in BPD, including depression, anxiety, and anger, but also for impulsivity, suicidality, and (to a lesser extent) behavioral dyscontrol. Although empiric evidence for the efficacy of MAOI antidepressants is strong, difficulties in managing the borderline patient on MAOI antidepressants may lead the clinician to consider the SSRI antidepressants as the first line of treatment. Empiric support for SSRI efficacy against depressed mood, anger, and impulsive–aggression in BPD is supported by these studies. It is apparent, however, that more double-blind, placebo-controlled trials are needed.

ANTICONVULSANTS

Background

Brief, reactive episodes of rage, affective and behavioral dyscontrol are among the core characteristics of BPD. Transient experiences of derealization, depersonalization, illusions, hallucinations, and other perceptual distortions also are commonly reported. These transient distortions in perception, mood and impulse bear a superficial resemblance to symptoms commonly found in temporal lobe epilepsy. Neurologically minded psychiatrists, noting the resemblance, postulated a limbic system cause for some symptom manifestations of BPD. Early clinical trials of phenytoin, an anticonvulsant, produced some improvement in these symptoms. (R Davies, MD, unpublished observations). At NIMH, Kellner et al[31] found that a limbic system stimulant, procaine, which provokes temporal lobe phenomena, produced a typical dysphoric reaction in some patients with BPD. This finding inspired clinical trials of carbamazepine, an anticonvulsant useful in temporal lobe epilepsy.[14]

Recent studies have failed to substantiate an epileptogenic etiology for symptoms of BPD, using EEG and sophisticated PET neuroimaging techniques.[17] Anticonvulsant medications have proven effective as mood stabilizers in the treatment of bipolar disorder, however, independent of any apparent anticonvulsant effects. Their application in BPD is directed toward regulation of mood lability or impulse dyscontrol, which may share a common neurobiology with similar symptoms in bipolar disorders. Among the anticonvulsant mood stabilizers, carbamazepine is the only medication studied in placebo-controlled trials. Divalproex has been studied in several open label trials. Clonazepam, a benzodiazepine anticonvulsant with mood stabilizing properties, is discussed later in this article in the antianxiety medications.

Studies

Cowdry and Gardiner[14] included carbamazepine (CBZ) in their double-blind, four-drug, placebo-controlled cross-over study (described earlier in text).[14] All patients were female, met diagnostic criteria for both BPD and hysteroid dysphoria, and gave clinical evidence of significant problems with behavioral impulsivity. Patients were referred by a psychotherapist and remained in concurrent psychotherapy during the medication trials, assuring some degree of clinical continuity and stability in the treatment. Patients took an average daily dosage of 820 mg of CBZ during the 6-week trial, titrated to therapeutic blood levels. The 14 carbamazepine trials were associated with significantly less behavioral dyscontrol, compared to 11 trials on placebo. Trials which were paired (i.e., same patient) showed less behavioral dyscontrol in 10 of 11 trials during the CBZ treatment. Seven of 11 placebo trials were discontinued for clinical worsening compared to only one of 14 CBZ trials. (24). An unexpected complication of CBZ treatment was the appearance of melancholic depression in three (of 17) patients, which improved when the medication was discontinued.[23]

De La Fuenta et al[15] conducted a double-blind, placebo-controlled trial of CBZ among 20 inpatients who met criteria for BPD but had no Axis I diagnoses, or evidence of "standard EEG traits of epilepsy." By conducting a traditional parallel comparison study, the authors avoided any concern with carry-over effects of medications inherent in the cross-over design used by Cowdry and Gardiner. Furthermore, they carefully screened patients for prior medication usage, requiring adequate washout times prior to entering the study (e.g., no neuroleptics for 2 months). The study was a 32-day trial with titration of drug to antiepileptic blood levels. All patients had concurrent psychotherapy. Although both groups improved with time on measures of depression (HRDS) and global symptomatology (BPRS), there were no significant differences between placebo and CBZ groups. Most importantly, there were no differences between groups on measures of behavioral dyscontrol. (Two CBZ patients dropped out of the study on days 24 and 29 because of wrist cutting and swallowing razor blades. There were no drop outs in the placebo condition.).

Most recently, interest has turned to divalproex sodium, an anticonvulsant with proven efficacy in bipolar disorders. In a series of open label studies, divalproex sodium has been found to be helpful in some criteria-defined patients with BPD in the areas of mood, anxiety, anger, impulsivity, rejection sensitivity, and global subjective irritability. Stein et al[59] conducted medication trials, (which were 8 weeks in duration), with borderline outpatients who had no comorbid major depression or history of bipolar disorder. Valproate was titrated to blood levels of 50 to 100 μg/mL. Only four of eight patients completing the trial reported significant improvement in mood and impulse symptoms. Wilcox[65] studied 30 borderline inpatients who had no comorbid psychiatric disorders, although five had EEG abnormalities (without overt seizures).[65] This relatively disturbed inpatient sample also received other concurrent medications and required periodic seclusion, which became a valuable dependent variable. With the addition of divalproex, patients improved globally (BPRS), especially in anxiety and tension, and required less time in seclusion. Both divalproex and a history of an abnormal EEG had predictive value for global improvement in BPRS and seclusion scores, with the divalproex contributing 25% of the variance and the abnormal EEG only minimally contributory.

Divalproex sodium has been shown to be useful against irritability and impulsive-aggressive behavior in patients who have failed treatment with an SSRI antidepressant, and across multiple personality diagnoses. Kavoussi and Coccaro[30] conducted open label, 8-week trials in 10 patients with a DSM–IV PD (five with BPD) who had failed prior medication trials with fluoxetine (at least 60 mg for 8 weeks).[30] Six of eight completers reported improvement on divalproex by the fourth week. These results support earlier findings of efficacy for divalproex for the disruptive behavior disorders of adolescents, i.e., adolescents with impulsive-aggression in the context of conduct disorder, oppositional or defiant disorder, and attention deficit hyperactivity disorder (ADHD).[18] Divalproex diminishes frequency of chronic temper outbursts and mood lability in this disruptive group and appears more specific for the biology of impulsive behavioral dyscontrol than for the diagnostic context.

Summary

In borderline patients with an effective presentation (e.g., hysteroid dysphoria) and histories of impulse dyscontrol, CBZ may be a useful treatment for behavior dyscontrol. This cannot be supported in BPD patients without affective or impulsive presentations. Divalproex may also be helpful in the specific context of impulsive aggression, although there are no placebo-controlled trials in the literature to confirm the open-label trials. Empiric support for the use of mood stabilizers in BPD has lagged far behind actual clinical use, which is widespread, although unguided by systematic research.

LITHIUM CARBONATE

Background

The mood lability of the borderline patient provides a rationale for the empirical use of lithium carbonate, a medication highly effective against mood lability in bipolar disorders. Early empirical trials with patients termed emotionally unstable character disorder (EUCD) (DSM–II) demonstrated efficacy against mood lability.[43] These patients were histrionic, adolescent girls with impulsive behaviors and *hedonistic* abuse of drugs and alcohol. Although there is some controversy as to whether EUCD fits into the modern classification of BPD, the efficacy of lithium carbonate against mood lability in the context of a personality disorder encouraged further experimentation. Lithium also was reported to have efficacy against impulsive-aggression in adult criminal subjects,[64] and in delinquent adolescents[47] in a series of double-blind placebo-controlled studies.

Studies

Although there have been case reports[47] and pilot studies[27] suggesting the usefulness of lithium in BPD, only one double-blind, placebo-controlled study has been published. Links et al[35] compared lithium carbonate (average daily dosage of 985.7 mg by week 3) to desipramine (average daily dosage of 162.5 mg) in a random assignment, double-blind, cross-over study, in which each patient had a 6-week treatment trial of each drug (with a 2-week washout in between trials). Patients were diagnosed by Gunderson's DIB (scaled score ≥7). Many had current or lifetime affective disorder comorbidity. This was a small sample study (n = 17), with only 10 patients completing two or more conditions. Neither lithium or desipramine demonstrated an antidepressant response compared to placebo. Therapist's rated their patients as more improved on lithium compared to placebo (PLC) on measures of irritability, anger and suicidal symptoms, an improvement not reported by patients themselves. There was also a trend for lithium to be superior to DMI on therapist's ratings in these areas. The suggested efficacy of lithium against irritability and anger is consistent with the antiaggressive properties reported in other personality disorders. Links et al[35] suggested that this efficacy against impulsive-aggression may be related to the action of lithium as a functional serotonin agonist.

Summary

Lithium carbonate may be a useful treatment for impulsive-aggression in the context of personality disorders, including BPD. Once again, despite widespread clinical use, an empirical database is sadly lacking. The need to monitor blood levels, and the toxicity of lithium carbonate in overdose, are practical considerations limiting the use of lithium in very impulsive patients with BPD.

ANXIOLYTIC AGENTS

Background

Anxiety is a common presenting complaint in patients with BPD. Although the diathesis to disruptive anxiety may be a chronic trait in the borderline patient, (historically called "pan-anxiety" or "free-floating" anxiety), the symptom presentation is most often acute and reactive to clear interpersonal stressors such as perceived rejection, or abandonment issues. In this setting, many clinicians rely on rapid acting benzodiazepine anxiolytics to treat both the acute presentations and the patient's chronic vulnerability.

Studies

Case reports attest to the possible use of clonazepam, a benzodiazepine anticonvulsant and antimanic agent with serotonin enhancing actions.[21] Clonazepam is associated with increase in serotonin levels, increased serotonin synthesis, and function.[6] Therefore, it shares some pharmacologic and antimanic properties with lithium carbonate, although the anticonvulsant properties resemble carbamazepine. Clonazepam may be useful as an adjunctive treatment for anxiety, anger, impulsivity, and dysphoric mood in the borderline patient. With a relatively long half-life of 18 to 50 hours, clonazepam can be used to establish a blood level for treatment of the borderline patient's chronic vulnerability to anxiety.

The high potency, short acting benzodiazepine, alprazolam, has also been reported as helpful in treating anxiety in individual borderline patients[19]; however, Gardiner and Cowdry[14] reported a significantly increased incidence of serious behavior dyscontrol as an adverse outcome of treatment with alprazolam in their four-drug, placebo-controlled cross-over trial. As noted earlier, this study included female borderline patients with comorbid hysteroid dysphoria and past histories of impulsive behavior. On an average daily dosage of 4.7 mg alprazolam, seven of 12 (58%) patients taking alprazolam had serious episodes of behavior dyscontrol compared to one of 13 (8%) taking placebo. Episodes of behavior dyscontrol involved drug overdoses, wrist and neck cuts, and throwing a chair at a child. Four alprazolam trials were stopped by the blind rater for dyscontrol while none of the placebo trials were discontinued.[22]

Summary

Despite widespread use, there are no random assignment, double-blind, placebo-controlled trials attesting to the efficacy of benzodiazepine anxiolytics in the patient with BPD. The one carefully conducted controlled trial reported very adverse outcomes (for alprazolam). Disinhibition has long been associated with the benzodiazepines as a possible adverse effect. In a disorder defined by a vulnerability to behavior dyscontrol, such reactions may be of greater clinical concern. Given the paucity of controlled studies on benzodiazepine use in BPD, a well-defined adverse risk profile, and the ever-present danger of abuse and dependence, the clinician would be well-advised to use caution prescribing alprazolam or other short acting benzodiazepines for the borderline patient. The serotonergic effects of clonazepam may make this long-acting benzodiazepine a better choice for treatment of anxiety in BPD. At present, there is no published literature addressing the use of the nonbenzodiazepine anxiolytics, such as buspirone, in BPD, though their action as serotonergic agonists and effects in anxiety disorders are promising.

PUTTING IT ALL TOGETHER: A SYMPTOM-SPECIFIC APPROACH

Target symptoms for pharmacotherapy of the borderline patient can be divided into three domains: cognitive-perceptual symptoms, affective dysregulation, and impulsive-behavioral dyscontrol. Clinical treatment algorithms may be developed for each symptom domain using the available empirical literature.[54] Although based on a small empiric database, algorithms for treatment of the BPD patient can offer initial guidance to the clinician.

Cognitive-perceptual symptoms include: suspiciousness, paranoid ideation, ideas of reference, dissociation, illusions, odd or eccentric thinking, and transitory (stress-related) hallucinations. Included with this group are anger and irritability related to cognitive symptoms. Neuroleptics are the treatment of first choice for this symptom presentation (Fig. 1). The literature supports the use of neuroleptics in low dose and

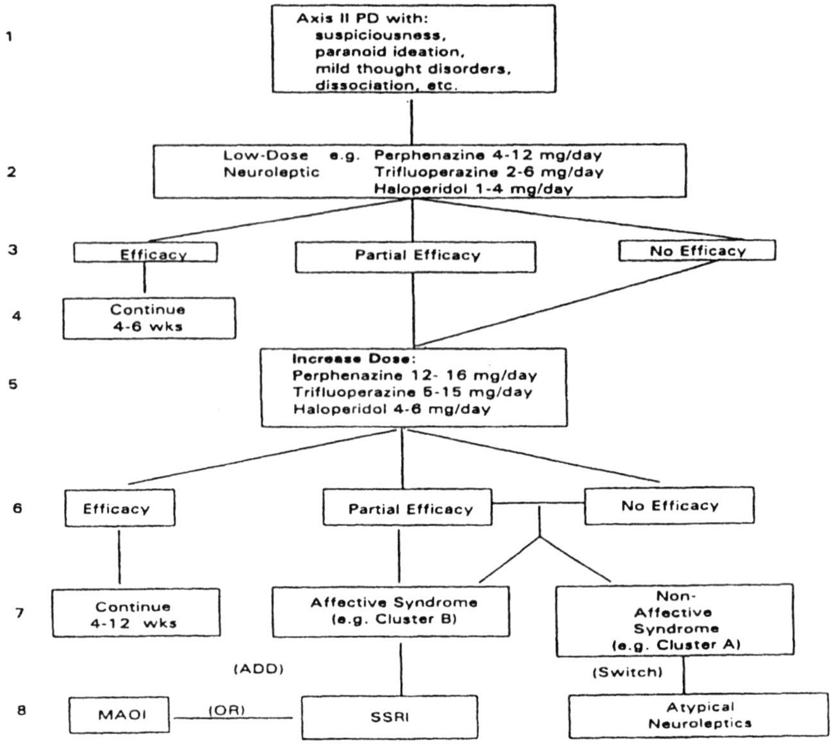

Figure 1. Algorithm for treatment of cognitive-perceptual symptoms in personality disorders. *From* Soloff PH: Algorithms for pharmacological treatment of personality dimensions: Symptom-specific treatments for cognitive-perceptual, affective, and impulsive-behavioral dysregulation. Bulletin of Menninger Clinic 62:195–214, 1998; reprinted by the permission of the Guilford Press.

for short time periods (weeks, not months). Continuation and maintenance therapies with low dose neuroleptics in BPD require careful assessment of the risk of tardive dyskinesia. A failure of rapid response of cognitive-perceptual symptoms to traditional neuroleptics should prompt consideration of atypical neuroleptics, which have been found helpful in patients with persistant psychotic features in the context of BPD. Failure of neuroleptic therapy should prompt a re-evaluation of diagnosis. If the cognitive symptoms are attributable to affective dysregulation, MAOI or SSRI antidepressants may prove more helpful.

The target symptoms of affective dysregulation include: lability of mood, rejection sensitivity, *mood crashes,* inappropriate intense anger, and temper outbursts. Borderline patients also commonly experience anxiety, chronic emptiness, dysphoria, loneliness, and anhedonia. The SSRI and related antidepressants are the treatment of first choice for the depressed, angry, labile, and anxious presentations of the borderline patient (Fig. 2). Failure of response with a first trial should prompt a second SSRI or

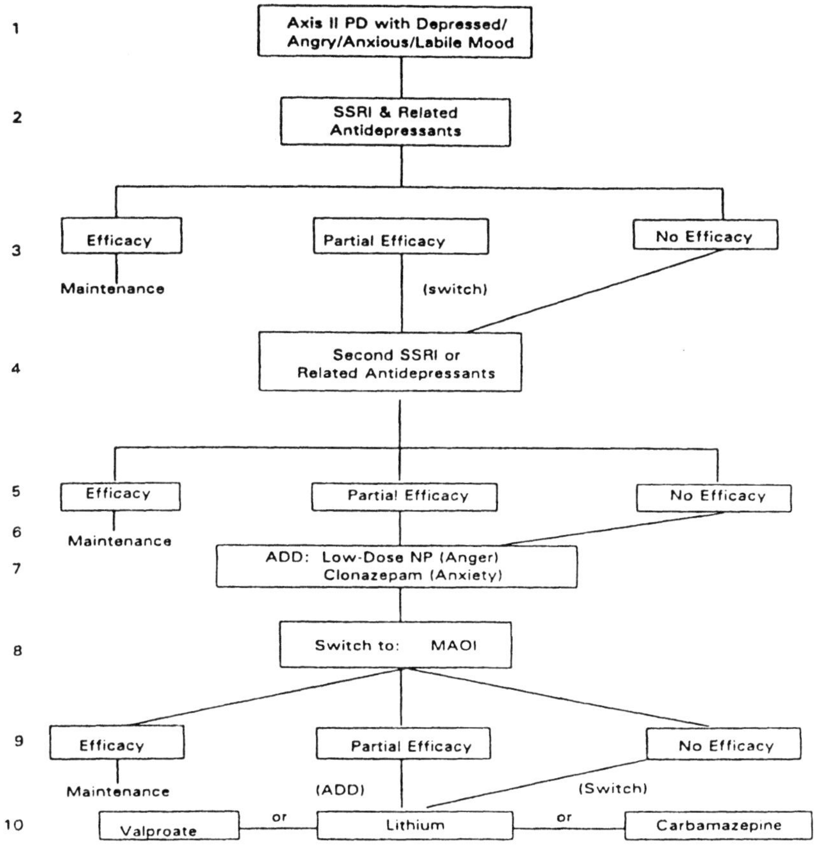

Figure 2. Algorithm for treatment of affective dysregulation in personality disorders. *From* Soloff PH: Algorithms for pharmacological treatment of personality dimensions: Symptom-specific treatments for cognitive-perceptual, affective, and impulsive-behavioral dysregulation. Bulletin of Menninger Clinic 62:195–214, 1998; reprinted by the permission of the Guilford Press.

related drug trial, because the "salvage strategy" has proven useful in BPD as well as in affective disorder studies. Failure of response to SSRI antidepressants should prompt consideration of an MAOI antidepressant, with supplementation (if needed) with a low dose neuroleptic for anger management or clonazepam for anxiety management. If this fails, the third line of treatment for the affective domain relies upon the mood stabilizers, lithium carbonate, valproate, or carbamazepine.

The impulsive-behavior symptom domain consists of recurrent suicidal threats, parasuicidal behaviors, impulsive-aggression, assaultiveness, property destruction, binge behaviors (on drugs, alcohol, sex, or food), and cognitive impulsivity with low frustration tolerance. SSRI and related antidepressants are the first line treatments for dysregulation

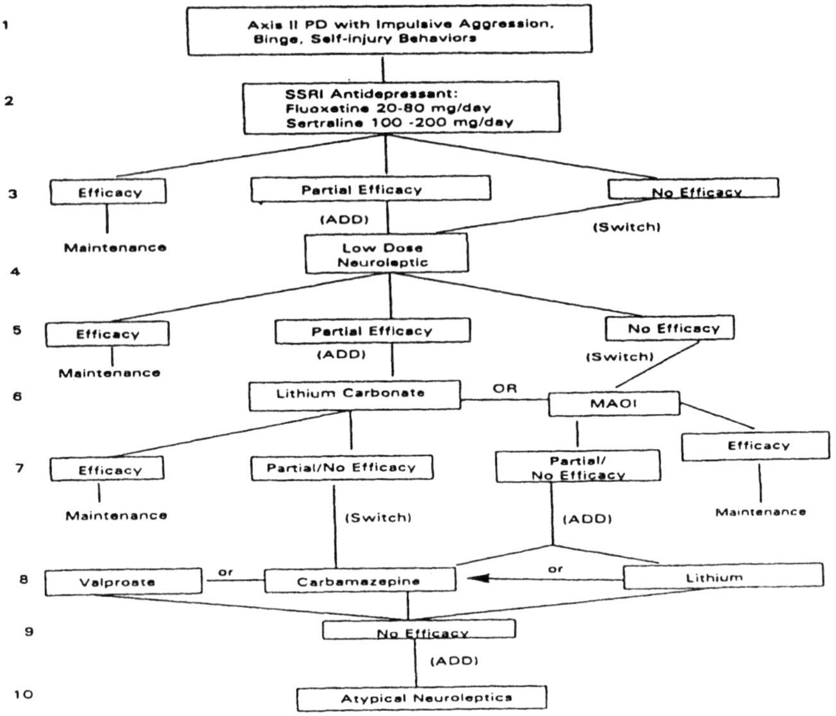

Figure 3. Algorithm for treatment of impulsive-behavioral symptoms in personality disorders. *From* Soloff PH: Algorithms for pharmacological treatment of personality dimensions: Symptom-specific treatments for cognitive-perceptual, affective, and impulsive-behavioral dysregulation. Bulletin of Menninger Clinic 62:195–214, 1998; reprinted by the permission of the Guilford Press.

of impulsive behavior as well as for affective dysregulation (Fig. 3). Failure of response should prompt consideration of low dose neuroleptics, which have a well-defined, but nonspecific, efficacy against impulsive behavior. Clinical urgency may require use of neuroleptics first, with gradual introduction of the SSRI antidepressant. Lithium carbonate or MAOI antidepressants would be considered after SSRI antidepressants, given the difficulties of management. Finally, consideration should be given to lithium carbonate or the anticonvulsant mood stabilizers. Atypical neuroleptics, especially clozapine, have been used "when all else has failed" and produced remission in some cases of psychotic symptoms or severe self-destructive behavior.

CONCLUSION

1. Pharmacotherapy should be viewed as an adjuvant to psychotherapy in the treatment of the borderline patient (i.e., diminish-

ing cognitive-perceptual, affective, and impulsive-behavioral symptom severity). Much of borderline psychopathology lies in the interpersonal domain, beyond the scope of medication management. Effective pharmacotherapy may make it possible for the patient to engage productively in psychotherapy; however, medications do not cure character and are never a substitute for the work of the therapist.

2. BPD is a multidimensional syndrome. No one medication is effective across all symptom domains. Treatments are symptom specific.
3. BPD is a chronic disorder. Treatment effects are modest in magnitude, and residual symptoms are the rule. Cure is not a realistic option. Reduction of symptom severity is a realistic goal of pharmacotherapy.
4. Current empirical guidelines are based on a small and inadequate database of studies. Empirical support through randomized controlled trials are lacking (or still awaiting replication) for widespread clinical practices involving the use of atypical neuroleptics, lithium carbonate, benzodiazepines, and anticonvulsant mood stabilizers in the borderline patient. The clinician should approach each treatment as an empirical trial, with the patient as co-investigator.

References

1. Akiskal HS: Sub-affective disorders: Dysthymic, cyclothymic and bipolar II disorders in the "borderline" realm. Psychiatr Clin North Am 4:25–46, 1981
2. American Psychiatric Association: Diagnostic and Statistical Manual of Mental Disorders, Ed 4. Washington, DC, APA Press, 1994, p 654
3. Brinkley J, Beitman D, Friedel R: Low dose neuroleptic regimens in the treatment of borderline patients. Arch Gen Psychiatry 36:319–326, 1979
4. Brown GL, Goodwin FK: Cerebrospinal fluid correlates of suicide attempts and aggression. Ann NY Acad Sci 487:175–188, 1986
5. Chengappa KN, Baker RW, Sirri C: The successful use of clozapine in ameliorating severe self mutilation in a patient with borderline personality disorder. J Personal Disord 9:76–82, 1995
6. Chouinard G: Clonazepam in acute and maintenance treatment of bipolar affective disorder. J Clin Psych 48:10, 1987
7. Cloninger CR, Svrakic DM, Przybeck TR: A psychobiological model of temperament and character. Arch Gen Psychiatry 50:975–990, 1993
8. Coccaro EF, Siever LJ: The Neuropsychopharmacology of Personality Disorders. *In* Bloom FE, Kupfer DJ (eds): Psychopharmacology: The Fourth Generation of Progress. New York, Raven Press. 1995, pp 1567–1579
9. Coccaro EF, Siever LJ, Klar HM, et al: Serotonergic studies in patients with affective and personality disorders: Correlates with suicidal and impulsive aggressive behavior. Arch Gen Psychiatry 46:587–599, 1989
10. Coccaro EF, Astill JL, Herbert JL, et al: Fluoxetine treatment of impulsive aggression in DSM III-R personality disorder patients. J Clin Psychopharmacol 10:373–375, 1990
11. Coccaro EF, Kavoussi RJ: Fluoxetine and Impulsive-Aggressive behavior in personality disordered subjects. Arch Gen Psychiatry 54:1081–1088, 1997

12. Cornelius JR, Soloff PH, Perel JM, et al: Fluoxetine trial in borderline personality disorder. Psychopharm Bull 26:151–154, 1990
13. Cornelius JR, Soloff PH, Perel JM, et al: Continuation pharmacotherapy of borderline personality disorder with haloperidol and phenelzine. Am J Psychiatry 150:1843–1848, 1993
14. Cowdry RW, Gardner DL: Pharmacotherapy of borderline personality disorder: Alprazolam, carbamazepine, trifluoperazine and tranylcypromine. Arch Gen Psychiatry 45:111–119, 1988
15. De La Fuenta JM, Lotstra F: A trial of carbamazepine in borderline personality disorder. Eur Neuropsychopharmacol 4:479–486, 1994
16. De La Fuenta JM, Goldman S, Stanus E, et al: Brain glucose metabolism in borderline personality disorder. J Psychiatr Res 31:531–541, 1997
17. De La Fuenta, Lotstra F, Goldman S, et al: Temporal glucose metabolism in borderline personality disorder. Psychiatry Research Neuroimaging. 55(4):237–245, 1994
18. Donovan SJ, Susser ES, Nunes EV, et al: Divalproex treatment of disruptive adolescents: A report of 10 cases. J Clin Psychiatry 58:12–15, 1997
19. Faltus F: The positive effect of alprazolam in the treatment of three patients with borderline personality disorder. Am J Psychiatry 141:802–803, 1984
20. Frankenburg FR, Zanarini MC: Clozapine treatment of borderline patients: A preliminary study. Compr Psychiatry 34:402–405, 1993
21. Freinhar JP, Alvarez WA: Clonazepam: (1986) A novel therapeutic adjunct. Int J Psychiatry Med 15:321–328, 1986
22. Gardner DL, Cowdry RW: Alprazolam induced dyscontrol in borderline personality disorder. Am J Psychiatry 142:98–100, 1985
23. Gardner DL, Cowdry RW: Development of melancholia during carbamazepine treatment in borderline personality disorder. J Clin Psychopharmacol 6:236–239, 1986
24. Gardner DL, Cowdry RW: Positive effects of carbamazepine on behavioral dyscontrol in borderline personality disorder. Am J Psychiatry 143:519–522, 1986
25. Gardner DL, Lucas PB, Cowdry RW: CSF metabolites in borderline personality disorder compared with normal controls. Biol Psychiatry 28:247–254, 1990
26. Goldberg SC, Schulz SC, Schulz PM, et al: Borderline and schizotypal personality disorders treated with low-dose thiothixene vs placebo. Arch Gen Psychiatry 43:680–686, 1986
27. Goldberg SC: Prediction of change in borderline personality disorder. Psychopharmacol Bull 25(4):550–555, 1989
28. Jensen HV, Anderson J: An open, noncomparative study of amoxapine in borderline disorders. Acta Psychiatr Scand 79:89–93, 1989
29. Kavoussi RJ, Liu J, Coccaro EF: An open trial of sertraline in personality disordered patients with impulsive aggression. J Clin Psychiatry 55(4):137–141, 1994
30. Kavoussi RJ, Coccaro EF: Divalproex Sodium for impulsive aggressive behavior in patients with personality disorder. J Clin Psychiatry 59:676–680, 1998
31. Kellner CH, Post RM, Putnam F, et al: Intravenous procaine as a probe of limbic system activity in psychiatric patients and normal controls. Biol Psychiatry 22:1107–1126, 1987
32. King R, Clark D, Mefford I: Neurochemical studies of impulsive-aggressive personality traits. *In* Carroll BJ, Barrett JE (eds): Psychopathology and the Brain. New York, Raven Press, 1991, pp 169–178
33. Kutcher S, Papatheodorou G, Reiter S, et al: The successful pharmacologic treatment of adolescents and young adults with borderline personality disorder: A preliminary open trial of flupenthixol. J Psychiatr Neurosci 20(2):113–118, 1995
34. Leone NF: Response of Borderline Patients to loxapine and chlorpromazine. J Clin Psychiatry 43:148–150, 1982
35. Links P: Lithium therapy for borderline patients. J Personal Disord 4:173–181, 1990
36. Linnoila A, Virkkunen M, Scheinin M, et al: Low cerebrospinal fluid 5-hydroxy-indole acetic acid concentrations differentiate impulsive from non-impulsive violent behavior. Life Sci 33:2609–2614, 1983
37. Markovitz PJ, Calabrese JR, Schulz SC, et al: Fluoxetine in the treatment of borderline and schizotypal personality disorders. Am J Psychiatry 148:1064–1067, 1991

38. Markovitz PJ, Wagner SL: Venlafaxine in the treatment of borderline personality disorder. Psychopharmacol Bull 31(4):773–777, 1995
39. Markovitz PJ: Pharmacotherapy of impulsivity, aggression and related disorders. *In* Hollander E, Stein D (eds): Impulsivity and Aggression. Surrey, UK, Wiley, 1995, pp 263–287
40. Montgomery SA, Montgomery D: Pharmacologic prevention of suicidal behavior. J Affect Disord 4:291–298, 1982
41. Norden MJ: Fluoxetine in borderline personality disorder. Prog Neuropsychopharmacol Biol Psychiatry 13:885–893, 1989
42. Parsons B, Quitkin FM, McGrath PJ, et al: Phenelzine, imipramine and placebo in borderline patients meeting criteria for atypical depression. Psychopharmacol Bull 25:524–534, 1989
43. Rifkin A, Levitan SJ, Galewski J, et al: Emotionally unstable character disorder: A follow-up study. Biol Psychiatry 4:65–79, 1972
44. Salzman C, Wolfson AN, Schatzberg A, et al: Effect of fluoxetine on anger in symptomatic volunteers with borderline personality disorder. J Clin Psychopharmacol 15:23–29, 1995
45. Schulz SC, Cornelius J, Schulz PM, et al: The amphetamine challange test in patients with borderline personality disorder. Am J Psychiatry 145:809–814, 1988
46. Serban G, Siegel S: Response of borderline and schizotypal patients to small doses of thiothixene and haloperidol. Am J Psychiatry 141:1455–1458, 1984
47. Shader RI, Jackson AH, Dodes LM: The anti-aggressive effects of lithium in man. Psychopharmacologia (Berl) 40:17–24, 1974
48. Sheard MH: Lithium in the treatment of aggression. J Nerv Ment Dis 160:108–118, 1975
49. Siever LJ, Trestman R: Multifactorial models of neurotransmitter mediated disorders. Int Clin Psychopharmacol 8:33–39, 1993
50. Siever LJ, Trestman RL, New AS, et al: PET studies and fenfluramine in impulsive patients. 5th International Congress on the Disorders of Personality (abstract). Vancouver, Canada. June 25–27, 1997, p 161
51. Soloff PH, Lis JA, Kelly T, et al: Risk factors for suicidal behavior in borderline personality disorder. Am J Psychiatry 151:1316–1323, 1994
52. Soloff PH, Cornelius JH, George A: The depressed borderline: One disorder or Two? Psychopharmacol Bull 27(1):23–30, 1991
53. Soloff PH, Nathan RS, George A, et al: Characterizing depression in borderline patients. J Clin Psychiatry 48:155–157, 1987
54. Soloff PH: Algorithms for pharmacological treatment of personality dimensions: Symptom specific treatments for cognitive-perceptual, affective, and impulsive-behavioral dysregulation. Bull Menninger Clin 62(2):195–214, 1998
55. Soloff PH, Cornelius J, George A, et al: Efficacy of phenelzine and haloperidol in borderline personality disorder. Arch Gen Psychiatry 50:377–385, 1993
56. Soloff PH, George A, Nathan RS, et al: Amitriptyline vs haloperidol in borderlines: Final outcomes and predictors of response. J Clin Psychopharmacol 9(4):238–246, 1989
57. Soloff PH, George A, Nathan RS, et al: Paradoxical effects of amitriptyline in borderline patients. Am J Psychiatry 143:1603–1605, 1986
58. Soloff PH, George A, Nathan S, et al: Progress in pharmacotherapy of borderline disorders. Arch Gen Psychiatry 3:691–697, 1986
59. Stein DJ, Simeon D, Frenkel M, et al: An open trial of valproate in borderline personality disorder. J Clin Psychiatry 56:506–510, 1995
60. Sternberg DE: Pharmacotherapy and affective syndromes in borderline personality disorder. Paper presented at the 140th annual meeting of the American Psychiatric Association. Chicago, IL, May 12, 1989
61. Stone MH: The course of borderline personality disorder. *In* Tasman A, Hales RE, Frances AJ (eds): Review of Psychiatry, Vol 8. Washington, DC, American Psychiatric Press, 1989, pp 103–123
62. Stone MH: Contemporary shift in the borderline concept from a subschizophrenic disorder to a subaffective disorder. Psychiatr Clin North Am 2:577–594, 1979
63. Traskman-Benz L, Asberg M, Schalling D: Serotonergic function and suicidal behavior in personality disorders. Ann NY Acad Sci 487:174–188, 1986

64. Tupin JP, Smith DB, Clanon TL, et al: Long-term use of lithium in aggressive disorders. Compr Psychiatry 14:311–317, 1973
65. Wilcox JA: Divalproex sodium as a treatment for borderline personality disorder. Ann Clin Psychiatry 7(1):33–37, 1995
65. Zisook S, Goff A, Sledge P, et al: Reported suicidal behavior and current suicidal ideation in a psychiatric outpatient clinic. Ann Clin Psychiatry 6(1):27–31, 1994

Address reprint requests to

Paul H. Soloff, MD
Western Psychiatric Institute and Clinic
3811 O'Hara Street
Pittsburgh, PA 15213

Acknowledgments

Cloninger, C.R. "A Systematic Method for the Clinical Description and Classification of Personality Variants." *Arch Gen Psychiatry* 44 (1987): 573–588. Reprinted with the permission of American Medical Association.

Costa, P.T., and McCrae, R.R. "The Five-Factor Model of Personality and Its Relevance to Personality Disorders." *Journal of Personality Disorders* 6 (1992): 343–359. Reprinted with the permission of Guilford Publications, Inc.

Goldberg, L.R. "An Alternative 'Description of Personality': The Big-Five Factor Structure." *J Pers Soc Psychol* 59 (1990): 1216–1229. Copyright © 1990 by the American Psychological Association. Reprinted with permission.

Gunderson, J.G., and Sabo, A. "The Phenomenological and Conceptual Interface of Borderline and Posttraumatic Stress Disorder." *Am J Psychiatry* 150 (1993): 19–27. Copyright 1993, the American Psychiatric Association. Reprinted by permission.

Mischel, W., and Shoda, Y. "Reconciling Processing Dynamics and Personality Dispositions." *Annu Rev Psychol* 49 (1998): 229–258. Reprinted with permission from the Annual Review of Psychology, Volume 49,© 1998, by Annual Reviews www.AnnualReviews.org.

Moffitt, T.E. "Adolescence-Limited and Life-Course Persistent Antisocial Behavior: A Developmental Taxonomy." *Psychol Review* 100 (1993): 674–701. Copyright © 1993 by the American Psychological Association. Reprinted with permission.

Widiger, T.A., and Costa, P.T., Jr. "Personality and Personality Disorders." *J Abnorm Psychol* 103 (1994): 78–91. Copyright 1994 by the American Psychological Association. Reprinted by permission.

Torgersen, S., Kringlen, E., and Cramer, V. "The Prevalence of Personality Disorders in a Community Sample." *Arch General Psychiatry* 58 (2001): 590–596. Reprinted with the permission of American Medical Association.

Bouchard, T.J., Jr., Lykken, D.T., McGue, M., Segal, N.L., and Tellegen, A. "Sources of Human Psychological Differences: The Minnesota Study of Twins Reared Apart." *Science* 250 (1990): 223–228. Reprinted with permission from "Sources of Human Psychological Differences: The Minnesota Study of Twins Reared Apart." *Science* 250 (1990): 223–228. Copyright 1990 American Association for the Advancement of Science.

Eaves, L., Heath, A., Martin, N., Maies, H., Neale, M., Kendler, K., Kirk, K., and Corey, L. "Comparing the Biological and Cultural Inheritance of Personality and Social Attitudes in the Virginia 30,000 Study of Twins and Their Relatives." *Twin Research* 2 (1999): 62–80. Reprinted with the permission of Nature Publishing Group.

Hewitt, J.K., Silberg, J.L., Rutter, M., Simonoff, E., Meyer, J.M., Maes, H., Pickles, A., Neale, M.C., Loeber, R., Erickson, M.T., Kendler, K.S., Heath, A.C., Truett, K.R., Reynolds, C.A., and Eaves, L.J. "Genetics and Developmental Psychopathology: 1. Phenotypic Assessment in the Virginia Twin Study of Adolescent Behavioral Development." *J Child Psychol Psychiatry* 38 (1997): 943–963. Reprinted with the permission of Cambridge University Press.

Johnson, J.G., Cohen, P., Brown, J., Smailes, E.M., and Bernstein, D.P. "Childhood Maltreatment Increases Risk for Personality Disorders during Early Adulthood." *Arch Gen Psychiatry* 56 (1999): 600–606. Reprinted with the permission of American Medical Association.

Kendler, K.S., Neale, M.C., Kessler, R.C., Heath, A.C., and Eaves, L.J. "A Test of the Equal-Environment Assumption in Twin Studies of Psychiatric Illness." *Behav Genet* 23 (1993): 21–27. Reprinted with the permission of Kluwer Academic/Plenum Publishers.

Maccoby, E.E. "Parenting and Its Effects on Children: On Reading and Misreading Behavior Genetics." *Annu Review Psychology* 51 (2000): 1–27. Reprinted with permission from the Annual Review of Psychology, Volume 51, © 2000, by Annual Reviews www.AnnualReviews.org.

Plomin, R. "The Role of Inheritance in Behavior." *Science* 248 (2000): 183–188. Reprinted with permission from "The role of inheritance in behavior." *Science* 248 (2000): 183–188. Copyright 2000 American Association for the Advancement of Science.

Tellegen, A., Lykken, D.R., Bouchard, T.J., Wilcox, K.J., Segal, N.L., and Rich, S. "Personality Similarity in Twins Reared Apart and Together." *J Personality and Social Psychology* 54 (1988): 1031–1039. Copyright © 1988 by the American Psychological Association. Reprinted with permission.

Torgersen, S., Lygren, S., Olien, P.A., et al. "A Twin Study of Personality Disorders." *Compr Psychiatry* 41 (2000): 5416–5425. Reprinted with the permission of W.B. Saunders Company.

Harris, J.R. "Where Is the Child's Environment? A Group Socialization Theory Development." *Psychol Rev* 102 (1995): 458–489. Copyright © 1995 by the American Psychological Association. Reprinted with permission.

Bechara, A., Damasio, A.R., Damasio, H., and Anderson, S.W. "Insensitivity to Future Consequences following Damage to Human Prefrontal Cortex." *Cognition* 40 (1994): 7–15. Reprinted with the permission of Elsevier Science BV.

Damasio, A.R., Tranel, D., and Damasio, H. "Individuals with Sociopathic Behavior Caused by Frontal Damage Fail to Respond Autonomically to Social Stimuli." *Behav Brain Res* 41 (1990): 81–94. Reprinted with the permission of Elsevier Science BV.

Davidson, R.J., Putnam, K.M., and Larson, C.L. "Dysfunction in the Neural Circuitry of Emotion Regulation--a Possible Prelude to Violence." *Science* 289 (2000): 591-594. Reprinted with permission from "Dysfunction in the neural circuitry of emotion regulation--a possible prelude to violence." *Science* 289 (2000): 591-594. Copyright 2000 American Association for the Advancement of Science.

Koerner, K., and Linehan, M.M. "Research on Dialectical Behavior Therapy for Patients with Borderline Personality Disorder." *Psychiatr Clin North Am* 23, 1 (2000): 151-167. Reprinted with the permission of the W.B. Saunders Company.

Soloff, P.H. "Psychopharmacology of Borderline Personality Disorder." *Psychiatr Clin North Am* 23 (2000): 169-192. Reprinted with the permission of the W.B. Saunders Company.